RANDOM HOUSE
ATLAS
— of the —
WORLD

RANDOM HOUSE
ATLAS
— of the —
WORLD

RANDOM HOUSE
REFERENCE

ISBN 0-375-72037-5
10 9 8 7 6 5 4 3 2 1
Printed and bound in Italy by Giunti Industrie Grafiche

Editorial Director: Hilary McGlynn
Head of Cartography: Chris Moore
Cartographic Production Manager: Caroline Beckley
Cartographers: Ben Brown, Rachel Hopper, Adam Meara, Nikki Sargeant
Technical Editors: Tracey Auden, Claire Lishman
Production Manager: John Normansell
Production Controller: Stacey Penny
Editor: Alexa Stace
Copy Editor: Robert Armstrong
Illustration: Sienna Artworks
Text Design: Michael Leaman, Paul Saunders

Photograph credits: p8/9 Ecoscene, p11 NASA, p13 R Roger/Science Photo Library,
p15 R Edmaier/Science Photo Library, p17 K Svenson/Science Photo Library,
p18 N Kamine/Science Photo Library, p32/33 PhotoDisk, p40/41 R Stephey/Helicon

CONTENTS

Page		Scale
6	**KEY MAP**	
8-31	**THE CHANGING WORLD**	
10	Our star and our neighbours	
12	The Earth and the Moon	
14	A world in motion	
16	Shaping the Earth	
18	Contrasting conditions	
20	Peopling the globe	
22	The population explosion	
24	Belief and understanding	
26	The world at work	
28	On the move	
30	The legacy of industry	
32-39	**THE BRITISH ISLES**	
33	Key to map symbols	
34	Administrative areas of Great Britain	
35	Ireland	1:1 750 000
36	Great Britain: North	1:1 750 000
38	Great Britain: South	1:1 750 000
40-43	**THE WORLD**	
41	Key to map symbols	
42	World	1:112 000 000
44-71	**EUROPE**	
46	Europe	1:20 200 000
48	Scandinavia	1:5 800 000
50	Central Europe	1:3 450 000
52	Germany	1:2 600 000
54	Benelux	1:2 300 000
56	British Isles	1:3 450 000
58	France	1:3 450 000
60	Spain and Portugal	1:3 450 000
62	The Alpine States	1:2 600 000
64	Italy	1:3 450 000
66	The Balkans	1:3 450 000
68	Greece and Western Turkey	1:3 450 000
70	European Russia	1:10 400 000
72-95	**ASIA**	
74	Asia	1:32 900 000
76	Northwest Asia	1:13 800 000
78	Northeast Asia	1:13 800 000
80	Eastern China	1:11 600 000
82	Japan and Korea	1:5 800 000
84	Southeast Asia	1:11 600 000
86	Malaysia and Indonesia	1:11 600 000
88	Southern Asia	1:11 600 000
90	The Middle East	1:12 700 000
92	Turkey	1:5 800 000
94	Israel and the Gulf States	1:2 850 000
96-109	**AFRICA**	
98	Africa	1:30 000 000
100	Northeast Africa	1:11 600 000
102	Northwest Africa	1:11 600 000
104	West Africa	1:11 600 000
106	Central Africa	1:11 600 000
108	Southern Africa	1:11 600 000
110-117	**OCEANIA**	
112	Oceania	1:40 500 000
114	Australia	1:13 800 000
116	New Zealand	1:4 650 000
118-135	**NORTH AMERICA**	
120	North America	1:34 700 000
122	Canada	1:13 800 000
124	United States	1:15 500 000
126	Northwest United States	1:7 200 000
128	Northeast United States	1:7 200 000
130	Southeast United States	1:7 200 000
132	Southwest United States	1:7 200 000
134	Central America and the Caribbean	1:16 100 000
136-143	**SOUTH AMERICA**	
138	South America	1:28 000 000
140	Northern South America	1:16 100 000
142	Southern South America	1:16 100 000
144	**POLAR REGIONS**	
145-176	**NATIONS OF THE WORLD**	
177-244	**INDEX**	
177	How to use the index	
178	Glossary	
179	Index	

KEY MAP

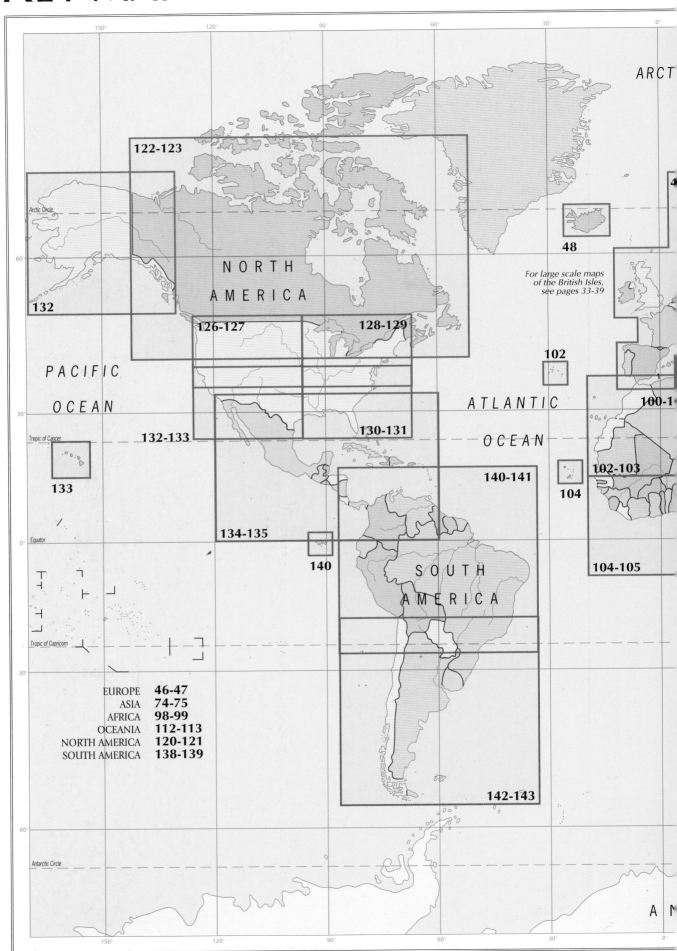

ARCT

122-123

132

48

For large scale maps of the British Isles, see pages 33-39

NORTH
AMERICA

126-127

128-129

102

PACIFIC

OCEAN

ATLANTIC

100-1

30°

OCEAN

Tropic of Cancer

132-133

130-131

133

140-141

102-103

104

Equator

134-135

140

SOUTH

104-105

AMERICA

Tropic of Capricorn

30°

EUROPE	46-47
ASIA	74-75
AFRICA	98-99
OCEANIA	112-113
NORTH AMERICA	120-121
SOUTH AMERICA	138-139

142-143

60°

Antarctic Circle

A

150°

120°

90°

60°

30°

0°

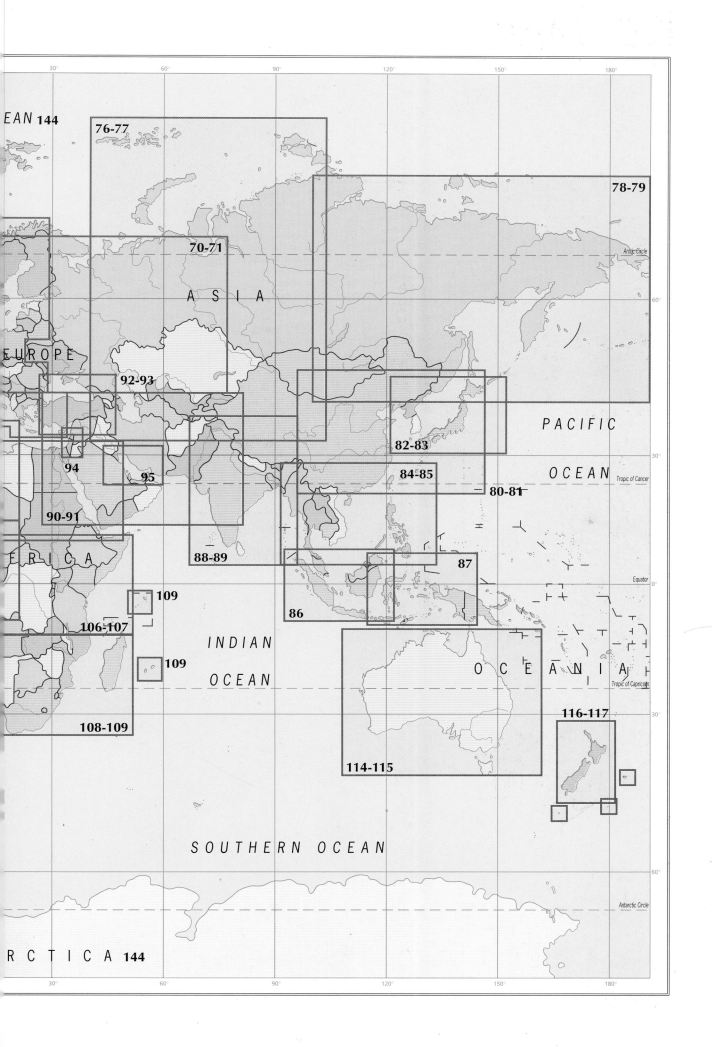

EAN **144**

76-77

78-79

Arctic Circle

60°

A S I A

70-71

EUROPE

92-93

PACIFIC

94

95

OCEAN

30°

Tropic of Cancer

82-83

84-85

80-81

90-91

RICA

88-89

87

86

Equator 0°

109

106-107

INDIAN

109

O C E A N I A

OCEAN

Tropic of Capricorn

30°

108-109

114-115

116-117

SOUTHERN OCEAN

60°

Antarctic Circle

RCTICA **144**

30°   60°   90°   120°   150°   180°

THE CHANGING WORLD

OUR STAR & OUR NEIGHBOURS

THE EARTH IS ONE MEMBER of a Solar System of nine planets orbiting our local star – the Sun. All these bodies formed from a single cloud of gas and dust around 4.5 billion years ago as it was compressed, possibly by shockwaves from a giant supernova explosion. The centre of the cloud collapsed most rapidly, becoming denser and attracting more material until eventually it reached a point so hot and dense that nuclear reactions began inside it. These reactions continue today and are the source of the sunlight that heats our planet and sustains life. The Sun is critical to the regulation of our climate and environment – fine alterations in Earth's orbit are thought to cause periodic ice ages, so we are fortunate that the Sun is not likely to change drastically for another 5 billion years.

On a shorter scale, the Sun's output does have slight fluctuations. A cycle of sunspot formation (comparatively cool regions of the Sun's surface caused by magnetic activity), reaches a maximum every 11 years. From 1645–1705 almost no sunspots were seen, a dip in solar activity which coincided with a 'mini-Ice Age' of unusually low temperatures on Earth.

Once the Sun had formed, a disk of material would have been left outside the newly-formed star, which condensed to form the planets. Particles in the gas and dust cloud collided and stuck together, becoming increasingly larger bodies. Eventually these 'proto-planets' were pulled into a spherical shape by their increasing gravity.

The Solar System we see today reflects the composition of that gas and dust cloud, and divides into two regions. The inner portion contains the four terrestrial (Earth-like) planets – from Mercury orbiting close to the Sun, through Venus and Earth, to Mars. Beyond the orbit of Mars lies the asteroid belt, a ring of rocky debris, outside which are the gas giants, enormous planets created where the cloud bulged with huge quantities of gas.

The inner rocky worlds
The terrestrial planets are all very different. Mercury is a small, baking world, quite similar to our own Moon, and covered in craters. Venus is shrouded in a thick atmosphere of carbon

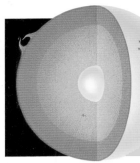

▶ THE SUN
The Sun is a massive ball of hydrogen gas [B], 1.39 million km across. Energy is generated at its heart, where temperatures exceed 15 million°C, by nuclear fusion – the joining together through a chain reaction of two hydrogen atoms to form one helium. In the process, a large amount of excess energy is released, carried to the surface of the Sun in giant convection cells, and then radiated across the Solar System from the top of

the 'photosphere' – the visible disk of the Sun, with a temperature of 5500°C.

◀ THE SOLAR SYSTEM
The solar system consists of 9 planets [A]: Pluto [1], the smallest, is the furthest away from the Sun, though once in every 248.6 years its orbit crosses inside Neptune's path. Neptune [2], the outermost of the gas giants, has a diameter of 49,400km, and orbits every 164.8 years.

Uranus [3] is similar in size to Neptune and orbits every 84 years. All the gas giants have ring systems, but Uranus's are second only to Saturn's. The planet is tilted at over 98° to the plane of the

A

dioxide and toxic molecules, with a surface pressure 95 times that of Earth's atmosphere, and temperatures of 470°C. Beyond the Earth's orbit, Mars is famous as the Red Planet – a colour given by rust in its surface dust. Although smaller than Earth, there is evidence that Mars once had a thick atmosphere, and that water ran on its surface – although now it is frozen into polar ice-caps.

The gas giants

The outer Solar System contains worlds quite different from those nearer the Sun – the gas giants. Largest of these is Jupiter, more massive than all the other planets in the Solar System put together, with churning weather systems that include the Great Red Spot, a storm large enough to engulf Earth. Beyond Jupiter lies Saturn, with its spectacular ring system of icy particles, and then the smaller giants Uranus and Neptune. Space probes have shown that Jupiter, Uranus and Neptune also have thin ring systems, although these are nothing to match Saturn's spectacle.

All four of these worlds have large families of moons orbiting round them. Jupiter has a vast family of moons, including Io, the most volcanic body in the Solar System, whose eruptions launch yellow plumes of sulphur into space, scarring its surface with streaks. The most interesting member of Uranus's satellite system is Miranda – a small, deeply-cratered world which displays so many variations in terrain that it must have suffered some great cataclysm in the past. Neptune's giant satellite Triton has active geysers shooting water, ammonia and methane 8km above its surface.

surface in its past. Next in towards the Sun is our own blue planet, the Earth [8], with a diameter of 12,700km. Within the orbit of the Earth lies its near twin Venus [9], circling the Sun in 225 days, and with a diameter of 12,100km. The atmosphere of Venus, however, is a poisonous mixture of carbon dioxide and other gases, with clouds of sulphuric acid. Mercury [10] is the second smallest planet with a diameter of only 4,880km, and a solar orbit that lasts 88 days. Its proximity to the Sun (58 million km) makes it a scorched world with no atmosphere, and a cratered surface similar to that of the Moon. It orbits the Sun once every 88 days.

Solar System, so it seems to roll around its orbit. Saturn [4] is noted for its spectacular ring system – the planet has a diameter of 105,000km, while the rings stretch out to 300,000km. It orbits the Sun every 29.5 years, and has a huge family of satellites.

Jupiter [5] orbits the Sun every 11.9 years. With a diameter of 137,400km it is the largest planet in the Solar System. It has complex weather systems, including the Great Red Spot, a storm with a diameter larger than the Earth's.

Between Jupiter and Mars is the asteroid belt [6], rocky debris left over from the Solar System's formation. Inside it lie the terrestrial planets. Mars [7], the red planet, circles the Sun in 1.9 years, and has a diameter of 6790km. Its surface is scoured by massive dust storms, and it shows evidence of running water on the

◀ *The Sun is just one of over 200 billion stars in the vast spiral of the Milky Way galaxy, like every other star that we see with the naked eye in the night sky. It lies roughly two-thirds of the way towards the edge of the galactic disc, orbiting the centre at a speed of 250 kilometres per second, taking 200 million years to complete each revolution. This view is what the galaxy would look like to an observer outside. But because of our position in the plane, we see the dense star clouds as a pale band across the sky.*

THE EARTH & THE MOON

THE EARTH'S SATELLITE, THE MOON, IS SO LARGE by comparison with our own world (at 3746km, it is over one-quarter the Earth's diameter) that astronomers consider the two together as a 'double planet'. This massive size and proximity means that the Moon has a great influence on the Earth itself, for example through the tides.

The origins of the Moon are open to debate – some believe that the Moon is a chunk of debris flung off when the still-molten Earth collided with another body the size of Mars, in the early days of the Solar System. Since then, the two bodies have had very different histories. The Moon's small size meant that it cooled more quickly and its low gravity made it unable to hold onto an atmosphere – the factor which has been crucial in shaping our own planet's terrain. In fact, the Moon has altered so little that it provides valuable information about the history of the early Solar System. The lack of an atmosphere also means that, unlike Earth, the Moon is not shielded from the extremes of heat from the Sun. Temperatures at noon climb to 150°C, while at night they can plummet to -200°C. These acute differences can even cause moonquakes as the surface stretches and contracts.

A familiar face

The Moon's surface divides into two distinct types of terrain, which can be easily distinguished with the naked eye from Earth. The bright highlands are highly cratered areas created more than 4 billion years ago during an era of bombardment by rock particles from space. The numbers of these particles dwindled until only a few massive chunks were left, which created enormous impact basins as they crashed into the Moon's surface. The gnarled highlands contrast sharply with the smoother, darker Maria (from the Latin for seas). After the cratering had died away, the Moon seems to have undergone a brief period of intense volcanic activity. Red-hot fissures opened up across its surface, out of which huge volumes of lava poured, flooding low-lying areas. These lava lakes solidified to form the Maria, marked by only a few, very small craters.

Lunar attraction

The changing direction of the Sun and Moon from Earth cause our monthly cycle of tides. Twice a month, at full and new moon, the high Spring Tides occur, with Moon and Sun lined up, or directly opposed, so the tidal effect is at its strongest. Such tidal effects have influenced the Earth-Moon system as a whole. Over millions of years, the friction of the oceans' movement has slowed the lunar 'day', so it now lasts exactly as long as the time the Moon takes to orbit Earth,with the result that it always keeps the same face turned towards us. Fossil records show that there were once 400 days in each Earth year, so the same effect must also be

▶ STRUCTURE OF THE MOON

The Earth's satellite, the Moon **[B]**, has a structure that reflects its different size, and possibly origin. Because it is a much smaller body – around one-twentieth the volume of the Earth – it has a higher surface area to volume ratio. It cooled down more rapidly early in the history of the Solar System, and is now inactive. The lunar crust [1] is actually thicker than Earth's – an average of 70km, though it is thinner on the Earth-facing side, possibly due to the tidal effects of the Earth's gravity. This could be a possible explanation of why the smooth 'seas' are found far more on this side, formed from eruptions of lava through the thin crust. Beneath this lie layers of solidified, cold rock, which decrease in rigidity. At the centre there may be a cold core [2], although its existence is still debated.

Sunlight

4

Earth

THE STRUCTURE OF THE EARTH

The Earth has the shape of a squashed ball or a spheroid [A]. It has a diameter at the poles of 12,703km, but is wider at the Equator, thrown outward by the rapid daily spin which causes a 'bulge'. The crust [1], on which lie the continents and oceans, is a thin layer of rock varying in depth between 10 and 20km. Below this lies a mantle [2], divided into two regions. The upper mantle extends down to 3000km, and divides into the mainly solid lithosphere and the mostly molten aesthenosphere. Beyond this, the molten rock of the upper and lower mantle extends down towards the molten outer [3] and solid inner [4] cores of iron and nickel, around 7000km across, at the centre of the Earth. It is the rotation of this core that is believed to generate the Earth's magnetic field, in an effect similar to that of a dynamo.

▶ THE EARTH'S SEASONS

The Poles of the Earth are tilted at 23.5° [C]. As it orbits the Sun, different parts of the globe receive a varying amount of sunlight through the year-long cycle of the seasons [3]. For six months of the year, the Northern Hemisphere is tilted towards the Sun, which therefore appears higher in the sky, giving warmer temperatures and longer days [1]. Six months later, when the Northern Hemisphere is tilted in the other direction, the days are shorter

Spring

Winter

Sun

Autumn

Summer

and the Sun stays closer to the horizon [2]. The situation is reversed in the Southern Hemisphere. The Tropics of Cancer and Capricorn are lines

around the globe at the lines of latitude +/- 23.5°. They mark the northernmost and southern-most points where the Sun appears directly overhead.

slowing its rotation as well. Hence in the distant future, the spin of the Earth could be so slow that its day and year are equal, so that one scorched side of the planet will permanently face the Sun.

Complete coverage

Very occasionally, as the Moon orbits around the Earth and it in turn moves around the Sun, all three bodies – Sun, Earth and Moon – line up exactly and an eclipse is seen. If the Earth blocks out the Sun shining onto the full Moon, a rather unspectacular lunar eclipse happens. Far more spectacular are solar eclipses, when the new Moon passes right across the face of the Sun. By chance the Moon and Sun have discs in the sky that are almost the same size. This means that total solar eclipses can only be seen for short periods of time from tiny regions of the Earth. The effect is breathtaking as the Moon covers the bright central disk of the Sun, and reveals the wispy white corona of gas streaming out from the Sun's surface.

D

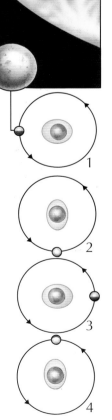

◀ HOW THE MOON BEGAN

The Moon orbits too far from the Earth to be a captured asteroid. Instead, it is thought to have been formed when a body the size of Mars collided with the still-molten Earth during the formation of the Solar System, some 5 billion years ago [1].

The collision resulted in a stream of debris being thrown off into orbit round the Earth [2], and this eventually condensed to form the Moon [3]. The iron-rich cores of the two original bodies combined and remained within the Earth, becoming its very dense central region, whilst the Moon formed from the two lighter outer sections.

This may explain why the Earth is thought to have a more complicated structure than the Moon, and also the lack of iron in Moon rock.

◀ HOW THE MOON AFFECTS THE EARTH'S TIDES

The proximity of the Moon to the Earth, coupled with its size, causes strong gravitational forces between the two worlds, which is shown in the tides [D].

As the Moon exerts a gravitational pull on the Earth, it draws the seas towards it, and creates a bulge in the seawater on one side of the planet. At the same time, the Earth itself is attracted towards the Moon, pulling it away from the sea on the opposite side of the globe

and creating a smaller tidal bulge on the opposite side. Because the Moon is relatively slow-moving, the tidal bulges in the sea remain in almost the same place, while the Earth rotates under them [1,2,3,4]. As each bulge passes a point on the Earth roughly once each day, seashores experience two high and two low tides each day (although the shape of an inlet can alter their spacing). As the Moon circles the Earth once a month, the tides occur at different times each day.

▼ During the brief minutes of the eclipse, the corona of the Sun can be seen.

Normally this is an invisible halo, made up of two distinct regions of gas which overlap, the K-corona and the F-corona. The latter reaches out many millions of kilometres from the Suns surface while the K-corona extends for a mere 75,000km.

A WORLD IN MOTION

WE THINK OF THE GROUND AS BEING STEADY AND IMMOVABLE: in fact the surface of the Earth is in a constant state of movement, propelled by the intense heat of the interior. Although our planet is 12,700km wide, the crust on which the continents and oceans lie is only a few tens of kilometres thick at its deepest. This thin crust is broken into slabs or plates, which float on top of an inner molten layer, the mantle. Where these plates collide with each other or slowly draw apart are areas of violent activity, subject to earthquakes and studded with volcanoes. This drama is not restricted to dry land: satellite photography has shown that the two-thirds of Earth's surface under the ocean is just as fascinating, with features such as chains of volcanic mountains that stretch for 60,000km around the globe.

The idea that the continents are slowly moving was first put forward to explain how the coastlines of different continents appear to fit together like pieces of a jigsaw puzzle. For example, the eastern coast of South America nestles snugly into the western coast of Africa. Such continental drifts can be traced back to a point around 250 million years ago, when all the land masses on Earth were joined into a supercontinent called Pangaea (from the Greek for all earth), surrounded by a single vast sea, the Tethys Ocean. This supercontinent slowly disintegrated into the major land masses we know today.

Geologists call their model for the movements of the Earth's crust plate tectonics. This describes the surface, both continents and ocean floor, as being split into plates whose movements are driven by the churning of the molten rock in the inner mantle. The largest plates are as wide as the Pacific Ocean, while others are much smaller. Their thickness varies from around 10km beneath the oceans, to 30km under major land masses, and up to 60km where a plate has to support the weight of a mountain range. In general, ocean floor plates are made of dense basaltic rocks, while the continents are formed from less dense granite.

Earthquakes

Most of the areas where plates are separating are hidden beneath the ocean. At the fault between the plates molten rock wells up through a fissure and solidifies, creating new ocean floor. Only in a few places can this process be seen on dry land, notably in the volcanoes of Iceland, which sits on a fault called the Mid-Atlantic Ridge.

Plates can meet in a number of ways. At earthquake zones they grind past each other in opposite directions, being compressed so that they store huge amounts of energy. This is released in calamitous movements of the ground – earthquakes. The most famous earthquake zone of all, the San Andreas Fault in California, is a region where the North American and Pacific Plates are moving past each other. Earthquake prediction hinges on the theory that major quakes are preceded by 'quiet' periods during which the plates lock together, and store up the energy. Not all the plate boundaries are earthquake or volcano zones – the Himalayas are the result of a head-on collision between the relatively fast-moving Indo-Australian Plate, and the Eurasian Plate. These two continental plates buckled upwards, forming the mountain range, and halting the Indo-Australian plate's movement.

Conversely, not all volcanoes are at plate boundaries. The volcanic Hawaiian Islands, for

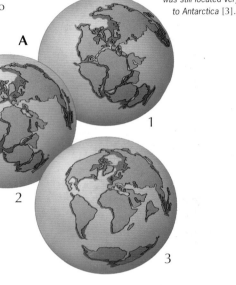

▼ PANGAEA
The continents of the world have not always looked as they do today **[A]**. *The process of plate tectonics means that that they have migrated across the surface of the Earth. 200 million years ago, in the Jurassic era, all the land masses were joined in a single supercontinent, Pangaea [1].*

Eventually, 120 million years ago,

Pangaea split in two, the northern Laurasia made up of present-day North America and Eurasia, and the southern Gondwana, comprising South America, Africa, Australia and India [2].

By 40 million years ago the world had taken on a familiar look, although India had yet to collide with Eurasia (and create the Himalayas in the process) and Australia was still located very close to Antarctica [3].

▼ PLATE TECTONICS
The processes of plate tectonics can be seen most clearly on a section of ocean floor **[B]**. *At a subduction zone [1], an oceanic plate meets a much thicker continental plate and is forced down into the Earth's upper mantle. The heat in this zone melts the upper basalt layer of the oceanic plate, forming liquid magma which then rises to the surface and is vented through volcanoes.*

At a mid-oceanic ridge [2] new crust is constantly being generated where two plates are separating. Magma rises up from the Earth's mantle, forcing its way through cracks in the crust, and solidifying.

As the cracks expand, a striated ocean floor is formed. When the new crust solidifies, traces of iron in it align with the Earth's magnetic field and so preserve a record of the various reversals in the field over millions of years.

A hot spot volcano [3] forms where the crust thins above a hot plume rising from the inner mantle. It is only the latest in a string of volcanoes that form as the oceanic plate moves over the stationary plume. The earlier volcanoes become extinct, subsiding to volcanic islands with coral fringes, and eventually become atolls, where only the ring of coral remains above the surface of the ocean.

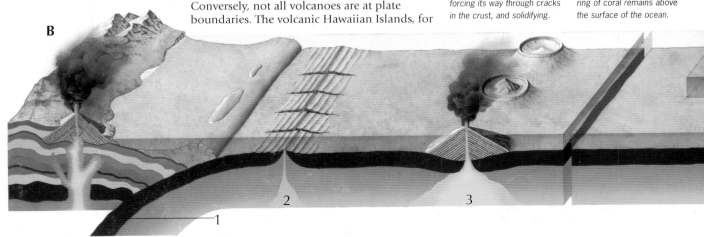

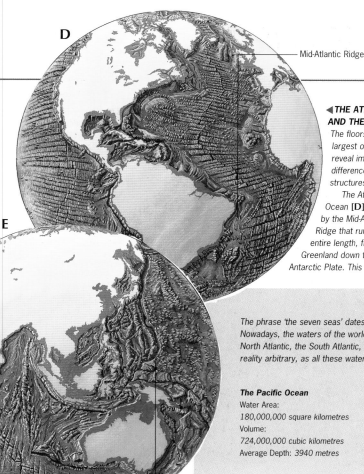

D

Mid-Atlantic Ridge

E

◄ THE ATLANTIC AND THE PACIFIC

The floors of the two largest oceans reveal important differences in their structures.

The Atlantic Ocean **[D]** is divided by the Mid-Atlantic Ridge that runs for its entire length, from Greenland down to the Antarctic Plate. This is a region where the Earth's crust is stretching, new floor being pumped out so that the Atlantic is gradually widening. As the rock is pulled apart, large slabs sink, creating the series of rifts that run parallel to the ridge along its length. Only in a few places does the ridge emerge above the sea, most spectacularly in Iceland, the shape of which is constantly being redefined by volcanic activity.

In contrast, the floor of the Pacific Ocean **[E]** shows signs of many different seismic activities. It is surrounded by the so-called 'ring of fire' – volcanic zones where the oceanic plates dive below continental ones and create volcanoes. At other places, oceanic plates converge, creating trenches where one plate dives below the other, such as the Marianas Trench, the deepest place on Earth.

THE SEVEN SEAS

The phrase 'the seven seas' dates back to the seas known to Muslim voyagers before the fifteenth century. Nowadays, the waters of the world are divided into seven oceans – the North Pacific, the South Pacific, the North Atlantic, the South Atlantic, the Indian, the Arctic and the Antarctic. But divisions such as these are in reality arbitrary, as all these waters can just as easily be considered as parts of one continuous global ocean.

The Pacific Ocean
Water Area:
180,000,000 square kilometres
Volume:
724,000,000 cubic kilometres
Average Depth: 3940 metres

The Atlantic Ocean
Water Area:
106,000,000 square kilometres
Volume:
355,000,000 cubic kilometres
Average Depth: 3310 metres

The Indian Ocean
Water Area:
75,000,000 square kilometres
Volume:
292,000,000 cubic kilometres
Average Depth: 3840 metres

Marianas Trench

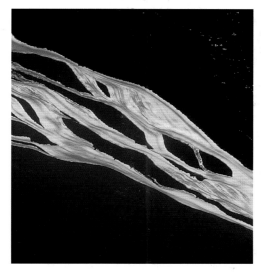

◄ Lava which erupts from the earth's surface can take on a number of forms Aa, or block lava, is runny, and quickly forms a hard pastry-like crust when it cools. Pahoehoe lava has a sheen to it like satin and often consolidates in rope-like forms. When this kind of lava comes into contact with the sea it takes on the form of a jumbled heap of pillows, hence its name pillow lava.

▼ SEA CHANGE

A coastal region **[C]** is shaped by the forces of longshore drift. Sand is pushed along the shore by ocean currents to build up spits [1], bars [2] and sometimes enclosing bays to form lagoons.

A river carries vast amounts of sediment out to sea, which is deposited to form a delta [3]. Under the sea, the accumulation of sediment forms the continental shelf [4], a region that slopes gently out from the coastline for about 75km, to depths of 100-200m. In places it is cut through by submarine gorges, formed either by rivers when the sea level was lower or by the undercutting effect of river currents flowing out to sea. The shelf gives way to the steep continental slope, which dives to depths of several kilometres. From the base of the slope, the continental rise extends up to 1000km from the coast into the ocean.

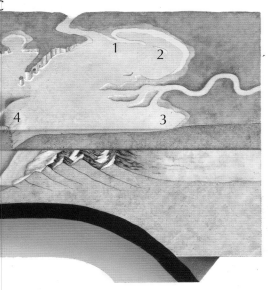

C

1

2

4

3

instance, lie in the middle of the Pacific Plate. This chain of volcanic mountains is caused by a semi-permanent 'hot spot' where molten magma rises from the depths of the mantle through the crust, and spews out of a volcano. Although the hot spot in the mantle is stationary, the Pacific Plate, and with it the volcano, is continually moving. Hawaii itself is only the most recent in a chain of 107 volcanic vents formed by the plume. As the plate moves on, each volcano becomes extinct, and a new one forms further along the chain. Many thousands of these 'hot spot' volcanoes are known – mostly beneath the ocean surface – so there must be hundreds of hot plumes in the mantle to have created them all.

While plates are being destroyed in the subduction zones where they collide, new plate material is being produced all the time deep beneath the ocean surface. The sea floor is just as geologically fascinating as the continental land surface, and is still awaiting full exploration.

Occasionally, the volcanic activity of the mid-oceanic ridges reaches the surface, and forms islands. At other places, hot gases venting from the depths of the Earth create pools of warmth on the ocean floor, where life can flourish.

SHAPING THE EARTH

OVER BILLIONS OF YEARS, THE HARSH landscape created by geological activity such as plate tectonics and volcanism has been softened and sculpted by the eroding forces of ice, water and air. Glaciers have ground out valleys, and rivers have carved huge gorges, including America's Grand Canyon. At the same time the steady pounding of the seas and oceans eats away and remodels coastlines.

Studies of the changing climate in the past show that the Earth has gone through periodic 'ice ages' when the ice-caps pushed into temperate regions closer to the Equator. These periods were critical in shaping the landscape that we see today – during the last Ice Age, which ended 10,000 years ago, an ice sheet covered most of Northern Europe, Asia and North America. The ice ages can be dated by drilling out an ice core from a polar cap. Each year a layer of new ice is laid down, which in colder years – during ice ages – is thicker. These records surprisingly reveal that over the last 4 million years, successive ice ages have gripped Earth for longer than the warmer periods in between.

Variations in the Earth's climate are thought to be the result of cyclical changes in its orbit, which becomes more, then less, elongated. According to these models the Earth's average temperature should currently be on the increase – which means that the measured increases in temperature cited as evidence of global warming and the greenhouse effect may have a natural cause.

Getting in shape

During the ice ages, massive glaciers formed across the globe. As these vast, slow-moving rivers of ice rolled forward, the sheer weight of ice ground down rocks in their paths, leaving a softened, altered landscape once they had retreated. These forces are still at work today: on Greenland and in Antarctica there are many glaciers which eventually find their way to the sea, where they break up into icebergs.

Although glaciers are the most dramatic form of erosion, there are others: over longer periods, rivers and seas can cut through rock and carve out valleys. Even rain has a profound cumulative effect on rock. Raindrops dissolve gases from the atmosphere and become dilute acid, chemically attacking igneous rocks formed from volcanic lava. In time, the particles broken off build up to great depths and are converted by pressure and heat into sedimentary rocks such as limestone. When these are subjected to the intense heat of the Earth's crust they become metamorphic rocks, such as marble and slate.

▶ **EARTH SCRAPER**
Glaciers [A] *are dramatic rivers of ice slowly creeping down valleys and carving mountain ranges into a series of sharp peaks. They usually originate where ice or hard-packed snow builds up in a cirque* [1], *a basin near a mountain top. After a sufficient mass has built up, it will start to move under its own gravity, wearing down rocks by pressure, scraping and frost action, to form glacial spoil called 'moraines'. The boulders of moraine underneath the glacier act as abrasives, scouring the landscape. Lateral moraines* [2] *are rocks cut away and pulled along at the sides of the glacier. Where two ice-rivers meet, the lateral moraines can join to form a medial moraine* [3] – *a stripe of rubble down the centre of the glacier. As the glacier grinds along over rocks and boulders, the stresses induced can open up deep and jagged splits called crevasses* [4]. *A glacier terminates at a snout* [5] *which may empty into the sea, or a great lake. On dry land the shape of the snout depends on the climatic conditions, and especially the rate at which the snout melts compared with the rate at which the glacier advances. If the the two rates are exactly*

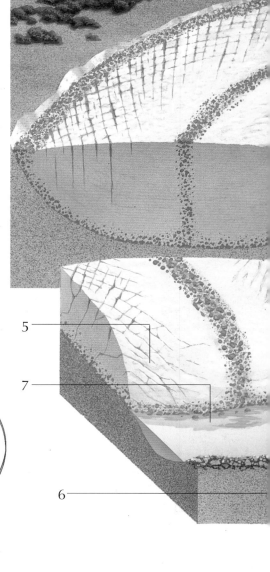

▼ **A WOBBLING WORLD**
The climate of the Earth is not constant but gradually varies over time in cycles of thousands of years [B]. *The shape of the Earth's orbit around the Sun can vary between an almost perfect circle* [1] *and a pronounced ellipse* [2] *over a cycle of around 100,000 years. When the orbit is more elliptical, the climate of the Earth is more extreme. At the same time, another cycle changes the angle of tilt of the planet between a minimum 21.8° and a maximum 24.4°* [C]. *At the maximum inclination, every 22,000 years, the climate is most extreme, and the seasons are especially marked, with the Poles pointing further away from the Sun during winter. When the effects of these cycles are combined, they lead to ice ages of varying severity, the last of which ended around 10,000 years ago.*

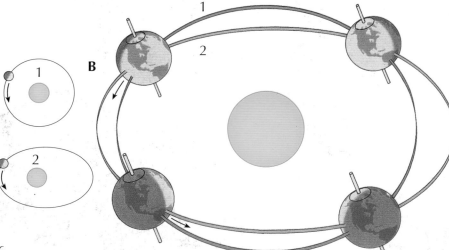

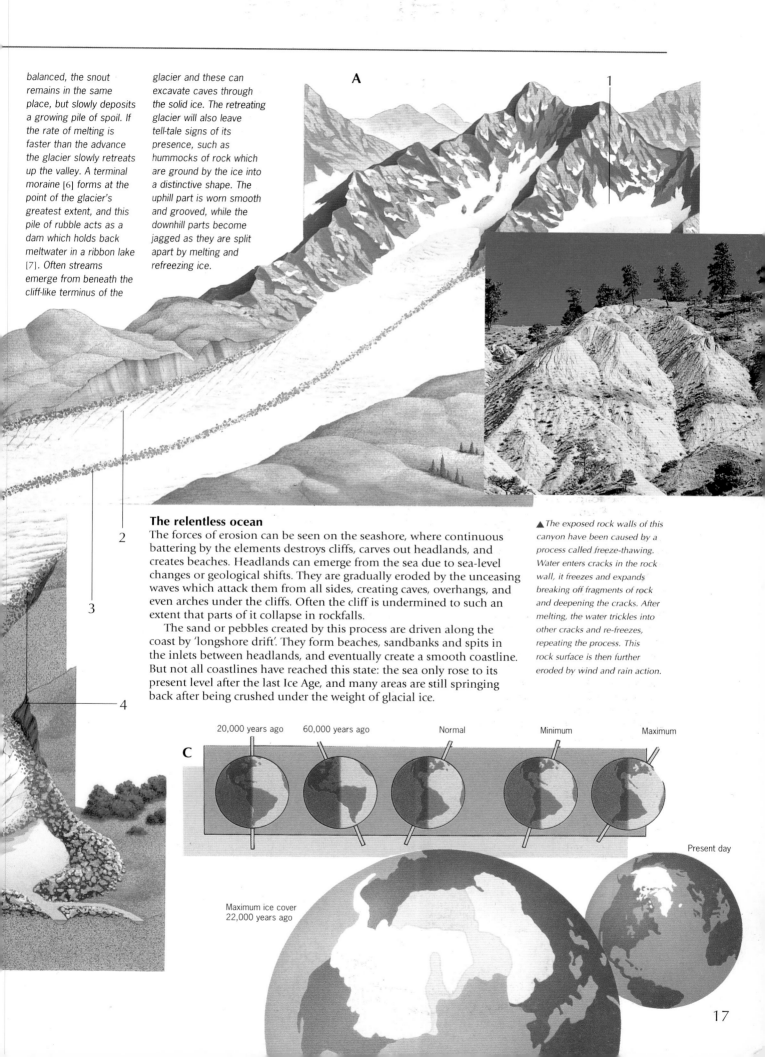

balanced, the snout remains in the same place, but slowly deposits a growing pile of spoil. If the rate of melting is faster than the advance the glacier slowly retreats up the valley. A terminal moraine [6] forms at the point of the glacier's greatest extent, and this pile of rubble acts as a dam which holds back meltwater in a ribbon lake [7]. Often streams emerge from beneath the cliff-like terminus of the glacier and these can excavate caves through the solid ice. The retreating glacier will also leave tell-tale signs of its presence, such as hummocks of rock which are ground by the ice into a distinctive shape. The uphill part is worn smooth and grooved, while the downhill parts become jagged as they are split apart by melting and refreezing ice.

The relentless ocean

The forces of erosion can be seen on the seashore, where continuous battering by the elements destroys cliffs, carves out headlands, and creates beaches. Headlands can emerge from the sea due to sea-level changes or geological shifts. They are gradually eroded by the unceasing waves which attack them from all sides, creating caves, overhangs, and even arches under the cliffs. Often the cliff is undermined to such an extent that parts of it collapse in rockfalls.

The sand or pebbles created by this process are driven along the coast by 'longshore drift'. They form beaches, sandbanks and spits in the inlets between headlands, and eventually create a smooth coastline. But not all coastlines have reached this state: the sea only rose to its present level after the last Ice Age, and many areas are still springing back after being crushed under the weight of glacial ice.

▲ The exposed rock walls of this canyon have been caused by a process called freeze-thawing. Water enters cracks in the rock wall, it freezes and expands breaking off fragments of rock and deepening the cracks. After melting, the water trickles into other cracks and re-freezes, repeating the process. This rock surface is then further eroded by wind and rain action.

A

1

2

3

4

C

20,000 years ago 60,000 years ago Normal Minimum Maximum

Present day

Maximum ice cover 22,000 years ago

17

CONTRASTING CONDITIONS

WE TALK SO MUCH ABOUT THE WEATHER because of its infinite changeability. As the Sun's radiation heats up the Equatorial zones of the planet much more than the Polar regions, it creates wide temperature contrasts. The hottest places on Earth can be a blistering 50°C in the shade, while in the depths of an Antarctic winter, levels as low as -70°C have been recorded. This variable heat produces hot air at the Equator, which rises, while cooler air further north and south sinks under it, producing wind patterns that stretch across the globe. These in turn create swirling eddies of air that can absorb water vapour over the sea, forming clouds, and deposit it as rain over land. Such air currents couple with the variable heat of the Sun to produce the wide variety of climates found on Earth, ranging from hot, rainless deserts to cool, wet, temperate coastal regions.

The atmosphere of the Earth just after it formed was an unbreatheable mixture of hydrogen and helium. In time this was replaced by an equally unbreatheable mixture belched out from volcanoes, which in turn has been modified by lifeforms to the air we breathe today. This is made up of 78 per cent nitrogen, 21 per cent oxygen, and a small proportion of carbon dioxide, which plants then recycle into oxygen. The remainder of the atmosphere is water vapour and small traces of other gases. The balance is a delicate one, perfectly suited to life as it has evolved, and the entire planet – both living things and minerals – is needed to maintain it.

The outer limits of the atmosphere stretch 2400 km above the surface, but the lower 15km, the troposphere, is the densest, holding nearly all the atmosphere's water vapour – which condenses under different conditions to create clouds. Beyond this region, up to 40 km high, lies the stratosphere, which contains a thin ozone layer that blocks out harmful ultraviolet radiation.

Climate types

Land near the Equator has weather patterns typified by those of southern Asia. For six months of the year cold dry winds blow from the land out to sea, giving arid conditions and little rain. In the summer the wind reverses direction and starts to blow warm air off the ocean. This air is heavy with water vapour and triggers torrential rainstorms over land.

Weather in the temperate latitudes of northern Europe is dominated by the jet stream, a band of high winds at altitudes of about 12km. It forms where warm air from the tropics meets cold Polar air, creating a jet of air travelling at speeds around 200kmh in summer, 400kmh in winter. The jet stream's direction develops in a similar way to a slowly flowing river, meandering and forming eddies. These are seen as high-pressure anticyclones, wind systems that create clear, dry weather, or low pressure depressions with associated clouds and weather fronts.

The circulation patterns of the oceans are just as important in regulating climate. In general, the oceans circulate in large eddies, clockwise in the Northern Hemisphere, anticlockwise in the Southern. One of the

— Hadley cell

A

▲ **CREATING WINDS**
The amount of heat absorbed at the Equator is much greater than at the Poles. The temperature difference creates giant circulation cells which transfer heat from the Equator to the Poles [A]. The Hadley cell is driven by hot air rising from the Equator which cools and returns to the surface at 30° latitude. Some of this returning air is drawn back towards the Equator, creating the trade winds. The Ferrel cell guides warm air towards the Poles, creating winds which

the Earth's rotation skews to become the Westerlies. Where these winds meet cold air blowing directly from the Pole, frontal depressions form giving unsettled weather. At the cell boundaries jet streams form – channels of high winds which encircle the planet. This circulation from the Equator to the Poles is complicated by the Earth's rotation, creating the Coriolis force which bends winds to the right in the Northern Hemisphere, and to the left in the Southern Hemisphere.

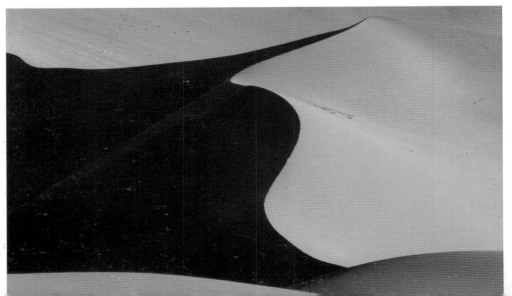

▶ Deserts can be created in many ways, and they may be hot or cold. The Antarctic, being one of the driest places in the world, is classed as a cold desert. The Sahara and the Arabian Deserts are classic examples of hot deserts. The photograph shows a sand dune system in the Namib Desert in Southern Africa.
Winds blowing over the land constantly shift dunes in ever changing patterns.

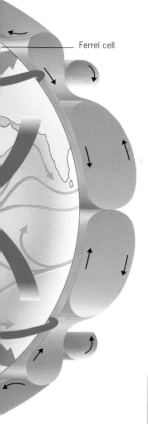

Ferrel cell

▶ *A tornado can form during a very severe thunderstorm* **[C]**. *Hot air evaporating off land or sea rises rapidly through the atmosphere, condensing to form clouds. As surface air rushes inward the low pressure at the centre of the storm, the spin of the Earth makes the whole complex spin, producing a typhoon or hurricane (right). Tornadoes occur when the fast-rising thermals, which create a storm, begin to spin even more quickly, perhaps in response to the local geography. As the thermal winds up on itself, it draws a funnel of cloud down from the bottom of the storm towards the ground, where the winds often exceed 200kmh. The extreme low pressure sucks up material from the ground, flinging it out at the top of the* tornado, *sometimes to land several kilometres away. Waterspouts are similar vortices that form over water.*

C

▶ VARIETY OF CLIMATE

The patterns of rainfall and temperature around the world divide the Earth into different regions of vegetation **[B]**. *Seven cities around the world illustrate the wide variety of weather these produce.*

New York has an east coast continental climate, with cold winters, hot summers and steady rainfall all year round. London's climate is marine west coast, similarly wet to New York's but with less variation between summer and winter temperatures. Omsk has typical steppe climate, with low rainfall and very cold winters followed by hot summers. Singapore's tropical climate gives almost constant hot and very wet weather. Manaus in Brazil's region of tropical savanna has constant high temperatures, with very dry summer months. A desert climate like that of Alice Springs has very high average temperatures (with a slight dip during the southern winter months), but almost no rain throughout the year. The Nigerian capital, Lagos, has a constantly hot tropical rainforest climate, characterized by its extremely wet summer months.

B

New York | London | Omsk | Singapore

Rainfall cm: 45 40 35 30 25 20 15 10 5
Temperature C: 40 30 20 10 0 -10

Manaus | Alice Springs | Lagos

Rainfall cm: 45 40 35 30 25 20 15 10 5
Temperature C: 40 30 20 10 0 -10

- Deciduous forest
- Steppe
- Evergreen forest
- Tropical rainforest
- Tropical savanna
- Desert
- Tundra

best-known currents is the Gulf Stream, which crosses the Atlantic towards northern Europe, moderating the climate with warm water carried from the Gulf of Mexico, counteracting the Polar air blowing over the rest of the continent.

Another example of the oceanic effect on the weather is El Niño. Normally, the circulation of the Pacific Ocean creates cold, dry weather on the west coast of South America, and rain on the east coast of Australia. Air and water currents circulate warm surface water westwards to Australia, raising sea levels and creating an upwelling of deep cold water off South America. But as the warm water spreads eastwards it destabilizes the trade winds, which reverse their direction. The ocean circulation reverses as well, with warm water off South America preventing the cold upwelling which brings up nutrients vital to fish stocks. On land, Australia experiences drought, and South America suffers torrential rain. Such drastic climatic changes show how delicate the balance is between climate and the environment.

Major volcanic eruptions can also affect the climate, throwing dust particles high into the upper atmosphere, where they block out sunlight. Sudden climate changes are believed to have caused mass extinction of life on Earth in the past, and as yet there is little humanity can do to counter, or even predict, these changes.

PEOPLING THE GLOBE

THE ORIGINS OF HUMANKIND ARE VERY HARD TO DETERMINE. The fossil record of our ancestors is very patchy, and thus the story involves large amounts of guesswork. Archaeologists believe that between 7 and 10 million years ago, a human ancestor, called Ramapithecus, developed from the same stock as chimpanzees and gorillas. The route from these creatures to modern man can be traced in terms of changing skeletons. Bipedal motion required a sturdy pelvis, while the increasing intelligence of these progenitors can be followed through increasing brain capacities. Ramapithecus was succeeded by Australopithecus, whose later form is named Homo habilis, the handy man, because fossil evidence shows that it used simple tools.

Homo erectus appeared in Africa 1.7 million years ago and spread to the rest of the world roughly 1 million years ago. They were almost as tall as modern humans, with skull capacities twice as large as Homo habilis. This species lived longer in Asia than in Africa – it includes Peking Man, who lived 250,000 years ago. It was gradually succeeded by our species, Homo sapiens, which appeared in Africa more than 500,000 years ago. The expansion was a slow drift as bands of hunter-gatherers followed prey animals. There can have been no population pressure: 10,000 years ago the world population was between 5 and 10 million, about the population of New York City today. As people settled in various places, climate and food sources led them to evolve differently. For example, those in very hot Equatorial countries kept a dark skin to protect them from ultraviolet sunlight; those in colder climates developed lighter skins to maximize the effect of a weaker sun – vitamin D, essential to bone growth, is gained from sunlight.

At first only Africa, Asia and the warmer parts of Europe were colonized: America and Australia remained empty for thousands of years. Movement between continental land masses was made possible by climate changes. During the last Ice Age, much of the world's water was locked into the ice caps. Sea levels dropped dramatically, what is now the Bering Strait became a land passage, and vast stretches of ocean became navigable by small boats.

Hunters to farmers

For two million years, human ancestors lived as hunter-gatherers, following a nomadic pattern of life, with a diet of animals and seasonal fruits. This changed between 20,000 and 10,000 years ago with the development of agriculture. About 15,000 years ago, as temperatures rose, primitive

▼ THE ICE AGE

In the Ice Age, parts of Europe were covered in glacial sheets and the North Sea was a great plain [A]. The climate and terrain were very like Alaska today, and herds of reindeer roamed the area. These were a main food source for groups of hunter-gatherers, traces of whom have been found in Europe, mostly in the warmer areas (southern Spain, south-west France and along main rivers). These people followed the deer herds on their grazing migrations, augmenting their diet with small game as well as vegetables, berries and grains. As the climate became warmer various groups settled near coasts to become fisher-gatherers.

A

● Hunter-gatherers
● Fisher-gatherers

◄ HOMO SAPIENS

From central and southern Africa Homo sapiens spread out to populate the whole world [B]. The first migration spread from Africa eastwards across to Asia. Routes branched off to northern Africa and southern Europe. A second wave occurred 15,000 years ago, when glaciation provided a land bridge across the Bering Strait, allowing movement from northern Asia to the Americas.

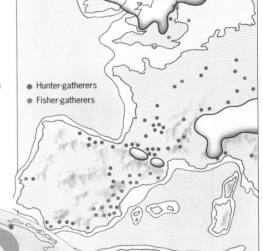

● Evidence of Homo sapiens

▲ Prehistoric Americans

B

C

◄ THE FIRST FARMERS

The first farming settlements, which developed into the first cities, were probably founded around 10,000 years ago in the 'Fertile Crescent' [C], a band of land stretching from the Mediterranean to the rivers Tigris and Euphrates, in modern Jordan, Lebanon, Syria, Turkey and Iraq. Civilisation also flowered along the banks of the river Nile, similarly suited to agriculture. From simple farmsteads grew villages, towns, cities and eventually whole civilisations.

○ Early settlements

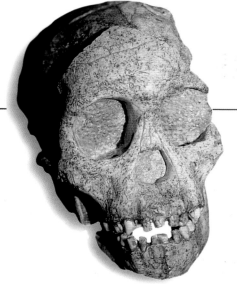

▲ This skull of Australopithicus africanus *is over 2 million years old.* Africanus *was the first hominid to leave the forest for the open plain.*

farming practices began to appear wherever the climate allowed it. The most important of these were Mesopotamia, the crescent between the rivers Tigris and Euphrates in modern Iraq, south-eastern Turkey and eastern Syria, the Nile valley, Central America and north-east China. Once wandering groups settled down the population soared, increasing from 5 to 300 million in 8000 years.

Small farming settlements developed into villages, then towns, then cities. Social and political organisations developed to control large groups of people. Gradually, the great civilisations grew, in the fertile fields of these first settlements. Along the Nile Valley, the Egyptians started to build a sophisticated culture around 3000BC, at the same time as the Sumerians were developing a system of city states in Mesopotamia. Similar civilisations appeared in China and Central America. Influences from these civilisations rippled outwards, laying down the pattern for the shape of the modern world.

▶ **OUT OF AFRICA**

It is now considered that the ancestors of humankind first appeared in Africa **[D]**. As well as indications of early Homo sapiens, the evidence for Africa's claims to be the cradle of humanity comes from fossils of Australopithecus and Homo erectus found in South Africa, Olduvai Gorge in Kenya, and Ethiopia. These are older than any others so far discovered in the world and so it seems likely that the human beings who evolved in Africa gradually spread out to other parts of the world. This is corroborated by fossils of a later date found in India, Java and China which indicate the direction of migration out of Africa. Early Homo sapiens fossils have also been found in China, southern Europe, North and South America and the Middle East. In Europe, the fossils found so far are confined to early forms of Homo sapiens and Neanderthal man, whose traces have been found in Germany, Hungary, France, Belgium, Greece, Czechoslovakia, Russia and the Middle East.

D

▲ Homo erectus
▲ Homo habilis
● Australopithecus
■ Early paleolithic

E

○ Caucasian
○ Mongol
○ Negroid
○ Indian/Caucasian
○ Aboriginal
○ Caucasian/Mongol
○ Negroid/Caucasian

▲ **FIRST MIGRATIONS**

Human beings it seems could not stay long in one place **[E]**. At first, migrations were slow and took place over thousands of years. From their African prototype, people adapted physically, in response to extremes of climate, gradually evolving into the various races that populate the world today. These races developed in certain areas, as shown on the map above, however, the forces of the modern world from the age of discovery onwards created later movements that have spread people around the world. These modern migrations, some voluntary, others enforced as in the slave trade, are also shown.

THE POPULATION EXPLOSION

HERE ARE 6 BILLION PEOPLE IN THE
WORLD TODAY. This figure is rising at a rate
of 140 million each year, an increase of
more than the population of Japan. But until
comparatively recently, the rate of increase of
the world population was low. Two thousand years ago,
there were an estimated 300 million people on Earth; by
1650 this had increased to a mere 500 million. Then in only
200 years this number had doubled, and in the 150 years
since then it has increased five-fold. In spite of recurrent
famine and war, the world population seems set on an
inexorable upward curve, doubling every 39 years.

This population explosion is a result of social developments
since the Industrial Revolution. Proportionally there are the same
number of births each year – or perhaps fewer. But the advances of
improved sanitation and nutrition made possible by the industrial and
scientific advances of the 18th and 19th centuries meant that fewer babies
died at birth and that people lived longer.

At first these changes were confined to the
countries of the developed world, in Europe and
America, but as they have spread around the world,
the population has ballooned. Now in most
European countries the population remains stable,
mainly because of the availability of reliable
contraception. Indeed, in some countries the birth rate
has fallen below the number needed to maintain
stability; this will result in a top-heavy 'age pyramid', with too many
grandparents and not enough grandchildren to support them. Some
countries, such as France and Sweden, have tried to encourage people to
have more babies through maternity payments and tax discounts for large
families.

In the developing world the situation is different. There are many
cultural and religious objections to the use of contraception. In a
traditional agricultural community, too, a large family was desirable.
As well as ensuring that the parents would have surviving children to look
after them, many children provided a workforce to farm the land. But
fewer people now live on the land, as farming becomes mechanized; and a
large family in an urban industrialized setting just creates more mouths to
feed. China, the most populated country in the world, has solved the
problem, rationing families to one child each.

The rush to the cities
All over the world, more people live in cities than in the country, because
it is no longer possible to make a living working on the land.
As a consequence cities have proliferated. The process is not a new one:
after the Industrial Revolution industrial towns gradually expanded until
they merged to form huge conurbations. In terms of
population density, a vast swathe of northern Europe

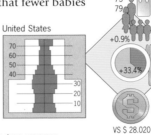

United States

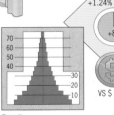

Brazil

B

>100   No of peo
        per sq. kn
11-100
8-10
<2

A

▲ **GLOBAL POPULATION**
The global population is
distributed in clumps and
clusters around the world.
In hotter countries, most
people live on a narrow ribbon
along the coast, leaving vast
arid inner tracts of land
underpopulated. In cooler
countries, the population is
able to spread itself more
evenly about the landmass.
The map makes clear the
huge numbers of people living
all across China and India, in
contrast with the comparatively
sparse population of much of
the United States. The graphics
around illustration [A] show
for each continent the rate of
population growth, the average
longevity of men and women,
the gross national product per
capita (a measure of wealth),
and the calorific intake per

head as a percentage of an
adult's average daily
requirement. These
illustrate the gap in health
and wealth between the
developed world and the
developing nations.

1750

1900

2000

D

▲ **GROWTH 1750–2000**
The growth of the human population
can be shown [D] by demonstrating
the number of people that would
occupy each 2km² of land of the
Earth's surface at various eras:
1750, 1900 and an estimation of
the figure for the year 2000.

▶ **POPULATION GROWTH**
The Earth's population has
swollen from a mere 250
million 1000 years ago (roughly
the present-day population
of the United States) to
6 billion today.

For most of the intervening
period growth was very slow,
and there were even slight
declines caused by plagues

such as the Black Death.
However, from about the time
of the Industrial Revolution the
rate of growth increased,
accelerating further with each
improvement in hygiene and
healthcare.

A graph of world population
growth over the past 300
years [C] can be split to show
how the relative increases in

each continent have been
staggered. Throughout recorded
history, the population of Asia
has been greater than that
of all the other continents
combined. However, during
the 19th century the population
of Europe grew at twice the
rate of Asia's, thanks mainly to
the improvements in living
conditions brought about by

scientific advances and the
Industrial Revolution. This rate
of growth has slowed in
Europe this century, whereas
that of Asia has accelerated
spectacularly – its population
seems likely to have tripled in
the fifty years from 1950.
Over the last two centuries
the populations of North and
South America have been

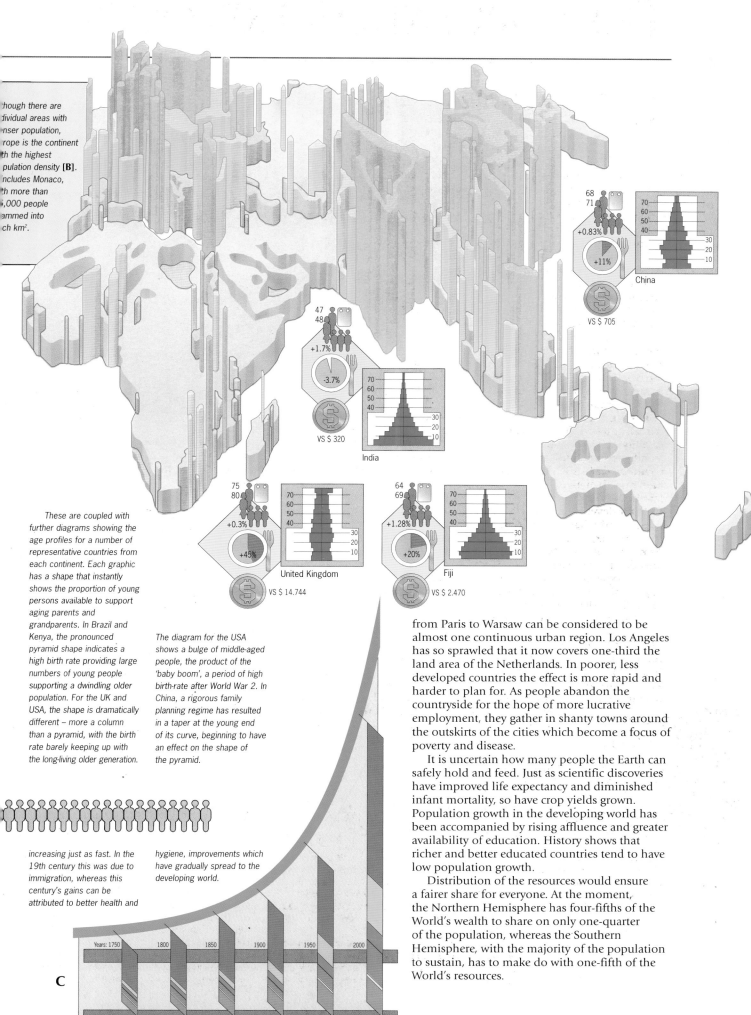

though there are
individual areas with
denser population,
Europe is the continent
with the highest
population density **[B]**.
It includes Monaco,
with more than
5,000 people
rammed into
each km².

68
71
+0.83%
+11%
VS $ 705
China

47
48
+1.7%
-3.7%
VS $ 320
India

75
80
+0.3%
+45%
VS $ 14.744
United Kingdom

64
69
+1.28%
+20%
VS $ 2.470
Fiji

These are coupled with
further diagrams showing the
age profiles for a number of
representative countries from
each continent. Each graphic
has a shape that instantly
shows the proportion of young
persons available to support
aging parents and
grandparents. In Brazil and
Kenya, the pronounced
pyramid shape indicates a
high birth rate providing large
numbers of young people
supporting a dwindling older
population. For the UK and
USA, the shape is dramatically
different – more a column
than a pyramid, with the birth
rate barely keeping up with
the long-living older generation.

The diagram for the USA
shows a bulge of middle-aged
people, the product of the
'baby boom', a period of high
birth-rate after World War 2. In
China, a rigorous family
planning regime has resulted
in a taper at the young end
of its curve, beginning to have
an effect on the shape of
the pyramid.

from Paris to Warsaw can be considered to be
almost one continuous urban region. Los Angeles
has so sprawled that it now covers one-third the
land area of the Netherlands. In poorer, less
developed countries the effect is more rapid and
harder to plan for. As people abandon the
countryside for the hope of more lucrative
employment, they gather in shanty towns around
the outskirts of the cities which become a focus of
poverty and disease.

It is uncertain how many people the Earth can
safely hold and feed. Just as scientific discoveries
have improved life expectancy and diminished
infant mortality, so have crop yields grown.
Population growth in the developing world has
been accompanied by rising affluence and greater
availability of education. History shows that
richer and better educated countries tend to have
low population growth.

Distribution of the resources would ensure
a fairer share for everyone. At the moment,
the Northern Hemisphere has four-fifths of the
World's wealth to share on only one-quarter
of the population, whereas the Southern
Hemisphere, with the majority of the population
to sustain, has to make do with one-fifth of the
World's resources.

increasing just as fast. In the
19th century this was due to
immigration, whereas this
century's gains can be
attributed to better health and

hygiene, improvements which
have gradually spread to the
developing world.

C

Years: 1750   1800   1850   1900   1950   2000

World population   790 million   980   1260   1650   2500   6200

BELIEF & UNDERSTANDING

MODERN COUNTRIES HAVE BEEN SHAPED POLITICALLY by many forces and movements, the most important being religion and language. Religion has been a central aspect of human society since before the earliest written records – fertility sculptures dating from the Ice Age indicate a need to recognize and pacify a spirit that brought forth the sun and rain, made crops grow and ensured a plentiful supply of food. The ancient Near-Eastern civilisations, particularly Egypt, had a multitude of different gods for each aspect of human life or death. This polytheism was continued in the Greek and Roman traditions, in contrast with monotheism, belief in a single all-powerful god, exemplified by Judaism and first recorded around 1200BC.

Today there are eleven major formal religions in the world: Christianity; Judaism; Islam; Hinduism; Buddhism and Jainism; Zoroastrianism; Confucianism; Taoism; Shinto and Sikhism. Of these Christianity is the most widespread, with over a billion followers. It has three major divisions: Roman Catholic, Protestant and Greek Orthodox, and 300 different denominations.

Christianity staked a political claim very early in the history of the developed world, being adopted as the official religion of the Roman Empire in AD324 by the emperor Constantine. The religion instantly changed from being a local Near-Eastern cult to the majority religion of Europe. It became more widespread over 1000 years later through the zeal of European colonists. The Portuguese and Spanish took Catholicism to South America, while the French, English and Dutch brought a variety of denominations to North America. The British took Anglicanism to Africa, India and China and the Dutch took Calvinism to South Africa and Malaysia.

More than words

There are over 3000 spoken languages in the world, a figure that does not include dialects. Of these, just over 100 have more than a million speakers, and only 13 have over 50 million speakers. Some of these are spoken by very large numbers of people (more than 800 million people speak Mandarin Chinese) concentrated in one country. Others – notably Portuguese, Spanish and English – are spoken in many places as a result of the colonial past. Just as explorers brought their religion with them, they also brought their language. Languages spread across the world through different mechanisms today. The growth of international trade has meant that a few languages – mostly English, and to a lesser extent French, Spanish and German – have become standard for business.

The film, television and music industries have been instrumental in making American English understood almost worldwide. American English is also the language of electronics and computing. As electronic communication grows through the Internet and other networks, it is interesting to speculate on what will happen to language in the freedom of cyberspace; perhaps a new, worldwide lingua franca of the Internet will emerge, allowing everyone to communicate as long as they have the technology.

| Christendom |
| Islam |
| Hinduism |
| Local cult |
| Confucianism |
| Buddhism |

▲ **MAIN BELIEF SYSTEMS**
The main illustration shows the distribution of the adherents to the main belief systems of the world [A]. The areas that carry no shading are not dominated by any of these main systems of belief: this does not mean that they are free of religion, merely that they are dominated by local or tribal traditions.

▶ **SPREAD OF RELIGIONS**
The great religions all originated in a comparatively small area of the globe [B], but have spread in different directions to be practised by the majority of the world's population.

Hinduism and Buddhism are the world's oldest religions. Hinduism arose in prehistoric India. Strictly speaking it is not a single religion, but a group of different bodies of belief. Today there are roughly 733 million Hindus worldwide.

Buddhism was founded in the 6th century BC, also in India, but spread eastwards and is now practised in various forms all over East Asia with large numbers of adherents in Tibet, China and Japan. The number of Buddhists in the world has been estimated at 315 million.

Judaism can be traced from before 1200BC. Jewish people have spread sorldwide from Israel, partly driven by periodic persecution. In particular, during the Nazi holocaust, 6 million Jews perished. Today Jews number 18 million worldwide.

Islam was was created in Arabia in the 7th century, and spread through migration, conversion and conquest. There are an estimated 1 billion Muslims worldwide.

Christianity, which also began in Palestine as a Jewish sect, has spread most around the world, through conquest and conversion. Today it is the most popular religion worldwide, the different denominations numbering 1.8 billion adherents.

| Christendom |
| Hinduism |
| Islam |
| Buddhism |
| Judaism |

B

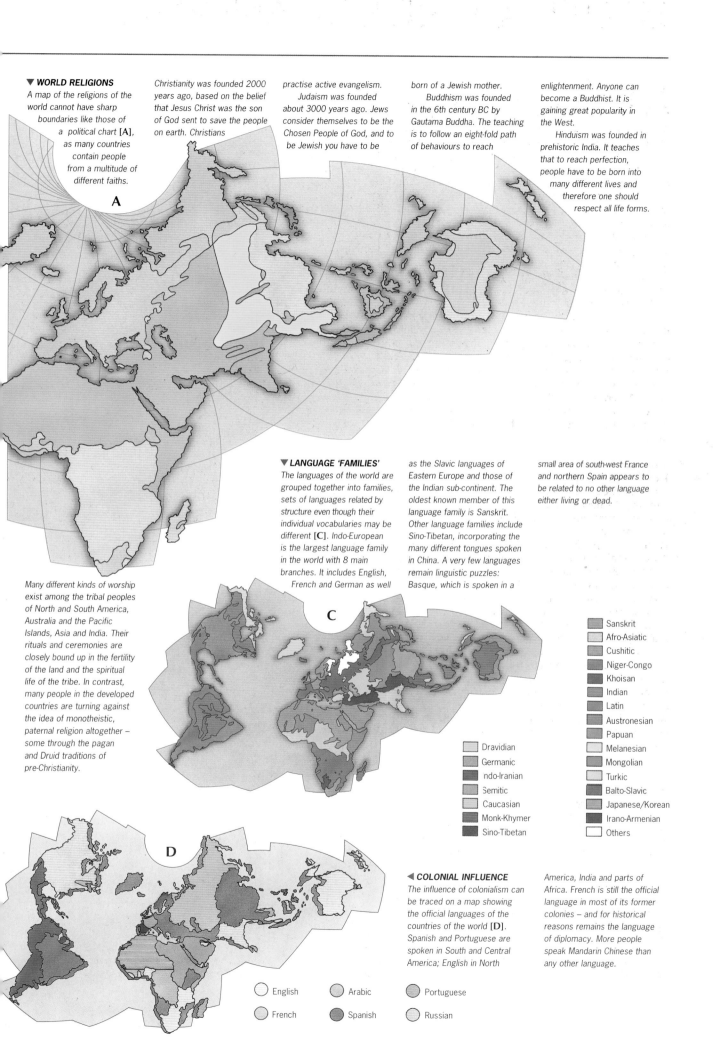

▼ WORLD RELIGIONS

A map of the religions of the world cannot have sharp boundaries like those of a political chart [A], as many countries contain people from a multitude of different faiths.

A

Christianity was founded 2000 years ago, based on the belief that Jesus Christ was the son of God sent to save the people on earth. Christians practise active evangelism.

Judaism was founded about 3000 years ago. Jews consider themselves to be the Chosen People of God, and to be Jewish you have to be born of a Jewish mother.

Buddhism was founded in the 6th century BC by Gautama Buddha. The teaching is to follow an eight-fold path of behaviours to reach enlightenment. Anyone can become a Buddhist. It is gaining great popularity in the West.

Hinduism was founded in prehistoric India. It teaches that to reach perfection, people have to be born into many different lives and therefore one should respect all life forms.

Many different kinds of worship exist among the tribal peoples of North and South America, Australia and the Pacific Islands, Asia and India. Their rituals and ceremonies are closely bound up in the fertility of the land and the spiritual life of the tribe. In contrast, many people in the developed countries are turning against the idea of monotheistic, paternal religion altogether – some through the pagan and Druid traditions of pre-Christianity.

▼ LANGUAGE 'FAMILIES'

The languages of the world are grouped together into families, sets of languages related by structure even though their individual vocabularies may be different [C]. Indo-European is the largest language family in the world with 8 main branches. It includes English, French and German as well as the Slavic languages of Eastern Europe and those of the Indian sub-continent. The oldest known member of this language family is Sanskrit. Other language families include Sino-Tibetan, incorporating the many different tongues spoken in China. A very few languages remain linguistic puzzles: Basque, which is spoken in a small area of south-west France and northern Spain appears to be related to no other language either living or dead.

C

- Dravidian
- Germanic
- ndo-Iranian
- Semitic
- Caucasian
- Monk-Khymer
- Sino-Tibetan

- Sanskrit
- Afro-Asiatic
- Cushitic
- Niger-Congo
- Khoisan
- Indian
- Latin
- Austronesian
- Papuan
- Melanesian
- Mongolian
- Turkic
- Balto-Slavic
- Japanese/Korean
- Irano-Armenian
- Others

D

◄ COLONIAL INFLUENCE

The influence of colonialism can be traced on a map showing the official languages of the countries of the world [D]. Spanish and Portuguese are spoken in South and Central America; English in North America, India and parts of Africa. French is still the official language in most of its former colonies – and for historical reasons remains the language of diplomacy. More people speak Mandarin Chinese than any other language.

- English
- French
- Arabic
- Spanish
- Portuguese
- Russian

THE WORLD AT WORK

THE DEVELOPMENT OF SOCIETY can be looked at as a series of industrial revolutions, as man has learned to use the Earth's resources. Ancient history divides up into three such stages: the Stone Age, when humans first learned to make stone tools and began to practise agriculture; the Bronze Age, when pure metals were first refined and used; and the Iron Age, when man discovered how to extract iron from rock and cast or forge it into tools and weapons.

The greatest industrial leaps have come in the past three centuries. New scientific discoveries led to the construction of the first steam engines, which transformed industry as well as transport. Iron was then overtaken by steel, and the chemical and electrical industries developed. Plastics, electrical transistors and silicon chips became part of everyday life. Each new wave of industries has had a far-reaching effect on society: employment rises and falls, new methods of transport become available and global trade opens up. With each 'revolution' a world economy is brought closer, fuelling an ever-increasing demand for energy.

The source of power

The first Industrial Revolution depended on coal to produce the iron and fire the steam engines. Today, the vast majority of the world's energy still comes from fossil fuels such as coal, oil and natural gas which are a finite resource. Coal is still burnt to generate electricity, supplying about 28 per cent of our total energy needs. The internal combustion engine has created an insatiable demand for petroleum. Today, oil reserves supply 40 per cent of the world's energy, and natural gas 20 per cent. As well as being a finite resource, fossil fuels are a major source of pollution, contributing to the greenhouse effect and the global warming that it brings. In the long term, other sources of energy will have to be found.

Energy alternatives

Nuclear power comes from the splitting of heavy uranium atoms, accompanied by the release of energy in a process called 'fission'. In many countries this energy has been harnessed to electricity needs, but there are many problems, particularly the long-term storage of waste products. Research continues into nuclear fusion, the process which powers the Sun. Although much more difficult to achieve, this could be a cleaner way of generating cheap energy. There are pollution-free energy sources. Hydro-electric power is used in countries such as Switzerland, where water provides more than half of all energy requirements, but it can have a great impact on the environment, flooding valleys and destroying eco-systems. Tidal power exploits the energy of the sea in a similar way. Windmills were one of our earliest sources of power. Today, wind-farms are sited on exposed coasts or on offshore spits, and some countries hope to be able to generate 10–20 per cent of energy needs in this way in the next decade or so. California, for instance, has tens of thousands of wind turbines.

The demand for energy is highest in the USA and western Europe, which are heavily industrialized and also have a large consumer society. At the same time, increasing consumption of oil has led to the rise in power and wealth of Middle-Eastern countries where two-thirds of the world's reserves are located.

A

▲ THE GLOBAL ECONOMY
The engine-houses of today's global economy are those countries that produce the most consumer goods. Map [A] is shaded according to the percentage of each country's total exports that are manufactured goods. It clearly demonstrates that the most successful manufacturing economies are concentrated in the richer northern hemisphere of the world. Almost the whole of Europe and North America have figures over 50%, but the best performers are in Central Europe and the Far East. These include traditionally industrial nations, such as Germany and Japan, as well as fast-growing economies like Korea, Taiwan and the Czech Republic.

The world's biggest producers of food are its largest countries in terms of area and population. However, although there is an overall excess of food, some countries, particularly in Africa, are still susceptible to famine. The reasons for this are both political and environmental. Traditionally farmed areas of land are often cleared to make way for so-called 'cash crops', and instead of using the land for self-sufficiency, an export-driven economy is created, with newly-displaced farmers to support. At the other extreme, the United States farms staple crops successfully on a massive scale, producing surpluses which can then be sold on to smaller countries.

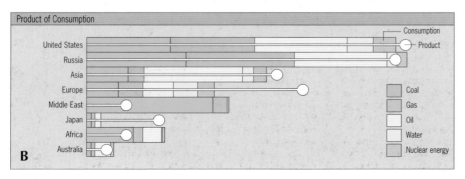

◀ ENERGY
The driving-force of an economy is energy, [B] so the balance between the energy a country produces – in the form of coal, oil and other fuels – and the amount it consumes is vital. This table shows the ratio for the main regions of the world. In many areas the balance is even, but some, such as Europe, produce 12% of world energy, but consume 17%.

▲ Wind turbines, pictured here in Palm Springs in California USA, are being viewed as an increasingly viable way of producing energy. Europe, especially Holland and Germany, has a number of these eco-friendly farms.

Map A legend:
<10%
11-25%
26-50%
51-74%
<75%

Chart B:
Product of Consumption

United States
Russia
Asia
Europe
Middle East
Japan
Africa
Australia

Consumption
Product

Coal
Gas
Oil
Water
Nuclear energy

B

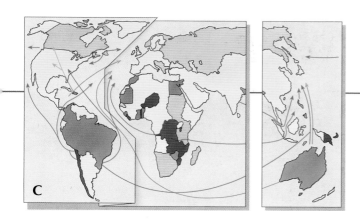

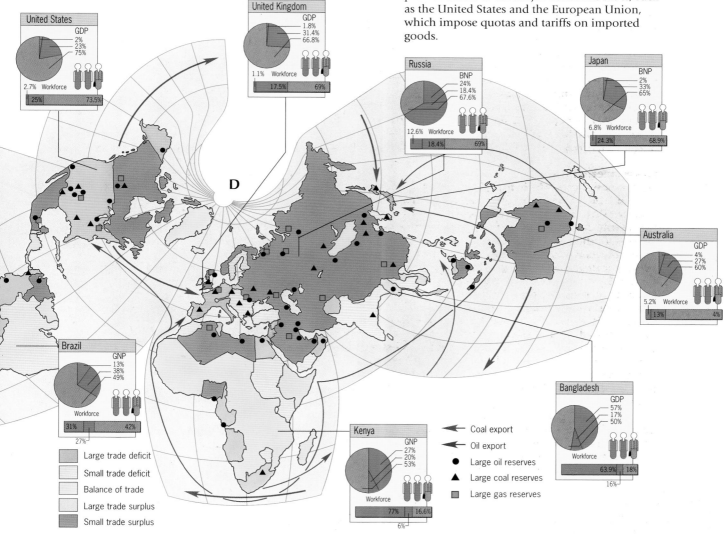

Legend (top):
→ Copper
→ Iron
→ Bauxite

5-9% | >5% | >50% | 10-49%

C

The Industrial Revolution, which began in Britain, soon spread through the rest of Europe. Apart from America, the industrialisation of the rest of the world was the result of investment by colonial European powers, taking advantage of cheap labour and raw materials, and faster, cheaper transport which turned the world into a single complex economy.

In the last fifty years the rest of the world has also developed major industries, overtaking the West. Japan became one of the world's great economic powers by heavy investment in new technology, and other nations are following its example. The pattern is now reversed as Far-Eastern companies open manufacturing plants in the West to provide goods for the lucrative consumer markets. Often, these plants assemble imported components, but they also provide access to the major economic blocs, such as the United States and the European Union, which impose quotas and tariffs on imported goods.

▲ MINERALS

Mineral deposits can often be the key to a nation's economy [C]. Jamaica has extensive bauxite and alumina deposits – the raw material for the production of aluminium – which account for almost half the country's total exports.

Mineral deposits are not only valued for their practical uses: gemstones can also bring in considerable income. Central and Southern Africa were the world's largest producers but are now threatened by the deposits in Australia, and those in Russia which have yet to be fully exploited, but which could flood and destabilize the market. If in the future the market is flooded with Russian diamonds, the market could collapse.

Many other minerals and metal ores are concentrated only in rocks which have undergone extensive weathering, or around mountain ranges, which have seen intense metamorphic processes in the past.

United States
GDP
2%
23%
75%
2.7% Workforce
25% | 73.5%

United Kingdom
GDP
1.8%
31.4%
66.8%
1.1% Workforce
17.5% | 69%

Russia
BNP
24%
18.4%
67.6%
12.6% Workforce
18.4% | 69%

Japan
BNP
2%
33%
65%
6.8% Workforce
24.3% | 68.9%

Australia
GDP
4%
27%
60%
5.2% Workforce
13% | 4%

D

Brazil
GNP
13%
38%
49%
Workforce
31% | 42%
27%

Bangladesh
GDP
57%
17%
50%
Workforce
63.9% | 18%
16%

Kenya
GNP
27%
20%
53%
Workforce
77% | 16.6%
6%

← Coal export
← Oil export
● Large oil reserves
▲ Large coal reserves
■ Large gas reserves

Large trade deficit
Small trade deficit
Balance of trade
Large trade surplus
Small trade surplus

▲ THE LABOUR FORCE

The relative economic development of various countries can be seen by comparing the numbers of people employed in different types of work, and the contribution to the gross domestic product (GDP) made by each [D]. Developing countries such as Bangladesh have a high proportion of labour involved in agriculture, which is responsible for a comparatively high proportion of GDP. Nigeria is similar, but its extensive oil reserves account for a higher industrial contribution to GDP.

As countries make more use of natural resources, more of the population is employed in heavy industry, creating more wealth, while improvements in agriculture lead to increased efficiency, and a reduction in the numbers employed. The agricultural output tends to remain steady, so that its contribution as a percentage of GDP decreases. In the most developed nations the majority of the workforce is employed in the manufacture and service sectors.

The graphics in the illustration [C] show the labour forces of several countries. The bar at the bottom gives the percentage involved in the agricultural (brown), industrial (blue) and service (grey) sectors, while the pie chart shows the contribution that each of these sectors makes to the GDP of that country.

ON THE MOVE

ONCE THE MAJORITY OF HUMANITY HAD SETTLED DOWN INTO PERMANENT VILLAGES, towns and cities, they began to devise ways to travel between them to trade and treaty. It was quickly realized that whoever controlled trade routes or devised the quickest means of transport would be at an advantage. Just as today, communications were all-important.

At first, people could only move as far as they could walk in a day, at most 32km. Around 8000 years ago, as farming was becoming established, some domesticated animals were employed as a means of transport. This did not make travel much faster, but enabled more goods to be carried or pulled along on sleds.

The great transportation breakthrough was of course the wheel, which was invented about 5000 years ago somewhere in the eastern Mediterranean. The earliest known example of wheeled transport is an Egyptian chariot, built about 2000BC. Horsedrawn chariots formed a rapid transport communications network in all the great empires and kingdoms, where rulers needed to know what was going on all over their territory.

Chariots could go faster if they had straight roads to run along. The first road network was established c1122BC in China under the emperor Chou, but the most famous road system, traces of which still exist today, was established in the Roman Empire. In engineering terms, probably the most impressive road system was built by the Incas of Peru. Built entirely of dry stone, the 4800km system wound over the steep slopes of the western Andes. These roads were for messengers on horse or foot: the Incas never used the wheel for transport.

Ships and the sea

The development of sea travel parallels that of roads. Empires that needed good internal communications along roads also needed to reach trading partners quickly and efficiently by sea. The oar was developed around the same time and in the same part of the world as the wheel. At once a propellant and a steering device, the oar made it possible to control speed and direction. The Phoenicians, a people from the eastern Mediterranean, combined oars with sail power in the galley, a long ship powered by a row of oars along each side. This eventually developed into the the Greek and Roman trireme, with three rows of oars on each side, which needed 200 rowers to power it.

Between the 14th and the 17th centuries ships and sea trading shaped the world. In 1300 northern European shipbuilders invented the rudder: before that, ships had been steered by a set of oars at the stern. In the mid-1400s, the Portuguese developed the three-masted ship, which at once increased sail-power, but kept the sails small enough to be easily handled. From the 15th to 17th centuries, these ships were used and developed by many nations, and oceans were criss-crossed by Portuguese, Dutch, Spanish and English ships claiming new colonies and discovering new trade routes.

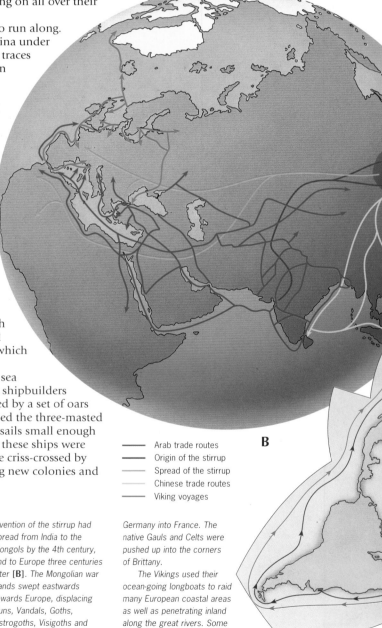

Roman roads
Roman Empire
Chinese Empire

▲ EARLY ROAD SYSTEMS
In the first few centuries of the Christian era, the landmass of Eurasia was dominated by empires at its east and west extremes [A]. Transport was central to both these realms. In Europe, the Romans built an extensive network of roads which allowed troops, administrators, tax-collectors and traders to travel quickly from one end of the empire to the other.

Under the Han dynasty, China began extensive trade. As well as extensive sea trading routes, there was the old Silk Road linking oases across the deserts of central Asia, along which caravans carried China's silks and spices as far as the Greek and Roman worlds.

Arab trade routes
Origin of the stirrup
Spread of the stirrup
Chinese trade routes
Viking voyages

▲ THE DARK AGES
The fall of the Roman Empire was a signal for mass movement across the known world. Arab traders opened trade routes that extended from Spain to China.

During the Dark Ages, both Europe and Asia were subject to raids by the Mongols, whose use of the stirrup gave them a mastery of warfare on horseback. The invention of the stirrup had spread from India to the Mongols by the 4th century, and to Europe three centuries later [B]. The Mongolian war bands swept eastwards towards Europe, displacing Huns, Vandals, Goths, Ostrogoths, Visigoths and Alans who moved into the western part of Europe, in turn displacing the Franks who moved from what is now Germany into France. The native Gauls and Celts were pushed up into the corners of Brittany.

The Vikings used their ocean-going longboats to raid many European coastal areas as well as penetrating inland along the great rivers. Some may have even reached the coast of North America.

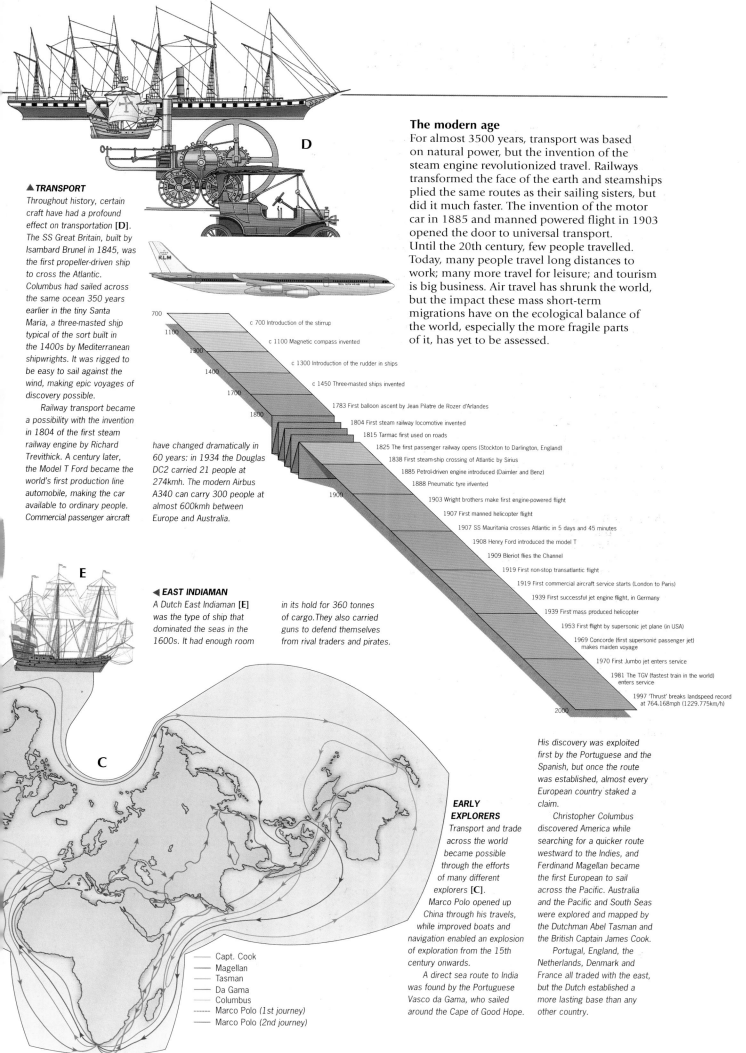

▲ TRANSPORT

Throughout history, certain craft have had a profound effect on transportation [D]. The SS Great Britain, built by Isambard Brunel in 1845, was the first propeller-driven ship to cross the Atlantic. Columbus had sailed across the same ocean 350 years earlier in the tiny Santa Maria, a three-masted ship typical of the sort built in the 1400s by Mediterranean shipwrights. It was rigged to be easy to sail against the wind, making epic voyages of discovery possible.

Railway transport became a possibility with the invention in 1804 of the first steam railway engine by Richard Trevithick. A century later, the Model T Ford became the world's first production line automobile, making the car available to ordinary people. Commercial passenger aircraft

have changed dramatically in 60 years: in 1934 the Douglas DC2 carried 21 people at 274kmh. The modern Airbus A340 can carry 300 people at almost 600kmh between Europe and Australia.

The modern age

For almost 3500 years, transport was based on natural power, but the invention of the steam engine revolutionized travel. Railways transformed the face of the earth and steamships plied the same routes as their sailing sisters, but did it much faster. The invention of the motor car in 1885 and manned powered flight in 1903 opened the door to universal transport.

Until the 20th century, few people travelled. Today, many people travel long distances to work; many more travel for leisure; and tourism is big business. Air travel has shrunk the world, but the impact these mass short-term migrations have on the ecological balance of the world, especially the more fragile parts of it, has yet to be assessed.

700
1100
1300
1400
1700
1800
1900
2000

c 700 Introduction of the stirrup
c 1100 Magnetic compass invented
c 1300 Introduction of the rudder in ships
c 1450 Three-masted ships invented
1783 First balloon ascent by Jean Pilatre de Rozer d'Arlandes
1804 First steam railway locomotive invented
1815 Tarmac first used on roads
1825 The first passenger railway opens (Stockton to Darlington, England)
1838 First steam-ship crossing of Atlantic by Sirius
1885 Petrol-driven engine introduced (Daimler and Benz)
1888 Pneumatic tyre invented
1903 Wright brothers make first engine-powered flight
1907 First manned helicopter flight
1907 SS Mauritania crosses Atlantic in 5 days and 45 minutes
1908 Henry Ford introduced the model T
1909 Bleriot flies the Channel
1919 First non-stop transatlantic flight
1919 First commercial aircraft service starts (London to Paris)
1939 First successful jet engine flight, in Germany
1939 First mass produced helicopter
1953 First flight by supersonic jet plane (in USA)
1969 Concorde (first supersonic passenger jet) makes maiden voyage
1970 First Jumbo jet enters service
1981 The TGV (fastest train in the world) enters service
1997 'Thrust' breaks landspeed record at 764.168mph (1229.775km/h)

◄ EAST INDIAMAN

A Dutch East Indiaman [E] was the type of ship that dominated the seas in the 1600s. It had enough room in its hold for 360 tonnes of cargo. They also carried guns to defend themselves from rival traders and pirates.

Capt. Cook
Magellan
Tasman
Da Gama
Columbus
Marco Polo *(1st journey)*
Marco Polo *(2nd journey)*

EARLY EXPLORERS

Transport and trade across the world became possible through the efforts of many different explorers [C].

Marco Polo opened up China through his travels, while improved boats and navigation enabled an explosion of exploration from the 15th century onwards.

A direct sea route to India was found by the Portuguese Vasco da Gama, who sailed around the Cape of Good Hope.

His discovery was exploited first by the Portuguese and the Spanish, but once the route was established, almost every European country staked a claim.

Christopher Columbus discovered America while searching for a quicker route westward to the Indies, and Ferdinand Magellan became the first European to sail across the Pacific. Australia and the Pacific and South Seas were explored and mapped by the Dutchman Abel Tasman and the British Captain James Cook.

Portugal, England, the Netherlands, Denmark and France all traded with the east, but the Dutch established a more lasting base than any other country.

THE LEGACY OF INDUSTRY

ODERN INDUSTRIAL SOCIETY PLACES GREAT DEMANDS ON THE EARTH'S NATURAL RESOURCES and the environment, constantly increasing demand for materials and energy. Not only is our way of life diminishing our planet's resources rapidly, but industry often produces harmful by-products. One of the best-known examples is the hole in the ozone layer. Aerosol spray cans were invented in the 1950s, using chlorofluorocarbons (CFCs) as propellants. The harmful effect on the environment was only realized after the discovery of a hole forming in the ozone layer high above the Antarctic. Ozone exists mainly at high altitudes where it absorbs harmful ultra-violet light from the Sun – radiation so intense that it would render the Earth uninhabitable if it reached the surface unchecked. CFC molecules break down the ozone molecules, but remain unaltered themselves, so that one CFC molecule can destroy many ozone molecules. An international agreement has now banned the manufacture of CFCs, but it will be several more years before the expansion of the ozone hole comes to a halt.

Global greenhouse

Industrialisation and our increasingly energy-hungry society have lead to the production of high levels of carbon dioxide (CO_2). The major effect is to trap heat near the Earth's surface, and prevent its reflection into space. The average temperature of the planet may rise, melting some of the Polar ice-caps and raising sea levels, posing major problems for low-lying countries in the next century. First predictions suggested that the sea level would rise up to 60cm in the next century, compared to around 15cm this century.

Ironically, these predictions are now being revised downward because of a newly-discovered 'benefit' of a different industrial pollutant. Oxides of sulphur in the atmosphere, a by-product of coal burning, actually have a cooling effect on the Earth, but they create another major problem – acid rain. Many industrial processes produce oxides of sulphur and nitrogen, which rise high into the atmosphere and are carried over great distances by the wind. Acid rain forms when the molecules come into contact with water, falling on land up to 1000km away. It can slowly poison and kill entire forests and wipe out fish stocks in lakes.

The Scandinavian countries have been particularly affected by this problem – prevailing winds from heavily industrialized countries such as Britain blow the pollution towards them. Evergreen forests have been badly damaged as the acid rainfall not only acidifies the soil, but also increases the take-up of alkaline molecules, draining the soil even more. Nutrients are washed out of the acidified soil, and poisonous metals released. Because the acidity affects the soil first, the effects can spread through an entire forest before they start to show up in dying trees.

▼ CAUSE AND EFFECT
The effects of human activity on a landscape can be seen by examining the changes in a fictional town over 2 centuries of industrialisation [A]. Where there was once a village on a riverbank [1] there is now an urban sprawl, suffering from pollution. This comes from many sources: industrial effluent and gas emissions; agricultural run-off of pesticides and fertilizers into the water course; exhaust emissions from road transport; the waste of the chemical and oil industries; and the possible radioactive poisoning of the environment from nuclear power stations.

At sea and in ports, oil spills are common. Even in the air, jet aircraft can leave lingering trails of exhaust gas, as well as habitually dumping unused fuel over built-up areas. And they add to a further taint of urban life – all-pervading noise pollution.

Agriculture
- Pesticides and herbicides can affect farmers' health and leave residues on food.
- Fertilizers percolate through to groundwater, raising nitrate levels in tapwater.

Transport
- Petrol engines produce roughly 300 million tonnes of poisonous carbon monoxide each year.
- Diesel engines create particulates, tiny granules of soot that can cause respiratory problems.

Chemical Industry
- Oil slicks are visible in every ocean and along the coast of most continents.
- Most plastics do not break down readily. Beaches covered with plastic flotsam are now a familiar but un-welcome sight.

Industrial pollution
- Carbon dioxide emissions contribute to the greenhouse effect.
- Poisonous heavy metals from industrial processes flow into rivers and enter the food chain.

Nuclear Power
- Each year nuclear power stations in the USA produce 15,000 tonnes of high-level waste, which needs to be stored for 10,000 years before it is safe – longer than any human civilisation has lasted.

A

▲ Smoke pours out of an industrial complex and pollutes the atmosphere. Governments across the globe have brought in legislation in an attempt to control them but there is little success, especially in Asia.

▶ THE GREENHOUSE EFFECT

Carbon dioxide (CO_2), makes up only 0.035% of the Earth's atmosphere but is an important component as it traps the heat of the Sun in the greenhouse effect [B]. Of incoming sunlight, 25% is reflected back into space by gases in the upper atmosphere [1]. A further 25% of the radiation is reflected back or absorbed by clouds [2]. Roughly 5% is immediately reflected by the Earth's surface [3], leaving 45% which is absorbed. The sunlight enters the atmosphere as relatively short wavelength ultraviolet and visible radiation, to which CO_2 is transparent. It is re-emitted by the Earth as longer wavelength infrared radiation, which CO_2 does absorb. This means that only 12% of the re-emitted radiation escapes into space [4] but 88% is reflected back to the ground, conserving the planet's heat [5]. The graph [C] shows how the average surface temperature of the Earth has been increasing over the last few years [D], an effect that some scientists attribute to the increasing amount of CO_2 in the atmosphere due to the burning of fossil fuels. The warming may simply be part of a natural cycle, and could be countered by the cooling effects of other pollutants.

▲ THE OZONE HOLE

In 1985 it was discovered that the level of protective ozone in the stratosphere above Antarctica had dropped dramatically. This 'hole' was caused by refrigerants called CFCs, whose production has now been banned.

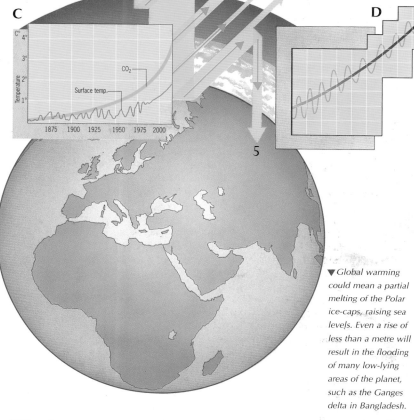

Water tables and rivers can be tainted either by leakage from industrial sites, or by 'run-off' of pesticides and fertilizers from agricultural land. Ground water is particularly vulnerable. In some places rainwater soaks into the ground and collects in underground reservoirs called aquifers. Aquifers provide a large proportion of water supplies, but can easily absorb agricultural chemicals, sewage or industrial waste soaking into the ground. Once polluted, they are difficult to clean up.

Not all ecological problems are caused by heavy industry. Across the world, deserts are spreading, not just because of changing climate, but because of the increasing needs of farmers who depend on the land that borders them. Constant grazing and cropping without ever giving the soil a chance to recover saps it of nutrients and moisture. Winds then blow away the topsoil, leaving an arid, infertile wasteland, which in turn prevents cloud formation and rain in the area. The deforestation of the rainforests also leaves topsoil which can only be farmed for a short time before becoming exhausted.

A hopeful future

We are still discovering many of the side-effects of modern industry. But recognising the problems is the first step towards solving them through methods such as recycling and the development of alternative energy sources and manufacturing processes.

▼ Global warming could mean a partial melting of the Polar ice-caps, raising sea levels. Even a rise of less than a metre will result in the flooding of many low-lying areas of the planet, such as the Ganges delta in Bangladesh.

THE BRITISH ISLES

KEY TO MAP SYMBOLS

Political regions

UNITED KINGDOM	country
SCOTLAND	nation or principality
━━━━━━━━	international boundary
━━━━━━━━	national boundary

Communications

━━━━━━━━	motorway
━━━━━━━━	main road
━━━━━━━━	other road
━━━━━━━━	main railway
━━━━━━━━	other railway
✈	major airport
✈	other airport

Hydrographic features

～～～	river
～⊢～	canal
⬭	lake, reservoir

Cities, towns & capitals

■ **LONDON**	over 3 million
▣ **DUBLIN**	1–3 million
▢ **SHEFFIELD**	500 000–1 million
○ **Swansea**	100 000–500 000
● Guildford	50 000–100 000
○ Cashel	20 000–50 000
▪ Dalbeattie	under 20 000
LONDON	country capital
Belfast	national capital
	urban area

Cultural features

DARTMOOR	National Park
⸪ Stonehenge	ancient site or ruin
▪▪▪▪▪▪▪▪▪▪	ancient wall

Topographic features

Lochnagar ▲1155	elevation above sea level (in metres)
2	elevation of land below sea level (in metres)

Each page also features a guide to relief colours

BRITISH ISLES: POLITICAL

- Great Britain comprises England, Scotland and Wales, and is the largest island in Europe.

- The United Kingdom of Great Britain and Ireland was formed in 1801, when Great Britain and the island of Ireland were united by Act of Parliament.

- The United Kingdom of Great Britain and Northern Ireland and the Republic of Ireland both came into being in 1921, when Ireland was partitioned. Northern Ireland, which remained within the Union, comprises six of the former counties of the former Irish province of Ulster. The Republic of Ireland is that part of Ireland which left the Union, and comprises most (about four fifths) of the island's territory.

- The Channel Islands (comprising Jersey, Guernsey, Alderney and Sark) and the Isle of Man are not part of the United Kingdom; they are direct dependencies of the Crown.

- In May 1999, the devolution of government in Scotland and Wales led to the formation of a Scottish Parliament (based in Edinburgh) and a Welsh Assembly (based in Cardiff), giving the two much greater autonomy.

- Ever since Partition in Ireland, bitter conflicts have divided the community. Years of lengthy negotiations aimed at establishing a political settlement to these culminated on 10 May 1998, in the signing of the Good Friday Agreement. On 2 December 1999, the major step towards full implementation of this agreement was finally taken, with the devolution of government in Northern Ireland.

ENGLAND
1 Bath & NE Somerset
2 Blackburn with Darwen
3 Bournemouth
4 Bracknell Forest
5 Bristol
6 Darlington
7 Derby City
8 Halton
9 Leicester City
10 Luton
11 Medway Towns
12 Milton Keynes
13 North Somerset
14 Nottingham City
15 Poole
16 Portsmouth
17 Reading
18 Rutland
19 Slough
20 Southampton
21 South Gloucestershire
22 Stockton-on-Tees
23 Stoke-on-Trent
24 Swindon
25 Telford & Wrekin
26 Thurrock
27 Warrington
28 Windsor & Maidenhead

SCOTLAND
1 City of Edinburgh
2 Clackmannanshire
3 East Dunbartonshire
4 East Lothian
5 East Renfrewshire
6 Falkirk
7 Glasgow City
8 Inverclyde
9 Midlothian
10 North Ayrshire
11 North Lanarkshire
12 Renfrewshire
13 West Dunbartonshire
14 West Lothian

NORTHERN IRELAND
1 Antrim
2 Ards
3 Ballymena
4 Ballymoney
5 Banbridge
6 Belfast
7 Carrickfergus
8 Castlereagh
9 Coleraine
10 Cookstown
11 Craigavon
12 Derry
13 Dungannon
14 Larne
15 Limavady
16 Lisburn
17 Magherafelt
18 Moyle
19 Newtownabbey
20 North Down

WALES
1 Blaenau Gwent
2 Bridgend
3 Caerphilly
4 Cardiff
5 Swansea
6 Denbighshire
7 Flintshire
8 Merthyr Tydfil
9 Monmouthshire
10 Neath Port Talbot
11 Newport
12 Rhondda Cynon Taff
13 Vale of Glamorgan
14 Torfaen
15 Wrexham

Administrative boundaries are not shown within Greater London. The Greater London Authority (GLA) comprises a London-wide assembly and a mayor (both elected every 4 years). The GLA has responsibility for strategic planning and economic development of London as a whole whereas the 32 borough councils continue to provide day to day services.

Scale 1 : 1 750 000

25   50   75   100 km
25   50 miles

ATLANTIC OCEAN

Tory
Tory Sound
Bloody Foreland
Dunfanaghy
Inishowen
Malin Head
Inishtrahull
Rathlin
Aran
GLENVEAGH
Derryveagh Mts.
Moville
Buncrana
Lough Foyle
Portrush
Fair Head
Ballycastle
North Channel
Dungloe
Blue Stack Mts.
Letterkenny
Londonderry
Coleraine
Ballymoney
Cushendall
Garron Pt
Gweebarra Bay
Lifford
Strabane
Dungiven
Limavady
Ballymena
Larne
Rossan Point
Ballybofey
Newtownstewart
Sperrin Mts.
Maghera
Island Magee
Killybegs
Donegal
Omagh
Magherafelt
Randalstown
Antrim
Ballyclare
Whitehead
Carrickfergus
UNITED KINGDOM
Donegal Bay
Ballyshannon
Belleek
Lower Lough Erne
Irvinestown
Enniskillen
Cookstown
Lough Neagh
Dungannon
NORTHERN IRELAND
Ballygawley
Armagh
Tandragee
Belfast
Newtownabbey
Holywood
Bangor
Comber
Lisburn
Newtownards
Ards Pen.
Inishmurray
Grange
Manorhamilton
Craigavon
Lurgan
Portadown
Dromore
Ballynahinch
Strangford Lough
Portaferry
Sligo
Colloony
Lough Allen
Lisnaskea
Upper Lough Erne
Newtownbutler
Clones
Monaghan
Rathfriland
Banbridge
Castlewellan
Downpatrick
Sligo Bay
Downpatrick Head
Killala Bay
Castleblayney
Newry
Newcastle
Dundrum Bay
Erris Head
Belmullet
Bangor Erris
Ballina
Charlestown
Boyle
Carrick-on-Shannon
Cavan
Carrickmacross
Mourne Mts.
Warrenpoint
Rostrevor
Kilkeel
Blacksod Bay
Achill Head
Achill
Nephin Beg Mts.
Lough Conn
Swinford
Ballaghaderreen
Virginia
Ardee
Clogher Head
Dundalk
Dundalk Bay
Corraun Peninsula
Clew Bay
Newport
Castlebar
Lough Carra
Ballyhaunis
Castlerea
Strokestown
Longford
Granard
Lough Sheelin
Kells
Slane
Drogheda
Clare
Westport
Lough Mask
Claremorris
Roscommon
Lough Derravaragh
Navan
Julianstown
Inishturk
Ballinrobe
Lough Ree
Mullingar
Lough Owel
Dunshaughlin
Balbriggan
Inishbofin
Inishshark
Connaught
Tuam
Ballygar
Athlone
Lough Ennell
Moate
Kinnegad
Royal Canal
Lambay
Swords
Malahide
Clifden
CONNEMARA
Oughterard
Lough Corrib
Claregalway
Ballinasloe
Kilbeggan
Grand Canal
Tullamore
Bog of Allen
Lucan
DUBLIN (BAILE ÁTHA CLIATH)
Slyne Head
Gorumna
Galway
Oranmore
Loughrea
Shannon
Cloghan
Kilcormac
Slieve Bloom Mts.
Mountmellick
Rathcoole
Naas
Dalkey
Dublin Bay
Dún Laoghaire
Inishmore
Galway Bay
Gort
Birr
Borrisokane
Mountrath
Port Laoise
Monasterevin
Kildare
Blessington Lakes
Bray
Inishmaan
Aran Islands
Inisheer
The Burren
Slieve Aughty Mts.
Lough Derg
Roscrea
REPUBLIC OF IRELAND
Nore
Castletown
Athy
WICKLOW MOUNTAINS
Wicklow
Ennistymon
Ennis
Nenagh
Abbeyleix
926 Lugnaquilla
Rathdrum
Wicklow Head
Liscannor Bay
Durrow
Carlow
Tullow
Arklow
Kilkee
Kilrush
Silvermine Mts.
Templemore
Thurles
Bagenalstown
Gorey
Loop Head
Tarbert
Limerick
Adare
Golden Vale
Slieveardagh Hills
Kilkenny
Callan
Thomastown
Enniscorthy
Cahore Point
Mouth of the Shannon
Listowel
Rathkeale
Newcastle West
Tipperary
Cashel
New Ross
Wexford
Rath Luirc
Caher
Carrick-on-Suir
Wexford Harbour
950 Brandon Mt.
Tralee Bay
Tralee
Castleisland
Mitchelstown
Clonmel
Waterford
Rosslare Harbour
Dingle
Abbeyfeale
Mallow
Blackwater
Carnsore Point
Dingle Bay
Killorglin
Lough Leane
Killarney
Fermoy
Tallowbridge
Dungarvan
Dungarvan Harbour
Hook Head
Saltee Islands
Cahersiveen
1040 Macgillycuddy's Reeks
KILLARNEY
Boggeragh Mts.
Macroom
Lee
Cork
Youghal
Youghal Bay
Kenmare
Ballincollig
Douglas
Cobh
Kinsale
Cork Harbour
Caha Mts.
Dunmanus Bay
Schull
Ballincollig
Old Head of Kinsale
Kenmare River
Bear I.
Bantry Bay
Bantry
Clonakilty
Clonakilty Bay
Dursey
Mizen Head
Roaringwater Bay
Sherkin Island
Cape Clear
Clear Island
Celtic Sea

IRISH SEA

metres / feet
1000 / 3280
500 / 1640
200 / 656
100 / 328
50 / 164
100 / 328
200 / 656
1000 / 3280
2000 / 6560

38 39

elicon Publishing Ltd

Scale 1 : 1 750 000

0   40   80   120 km
0   20   40   60 miles

© Helicon Publishing Ltd

metres feet
1000 3280
500   1640
200   656
100   328
0   0
50   164
100   328
200   656
1000 3280
2000 6560
metres feet

Shetland Islands (inset)

Herma Ness
Haroldswick
Unst
Fetlar
Mid Yell
Yell
Out Skerries
Whalsay
SHETLAND ISLANDS
Bressay
Isle of Noss
Lerwick
Yell Sound
Brae
Mousa
North Roe
449 Ronas Hill
Muckle Roe
Sumburgh
Hillswick
West Burra
Sumburgh Head
St. Magnus Bay
Papa Stour
Mainland
Foula
Fair Isle

Main map labels

Fair Isle

ATLANTIC OCEAN

North Ronaldsay
Papa Westray
Westray
Sanday
Stronsay
The North Sound
Eday
Shapinsay
ORKNEY ISLANDS
Rousay
Kirkwall
Hoy
Scapa Flow
South Ronaldsay
Twatt
Stromness
Mainland
Duncansby Head
Stroma
John o' Groats
Pentland Firth
Dunnet Head
Sinclair's Bay
Wick
Thurso
Strathy
Halkirk
Lybster
Caithness
Helmsdale
Strathy Point
Bettyhill
Kinbrace
Brora
Tongue
Ossian
Loch Eriboll
962 Ben Kilbreck
Laing
Dornoch Firth
Durness
927 Ben Hope
Loch Shin
Tarbat Ness
Cape Wrath
Sule Skerry
Stack Skerry
998 Ben More Assynt
Dornoch
Tain
Moray Firth
Lossiemouth
Scourie
Elphin
Lochinver
Easter Ross
Invergordon
Dingwall
Elgin
Forres
Nairn
Buckie
Cullen
Sula Sgeir
Eddrachillis Bay
Enard Bay
1108 Sgurr Mòr
Ullapool
1046 Ben Wyvis
Muir of Ord
Inverness
Black Isle
Rona
Gruinard Bay
Loch Broom
Achnasheen
Beauly
Grantown-on-Spey
Aviemore
Cairngorm Mts.
Gairloch
Loch Maree
Wester Ross
Kinlochewe
Strathcarron
Drumnadrochit
Monadhliath Mts.
Newtonmore
1309 Ben Macdui
Braemar
Butt of Lewis
Port Nis
Loch Ewe
Torridon
Shieldaig
Shel Bridge
Fort Augustus
941 Carn Bàn
1148 Ben Alder Erioch
Barabhas
Stornoway
Shiant Islands
Applecross
Kyle of Lochalsh
Loch Ness
Kingussie
Lochcarron
Broadford
Loch Shiel
Laggan
Spean Bridge
Lewis
Portree
Skye
Cuillin Hills
Sligachan
Dunvegan
Loch Snizort
Raasay
Sound of Raasay
Inner Sound
Scalpay
Soay
Loch Morar
Fort William
1343 Ben Nevis
Baile Ailein
Sound of Harris
North Harris
Tarbert
South Harris
Scalpay
Little Minch
Eigg
Rum
Muck
Canna
Point of Ardnamurchan
Sound of Arisaig
Glenfinnan
Mallaig
Sound of Sleat
The Minch
Gallan Head
Taransay
Scarp
Sea of the Hebrides
Berneray
Pabbay
Ronay
Wiay
Lochmaddy
North Uist
Benbecula
South Uist
Lochboisdale
Sound of Barra
Castlebay
Barra
Vatersay
Sandray
Mingulay
Monach Islands
Eriskay
Flannan Islands

Kinnaird Head
Peterhead
Fraserburgh
Mintlaw
Buchan
Elton
Turriff
Macduff
Banff
Aberdeen
Girdle Ness
Rhynie
Huntly
Insch
Inverurie
Kintore
Dee
Banchory
Stonehaven
Inverbervie
Rhynie
Keith
Charlestown of Aberlour
Ballater
1155 Lochnagar
Aboyne
Laurencekirk
Brechin
Montrose
Spey Bay
Elgin
Grampian Mountains
Strathspey
Cabrach
Speyside
Badenoch
Kirriemuir
1148 Ben Alder Erioch
North West Highlands
Glen Mor
Glen More
Loch Lochy
Loch Nevis
Loch Arkaig
Anaheilt

Sound of Barra
57° N

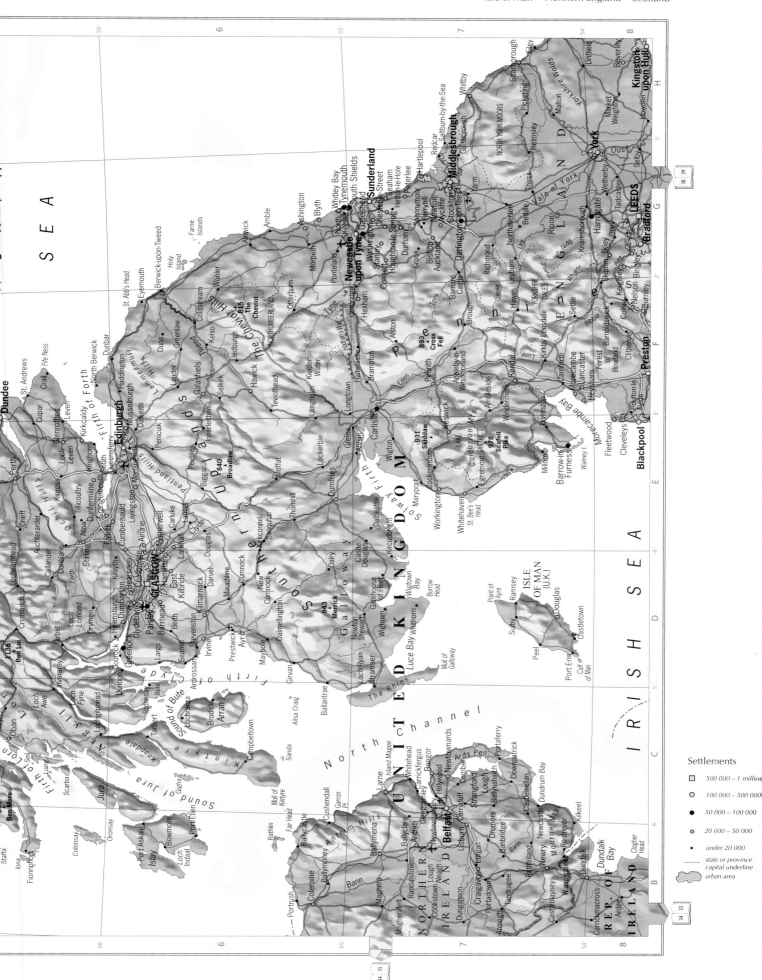

Settlements

☐	500 000 – 1 million
○	100 000 – 500 000
●	50 000 – 100 000
◎	20 000 – 50 000
•	under 20 000
——	state or province
capital underline	
	urban area

Scale 1 : 1 750 000

| 0 | 40 | | 80 | | 120 km |

metres / feet scale:
1000 / 3280
500 / 1640
200 / 656
100 / 328
0 / 0
50 / 164
100 / 328
200 / 656
1000 / 3280
2000 / 6560
metres / feet

ISLE OF MAN (U.K.)
Peel
Port Erin
Castletown
Calf of Man
Douglas

IRISH SEA

Millom
Liverston
Barrow-in-Furness
Walney I.
Morecambe Bay
Carn...
Morecambe
Lancas...
Heysham
Bo...
Fleetwood
Cleveleys
Blackpool
Poulton-le-Fylde
Lytham St. Anne's
Leyland
Southport
Burscough Bridge
Ormskirk
Skelmersdale
Formby
Crosby
Kirkby
Bootle
Liverpool Bay
LIVERPOOL
St. Helen...
Wallasey
Birkenhead
West Kirby
Bebington
Neston
Ellesmere Port
Chester

Dundalk Bay
Virginia
Ardee
Ceanannus Mør
Clogher Head
Slane
Drogheda
Navan
Julianstown
Balbriggan
Boyne
Dunshaughlin
Royal Canal
Lambay
Kinnegad
Swords
Malahide
Grand Canal
Bog of Allen
DUBLIN
(BAILE ÁTHA CLIATH)
Lucan
Dublin Bay
Rathcoole
Dalkey
Dún Laoghaire
Naas
Kildare
Bray
Monasterevin
Blessington Lakes
WICKLOW MOUNTAINS
Athy
926 Lugnaquilla
Wicklow
Wicklow Head
REPUBLIC OF
Carlow
Rathdrum
Tullow
Bagenalstown
Arklow
IRELAND
Gorey
Enniscorthy
Cahore Point
New Ross
Wexford
Wexford Harbour
Rosslare Harbour
Carnsore Point
Hook Head
Saltee Islands

Carmel Head
Amlwch
Great Ormes Head
Holyhead
Anglesey
Llandudno
Holy Island
Conwy Bay
Conwy
Colwyn Bay
Rhyl
Menai Bridge
Bangor
Denbigh
Connah's Quay
Menai Str.
Caernarfon
Llanrwst
Ruthin
Mold
Caernarfon Bay
1085 Snowdon
Betws-y-Coed
Wrexham
Nefyn
Blaenau Ffestiniog
Llangollen
Oswestry
Ellesmere
Lleyn Peninsula
Porthmadog
Ffestiniog
Bala
UNI...
Pwllheli
SNOWDONIA
Braich y Pwll
Tremadog Bay
Harlech
Dee
Bardsey
Barmouth
Dolgellau
Shrewsbury
Barmouth Bay
892 Cadair Idris
Welshpool
Machynlleth
Newtown
Church Stretton
Cardigan Bay
WALES
Aberystwyth
Llanidloes
Ludlow
Rhayader
Knighton
Aberaeron
Cambrian Mountains
Llandrindod Wells
Leominster
Tregaron
Kington
Lampeter
Builth Wells
Hereford
Cardigan
Llanwrtyd Wells
Wye
Newcastle Emlyn
Goodwick
Llandovery
Black Mts.
Fishguard
Ross-o...
St. David's Head
Pen y Fan 886
St. David's
BRECON BEACONS
Tretower
Llandeilo
Abergavenny
St. Brides Bay
Carmarthen
Ystradgynlais
Ebbw Vale
Monmout...
Haverfordwest
Narberth
Merthyr Tydfil
Tredegar
Usk
Milford Haven
Ammanford
Aberdare
Abertillery
Pontypool
Pembroke Dock
Llanelli
Rhymney
Chepsto...
PEMBROKESHIRE COAST
Pembroke
Carmarthen Bay
Neath
Rhondda
Cwmbran
St. Govan's Head
Gower
Swansea
Pontypridd
Caerphilly
Newport
Port Talbot
Bri...
Swansea Bay
Bridgend
Cardiff
Porthcawl
Cowbridge
Penarth
Barry
Clevedon
Severn Estuary
Bristol Channel
Weston-super-Mare
Cheddar
We...
Glastonbury

Celtic Sea

St. George's Channel

① F   2°   G
Alderney
Cap de la Hague
Passage de la Déroute
Cherbourg
Guernsey
Herm
Sark
FRANCE
St. Peter Port
CHANNEL ISLANDS (U.K.)
Jersey
St. Helier
F   2° W   G

Lundy
Ilfracombe
Lynton
Foreland Pt
Hartland Point
Braunton
Minehead
Bridgwater Bay
EXMOOR
Bridgwater
Barnstaple or Bideford Bay
Barnstaple
Taunton
Bideford
Wellington
Great Torrington
Tiverton
Crewker...
Holsworthy
Crediton
Chard
Bude
Bude Bay
Honiton
Ye...
Exe
S. Do...
Okehampton
Exeter
Seaton
Launceston
Sidmouth
Lyme Regis
Tamar
DARTMOOR
Exmouth
Lyme Bay
Bodmin Moor
Newton Abbot
Teignmouth
Padstow
Tavistock
Torquay
Wadebridge
Bodmin
Paignton
Torbay
Liskeard
Totnes
Brixham
Newquay
Looe
Whitsand Bay
Ivybridge
St. Austell
Fowey
Plymouth
Dartmouth
St. Austell Bay
Kingsbridge
Redruth
Truro
Saltash
Salcombe
St. Ives Bay
St. Ives
Camborne
Falmouth
Start Point
Penzance
Helston
Falmouth Bay
Prawle Point
Mount's Bay
Hugh Town
Isles of Scilly
Land's End
Lizard
Lizard Point

ATLANTIC OCEAN

© Helicon Publishing Ltd

Settlements

- ■ over 3 million
- ▣ 1 – 3 million
- ▢ 500 000 – 1 million
- ○ 100 000 – 500 000
- • 50 000 – 100 000
- ◦ 20 000 – 50 000
- · under 20 000
- — country capital underline
- — state or province capital underline
- urban area

THE WORLD

KEY TO MAP SYMBOLS

Political regions

CANADA   country

ONTARIO   state or province

——————   international boundary (physical regional maps)

——————   international boundary (political continental maps)

——————   state or province boundary

—·—·—·—   undefined/disputed boundary or ceasefire/demarcation line

Communications

——————   motorway

——————   main road

——————   other road

– – – – –   track

——————   railway

✈   international airport

Hydrographic features

river, canal

seasonal river

Niagara Falls   *Kariba Dam*   waterfall, dam

lake, seasonal lake

salt lake, seasonal salt lake

ice cap or glacier

Cities, towns & capitals

▣ **CHICAGO**   over 3 million

▢ **HAMBURG**   1–3 million

◉ **Bulawayo**   250 000–1 million

● Antofogasta   100 000–250 000

◦ Ajaccio   25 000–100 000

· Indian Springs   under 25 000

LONDON   country capital

<u>Columbia</u>   state or province capital

urban area

Cultural features

.· Persepolis   ancient site or ruin

▪▪▪▪▪▪▪▪▪▪▪▪   ancient wall

Topographic features

▲ **Mount Ziel**   elevation above sea level (in metres)
▲ 1510

▾ 133   elevation of land below sea level (in metres)

⋈ **Khyber Pass**   mountain pass (height in metres)
1080

Each page also features a guide to relief colours

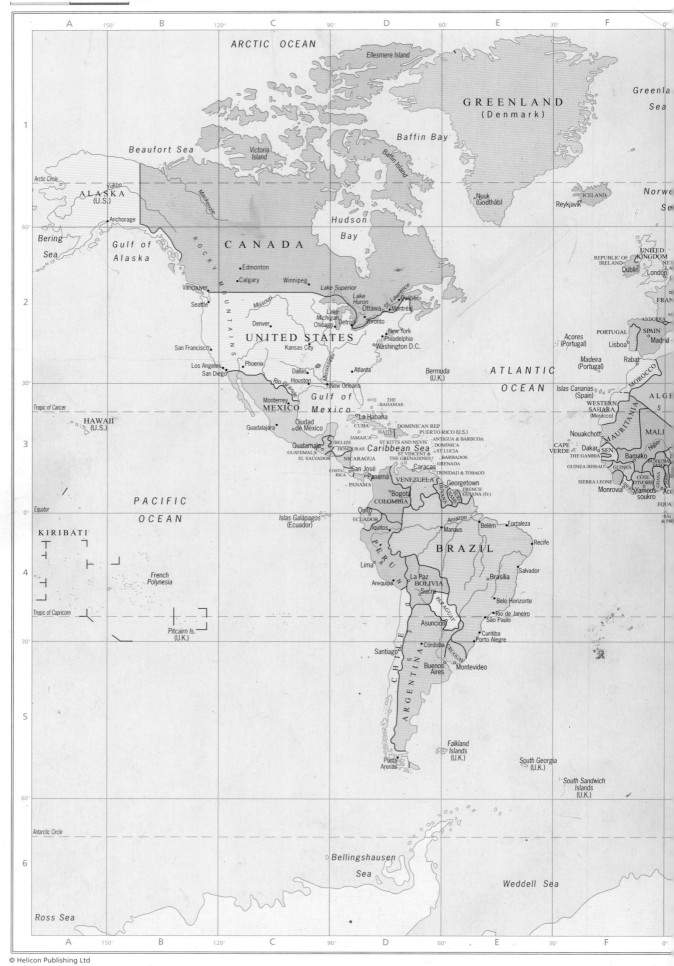

Equatorial Scale 1 : 112 000 000

0   1000   2000   3000   4000 km

0   1000   2000 miles

ARCTIC OCEAN

Ellesmere Island

GREENLAND
(Denmark)

Greenla
Sea

Baffin Bay

Beaufort Sea

Victoria
Island

Baffin Island

Arctic Circle

ALASKA
(U.S.)

Yukon

Mackenzie

Nuuk
(Godthåb)

ICELAND

Norwe
Sea

Reykjavik

Anchorage

Hudson
Bay

Bering
Sea

Gulf of
Alaska

CANADA

Edmonton

Calgary   Winnipeg   Lake Superior

REPUBLIC OF
IRELAND

UNITED
KINGDOM

Dublin   London
NE

Vancouver

Seattle

R O C K Y   M O U N T A I N S

Missouri

Lake
Huron   St. Lawrence   Québec

Lake
Michigan   Ottawa   Montréal

Chicago   Detroit   Toronto

FRAN

ANDORRA

San Francisco

Denver

UNITED STATES

Kansas City

New York

Philadelphia

Washington D.C.

Açores
(Portugal)

PORTUGAL

Lisboa

SPAIN

Madrid

Los Angeles

San Diego

Phoenix

Dallas

Houston

Rio Grande

Atlanta

Bermuda
(U.K.)

ATLANTIC

Madeira
(Portugal)

Rabat

MOROCCO

Monterrey

MEXICO

New Orleans

Mississippi

Gulf of
Mexico

THE
BAHAMAS

OCEAN

Islas Canarias
(Spain)

ALG

Tropic of Cancer

HAWAII
(U.S.)

Guadalajara

Ciudad
de México

La Habana

CUBA

DOMINICAN REP

PUERTO RICO (U.S.)

WESTERN
SAHARA
(Morocco)

MAURITANIA

S

Guatemala

BELIZE

HAITI

JAMAICA

ST KITTS AND NEVIS

ANTIGUA & BARBUDA

DOMINICA

Nouakchott

MALI

GUATEMALA   HONDURAS   Caribbean Sea   ST LUCIA

EL SALVADOR   NICARAGUA   ST VINCENT &   BARBADOS

THE GRENADINES   GRENADA

CAPE
VERDE

Dakar

SEN

THE GAMBIA

GUINEA-BISSAU   GUINEA

Bamako

BURKINA

Niger

COSTA
RICA   San José   Caracas   TRINIDAD & TOBAGO

PANAMA   Panamá   VENEZUELA   Georgetown

Bogotá   GUYANA   FRENCH
GUIANA (Fr.)

SIERRA LEONE

Monrovia

CÔTE
D'IVOIRE

Yamous-
soukro

GHANA

Ac

PACIFIC

OCEAN

COLOMBIA

Quito

ECUADOR

Amazon

Belém   Fortaleza

EQUAT

SÃO
& S

KIRIBATI

Islas Galápagos
(Ecuador)

Iquitos   Manaus

BRAZIL

Recife

Equator

French
Polynesia

P E R U

Lima

La Paz

BOLIVIA

Brasília

Salvador

Belo Horizonte

Arequipa

Sucre

PARAGUAY

Rio de Janeiro

São Paulo

Tropic of Capricorn

Pitcairn Is.
(U.K.)

Asunción

Curitiba

Porto Alegre

Santiago

Córdoba

URUGUAY

C H I L E

A R G E N T I N A

Buenos
Aires   Montevideo

Punta
Arenas

Falkland
Islands
(U.K.)

South Georgia
(U.K.)

South Sandwich
Islands
(U.K.)

Antarctic Circle

Bellingshausen
Sea

Weddell Sea

Ross Sea

© Helicon Publishing Ltd

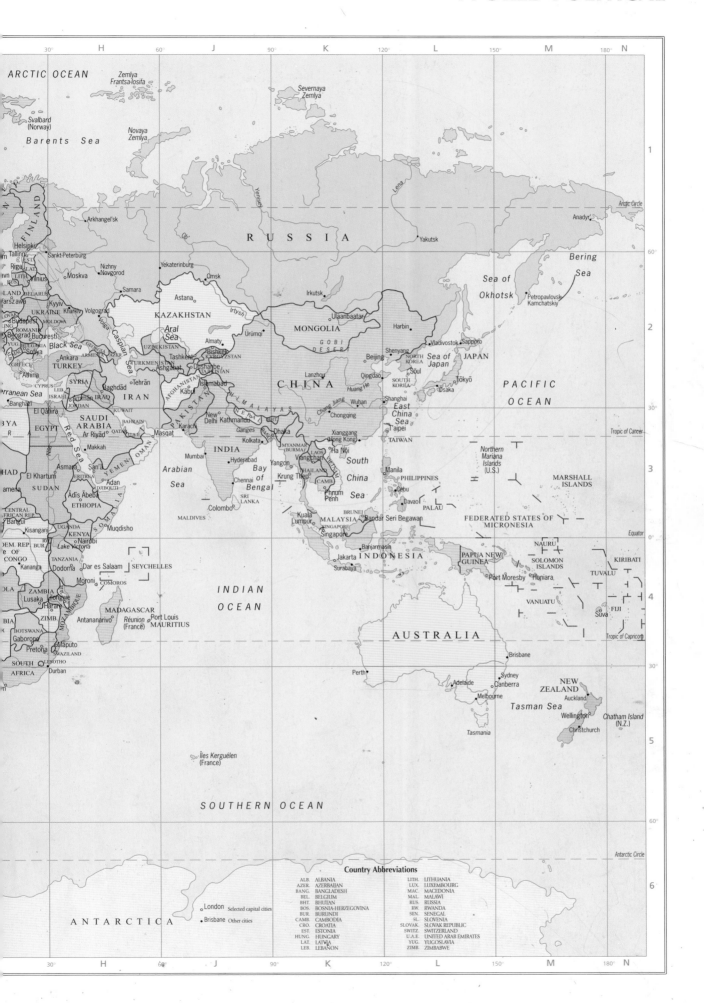

ARCTIC OCEAN

Svalbard (Norway)

Zemlya Frantsa-Iosifa

Novaya Zemlya

Severnaya Zemlya

Barents Sea

FINLAND

Helsinki
Tallinn
EST
Riga
LATV
LITH. Vilnius
BELARUS
Warszawa
UKRAINE
Kyyiv
MOLDOVA
SLOVAK.
Budapest
HUNG.
ROMANIA
Beograd
Bucuresti
YUG.
BULGARIA
Sofiya
GREECE
Athina
CYPRUS
LEB.
rranean Sea
ISRAEL
JORDAN
El Qâhira
LIBYA
EGYPT
Makkah
Ar Riyâd
SAUDI ARABIA

Sankt-Peterburg
Moskva
Nizhny Novgorod
Samara
Volgograd
Kharkiv
GEORGIA
ARMENIA AZER.
Ankara
TURKEY
SYRIA
Baghdâd
IRAQ
KUWAIT
BAHRAIN
QATAR
U.A.E.

Arkhangel'sk

R U S S I A

Yekaterinburg
Omsk
Astana

Arkhangel'sk

KAZAKHSTAN

Aral Sea
Caspian Sea
UZBEKISTAN
Tashkent
TURKMENISTAN
Ashgabat
Tehrân
Dushanbe TAJIKISTAN
IRAN
AFGHANISTAN
Kâbul
Islâmâbâd
PAKISTAN
Masqat
OMAN
YEMEN
San'â
Asmara
ERITREA
DJIBOUTI
Âdan

Bishkek
KYRGYZSTAN
Almaty
Ürümqi

MONGOLIA
Ulaanbaatar
GOBI DESERT

Irkutsk

Yakutsk

Arctic Circle

Anadyr'

Bering Sea

Sea of Okhotsk
Petropavlovsk-Kamchatskiy

Harbin
Shenyang
Beijing
NORTH KOREA
Vladivostok
Sapporo
Sea of Japan
JAPAN

Lanzhou
Huang He
CHINA
Chang Jiang
Chongqing
Wuhan
Shanghai
Qingdao
SOUTH KOREA
Sôul
Ôsaka
Tôkyô

East China Sea
Taipei
TAIWAN

New Delhi
Kathmandu
NEPAL
BHT.
Ganges
Dhaka
BANG.
Kolkata
MYANMAR (BURMA)
Xianggang (Hong Kong)

Tropic of Cancer

PACIFIC OCEAN

Northern Mariana Islands (U.S.)

MARSHALL ISLANDS

HIMALAYAS

Karâchi
Mumbai
INDIA
Hyderabad
Chennai
Arabian Sea
Bay of Bengal
SRI LANKA
Colombo
MALDIVES

Yangon
Krung Thep
THAILAND
LAOS
Vientiane
Ha Nôi
VIETNAM
CAMB.
Phnum Penh
South China Sea

Manila
PHILIPPINES
Cebu
Davao
PALAU

FEDERATED STATES OF MICRONESIA

Kuala Lumpur
MALAYSIA
BRUNEI
Bandar Seri Begawan
SINGAPORE
Singapore

Banjarmasin
Jakarta
INDONESIA
Surabaya

PAPUA NEW GUINEA
Port Moresby

NAURU
SOLOMON ISLANDS
Honiara

Equator

KIRIBATI
TUVALU

INDIAN OCEAN

SEYCHELLES

VANUATU
FIJI
Suva

Tropic of Capricorn

MADAGASCAR
Antananarivo
Réunion (France)
Port Louis
MAURITIUS
COMOROS
Moroni

AUSTRALIA

Brisbane
Perth
Adelaide
Sydney
Canberra
Melbourne

Tasman Sea
Tasmania

NEW ZEALAND
Auckland
Wellington
Christchurch
Chatham Island (N.Z.)

Îles Kerguélen (France)

SOUTHERN OCEAN

A N T A R C T I C A

Country Abbreviations

ALB.	ALBANIA	LITH.	LITHUANIA
AZER.	AZERBAIJAN	LUX.	LUXEMBOURG
BANG.	BANGLADESH	MAC.	MACEDONIA
BEL.	BELGIUM	MAL.	MALAWI
BHT.	BHUTAN	RUS.	RUSSIA
BOS.	BOSNIA-HERZEGOVINA	RW.	RWANDA
BUR.	BURUNDI	SEN.	SENEGAL
CAMB.	CAMBODIA	SL.	SLOVENIA
CRO.	CROATIA	SLOVAK.	SLOVAK REPUBLIC
EST.	ESTONIA	SWITZ.	SWITZERLAND
HUNG.	HUNGARY	U.A.E.	UNITED ARAB EMIRATES
LAT.	LATVIA	YUG.	YUGOSLAVIA
LEB.	LEBANON	ZIMB.	ZIMBABWE

○ London Selected capital cities
● Brisbane Other cities

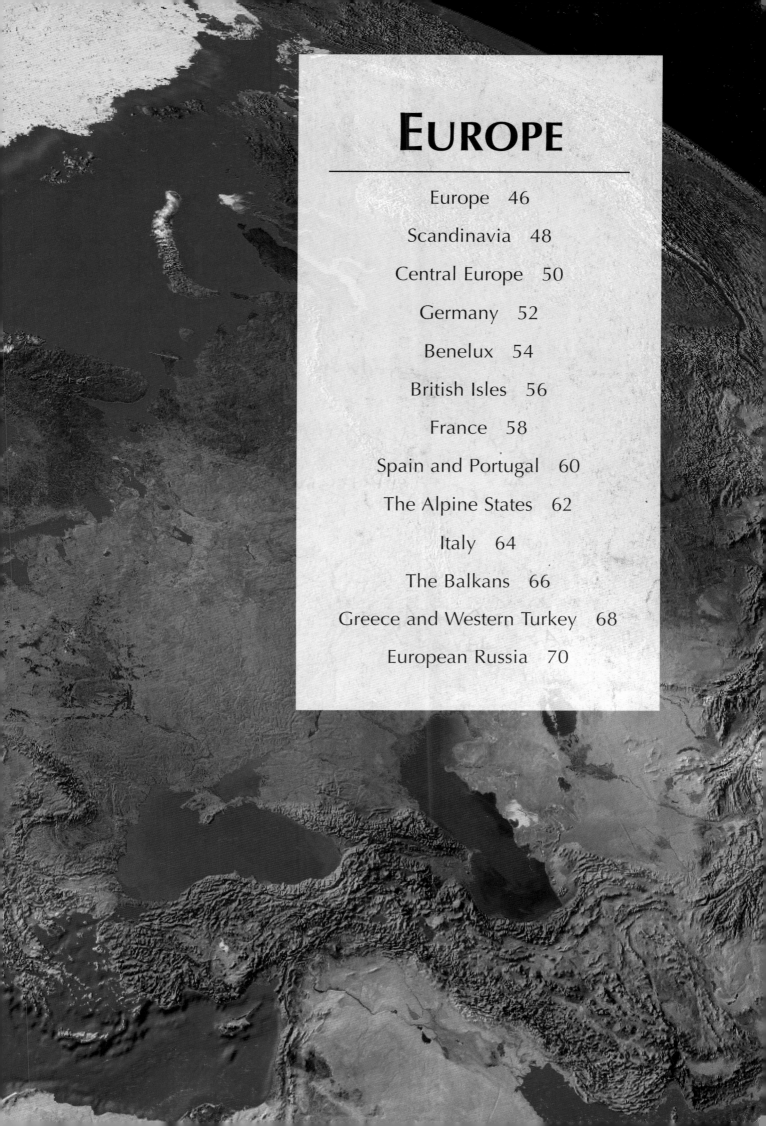

EUROPE

Europe 46

Scandinavia 48

Central Europe 50

Germany 52

Benelux 54

British Isles 56

France 58

Spain and Portugal 60

The Alpine States 62

Italy 64

The Balkans 66

Greece and Western Turkey 68

European Russia 70

Scale 1 : 20 200 000

0	250		500	750 km	
0	100	200	300 miles		

60° N   A   1   30° W   B   20°   C   70° 10°   D   0°   E   10°   F   20°

Arctic Circle

Reykjavík • **ICELAND**

N o r w e g i a n

Tromsø

Sea

Kir

Faeroes
(Denmark)

N O R W A Y

S W E D E N

Trondheim

Shetland Is.
(U.K.)

Rockall

Bergen

Oslo

Stavanger

Gulf of Both

Sundsvall

Tampe

Outer
Hebrides

Orkney Is.

SCOTLAND

Glasgow

Edinburgh

Stockholm

Vänern

Ta

North

NORTHERN
IRELAND

Belfast

Sea

Göteborg

Gotland

DENMARK

Århus

LIT

Ka

**REP. OF
IRELAND**

**DUBLIN
(BAILE ÁTHA CLIATH)**

UNITED

WALES

KINGDOM

**København
(Copenhagen)**

Bornholm

RUSSIA

Kalinir

A T L A N T I C

BIRMINGHAM

Cardiff

ENGLAND

Plymouth

LONDON

Amsterdam

HAMBURG

Gdańsk

Wisła

Hroc

Ems

's-Gravenhage
(The Hague)

**NETHER-
LANDS**

Hannover

Elbe

BERLIN

**WARSZAWA
(WARSAW)**

O C E A N

*Channel
Islands*

English Channel

Bruxelles
(Brussels)

BELGIUM

Rhine

Bonn

Frankfurt

GERMANY

Odra (Oder)

POLAND

Vistula

Luxembourg

LUXEMBOURG

Seine

PARIS

Strasbourg

**PRAHA
(PRAGUE)**

CZECH REP.

*Bay
of
Biscay*

Loire

FRANCE

**MÜNCHEN
(MUNICH)**

Danube

**WIEN
(VIENNA)**

SLOVAK REP.

Bratislava

Cabo Fisterra

Bordeaux

Lyon

Bern

Vaduz

LIECHTENSTEIN

AUSTRIA

BUDAPEST

Clu
Napoc

PORTUGAL

Massif

4808
Mt.
Blanc

SWITZERLAND

A l p s

SLOVENIA

HUNGARY

Central

Andorra
la Vella

Genova
(Genoa)

**MILANO
(MILAN)**

Ljubljana

Zagreb

R

Lisboa
(Lisbon)

Ebro

MADRID

Pyrenees

ANDORRA

Marseille

CROATIA

Rhône

**SAN
MARINO**

Tagus

MONACO

**BOSNIA-
HERZEGOVINA**

**BEOGRA
(BELGRA**

SPAIN

BARCELONA

*Corse
(Corsica)
(France)*

Ajaccio

**VATICAN
CITY**

Sarajevo

YUGOSLAVIA

*Cabo de
São Vicente*

Valencia

*Islas Baleares
(Balearic Islands)*

Menorca

**ROMA
(ROME)**

ITALY

Appennino

**SOFIYA
(SOFIA)**

Strait of Gibraltar

Gibraltar (U.K.)

Eivissa

Mallorca

*Sardegna
(Sardinia)
(Italy)*

**NAPOLI
(NAPLES)**

Adriatic Sea

Tiranë
(Tirana)

MACEDON

Skopje

Ceuta
(Spain)

Cagliari

*Tyrrhenian
Sea*

Taranto

ALBANIA

RABAT

Melilla
(Spain)

M e d i t e r r a n e a n

Kerkyra
(Corfu)

GREE

**ALGER
(ALGIERS)**

Palermo

*Sicilia
(Sicily)*

Mte. Etna
3340

*Ionian
Sea*

Ath
(Ath

Tunis

S e a

Valletta

MALTA

A F R I C A

**Tarābulus
(Tripoli)**

Banghāzī

D   0°   E   10°   F   20°

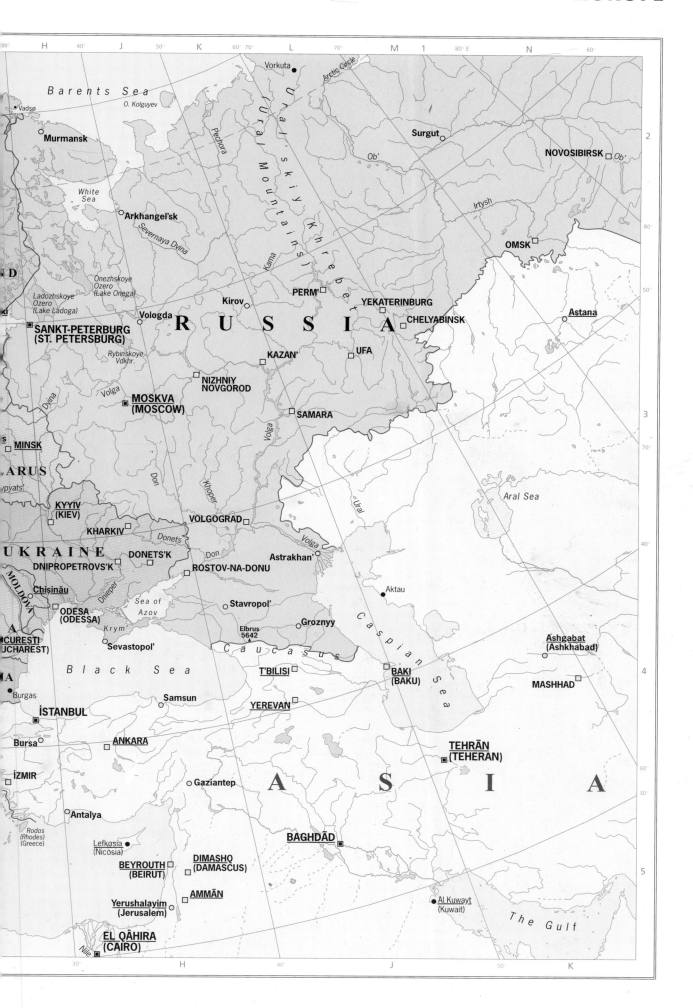

Barents Sea

Vadsø

Murmansk

O. Kolguyev

White Sea

Arkhangel'sk

Severnaya Dvina

Onezhskoye Ozero (Lake Onega)

Ladozhskoye Ozero (Lake Ladoga)

Vologda

SANKT-PETERBURG (ST. PETERSBURG)

Rybinskoye Vdkhr.

R U S S I A

Vorkuta

Ural'skiy Khrebet (Ural Mountains)

Pechora

Surgut

NOVOSIBIRSK   Ob'

Ob'

Irtysh

OMSK

Kama

PERM'

Kirov

YEKATERINBURG

CHELYABINSK

Astana

KAZAN'

UFA

Dvina

NIZHNIY NOVGOROD

Volga

MOSKVA (MOSCOW)

SAMARA

MINSK

Volga

ARUS

pyats'

KYYIV (KIEV)

Don

Khoper

VOLGOGRAD

Aral Sea

KHARKIV

Donets

Ural

UKRAINE

DONETS'K

Don

ROSTOV-NA-DONU

Astrakhan'

Volga

DNIPROPETROVS'K

MOLDOVA

Chişinău

Dnieper

Sea of Azov

Stavropol'

Aktau

ODESA (ODESSA)

Krym'

Elbrus 5642

Groznyy

Caspian Sea

Ashgabat (Ashkhabad)

CURESTI (UCHAREST)

Sevastopol'

C a u c a s u s

T'BILISI

BAKI (BAKU)

MASHHAD

A

Burgas

Black Sea

Samsun

YEREVAN

İSTANBUL

Bursa

ANKARA

TEHRĀN (TEHERAN)

İZMIR

Gaziantep

A   S   I   A

Antalya

Rodos (Rhodes) (Greece)

Lefkosia (Nicosia)

BAGHDĀD

BEYROUTH (BEIRUT)

DIMASHQ (DAMASCUS)

Yerushalayim (Jerusalem)

AMMĀN

Al Kuwayt (Kuwait)

EL QÂHIRA (CAIRO)

Nile

The Gulf

Arctic Circle

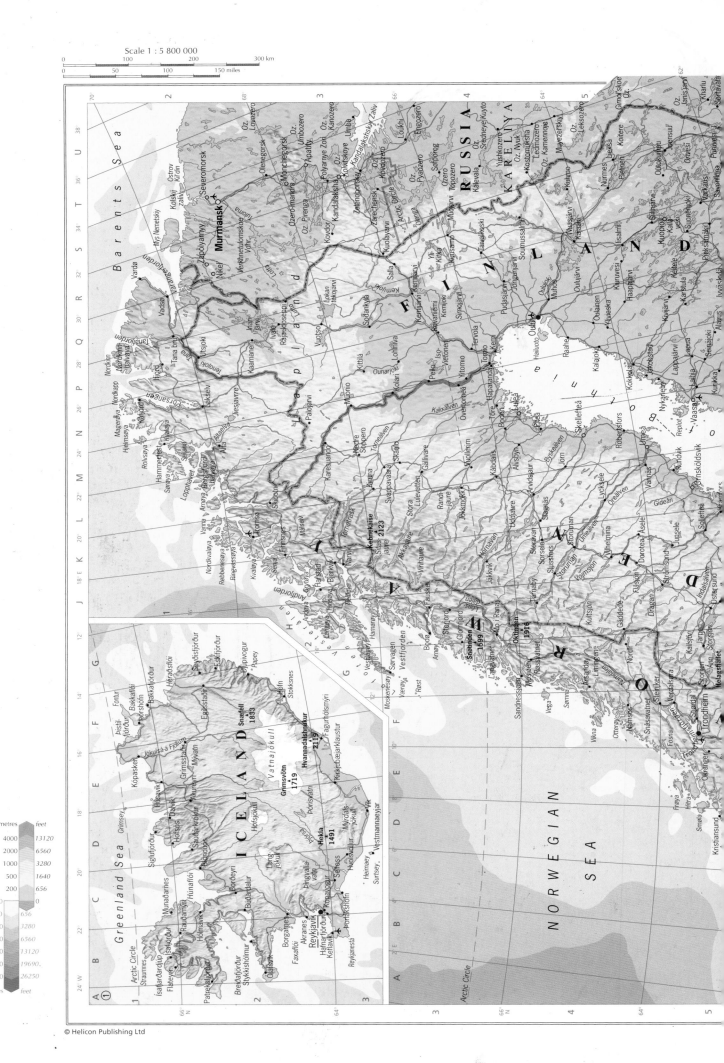

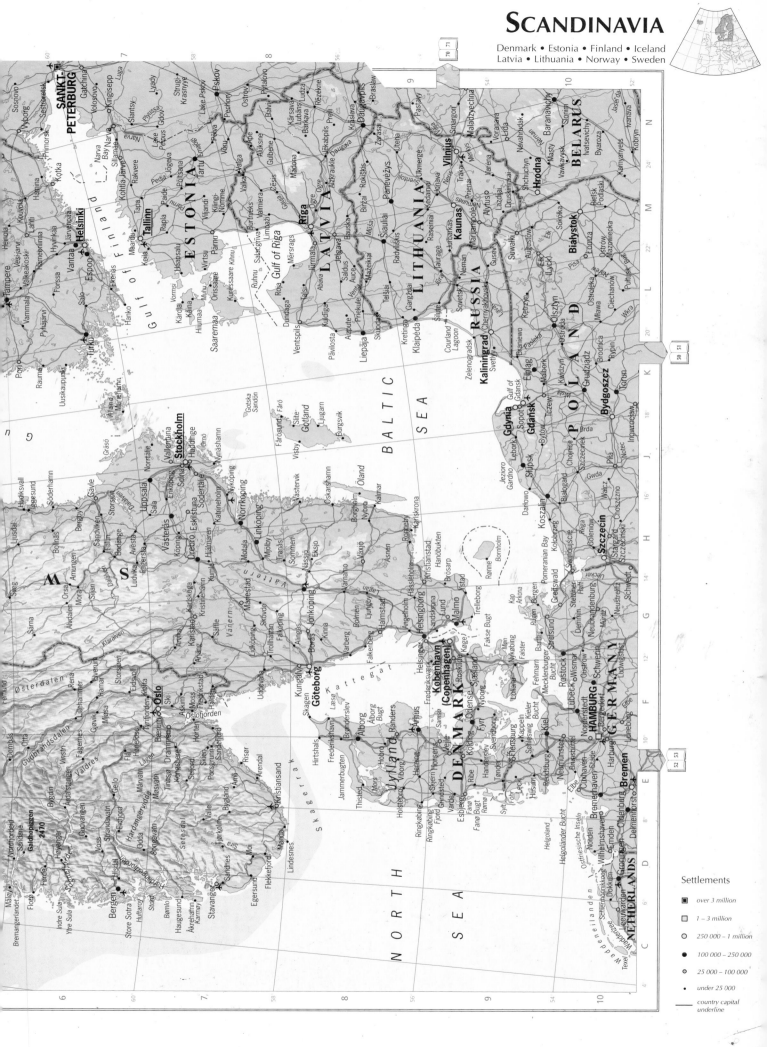

SCANDINAVIA

Denmark • Estonia • Finland • Iceland
Latvia • Lithuania • Norway • Sweden

SANKT-
PETERBURG

Helsinki

Tallinn

ESTONIA

Gulf of Finland

LATVIA

Rīga

Gulf of Riga

LITHUANIA

Vilnius

Kaunas

RUSSIA

Hrodna

BELARUS

Kaliningrad

Gdynia
Sopot
Gdańsk

POLAND

Białystok

Bydgoszcz

Szczecin

BALTIC
SEA

Gotland

Bornholm

Stockholm
Huddinge

Uppsala

Gävle

S
W
E
D
E
N

Göteborg

København
(Copenhagen)

Malmö

Kattegat

DENMARK

Jylland

Kiel

HAMBURG

Bremen

GERMANY

HRODNA

Oslo

NORTH
SEA

Skagerrak

Bergen

Galdhøpiggen
2470

N
O
R
W
A
Y

NETHERLANDS

Settlements

■	over 3 million
□	1 – 3 million
◉	250 000 – 1 million
●	100 000 – 250 000
○	25 000 – 100 000
•	under 25 000
___	country capital underline

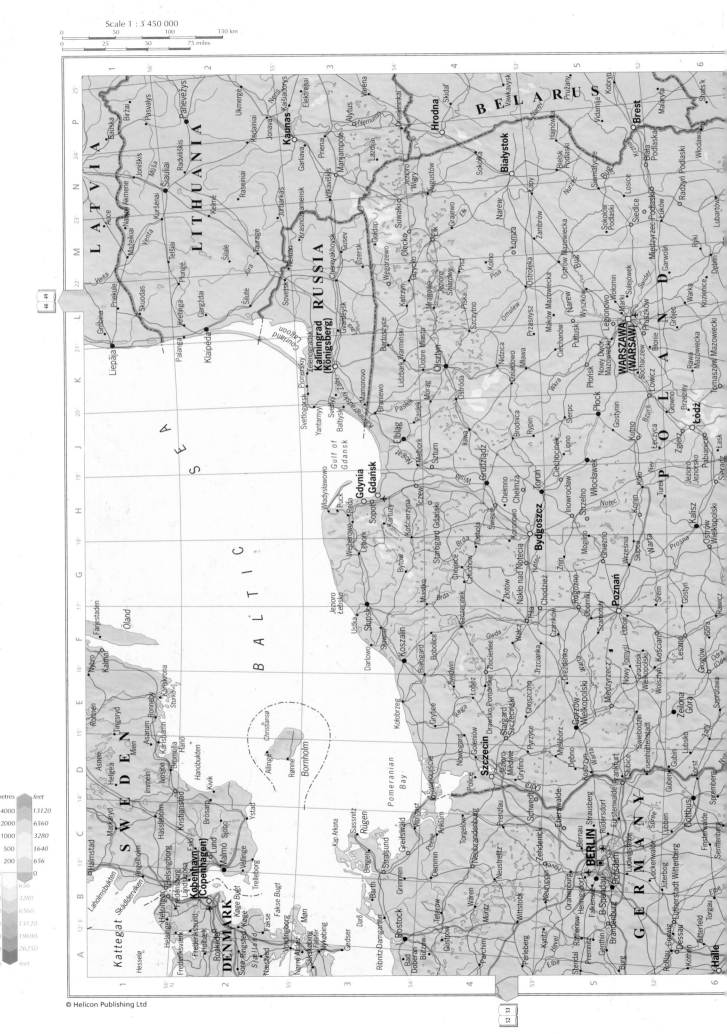

Scale 1 : 3 450 000

© Helicon Publishing Ltd

Countries / regions (large labels): UKRAINE, ROMANIA, SLOVAK REPUBLIC, HUNGARY, CZECH REPUBLIC, AUSTRIA, YUGOSLAVIA, CROATIA, SLOVENIA, ITALY, Carpathian Mountains, Böhmerwald, Nieder Tauern

Capitals / major cities: L'viv, Kraków, Praha (Prague), Ostrava, Brno, Wien (Vienna), Bratislava, Budapest, Zagreb, Ljubljana, Timişoara, Cluj-Napoca, Chemnitz

Peaks: 2043 Ďumbier, 1014 Kékes, 2995 Hohe Dachstein, 2864 Triglav, 1456 Großer Arber, 3798 Großglockner

Settlements

■	over 3 million
□	1 – 3 million
○	250 000 – 1 million
●	100 000 – 250 000
◉	25 000 – 100 000
•	under 25 000
—	country capital underline
~	urban area

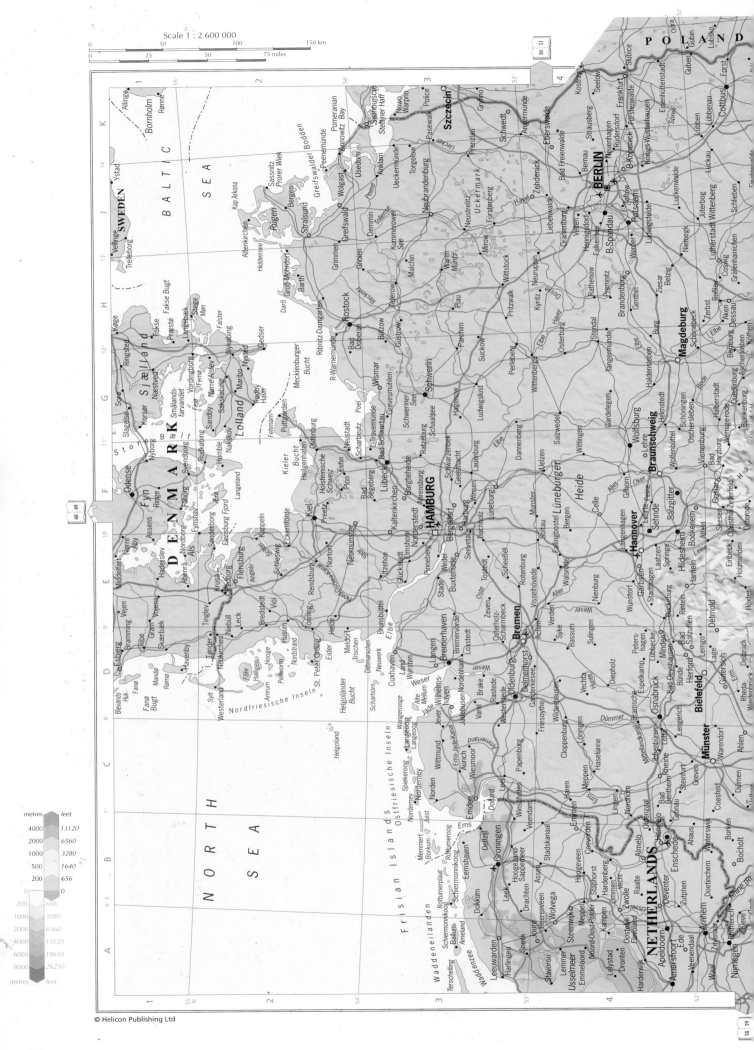

Scale 1 : 2 600 000

0   50   100   150 km
0   25   50   75 miles

© Helicon Publishing Ltd

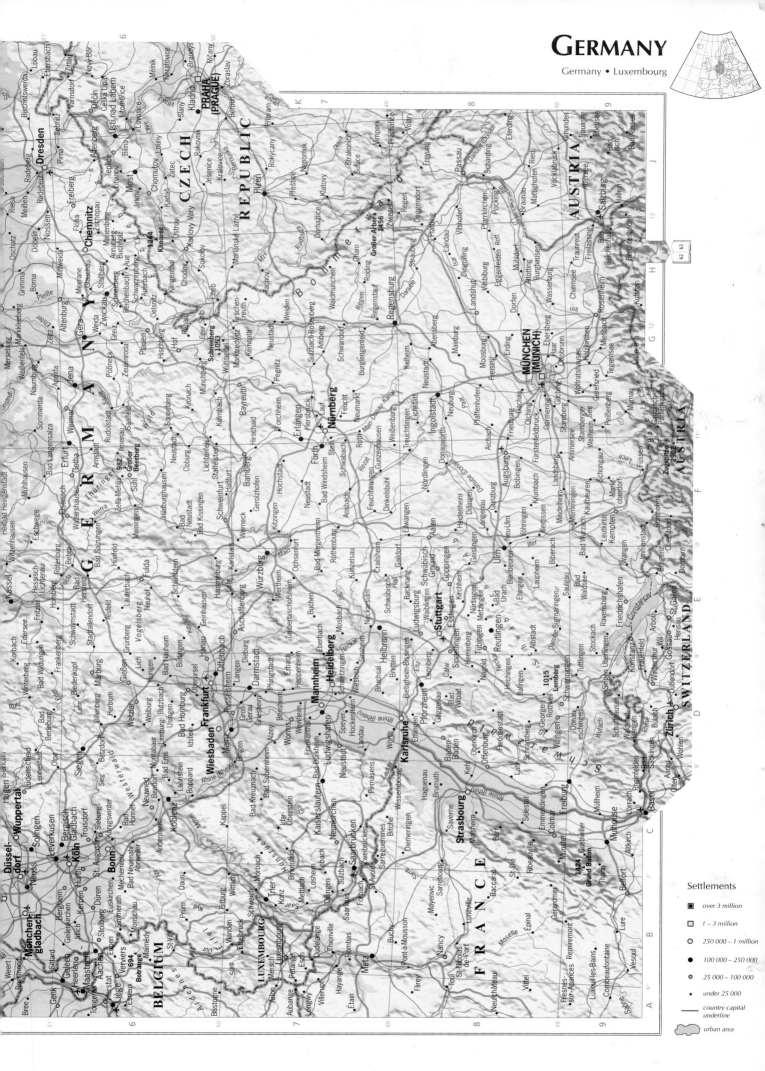

GERMANY

Germany • Luxembourg

Settlements

■ over 3 million

□ 1 – 3 million

○ 250 000 – 1 million

● 100 000 – 250 000

◦ 25 000 – 100 000

· under 25 000

— country capital
underline

urban area

Scale 1 : 2 300 000

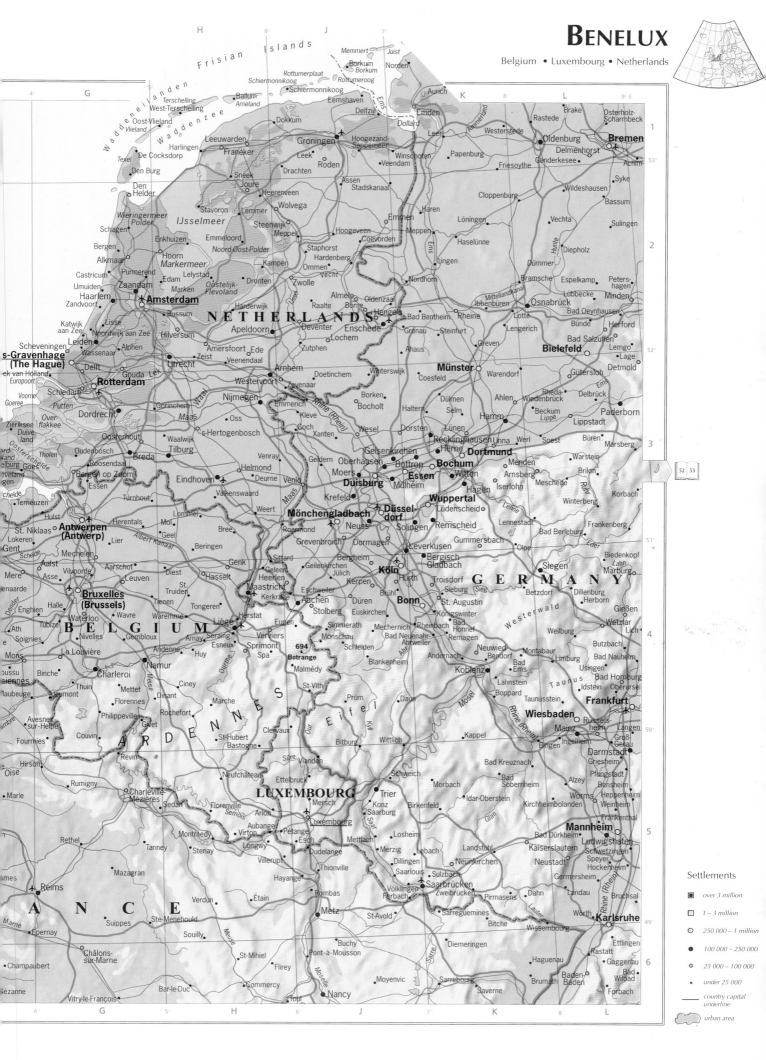

Frisian Islands

Memmert
Borkum
Borkum
Juist
Norden
Rottumerplaat
Schiermonnikoog
Rottumeroog
Schiermonnikoog
Aurich

Waddeneilanden
Terschelling
West-Terschelling
Ameland
Ballum
Eemshaven
Delfzijl
Emden
Leer
Rastede
Brake
Osterholz-Scharmbeck
Oost-Vlieland
Vlieland
Waddenzee
Harlingen
Dokkum
Hoogezand-Sappemeer
Dollard
Westerstede
Oldenburg
Delmenhorst
Bremen
Texel
De Cocksdorp
Leeuwarden
Franeker
Groningen
Winschoten
Papenburg
Friesoythe
Ganderkesee
Achim
Den Burg
Den Helder
Sneek
Joure
Leek
Roden
Veendam
Assen
Stadskanaal
Cloppenburg
Wildeshausen
Syke
Bassum
Sulingen

Wieringermeer Polder
Schagen
Heerenveen
Wolvega
Haren
Löningen
Vechta
Diepholz
Hunte
Bergen
Alkmaar
Castricum
IJmuiden
Zaandam
Haarlem
Zandvoort
Enkhuizen
Hoorn
Markermeer
Edam
Marken
Purmerend
Stavoren
Lemmer
Emmeloord
Noord-Oost-Polder
Steenwijk
Meppel
Staphorst
Hoogeveen
Coevorden
Emmen
Meppen
Haselünne
Lingen
Nordhorn
Bramsche
Espelkamp
Dümmer
Petershagen
Minden

IJsselmeer
Amsterdam
Zaandam
Lelystad
Oostelijk-Flevoland
Dronten
Zwolle
Raalte
Oldenzaal
Almelo
Borne
Ibbenbüren
Mittellandkanal
Osnabrück
Lübbecke
Bünde
Bad Oeynhausen
Herford

NETHERLANDS
Harderwijk
Apeldoorn
Deventer
Hengelo
Enschede
Gronau
Ahaus
Steinfurt
Greven
Bielefeld
Lage
Detmold
's-Gravenhage (The Hague)
Scheveningen
Leiden
Wassenaar
Katwijk aan Zee
Noordwijk aan Zee
Alphen
Hilversum
Amersfoort
Ede
Zeist
Veenendaal
Arnhem
Doetinchem
Winterswijk
Coesfeld
Münster
Warendorf
Gütersloh
Bad Salzuflen
Lemgo

Delft
Gouda
Lek
Utrecht
Westervoort
Zevenaar
Borken
Ahlen
Rheda-Wiedenbrück
Delbrück
Rotterdam
Schiedam
Europoort
ek van Holland
Nijmegen
Emmerich
Rhine (Rhein)
Wesel
Dorsten
Haltern
Dülmen
Selm
Lünen
Hamm
Beckum
Lippe
Paderborn
Lippstadt

Voorne
Goeree
Putten
Dordrecht
Gorinchem
Waal
Maas
s-Hertogenbosch
Oss
Kleve
Goch
Xanten
Gelsenkirchen
Recklinghausen
Unna
Werl
Soest
Büren
Marsberg

Zierikzee
Duiveland
Overflakkee
Oosterhout
Waalwijk
Tilburg
Venray
Geldern
Oberhausen
Bottrop
Herne
Dortmund
Menden
Warstein
Brilon

Tholen
Goes
Roosendaal
Breda
Helmond
Deurne
Moers
Duisburg
Mülheim
Essen
Witten
Bochum
Arnsberg
Iserlohn
Mescheide
Korbach

Bergen op Zoom
Essen
Eindhoven
Valkenswaard
Weert
Venlo
Krefeld
Hagen
Lüdenscheid
Winterberg

Terneuzen
Hulst
St. Niklaas
Antwerpen (Antwerp)
Turnhout
Herentals
Lier
Mol
Geel
Bree
Roermond
Mönchengladbach
Neuss
Düsseldorf
Solingen
Remscheid
Wuppertal
Lennestadt
Bad Berleburg
Frankenberg

Lokeren
Gent
Mechelen
Aarschot
Diest
Lommel
Beringen
Genk
Sittard
Geilenkirchen
Jülich
Grevenbroich
Dormagen
Leverkusen
Bergheim
Bergisch Gladbach
Gummersbach
Olpe
Biedenkopf
Lahn
Marburg

Aalst
Mere
Asse
Vilvoorde
Leuven
Hasselt
Heerlen
Eschweiler
Kerpen
Brühl
Hürth
Köln
Troisdorf
Siegburg
Sieg
Siegen
Betzdorf
Dillenburg
Herborn
Gießen
Wetzlar
Lich

enaarde
Enghien
Waterloo
Bruxelles (Brussels)
Wavre
St. Truiden
Tienen
Tongeren
Maastricht
Kerkrade
Aachen
Düren
Euskirchen
Bonn
St. Augustin
Königswinter
Westerwald
Weilburg
Butzbach
Bad Nauheim
Bad Homburg

Ath
Soignies
Nivelles
Gembloux
Andenne
Amay
Seraing
Liège
Herstal
Eupen
Verviers
Simmerath
Monschau
Mechernich
Rheinbach
Bad Honnef
Remagen
Neuwied
Bendorf
Montabaur
Limburg
Usingen
Idstein
Oberursel

Mons
Binche
Thuin
Mettet
Ciney
Huy
Esneux
Sprimont
Spa
694
Botrange
Malmédy
Schleiden
Blankenheim
Ahr
Andernach
Koblenz
Bad Ems
Lahnstein
Boppard
Taunusstein
Taunus
Frankfurt

oussu
Charleroi
Namur
Dinant
Rochefort
Marche
St-Vith
Prüm
Eifel
Daun
Kyll
Mosel
Wiesbaden
Mainz
Rüsselsheim
Langen

iennes
aubeuge
Philippeville
Florennes
Givet
Couvin
Beauraing
Clervaux
Bitburg
Wittlich
Kappel
Bad Kreuznach
Rhine (Rhein)
Bingen
Ingelheim
Groß-Gerau
Darmstadt
Pfungstadt
Bensheim

Oise
Marle
Avesnes-sur-Helpe
Fourmies
Hirson
Rumigny
Revin
Charleville-Mézières
Sedan
St-Hubert
Bastogne
Neufchâteau
Vianden
Ettelbruck
Sûre
Schweich
Morbach
Idar-Oberstein
Bad Sobernheim
Alzey
Worms
Heppenheim
Weinheim

Rethel
Mazagran
Montmedy
Stenay
Tanney
Florenville
Semois
Arlon
Aubange
Virton
Longwy
LUXEMBOURG
Mersch
Luxembourg
Pétange
Esch
Dudelange
Trier
Konz
Saarburg
Saar
Birkenfeld
Mettlach
Losheim
Landstuhl
Merzig
Kirchheimbolanden
Frankenthal
Mannheim
Ludwigshafen
Schwetzingen
Speyer
Hockenheim

Reims
Champaubert
Épernay
Châlons-sur-Marne
Suippes
Ste-Menehould
Souilly
Villerupt
Thionville
Hayange
Rombas
Metz
St-Avold
Völklingen
Forbach
Saarbrücken
Zweibrücken
Sarreguemines
Bitche
Wissembourg
Karlsruhe
Germersheim
Landau
Bruchsal
Wörth
Bad Wildbad
Forbach

Vitry-le-François
ézanne
Marne
Bar-le-Duc
Flirey
Commercy
Pont-à-Mousson
Toul
Nancy
Buchy
Moyenvic
Sarrebourg
Diemeringen
Haguenau
Brumath
Baden-Baden
Rastatt
Ettlingen
Gaggenau
Bad Wildbad

ANCE
BELGIUM
ARDENNES
GERMANY
FRANCE

Settlements

- ▣ over 3 million
- □ 1 – 3 million
- ○ 250 000 – 1 million
- ● 100 000 – 250 000
- ○ 25 000 – 100 000
- • under 25 000
- —— country capital underline
- urban area

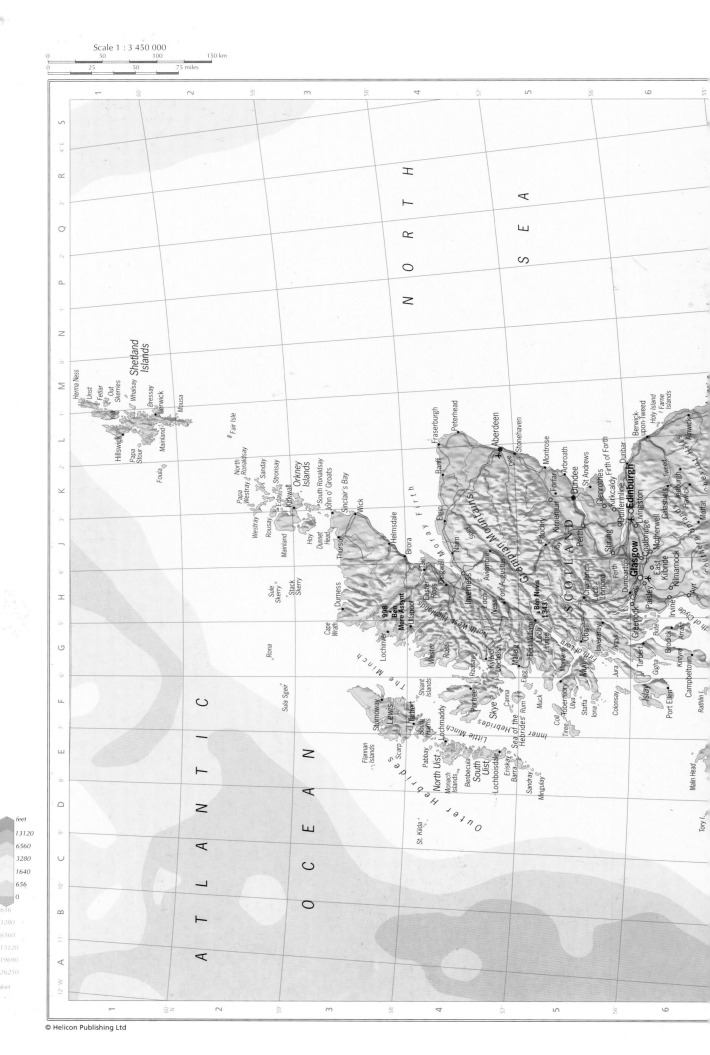

Scale 1 : 3 450 000

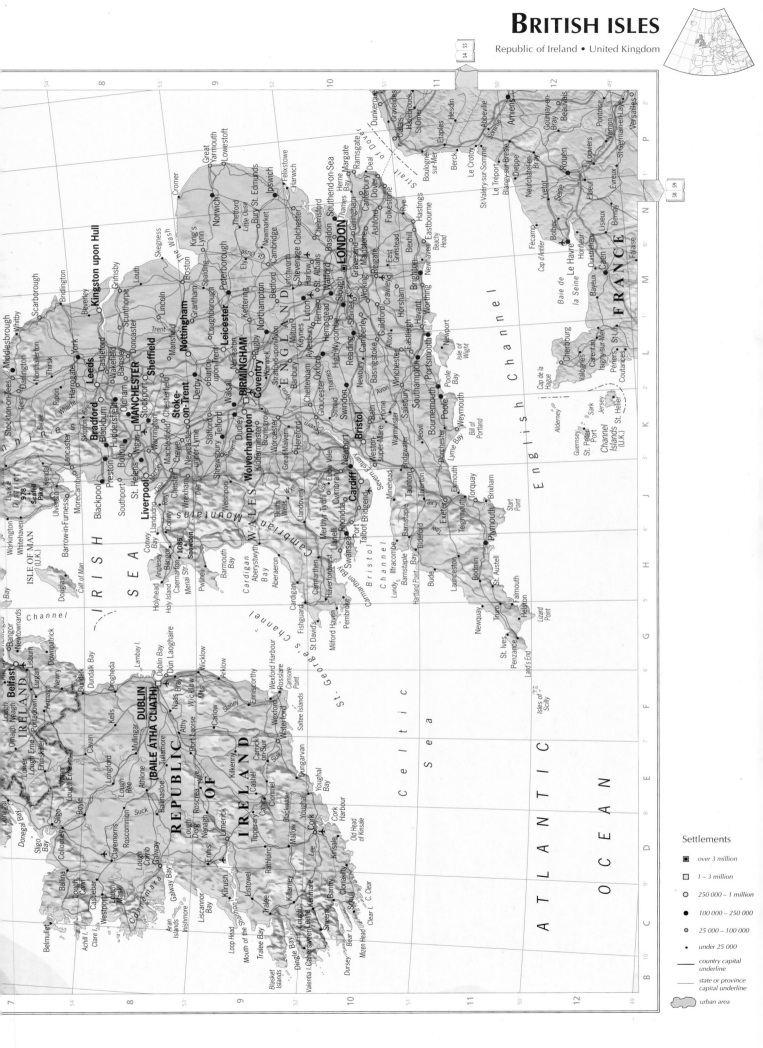

Settlements

◼ over 3 million

◻ 1 – 3 million

◯ 250 000 – 1 million

● 100 000 – 250 000

◉ 25 000 – 100 000

• under 25 000

— country capital underline

— state or province capital underline

⬭ urban area

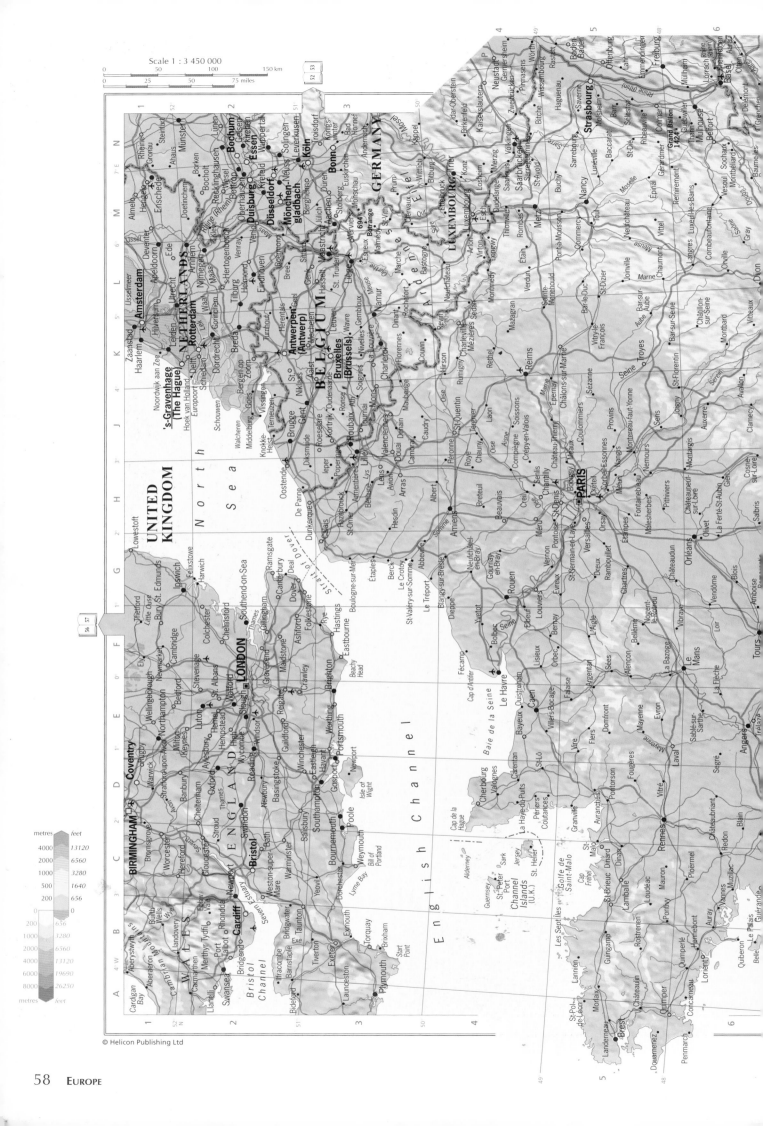

© Helicon Publishing Ltd

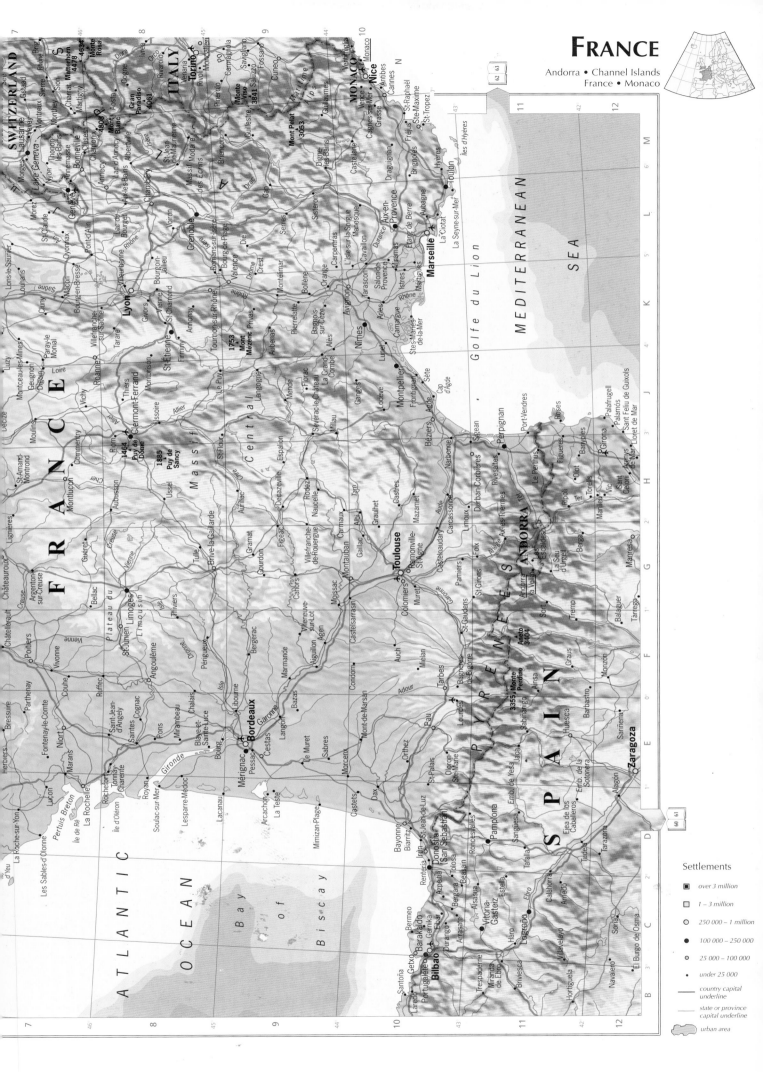

FRANCE

Andorra • Channel Islands
France • Monaco

Settlements

■ over 3 million

□ 1 – 3 million

◉ 250 000 – 1 million

● 100 000 – 250 000

◍ 25 000 – 100 000

· under 25 000

— country capital
underline

— state or province
capital underline

urban area

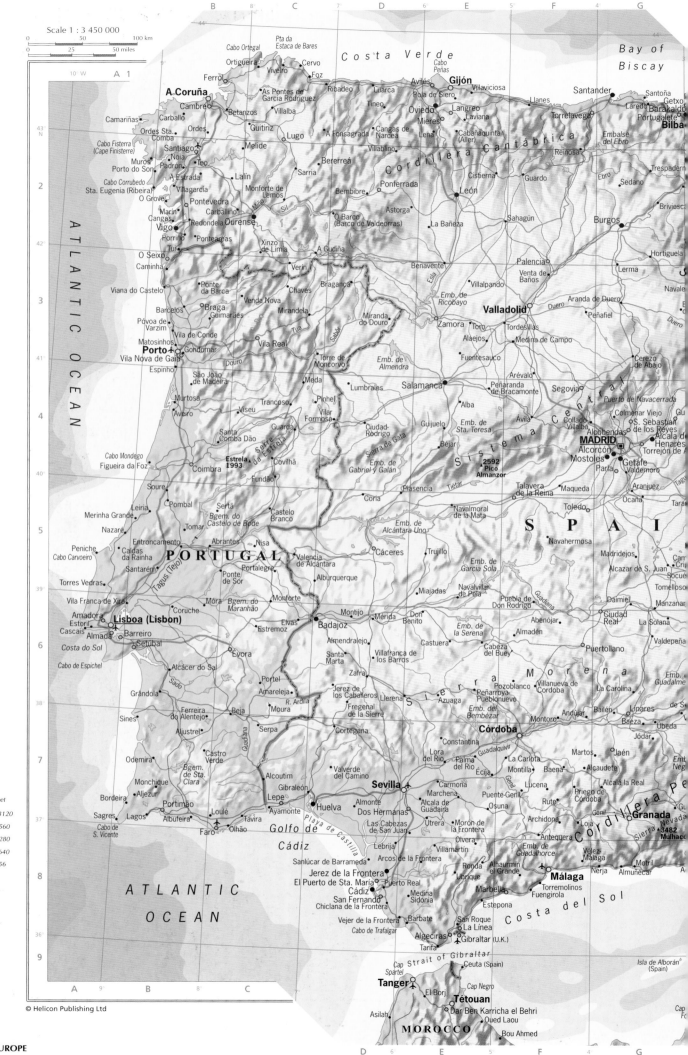

Scale 1 : 3 450 000

© Helicon Publishing Ltd

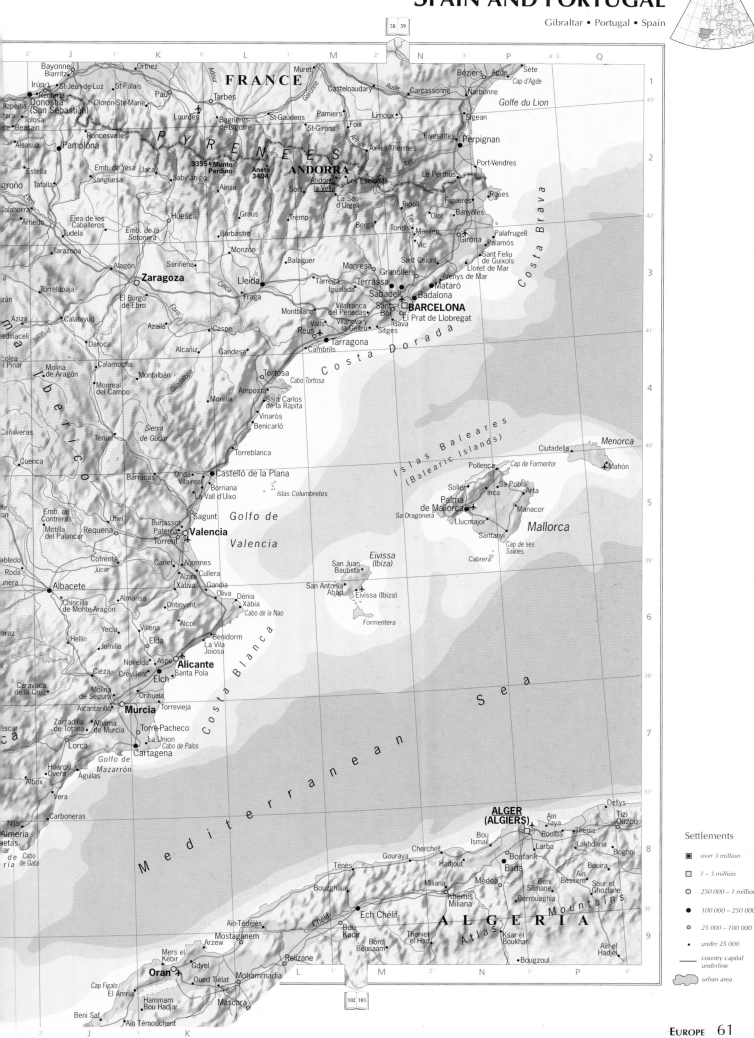

Settlements

■	over 3 million
□	1 – 3 million
○	250 000 – 1 million
●	100 000 – 250 000
○	25 000 – 100 000
•	under 25 000
—	country capital underline
	urban area

Scale 1 : 2 600 000

© Helicon Publishing Ltd

52 53

CZECH REPUBLIC

SLOVAK REP.

AUSTRIA

HUNGARY

SLOVENIA

CROATIA

BOSNIA-HERZEGOVINA

SAN MARINO

WIEN (VIENNA)

Bratislava

Zagreb

Ljubljana

Venezia (Venice)

Salzburg · Linz · Graz · Maribor

Regensburg · Regen · Passau

Großglockner 3798

Triglav 2864

Snežnik 1796

Vaganski Vrh 1758

Niedere Tauern · Hohe Tauern · Karnische Alpen · Dinaric Alps

Golfo di Venezia · *Golfo di Trieste*

Adriatic Sea

66 67

64 65

Settlements

▫	1 – 3 million
○	250 000 – 1 million
●	100 000 – 250 000
◦	25 000 – 100 000
·	under 25 000
——	country capital underline
〰	urban area

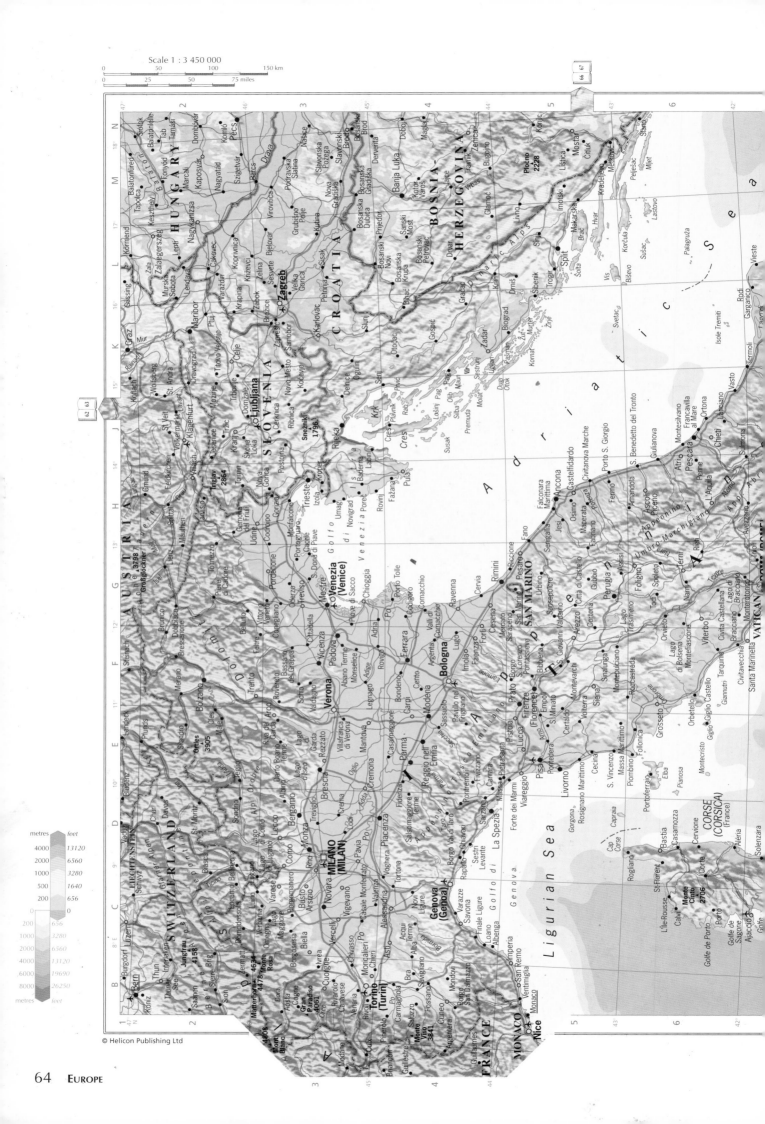

ITALY

Corsica • Italy • Malta • San Marino • Vatican City

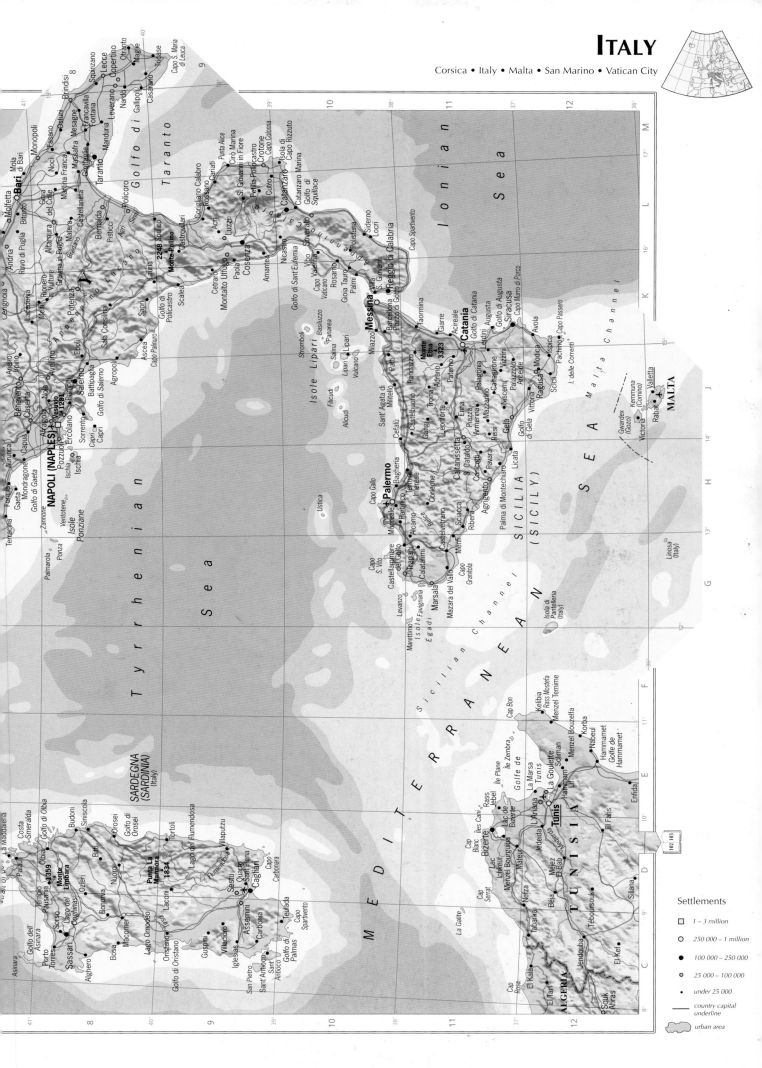

Otranto Maglie Tricase Capo S. Maria di Leuca
Squinzano Lecce Copertino
Brindisi Leverano Nardò Gallipoli
Mesagne Francavilla Fontana Manduria Casarano
Ostuni Martina Franca
Cisternino Grottaglie
Mola di Bari Taranto
Monopoli Noci
Bari Castellaneta Golfo di Taranto
Bitonto Palagianello
Molfetta Gioia del Colle Bernalda Pisticci
Ruvo di Puglia Altamura Matera Policoro
Andria Gravina in Puglia Grassano Punta Alice
Corato Montalbano Jonico Ciró Marina
Cerignola Melfi Rionero in Vulture Spinazzola Ciró
Lacedonia Potenza Acri S. Giovanni in Fiore
Laurenzana Castrovillari Crotone Capo Colonna
Ariano Irpino **2248 Monte-Pollino** Cosenza Cutro
Benevento Avellino Sala Consilina Paola Catanzaro Capo di
Nola Eboli Cetraro Luzzi Soverato Squillace
NAPOLI (NAPLES) Agropoli Scalea Nicastro Siderno
Caserta Salerno Montalto Uffugo Rosarno Locri
Capua Battipaglia Golfo di Policastro Capo Vaticano Capo Spartivento
Aragona **Vesuvio 1281** Sapri Vibo Valentia Gioia Tauro
Pozzuoli Ercolano Ascea Capo Palinuro Palmi S. Giovanni
Sorrento Capri **Messina** Reggio di Calabria Pozzo di Gotto
Ischia Capri Stromboli Milazzo Barcellona Taormina
Isole Lipari Basiluzzo Giarre
Panarea Salina Randazzo Acireale
Filicudi Lipari Vulcano **Monte Etna 3323** **Catania**
Alicudi Sant'Agata di Militello Troina Adrano Paternò Golfo di Catania
Cefalù Castelbuono Gangi Leonforte Lentini Augusta
Ustica Termini Nicosia Enna Piazza Vizzini Siracusa
Palermo Imerese Caltanissetta Armerina Caltagirone Capo Murro di Porco
Monreale Bagheria S. Cataldo Canicatti Palazzolo Avola
Partinico Corleone Gela Acreide Capo Passero
Alcamo Sciacca Agrigento Favara Licata Vittoria Pachino Capo Passero
Castelvetrano Ribera Palma di Montechiaro Golfo di Gela Modica I. delle Correnti
Menfi Scicli Ispica
Mazara del Vallo Comiso Ragusa
Marsala Campobello **SICILIA (SICILY)**
Calatafimi Trapani
Castellammare del Golfo Capo S. Vito
Levanzo **MALTA**
Marettimo **Isole Égadi** Favignana Gwardex (Gozo) Kemmuna (Comino)
Isola di Pantelleria (Italy) Victoria Rabat **Valletta**
Linosa (Italy)

Tyrrhenian Sea

Ionian Sea

Malta Channel

MEDITERRANEAN SEA

Mediterranean Sea

Sicilian Channel

Sardegna (SARDINIA) (Italy)

Costa Smeralda Golfo di Olbia
La Maddalena Olbia
Porto Torres Siniscola
Sassari Budoni Orosei
Alghero Bitti Golfo di Orosei
Bonorva Nuoro
Bosa Macomer **Punta La Marmora 1834**
Monte Limbara 1359 Tortolì
Tempio Pausania Oristano Lago del Flumendosa
Sorso Lago di Coghinas Villaputzu
Ozieri Laconi Sant'Elena
Golfo di Oristano Lago Omodeo Muravera
Guspini Quarto Cagliari
Villacidro Sant'Elena Golfo di Cagliari
Iglesias Assemini Carbonia
San Pietro Sant'Antioco Capo Carbonara
Sant'Antioco Golfo di Palmas Capo Spartivento
Carbonara

TUNISIA
Tunis La Goulette La Marsa
Bizerte Ariana Soliman
Menzel Bourguiba Hammam Hammamet
Mateur Lif Golfe de Hammamet
Béja Menzel Temime
Medjez Nabeul Korba
El Bab Grombalia
Nefza Soliman
Tabarka Mejez El Fahs
Jendouba Siliana
Tébourouk Enfida
ALGERIA El Kef
Souk El Tarf Cap Bon
Ahras Kelibia Rass Mostéfa Menzel Bouzelfa
Ras Jebel Îles Cani Golfe de Tunis
Cap Blanc Cap Serrat Îlot Plane Île Zembra
Lac de Bizerte Lac Ichkeul
Cap Negro Cap Rosa La Galite

EUROPE 65

Settlements

☐ 1 – 3 million
◯ 250 000 – 1 million
● 100 000 – 250 000
◉ 25 000 – 100 000
· under 25 000
—— country capital underline
⬡ urban area

102 103

© Helicon Publishing Ltd

UKRAINE

MOLDOVA

ROMANIA

ODESA
(ODESSA)

Chişinău

Cluj-Napoca

Târgu Mureş

BUCUREŞTI
(BUCHAREST)

Craiova

Ploieşti

Constanţa

Varna

BLACK

SEA

Burgas

SOFIJA
(SOFIA)

BULGARIA

Plovdiv

Edirne

TURKEY

İSTANBUL

Kartal

GREECE

Marmara Denizi
(Sea of Marmara)

Settlements

▣	over 3 million
▢	1 – 3 million
○	250 000 – 1 million
●	100 000 – 250 000
◎	25 000 – 100 000
•	under 25 000
──	country capital underline
──	state or province capital underline
⬡	urban area

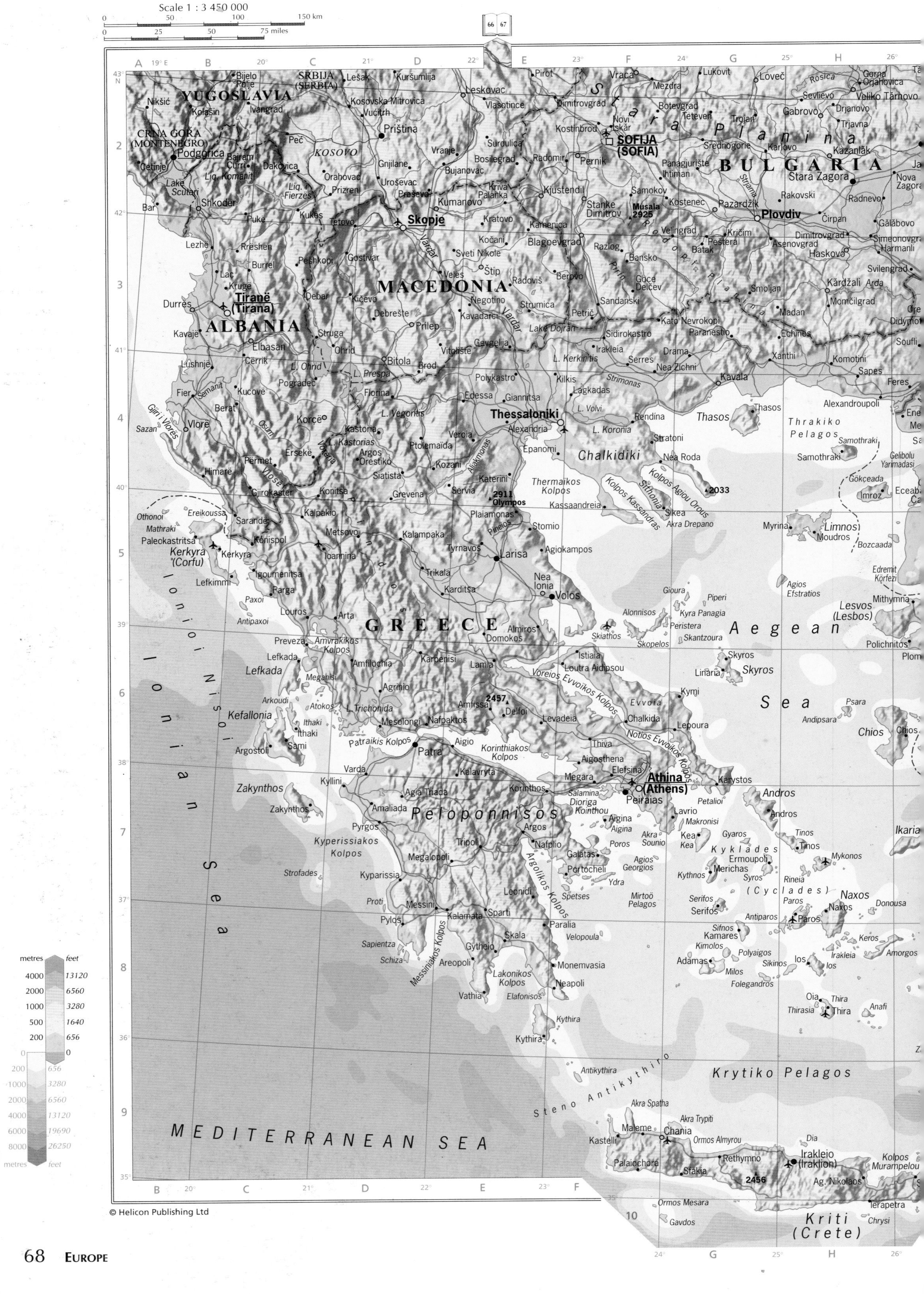

Scale 1 : 3 450 000

0   50   100   150 km
0   25   50   75 miles

66 67

YUGOSLAVIA

SRBIJA (SERBIA)

Bijelo Polje
Nikšić
Kolašin
Ivangrad
Peč
Lešak
Kuršumlija
Leskovac
Pirot
Vraca
Mezdra
Lukovit
Loveč
Rosica
Gorna Orjahovica
Veliko Tărnovo

CRNA GORA (MONTENEGRO)
Podgorica
Cetinje
Bairam Curri
Dakovica
Kosovska Mitrovica
Vučitrn
Priština
KOSOVO
Vranje
Bosilegrad
Surdulica
Radomir
Pernik
Kostinbrod
Novi Iskăr
SOFIJA (SOFIJA)
Botevgrad
Teteven
Trojan
Gabrovo
Drjanovo
Srednogorie
Karlovo
Kazanlăk
BULGARIA

Bar
Lake Scutari
Liq. i Komanit
Shkodër
Puke
Liq. i Fierzës
Prizren
Uroševac
Gnjilane
Preševo
Kumanovo
Kriva Palanka
Kjustendil
Stanke Dimitrov
Samokov
Kostenec
Pazardžik
Rakovski
Radnevo
Musala 2925
Panagjurište
Ihtiman
Velingrad
Peštera
Batak
Asenovgrad
Haskovo
Simeonovgrad
Harmanli
Plovdiv
Dimitrovgrad
Svilengrad
Čirpan
Gălăbovo
Stara Zagora
Nova Zagora

Lezhe
Rrëshen
Burrel
Tetovo
Skopje
Kratovo
Kočani
Berovo
Razlog
Bansko
Goce Delčev
Smoljan
Kărdžali
Arda
Madan
Momčilgrad

Lac
Krujë
Tiranë (Tirana)
Peshkopi
Gostivar
Kičevo
Debar
Debrešte
MACEDONIA
Veles
Štip
Radoviš
Strumica
Petrič
Sandanski
Kato Nevrokopi
Paranestio
Echinos
Xanthi
Komotini

Durrës
ALBANIA
Kavaje
Elbasan
Cërrik
Struga
Ohrid
Prilep
Negotino
Kavadarci
Gevgelija
L. Dojran
Sidirokastro
Serres
Drama
Nea Zichni
Sapes
Feres

Fier
Lushnjë
Berat
Pogradec
L. Ohrid
L. Prespa
Bitola
Brod
Vitoliste
Polykastro
Kilkis
Lagkadas
Strimonas
Kavala

Semani
Kucovë
Korcë
Florina
Edessa
Giannitsa
L. Kerkinitis
Thasos
Thrakiko Pelagos
Thasos
Alexandroupoli

Vlorë
Sazan
Gjiri i Vlores
Osum
L. Vegoritis
Kastoria
Ptolemaida
Veroia
Thessaloniki
Epanomi
L. Volvi
Rendina
Stratoni
Samothraki
Samothraki
Gökceada
Eceab

Himarë
Permet
Ersekë
L. Kastorias
Argos Orestiko
Siatista
Kozani
Servia
Alexandria
Chalkidiki
Nea Roda
Akra Drepano
Sikea
Imroz

Gjirokaster
Konitsa
Grevena
2911 Olympos
Katerini
Thermaikos Kolpos
Kassaandreia
Kolpos Kassandras
Kolpos Agiou Orous
Sithonia
2033

Othonoi
Ereikoussa
Mathraki
Paleokastritsa
Sarande
Kerkyra (Corfu)
Kerkyra
Metsovo
Kalpaki
Plaiamonas
Pinelos
Stomio
Agiokampos
Myrina
Limnos
Moudros
Bozcaada

Konispol
Igoumenitsa
Ioannina
Kalampaka
Tyrnavos
Larisa
Edremit Körfezi

Lefkimmi
Paxoi
Antipaxoi
Parga
Trikala
Karditsa
Nea Ionia
Volos
Gioura
Piperi
Kyra Panagia
Peristera
Agios Efstratios
Lesvos (Lesbos)
Mithymna

Loutros
Arta
G R E E C E
Almiros
Domokos
Alonnisos
Skantzoura
Skyros
Skyros
Linaria
Polichnitos

Preveza
Amvrakikos Kolpos
Amfilochia
Karpenisi
Lamia
Istiaia
Loutra Aidipsou
Skiathos
Skopelos
Kymi
Aegean Sea

Lefkada
Lefkada
Megablisi
Agrinio
Amfissa **2457**
Delfoi
Levadeia
Chalkida
Lepoura
Psara
Andipsara
Chios
Chios

Arkoudi
Atokos
Trichonida
Mesolongi
Nafpaktos
Thiva
Evvoia
Voreios Evvoikos Kolpos
Notios Evvoikos Kolpos

Kefallonia
Ithaki
Ithaki
Sami
Patraikis Kolpos
Aigio
Korinthiakos Kolpos
Aigosthena
Megara
Elefsina
Athina (Athens)
Karystos
Andros

Argostoli
Patra
Varda
Kalavryta
Korinthos
Salamina
Dioriga Ko**inthou**
Peiraias
Lavrio
Petalioi
Andros

Zakynthos
Kyllini
Agia Triada
Argos
Nafplio
Aigina
Aigina
Akra Sounio
Makronisi
Kea
Kea
Tinos
Tinos
Mykonos
Ikaria

Zakynthos
Peloponnisos
Amaliada
Pyrgos
Tripoli
Argolikos Kolpos
Galatas
Poros
Ydra
Agios Georgios
Gyaros
Kythnos
Merichas
Syros
Ermoupoli
Rineia
Kyklades (Cyclades)
Naxos

Kyperissiakos Kolpos
Megalopoli
Kyparissia
Spetses
Mirtoö Pelagos
Serifos
Serifos
Paros
Naxos
Naxos
Donousa
Antiparos
Paros
Keros
Amorgos

Strofades
Proti
Leonidi
Sifnos
Kamares
Kimolos
Polyaigos
Ios
Irakleia

Messini
Kalamata
Sparti
Paralia
Velopoula
Adamas
Milos
Sikinos
Ios
Folegandros

Pylos
Sapientza
Schiza
Gytheio
Skala
Monemvasia
Neapoli
Oia
Thira
Thirasia
Thira
Anafi

Messiniakos Kolpos
Areopoli
Lakonikos Kolpos
Elafonisos
Vathia
Kythira
Kythira

Antikythira
Krytiko Pelagos
Akra Spatha
Akra Trypiti
Steno Antikythiro
Gavdos
Chrysi

M E D I T E R R A N E A N   S E A

Kastelli
Palaiochora
Maleme
Chania
Stakia **2456**
Rethymno
Ormos Almyrou
Dia
Irakleio (Iraklion)
Kolpos Murampelou
Ag. Nikolaos
Ierapetra
Ormos Mesara

Kriti (Crete)

Ionioi Nisia
Ionian Sea

metres / feet
4000 / 13120
2000 / 6560
1000 / 3280
500 / 1640
200 / 656
0 / 0
200 / 656
1000 / 3280
2000 / 6560
4000 / 13120
6000 / 19690
8000 / 26250
metres / feet

© Helicon Publishing Ltd

Stara planina

Rodopi planina

Pirin

Albania • Greece • Macedonia • Western Turkey

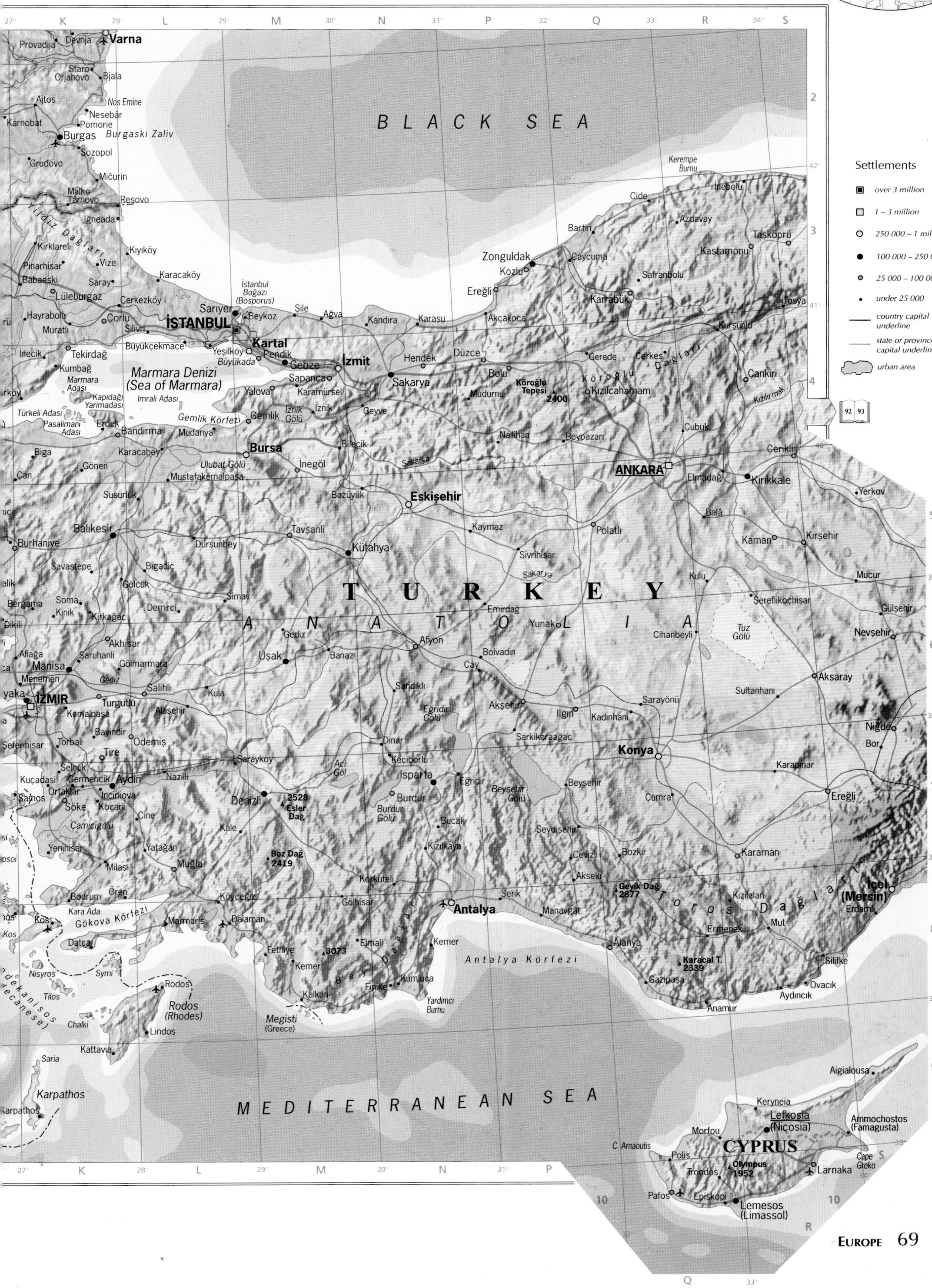

Settlements

▣	over 3 million
▢	1 – 3 million
○	250 000 – 1 million
●	100 000 – 250 000
○	25 000 – 100 000
•	under 25 000
▬	country capital underline
▬	state or province capital underline
	urban area

92 93

BLACK SEA

Provadija • Devnja • **Varna**
Staro Orjahovo • Bjala
Ajtos • Nos Emine • Nesebâr • Pomorie
Karnobat • **Burgas** • Burgaski Zaliv • Sozopol
Grudovo • Mičurin
Malko Tărnovo • Resovo
Yıldız Dağları • İğneada
Kırklareli • Vize • Kıyıköy
Pınarhisar • Saray • Karacaköy
Babaeski • Lüleburgaz • Çerkezköy
Hayrabolu • Çorlu • Silivri • **İSTANBUL** • Sarıyer • Beykoz • İstanbul Boğazı (Bosporus) • Şile • Ağva
Muratlı • Büyükçekmece • **Kartal** • Yeşilköy • Pendik • Gebze • **İzmit**
Tekirdağ • Büyükada • Kandıra • Karasu • Akçakoca
Kumbağ • Marmara Adası • Sapanca • Karamürsel • **Sakarya** • Hendek • Düzce
Türkeli Adası • Kapıdağı Yarimadası • İmralı Adası • Yalova • Geyve • Mudurnu • Bolu
Erdek • Bandırma • Gemlik Körfezi • Gemlik • İznik Gölü • İznik
Biga • Karacabey • Mudanya • **Bursa** • Bilecik • Sakarya
Çan • Gönen • Ulubat Gölü • İnegöl • Bozüyük • **Eskişehir** • Kaymaz • Polatlı
Mustafakemalpaşa • **ANKARA** • Elmadağ • **Kırıkkale**
Susurluk • Tavşanlı • Balâ • Yerköy
Balıkesir • Dursunbey • **Kütahya** • Sivrihisar • Kaman • Kırşehir • Mucur
Burhaniye • Bigadiç • Simav • Kulu • Şereflikoçhisar • Gülşehir
Savaştepe • Gölcük • **T U R K E Y A N A T O L I A** • Tuz Gölü • Nevşehir
Bergama • Soma • Demirci • Gediz • Emirdağ • Yunak • Cihanbeyli
Kınık • Kırkağaç • **Afyon** • Bolvadin • Sultanhanı • Aksaray • Niğde
Dikili • Akhisar • Uşak • Banaz • Çay • Sandıklı • Akşehir • Sarayönü • Bor
Allağa • Manisa • Saruhanlı • Gölmarmara • Gediz • İlgın • Kadınhanı
Menemen • Salihli • Kula • Eğridir Gölü • **Konya** • Karapınar
İZMİR • Turgutlu • Alaşehir • Dinar • Keçiborlu • Çumra • **Ereğli**
Kemalpaşa • Bayındır • Ödemiş • Sarayköy • Isparta • Eğridir • Beyşehir Gölü • Beyşehir • Karaman
Seferihisar • Torbalı • Tire • **Denizli** • Burdur • Bucak • Seydişehir
Selçuk • Germencik • **Aydın** • Nazilli • Kale • Burdur Gölü • Kızılkaya • Cevizli • Bozkır • Karaman
Kuşadası • Ortaklar • İncirliova • Çine • Akseki
Samos • Söke • Koçarli • Yatağan • Muğla • Korkuteli • Serik • **İçel (Mersin)**
Çamiçigölu • Milas • Ören • Köyceğiz • Gölhisar • **Antalya** • Manavgat • Ermenek • Mut • Erdemli
Yenihisar • Bodrum • Kara Ada • Gökova Körfezi • Marmaris • Dalaman • Elmalı • Kemer • Alanya • Gazipaşa • Silifke
Kos • Datça • Fethiye • Kemer • Kumluca • Antalya Körfezi • Anamur • Ovacık • Aydıncık
Nisyros • Symi • Rodos • Kalkan • Finike • Yardımcı Burnu
Tilos • Rodos (Rhodes) • Megisti (Greece) • Lindos
Chalki • Kattavia
Saria • Aigialousa
Karpathos • Keryneia • **Lefkosia (Nicosia)** • Ammochostos (Famagusta)
Morfou • **CYPRUS** • Cape Greko
C. Arnaoutis • Polis • Larnaka
Pafos • Olympus 1952 • Troodos • Episkopi • **Lemesos (Limassol)**

MEDITERRANEAN SEA

Kerempe Burnu • Cide • İnebolu
Azdavay • Taşköprü • Kastamonu
Bartın • Safranbolu • Tosya
Zonguldak • Kozlu • Çaycuma • Karabük • Kurşunlu
Ereğli • Koröğlü Dağları • Gerede • Çerkeş • Çankırı
Koröğlü Tepesi 2400 • Kızılcahamam • Kızılırmak • Çerikli
Nallıhan • Beypazarı • Çubuk

2528 Esler Dağ
Boz Dağ 2419
3073
Geyik Dağ 2877
Karacal T. 2339

Scale 1 : 10 400 000

0   200   400   600 km
0   100   200   300 miles

Norwegian Sea

NORWAY

2470 Galdhøpiggen   1796 Helagsfjället

SWEDEN

FINLAND   **KARELIYA**

Kristiansund · Molde · Trondheim · Namsos · Verdalsøra · Enafors · Dombås · Røros · Fagernes · Lillehammer · Mjøsa · Hamar · Hønefoss · Oslo · Moss · Arvika · Borlänge · Falun · Ludvika · Gävle · Vänern · Örebro · Västerås · Uppsala · Skövde · Motala · Eskilstuna · Norrköping · Södertälje · Borås · Jönköping · Linköping · Nyköping · Norrtälje · **Stockholm** · Varnamo · Västervik · Växjö · Karlskrona · Kalmar · Öland · Gotland

Tärnaby · Jokkmokk · Storavan · Gäddede · Storuman · Arvidsjaur · Boden · Luleå · Vilhelmina · Lycksele · Skellefteå · Åsele · Östersund · Strömsund · Umeå · Ljusdal · Sundsvall · Härnösand · Söderhamn · Hudiksvall · Mora · Ljusnan · Särna · Ånge · Kramfors · Örnsköldsvik

Gulf of Bothnia

Oulu · Kokkola · Jakobstad · Vaasa · Seinäjoki · Kristinestad · Pori · Turku · Tampere · Jyväskylä · Kuopio · Joensuu · Mikkeli · Hämeenlinna · Lahti · Kouvola · Kotka · **Helsinki** · Espoo · Vantaa · Hanko · Hameenlinna · Lappeenranta · Imatra · Savonlinna · Vyborg

Gulf of Finland

Kemi · Tornio · Rovaniemi · Kemijärvi · Salla · Sodankylä · Pello · Kalixälven · Overtorneå · Suomussalmi · Kuusamo · Pudasjärvi · Oulujoki · Iisalmi · Nurmes · Pielinen · Oz. Topozero · Kalevala · Loukhi · Yushkozero · Kem' · Belomorsk · Segezha · Onega · Medvezh'yegorsk · Oz. Vygozero · Pyal'ma · Porosozero · Suoyarvi · Kondopoga · Onezhskoye Ozero · **Petrozavodsk** · Pudozh · Sortavala · Pitkyaranta · Ladozhskoye Ozero (Lake Ladoga) · Olonets · Lodeynoye

Monchegorsk · Apatity · Kandalaksha · Zelenoborskiy · Oz. Pyaozero · Umba · **Kolskiy Poluostrov** · Kandalakshskiy Zaliv · Kuzomen · Morzhovets · **Beloye More (White Sea)** · Dvinskaya Guba · Kuya · **Severodvinsk** · **Arkhan[gelsk]** · Kargopol' · Nyandoma · Konosha · Vel'sk · Plesetsk · Bereznik

Barents Sea

ESTONIA

Tallinn · Haapsalu · Hiiumaa · Saaremaa · Pärnu · Viljandi · Tartu · Rakvere · Kohtla-Järve · Narva · Pushkin · **SANKT-PETERBURG (ST. PETERSBURG)** · Gatchina · Volkhov · Kirishi · Tikhvin · Babayevo · Belozersk · Lake Slantsy · Pskov · Ostrov · Opochka · Velikiye Luki · Lake Peipus · Valga · Võru · L. Pskov · Novgorod · Staraya Russa · Dno · Sol'tsy · Oz. Il'men' · Borovichi · **Cherepovets** · Gryazovets · **Vologda** · Sokol · Tot'ma · Syamzha · Kharovsk · Kirillov · Rybinskoye Vodokhranilishche · Poshekhon'ye · **Rybinsk** · Danilov · Buy · Galich · **Yaroslavl'** · **Kostroma** · Makar'yev · Kineshma

BALTIC SEA

Ventspils · Talsi · Liepāja · Jūrmala · **Riga** · Gulf of Riga · Valmiera · Jelgava · Ventа · Gulbene · **LATVIA** · Jēkabpils · Rēzekne · Daugava · Šiauliai · Telšiai · Klaipēda · **LITHUANIA** · Panevėžys · Daugavpils · Polatsk · Navapolatsk · Hlybokaye · Zap. Dvina · Nelidovo · Rzhev · Zubtsov · Staritsa · Ostashkov · Torzhok · **Tver'** · Dubna · Kimry · Klin · Zelenograd · Sergiyev Posad · Uglich · Rostov · Ivanovo · Shuya · Teykovo · Yur'yev · **Dzerzhinsk** · Kovrov · **Vladimir** · Murom · Vyksa · NOV[gorod]

RUSSIA

Słupsk · Koszalin · **Gdynia** · **Gdańsk** · Tczew · Kaliningrad · Chernyakhovsk · Chojnice · Elbląg · Olsztyn · Suwałki · Ełk · Grudziądz · **Bydgoszcz** · Toruń · Kalisz · **POLAND** · Włocławek · Płock · Ostrołęka · Piotrków Trybunalski · **Łódź** · Siedlce · **WARSZAWA (WARSAW)** · **Białystok** · **Częstochowa** · Radom · Puławy · **Katowice** · Kielce · **Lublin** · **Kraków** · Tarnów · Stalowa Wola · Zamość · Nowy Sącz · Rzeszów · Kovel' · **SLOVAK REP.** · Prešov · Košice · Poprad · Sambir · Drohobych · Uzhhorod · Mukacheve · **HUNGARY** · Nyíregyháza · Debrecen · Satu Mare · Oradea · Baia Mare · Zalău

Kaunas · Marijampolė · Alytus · Lazdijai · Kėdainiai · **Vilnius** · Hrodna · Lida · **MINSK** · Baranavichy · Maladzyechna · Vitsyebsk · **Smolensk** · Orsha · Barysaw · Safonovo · Pochinok · Yartsevo · Vyaz'ma · **MOSKVA (MOSCOW)** · Podol'sk · Obninsk · Serpukhov · Orekhovo-Zuyevo · Noginsk · Kolomna · Stupino · **Ryazan'** · Kasimov · **Kaluga** · Venev · Mithaylov · Shilovo · **Tula** · Novomoskovsk · Shatsk · **MORDOV[IYA]** · **BELARUS** · Slonim · Slutsk · Salihorsk · Kobryn · Brest · Pinsk · Stolin · Mazyr · **Mahilyow** · Babruysk · Krychaw · Svyetlahorsk · Rechytsa · Klintsy · Navlya · Novozybkov · **Bryansk** · **Orel** · Mtsensk · Novosil' · Plavsk · Dankov · Morshansk · Ryazhsk · Yefremov · Yelets · Livny · Zadonsk · **Lipetsk** · Michurinsk · Kirsanov · **Tambov** · Usman · Gryazi · Rtishchevo

UKRAINE

Luts'k · Rivne · Sarny · Chervonohrad · **L'viv** · Ternopil' · Shepetivka · Novohrad Volyns'kyy · **Zhytomyr** · Berdychiv · Khmel'nyts'kyy · Ivano-Frankivs'k · Kolomyya · Chernivtsi · Kam"yanets'-Podil's'kyy · Vinnytsya · **KYYIV (KIEV)** · Brovary · Pryluky · Romny · **Sumy** · Okhtyrka · Oboyan' · Bila Tserkva · Korosten' · Chornobyl' · Nizhyn · Konotop · Ryl'sk · Shchigry · **Kursk** · Shostka · Hlukhiv · **Chernihiv** · **Belgorod** · Staryy Oskol · Liski · Pavlovsk · **Voronezh** · Anna · Zherdevka · Borisoglebsk · Balasho[v] · Uryupinsk · Novoanninskiy · Povorino · Arkada[k]

Zhovkva · Dunayivtsi · Bal'ti · **MOLDOVA** · **Chişinău** · Tiraspol · Tighina · Căhul · Ribniţa · Kotovs'k · Pervomays'k · **Kirovohrad** · Oleksandriya · **Cherkasy** · **Poltava** · Kremenchuk · Smila · Uman' · **KHARKIV** · Kup"yans'k · Izyum · Valuyki · Rossosh' · Kalach · Kantemirovka · Mikhaylovka · Frolovo · **Dniprodzerzhyns'k** · **DNIPROPETROVS'K** · Pavlohrad · Slov"yans'k · Kramators'k · Svatove · Lysychans'k · Stakhanov · Kamensk-Shakhtinskiy · Kalач-na-Donu · Surovikino · Vol[gograd] · **VOLGO[GRAD]**

ROMANIA

Cluj-Napoca · Bistriţa · Suceava · Botoşani · Mureş · Târgu Mureş · Piatra-Neamţ · Alba Iulia · Deva · Sibiu · Iaşi · Bârlad · Bacău · Vaslui · Petroşani · Braşov · Târgu Jiu · Râmnicu Vâlcea · Târgovişte · Piteşti · Ploieşti · Focşani · Galaţi · Buzău · Brăila · **BUCUREŞTI (BUCHAREST)** · Alexandria · Giurgiu · Călăraşi · Lom · Montana · Vraţa · Pleven · Ruse · Lovech · Razgrad · Silistra · **Constanţa** · **BULGARIA**

Odesa · **ODESA (ODESSA)** · Bilhorod-Dnistrovs'kyy · Izmayil · **Mykolayiv** · Kryvyy Rih · Vodoskhovyshche · **Zaporizhzhya** · **Kherson** · Nikopol' · Kakhovs'ke · Melitopol' · Berdyans'k · Karkinits'ka Zatoka · Chornomors'ke · Mys Prubiynyy · Yevpatoriya · **Krym** · **Simferopol'** · **Sevastopol'** · Balaklava · Yalta · Sudak · Feodosiya · **Makiyivka** · **DONETS'K** · Yenakiyeve · **Luhans'k** · **Mariupol'** · **Taganrog** · Taganrogskiy Zaliv · Yeysk · **Sea of Azov** · Kerch · Temryuk · Anapa · **Novorossiysk** · Tuapse

Black Sea

Shakhty · **Novocherkassk** · **ROSTOV-NA-DONU** · Volgodonsk · Tsimlyanskoye Vodokhranilishche · Millerovo · Kotel'nikovo · Dubovskoye · **Stavropol'skaya Vozvyshennost'** · Sal'sk · Proletarsk · Ipatovo · Svetlograd · Tikhoretsk · **Krasnodar** · Kropotkin · Novoaleksandrovsk · **Armavir** · Labinsk · Maykop · **KARACHAYEVO-CHERKESIYA** · Cherkessk · Psebay · **Stavropol'** · **KAL[MYKIYA]** · Elista · Yashk[ul'] · Nevinnomyssk · Budenn[ovsk] · Neftekumsk · Zelenokumsk

292 · 246 · 239

© Helicon Publishing Ltd

48 49 · 92 93

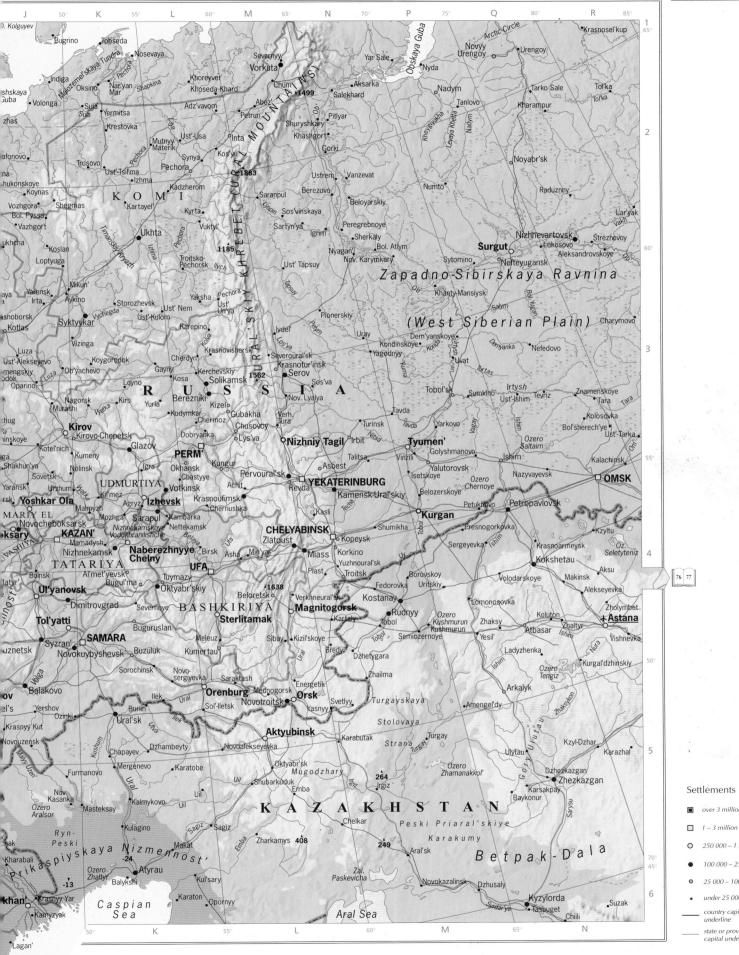

J 50° K 55° L 60° M 65° N 70° P 75° Q 80° R 85°

O. Kolguyev
Bugrino
Tobseda
Nosevaya
Krasnosel'kup

Indiga
Oksino
Nar'yan Mar
Shapkina
Severnyy
Vorkuta
•1499
Yar Sale
Obskaya Guba
Nyda
Nadym
Tarko Sale
Tol'ka
Tol'ka

shskaya Guba
Volonga
Malozemel'skaya Tundra
Pechora
Khoreyver
Khoseda Khard
Abez'
Chum
Aksarka
Salekhard
Novyy Urengoy
Urengoy
Kharampur

zhas
Sula
Yermitsa
Adz'vavom
Petrun
Shuryshkary
Pitlyar
Tanlovo
Noyabr'sk

afonovo
Trusovo
Ust'-Usa
Izhma
Inta
•1883
Khashgort
Gorki
Ustrem
Vanzevat
Numto
Raduzhnyy

hukonskoye
Koynas
Ust'-Tsil'ma
Pechora
Synya
Kos'yu
Berezovo
Beloyarskiy
Sos'vinskaya
Peregrebnoye
Nizhnevartovsk
Lar'yak
Yakh
Strezhevoy

Vozhgora
Shegmas
Kartayel'
Kyrta
Vuktyl
Sartyn'ya
Igrim
Bol. Atlym
Nov. Karymkary
Surgut
Lokosovo
Aleksandrovskoye

Bol. Pyssa
Vazhgort
Ukhta
•1185
Troitsko-Pechorsk
Ilych
Ust' Tapsuy
Nyagan'
Sherkaly
Sytomino
Nefteyugansk

ukhcha
Koslan
Loptyuga
Kadzherom
Yaksha
Krasnovishersk
Ust' Un'ya
Pechora
Ivdel'
Uray
Kondinskoye
Yagodnyy
Khanty-Mansiysk
Salym
Zapadno-Sibirskaya Ravnina

Yarensk
Mikun'
Aykino
Storozhevsk
Karepino
Kova
Los'ya
Pelym
Dem'yanskoye
Konda
Uvat
Derbyanka
Nefedovo
Charymovo

aya
Irta
Vychegda
Ust' Nem
Cherdyn
Kosa
Severoural'sk
Krasnotur'insk
Yagodnyy
Uvat
Turtas
(West Siberian Plain)

snoborsk
Syktyvkar
Vizinga
Koygorodok
Solikamsk
•1562
Serov
Sos'va
Tobol'
Sumkino
Ust'-Ishim
Tevriz
Znamenskoye
Tara

Luza
Ust'-Alekseyevo
mengskiy
Oparino
Loyno
Kosa
Yurla
Berezniki
Kizel
Nov. Lyalya
Tavda
Yarkovo
Irtysh
Vagay
Ishim
Kolosovka
Bol'sherech'ye
Ust'-Tarka

odk
Nagorsk
Murashi
Vyatka
Kirs
Kudymkar
Chermoz
Gubakha
Chusovoy
Verh. Tura
Turinsk
Nitsa
Tavda
Ozero Saltaim

Kirov
Kirovo-Chepetsk
Glazov
Dobryanka
Lys'va
Nizhniy Tagil
Irbit
Tyumen'
Golyshmanovo
Ishim
Nazyvayevsk
Kalachinsk
OMSK

hug
Kotel'nich
Kumeny
Igra
Okhansk
Kungur
Pervoural'sk
Asbest
Talitsa
Vinzili
Yalutorovsk
Isetskoye
Belozerskoye
Petukhovo
Petropavlovsk

inskoye
Shakhun'ya
Nolinsk
Chastyye
Achit
Revda
YEKATERINBURG
Kamensk-Ural'skiy
T-cha
Ozero Chernoye

Yaransk
Sovetsk
Urzhum
UDMURTIYA
Votkinsk
Krasnoufimsk
Chernushka
Kasli
Kurgan
Shumikha
Tobol
Presnogorkovka
Sergeyevka
Krasnoarmeysk
Oz. Seletyteniz

YOSHKAR OLA
Malmyzh
Kil'mez
Izhevsk
Agryz
Kambarka
Belaya
Kopeysk
Yuzhnoural'sk
Borovskoy
Uritskiy
Volodarskoye
Kokshetau
Aksu
Kzyltu

MARIY EL
Novocheboksarsk
Mozhga
Sarapul
Nizhnekamskoye Vodokhranilishche
Neftekamsk
CHELYABINSK
Zlatoust
Korkino
Troitsk
Fedorovka
Makinsk
Alekseyevka

ksary
KAZAN'
Nizhnekamsk
Mamadysh
Birsk
Asha
Miass
Plast
Ul
Astana
Zholymbet

TATARIYA
Buinsk
Al'met'yevsk
UFA
Tuymazy
Min'yar
Beloretsk
•1638
Kostanay
Rudnyy
Lomonosovka
Koluton
Zhaltyr
Vishnevka

Ul'yanovsk
Bugul'ma
Oktyabr'skiy
BASHKIRIYA
Verkhneural'sk
Magnitogorsk
Kartaly
Tobol
Ozero Kushmurun
Zhaksy
Atbasar
Ladyzhenka
Kurgal'dzhinskiy

Dimitrovgrad
Severnoye
Sterlitamak
Sibay
Kizil'skoye
Tobol
Semiozernoye
Yesil'
Ishim
Nura

Tol'yatti
Syzran'
SAMARA
Buguruslan
Meleuz
Kumertau
Bredy
Dzhetygara
Zhailma
Ozero Tengiz
Arkalyk
Kurgal'dzhinskiy

uznetsk
Novokuybyshevsk
Buzuluk
Sorochinsk
Novo-sergiyevka
Saraktash
Energetik
Svetlyy
Turgayskaya
Stolovaya
Amengel'dy
Zhaksykon
Gory Ulutau

ov
Balakovo
Ilek
Ural
Orenburg
Mednogorsk
Orsk
Yasnyy
Strana
Turgay
Kzyl-Dzhar
Karazhal

el's
Yershov
Ozinki
Burlin
Sol'-Iletsk
Novotroitsk
Kumtau
Turgay
Ozero Zhamanakkol
Ulytau
Dzhezkazgan
Karazhal

Krasnyy Kut
Ural'sk
Ilek
Aktyubinsk
Karabutak
Karsakpay
Zhezkazgan

Novouzensk
Chapayev
Dzhambeyty
Novoalekseyevka
Oktyabr'sk
Mugodzhary
264 Irgiz
Ozero Zhamanakkol
Baykonur
Dzhezkazgan

Nov. Kasanka
Mergenevo
Karatobe
Shubarkuduk
Emba
Irgiz
Karsakpay
Sarysu

Furmanovo
Kulagino
Kalmykovo
Uil
Uil
KAZAKHSTAN
Chelkar
Peski Priaral'skiye Karakumy
Novokazalinsk
Dzhusaly

Ryn-Peski
Masteksay
Sagiz
Sagiz
Zharkamys
408
249
Aral'sk
Betpak-Dala
Kyzylorda
Suzak

Ozero Aralsor
Kulsary
Emba
Zal. Paskevicha
Syzdar'ya
Tasbuget
Chilli

Prikaspiyskaya Nizmennost'
Ozero Zhaltyr
-24
Atyrau
Kul'sary
Oporniy
Aral Sea

khan'
Krasnyy Yar
-13
Balykshi
Karaton
Kamyzyak
Caspian Sea

Settlements

- ■ over 3 million
- □ 1 – 3 million
- ○ 250 000 – 1 million
- ● 100 000 – 250 000
- ◉ 25 000 – 100 000
- • under 25 000
- —— country capital underline
- —— state or province capital underline

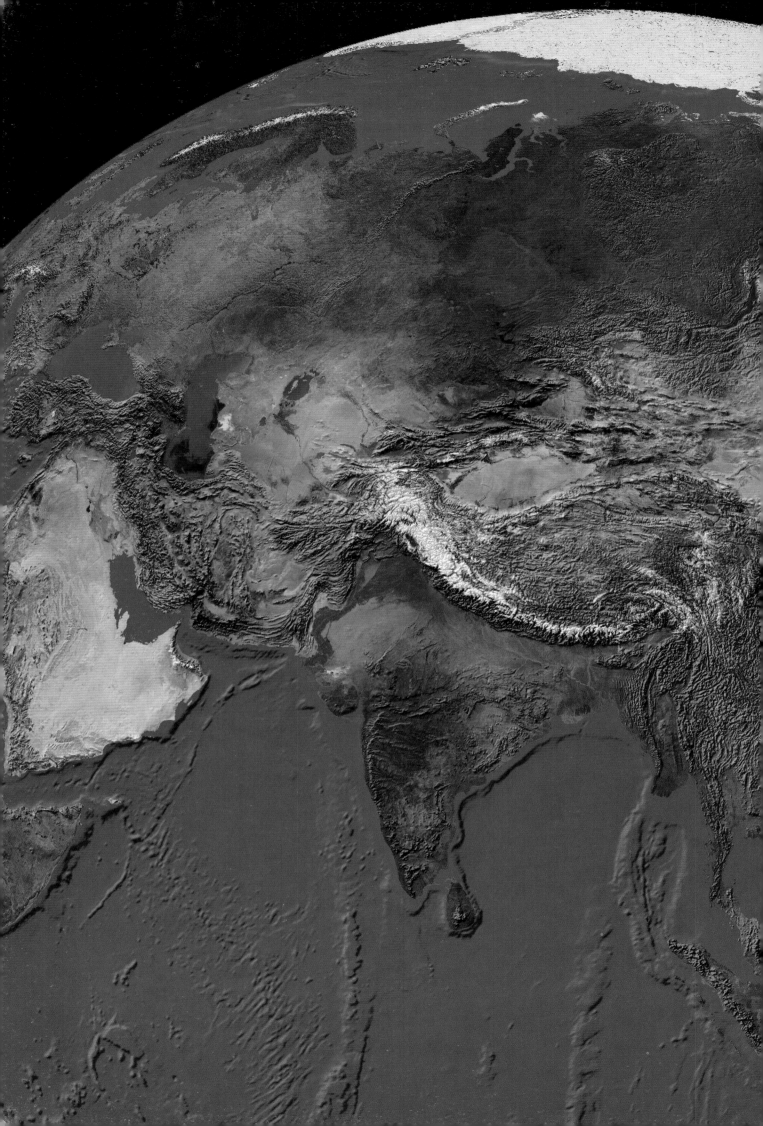

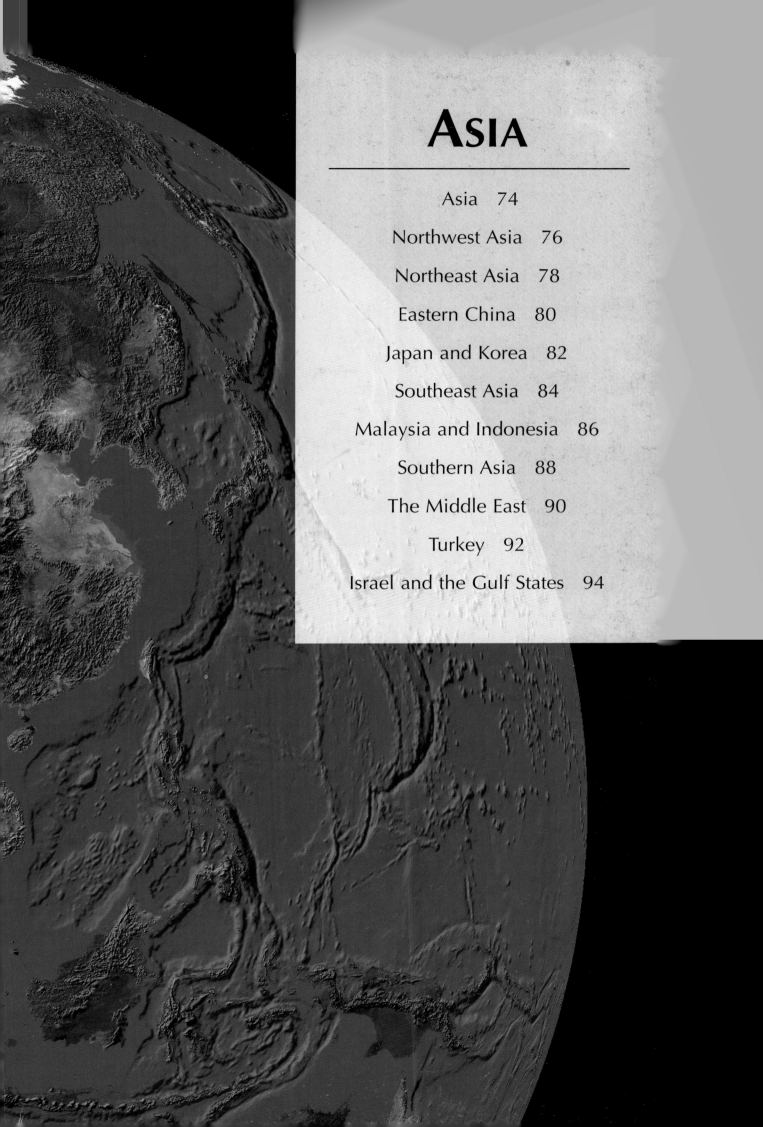

ASIA

Asia   74

Northwest Asia   76

Northeast Asia   78

Eastern China   80

Japan and Korea   82

Southeast Asia   84

Malaysia and Indonesia   86

Southern Asia   88

The Middle East   90

Turkey   92

Israel and the Gulf States   94

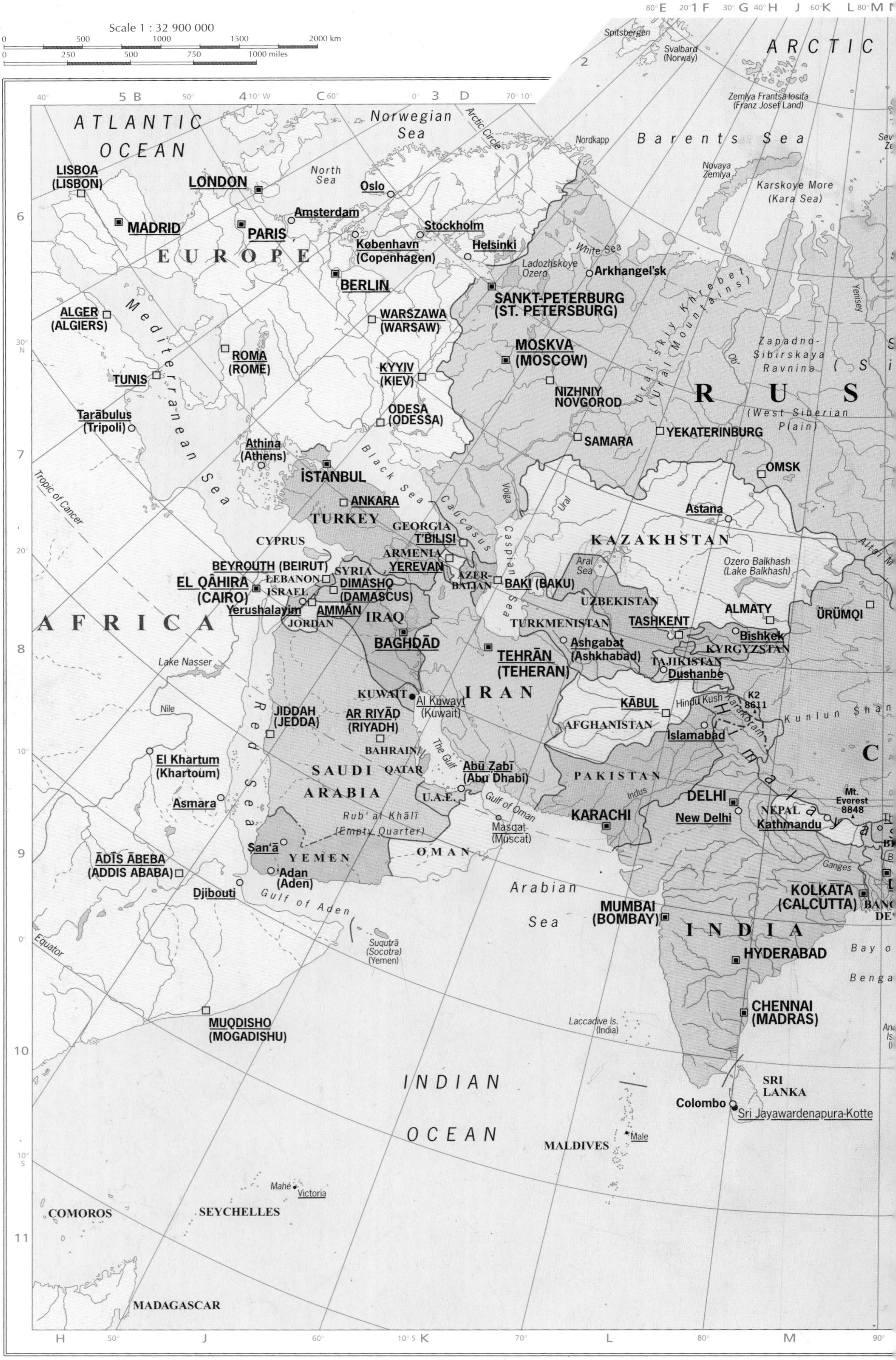

Scale 1 : 32 900 000

0   500   1000   1500   2000 km
0 250 500 750 1000 miles

ATLANTIC
OCEAN

ARCTIC

Spitsbergen
Svalbard
(Norway)

Zemlya Frantsa-Iosifa
(Franz Josef Land)

Nordkapp

Barents Sea

Norwegian
Sea

Arctic Circle

Sev

Novaya
Zemlya

Karskoye More
(Kara Sea)

LISBOA
(LISBON)

LONDON

Oslo

North
Sea

MADRID

Amsterdam

Stockholm

EUROPE

PARIS

København
(Copenhagen)

Helsinki

White Sea

Arkhangel'sk

Ladozhskoye
Ozero

BERLIN

SANKT-PETERBURG
(ST. PETERSBURG)

ALGER
(ALGIERS)

WARSZAWA
(WARSAW)

MOSKVA
(MOSCOW)

NIZHNIY
NOVGOROD

R U S

Yenisey

ROMA
(ROME)

Zapadno-
Sibirskaya
Ravnina (S

KYYIV
(KIEV)

SAMARA

YEKATERINBURG

(West Siberian
Plain)

TUNIS

Tarābulus
(Tripoli)

ODESA
(ODESSA)

Mediterranean Sea

Tropic of Cancer

Athina
(Athens)

Black Sea

İSTANBUL

Volga

OMSK

Ural

ANKARA

Caucasus

TURKEY

Astana

KAZAKHSTAN

Altai

ÜRÜMQI

CYPRUS

GEORGIA
T'BILISI

ARMENIA
YEREVAN

Caspian Sea

BEYROUTH (BEIRUT)

SYRIA

AZER-
BAIJAN

BAKI (BAKU)

Aral
Sea

Ozero Balkhash
(Lake Balkhash)

UZBEKISTAN

EL QÂHIRA
(CAIRO)

LEBANON

DIMASHQ
(DAMASCUS)

ISRAEL

Yerushalayim

AMMĀN

JORDAN

IRAQ

BAGHDĀD

TURKMENISTAN

TASHKENT

ALMATY

AFRICA

I R A N

TEHRĀN
(TEHERAN)

Ashgabat
(Ashkhabad)

TAJIKISTAN

BISHKEK

KYRGYZSTAN

Lake Nasser

Nile

KUWAIT

Al Kuwayt
(Kuwait)

Dushanbe

KĀBUL

K2
8611

Hindu Kush

Karakoram

Kunlun Shan

C

JIDDAH
(JEDDA)

AR RIYĀD
(RIYADH)

AFGHANISTAN

Islamabad

El Khartum
(Khartoum)

BAHRAIN

QATAR

The Gulf

Abū Zabī
(Abu Dhabi)

PAKISTAN

Indus

Mt.
Everest
8848

DELHI

NEPAL

Asmara

SAUDI

ARABIA

U.A.E.

Gulf of Oman

KARACHI

New Delhi

Kathmandu

Rub' al Khālī
(Empty Quarter)

Masqat
(Muscat)

Ganges

B

ĀDĪS ĀBEBA
(ADDIS ABABA)

San'ā

YEMEN

OMAN

KOLKATA
(CALCUTTA)

BANG
DE

Red Sea

Adan
(Aden)

Djibouti

Gulf of Aden

Arabian
Sea

MUMBAI
(BOMBAY)

I N D I A

Bay o

Equator

Suqutrā
(Socotra)
(Yemen)

HYDERABAD

Benga

MUQDISHO
(MOGADISHU)

Laccadive Is.
(India)

CHENNAI
(MADRAS)

An
Is.

INDIAN

SRI
LANKA

OCEAN

Colombo

Sri Jayawardenapura-Kotte

MALDIVES

Male

Mahé

Victoria

COMOROS

SEYCHELLES

MADAGASCAR

H 50° J 60° 10° S K 70° L 80° M 90°

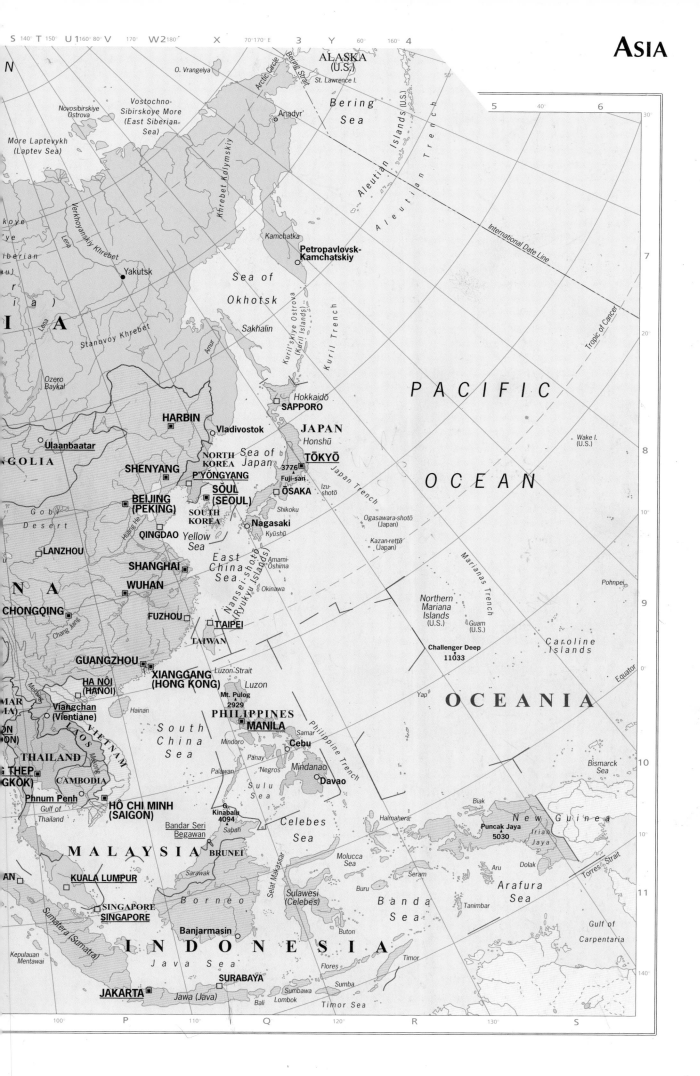

S 140° T 150° U 1 160° 80° V 170° W 2 180° X 70° 170° E 3 Y 60° 160° 4

N

ALASKA
(U.S.)

O. Vrangelya
Arctic Circle
Bering Strait
St. Lawrence I.

Novosibirskiye Ostrova

Vostochno-Sibirskoye More (East Siberian Sea)

Bering Sea

More Laptevykh (Laptev Sea)

Anadyr'

Aleutian Islands (U.S.)

Aleutian Trench

Khrebet Kolymskiy

I A

Kamchatka

International Date Line

5 40° 6

30°

Stanovoy Khrebet

Verkhoyanskiy Khrebet

Lena

Siberian

Yakutsk

Amur

Petropavlovsk-Kamchatskiy

Sea of Okhotsk

7

Tropic of Cancer

20°

Ozero Baykal

Sakhalin

Kuril'skiye Ostrova (Kuril Islands)

Kuril Trench

PACIFIC

Hokkaidō
SAPPORO

HARBIN

Vladivostok

JAPAN
Honshū

Wake I.
(U.S.)

OCEAN

8

MONGOLIA

Ulaanbaatar

SHENYANG

NORTH KOREA

P'YŎNGYANG

Sea of Japan

3776 ▲
Fuji-san

TŌKYŌ

Japan Trench

BEIJING
(PEKING)

SŎUL
(SEOUL)

ŌSAKA

Izu-shotō

10°

Gobi Desert

SOUTH KOREA

Shikoku

QINGDAO

Yellow Sea

Nagasaki

Kyūshū

Amami-Ōshima

*Ogasawara-shotō
(Japan)*

LANZHOU

C H I N A

SHANGHAI

East China Sea

WUHAN

Nansei-shotō

Ryukyu Islands

Okinawa

*Kazan-rettō
(Japan)*

Marianas Trench

Pohnpei

9

0°

CHONGQING

Chang Jiang

FUZHOU

T'AIPEI

TAIWAN

Luzon Strait

GUANGZHOU

XIANGGANG
(HONG KONG)

Hainan

Luzon

Mt. Pulog
2929 ▲

Northern Mariana Islands
(U.S.)

Guam (U.S.)

Challenger Deep
11033

Caroline Islands

HA NÔI
(HANOI)

VIETNAM

Viangchan
(Vientiane)

LAOS

PHILIPPINES

MANILA

Yap

OCEANIA

Equator
0°

MYANMAR

THAILAND

South China Sea

Mindoro

Samar

Cebu

Philippine Trench

10°

KRUNG THEP
(BANGKOK)

CAMBODIA

Palawan

Panay

Negros

Mindanao

Bismarck Sea

Phnum Penh

Gulf of Thailand

HÔ CHI MINH
(SAIGON)

G. Kinabalu
4094 ▲

Sulu Sea

Davao

Celebes Sea

Halmahera

Biak

New Guinea

Puncak Jaya
5030 ▲

Irian Jaya

Mekong

MALAYSIA

Sabah

BRUNEI

Bandar Seri Begawan

Sarawak

Selat Makassar

Molucca Sea

Seram

Aru

Dolak

Torres Strait

10°

KUALA LUMPUR

Borneo

Buru

SINGAPORE
SINGAPORE

*Sulawesi
(Celebes)*

Banda Sea

Arafura Sea

11

Sumatera (Sumatra)

Banjarmasin

I N D O N E S I A

Buton

Gulf of Carpentaria

Kepulauan Mentawai

Java Sea

Timor

140°

SURABAYA

Jawa (Java)

Flores

Sumba

JAKARTA

Bali
Lombok

Sumbawa

Timor Sea

100° P 110° Q 120° R 130° S

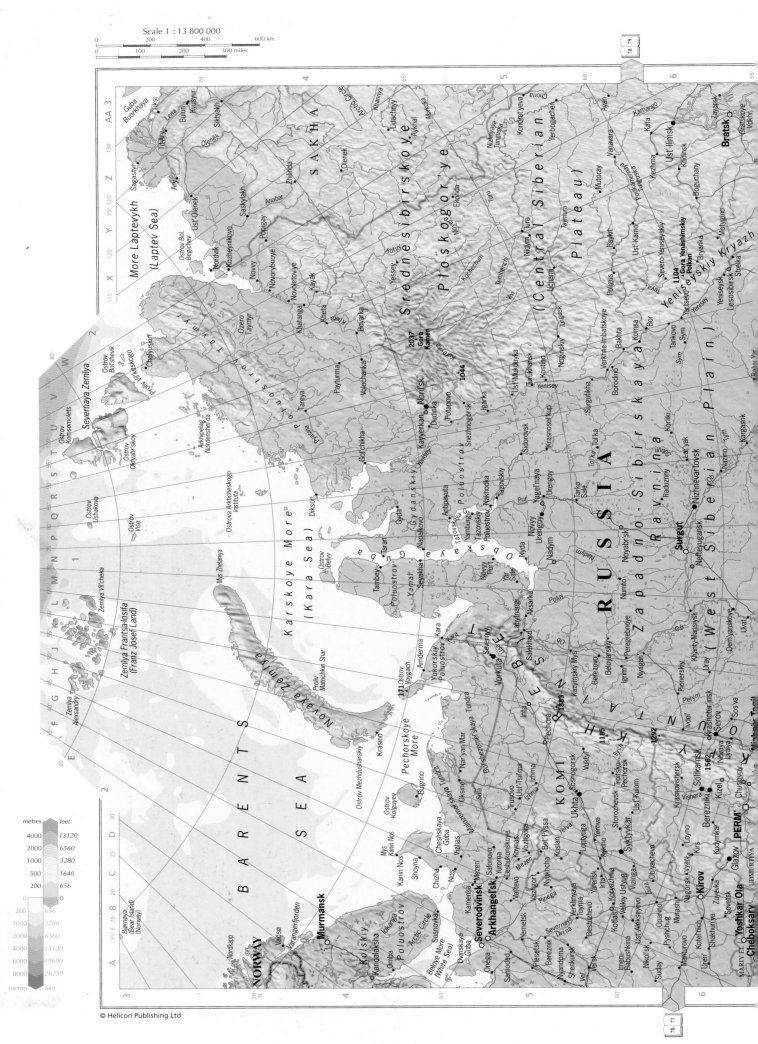

Scale 1 : 13 800 000

© Helicon Publishing Ltd

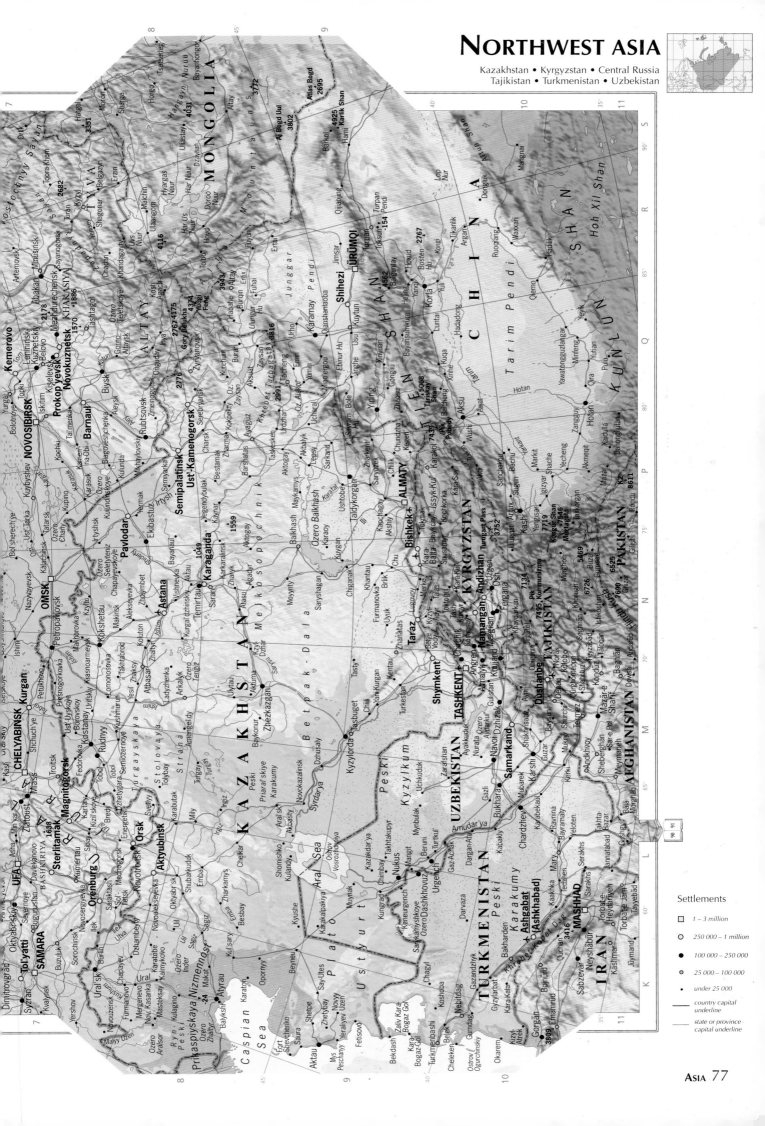

Mongolia • Eastern Russia

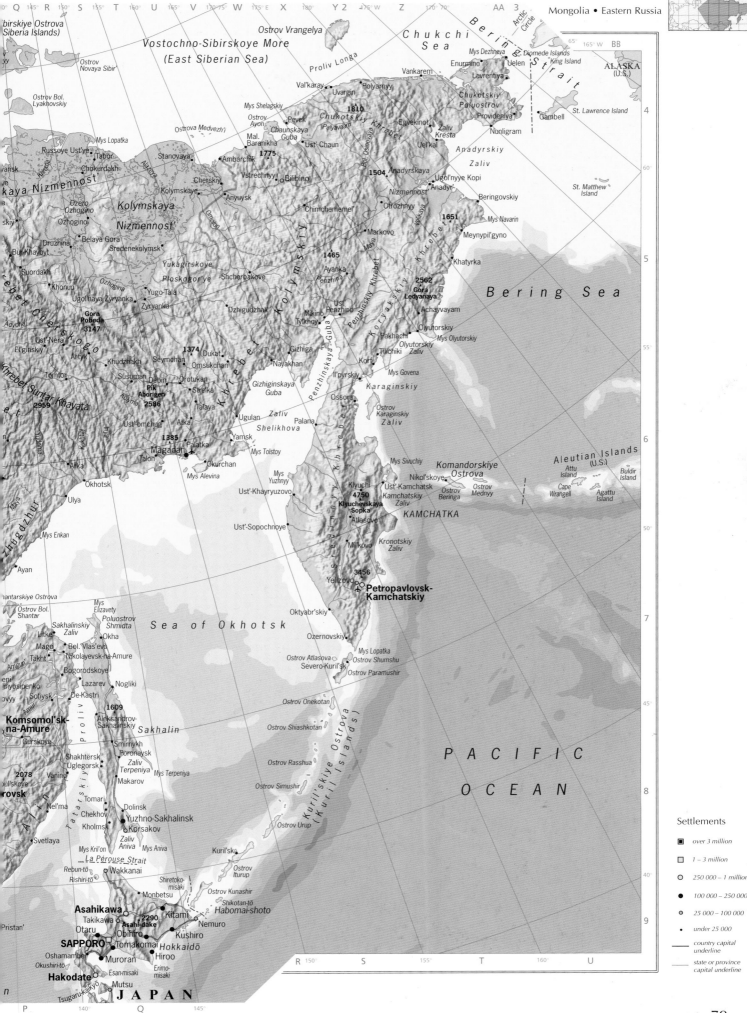

Scale 1 : 11 600 000

© Helicon Publishing Ltd

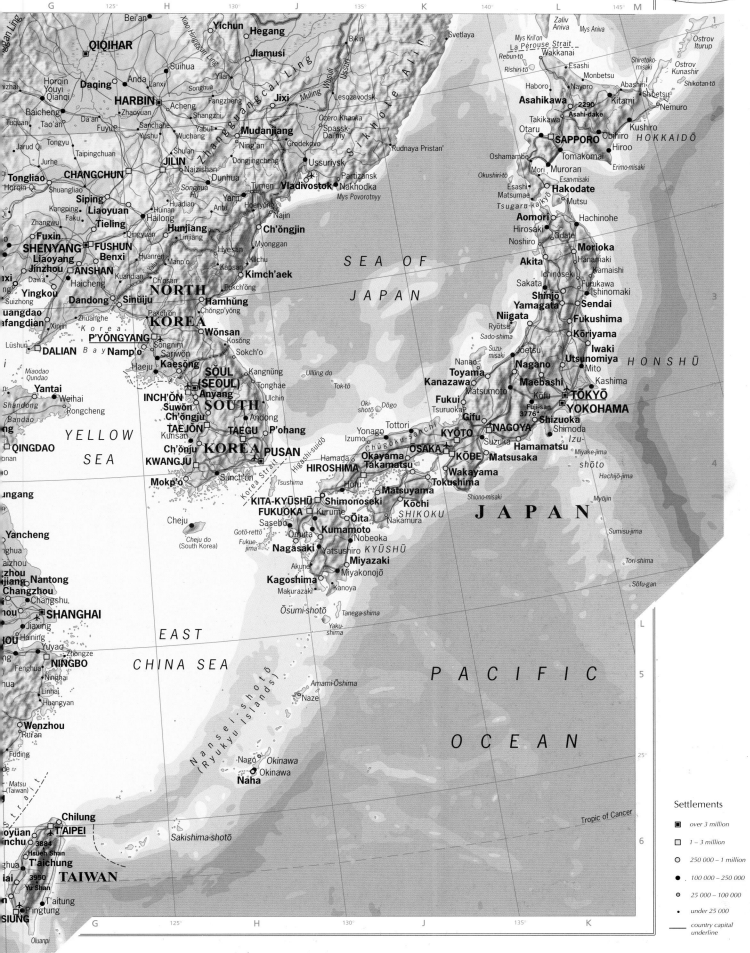

G 125° H 130° J 135° K 140° L 145° M

Bei'an
Yichun
Hegang
QIQIHAR
Suihua
Jiamusi
Anda Lanxi
Horqin Daqing
Youyi Qianqi
Baicheng Zhaoyuan
Tao'an HARBIN Acheng Fangzheng Yilan
Da'an Sanchahe Shangzhi Jixi
Jurhe Fuyu Yushu Wuchang Ning'an Mudanjiang
Jarud Qi Taipingchuan Shulan Dongjingcheng
Tongyu Naizishan Ussuriysk
Tongliao Huadian Tumen Vladivostok
Horqin Qi CHANGCHUN Dunhua Yanji Nakhodka
Shuangliao Antu Hunchun
Siping Huinan Hailong Yanbian Najin
Liaoyuan Qingyuan Ch'ŏngjin
Zhangwu Tieling Linjiang
Kangping Faku Hunjiang Kimch'aek
Fuxin Hyesan
SHENYANG FUSHUN Manp'o
Liaoyang ANSHAN Huanren Kapsan Kilchu
Jinzhou Benxi Kuandian Ch'osan
Haicheng Pukch'ŏng
Yingkou Dandong Sinŭiju NORTH Hamhŭng
Dawa Zhuanghe Chŏngp'yŏng
Xinjin Pakchŏn KOREA Wŏnsan
DALIAN Songnim P'YŎNGYANG
Nampo Sariwŏn Kosŏng
Haeju Kaesŏng
Yantai Weihai SŎUL Kangnŭng
QINGDAO INCH'ŎN (SEOUL) Tonghae
Suwŏn Anyang SOUTH Ulchin
Ch'ŏngju KOREA Andong
TAEJŎN TAEGU P'ohang
Kunsan Ch'ŏnju PUSAN
KWANGJU Sunch'ŏn
Mokp'o
Cheju
TAIPEI TAIWAN
T'aichung
KAOHSIUNG

SEA OF JAPAN
YELLOW SEA
EAST CHINA SEA
PACIFIC OCEAN

HOKKAIDŌ
Wakkanai
Asahikawa
SAPPORO
Hakodate
Aomori
Morioka
Akita
Sendai
Niigata
Fukushima
Nagano
TŌKYŌ
YOKOHAMA
KYŌTO
NAGOYA
ŌSAKA
KŌBE
HIROSHIMA
FUKUOKA
KITA-KYŪSHŪ
Kumamoto
Nagasaki
Kagoshima
Miyazaki
JAPAN
SHIKOKU
KYŪSHŪ
HONSHŪ

Nansei-shotō (Ryukyu Islands)
Okinawa
Naha

Tropic of Cancer

Settlements

■ over 3 million
□ 1 – 3 million
○ 250 000 – 1 million
● 100 000 – 250 000
◉ 25 000 – 100 000
• under 25 000
— country capital underline

Scale 1 : 5 800 000

| 0 | 100 | 200 | 300 km |
| 0 | 50 | 100 | 150 miles |

metres / *feet*

metres	feet
4000	13120
2000	6560
1000	3280
500	1640
200	656
0	0
200	656
1000	3280
2000	6560
4000	13120
6000	19690
8000	26250

metres / feet

RUSSIA

CHINA

NORTH KOREA

SOUTH KOREA

JAPAN

Tongliao
CHANGCHUN
JILIN
Golin Baixing
Fuyu
Sanchahe
Shangzhi
Linkou
Jixi
Muling
Lesozavodsk
Tongyu
Taipingchuan
Nong'an
Yushu
Wuchang
Ning'an
Mudanjiang
Turiy Rog
Ozero Khanka
Kamen Rybolov
Spassk-Dal'niy
Jurhe
Shuangliao
Shulan
Songhua Hu
Dongjingcheng
Suifenhe
Grodekovo
Poltavka
Siping
Kangping
Zhangwu
Faku
Liaoyuan
Huinan
Huadian
Songhua Hu
Dunhua
Tianqiaoling
Ussuriysk
Razdol'noye
Artem
Tieling
Qingyuan
Hailong
Antu
Yanji
Tumen
Hunchun
Vladivostok
Partizansk
SHENYANG
FUSHUN
Xinmin
Benxi
Tianshifu
Fengcheng
Huanren
Fusong
Dalizi
Paekdu San 2750
Kambo Ho 2541
Ch'ŏngjin
Myŏnggan
Najin
Slavyanka
Nakhodka
Mys Povorotnyy
Hoeryŏng
Kilchu
Liaoyang
Anshan
Haicheng
Kuandian
Ch'osan
Kanggye
Mt.Tuun 2487
Hyesan
Kapsan
Helong
Onsŏng
Laotougou
Yingkou
Dawa
Gai Xian
Fengcheng
Pyŏktong
Mrano'o
2310
P'ungsan
Tanch'ŏn
Kimch'aek
Wafangdian
Zhuanghe
Uiju
Sakchu
Huich'ŏn
Pukch'ŏng
Dandong
Donggou
Sinŭiju
Chŏngju
Pakch'ŏn
Sinanju
Hamhŭng
Hŭngnam
Namp'o
P'YŎNGYANG
Yangdok
Wŏnsan
Chŏngp'yŏng
Yŏnghŭng
SEA
Korea Bay
Sariwŏn
Songnim
Hoeyang
Kosŏng
JAP
Haeju
Kaesŏng
P'yŏnggang
Sokch'o
1708
Ullŭng do
Chengshan Jiao
Rongcheng
Ongjin
Tongduch'ŏn
Ch'unch'ŏn
Kangnŭng
SOUL (SEOUL)
Puch'ŏn
Songnam
INCH'ŏN
Anyang
Wŏnju
Tonghae
Suwŏn
Ch'ungju
1321
Ulchin
Sŏsan
Ch'ŏnan
Oki-shotō
Dōgo
Saigo
Yellow Sea
Taech'ŏn
Ch'ŏngju
SOUTH
Andong
P'ohang
TAEJŎN
KOREA
Kyŏngju
Matsue
Tottori
Toyooka
Kunsan
Ch'ŏnju
TAEGU
Yonago
Fukuchiyama
Izumo
Tsuyama
KYŌ
KWANGJU
Chŏngup
Kŏch'ang
Namwŏn
Masan
Ulsan
Ōda
Tōjō
Himeji
OSAKA
Naju
Sunch'ŏn
Chinju
PUSAN
Hamada
Miyoshi
Kurashiki
Akashi
Mokp'o
Chin do
Posŏng
Yŏsu
Samch'ŏnp'o
Kamitsushima
Yamaguchi
HIROSHIMA
Harima-nada
Awaji-shima
Haenam
Wando
Tsushima
Higashi-suidō
Izuhara
Korea Strait
Shimonoseki
Hōfu
Kure
Imabari
Takamatsu
Huiuchi-nada
Fukuyama
Cheju
Cheju do (South Korea)
KITA-KYŪSHŪ
Ube
Tokuyama
Matsuyama
Tokushima
FUKUOKA
Iki
Suō-nada
Nakatsu
Iyo-nada
Kōchi
Nankoku
Anan
Karatsu
Usa
Uwajima
Gobo
Sasebo
Kurume
Ōita
Usuki
Tosa-wan
Tanabe
Gotō-rettō
Ōmura
Saga
Saiki
SHIKOKU
Murota
Fukue-jima
Isahaya
Ōmuta
1788
Kushimo
Fukue
Nagasaki
Shimabara
Kumamoto
Nobeoka
Ashizuri-misaki
Nomo-saki
Yatsushiro
Hyūga
Amakusa-Shimo-shima
Kyūshū-sanchi
East China Sea
Akune
Hitoyoshi
Shimo-Koshiki-jima
Kushikino
KYŪSHŪ
Miyazaki
Kagoshima
Miyakonojō
Noma-misaki
Kanoya
Toi-misaki
Makurazaki
Ōsumi-kaikyō
Ōsumi-shotō
Nishinoomote
Kamiyaku
Tanega-shima
Yaku-shima
Kukinaga

Zhangguangcai Ling

© Helicon Publishing Ltd

82 ASIA

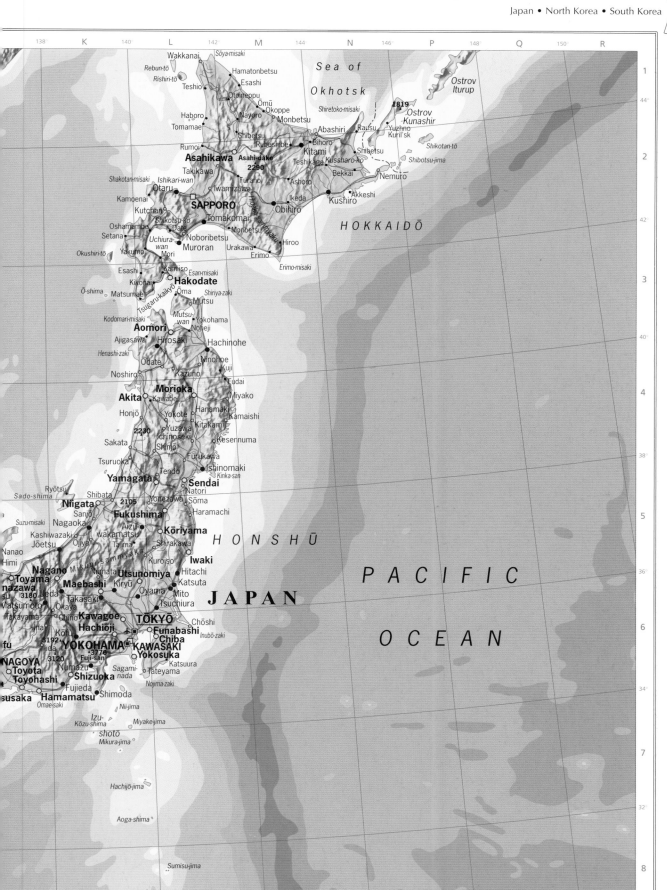

Wakkanai
Sōya-misaki
Rebun-tō
Rishiri-tō
Hamatonbetsu
Teshio
Esashi
Otoineppu
Ōmū
Haboro
Nayoro
Okoppe
Monbetsu
Tomamae
Shibetsu
Rumoi
Rubeshibe
Bihoro
Asahikawa
Asahi-dake
2290
Takikawa
Kitami
Teshikaga
Kussharo-ko
Shakotan-misaki
Furano
Iwamizawa
Ashoro
Bekkai
Kamoenai
Otaru
SAPPORO
Tomakomai
Obihiro
Ikeda
Nemuro
Kutchan
Shikotsu-ko
Date
Monbetsu
Kushiro
Akkeshi
Oshamambe
Noboribetsu
Setana
Yakumo
Muroran
Urakawa
Erimo
Hiroo

Sea of Okhotsk
Shiretoko-misaki
Rausu
Abashiri
Shibetsu
1819
Ostrov Kunashir
Yuzhno Kuril'sk
Shikotan-tō
Shibotsu-jima

HOKKAIDŌ
Ostrov Iturup

Okushiri-tō
Esashi
Kamiiso
Esan-misaki
Kikonai
Hakodate
Ō-shima
Matsumae
Ōma
Shiriya-zaki
Kodomari-misaki
Mutsu
Yokohama
Mutsu-wan
Nōheji
Aomori
Ajigasawa
Hirosaki
Henashi-zaki
Ōdate
Ninohe
Hachinohe
Noshiro
Kazuno
Kuji
Fudai
Morioka
Akita
Kawabe
Miyako
Honjō
Yokote
Hanamaki
Kamaishi
2230
Yuzawa
Kitakami
Kesennuma
Sakata
Ichinoseki
Tsuruoka
Shinjō
Furukawa
Tendō
Ishinomaki
Kinka-san
Yamagata
Sendai
Ryōtsu
Shibata
Natori
Sado-shima
Yonezawa
Sōma
Suzu-misaki
2105
Haramachi
Niigata
Sanjō
Fukushima
Nagaoka
Aizu
Kōriyama
Kashiwazaki
wakamatsu
Jōetsu
Oiya
Shirakawa
Nanao
Tairai
Himi
Kuroiso
Nagano
Miyaka
Iwaki
Toyama
Numata
Utsunomiya
Hitachi
nazawa
3180
Ueda
Maebashi
Kiryū
Katsuta
Matsumoto
Okaya
Takasaki
Mito
akayama
Chino
Ōyama
Tsuchiura
inar
Kawagoe
Kōfu
3192
Hachiōji
Chōshi
ifu
Iida
YOKOHAMA
TŌKYŌ
Inubō-zaki
NAGOYA
3120
Fuji-san
Funabashi
Toyota
Numazu
3776
Chiba
Shizuoka
KAWASAKI
Toyohashi
Fujieda
Yokosuka
usaka
Hamamatsu
Shimoda
Katsuura
Ōmae-saki
Sagami-nada
Tateyama
Izu-
Nojima-zaki
Kōzu-shima
Nii-jima
shotō
Miyake-jima
Mikura-jima

HONSHŪ

JAPAN

PACIFIC OCEAN

Hachijō-jima

Aoga-shima

Sumisu-jima

Tori-shima

Settlements

- ■ over 3 million
- □ 1 – 3 million
- ○ 250 000 – 1 million
- ● 100 000 – 250 000
- ◉ 25 000 – 100 000
- • under 25 000
- — country capital underline

Pangin · Zayu · Deqen · 95° E · B · 100° · C · 105° · D · Jis

BHUTAN
Tashigang · Hāpoli · Dibrugarh · Tinsukia · Tazungdam · Gongshan · Zhongdian · Xichang · **Zunyi** · Huaihua

Itanagar · Brahmaputra · Rutao · Weixi · Lijiang · Liupanshui · **GUIYANG**
Barpeta · Goalpara · Nagaon · Jorhat · Golaghat · Tabong · **Dukou** · Weining · Anshun · Duyun · Kaili
Guwahati · **I N D I A** · Kohima · Maingkwan · Yongren · Qujing · Xingyi · Guanling · **CH**

Shillong · Dimapur · Myitkyina · Yun Xian · **KUNMING** · Hechi · Yang
Sylhet · Imphal · Mogaung · Baoshan · Dali · **Chuxiong** · Nanpan
Silchar · Hopin · **Bose**
Bhairab Bazar · Tropic of Cancer · Aizawl · Bhamo · Mông Yu · Lincang · Gengma · Cangyuan · Jinggu · Kaiyuan · Yanshan · Heshan
Comilla · Karnafuli Reservoir · Kalemyo · Mabein · Lashio · Lai Chau · Cao Bang · Jingxi · Pingguo · Binyang
Feni · Saiha · Haka · Chindwin · Shwebo · Mogok · Mong Yai · Simao · Yuanjiang · Lao Cai · Tuyen Quang · **Pingxiang** · Qinzhou · **Nanning** · Wuxu
CHITTAGONG · **BANGLADESH** · Monywa · **MANDALAY** · Mong Kung · Kengtung · Jinghong · Phongsali · Nole · Thai Nguyen · Hepu
Cox's Bazar · Amarapura · Kyaukse · Kunhing · Muang Sing · Louang Namtha · Muang Khoua · Xam Nua · Tuên Giao · Son La · **HA NÔI** · Tiên Yen · **Zhanj**
Paletwa · 3053 · Pakokku · Meiktila · Taung-gyi · Wan Hsa-la · Phôngsali · **(HANOI)** · Moc Chau · Beihai · **Zhanj**

MYANMAR · Mt. Victoria · Chauk · Salween · Viêt Tri · Ninh Binh · Nam Dinh · **HAI PHONG**
(BURMA) · Magwe · Taungdwingyi · Loikaw · Chiang · Nan · Louangphrabang · Ban · Thanh Hoa · *Gulf of* · Dan Xian · *Haik*
Kyaukpyu · Minbu · Sinbaungwe · Pyinmana · Toungoo · Pasawng · Rai · Mekong · Xiênghoang · Ban · *Tongking* · Dongfang · *Hainan*
Ramree Island · Taungup · Pyè · Mae Hong Son · **L A O S** · Muang Pakxan · Ha Tinh · Vinh · Tongshi
Bay of · Sandoway · Zigon · Chiang Mai · Siri Kit Dam · Muang Khoua · Dông Hôi · Sanya
Bengal · Cheduba Island · Kyeintali · **Chiang Mai** · Lampang · Nan · Chiang Khan · Nong Khai · Khamkeut · **Huê** · **Da Nang**
Henzada · Pegu · Mae Suriang · Uttaradit · Loei · Udon Thani · Muang Khammouan · Quang Tri · Hôi An
Bassein · Insein · Thaton · Nam Ping · Chum Phae · Sakhon Nakhon · Muang Phin · Quang Ng
Myaungmya · **YANGON** · Moulmein · Phitsanulok · Phichit · Khon Kaen · Mukdahan · Savannakhet
Cape Negrais · Bogale · Labutta · **(RANGOON)** · Kawkareik · Chaiyaphum · Roi Et · Khemmarat · Ban · Kon Tum
Mouths of the Irrawaddy · *Gulf of Martaban* · Ye · Nakhon Sawan · Lam Chi · Suwannaphum · Ubon Ratchathani · Pakxé · Quang Ng
Sangkhla · Bun · **Nakhon** · Chainat · Mae Nam Mun · Surin · Det Udom · Attapu · Play Cu · Qui N
Preparis North Channel · **Ratchasima** · Ayutthaya · **THAILAND** · Phumi Sâmraông · M. Không · Virôchey
Preparis Island · Sara Buri · Siĕmréab · Stoeng Treng · **Buôn Mê** · Tuy Ho
Preparis South Channel · Tavoy · **KRUNG THEP** · Aranyaprathet · Sisôphôn · **Thuôt** · Ninh H
Coco Channel · **(BANGKOK)** · Bătdâmbâng · Tônlé Sap · Plây Cu · Nha · Cam R
Rat Buri · Phet Buri · **CAMBODIA** · Kâmpóng Chhnăng · Kâmpóng Cham · Da Lat · **Nha** · Phan Ra
North Andaman · Pattaya · Rayong · Ko Chang · Da Lat · Bao Lôc · Phan Thiêt
Andaman Islands · Palaw · Ban Hua Hin · Chânthaburi · Krông Kaôh Kông · Chon Thanh · Bao Lôc · Phan Ra
(India) · Mergui · Prachuap Khiri Khan · **Phnum Penh** · Ta Khmau · Tay Ninh · Biên Hoa
Middle Andaman · Bang Saphan Yai · Kâmpôt · Kâmpông Cham · **HÔ CHI MINH** · Phan Thiêt
Ritchie's Archipelago · *Gulf* · Sihanoukville · **(SAIGON)** · My Tho · Vung Tau
South Andaman · Chumphon · *of* · Dao Phu Quôc · Long Xuyên · Rach Gia
Port Blair · Kawthaung · *Thailand* · **Cân Tho**
Duncan Passage · Ranong · Ca Mau · Bac Liêu · *Mouths of the Mekong*
A n d a m a n · Takua Pa · Surat Thani · Ko Samui · Nam Can · Côn Son
Little Andaman · Phuket · Krabi · **Nakhon Si Thammarat**
Ten Degree Channel · *S e a* · Thung Song · Phatthalung
Car Nicobar · Trang · Thale Luang · Songkhla
Katchall · Nicobar Islands · Satun · Hat Yai · Pattani
Little Nicobar · (India) · Langkawi · Kangar · Yala · Narathiwat
Great Nicobar · Sabang · Alor Setar · **Kota Bharu** · **M A L A**
Banda Aceh · Sungei Petani · Ban Betong · Kuala Kerai
Bireun · **George Town** · Gerik · Kuala Terengganu
Lhokseumawe · Pinang · Taiping · G. Korbu · Kuala Lipis · Dungun · *Laut*
Langsa · 2182 · Kemasik
Takengon · **Ipoh** · Kuala Lipis · *Malay* · Kuantan · *Natuna Besar* · Panarik
Meulaboh · **MEDAN** · Bagun Datuk · Bentong · Temerloh · *Peninsula* · **Kepulauan Natuna**
S U M A T E R A · 3145 · Tebingtinggi · Kuala Lumpur · Kuantan
(SUMATRA) · Gunung Leuser · Pematangsiantar · **KUALA LUMPUR** · Seremban · Jemaja · **Kepulauan Anambas** · Subi Besar
Sibigo · Danau Toba · Prapat · Melaka · Segamat · Mersing · (Indonesia)
Simeulue · Sinabang · Barus · Bagansiapiapi · Dumai · Muar · Keluang · Tanjun Datu
Singkilbaru · Gunungsitoli · Baligé · Kotapinang · Batu Pahat · **SINGAPORE** · Sambas
Sibolga · Nias · **INDONESIA** · Duri · **Johor Bahru** · **SINGAPORE** · Pemangkat · Sliuas

INDIAN OCEAN
Bay of Bengal
Strait of Malacca

metres / feet
4000 / 13120
2000 / 6560
1000 / 3280
500 / 1640
200 / 656
0 / 0
200 / 656
1000 / 3280
2000 / 6560
4000 / 13120
6000 / 19690
8000 / 26250
metres / feet

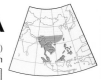

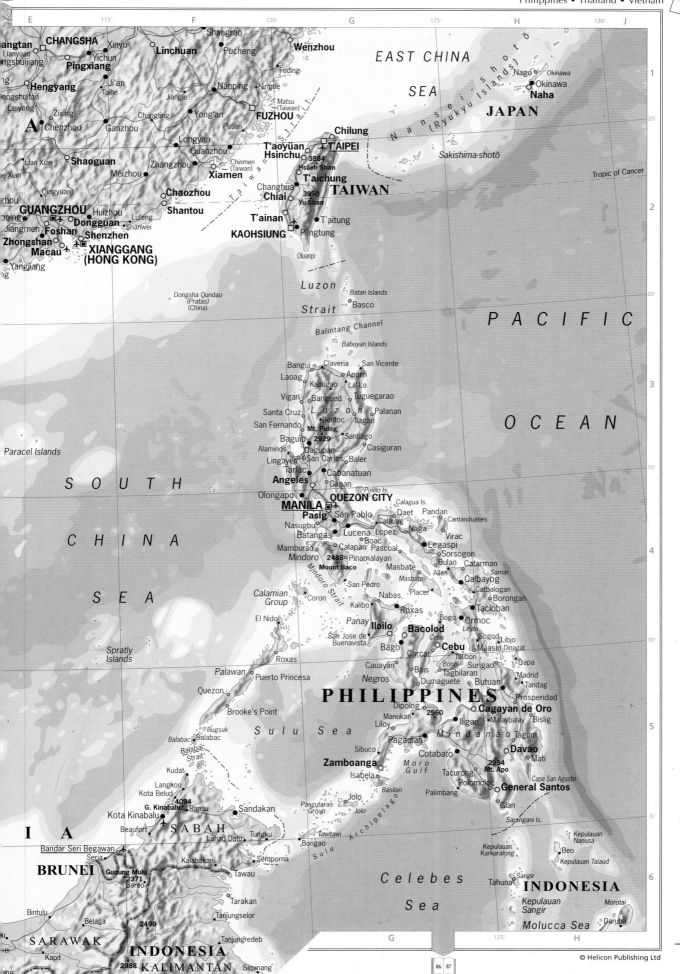

CHANGSHA

81

E 115° F 120° G 125° H 130° J

angtan
Xinyu
Shangrao
CHANGSHA
Yichun **Linchuan**
Pucheng
Wenzhou
ngshuijiang
Pingxiang
Ji'an
Nanping
Ningde
Fuding
Hengyang
Taihe
Changting
Yong'an
Jiangle
Matsu
(Taiwan)
FUZHOU
Putian
Chilung
ngshuitan
Leiyang
Zixing
Longyan
Quanzhou
Putian
T'aoyüan
T'AIPEI
A Chenzhou
Ganzhou
Xiamen
Changhua
Hsinchu 3884
Hsüeh Shan

EAST CHINA
SEA
Nago Okinawa
Okinawa
Naha
JAPAN

25°
Tropic of Cancer

Lian Xian **Shaoguan**
Meizhou
Zhangzhou
(Chinmen)
(Taiwan)
Changhua **T'aichung**
e Xian
Qingyuan
Chaozhou
Chiai 3950
Yu Shan
TAIWAN
hou
GUANGZHOU
Huizhou
Shantou
T'ainan
T'aitung

Dongguan
Lufeng
KAOHSIUNG P'ingtung
20°
Zhongshan Foshan
Shanwei
Macau Shenzhen
Yangjiang
**XIANGGANG
(HONG KONG)**
Oluanpi

Luzon
Batan Islands
PACIFIC

Strait
Basco

Balintang Channel
Babuyan Islands

Paracel Islands
Bangui Claveria San Vicente
Laoag Aparri
Kabugao Lal-lo
Vigan Bangued Tuguegarao
OCEAN

S
Santa Cruz *Luzon* Palanan
San Fernando Bontoc Ilagan
Mt. Pulog
O
Baguio 2929 Santiago
Alaminos Casiguran

U
Dagupan
Lingayen San Carlos Baler

T
Tarlac Cabanatuan
Angeles Gapan
H
Olongapo Polillo Is.
QUEZON CITY Calagua Is.
MANILA Daet Pandan
Pasig San Pablo Naga *Cantanduanes*
C
Nasugbu Calauag
Batangas Lucena Lopez Virac
H
Mamburao Boac Legaspi
Calapan Pascual Sorsogon
I
Mindoro 2488 Pinamalayan Bulan Catarman
Mount Baco Masbate *Samar*
N
Mindoro Strait Masbate Allen Catbalogan
San Pedro Calbayog
A
Calamian Nabas Borongan
Group Coron Placer Tacloban
Kalibo Ormoc
El Nido Roxas *Leyte*
S
Panay **Iloilo** Bogo
San Jose de **Bacolod** **Cebu** Sogod Libjo
E
Buenavista *Cebu* Maasin *Dinagat*
Bago Carcar Talibon Dapa
A
Spratly Roxas Cauayan Bais *Bohol* Surigao
Islands Bago Tagbilaran Madrid
Palawan Dumaguete Butuan Tandag
Negros Prosperidad
Quezon Dipolog
PHILIPPINES
Brooke's Point Manukan **Cagayan de Oro**
2560 Iligan Malaybalay Bislig
Liloy
Sulu Sea Pagadian *Mindanao* Tagum
Bugsuk Sibuco Cotabato **Davao** Mati
Balabac Balabac Isabela *Moro* Tacurong 2954
Zamboanga *Gulf* Polomoloc Mt. Apo
Balabac Palimbang **General Santos**
Strait Jolo *Cape San Agustin*
Kudat Jolo Glan
Langkon *Pangutaran* *Sarangani Is.*
Kota Belud *Group*
4094
G. Kinabalu Ranau Sandakan
Kota Kinabalu Tawi-Tawi *Kepulauan*
SABAH Tungku Bongao *Nanusa*
Beaufort Lahad Datu *Sulu* Beo
I A *Archipelago* *Kepulauan*
Bandar Seri Begawan Kalabakan *Karkaralong*
Seria Semporna *Celebes* Tahuna **INDONESIA**
BRUNEI *Gunung Mulu* Tawau *Sea* Sangir
2371 Tarakan *Kepulauan*
Bareo *Sangir*
Bintulu Belaga 2499 Tanjungselor *Molucca Sea* Daruba
SARAWAK Tanjungredeb Morotai
Kapit *Muarawahau*
kei **INDONESIA** Sepinang
2988 **KALIMANTAN** Sangkulirang

E 115° F G 125° H

South

China

Sea

86 87

© Helicon Publishing Ltd

Settlements

■ over 3 million
□ 1 – 3 million
○ 250 000 – 1 million
● 100 000 – 250 000
◉ 25 000 – 100 000
· under 25 000
— country capital underline

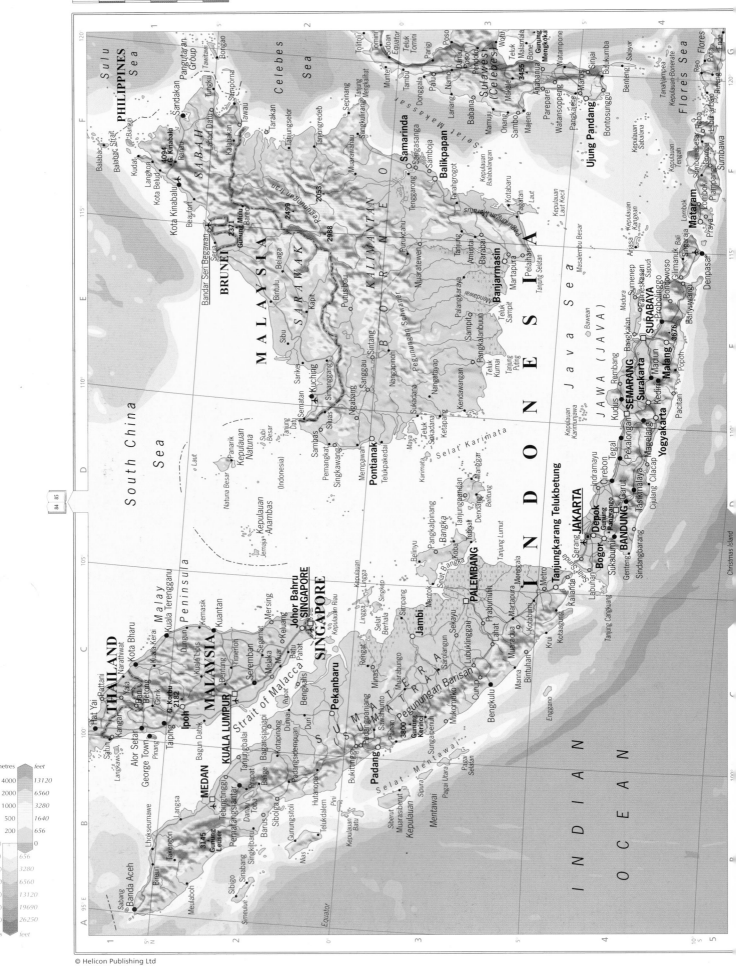

Scale 1 : 11 600 000

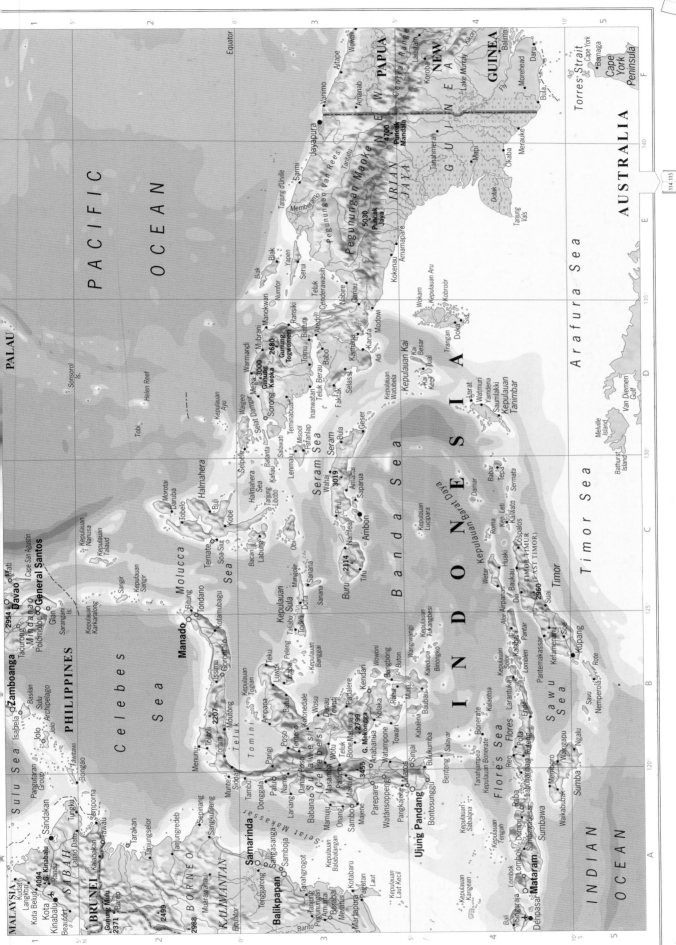

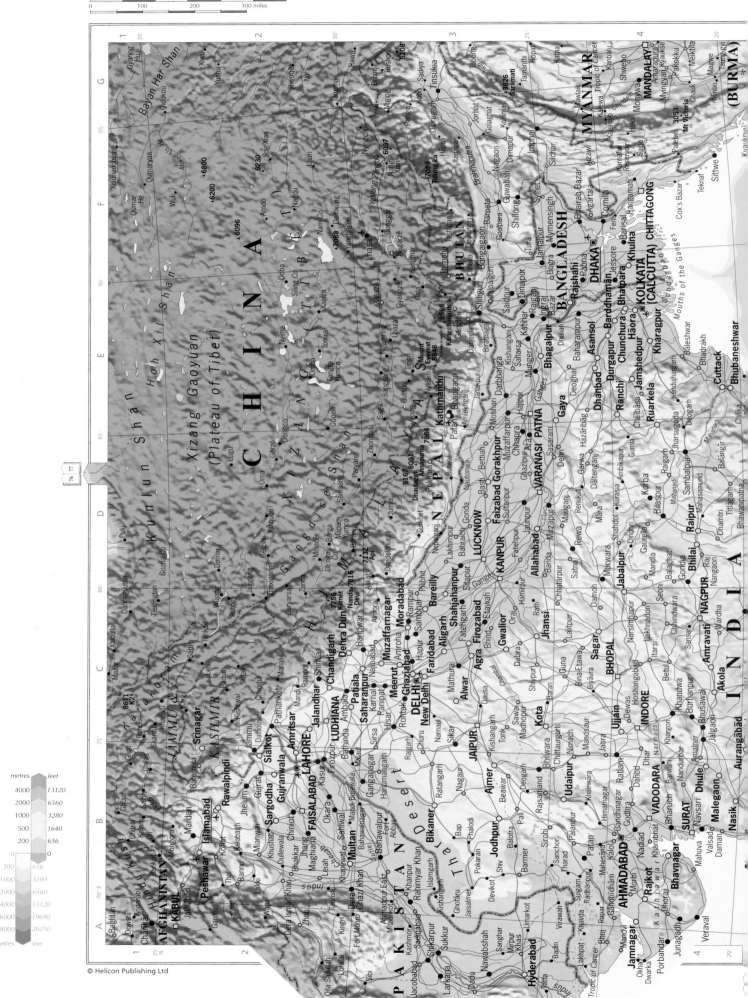

Scale 1 : 11 600 000

© Helicon Publishing Ltd

88 ASIA

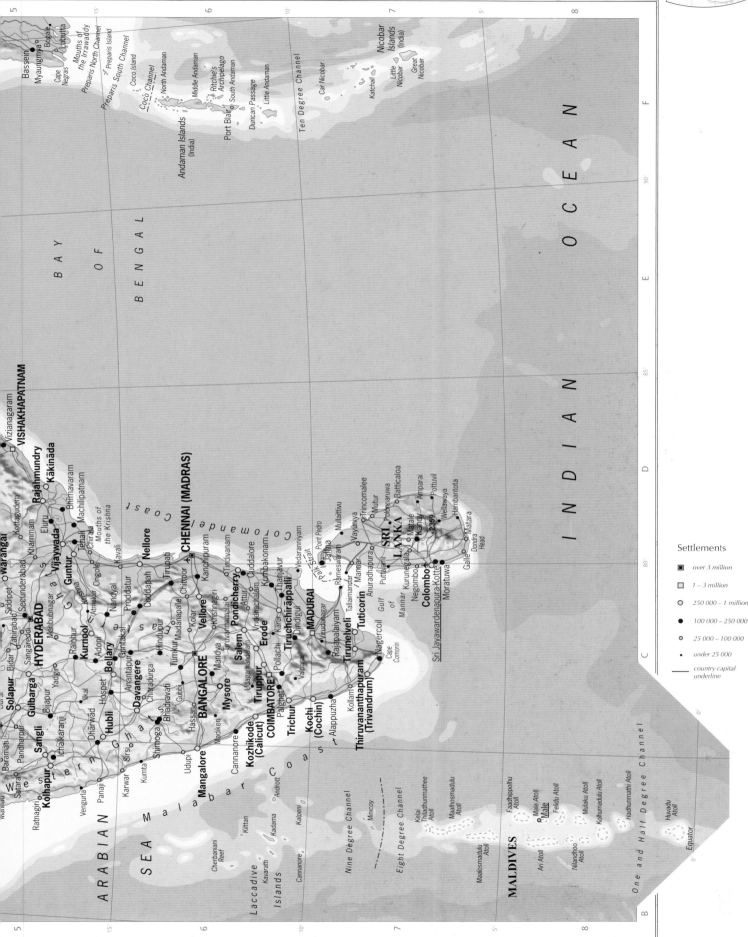

Settlements

■	*over 3 million*
□	*1 – 3 million*
○	*250 000 – 1 million*
●	*100 000 – 250 000*
◦	*25 000 – 100 000*
·	*under 25 000*
——	*country capital underline*

Scale 1 : 12 700 000

0   200   400   600 km
0 100 200 300 miles

RUSSIA

GEORGIA
T'BILISI

ARMENIA   **AZERBAIJAN**
YEREVAN   BAKI (BAKU)

Black Sea

Sochi · Pyatigorsk
Cherkessk · Kislovodsk
Elbrus 5642 · Nal'chik · Groznyy · Makhachkala
Nazran · Vladikavkaz · Kaspiysk
Izberbash
Och'amch'ire · Zugdidi · K'ut'aisi · Derbent
Sokhumi · Bat'umi · Samtredia · Vachi
Ordu · Trabzon · Rize · Artvin · Oltu · Ardahan · Kars · Gyumri · Vanadzor
Caspian Sea
Sumqayit

TURKEY

Haskovo · Edirne · Kurdzhali · Lüleburgaz
İSTANBUL · Zonguldak · Bartın · İnebolu · Sinop · İnce Burun
Bosporus · Gebze · İzmit · Düzce · Bolu · Kastamonu · Bafra · Samsun
Marmara · Denizli · Sakarya · Koroğlu Dağları · Çankırı · Çorum · Amasya · Ordu
Çanakkale · Bursa · Eskişehir · Beypazarı · **ANKARA** · Kırıkkale · Sorgun · Tokat · Turhal · Gümüşhane · Horasan · Erzurum
Edremit · Balıkesir · Kütahya · Afyon · Polatlı · Kulu · Kırşehir · Sivas · Divriği · Tunceli · Bingöl · Murat 4434 · Patnos · Erciş
İZMIR · Manisa · Uşak · Sandıklı · Aksaray · **Kayseri** · Gürün · Kesis Dağları · Elazığ · Muş · Van · Başkale · Hakkâri
Salihli · Denizli · Dinar · Isparta · Akşehir · Niğde · Göksun · Malatya · Diyarbakır · Siirt · Cizre
Aydın · Burdur · Konya · Karaman · Kahraman Maraş · Gaziantep · Mardin · Zakho
Bodrum · Muğla · Fethiye · Elmalı · Antalya · Alanya · Silifke · **ADANA** · Osmaniye · Nizip · Şanlıurfa · Al Qāmishlī · Al Mawşil
Rodos · Finike · Anamur · İçel · Tarsus · İskenderun · Antakya · Manbij · Tall 'Afar · Arbīl

CYPRUS
Lefkosia (Nicosia)
Lemesos (Limassol)

SYRIA
HALAB (ALEPPO) · Ar Raqqah · Sinjār · As Sulaymānīyah
Lādhiqīyah · İdlib · Hamāh · Dayr az Zawr · Kirkūk
Trâblous (Tripoli) · Hims (Homs) · Tadmur · Bayji
LEBANON · Tikrit
BEYROUTH (BEIRUT) · DIMASHQ (DAMASCUS) · Zahlé
Ba'qūbah
Hefa (Haïfa)

ISRAEL
Tel Aviv-Yafo · İrbid · Ar Ramādī · **BAGHDĀD**
Yerushalayim (Jerusalem) · Zarqā · **'AMMĀN** · Ar Rutba · Karbalā' · Al Kūt
Dead Sea · Al Hillah · Al 'Amārah
Beér Sheva' · Al Hadīthah · An Najaf · Masjed Soleymān
Al Jālamīd · Ad Dīwānīyah · Ahvāz

IRAQ

Badiyat ash Shām (Syrian Desert)

JORDAN
Ma'ān · Ar'ar · An Nāşirīyah · Al Başrah · Ābādān
Elat · Aqaba
Al Jawf · Sākākah · As Salmān
Al Humaydah · Rafhā · **KUWAIT**
Al Kuwayt (Kuwait)
Tabūk · Hafar al Bāţin · Al Fuhayhil
Ash Shu'bah · Būshehr (Bushire)

SAUDI ARABIA

An Nafud
Taymā · Hā'il
Al Wari'ah · Al Jubayl
Burayḍah · Al Artāwīyah
'Unayzah · Al Majma'ah · Rumāḥ · **Ad Dammām** · Al Manāmah · **BAHRAIN**
Ad Dawādimī · **AR RIYĀḌ (RIYADH)** · Al Mubarraz · Al Hufūf · **QATAR** · Ad Daw (Doha)
Al Kharj · Harad
Al Madīnah (Medina) · Afīf · **U.A.E.**
Ḥalabān · Qalamat Nadqān · Al 'Ubaylah
Rābigh · Qadīmah · Zalim
JIDDAH (JEDDA) · Usfān · Laylā
MAKKAH (Mecca) · At Ṭā'if
Al Lith · Qal'at Bīshah · As Sulayyil
Rub' al Khālī (Empty Quarter)
Al Qunfudhah
Abhā · Khamis Mushayt · Sharūrah · Thamūd
Zahrān · Najrān · Wuday'ah · Zamakh · Damq
Jīzān · Sa'dah · Hūth · Şan'ā · Ma'rib · Say'ūn · Tarīm · Qishn
As Zaydīyah · Amrān · Shabwah · Sayhūt

EGYPT

EL ISKANDARÎYA (ALEXANDRIA)
Bûr Sa'îd · Tanta · El Mansûra
Benha · EL QÂHIRA (CAIRO)
EL GÎZA · El Suweis
Helwan · Beni Suef
Beni Mazâr · El Minya · Mallawi · Asyût · Abnûb · Akhmîm · Sohâg · Girga · Qena · Qus · Luxor
Valley of the Kings · El Khârga · Isna · Idfu · Kom Ombo
Bâris · Aswân · Aswân Dam
Tropic of Cancer
Abu Simbel · Wadi Halfa · Lake Nasser
Sinai · Gebel Katherina 2637 · Ras Ghârib
Sharm el Sheikh · Hurghada · Bûr Safâga · Quseir · Marsa Alam · Ras Banâs
Dubâ · Al Wajh · Umm Lajj
Yanbu' al Bahr · Badr Ḥunayn
Râs Abu Shagara

RED SEA

ADMINISTERED BY SUDAN
Halaib · Bur Sudan (Port Sudan)
Suakin · Sinkat · Tokat

SUDAN

Nubian Desert
Merowe · Berber · Atbara · Haiya · Ras Kasar
Umm Durman · El Khartum Bahri · **El Khartum (Khartoum)** · Shendi
Kassala · Khashm el Girba · Akordat · Keren · Massawa
Wad Medani · Teseney · Barentu · **Asmara**
Ed Dueim · Sennar · Gedaref · Metema · Gallabat
Kosti · Rabak · Singa · Om Hajer · Himora
Bahr el Abiad · Bahr el Azraq

ERITREA

Dahlak Archipelago
Dèhalak Desèt
Agena · Algena
Sad'ah · Harad · Bayt al Faqīh
Āksum · Adigrat · Adīgrat
Ras Dashen Terara 4620 · Mek'elē · Ti'o · Al Hudaydah · **YEMEN** · Ar Rawdah · Ash Shihr · Al Mukallā
Maych'ew · Assab · Bāb al Mandab · Ibb 2514 · Jabal Thamar · Dhamār · Ta'izz · Shuqrah · Zinjibār
Bayt al Faqīh · Al Mukhā

ETHIOPIA

3760 Şan'ā
Jabal an Nabī Shu'ayb

DJIBOUTI
Djibouti · Tendaho · Lake Abbe · Dikhil · Sāylac
SOMALIA
'Adan (Aden) · Maydh · Boosaaso · Caluula · Raas Aseir · Bereeda

Gulf of Aden

Mediterranean Sea

metres / feet
4000 / 13120
2000 / 6560
1000 / 3280
500 / 1640
200 / 656
0 / 0
200 / 656
1000 / 3280
2000 / 6560
4000 / 13120
6000 / 19690
8000 / 26250
metres / feet

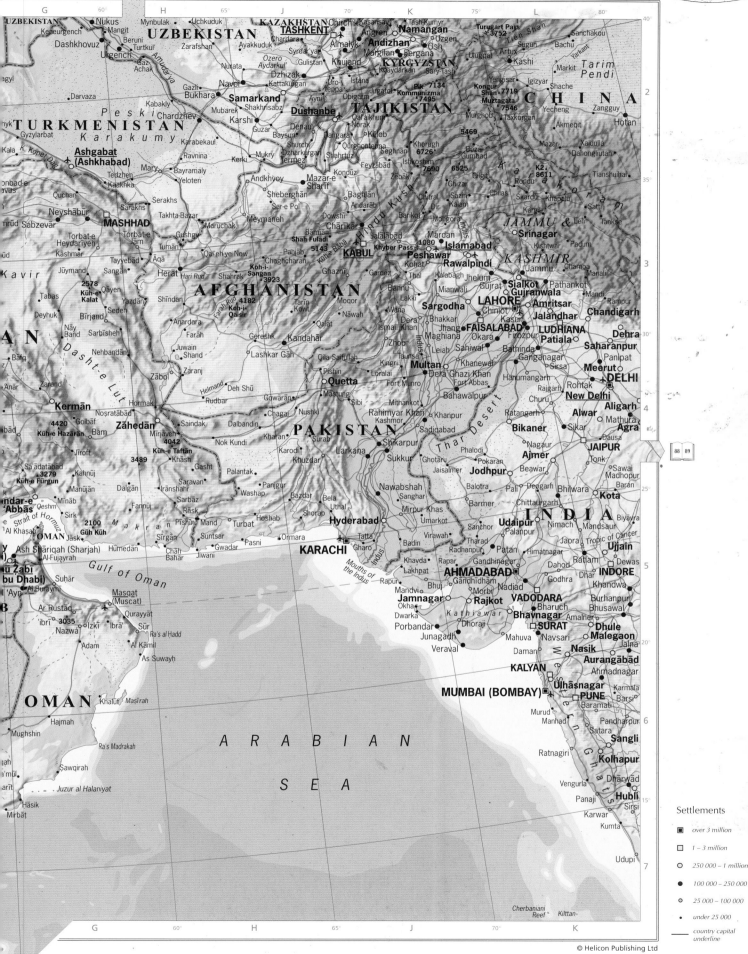

UZBEKISTAN

Nukus
Mynbulak
Uchkuduk
KAZAKHSTAN
Chirchik Kasansay
Mangit
Keneurgench
Zarafshan
Chardara
Angren
Namangan
Beruni
Turtkul
Ayakkuduk
Almalyk
Andizhan
Turkul
Ozero
Syrdar'ya
Osh
Dashkhovuz
Nurata
Gulistan
Uzgen
Fergana
Urgench
Aydarkul'
Khujand
Margilan
KYRGYZSTAN
Turagart Pass
Sanchakou
Gaz-
Achak
Navoi
Dzhizak
Uro-
teppa
Istana
Kbaydarkan
Sary-Tash
3752
Sugun
Bachu
Darvaza
Bukhara
Samarkand
Mubarek
Shakhrisabz
Obigarm
Jirgatol
Pik 7134
Kommunizma
7495
Uluqqat
Yengisar
Artux
Kashi
Markit
Igziyar
Shache
Yarkand
Tarim
Pendi

TURKMENISTAN
Peski
Chardzhev
Karshi
Guzar
Denau
Baysun
Shurchi
Dangara
Kulob
Khorugh 6726
Bzar
Gumbad
Mazar
Kongur
Shan 7719
Muztagata
7546
Yecheng
Zangguy
Akmeqit
Xaidulla
Qahongliutan
Hotan

CHINA

OMAN

ARABIAN

SEA

ASIA 91

Scale 1 : 5 800 000

0   100   200   300 km
0   50   100   150 miles

ROMANIA
Titu
Bolintin-
Vale
Urziceni
Babadag
Lacul
Razim
Videle
★ **BUCUREȘTI**
(BUCHAREST)
Slobozia
Ialomița
Hârșova
Danube
Lacul Sinoie
Alexandria
Giurgiu
Oltenița
Călărași
Medgidia
● **Constanța**
Zimnicea
Tutrakan
Danube
Silistra
Tervel
Mangalia
Ruse
Razgrad
Dobrič
Balčik
Bjala
Popovo
Novi Pazar
Târgoviște
Veliko Târnovo
● **Šumen**
Provadija
Nos
Kaliakra
Trjavna
✈
● **Varna**
BULGARIA
Nova
Zagora
Sliven
Aitos
Nesebăr
Nos Emine
Stara
Zagora
Jambol
Burgas
Pomorie
Elhovo
Grudovo
Sozopol
Burgaski Zaliv
Harmanli
Malko
Târnovo
Rezovo
Yıldız Dağları

BLACK   SEA

Edirne
Kırklareli
İğneada
İnce Burun
Uzunköprü
Saray
Kıyıköy
Meriç
Babaeski
Lüleburgaz
Karacaköy
İstanbul
Boğazı
(Bosporus)
Cide
İnebolu
Ayancık
Sinop
İpsala
Hayrabolu
Çorlu
Sarıyer
Zonguldak
Bartın
Kastamonu
Taşköprü
Alaçam
Bafra Burun
Keșan
Malkara
Tekirdağ
Yeşilköy
Silivri
● **İSTANBUL**
Ereğli
Karasu
Safranbolu
Boyabat
Vezirköprü
● **Samsun**
Şarköy
Gebze
İzmit
Düzce
Gerede
Kurșunlu
Çankırı
Osmancık
Havza
Çarşamba
Marmara Denizi
Yalova
Sakarya
Bolu
Kızılcahamam
Merzifon
Taşova
Gelibolu
Marmara Adası
Gemlik
İznik
2400
Köroğlu Dağları
Amasya
Çanakkale
Erdek
Bandırma
İznik Gölü
Sakarya
Beypazarı
Kızılırmak
Çorum
Turhal
Resadiye
Ezine
Bursa
İnegöl
Kalecik
Sungurlu
Tokat
Edremit
Balıkesir
Dursunbey
Tavșanli
Eskişehir
● **ANKARA**
Çerikli
Yıldızeli
Lesvos
Mytilini
Ayvalık
Bergama
Simav
Kütahya
Polatlı
Bala
Kırıkkale
Yerköy
Yozgat
Sorgun
Akdağmadeni
Plomari
Akhisar
ANATOLIA
Sivrihisar
Kaman
Kırşehir
Sarıkaya
Şarkışla
Aliağa
● **İZMİR**
Manisa
Salihli
Uşak
Banaz
Emirdağ
Yunak
Kulu
TURKEY
Șereflikoçhisar
Bünyan
Ulaş
Urla
Ödemiş
Kula
Afyon
Cihanbeyli
Tuz
Gölü
Nevşehir
● **Kayseri**
Samos
Samos
Fournoi
Aydın
Sarayköy
Sandıklı
Dinar
Akșehir
Eğridir
Gölü
Ilgın
Kadınhanı
Aksaray
Yeşilhisar
Pınarbașı
Leros
Söke
Denizli
Burdur
Isparta
Beyşehir
Gölü
● **Konya**
Niğde
Saimbeyli
Kalymnos
Kalymnos
Milas
Muğla
Kale
Bucak
Beyșehir
Seydişehir
2288
Ereğli
Ulukışla
● **Kahraman Maraş**
Kos
Nisyros
Bodrum
Gökova Körfezi
Marmaris
Datça
Korkuteli
Bozkır
Karaman
Kozan
Kadirli
Bahçe
Tilos
Symi
Rodos
Elmali
Antalya
Serik
Toros Dağları
Tarsus
● **ADANA**
Gaziantep
Osmaniye
GREECE
Chalki
Rodos
Fethiye
Kalkan
Finike
Antalya
Körfezi
Manavgat
Alanya
Mut
Ermenek
İskenderun
Megisti
(Greece)
Kumluca
Anamur
Silifke
Karatas
● **İçel
(Mersin)**
Karataş
Kırıkhan
Saria
Kattavia
Kasos
Karpathos
Karpathos
Antakya
Yayladağı
Afrin
HAL
(ALE

MEDITERRANEAN   SEA

C. Apostolos
Andreas
Aigialousa
Jisr ash Shughūr
İdlib
Ma'arr
an Nu'
Keryneia
Ammochostos
(Famagusta)
Al Lādhiqīyah
Jablah
C. Arnaoutis
Lefkosia
(Nicosia)
C. Greko
Bāniyās
Hamāh
Polis
Olympus
Troodos 1952
Larnaka
Tartūs
Pafos
Lemesos
(Limassol)
CYPRUS
Al Hamīdīyah
Tall
Kalakh
**Hims
(Hom**
Trâblous
(Tripoli)
Halba
3087
2464
Al
Qornet es
Saouda
2659
An Nab
2628
Taī'at
Mūsā
**BEYROUTH
(BEIRUT)**
Zablé
Jayrūd
Saida
LEBANON
Qaraoaoun
Sour
Qatana
**DIMASHQ
(DAMASC**
Qatana
Dūm

metres | feet
4000 | 13120
2000 | 6560
1000 | 3280
500 | 1640
200 | 656
0 | 0
200 | 656
1000 | 3280
2000 | 6560
4000 | 13120
6000 | 19690
8000 | 26250
metres | feet

H   40°   J   42°   K   44°   L   46°   M   48°   N

Slavyánsk-na-Kubani
Krasnodar
ymsk
Goryachiy Klyuch
rossiysk
zhik
haylovskiy
Tuapse
Sochi
Adler
Gagra
Gudaut'a
Sokhumi
Och'amch'ire
Zugdidi

Ust'-Labinsk
Armavir
Adygeysk
Maykop
Khadyzhensk
Belorechensk
Psebay
Teberda

Svetlograd
Stavropol'
Nevinnomyssk
Cherkessk
Kislovodsk
Pyatigorsk
Mineral'nyye Vody
Prokhladnyy

Blagodarnyy
Budennovsk

Neftekumsk
Yuzhno-Sukhokumsk
Kochubey

KALMYKIYA

Kutan
Kizlyarskiy Zaliv
Kraynovka

Os. Chechen'
Agrakhanskiy Poluostrov

1

44°

50°

R U S S I A

ADYGEYA
KARACHAYEVO-CHERKESIYA
Karachayevsk
Zelenokumsk
Mozdok
Terek
Nazran
KABARDINO-BALKARIYA
Nal'chik
5642 Elbrus
5203

Kargalinskaya
Babayurt

Kizlyar

Makhachkala
Kaspiysk
Buynaksk

CASPIAN

P

SEVERNAYA OSETIYA
Sadon
5047 Kazbek
Oni
INGUSHETIYA
Vladikavkaz
Gudermes
Urus Martan
CHECHNYA
Groznyy
4494 4276 Diklosmta
DAGESTAN
Khasavyurt
Gunib
Levashi
Kumukh

Izberbash
Derbent

2

42°

SEA

Tqvarch'eli
Lajanurpekhi
Ts'khinvali
K'ut'aisi
P'ot'i
Samtredia
GEORGIA
Gori
Kaspi
T'elavi
Ovareli
4131
Kasumkent
Qusar
Xacmaz
Quba
Davaci
Siyazan

Ozurget'i
Bat'umi
Hopa
Pazar
Rize
Trabzon
Giresun
Gümüshane

Khashuri
Borjomi
Arkhalts'ikhe
Akhalk'alak'i
Bolnisi
T'BILISI
Rust'avi
Dedoplis
Zaqatala
Qax
Şäki
Akhty
4466 Gora Bazardyuzi
Mingäcevir Su Anbarı
Mingäcevir
İsmayıllı
Gilazi

3

adolu
Trabzon
Artvin
Yusufeli
Ardahan
3937
Göle
Kars
Vanadzor
Dilijan
Tashir
Alaverdi
Qazax
Tovuz
Gäncä
Sämkir
Bärdä
Yevlax
AZERBAIJAN
Samaxı
Ağsu

Sumqayıt
BAKI (BAKU)

Daǧları
Bayburt
Gyumri
Hrazdan
ARMENIA
YEREVAN
Ejmiadzin
Sevana Lich
Vardenis
3724
Ağcabädi
Kürdämir
İmişli
Saatli
Äli Bayramlı

Salyan
Qazımämmäd
Sanqaçal

40°

Süşehri
Gümüshane
Erzincan
Aşkale
Erzurum
Tortum
Pasinler
Horasan
Ağri
Oltu
Sarıkamış
Vedi
Ararat
Mt. Ararat 5165
Sisian
Goris
Xankändi
Şuşa
Horadiz
Tazeh Kand
Biläsuvar
Neftçala

4

ivriği
Pülümür
Kemaliye
Tunceli
Ağın
Keban Baraji
Palu
Bingöl
Karakoçan
Varto
Solhan
Muş
Murat
Dogubeyazit
Patnos
Erciş
Muradiye
4434 Süphan Daği
AZER.
Sahbuz
Naxcivan
Culfa
Jolfa
Qazangöldag 3829
Minciван
Khodä Afarin
Avärsin
Calilabad
Masallı
Lerik
4810
Khiyav
Astara
Ardabīl
Länkäran

Elazığ
Fırat (Euphrates)
Maden
Silvan
Mus
Tatvan
Van Gölü
Van
Bitlis
Gevaş
Baskale
Ercek
Qotur
Salmas
Khvoy
Tasūj
Marand
Ahar
Bastānābād
Sarāb
Täläsh
Hashtpar
Bandar-e Anzalī

Malatya
Ergani
Siverek
Diyarbakır
Batman
Siirt
Catak
Yüksekova
Hakkari
Lura Shirin
Daryācheh-ye Orūmīyeh
3710 Kuh-e Sahand
Orūmīyeh
Āzarān
Miāneh
Nik Pey
Rasht

5

Kahta
isehir
Hilva
Viranşehir
Mardin
Nusaybin
Cizre
Sinak
Zākho
Amādiyah
Zebar
Haydarābād
Bonāb
Marāgheh
Miandowāb
Kirk Bulağ D. 3107
Zanjān

ozova
Sanliurfa
Akçakale
Kızıltepe
Al Qāmishlī
Dahūk
Tall 'Uwaynāt
Rawāndiz
Mahābād
Bowkan
Yangi Kand
Abhar

40°

râbulus
'Ayn 'Isā
Al Hasakah
Tall 'Afar
Sinjār
Ash Shadādah
Al Mawşil
Ranya
Saqqez
I R A N

Buhayrat al Asad
Ar Ruşafah
Koi Sānjaq
Sar Dasht
Bāneh
Dīvandarreh
Bījār
Zāgheh-ye Bālā

6

34°

Dayr az Zawr
Ar Raqqah
As Sulaymānīyah
Ash Sharqāt
Arbīl
Halabja
Pāveh
Marīvan
Sanandaj
Qorveh

MESOPOTAMIA
Kirkūk
Tuz Khurmātū
Kifrī
IRAQ
Karand
Ravānsar
Kāmyārān
Kermānshāh
Harsin

Settlements

RIA
As Sukhnah
Tadmur
Mayādīn
Āl Bū Kamāl
Rāwah
Anah
Al Hadīthah
Tikrīt
Baiji
Sāmarrā'
Buhayrat ath Tharthār
Tigris
Jalūlā
Gilan Garb
Eslāmābād e Gharb
Īlām
Mehrān
Kūhdasht

diyat ash Shām
(Syrian Desert)
Tadmur
Khān al Baghdādī
Hīt
Ar Ramādī
Habbānīyah
Al Khālis
Ba'qūbah
Al Muqdādīyah
BAGHDAD
Bar al Milh
Ar Rutba
Dehlorān
Mālavi

7

Settlements

■ over 3 million

□ 1 – 3 million

○ 250 000 – 1 million

● 100 000 – 250 000

◉ 25 000 – 100 000

· under 25 000

—— country capital underline

—— state or province capital underline

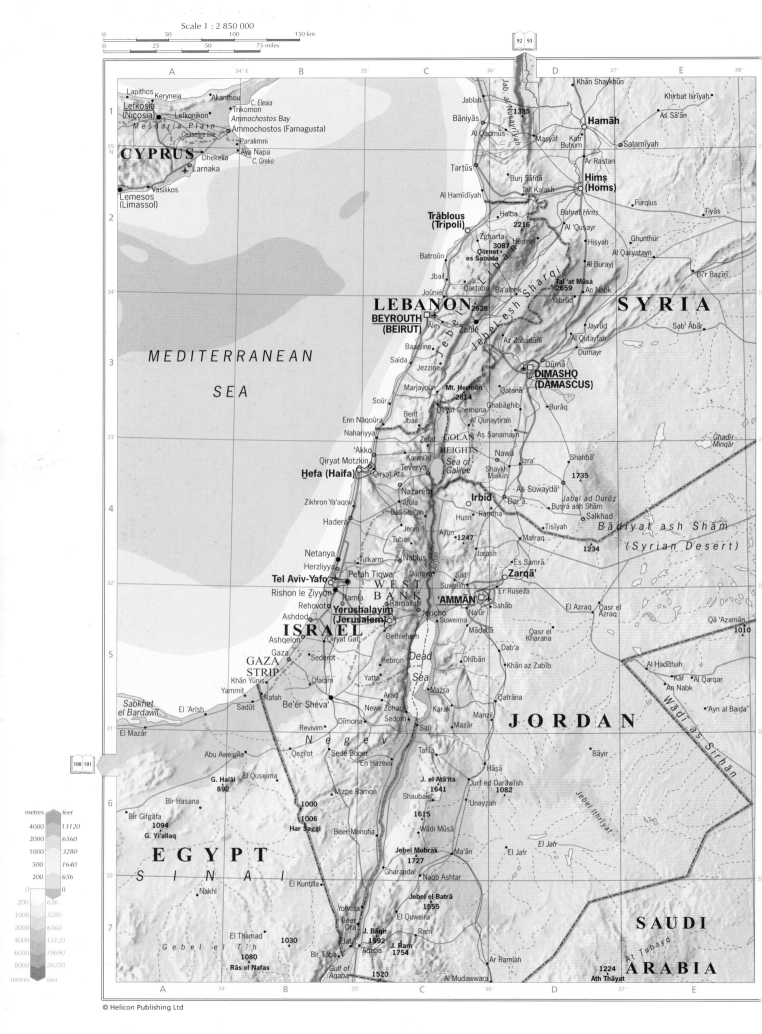

Scale 1 : 2 850 000

0   50   100   150 km
0   25   50   75 miles

92 | 93

| A | 34° E | B | 35° | C | 36° | D | 37° | E | 38° |

CYPRUS

Lapithos · Keryneia
Lefkosia
(Nicosia) · Lefkonikon · Akanthou · C. Eleaia
Mesaoria Plain · Ammochostos Bay
Trikomon
Paralimni · Ammochostos (Famagusta)
Ceasefire line
Aya Napa
Dhekelia · C. Greko
Larnaka

Lemesos
(Limassol) · Vasilikos

MEDITERRANEAN

SEA

Khān Shaykhūn
Khirbat Isrīyah
Jablah
Bāniyās · 1385
As Sā'an
Hamāh
Al Qadmūs · Masyāf · Kafr Buhum
Salamīyah
Tartūs · Ar Rastan
Burj Sāfitā · Tall Kalakh
Hims
(Homs)
Al Hamīdīyah · Bahrat Hims · Furqlus
Halba · Tiyās
Trâblous · 2216 · Al 'Qusayr
(Tripoli) · Zgharta · Hermel · Hisyah · Al Qaryatayn · Ghunthūr
3087 · Ghunthūr
Qornet · Ba'albek · Al Burayj
Batroûn · es Saouda · Bi'r Bazīrī
Jbail · Qartaba · Tal 'at Mūsá · An Nabk
Joûnié · 2659
LEBANON · 2628 · Yabrūd · **SYRIA**
BEYROUTH · Aley · Zahlé
(BEIRUT) · Az Zabadānī · Jayrūd · Sab' Ābār
Baaqline · Al Qutayfah
Saïda · Dūmā · Dumayr
Jezzine · **DIMASHQ** · (DAMASCUS)
Marjayoûn · Qatanā · Burāq
Soûr · Mt. Hermon · Ghabāghib
Berit · 2814 · Qiryat Shemona · Aş Sanamayn
Jbail · Al Qunaytirah · Nawā
Enn Nâqoûra · Zefat · Shaykh · Shahbā'
Nahariyya · **GOLAN** · Miskīn · 1735
HEIGHTS · Izra'
'Akko · Karmi'el · Nawā
Qiryat Motzkin · Sea of · Shaykh Miskīn
Teverya · Galilee · As Suwaydā'
Hefa (Haifa) · Qiryat Ata · Jabal ad Durūz
Nazareth · **Irbid** · Bar'a · Busrá ash Shām
Zikhron Ya'aqov · Afula · Husn · Rāmtha · Salkhad
Bet She'an · Ajlūn · Tisīyah · **Bādiyat ash Shām**
Hadera · Jenin · •1247 · Mafraq · 1234 · (Syrian Desert)
Tubas · Jarash · Es Samrā'
Netanya · Nablus · Jordan · Salt
Herzliyya · Tulkarm · Dāmiya · Suweilih · **Zarqā'** · Ghadīr-Minqār
Tel Aviv-Yafo · **WEST** · Er Ruseifa
Rishon le Ziyyon · **BANK** · **'AMMĀN** · El Azraq · Qasr el Azraq
Ramla · Ramallah · Sahāb
Rehovot · Jericho · Na'ūr
Ashdod · **Yerushalayim** · Suweima · Mādabā · Qasr el Kharana
(Jerusalem) · Bethlehem · Dab'a · Qā 'Azamān
ISRAEL · Qiryat Gat · 1010
Ashqelon · Dhībān · Khān az Zabīb
Gaza · Hebron · **Dead** · Al Hadītha
Sederot · **Sea** · Manzil · Kāf · Al Qarqar
GAZA · Ofaqim · Yatta · Mazra · Qatrāna · An Nabk
STRIP · Arad · Karak · 'Ayn al Baida'
Khān Yūnis · Newe Zohar
Yammit · Rafah · Dīmona · Sedom · Mazar
Sabkhet · Sadût · Be'ér Sheva' · Safi · **JORDAN**
el Bardawîl · El 'Arîsh · Revivim · Tafila · Bāyir
El Mazâr · **N e g e v** · Hāsā · Wādī as Sirhān
Abu Aweigîla · Qezi'ot · Sede Boqer · En Hazeva · J. el Atā'ita · Jurf ed Darāwīsh
G. Halâl · 1641 · 1082
892 · El Quseima · Mizpe Ramon · Shaubak · Jebel Ithrīyat
Bîr Hasana · 'Unayzah
Bîr Gifgâfa · 1000 · 1615
1094 · 1006 · Beer Menuha · Wādī Mūsá · El Jafr
G. Yi'allaq · Har Saggi · Ma'ān
EGYPT · Jebel Mubrak · El Jafr
S I N A I · 1727 · El Jafr
Gharandal · Naqb Ashtar
Nakhl · El Kuntilla · Jebel el Batrā · **SAUDI**
Yotvata · 1555 · El Quweira
Beer · Ram
El Thamad · Ora · **ARABIA**
1030 · J. Bâqir
El Quseima · 1592 · J. Ram · At Tubayq
1080 · Bîr Tâba · Elat · 1754
Râs el Nafas · Gulf of · 'Aqaba · 1224
Gebel el Tîh · Aqaba · Ath Thāyat
1520 · Al Mudawwara

metres | feet
4000 | 13120
2000 | 6560
1000 | 3280
500 | 1640
200 | 656
0 | 0
200 | 656
1000 | 3280
2000 | 6560
4000 | 13120
6000 | 19690
8000 | 26250
metres | feet

Bahrain • Israel • Jordan • Kuwait
Lebanon • Qatar • United Arab Emirates

Scale 1 : 5 800 000

100   200   300 km
50   100   150 miles

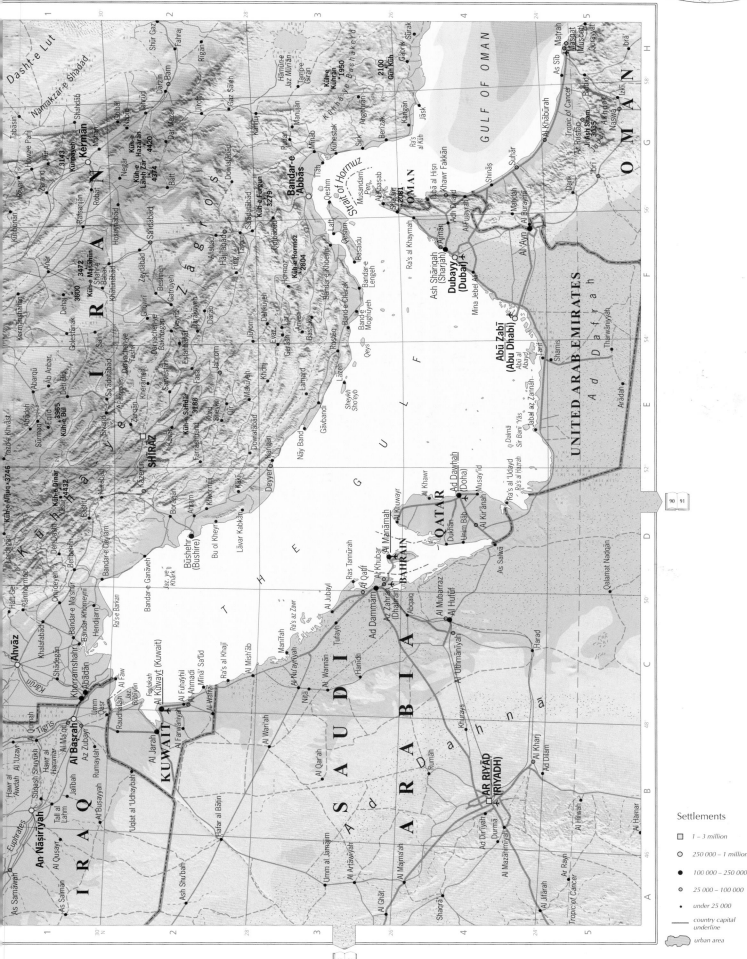

Settlements

□   1 – 3 million

○   250 000 – 1 million

●   100 000 – 250 000

◎   25 000 – 100 000

·   under 25 000

—   country capital underline

  urban area

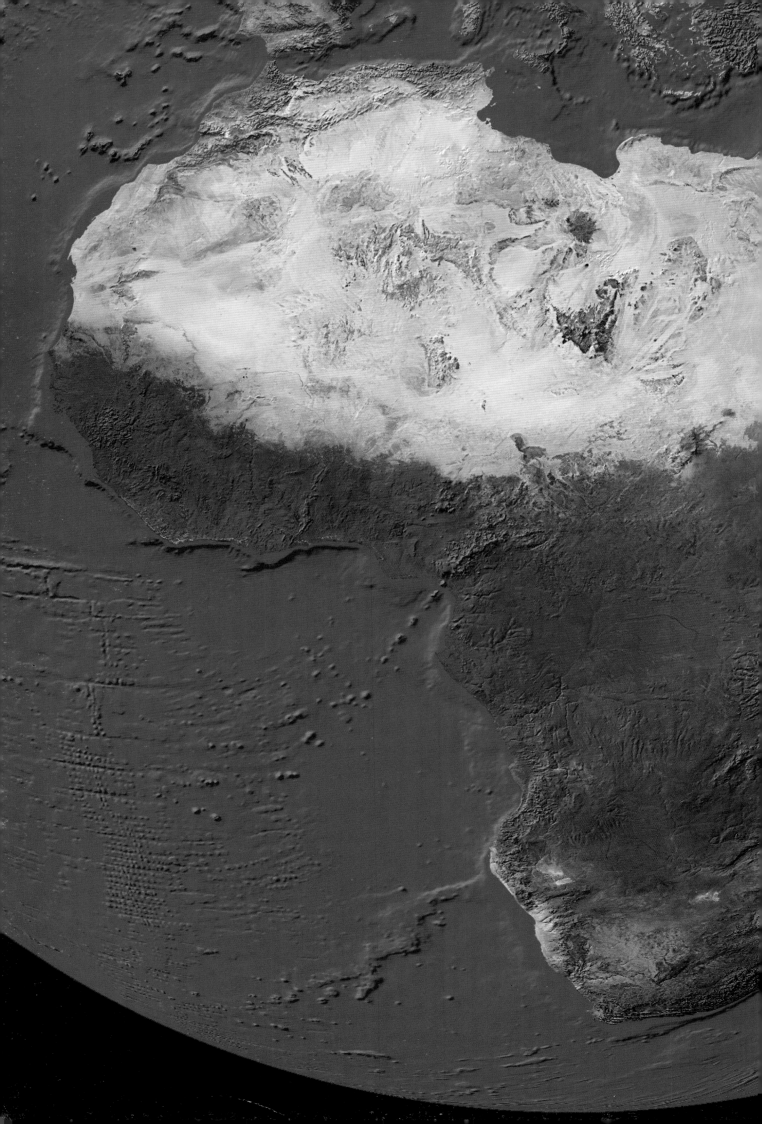

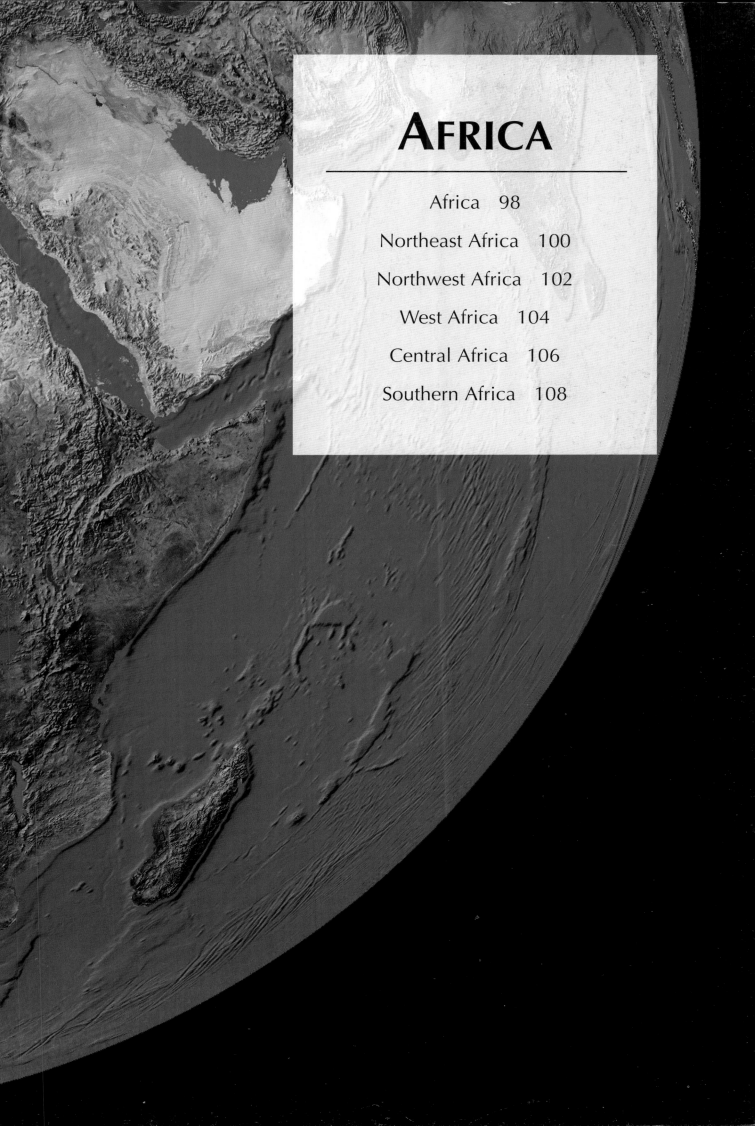

AFRICA

Africa   98

Northeast Africa   100

Northwest Africa   102

West Africa   104

Central Africa   106

Southern Africa   108

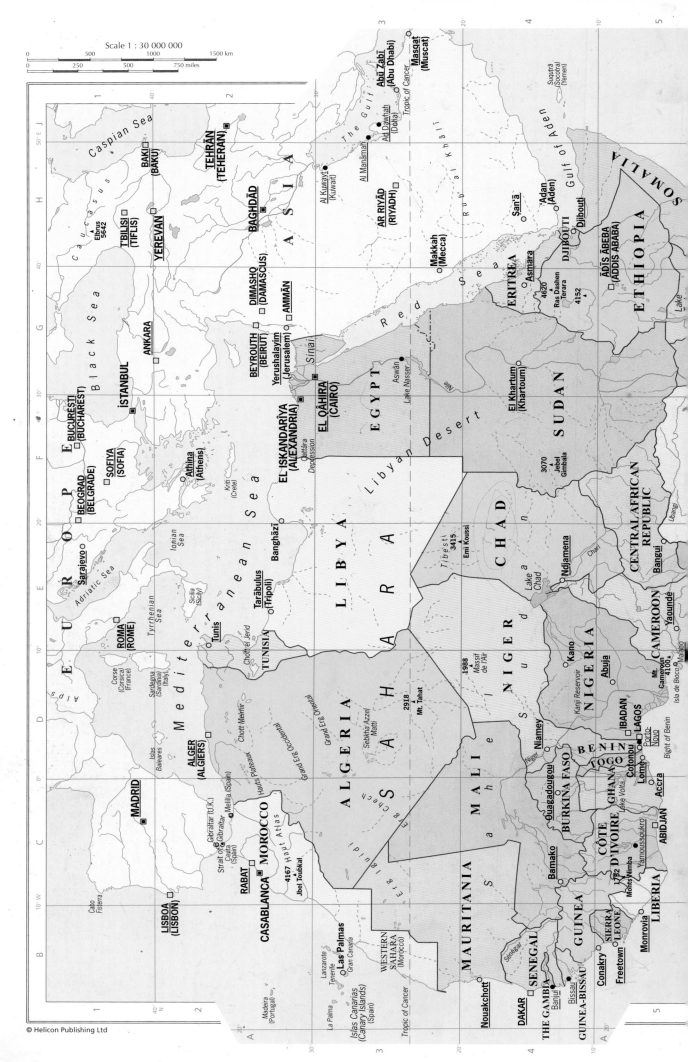

Scale 1 : 30 000 000

© Helicon Publishing Ltd

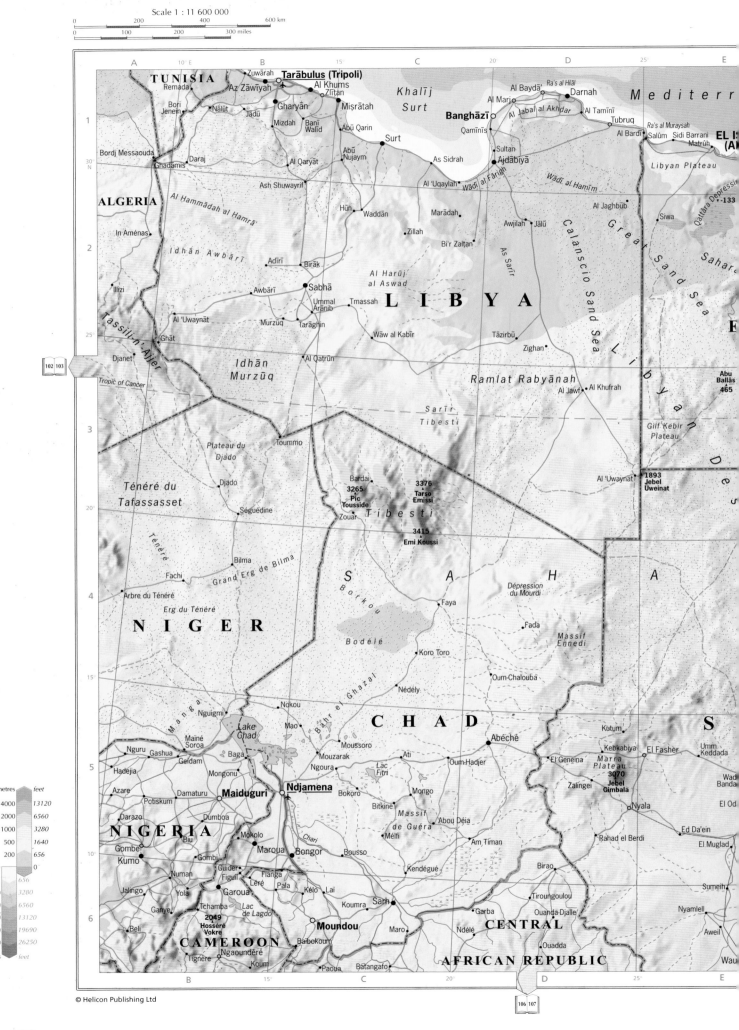

Scale 1 : 11 600 000

| 0 | 200 | 400 | 600 km |
| 0 | 100 | 200 | 300 miles |

TUNISIA
Zuwārah **Tarābulus (Tripoli)**
Remada Az Zāwīyah Al Khums
Bori Zlītan
Jenem Nālūt Jādū Gharyān Mişrātah
Mizdah Banī
Abū Qarin Walīd
Khalīj
Surt

Al Baydā' Ra's al Hilāl
Al Marj **Darnah**
Al Mario Al Jabal al Akhdar Al Tamīnī
Banghāzī Tubruq
Qamīnīs Ra's al Muraysah
Al Bardī Salūm Sidi Barrani
Mediterr
EL I'
(A

Bordj Messaouda Surt
Ghadamis Daraj Al Qaryāt Abū Ajdābiyā
Nujaym As Sidrah
30°N Ash Shuwayrif Al 'Uqaylah Wādī al Fārigh Wādī al Hamīm
ALGERIA Al Hammādah al Hamrā' Al Jaghbūb Siwa
In Aménas Hūn Waddān Marādah Awjilah Jālū **Libyan Plateau** Qattāra Depressi
-133
Idhān Awbārī Zillah Bi'r Zaltan As Sarīr **S a h a r a**
Adīrī Birāk Al Harūj Calanscio Sand Sea
al Aswad **L I B Y A** Tāzirbū Zighan **Great Sand Sea**
Illizi Awbārī **Sabhā** Tmassah Wāw al Kabīr **L i b y a n   D e**
Al 'Uwaynāt Umm al Taghrin Ramlat Rabyānah Abu
Ghāt Aranib Murzūq Al Jawf Al Khufrah Ballās
Djanet **Idhān** Al Qatrūn 465
Tropic of Cancer **Murzūq** **Sarīr** Gilf Kebir
Tibesti Plateau
3 Toummo 1893
Plateau du Al 'Uwaynāt Jebel
Djado Bardai 3376 Uweinat
Ténéré du Djado 3265 Tarso
Tafassasset Séguédine Pic Emissi
Toussidé **T i b e s t i**
Zouar 3415
Ténéré Emi Koussi
Bilma **S** **A** **H** **A**
Fachi Grand Erg de Bilma Dépression
Arbre du Ténéré Borkou du Mourdi Massif
N I G E R Erg du Ténéré Faya Ennedi
Bodélé Fada
Koro Toro
15° Oum-Chalouba Kutum
Nédély El Geneina El Fasher Umm
Nguigmi Nokou Kebkabiya Keddada
Manga Mao Bahr el Ghazal **C H A D** Abéché Marra
Lake Moussoro Plateau
Maïné Chad Ati Oum-Hadjer Zalingei 3070
Nguru Soroa Baga Ngoura Lac Jebel
Gashua Geldam Mongonu Mouzarak Fitri Mongo Gimbala Nyala
Hadejia Bokoro El Od
Azare Damaturu **Ndjamena** Bitkine Abou Déia Rahad el Berdi El Muglad
Potiskum Maïduguri Massif Wad
Darazo Dumboa de Guéra Am Tïman Banda
NIGERIA Mokolo Chari Mélfi Birao
Gombe Biu Maroua Bongor Bousso Kendégué Tiroungoulou Sumeih
Kumo Gombi Guider Flanga Kélo Laï Nyamlell
Jalingo Numan Figuil Léré Pala Koumra Sarh Garba
Yola Garoua Ouanda-Djalle Aweil
Ganye Tchamba Lac Koumra Maro Ndélé **CENTRAL** Nyamlell
Beli Hosséré de Lagdo **Moundou** Ouadda
2049 Vokre Baïbokoum **AFRICAN REPUBLIC** Wau
CAMEROON Tignère Ngaoundéré
Koum Paoua Bātangafo

metres feet
4000 13120
2000 6560
1000 3280
500 1640
200 656
0
200 656
1000 3280
2000 6560
4000 13120
6000 19690
8000 26250
metres feet

© Helicon Publishing Ltd

Chad • Egypt • Eritrea • Libya • Sudan

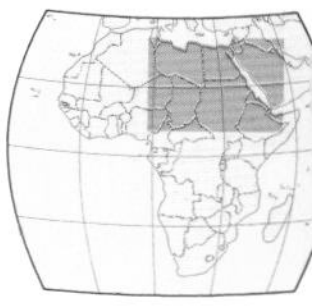

92 93

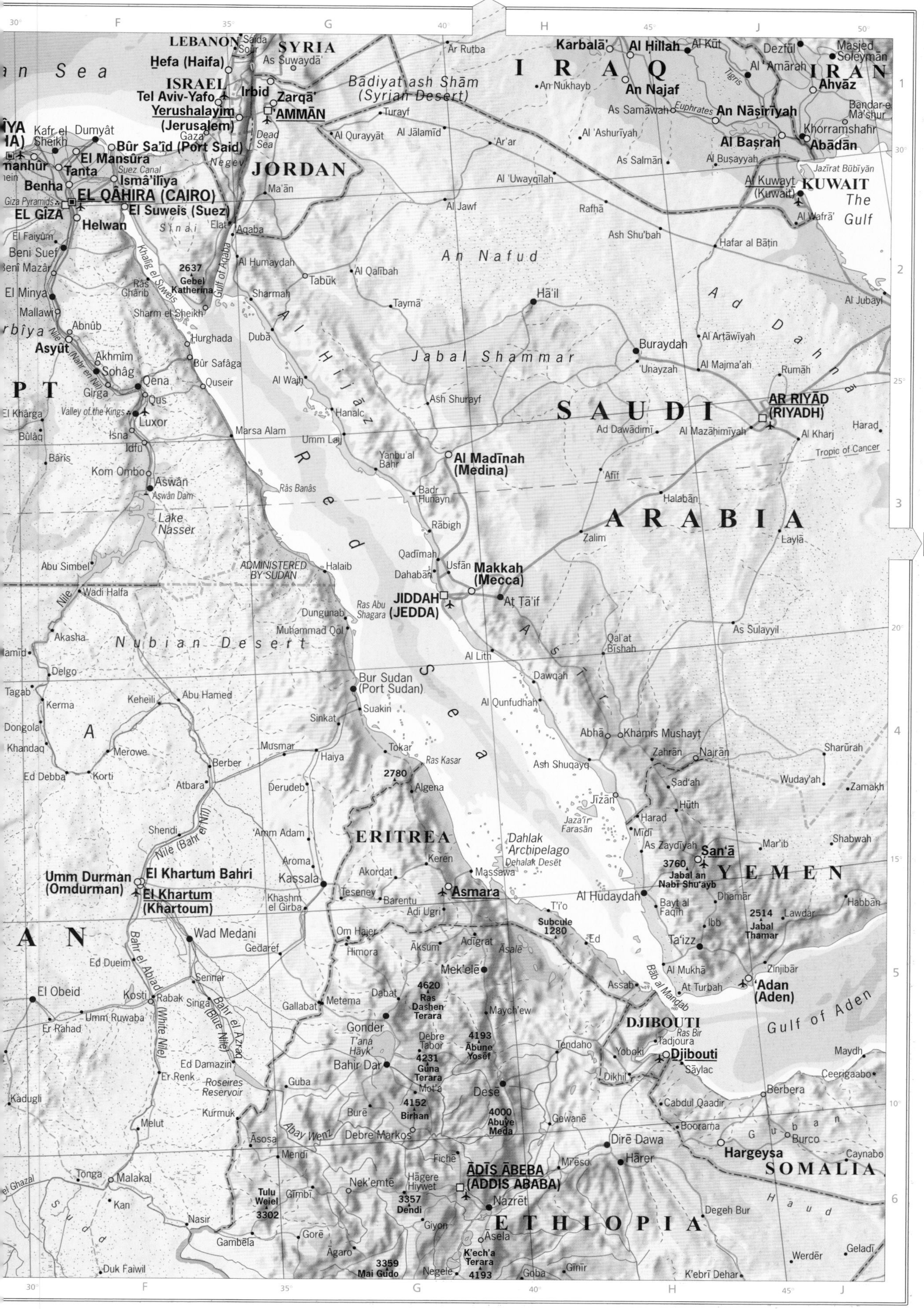

LEBANON
Saida
Sour
SYRIA
As Suwaydā'
Ar Rutba
Karbalā'
Al Hillah
Al Kūt
Dezfūl
Masjed Soleymān
IRAQ
IRAN
Hefa (Haifa)
ISRAEL
Tel Aviv-Yafo
Irbid
Zarqā'
Yerushalayim (Jerusalem)
AMMAN
Bādiyat ash Shām (Syrian Desert)
Turayf
An Nukhayb
An Najaf
Al 'Amārah
Ahvāz
Bandar-e Ma'shur
As Samāwah
Euphrates
Tigris
An Nāṣirīyah
Khorramshahr
Abādān
Al Baṣrah
Al Busayyah
Al 'Ashurīyah
As Salmān
Kafr el Sheikh
Dumyât
Bûr Sa'îd (Port Said)
El Mansûra
Tanta
Benha
Gaza
Dead Sea
Negev
JORDAN
Ma'ān
Al Qurayyāt
Al Jalāmīd
'Ar'ar
Al 'Uwayqīlah
Jazīrat Būbīyān
Al Kuwayt (Kuwait)
KUWAIT
The Gulf
Suez Canal
Ismâ'ilîya
EL QÂHIRA (CAIRO)
Giza Pyramids
EL GÎZA
El Suweis (Suez)
Helwan
Sinai
Elat
Aqaba
Al Jawf
Rafhā
Al Wafrā'
Ash Shu'bah
Hafar al Bātin
El Faiyûm
Beni Suef
Beni Mazâr
El Minya
Mallawi
Abnûb
Asyût
Akhmîm
Sohâg
Qena
Girga
Khalig el Suweis
Gulf of Aqaba
2637 Gebel Katherina
Râs Ghârib
Sharm el Sheikh
Al Humaydah
Tabūk
Al Qalībah
An Nafud
Sharmah
Taymā'
Ḥā'il
Ad Dahnā
Al Jubayl
Hurghada
Bûr Safâga
Quseir
Dubā
Al Hijāz
Al Wajh
Jabal Shammar
Buraydah
'Unayzah
Al Arṭāwīyah
Al Majma'ah
Rumāh
Nile
Nahr en Nil
Qus
Luxor
Valley of the Kings
El Khârga
Bûlâq
Isna
Idfu
Bârîs
Kom Ombo
Aswân
Aswân Dam
Lake Nasser
Hanak
Marsa Alam
Umm Lajj
Ash Shurayf
SAUDI ARABIA
Ad Dawādimī
Al Mazāḥimīyah
AR RIYĀD (RIYADH)
Al Kharj
Harad
Tropic of Cancer
Yanbu'al Bahr
Al Madīnah (Medina)
Afīf
Rās Banās
Badr Ḥunayn
Halabān
Red Sea
Rābigh
Zalim
Laylā
Abu Simbel
ADMINISTERED BY SUDAN
Halaib
Qadīmah
Dahabān
Usfān
Makkah (Mecca)
JIDDAH (JEDDA)
At Ṭā'if
Ras Abu Shagara
Wadi Halfa
Dungunab
Muhammad Qol
Akasha
Nubian Desert
Asīr
Qal'at Bīshah
As Sulayyil
Al Līth
Delgo
Tagab
Kerma
Keheili
Abu Hamed
Bur Sudan (Port Sudan)
Suakin
Dawqah
Al Qunfudhah
Dongola
Khandaq
Merowe
Sinkat
Tokar
Ras Kasar
Abhā
Khamīs Mushayṭ
Zahrān
Najrān
Sharūrah
Ed Debba
Korti
Berber
Musmar
Haiya
Ash Shuqayq
Atbara
Derudeb
2780
Algena
Ṣa'dah
Wuday'ah
Zamakh
Jīzān
Ḥūth
Shendi
Harad
Jaza'ir Farasān
Midī
'Amm Adam
ERITREA
Dahlak Archipelago
Dahalak Desēt
As Zaydīyah
Ṣan'ā
Mar'ib
Shabwah
Nile (Bahr el Nil)
Aroma
Keren
3760 Jabal an Nabī Shu'ayb
YEMEN
Umm Durman (Omdurman)
El Khartum Bahri
El Khartum (Khartoum)
Kassala
Akordat
Massawa
Asmara
Al Hudaydah
Dhamār
Habbān
Khashm el Girba
Teseney
Barentu
Adi Ugri
T'i'o
Bayt al Faqīh
2514 Jabal Thamar
Lawdar
Wad Medani
Om Hajer
Subcule 1280
Ibb
Gedaref
Himora
Ādīgrat
Āksum
Ed
Ta'izz
Bahr el Abiad
Ed Dueim
Āsale
El Obeid
Sennar
Mek'elē
Al Mukhā
Zinjibār
Kosti
Rabak
Singa
Bahr el Azraq (Blue Nile)
Dabat
4620 Ras Dashen Terara
Assab
Bāb al Mandab
At Turbah
'Adan (Aden)
Gallabat
Metema
Maych'ew
Gulf of Aden
Umm Ruwaba
Er Rahad
(White Nile)
Gonder
T'ana Hāyk'
Debre Tabor
4193 Ābune Yosef
4231 Guna Terara
DJIBOUTI
Ras Bir
Tadjoura
Tendaho
Yoboki
Djibouti
Sāylac
Maydh
Ed Damazin
Er Renk
Roseires Reservoir
Bahir Dar
Mot'a
Dikhil
Ceerigaabo
Berbera
Kadugli
Guba
Kurmuk
Burē
4152 Birhan
Desē
4000 Abuye Meda
Cabdul Qaadir
Melut
Āsosa
Abay Wenz
Debre Markos
Gewanē
Boorama
Guban
Burco
Hargeysa
Dirē Dawa
Mendī
Fichē
Mī'ēso
Hārer
SOMALIA
Caynabo
Bahr el Ghazal
Tonga
Malakal
ĀDĪS ĀBEBA (ADDIS ABABA)
Nek'emtē
Hāgere Hiywet
Tulu Weiel 3302
Gimbī
3357 Dendī
Nazrēt
ETHIOPIA
Kan
Sudd
Haud
Degeh Bur
Nasir
Gīyon
Asela
Gambēla
Gorē
Āgaro
K'ech'a Terara 4193
Werdēr
Geladī
Duk Faiwil
3359 Mai Gudo
Negele
Goba
Ginīr
K'ebrī Dehar
30°
35°
40°
45°
50°
30°
25°
20°
15°
10°
F
G
H
J
1
2
3
4
5
6

90 91

Settlements

- over 3 million
- 1 – 3 million
- 250 000 – 1 million
- 100 000 – 250 000
- 25 000 – 100 000
- under 25 000
- country capital underline

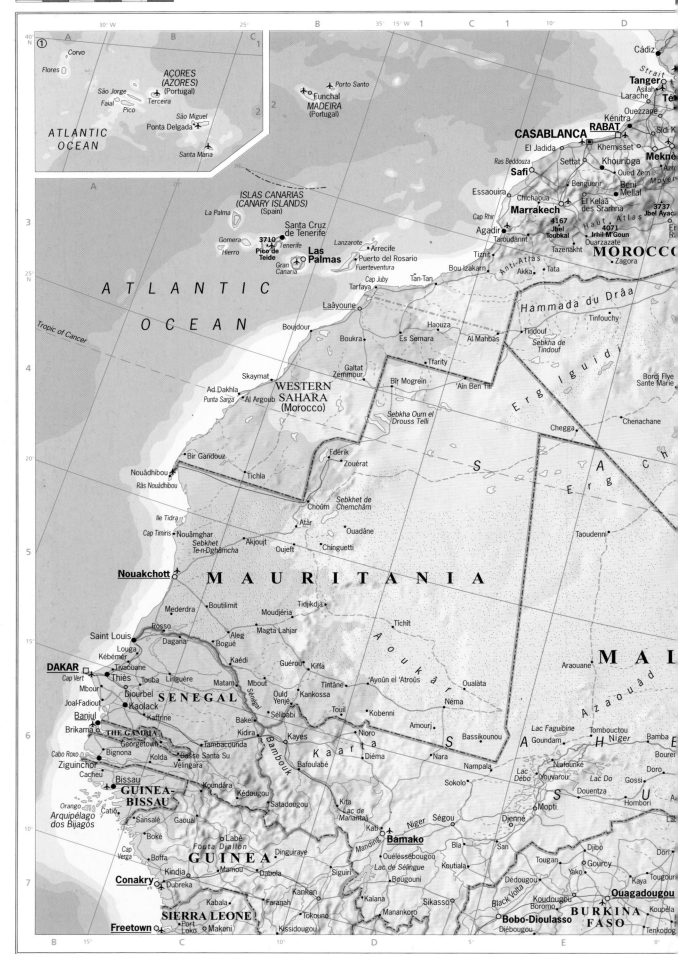

Scale 1 : 11 600 000

ATLANTIC OCEAN

① ATLANTIC OCEAN

Corvo

Flores

AÇORES
(AZORES)
(Portugal)

São Jorge
Faial   Terceira
    Pico
Graciosa

São Miguel
Ponta Delgada

Santa Maria

Porto Santo
Funchal
MADEIRA
(Portugal)

Cádiz
Strait
Tanger
Asilah
Larache   Té
Ouezzane
Kénitra
Sidi K
RABAT
CASABLANCA
El Jadida   Khemisset   Mekne
Ras Beddouza   Settat   Khouribga
Safi   Oued Zem   Azr
Benguerir   Beni   Moye
Essaouira   Chichaoua   El Kelaâ   Mellal
    des Srarhna   3737
Cap Rhir   Marrakech   4167   Jbel Ayac
    Jbel   4071
Agadir   Toubkal   Irhil M'Goun   MOROCCO
Taroudannt   Haut   Atlas
    Ouarzazate
Tiznit   Tazenakht
Bou Izakarn   Anti-Atlas   Tata
    Akka
Tan-Tan   Zagora
Cap Juby   Hammada du Drâa
Tarfaya
    Tinfouchy
Laâyoune   Haouza
    Tindouf
Boujdour   Es Semara
    Al Mahbas   Sebkha de
    Tindouf
Boukra   Tfarity   Bordj Flye
Galtat   Erg   Sante Marie
Skaymat   Zemmour   'Aïn Ben Tili   Iguidi
WESTERN   Bîr Mogrein
Ad Dakhla   SAHARA
Punta Sarga   (Morocco)   Chenachane
Al Argoub   Sebkha Oum el   Chegga
    Drouss Telli   S   A   Ch
Bir Gandouz   Fdérik   Erg
    Zouérat
Nouâdhibou   Tichla
Râs Nouâdhibou   Choûm   Taoudenni
    Sebkhet de
    Chemchâm
Ile Tidra   Atâr   Ouadâne
Cap Timiris   Nouâmghar   Akjoujt   Chinguetti
    Sebkhet   Oujeft
    Ten-Dghâmcha
Nouakchott   M A U R I T A N I A
Mederdra   Boutilimit   Tidjikdja
    Moudjéria   Tîchît
Rosso   Magta Lahjar   A
Saint Louis   Aleg   o   M A
Louga   Dagana   Boguê   u
Kébémèr   Kaédi   Guérou   k   Araouane
DAKAR   Tivaouane   Kiffa   â
Cap Vert   Thiès   Matam   'Ayoûn el 'Atroûs   r   Azaouad
Mbour   Diourbel   Mbout   Tintâne   Oualàta
Joal-Fadiout   Linguère   Sénégal   Kankossa   Néma
    SENEGAL   Ould   S
Kaolack   Yenjé   Kobenni   A
Banjul   Kaffrine   Sélibabi   Touil   Amourj   Bassikounou   Lac Faguibine
Brikama   Bakel   Kidira   Kayes   Nioro   Goundam   Tombouctou
THE GAMBIA   Nampala   Niger   Bamba
Georgetown   Kidira   Kayes   Nara   Sokolo   Niafounké   Bourei
Cabo Roxo   Bignona   Tambacounda   K   Diéma   Lac   Doro
Ziguinchor   Kolda   Basse Santa Su   a   Bafoulabé   Débo   Gossi
Cacheu   Vélingara   a   Lac Do   Hombori
    Koundara   r   Douentza   S
Bissau   t   U
GUINEA-   Kédougou   a   Mopti
BISSAU   Satadougou   Kita   Youvarou   Djenné
Arquipélago   Sansalé   Lac de   Niafounké
dos Bijagós   Gaoual   Manantali   Kati   Ségou   Bla   Djibo
    Boké   Kita   Bamako   San   Tougan
Cap   Labé   Dinguiraye   Niger   Ouéléssébougou   Djibo
Verga   Boffa   Fouta   Manding   Koutiala   Yako   Gourcy
    Djallon   Siguiri   Lac de Sélingue   Bougouni   OUAGADOUGOU
Conakry   Kindia   GUINEA   Dabola   Kalana   Sikasso   Dédougou   BURKINA
Dubreka   Mamou   Kankan   Koudougou   FASO
    Kabala   Faranah   Tokouno   Manankoro   Bobo-Dioulasso
SIERRA LEONE   Kissidougou   Diébougou   Tenkodo
Freetown   Port   Makeni
    Loko

MALI

metres   feet
4000   13120
2000   6560
1000   3280
500   1640
200   656
0   0
200   656
1000   3280
2000   6560
4000   13120
6000   19690
8000   26250
metres   feet

30° W   25° W   20° W   15° W   10°   5°   D
40° N
A   B   C   1   A   B   C   1   D
2   2
35°   15° W   1   C   1   10°
3
25° N
4
Tropic of Cancer
20°
5
15°
6
7
15°   10°   5°   E
B   C   D

© Helicon Publishing Ltd

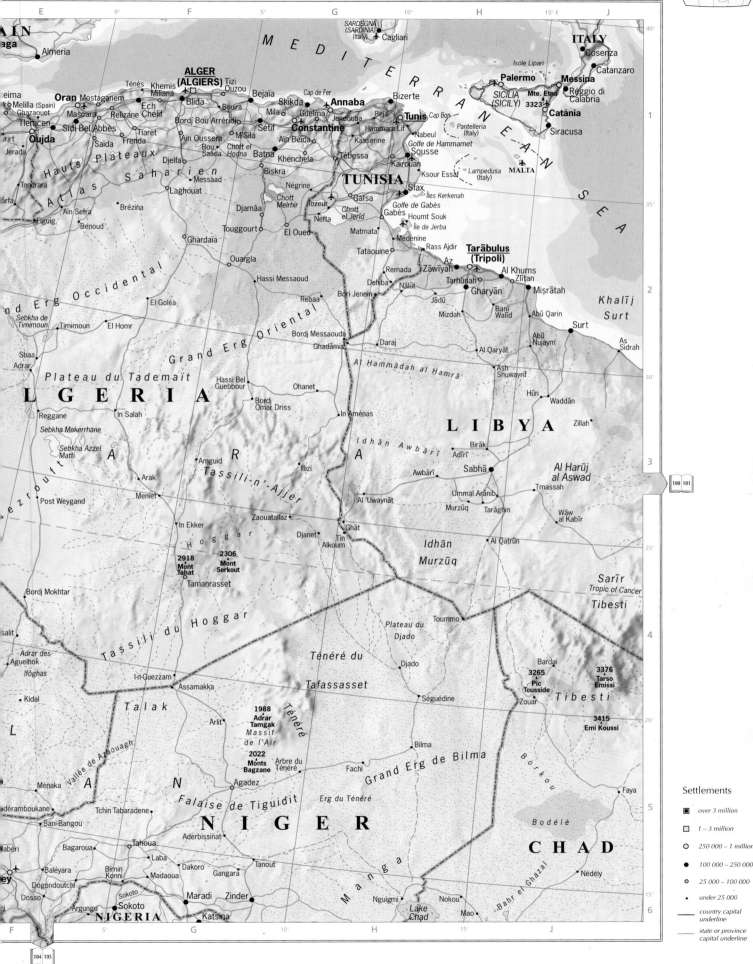

MEDITERRANEAN SEA

ITALY

SARDEGNA (SARDINIA) (Italy)
Cagliari
Cosenza
Catanzaro
Isole Lipari
Palermo
SICILIA (SICILY)
Messina
Reggio di Calabria
Mte. Etna 3323
Catánia
Siracusa

Almería
Melilla (Spain)
Ghazaouet
Tlemcen
Oujda
Jerada
árfa
Tendrara
Figuig
Benoud
Ain Sefra
Brézina

Oran Mostaganem
Mascara
Sidi Bel Abbès
Saïda
Frenda
Tiaret

ALGER (ALGIERS)
Ténès Khemis Miliana
Blida Bouira
Ech Chélif
Bordj Bou Arréridj
Ain Oussera
Bou Saâda
M'Sila
Sétif
Mila
Aïn Beïda
Khenchela
Batna
Biskra

Tizi Ouzou
Bejaïa
Skikda
Constantine
Annaba
Guelma
Béja
Jendouba
Hammam Lif
Kasserine
Tébessa

Cap de Fer
Bizerte
Tunis
Cap Bon
Nabeul
Golfe de Hammamet
Sousse

Pantelleria (Italy)
Lampedusa (Italy)
MALTA

Hauts plateaux
Atlas Saharien
Messaad
Laghouat
Djelfa
Chott el Hodna
Négrine
Chott Melrhir
Djamâa
Nefta
Tozeur
Gafsa
TUNISIA
Sfax
Îles Kerkenah
Kairouan
Ksour Essaf

Ghardaïa
Touggourt
El Oued
Chott el Jerid
Matmata
Medenine
Golfe de Gabès
Gabès
Houmt Souk
Île de Jerba

Grand Erg Occidental
Sebkha de Timimoun
Timimoun
El Homr
El Goléa
Hassi Messaoud

Rebaa
Bordj Messaouda
Ghadāmis
Daraj
Al Hammādah al Hamrā
Al Qaryāt
Abū Nujaym
As Sidrah

Bordj Jenein
Dehiba
Remada
Tataouine
Rass Ajdir
Az
Zāwīyah
Zlītan
Al Khums
Tarābulus (Tripoli)
Tarhūnah
Gharyān
Miṣrātah
Khalīj Surt
Surt

Jādū
Nālūt
Mizdah
Banī Walīd
Abū Qarin

Sbaa
Adrar
Reggane
In Salah
Sebkha Mekerrhane
Sebkha Azzel Matti

Plateau du Tademaït
Hassi Bel Guebbour
Ohanet
Bordj Omar Driss
In Aménas

ALGERIA
A
Z
R
A
Hoggar

LIBYA
Ash Shuwayrif
Hūn
Waddān
Zillah
Al Harūj al Aswad
Tmassah

Idhān Awbārī
Birāk
Adīrī
Awbārī
Sabhā
Ummal Aränib
Murzūq
Tarāghin
Wāw al Kabīr

Amguid
Arak
Meniet
Post Weygand
Illizi
Tassili-n'-Ajjer
Al 'Uwaynāt
Ghāt

2918 Mont Tahat
2306 Mont Serkout
In Ekker
Zaouatallaz
Djanet
Tin Alkoum
Ghāt
Idhān Murzūq
Al Qatrūn

Tamanrasset
Tassili du Hoggar
Sarīr
Tropic of Cancer
Tibesti

Bordj Mokhtar
Adrar des Ifoghas
Aguelhok
Kidal

Plateau du Djado
Toummo
Djado
Ténéré du Tafassasset
Séguédine
Bardai
3265 Pic Toussidé
Zouar
Tibesti
3376 Tarso Emissi

In-Guezzam
Assamakka
Talak
Arlit
1988 Adrar Tamgak
Massif de l'Aïr
2022 Monts Bagzane
Agadez
Bilma
3415 Emi Koussi
Borkou
Faya

Ménaka
Bani-Bangou
déramboukane

Vallée de Azaouagh
Falaise de Tiguidit
Erg du Ténéré
Grand Erg de Bilma
Bodélé

Kidal
Tchin Tabaradene
Aderbissinat
Fachi
Arbre du Ténéré

Abalak
Tahoua
Laba
MALI
NIGER
CHAD
Nédély

Bagaroua
Madaoua
Gangara
Tanout
Manga

Baléyara
Birnin Konni
Dakoro
Zinder
Nguigmi
Nokou
Mao
Faya

Dogondoutchi
Dosso
Sokoto
Maradi
Katsina
NIGERIA
Argungu
Lake Chad

100 101
104 105

Settlements

◼ over 3 million
◻ 1 – 3 million
◯ 250 000 – 1 million
● 100 000 – 250 000
◉ 25 000 – 100 000
∙ under 25 000
— country capital underline
— state or province capital underline

Scale 1 : 11 600 000

| 0 | 200 | 400 | 600 km |
| 0 | 100 | 200 | 300 miles |

A 15° W **B** 10° **C** 5° **D** 0°

Boutilimit
Moudjéria
Oualâta

Mederdra
Aoukâr
Néma

Rosso
Bogué
Aleg
M A U R I T A N I A
Kiffa
Ayoûn el 'Atroûs
Kobenni
Amourj
Bassikounou
Lac Faguibine
Tombouctou
Niger
Bamba
Bourem

Saint Louis
Dagana
Kaédi
Mbout
Kankossa
Nara
Nampala
Lac Débo
Youvarou
Lac Do Hombori
Gossi

Louga
Matam
Ould Yenjé
Nioro du Sahel
Sokolo
Douentza
Doro

Kébémer
Linguère
Sélibabi
Diéma
S

DAKAR
Thiès
Touba
Bakel
Kayes
Didiéni
Ségou
San
Mopti

Cap Vert
Diourbel
Kidira
SENEGAL
Kati
Bla
Tougan
Djibo
Dori

Mbour
Joal-Fadiout
Kaolack
Kaffrine
Tambacounda
Bafoulabé
Kaarta
Niger
Bamako
Koutiala
Dédougou
Koudougou
OUAGADOUGOU

Banjul
Georgetown
Lac de Manantali
Bamako
Ouéléssébougou
Boromo
Léo
Tenkodogo

Brikama
THE GAMBIA
Kolda
Vélingara
Satadougou
Bougouni
Sikasso
Diébougou
Lawra
Navrongo
Bolgatanga

Ziguinchor
Bignona
Kédougou
Kita
Lac de Sélingue
Kalana
Bobo-Dioulasso
Boromo

Cabo Roxo
Cachéu
I Koundára
Kankan
Manankoro
Wa

GUINEA-BISSAU
Bissau
Catió
Gaoual
Labé
Dinguiraye
Siguiri
Odienné
Quangolodougou
Ferkéssédougou
Bole

Arquipélago dos Bijagós
Sansalé
Boké
Dabola
Faranah
Tokounou
Boundiali
Korhogo
Bouna

Cap Verga
Boffa
Kindia
Mamou
Kissidougou
Niakaramandougou
Katiola
Bondoukou
Tanda
Kintampo

Conakry
Dubréka
Kabala
SIERRA LEONE
Guéckédou
Beyla
Touba
Man
Lac de Kossou
Bouaké
Techiman

Port Loko
Makeni
Koidu
Voinjama
Nzérékoré
1752 Monts Nimba
Daloa
Yamoussoukro
Agnibilékrou
Sunyani

Freetown
Bo
Kenema
Gbarnga
Sanniquellie
Toulépleu
Guiglo
Issia
Gagnoa
Abengourou
Kumasi
Obuasi

Bonthe
Zimmi
Mano River
LIBERIA
Zwedru
Soubré
Divo
Aboisso
Dunkwa
Accra

Sherbro Island
Bo
Kakata
Buchanan
Monrovia
CÔTE D'IVOIRE
ABIDJAN
Sekondi
Cape Coast
Takoradi

River Cess
Greenville
Gbaaka
Sassandra
Cape Three Points

Barclayville
Tabou
San-Pédro

Cape Palmas

G u l f   o

Equator

A T L A N T I C

O C E A N

Ascension (U.K.)

Cape Verde inset:
① A Ponta do Sol B
Santo Antão
Mindelo
São Vicente
Pedra Lume
Sal
Boa Vista
São Nicolau
Curral Velho
ATLANTIC OCEAN
São Tiago
Maio
Fogo
Porto Inglês
15° N
São Filipe
Praia
CAPE VERDE
25° W

metres	feet
4000	13120
2000	6560
1000	3280
500	1640
200	656
0	0
200	656
1000	3280
2000	6560
4000	13120
6000	19690
8000	26250
metres	feet

WEST AFRICA

Benin • Burkina Faso • Cameroon • Cape Verde • Congo • Côte d'Ivoire • Equatorial Guinea • Gabon • The Gambia
Ghana • Guinea • Guinea-Bissau • Liberia • Nigeria • São Tomé & Príncipe • Senegal • Sierra Leone • Togo

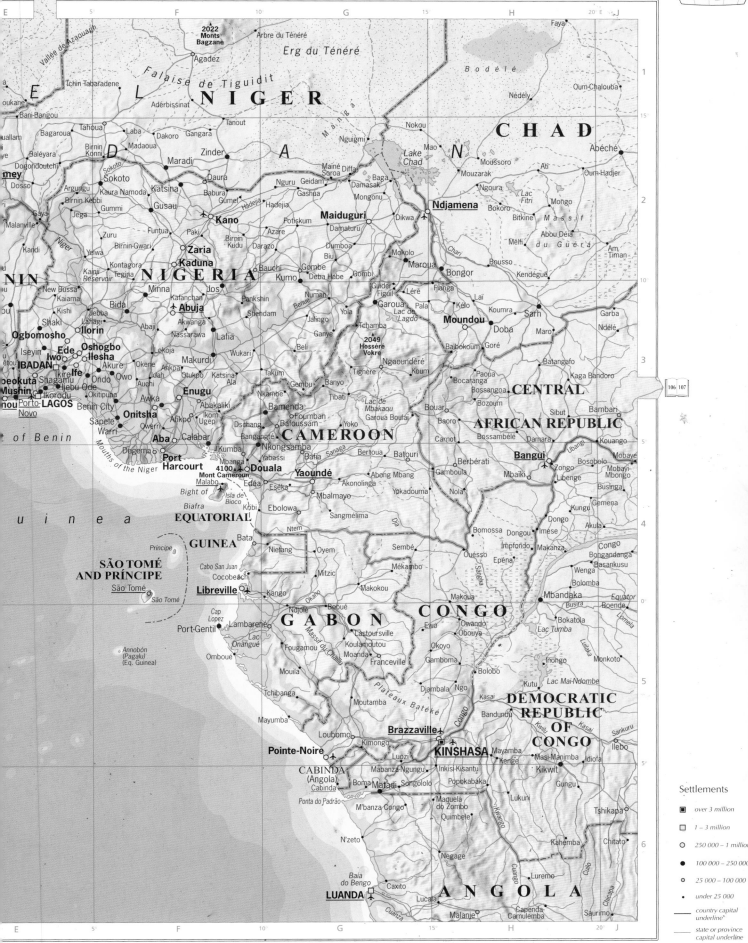

Settlements

■	over 3 million
□	1 – 3 million
○	250 000 – 1 million
●	100 000 – 250 000
◦	25 000 – 100 000
·	under 25 000
—	country capital underline
—	state or province capital underline

Scale 1 : 11 600 000

© Helicon Publishing Ltd

CENTRAL AFRICA

Angola • Burundi • Central African Republic • Democratic Republic of Congo
Djibouti • Ethiopia • Kenya • Rwanda • Somalia • Tanzania • Uganda

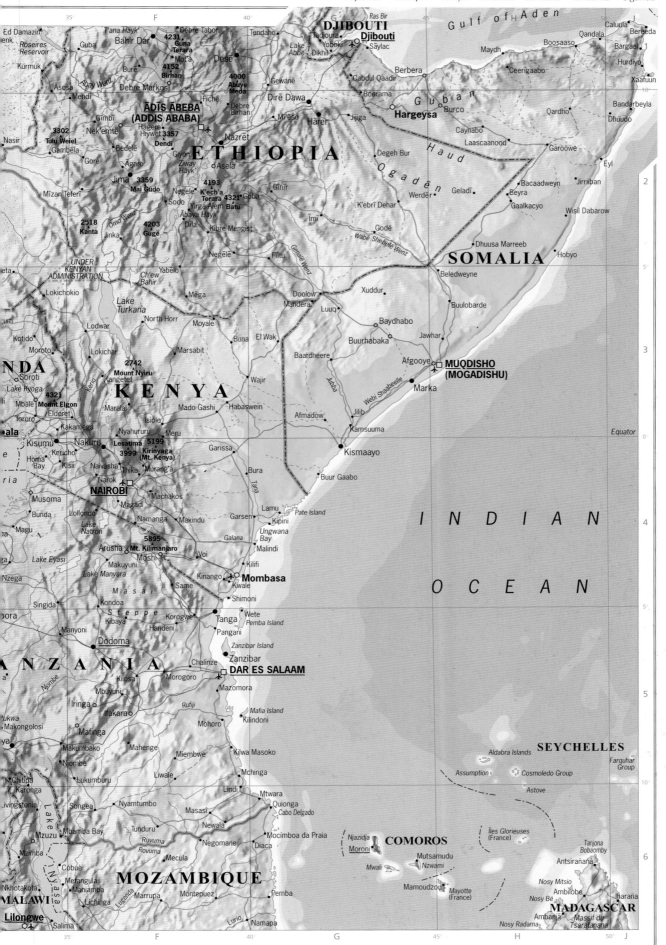

GULF of ADEN

DJIBOUTI

INDIAN OCEAN

ETHIOPIA

SOMALIA

KENYA

TANZANIA

MOZAMBIQUE

MALAWI

COMOROS

SEYCHELLES

MADAGASCAR

Settlements

- ◼ over 3 million
- ◻ 1 – 3 million
- ○ 250 000 – 1 million
- ● 100 000 – 250 000
- ◉ 25 000 – 100 000
- ∙ under 25 000
- — country capital underline

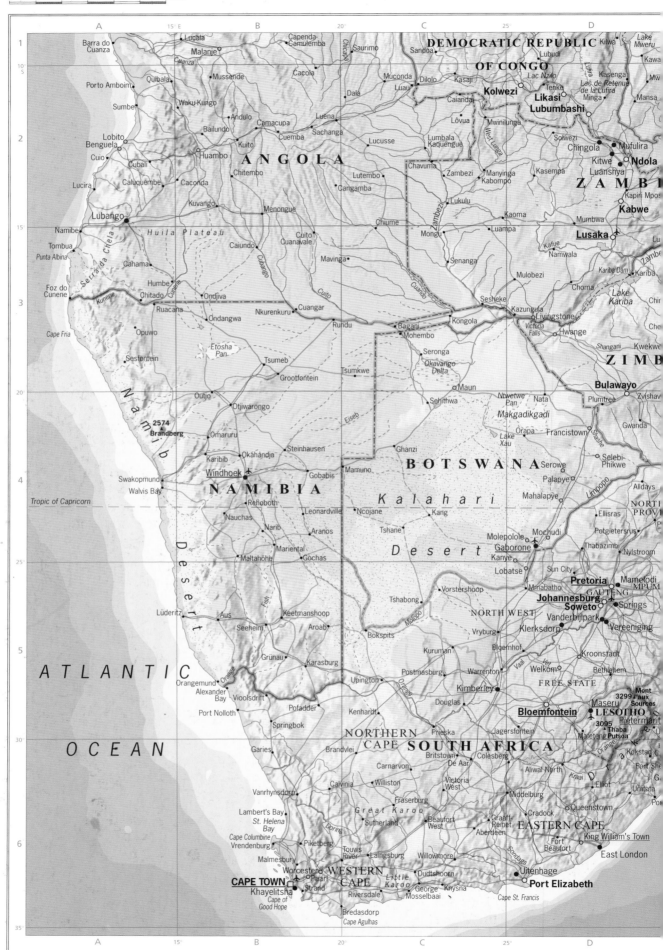

Scale 1 : 11 600 000

ATLANTIC

OCEAN

metres feet
4000 13120
2000 6560
1000 3280
500 1640
200 656
0 0
200 656
1000 3280
2000 6560
4000 13120
6000 19690
8000 26250
metres feet

© Helicon Publishing Ltd

SOUTHERN AFRICA

Botswana • Comoros • Lesotho • Madagascar • Malawi • Mauritius
Mozambique • Namibia • Seychelles • South Africa • Swaziland • Zambia • Zimbabwe

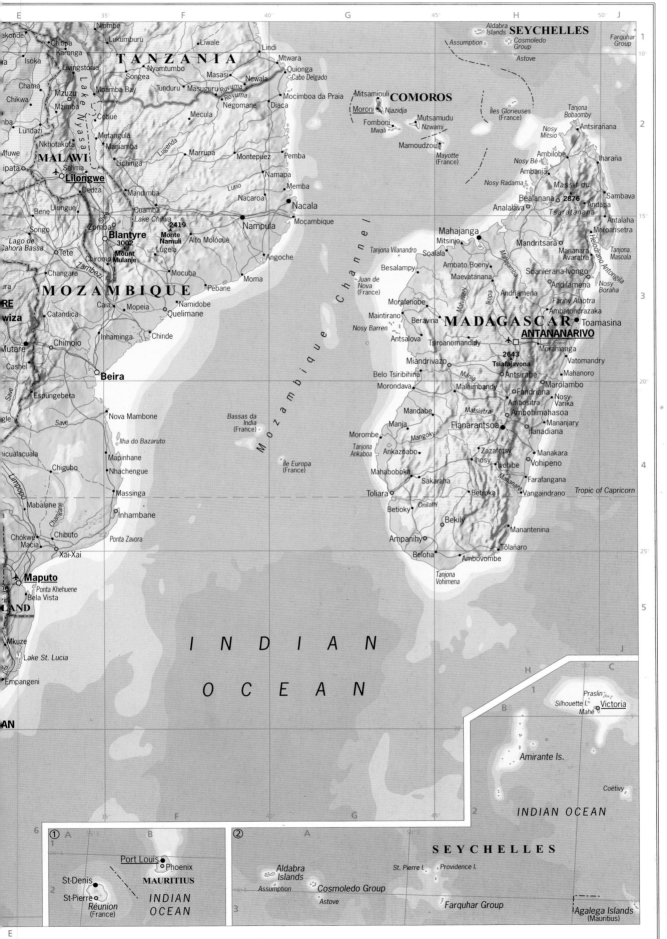

SEYCHELLES

Aldabra Islands
Assumption
Cosmoledo Group
Astove
Farquhar Group

TANZANIA

Njombe
Lukumburu
Liwale
Lindi
Chitipa
Isoka
Karonga
Nyamtumbo
Masasi
Mtwara
Livingstonia
Songea
Tunduru
Masuguru
Newala
Quionga
Cabo Delgado
Chama
Mbamba Bay
Ngomane
Rovuma
Diaca
Mocímboa da Praia
Chikwa
Mzuzu
Mzimba
Cobuè
Mecula
Mecula
Negomane
Mitsamiouli

COMOROS

Moroni
Njazidja
Lundazi
Metangula
Marrupa
Montepuez
Pemba
Fomboni
Mwali
Nzwarni
Mutsamudu
Mfuwe
Maniamba
Lichinga
Mamoudzou
ipata
MALAWI
Salima
Namapa
Mayotte (France)
Mandimba
Memba
Nosy Mitsio
Lilongwe
Dedza
Nacaroa
Nacala
Ambilobe
Antsiranana
Songo
Zomba
Cuamba
Moçambique
Nosy Bé
Ambanja
Tanjona Bobaomby
Bene
Uongue
Lake Chilwa
Blantyre
2419
Nampula
Nosy Radama
Bealanana
2876
Sambava
Andapa
Lago de
Cahora Bassa
Tete
3002
Monte Namuli
Alto Molócuè
Analalava
Massif du
Tsaratanana
Antalaha
Changara
Mount Mulanje
Lúgela
Mahajanga
Mandritsara
Maroansetra
Chiromo
Zambezi
Mocuba
Mitsinjo
Ambato Boeny
Soanierana-Ivongo
Tanjona Masoala
MOZAMBIQUE
Pebane
Soalala
Andilamena
Helodrano Antongila
wiza
Caia
Mopeia
Moma
Tanjona Vilanandro
Maevatanana
Farihy Alaotra
Nosy Boraha
Catandica
Quelimane
Besalampy
Ambatondrazaka
Chimoio
Inhaminga
Chinde
Morafenobe
Andriamena
Mutare
Juan de Nova (France)
Maintirano
Beravina
MADAGASCAR
Toamasina
Cashel
Nosy Barren
Antsalova
Tsiroanomandidy
ANTANANARIVO
Moramanga
Beira
Miandrivazo
2643
Tsiafajavona
Vatomandry
Espungebera
Belo Tsiribihina
Antsirabe
Mahanoro
Morondava
Malaimbandy
Marolambo
Nova Mambone
Mandabe
Matsiatra
Ambositra
Nosy-Varika
Ilha do Bazaruto
Manja
Mangoky
Ambohimahasoa
Mananjary
Mapinhane
Morombe
Fianarantsoa
Ifanadiana
Nhachengue
Tanjona Ankaboa
Ankazoabo
Zazafotsy
Manakara
icualacuala
Chigubo
Mahaboboka
Ihosy
Ivohibe
Vohipeno
Massinga
Sakaraha
Mofanana
Farafangana
Mabalane
Inhambane
Betroka
Vangaindrano
Tropic of Capricorn
Chókwè
Chibuto
Ponta Zavora
Toliara
Betioky
Onilahy
Bekily
Manantenina
Macia
Xai-Xai
Ampanihy
Beloha
Tôlañaro
Ambovombe
Maputo
Ponta Khehuene
Bela Vista
Tanjona Vohimena
LAND
Mkuze
Lake St. Lucia
Empangeni
AN

Mozambique Channel

INDIAN

OCEAN

SEYCHELLES

①

| A | B |

Port Louis
Phoenix
MAURITIUS
St-Denis
St-Pierre
Réunion (France)
INDIAN OCEAN

②

| A |

Aldabra Islands
Assumption
Cosmoledo Group
Astove
St. Pierre I.
Providence I.
Farquhar Group
Agalega Islands (Mauritius)

Praslin
Silhouette I.
Mahé
Victoria
Amirante Is.
Coëtivy
INDIAN OCEAN

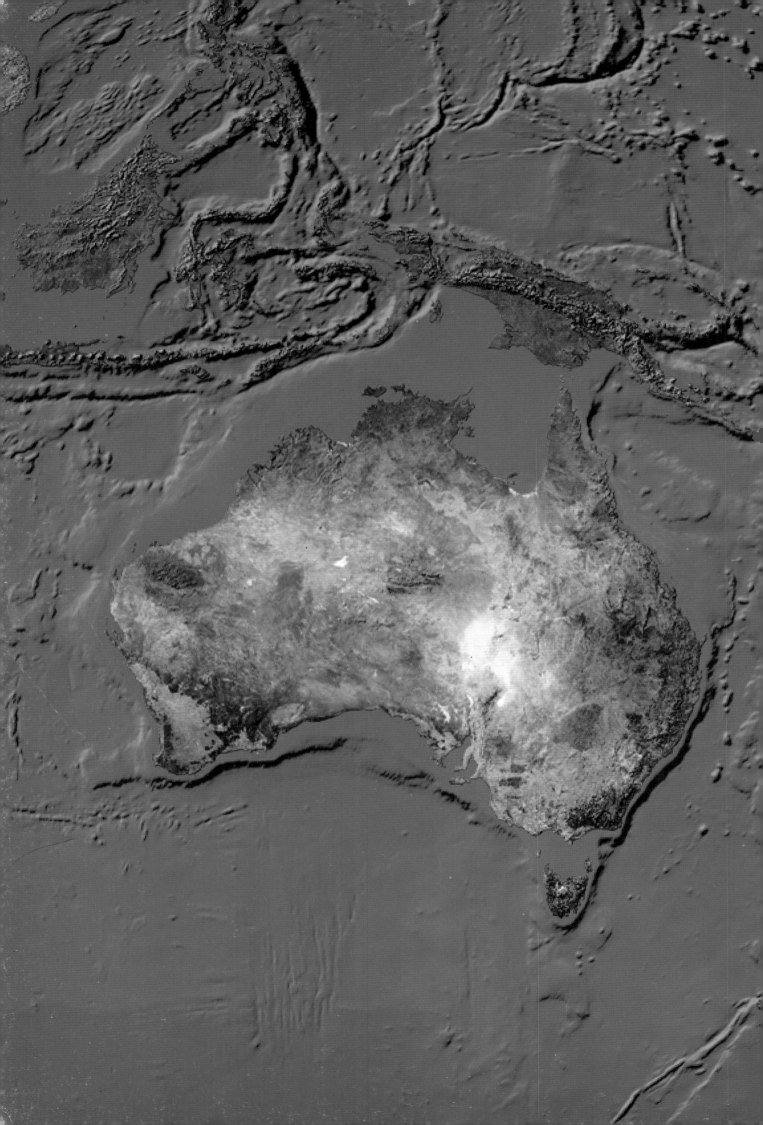

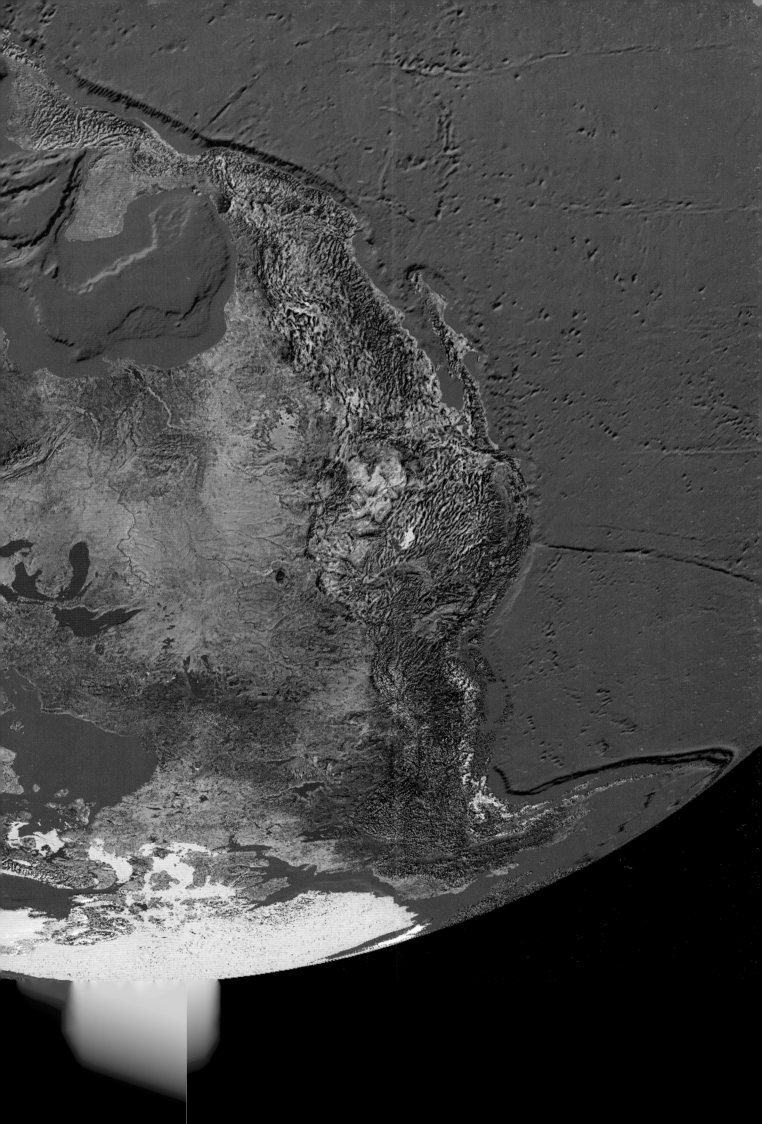

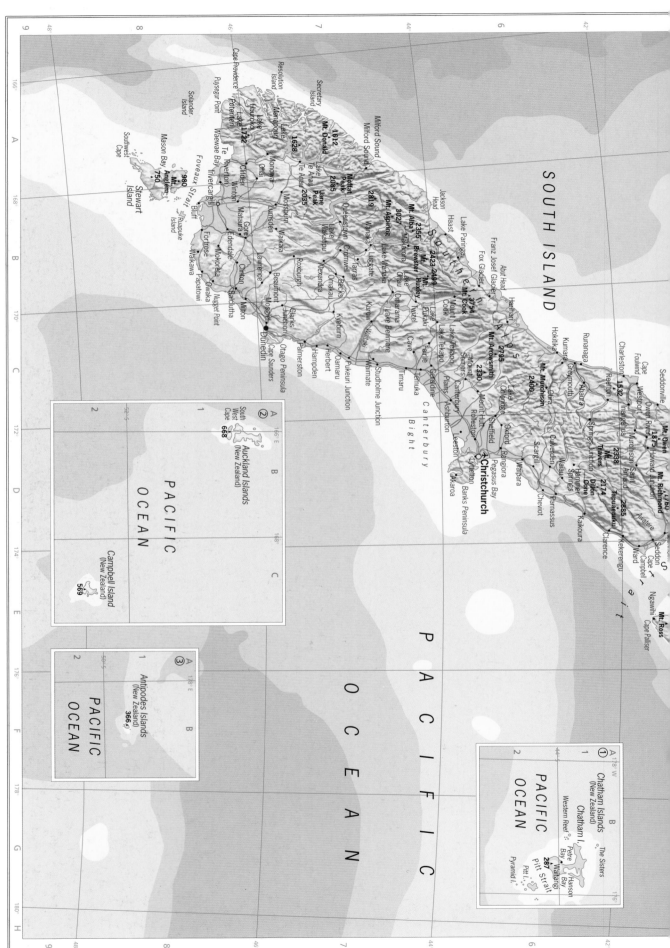

NEW ZEALAND

Antipodes Islands • Auckland Island • Chatham Islands
Campbell Island • Chatham Islands

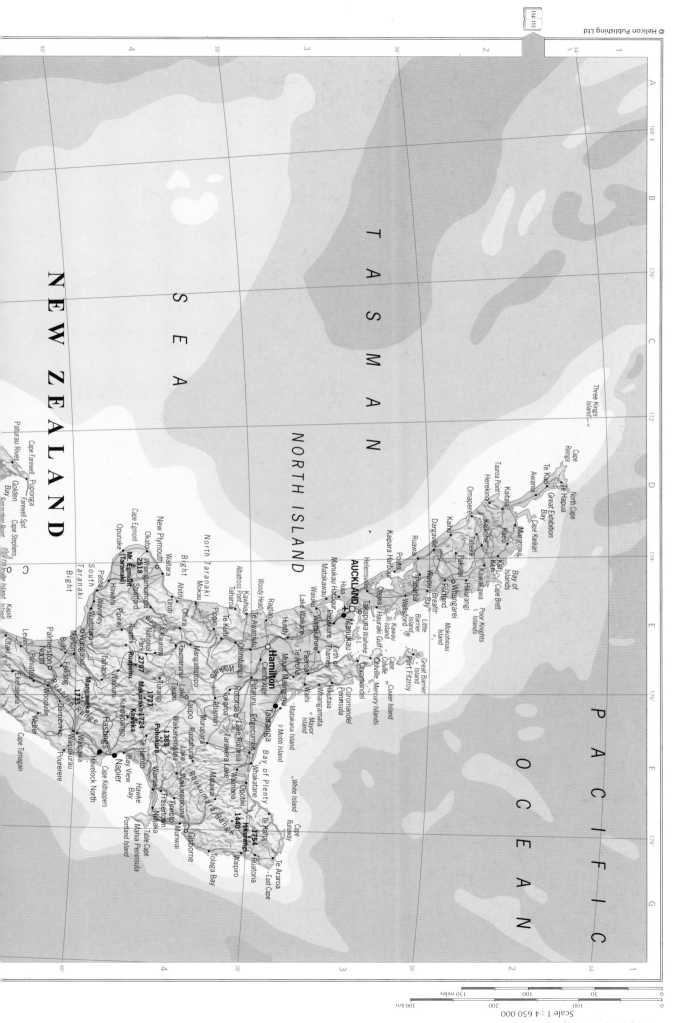

NEW ZEALAND

TASMAN SEA

NORTH ISLAND

PACIFIC OCEAN

Scale 1 : 4 650 000

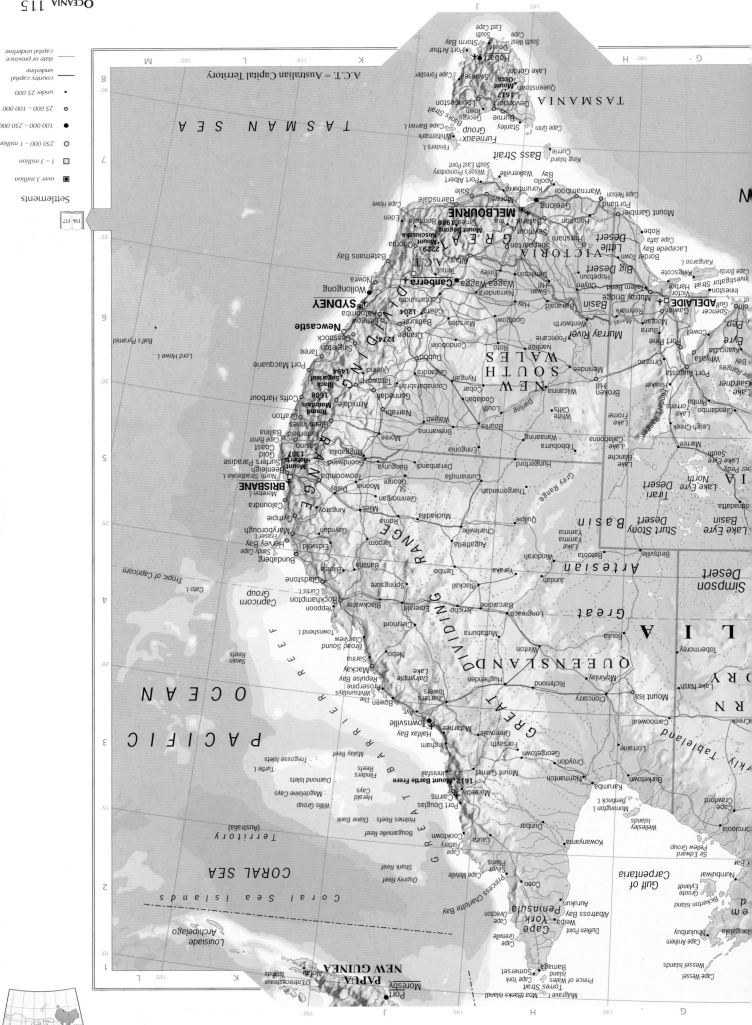

AUSTRALIA

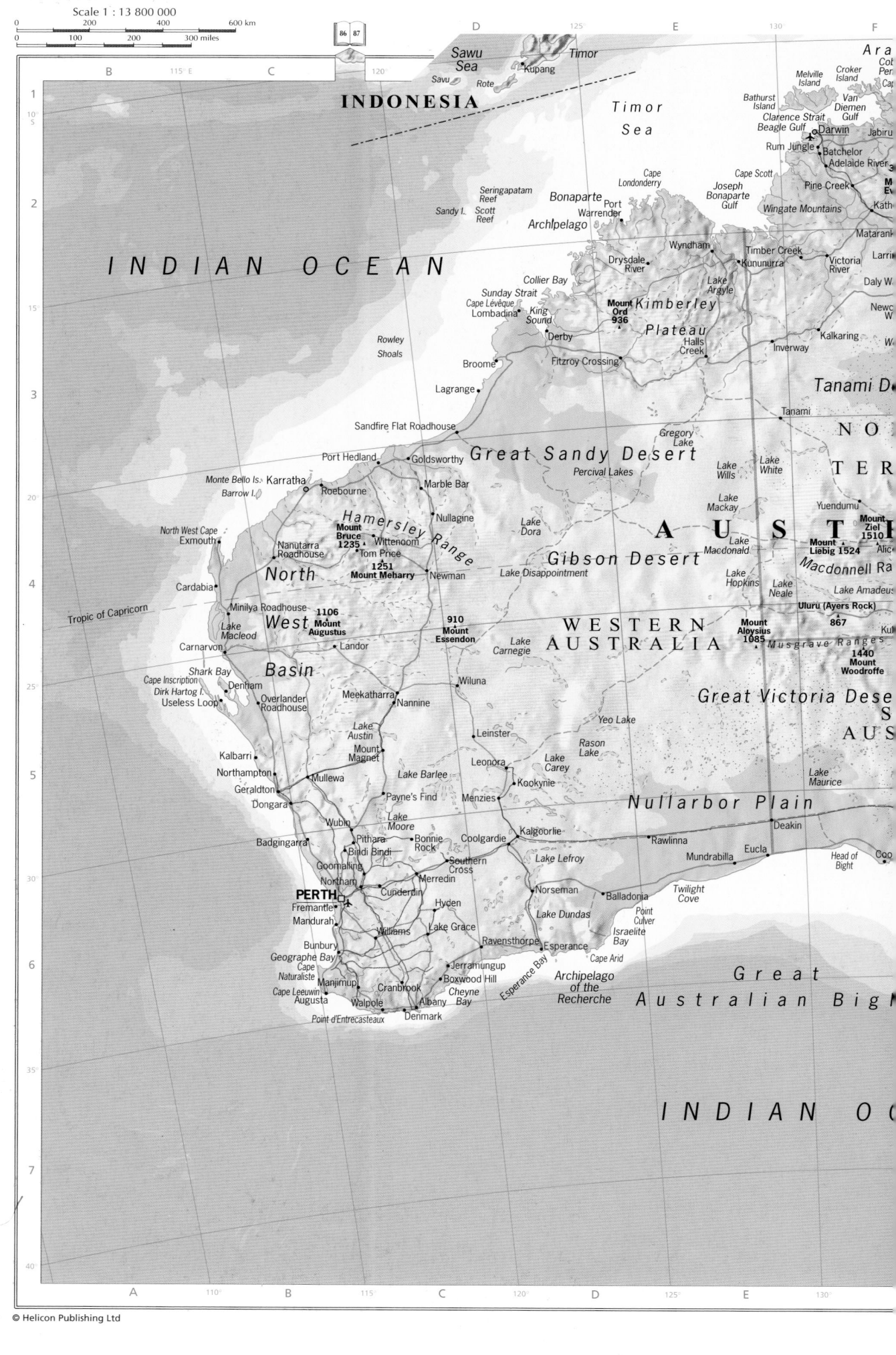

Scale 1 : 13 800 000

INDONESIA

Sawu Sea
Savu
Rote
Timor
Kupang

Timor Sea

Arafura

Melville Island
Croker Island
Cobourg Peninsula
Bathurst Island
Clarence Strait
Van Diemen Gulf
Beagle Gulf
Darwin
Jabiru
Rum Jungle
Batchelor
Adelaide River
Pine Creek
Katherine
Mataranka

INDIAN OCEAN

Cape Londonderry
Cape Scott
Seringapatam Reef
Sandy I.
Scott Reef
Bonaparte Archipelago
Port Warrender
Joseph Bonaparte Gulf
Wyndham
Kununurra
Victoria River
Daly River
Larrimah

Collier Bay
Sunday Strait
Cape Lévêque
Lombadina
King Sound
Mount Ord 936
Kimberley Plateau
Lake Argyle
Halls Creek
Inverway
Kalkaring
Newcastle Waters

Rowley Shoals
Derby
Fitzroy Crossing
Broome
Lagrange

Tanami Desert
Tanami

Sandfire Flat Roadhouse
Great Sandy Desert
Gregory Lake
Lake Wills
Lake White
NORTHERN TERRITORY

Port Hedland
Goldsworthy
Percival Lakes
Monte Bello Is.
Karratha
Barrow I.
Roebourne
Marble Bar
Nullagine
Lake Mackay
Yuendumu
Mount Ziel 1510

North West Cape
Exmouth
Hamersley Range
Mount Bruce 1235
Wittenoom
Tom Price
1251 Mount Meharry
Newman
Lake Dora
Gibson Desert
Lake Macdonald
Mount Liebig 1524
Alice Springs
Macdonnell Ranges

Nanutarra Roadhouse
North
West
Basin
Cardabia
Lake Disappointment
Lake Hopkins
Lake Neale
Lake Amadeus

Tropic of Capricorn
Minilya Roadhouse
1106 Mount Augustus
Landor
910 Mount Essendon
WESTERN AUSTRALIA
Mount Aloysius 1085
Uluru (Ayers Rock) 867
Musgrave Ranges
1440 Mount Woodroffe

Lake Macleod
Carnarvon
Lake Carnegie
Great Victoria Desert
SOUTH AUSTRALIA

Shark Bay
Cape Inscription
Dirk Hartog I.
Useless Loop
Denham
Overlander Roadhouse
Meekatharra
Nannine
Wiluna
Yeo Lake
Lake Maurice

Kalbarri
Lake Austin
Mount Magnet
Leinster
Leonora
Lake Carey
Rason Lake

Northampton
Mullewa
Lake Barlee
Menzies
Kookynie
Nullarbor Plain

Geraldton
Payne's Find
Kalgoorlie
Rawlinna
Deakin

Dongara
Lake Moore
Coolgardie
Lake Lefroy
Eucla

Wubin
Pithara
Bonnie Rock
Southern Cross
Mundrabilla
Head of Bight

Badgingarra
Bindi Bindi
Goomalling
Merredin
Norseman
Balladonia
Twilight Cove

PERTH
Northam
Cunderdin
Hyden
Lake Dundas
Point Culver

Fremantle
Mandurah
Williams
Lake Grace
Israelite Bay

Bunbury
Ravensthorpe
Esperance
Cape Arid

Geographe Bay
Jerramungup
Esperance Bay
Archipelago of the Recherche

Cape Naturaliste
Boxwood Hill
Great Australian Bight

Manjimup
Cranbrook
Cheyne Bay

Cape Leeuwin
Augusta
Walpole
Albany
Denmark

Point d'Entrecasteaux

INDIAN OCEAN

metres	feet
4000	13120
2000	6560
1000	3280
500	1640
200	656
0	0
200	656
1000	3280
2000	6560
4000	13120
6000	19690
8000	26250
metres	feet

OCEANIA

Scale 1 : 40 500 000

OCEANIA

Oceania 112

Australia 114

New Zealand 116

NORTH AMERICA

North America   120

Canada   122

United States   124

Northwest United States   126

Northeast United States   128

Southeast United States   130

Southwest United States   132

Central America and the Caribbean   134

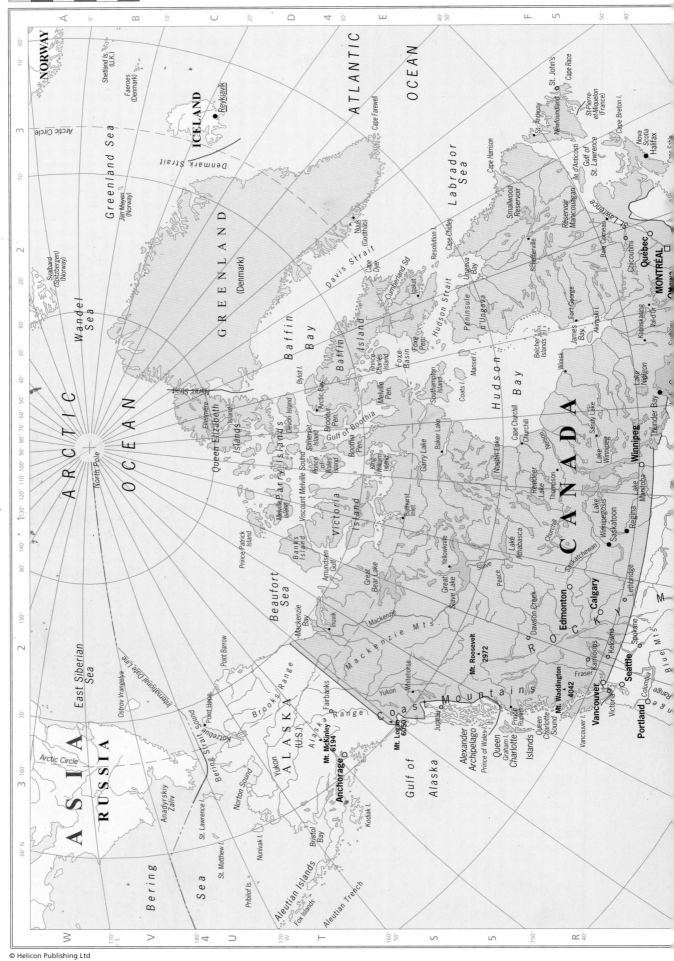

Scale 1 : 34 700 000

500   1000   1500 km

250   500   750 miles

NORWAY

Shetland Is. (U.K.)

Faeroes (Denmark)

ICELAND   Reykjavík

Arctic Circle

Greenland Sea

Jan Mayen (Norway)

Svalbard (Spitzbergen) (Norway)

Wandel Sea

GREENLAND (Denmark)

Denmark Strait

ATLANTIC   OCEAN

Cape Farewell

Labrador Sea

Cape Harrison

Cape Chidley

Resolution I.

Cape Dyer

Cumberland Sd

Davis   Strait

Nuuk (Godthåb)

Baffin   Bay

Nares Strait

Smallwood Reservoir

Schefferville

Ungava Bay

Péninsule d'Ungava

Hudson   Strait

St. Anthony

St-Pierre-et-Miquelon (France)

Newfoundland   Cape Race

Gulf of St. Lawrence

Île d'Anticosti

Cape Breton I.

Nova Scotia   Halifax

St. Lawrence

Québec   Chicoutimi

MONTRÉAL

Baie Comeau

Kapuskasing   Val-d'Or

Fort George

James Bay

Belcher Islands

Akimiski I.

Winisk

Lake Nipigon

Thunder Bay

ARCTIC   OCEAN

North Pole

Ellesmere Island

Queen Elizabeth Islands

Devon Island

Bylot I.

Arctic Bay

Baffin   Island

Brodeur Pen.

Somerset Island

Prince of Wales Island

King William Island

Boothia Pen.

Gulf of Boothia

Melville Pen.

Foxe Pen.

Prince Charles Island

Foxe Basin

Mansel I.

Southampton I.

Coats I.

Hudson   Bay

Cape Churchill

Churchill

Nelson

Nueltin Lake

Baker Lake

Reindeer Lake

Thompson

CANADA

Lake Winnipeg

Saskatoon

Regina

Lake Manitoba

Winnipeg

Lake Winnipegosis

Banks Island

Melville Island

Viscount Melville Sound

Prince of Wales Island

Victoria   Island

Bathurst Inlet

Prince Patrick Island

Beaufort Sea

Mackenzie Bay

Amundsen Gulf

Great Bear Lake

Yellowknife

Garry Lake

Lake Athabasca

Churchill

Saskatchewan

Slave

Great Slave Lake

Peace

Mackenzie

Mackenzie Mts

Mt. Roosevelt 2972

Edmonton

Calgary

Lethbridge

Dawson Creek

Kamloops

Fraser

R O C K Y

East Siberian Sea

Ostrov Vrangelya

International Date Line

Point Barrow

Point Hope

Kotzebue Sound

Brooks   Range

Range

Inuvik

Alaska Range

Fairbanks

Yukon

Whitehorse

Coast   Mountains

Mt. Logan 6050

Juneau

Mt. Waddington 4042

Prince Rupert

Queen Charlotte Islands

Graham I.

Prince of Wales I.

Alexander Archipelago

Vancouver I.

Victoria

Vancouver

Seattle

Spokane

Portland

Columbia

Blue Mts

Range

ASIA

RUSSIA

Arctic Circle

Anadyrskiy Zaliv

Bering   Strait   Sound

St. Lawrence I.

St. Matthew I.

Nunivak I.

Norton Sound

Yukon

ALASKA (U.S.)

Mt. McKinley 6194

Anchorage

Kodiak I.

Bristol Bay

Pribilof Is.

Bering   Sea

Aleutian Islands   Fox Islands

Aleutian Trench

Gulf of Alaska

Queen Charlotte Sound

Scale 1 : 13 800 000

© Helicon Publishing Ltd

122 NORTH AMERICA

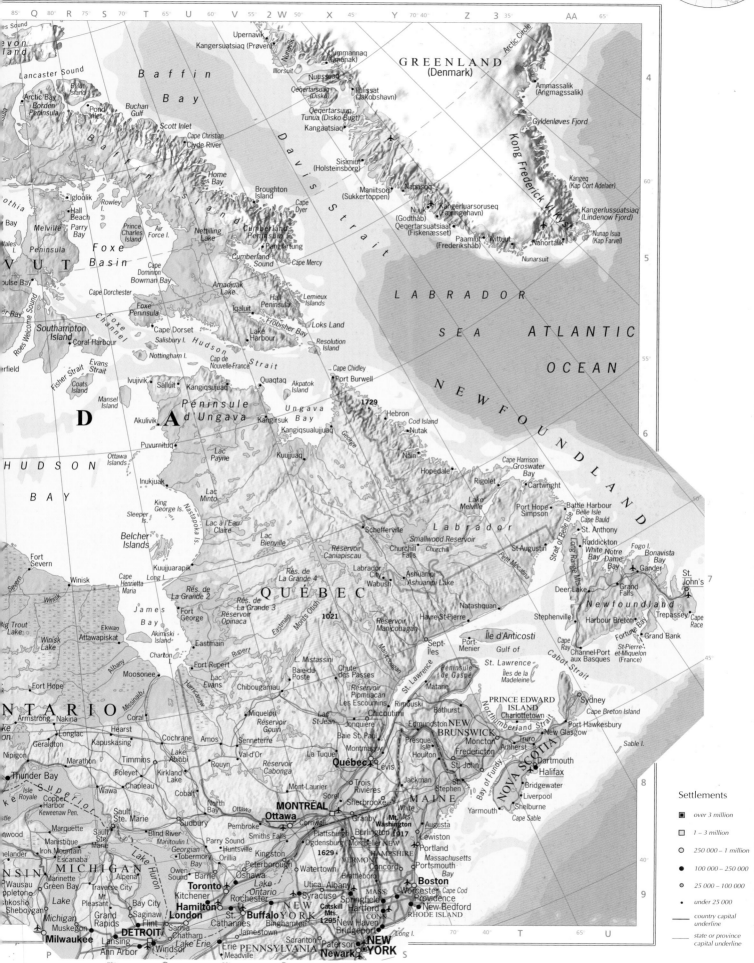

Settlements

- ▣ over 3 million
- ☐ 1 – 3 million
- ○ 250 000 – 1 million
- ● 100 000 – 250 000
- ◦ 25 000 – 100 000
- · under 25 000
- — country capital underline
- — state or province capital underline

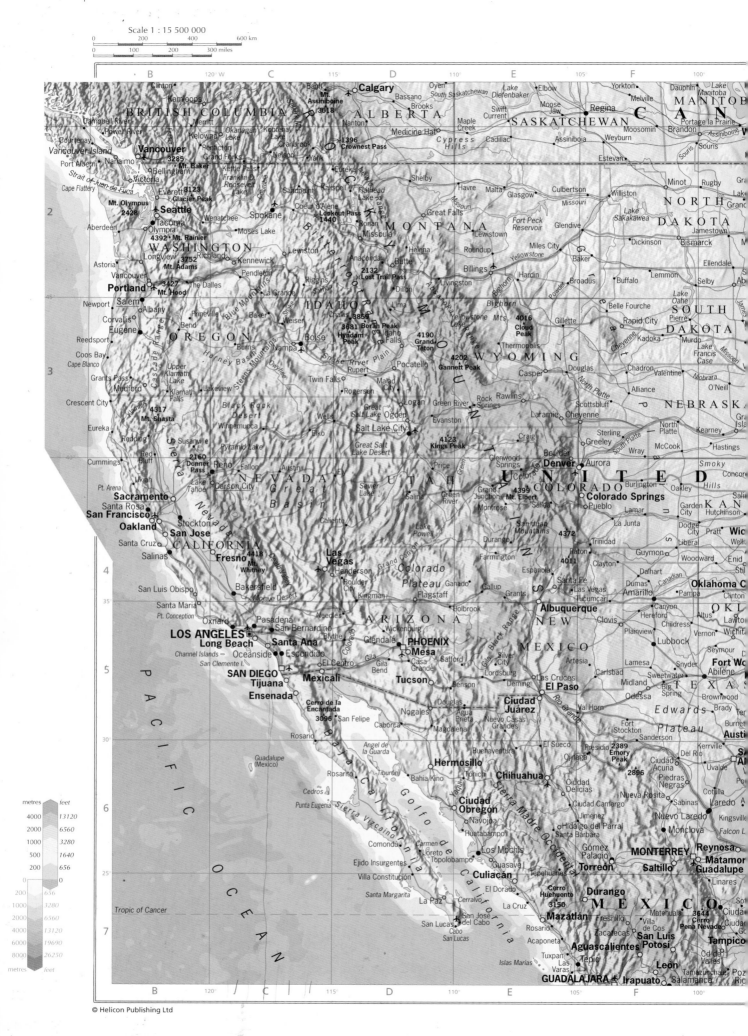

Scale 1 : 15 500 000

© Helicon Publishing Ltd

Scale 1 : 7 200 000

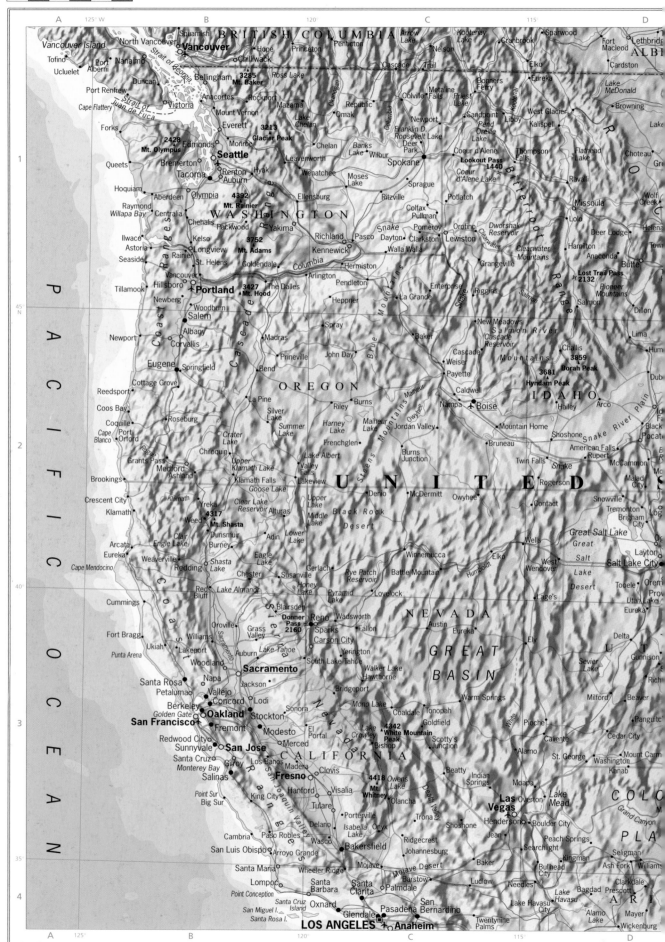

© Helicon Publishing Ltd

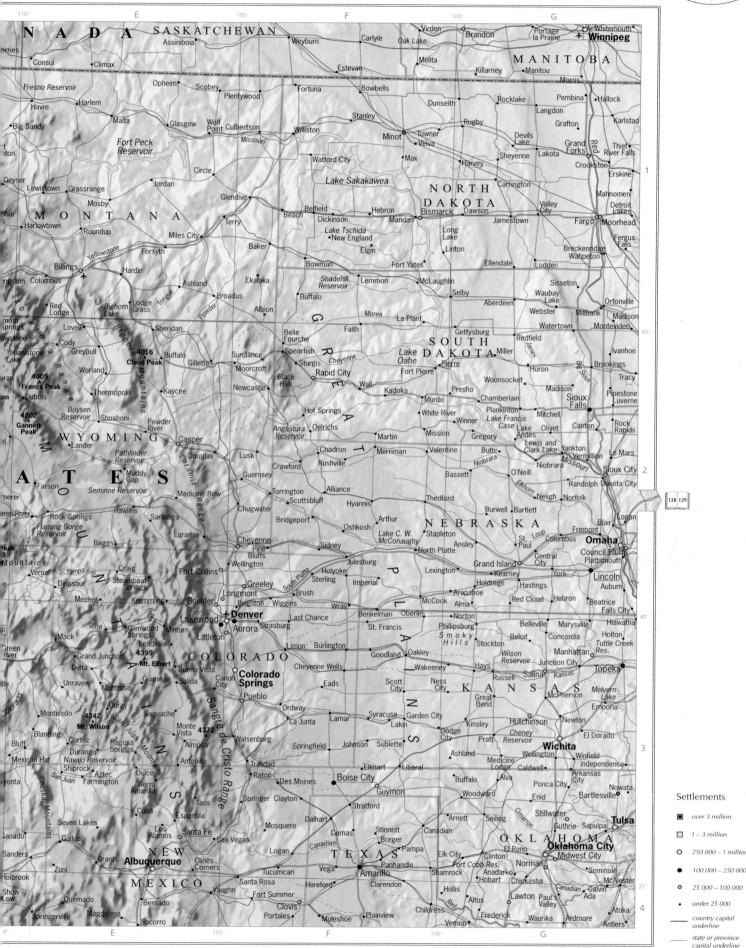

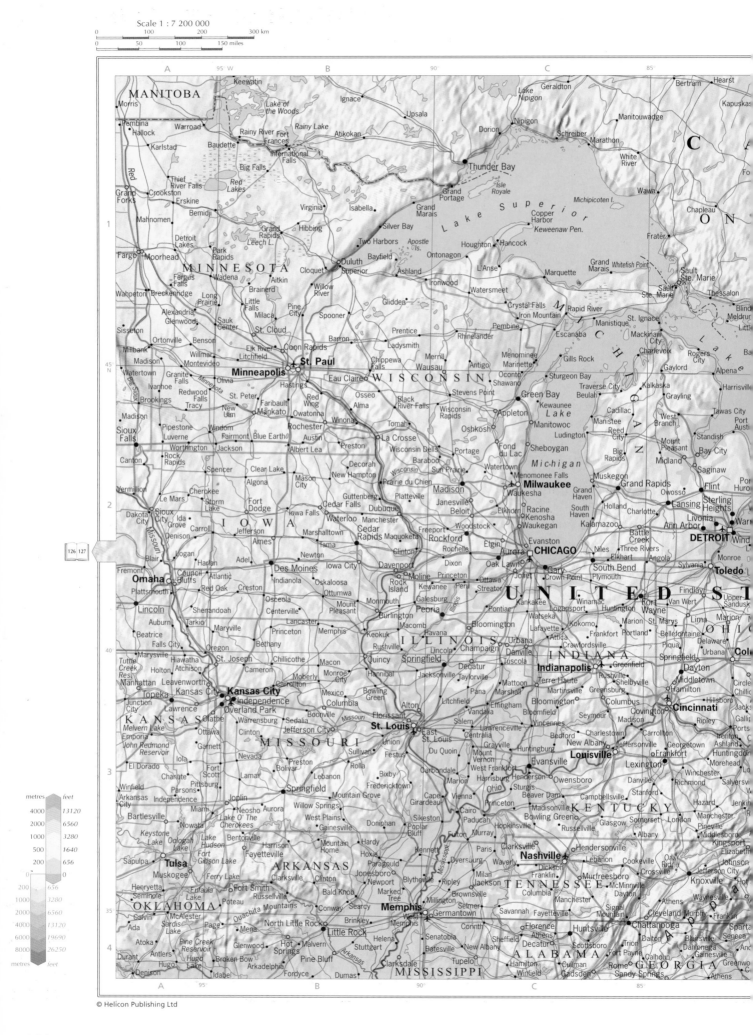

Scale 1 : 7 200 000

© Helicon Publishing Ltd

Connecticut • Delaware • District of Columbia • Illinois • Indiana • Iowa • Maine • Maryland • Massachusetts • Michigan • Minnesota • New Hampshire • New Jersey • New York • Ohio • Pennsylvania • Rhode Island • Vermont • West Virginia • Wisconsin

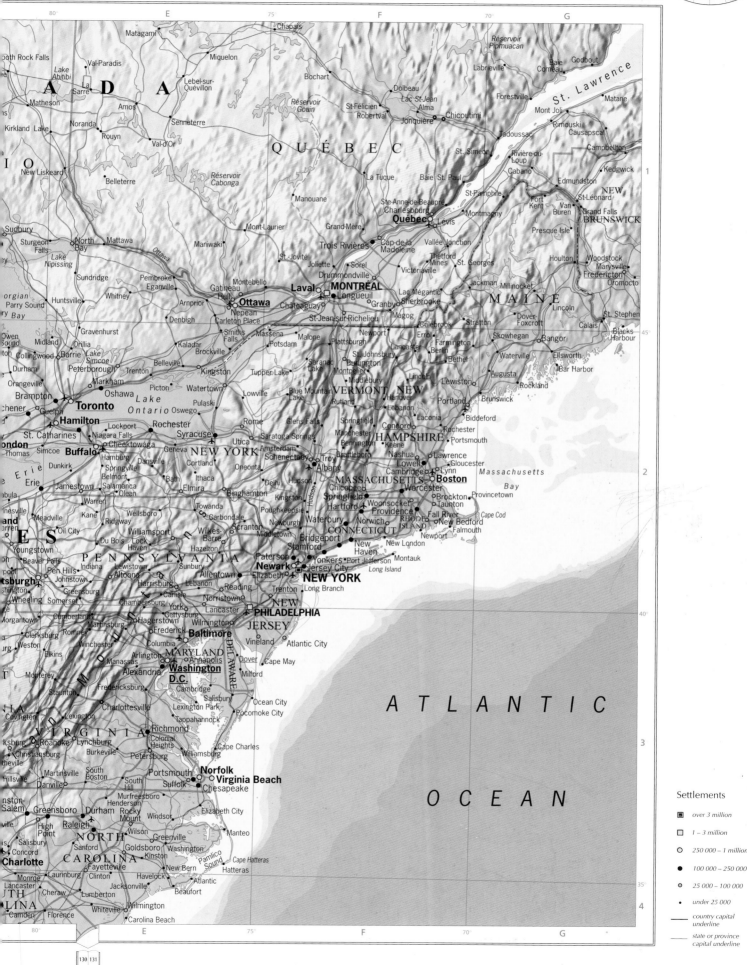

Settlements

- ◼ over 3 million
- ◻ 1 – 3 million
- ○ 250 000 – 1 million
- ● 100 000 – 250 000
- ◉ 25 000 – 100 000
- • under 25 000
- ___ country capital underline
- ___ state or province capital underline

Scale 1 : 7 200 000

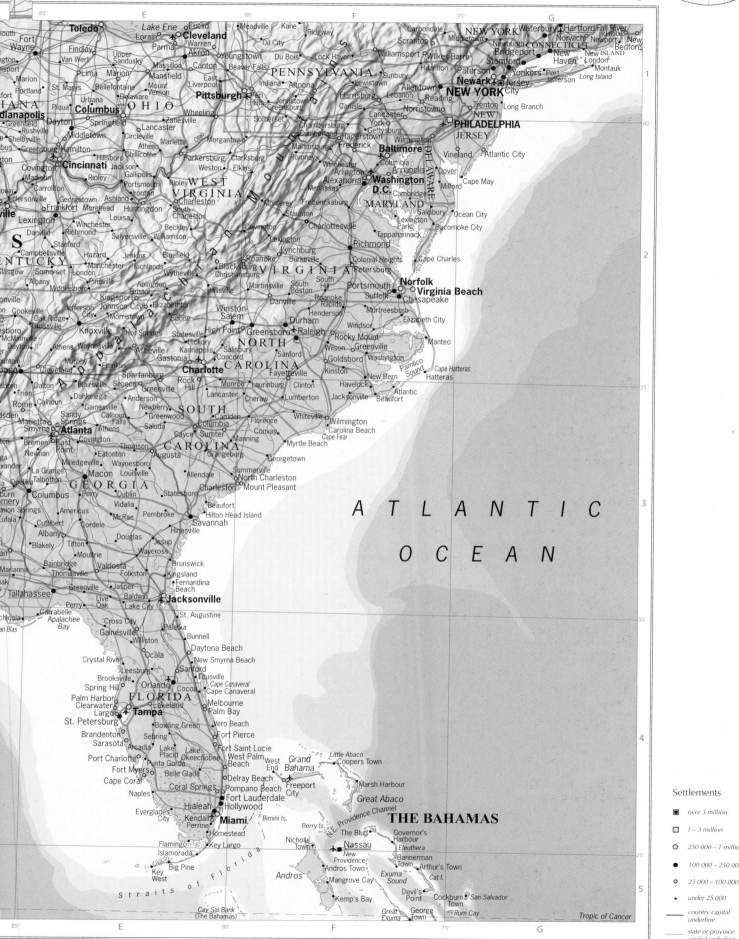

SOUTHEAST UNITED STATES
Alabama • Arkansas • The Bahamas • Florida • Georgia • Kentucky • Louisiana
Mississippi • Missouri • North Carolina • South Carolina • Tennessee • Texas • Virginia

128 129

Settlements

■	over 3 million
□	1 – 3 million
○	250 000 – 1 million
●	100 000 – 250 000
◦	25 000 – 100 000
•	under 25 000
‾	country capital underline
‾	state or province capital underline

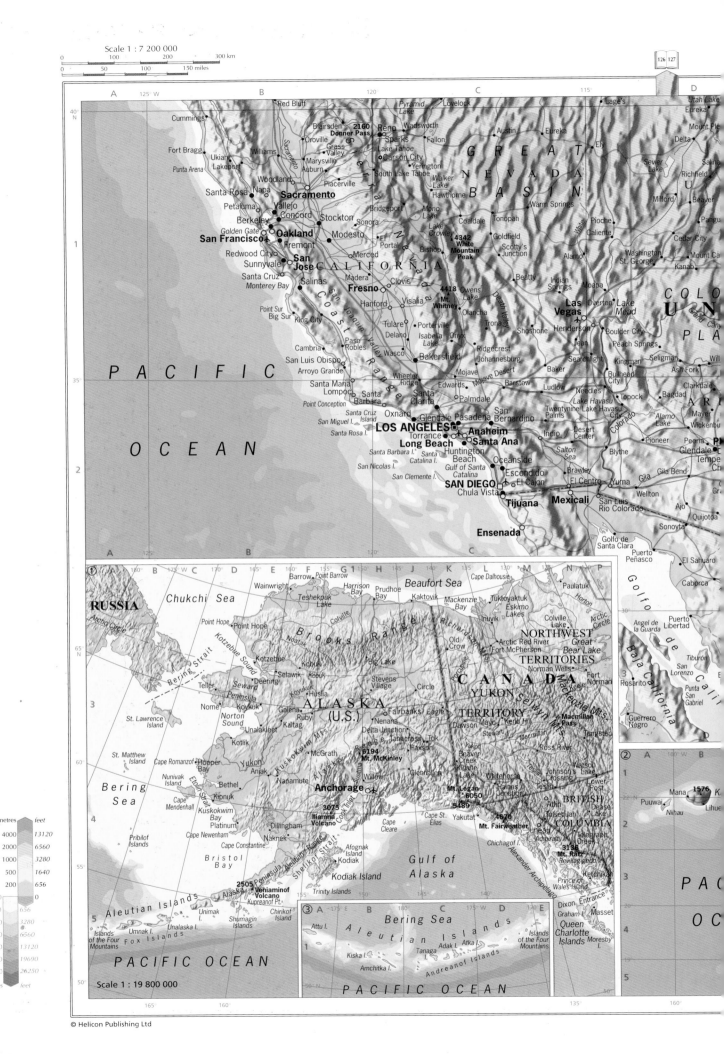

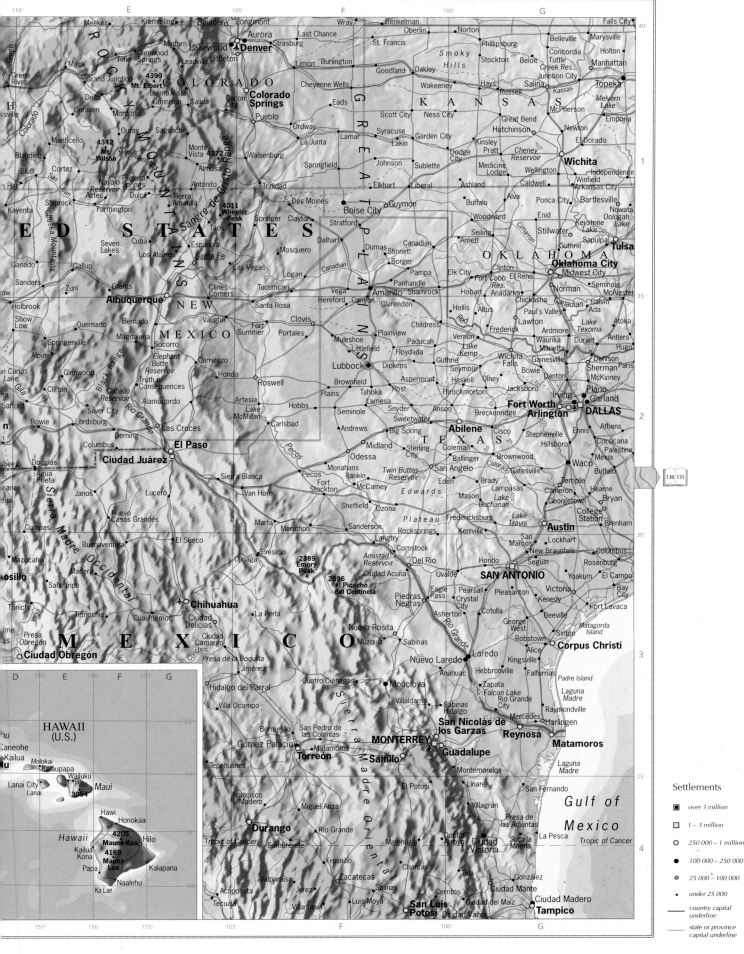

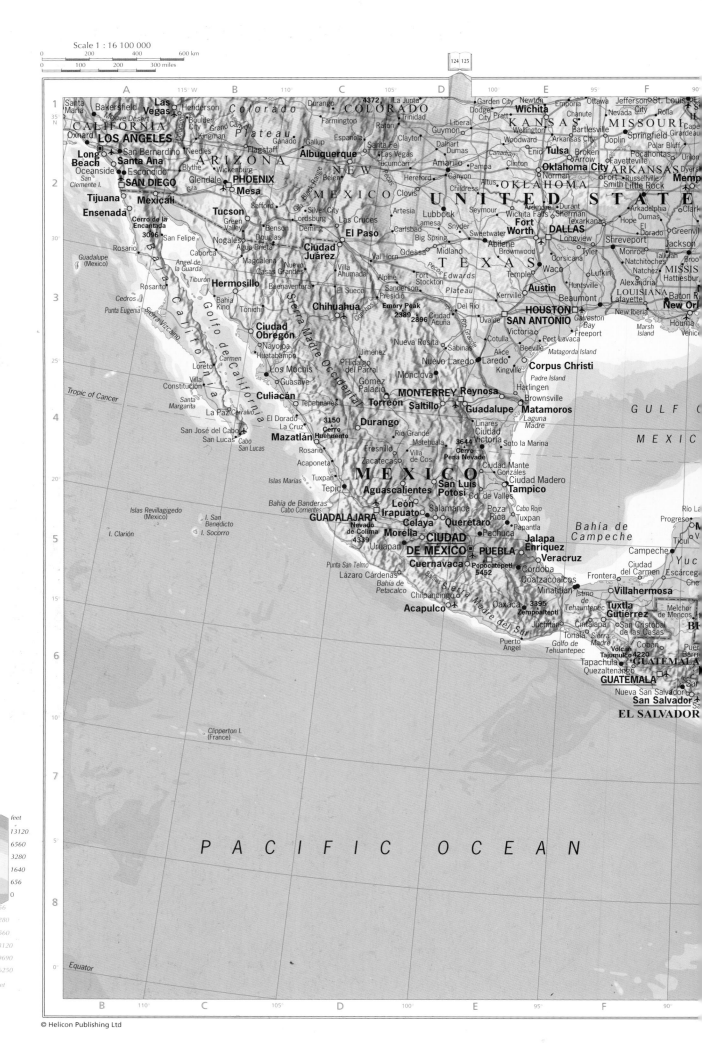

Scale 1 : 16 100 000

PACIFIC OCEAN

GULF OF MEXICO

metres / feet
4000 / 13120
2000 / 6560
1000 / 3280
500 / 1640
200 / 656
0 / 0
200 / 656
1000 / 3280
2000 / 6560
4000 / 13120
6000 / 19690
8000 / 26250
metres / feet

© Helicon Publishing Ltd

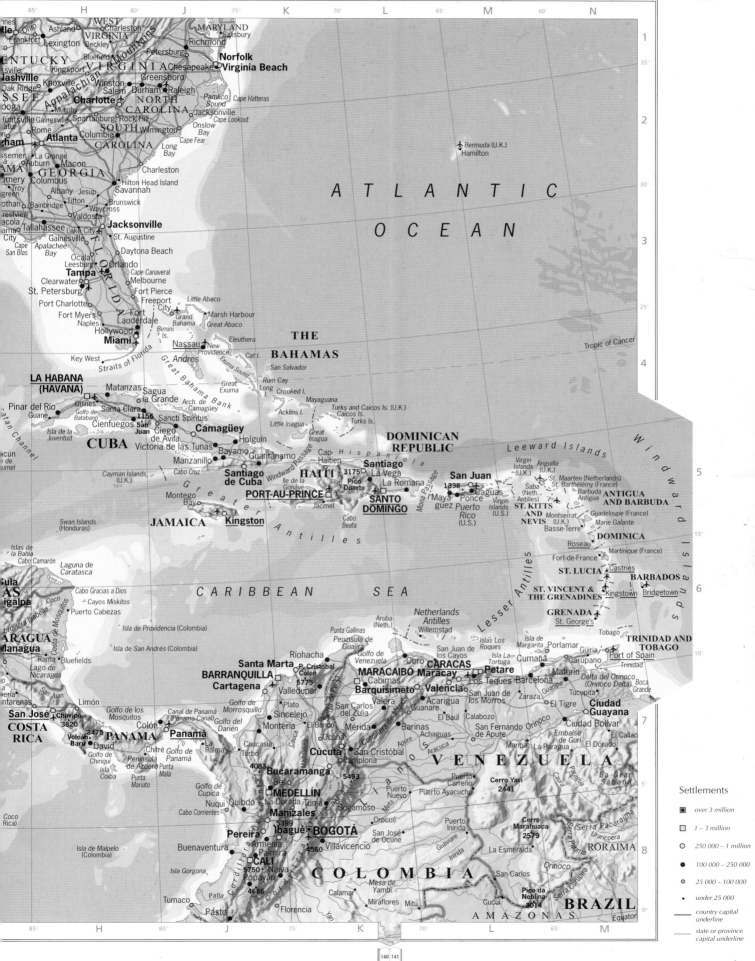

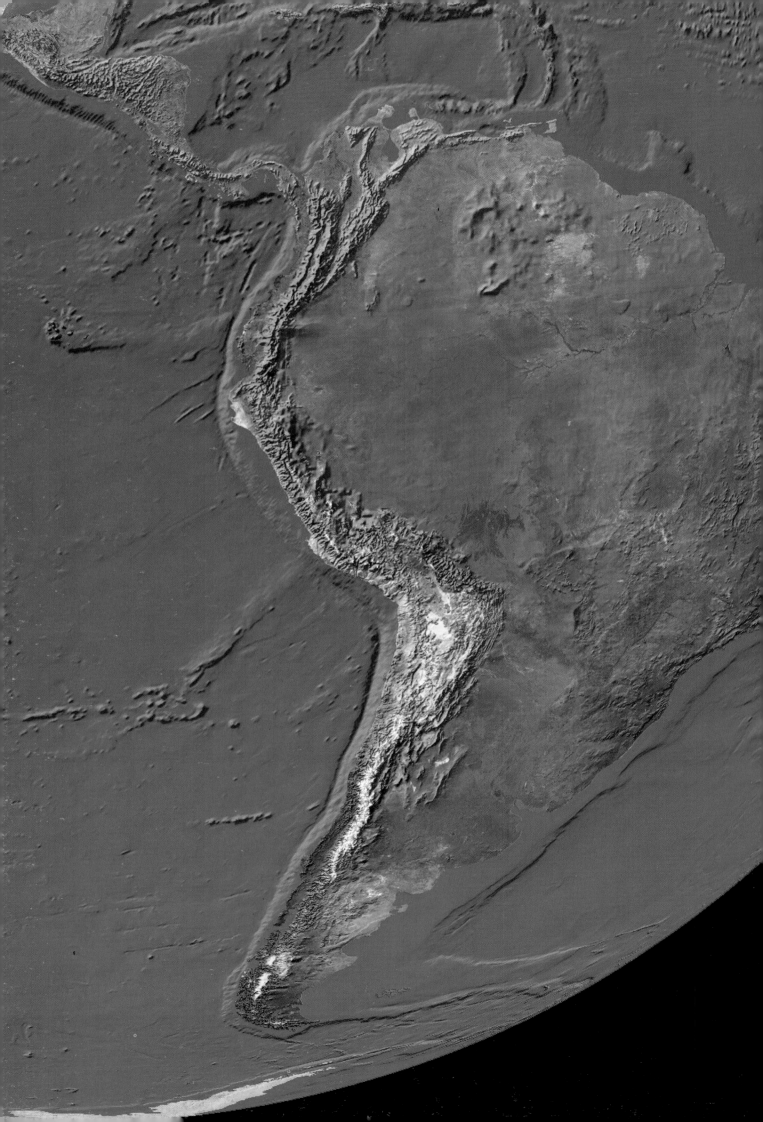

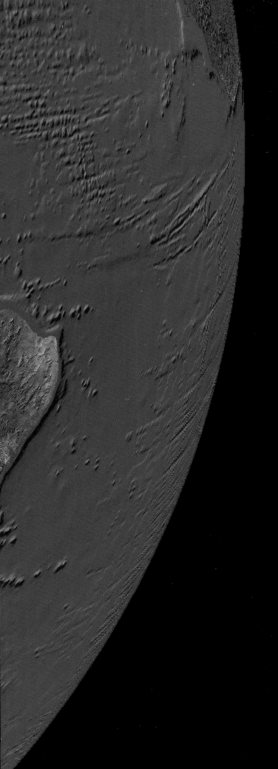

SOUTH AMERICA

South America   138

Northern South America   140

Southern South America   142

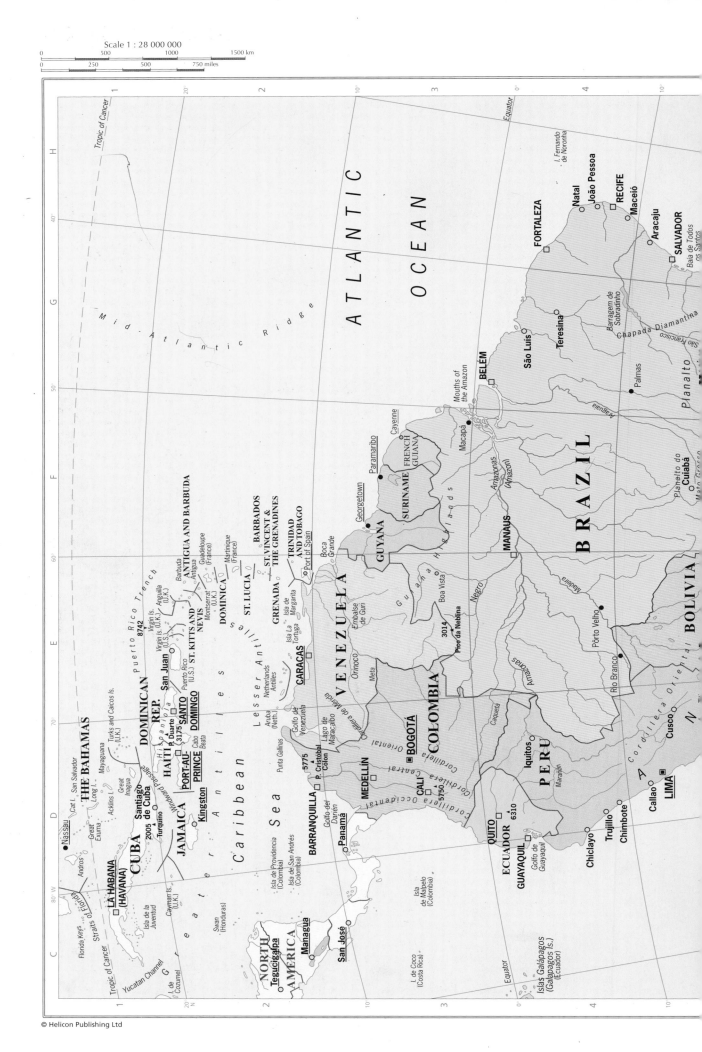

Scale 1 : 28 000 000

500   1000   1500 km

250   500   750 miles

Tropic of Cancer

ATLANTIC

OCEAN

Mid - Atlantic Ridge

Equator

I. Fernando de Noronha

João Pessoa
RECIFE
Natal
Maceió
Aracaju
FORTALEZA
SALVADOR
Baía de Todos os Santos

Barragem de Sobradinho
Chapada Diamantina

Teresina
São Luís
Palmas

BELÉM
Mouths of the Amazon
Macapá

Planalto do **Cuiabá**
Planalto de Mato Grosso

Cayenne

B R A Z I L

Paramaribo

Madeira

SURINAME FRENCH GUIANA

Georgetown

MANAUS
Amazonas (Amazon)

GUYANA

G u i a n a   H i g h l a n d s

Boa Vista

Negro

Pôrto Velho

Rio Branco

Boca Grande
Port of Spain
Isla de Margarita

Embalse de Guri

3014
Pico da Neblina

Purus

Juruá

Cordillera Oriental **BOLIVIA**

Orinoco
Meta

V E N E Z U E L A

Cusco

CARACAS
Isla La Tortuga

Golfo de Venezuela
Lago de Maracaibo

5775
P. Cristóbal Colón

Cordillera de Mérida

BOGOTÁ
COLOMBIA

Caquetá

Iquitos

P E R U

A   N   D   E   S

Cordillera Oriental

Marañón

Cordillera Central

MEDELLÍN
CALI
5750

Cordillera Occidental

LIMA
Callao

Chimbote
Trujillo
Chiclayo

6310
QUITO
ECUADOR
GUAYAQUIL
Golfo de Guayaquil

Islas Galápagos
(Galápagos Is.)
(Ecuador)

Equator

I. de Coco
(Costa Rica)

Isla de Malpelo
(Colombia)

Tropic of Cancer

Florida Keys
Straits of Florida

Yucatán Channel
I. de Cozumel

NORTH
Tegucigalpa
AMERICA

San José

Managua

L A   H A B A N A
(HAVANA)
Isla de la Juventud

C U B A

Nassau
Cat I., San Salvador
THE BAHAMAS
Andros I.
Long I.
Great Exuma
Mayaguana
Acklins I.
Great Inagua
Turks and Caicos Is.
(U.K.)

Santiago
de Cuba
2005
Turquino

JAMAICA
Kingston

Cayman Is.
(U.K.)

Swan (Honduras)

Isla de Providencia
(Colombia)
Isla de San Andrés
(Colombia)

Windward Passage

Hispaniola

HAITI
P. Duarte
3175
PORT-AU-
PRINCE

DOMINICAN
REP.
San Juan
SANTO
DOMINGO
Puerto Rico (U.S.)
Cabo Beata

Puerto Rico Trench
8742

Virgin Is. (U.K.)
Virgin Is. (U.S.)
Anguilla (U.K.)
ST. KITTS AND
NEVIS
Montserrat (U.K.)

Barbuda
ANTIGUA AND BARBUDA
Antigua

Guadeloupe
(France)

DOMINICA
Martinique
(France)

ST. LUCIA

BARBADOS

ST. VINCENT &
THE GRENADINES

GRENADA

TRINIDAD
AND TOBAGO

L e s s e r   A n t i l l e s
Netherlands Antilles
Aruba (Neth.)

G r e a t e r   A n t i l l e s

C a r i b b e a n   S e a

Punta Gallinas

BARRANQUILLA
Golfo del Darién
Panamá

Golfo de Venezuela

80 W

70

60

50

40

20

10

20 N

10

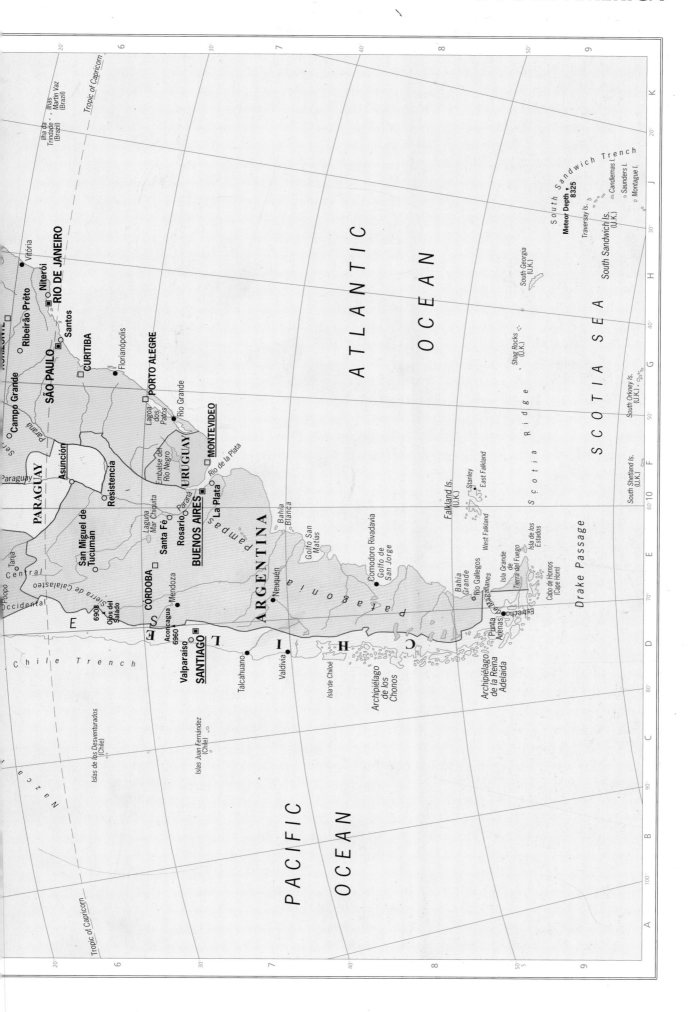

SOUTH AMERICA

Tropic of Capricorn

Ilha da Trindade (Brazil)
Ilhas Martin Vaz (Brazil)

Vitória
Niterói
Ribeirão Prêto
RIO DE JANEIRO
Santos
SÃO PAULO
CURITIBA
Campo Grande
Florianópolis
PORTO ALEGRE
Paraná
Lagoa dos Patos
Rio Grande
Asunción
PARAGUAY
Paraguay
MONTEVIDEO
URUGUAY
Embalse del Río Negro
Río de la Plata
Resistencia
Rosario
Santa Fé
Laguna Mar Chiquita
San Miguel de Tucumán
La Plata
BUENOS AIRES
Paraná
Uruguay
Tarija
CÓRDOBA
Mendoza
Ojos del Salado
6908
Sierra de Calalasteo
Central
Occidental
Poopó

Aconcagua
6960
Valparaíso
SANTIAGO
ARGENTINA
Bahía Blanca
Neuquén
Talcahuano
Valdivia
Isla de Chiloé
Chile Trench

Islas de los Desventurados (Chile)

Islas Juan Fernández (Chile)

Archipiélago de los Chonos
Archipiélago de la Reina Adelaida
Punta Arenas
Estrecho
Bahía Grande
Río Gallegos
Golfo San Matías
Golfo de San Jorge
Comodoro Rivadavia
Patagonia
CHILE

PACIFIC OCEAN

ATLANTIC OCEAN

Falkland Is. (U.K.)
Stanley
East Falkland
West Falkland
Isla de los Estados
Isla Grande de Tierra del Fuego
Cabo de Hornos (Cape Horn)
Drake Passage

Scotia Ridge
SCOTIA SEA
South Georgia (U.K.)
Shag Rocks (U.K.)
South Orkney Is. (U.K.)
South Shetland Is. (U.K.)
South Sandwich Trench
Meteor Depth 8325
Traversay Is.
Candlemas I.
Saunders I.
Montague I.
South Sandwich Is. (U.K.)

Nazca

Tropic of Capricorn

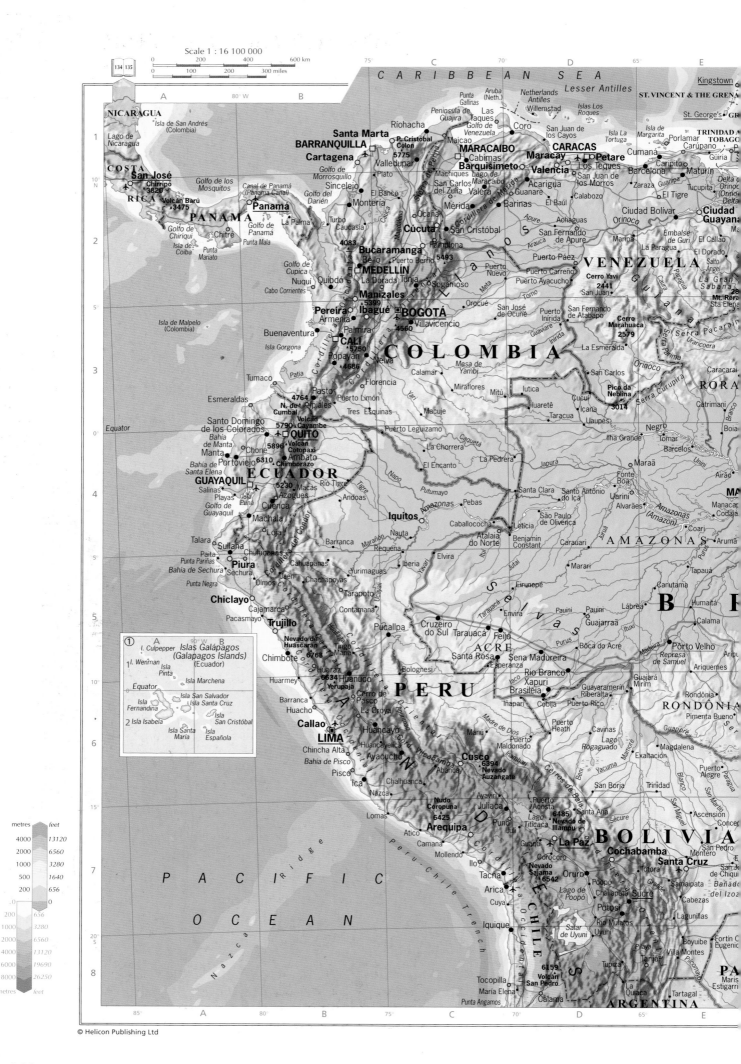

Scale 1 : 16 100 000

© Helicon Publishing Ltd

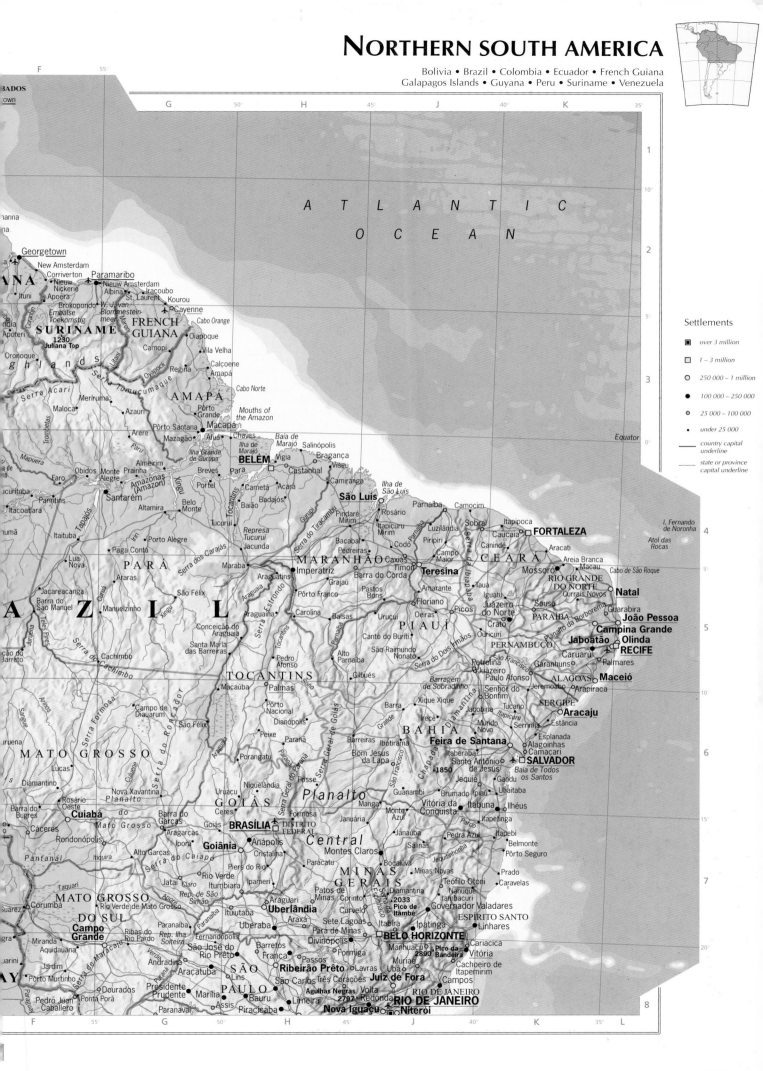

Settlements

■ over 3 million

□ 1 – 3 million

○ 250 000 – 1 million

● 100 000 – 250 000

◐ 25 000 – 100 000

• under 25 000

— country capital underline

— state or province capital underline

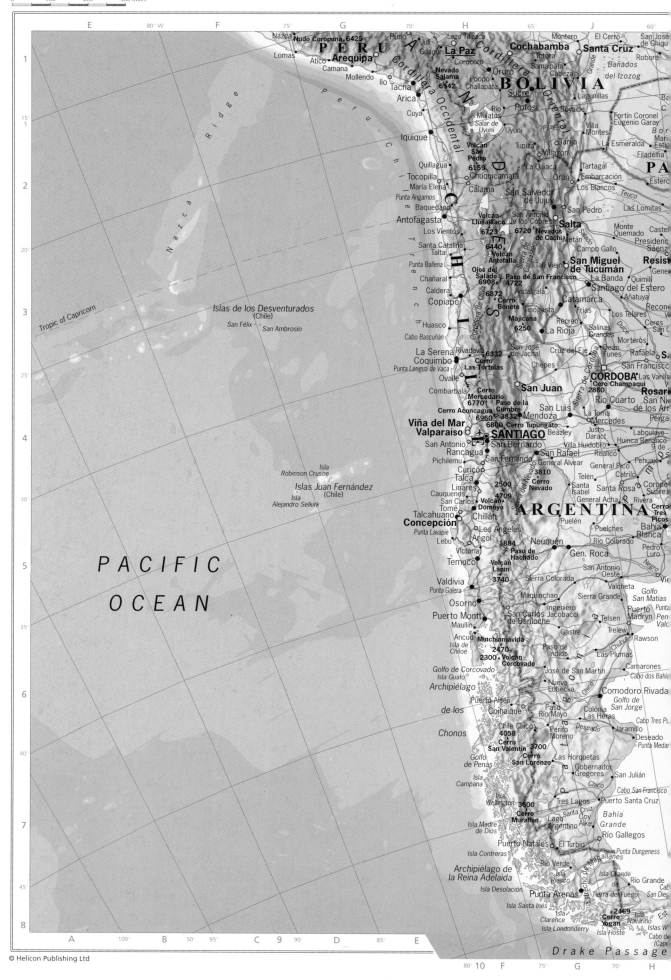

Scale 1 : 16 100 000

0   200   400   600 km
0   100   200   300 miles

PACIFIC

OCEAN

PERU
Nazca   Nudo Coropuna 6425
Lomas   Puno   Lago Titicaca
Atico   Arequipa   Juli   Guaqui   La Paz   Cochabamba   Montero   El Cerro   San José de Chigu
Camana   Corocoro   Totora   Santa Cruz   Roboré
Mollendo   Ilo   Oruro   Samaipata   Bañados del Izozog
Tacna   Nevado Sajama 6542   Poopó   Cabezas   Lagunillas
Arica   Challapata   BOLIVIA   Boyuibe
Cuya   Potosí   Sucre   Villa Montes   Fortín Coronel Eugenio Garay
Rio Mulatos   Tarija   Filadélfia   PA
Iquique   Salar de Uyuni   Uyoni   La Quiaca   Tartagal   Esmeralda   Mari   Esti
Volcán San Pedro   Tupiza   Orán   Embarcación   Estero
Quillagua   6159   Villazón   Los Blancos   Las Lomitas
Tocopilla   Chuquicamata   San Salvador de Jujuy   San Pedro   Teuco
María Elena   Calama   Volcán Llullaillaco   San Antonio de los Cobres   Salta   Metán   Monte Quemado   Presidencia Sáenz   Castel
Punta Angamos   Baquedano   6723   6720   Nevados de Cachi   Campo Gallo
Antofagasta   6440   Volcán Antofalla   Tafi Viejo   San Miguel de Tucumán   Resist   Gene
Los Vientos   Sierra de Calalaste   La Banda   Quimili
Santa Catalina   Ojos del Salado   Paso de San Francisco   Andalgalá   Santiago del Estero   Añatuya   Recon
Taltal   6908   4722   Catamarca
Punta Ballena   6872   Tinogasta   Frias   Los Telares   Ceres   San
Chañaral   Cerro Bonete   Majicana   Recreo   Salinas Grandes   Morteros
Caldera   Copiapó   6250   La Rioja   Dulce   San
Islas de los Desventurados   Huasco   Cerro Champaqui   San Francisco   San
(Chile)   Cabo Bascuñán   6332   San Jose de Jáchal   Cruz del Eje   Deán Funes   Rafaela   S
San Félix   San Ambrosio   La Serena   Rivadavia   Cerro Las Tórtolas   Chepes   CÓRDOBA   Las Varilla
Coquimbo   Punta Lengua de Vaca   2880   Rio Cuarto   Rosari
Ovalle   Cerro Champaqui   San Ni
Combarbalá   Cerro Mercedario   San Juan   San Luis   de los Arr
6770   Paso de la Cumbre   Río Cuarto   Perga
Cerro Aconcagua   6960   3832   Mendoza   La Toma   Mercedes
Isla   6800   Cerro Tupungato   Justo Daract   Laboulaye
Robinson Crusoe   Viña del Mar   Beazley   Villa Huidobro   Huinca Renancó   de
Valparaíso   SANTIAGO   San Rafael   Realicó
Islas Juan Fernández   San Antonio   San Bernardo   General Alvear   General Pico   Pehuajó
(Chile)   Rancagua   San Fernando   General Alvear
Isla   Pichilemu   3810   Telén   Catriló
Alejandro Selkirk   Curicó   Santa Isabel   Santa Rosa   Coronel Suárez
Talca   2500   Cerro Nevado   General Acha   Rivera   Cerro Tres Picos
Linares   ARGENTINA
Cauquenes   4709   Puelén   Puelches   Bahía Blanca
San Carlos   Volcán Domuyo   Pedro Luro
Tomé   Chillán   Neuquén   Río Colorado
Talcahuano   Los Angeles   1884   Negro
Concepción   Angol   Paso de Hachado   Gen. Roca   San Antonio Oeste
Punta Lavapie   Lebu   Victoria   Volcán Lanín   Sierra Colorada   Valcheta
Temuco   3740   San Antonio Oeste   Golfo San Matías
Valdivia   Maquinchao
Punta Galera   Sierra Grande
Osorno   Ingeniero Jacobacci   Telsen   Puerto Madryn
Puerto Montt   San Carlos de Bariloche   Gastre   Trelew   Puerto Val
Maullín   Ancud   Rawson
Isla de Chiloé   Minchinmávida   Paso de Indios   Chubut
2470   Las Plumas
2300   Volcán Corcovado   Camarones
Golfo de Corcovado   José de San Martín   Cabo dos Bahía
Isla Guafo   Nueva Lubecka   Comodoro Rivadavia
Archipiélago   Puerto Aisén   Colonia Las Heras   Golfo de San Jorge
de los   Coihaique   Paso Río Mayo   Deseado   Cabo Tres Pu
Chile Chico   Perito Moreno   Jaramillo
Chonos   4058   Deseado
Cerro San Valentín   Las Horquetas   Punta Medar
Golfo de Penas   3700   Gobernador Gregores
Isla Campana   Cerro San Lorenzo   San Julián
Chico   Cabo San Francisco
Isla Wellington   Tres Lagos   Puerto Santa Cruz
3600   Santa Cruz
Isla Madre de Dios   Cerro Murallón   Lago Argentino   Coy Aike   Bahía Grande
Puerto Natales   El Turbio   Río Gallegos
Isla Contreras   Punta Dungeness
Río Verde
Archipiélago de   Isla Riesco   Isla Grande   Río Grande
la Reina Adelaida   Tierra del Fuego   Cab
Isla Desolación   Punta Arenas   San Dieg
Isla Santa Inés   2469
Isla Clarence   Cerro Yogan   Isla Navarino
Isla Londonderry   Isla Hoste   Cabo (Cape)

Tropic of Capricorn

Drake Passage

metres   feet
4000   13120
2000   6560
1000   3280
500   1640
200   656
0   0
200   656
1000   3280
2000   6560
4000   13120
6000   19690
8000   26250
metres   feet

© Helicon Publishing Ltd

Taquari
GOIÁS
Itumbiara
Ipanieri
Teófilo Otoni
Nanuque
Prado
Rio Verde
de Mato Grosso
Araguari
Patos
Diamantina
Itambacuri
Caravelas
Apore
Ituiutaba
de Minas
Corinto
2033
Itambacuri
MATO GROSSO
Paranaíba
Uberlândia
Curvelo
Pico de
Governador Valadares
Fernandópolis
Uberaba
MINAS GERAIS
Itambé
Ipatinga
Linhares
DO SUL
Ribas do
Andradina
Grande
Araxá
Sete Lagoas
BELO HORIZONTE
ESPÍRITO
Rio Pardo
São José
Formiga
Divinópolis
2890
Cariacica
B R A Z I L
do Rio Prêto
Franca
Lavras
Pico da
SANTO
Murtinho
Presidente
Lins
Varginha
Bandeira
Vitória
Dourados
Prudente
SÃO PAULO
São Carlos
2797
RIO
Campos
Ponta Porã
Marília
Bauru
Limeira
Serra da Mantiqueira
Juiz de
DE
Amambaí
Paranavaí
Assis
Piracicaba
Agulhas Negras
Fora
JANEIRO
Cabo de São Tomé
Maringá
Campinas
Duque de Caxias
Petrópolis
Londrina
Soracaba
Nova Iguaçu
Niterói
Cabo Frio
Campo Mourão
SÃO PAULO
Santo
André
RIO DE JANEIRO
PARANÁ
São Vicente
Santos
Isla de São Sebastião
Castro
Jacupiranga
Cascavel
Paranaguá
Foz do Iguaçu
CURITIBA
Ponta
Lapa
Isla de São Francisco
Grossa
União da Vitória
Mafra
Joinville
Palmas
SANTA CATARINA
Itajaí
Eldorado
Chapecó
Blumenau
Erechim
Lajes
Florianópolis
Carazinho
Passo
Tubarão
Laguna
Cruz Alta
Fundo
Vacaria
Criciúma
RIO GRANDE
Santa
Caxias do Sul
Borja
Santiago
Maria
Novo Hamburgo
Uruguaiana
Cachoeira
PORTO ALEGRE
DO SUL
do Sul
Artigas
Santana do
Livramento
Lagoa dos Patos
Salto
Rivera
Bagé
Pelotas
Tacuarembó
Melo
Rio Grande
Paysandú
Lagoa Mirim
Albardão do
URUGUAY
Mercedes
Durazno
João Maria
Santa Vitória
Florida
do Palmar
Trinidad
Minas
Maldonado
Quilmes
MONTEVIDEO
La Plata
Rio de la Plata
Bahía
Samborombón
Punta Norte
Dolores
Pinamar
Mar del Plata
Necochea

Ilha da Trindade
(Brazil)

Ilhas Martin Vaz
(Brazil)

Tropic of Capricorn

ATLANTIC

OCEAN

Falkland Islands
(U.K.)
Mt.
Adam
705
Stanley
Mt.
East Falkland
Usborne

Scotia Ridge

Shag Rocks
(U.K.)

Cape Alexandra
Grytviken
2934
South Georgia (U.K.)
Mt. Paget
Cape Disappointment

SCOTIA SEA

Settlements

■ over 3 million

□ 1 – 3 million

◎ 250 000 – 1 million

● 100 000 – 250 000

◉ 25 000 – 100 000

• under 25 000

___ country capital
underline

___ state or province
capital underline

POLAR REGIONS

Scale 1 : 50 700 000

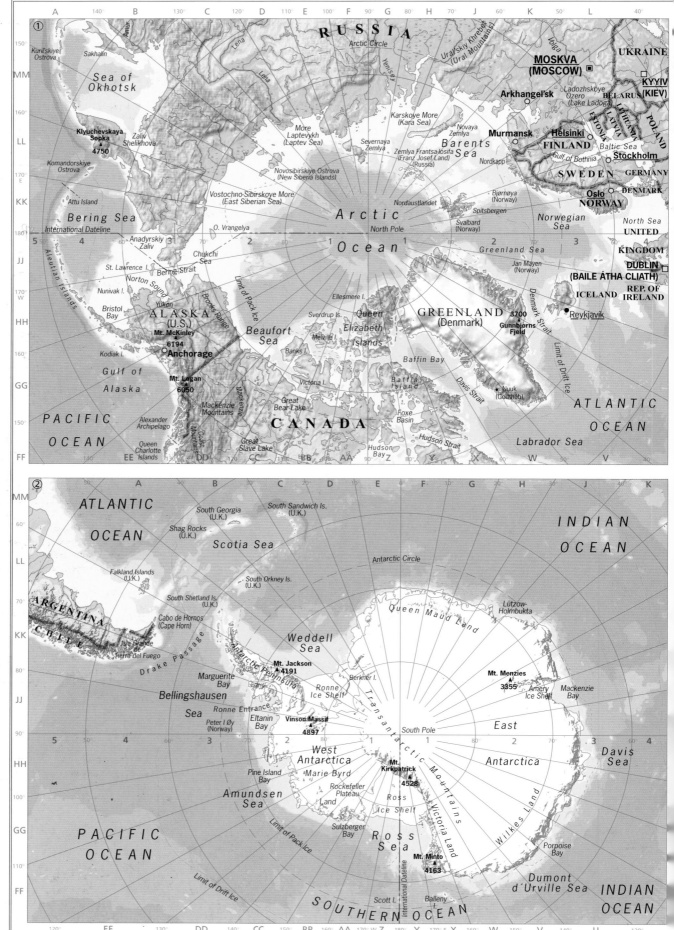

Map ① (Arctic)

RUSSIA

Arctic Circle

Ural'skiy Khrebet (Ural Mountains)

Amur
Sakhalin
Kuril'skiye Ostrova
Sea of Okhotsk
Zaliv Shelikhova
Komandorskiye Ostrova
Klyuchevskaya Sopka 4750
Attu Island
Bering Sea
International Dateline
Aleutian Islands
Anadyrskiy Zaliv
Chukchi Sea
St. Lawrence I.
Bering Strait
Norton Sound
Nunivak I.
Bristol Bay
Yukon
ALASKA (U.S.)
Brooks Range
Mt. McKinley 6194
Anchorage
Kodiak I.
Gulf of Alaska
Mt. Logan 6050
PACIFIC OCEAN
Alexander Archipelago
Queen Charlotte Islands
Coast Mountains
Mackenzie Mountains
Mackenzie
Great Bear Lake
Great Slave Lake
Victoria I.
Banks I.
Melville I.
Beaufort Sea
Limit of Pack Ice
Sverdrup Is.
Queen Elizabeth Islands
Ellesmere I.
CANADA
Hudson Bay
Hudson Strait
Foxe Basin
Baffin Island
Baffin Bay
Davis Strait
Labrador Sea
Nuuk (Godthåb)
GREENLAND (Denmark)
Gunnbjørns Fjeld 3700
Denmark Strait
Reykjavik
Limit of Drift Ice
ICELAND
REP. OF IRELAND
DUBLIN (BAILE ÁTHA CLIATH)
ATLANTIC OCEAN
North Sea
UNITED KINGDOM
Jan Mayen (Norway)
Greenland Sea
Norwegian Sea
Bjørnøya (Norway)
Svalbard (Norway)
Spitsbergen
Nordaustlandet
NORWAY
Oslo
DENMARK
GERMANY
Stockholm
Gulf of Bothnia
Baltic Sea
SWEDEN
POLAND
LATVIA
LITHUANIA
ESTONIA
Helsinki
FINLAND
Nordkapp
Murmansk
Arkhangel'sk
Ladozhskoye Ozero (Lake Ladoga)
Barents Sea
Zemlya Frantsa-Iosifa (Franz Josef Land) (Russia)
Novaya Zemlya
Severnaya Zemlya
Karskoye More (Kara Sea)
More Laptevykh (Laptev Sea)
Novosibirskiye Ostrova (New Siberia Islands)
Vostochno-Sibirskoye More (East Siberian Sea)
O. Vrangelya
Lena
Yenisey
Ob'
North Pole
Arctic Ocean
MOSKVA (MOSCOW)
UKRAINE
KYYIV (KIEV)
BELARUS
Volga

International Dateline

Map ② (Antarctica)

ATLANTIC OCEAN
INDIAN OCEAN
South Georgia (U.K.)
South Sandwich Is. (U.K.)
Shag Rocks (U.K.)
Scotia Sea
Falkland Islands (U.K.)
South Orkney Is. (U.K.)
Antarctic Circle
South Shetland Is. (U.K.)
Cabo de Hornos (Cape Horn)
Isla Grande de Tierra del Fuego
ARGENTINA
CHILE
Drake Passage
Antarctic Peninsula
Weddell Sea
Mt. Jackson 4191
Marguerite Bay
Bellingshausen Sea
Ronne Entrance
Eltanin Bay
Peter I Øy (Norway)
Ronne Ice Shelf
Berkner I.
Vinson Massif 4897
West Antarctica
Marie Byrd Land
Pine Island Bay
Amundsen Sea
Rockefeller Plateau
Sulzberger Bay
Ross Ice Shelf
Ross Sea
Mt. Minto 4163
Scott I.
Balleny
Queen Maud Land
Lützow-Holmbukta
Mt. Menzies 3355
Amery Ice Shelf
Mackenzie Bay
Transantarctic Mountains
South Pole
East Antarctica
Mt. Kirkpatrick 4528
Victoria Land
Wilkes Land
Davis Sea
Porpoise Bay
Dumont d'Urville Sea
INDIAN OCEAN
SOUTHERN OCEAN
PACIFIC OCEAN
Limit of Pack Ice
Limit of Drift Ice
International Dateline
Antarctic Circle

Settlements

- ■ over 3 million
- ▢ 1 – 3 million
- ○ 250 000 – 1 million
- ● 100 000 – 250 000
- — country capital underline

metres	feet
4000	13120
2000	6560
1000	3280
500	1640
200	656
0	0
200	656
1000	3280
2000	6560
4000	13120
6000	19690
8000	26250
metres	feet

NATIONS OF THE WORLD

This is an alphabetical listing of all the 192 sovereign nations of the world. A map page reference is included for each country. The statistics used are the latest available at the time of going to press. Place names are given in English where a popular form exists and otherwise are shown in their local form.

There is a list of useful web site links for each country denoted by the following symbol:

Sites for each country are listed below with the web address and a brief description on the site content. Certain sites cover many or all of the countries of the world. These are indicated by the abbreviations alongside the web site symbol. An explanation of these abbreviations together with the details of each site are given opposite:

■ CIA
World Factbook 2000
http://www.odci.gov/cia/publications/factbook/
Official Central Intelligence Agency Web site for The World Factbook. This site offers detailed and accurate statistics for all the countries of the world, including sections on geography, population, government, and economy. Although the site contains few graphics, a map of each country and an image of its flag are also included.

■ LC
Library of Congress: Country Studies
http://lcweb2.loc.gov/frd/cs/
Online version of a series of books published by the Federal Research Division of the US Library of Congress. Studies of over 100 countries are featured, covering such subjects as geography, economy, and government. There are also informative articles on each country's historical and social background, together with maps and timelines.

■ AN
Arabnet
http://www.arab.net/
Features detailed country data on all the major Arab nations, including sections on history, government, business, and culture. The site contains the latest Arab-related news worldwide, as well as a collection of articles written by leading journalists and editors from the Middle East. Although the site lacks graphics, this is compensated for by the large amount of information available.

■ LP
Lonely Planet Online
http://www.lonelyplanet.com/
From the makers of the Lonely Planet series comes a comprehensive resource for travellers. The 'World guide' section offers detailed

information on each country, with pages for attractions, health risks, and visa requirements. There is also regularly updated news, as well as a bulletin board for travellers to share advice.

■ RG
Rough Guides to Travel
http://travel.roughguides.com/
Well-designed resource from the makers of the Rough Guide travel series. The 'Travel talk' section allows users to share advice on travelling the world, with sections including 'First-time travel', and 'Travel partners'. The site features regular articles on selected destinations around the world, and the opportunity to sign up for weekly travel updates.

■ WTG
World Travel Guide
http://www.wtgonline.com/navigate/world.asp
Informative travel guide to the countries of the world. There are sections on history and government for every featured country, as well as advice aimed more specifically at the traveller. It will keep you up-to-date on visa and currency requirements, accommodation options, travel, and highlights not to be missed.

■ NA
New Africa
http://www.newafrica.com/
Extensive resource that features detailed information on each country in Africa, with subjects including health, economy, and population. The site also features the latest news events affecting Africa, as well as information on investment opportunities. Although the site's emphasis is primarily on statistical data, it also provides a useful insight into the continent's national parks and tourist attractions, as well as a travel guide for each country.

AFGHANISTAN
Map page 90

National name Dowlat-e Eslāmi-ye Afghānestān/Islamic State of Afghanistan
Area 652,225 sq km/251,825 sq mi
Capital Kābul
Major towns/cities Kandahār, Herāt, Mazār-e Sharīf, Jalālābād, Konduz, Qal'eh-ye Now
Physical features mountainous in centre and northeast (Hindu Kush mountain range; Khyber and Salang passes, Wakhan salient, and Panjshir Valley), plains in north and southwest, Amu Darya (Oxus) River, Helmand River, Lake Saberi
Currency afgháni
GNP per capita (PPP) (US$) 800 (1999 est)
Resources natural gas, coal, iron ore, barytes, lapis lazuli, salt, talc, copper, chrome, gold, silver, asbestos, small petroleum reserves
Population 22,720,000 (2000 est)
Population density (per sq km) 34 (1999 est)
Language Pashto, Dari (both official), Uzbek, Turkmen, Balochi, Pashai
Religion Muslim (84% Sunni, 15% Shiite), other 1%
Time difference GMT+4.5

 ■ CIA ■ LP ■ WTG

ALBANIA
Map page 68

National name Republika e Shqipërisë/Republic of Albania
Area 28,748 sq km/11,099 sq mi
Capital Tirana
Major towns/cities Durrës, Shkodër, Elbasan, Vlorë, Korçë
Major ports Durrës

Physical features mainly mountainous, with rivers flowing east–west, and a narrow coastal plain
Currency lek
GNP per capita (PPP) (US$) 2,892 (1999)
Resources chromite (one of world's largest producers), copper, coal, nickel, petroleum and natural gas
Population 3,113,000 (2000 est)
Population density (per sq km) 108 (1999 est)
Language Albanian (official), Greek
Religion Muslim, Albanian Orthodox, Roman Catholic
Time difference GMT +1

 ■ CIA ■ LC ■ LP ■ WTG

■ Albanian World Wide Web Page
http://www.albanian.com/main/
Facts, pictures, and maps help you explore Albania and the Albanian-populated regions of the Balkans. Historical, cultural, and travel information is provided, along with a small English–Albanian dictionary. A 'virtual tour' enables you to click on a map and visit places in Albania to find out about their history and tourist attractions.

■ Tirana
http://www.albania.co.uk/cityguide/tirana.html
Good introduction to the Albanian capital. There are descriptions of the city, its history, public buildings, and cultural and artistic institutions. There are a number of photographs to accompany the descriptions.

ALGERIA
Map page 102

National name Al-Jumhuriyyat al-Jaza'iriyya ad-Dimuqratiyya ash-Sha'biyya/Democratic People's Republic of Algeria
Area 2,381,741 sq km/919,590 sq mi
Capital Algiers (Arabic al-Jaza'ir)
Major towns/cities Oran, Annaba, Blida, Sétif, Constantine
Major ports Oran (Ouahran), Annaba (Bône)

Physical features coastal plains backed by mountains in north, Sahara desert in south; Atlas mountains, Barbary Coast, Chott Melrhir depression, Hoggar mountains
Currency Algerian dinar
GNP per capita (PPP) (US$) 4,753 (1999)
Resources natural gas and petroleum, iron ore, phosphates, lead, zinc, mercury, silver, salt, antimony, copper
Population 31,471,000 (2000 est)
Population density (per sq km) 13 (1999 est)
Language Arabic (official), Berber, French
Religion Sunni Muslim (state religion) 99%, Christian and Jewish 1%
Time difference GMT +/–0

 ■ CIA ■ LC ■ AN ■ LP ■ NA ■ WTG

■ Algeria
http://i-cias.com/m.s/algeria/index.htm
Colourful travelling guide to Algeria and some of its major cities. It includes sections on 'Getting there', 'Visas and passports', 'Climate', 'Health', 'What to buy', as well as a long, illustrated list of places to go.

ANDORRA
Map page 60

National name Principat d'Andorra/Principality of Andorra
Area 468 sq km/181 sq mi
Capital Andorra la Vella
Major towns/cities Les Escaldes
Physical features mountainous, with narrow valleys; the eastern Pyrenees, Valira River
Currency French franc and Spanish peseta
GNP per capita (PPP) (US$) 18,000 (1996 est)
Resources iron, lead, aluminium, hydroelectric power
Population 78,000 (2000 est)
Population density (per sq km) 146 (1999 est)
Language Catalan (official), Spanish, French
Religion Roman Catholic (92%)

Time difference GMT +1

 www. ■ CIA ■ LP ■ WTG

ANGOLA
Map page 98

National name República de Angolo/Republic of Angola

Area 1,246,700 sq km/ 481,350 sq mi

Capital Luanda (and chief port)

Major towns/cities Lobito, Benguela, Huambo, Lubango, Malanje, Namibe, Kuito

Major ports Huambo, Lubango, Malanje

Physical features narrow coastal plain rises to vast interior plateau with rainforest in northwest; desert in south; Cuanza, Cuito, Cubango, and Cunene rivers

Currency kwanza

GNP per capita (PPP) (US$) 632 (1999)

Resources petroleum, diamonds, granite, iron ore, marble, salt, phosphates, manganese, copper

Population 12,878,000 (2000 est)

Population density (per sq km) 10 (1999 est)

Language Portuguese (official), Bantu, other native dialects

Religion Roman Catholic 38%, Protestant 15%, animist 47%

Time difference GMT +1

 www. ■ CIA ■ LC ■ LP ■ NA ■ WTG

■ **Angola**
http://www.angola.org/

Angola's official Web site has a noticeable pro-government stance, but is well worth looking up for travel information; notes on the country's economy, geography, population, and history; and a virtual tour of Angola's historic buildings.

ANTIGUA AND BARBUDA
Map page 134

Area 440 sq km/169 sq mi (Antigua 280 sq km/108 sq mi, Barbuda 161 sq km/62 sq mi, plus Redonda 1 sq km/0.4 sq mi)

Capital St. John's (on Antigua) (and chief port)

Major towns/cities Codrington (on Barbuda)

Physical features low-lying tropical islands of limestone and coral with some higher volcanic outcrops; no rivers and low rainfall result in frequent droughts and deforestation. Antigua is the largest of the Leeward Islands; Redonda is an uninhabited island of volcanic rock rising to 305 m/1,000 ft

Currency East Caribbean dollar

GNP per capita (PPP) (US$) 8,959 (1999 est)

Population 68,000 (2000 est)

Population density (per sq km) 246 (1999 est)

Language English (official), local dialects

Religion Christian (mostly Anglican)

Time difference GMT –4

 www. ■ CIA ■ LP ■ RG ■ WTG

■ **Official Guide to Antigua and Barbuda**
http://www.interknowledge.com/antigua-barbuda/

Official Web site of Antigua and Barbuda's Department of Tourism aimed, naturally enough, at the prospective tourist, with sections on travel tips, activities, and accommodation.

ARGENTINA
Map page 142

National name República Argentina/Argentine Republic

Area 2,780,400 sq km/1,073,518 sq mi

Capital Buenos Aires

Major towns/cities Rosario, Córdoba, San Miguel de Tucumán, Mendoza, Santa Fé, La Plata

Major ports La Plata and Bahía Blanca

Physical features mountains in west, forest and savannah in north, pampas (treeless plains) in east-central area, Patagonian plateau in south; rivers Colorado, Salado, Paraná, Uruguay, Río de La Plata estuary; Andes mountains, with Aconcagua the highest peak in western hemisphere; Iguaçu Falls

Territories disputed claim to the Falkland Islands (Islas Malvinas), and part of Antarctica

Currency peso (= 10,000 australs, which it replaced in 1992)

GNP per capita (PPP) (US$) 11,324 (1999)

Resources coal, crude oil, natural gas, iron ore, lead ore, zinc ore, tin, gold, silver, uranium ore, marble, borates, granite

Population 37,032,000 (2000 est)

Population density (per sq km) 13 (1999 est)

Language Spanish (official) (95%), Italian (3%), English, German, French

Religion predominantly Roman Catholic (state-supported), 2% protestant, 2% Jewish

Time difference GMT –3

 www. ■ CIA ■ LP ■ WTG

■ **Introduction to Argentina**
http://www.interknowledge.com/argentina/index.html

Lively, illustrated guide to the six major regions which make up this country, and sections on such things as 'History & culture', 'Calendar of events', and 'Travel tips'.

■ **Buenos Aires, Argentina**
http://travel.lycos.com/Destinations/South_America/Argentina/Buenos_Aires/

Profile of Argentina's multi-ethnic capital, Buenos Aires. There is a general introduction to the city's main features, and four sections – 'Visitors' guide', 'Culture and history', 'News and weather', and 'Entertainment' – with links to photographs, and to further useful information in English and Spanish about the city and the country.

■ **Tierra del Fuego, Argentina**
http://www.tierradelfuego.org.ar/

General introduction to the 'land of fire', Tierra del Fuego, and its capital Ushuaia. This official site also includes photographs, and information on the activities available in the surrounding area, such as fishing and skiing.

ARMENIA
Map page 92

National name Hayastani Hanrapetoutioun/Republic of Armenia

Area 29,800 sq km/11,505 sq mi

Capital Yerevan

Major towns/cities Gyumri (formerly Leninakan), Vanadzor (formerly Kirovakan), Hrazdan, Aboyvan

Physical features mainly mountainous (including Mount Ararat), wooded

Currency dram (replaced Russian rouble in 1993)

GNP per capita (PPP) (US$) 2,210 (1999)

Resources copper, zinc, molybdenum, iron, silver, marble, granite

Population 3,520,000 (2000 est)

Population density (per sq km) 118 (1999 est)

Language Armenian (official)

Religion Armenian Orthodox

Time difference GMT +4

 www. ■ CIA ■ LC ■ LP ■ WTG

■ **Armenian Land and Culture Organization**
http://www.lcousa.org/

Armenian international organization intent on preserving their monuments and history. As well as providing an Armenian perspective on the history, culture, and sovereignty of this region of Azerbaijan, this site gives information about the organization's campaigns and how the organization operates.

AUSTRALIA
Map page 114

National name Commonwealth of Australia

Area 7,682,850 sq km/ 2,966,136 sq mi

Capital Canberra

Major towns/cities Adelaide, Alice Springs, Brisbane, Darwin, Melbourne, Perth, Sydney, Hobart, Newcastle, Wollongong

Physical features Ayers Rock; Arnhem Land; Gulf of Carpentaria; Cape York Peninsula; Great Australian Bight; Great Sandy Desert; Gibson Desert; Great Victoria Desert; Simpson Desert; the Great Barrier Reef; Great Dividing Range and Australian Alps in the east (Mount Kosciusko, 2,229 m/7,136 ft, Australia's highest peak). The fertile southeast region is watered by the Darling, Lachlan, Murrumbridgee, and Murray rivers. Lake Eyre basin and Nullarbor Plain in the south

Territories Norfolk Island, Christmas Island, Cocos (Keeling) Islands, Ashmore and Cartier Islands, Coral Sea Islands, Heard Island and McDonald Islands, Australian Antarctic Territory

Currency Australian dollar

GNP per capita (PPP) (US$) 22,448 (1999)

Resources coal, iron ore (world's third-largest producer), bauxite, copper, zinc (world's second-largest producer), nickel (world's fifth-largest producer), uranium, gold, diamonds

Population 18,886,000 (2000 est)

Population density (per sq km) 2 (1999 est)

Language English (official), Aboriginal languages

Religion Anglican 26%, Roman Catholic 26%, other Christian 24%

Time difference GMT +8/10

 www. ■ CIA ■ LP ■ RG ■ WTG

■ **Sydney Interactive Visitors Guide**
http://www.visitorsguide.aust.com/~tourism/sydney/index.html

Interactive guide to Sydney, Australia. The guide features the 'museums, art galleries, history, maps, attractions, tours, festivals, hotels, and fine dining for both visitors and residents of Sydney.'

■ **Melbourne City Search**
http://www.melbourne.vic.gov.au//

Searchable source of information on Australia's second city. Primarily designed for residents, this site is updated on a daily basis with news of local events, community groups, local government, cultural life, sport, and weather. For visitors there is information on accommodation and tourist attractions.

■ **Great Barrier Reef Marine Park Authority**
http://www.gbrmpa.gov.au/

Comprehensive official information on all aspects of the Great Barrier Reef and efforts to preserve this World Heritage Area. The online edition of the authority's quarterly Reef Research gives detail of current related scientific work.

■ **Destination Queensland**
http://www.qttc.com.au/

Large source of well-organized official tourist information on Australia's fastest growing state. The attractions of all regions of the vast state are described and easily accessible. Practical information is provided together with links to further sources. There is extensive information on the state's commitment to ecotourism and environmental protection.

■ **Tasmania – Discover Your Natural State**
http://www.tourism.tas.gov.au/nu_index.html

Official guide to Australia's island state. The quiet charms of 'Tassie' and local pride in its heritage, culture, and cuisine are evoked by informative text and a series of photographs. The history of the state is presented by means of quotes from famous visitors. All the regions of the state are covered.

■ **Australian Capital Territory**
http://www.act.gov.au/

Official guide to Australia's federal territory. There is information on government services, business life, local amenities, and the environment. This site also includes a guide to tourist attractions in Canberra and elsewhere in the territory.

AUSTRIA

Map page 62

National name Republik Österreich/
Republic of Austria
Area 83,859 sq km/32,367 sq mi
Capital Vienna
Major towns/cities Graz, Linz,
Salzburg, Innsbruck, Klagenfurt
Physical features landlocked
mountainous state, with Alps in west and south (Austrian Alps,
including Grossglockner and Brenner and Semmering passes,
Lechtaler and Allgauer Alps north of River Inn, Carnic Alps on
Italian border) and low relief in east where most of the population
is concentrated; River Danube
Currency schilling
GNP per capita (PPP) (US$) 23,808 (1999)
Resources lignite, iron, kaolin, gypsum, talcum, magnesite, lead,
zinc, forests
Population 8,211,000 (2000 est)
Population density (per sq km) 98 (1999 est)
Language German (official)
Religion Roman Catholic 78%, Protestant 5%
Time difference GMT +1

 ■ CIA ■ LC ■ LP ■ RG ■ WTG

■ **Vienna**
http://www.info-austria.net
Guide to Vienna. Aimed at the tourist, this site details what to do
before you go, and what to do when you get there. History,
geography, and travel information, as well as features on festivals,
make up the majority of the remaining information on this site,
but there are also details of local transport and a list of useful
telephone numbers.

■ **Information from Austria**
http://www.austria.gv.at/e/
Easily navigable official guide to Austria from the office of the
Chancellor. There is comprehensive information on Austrian
foreign policy, as well as education, electoral, parliamentary, and
social security systems. There is regularly updated news and
foreign ministry press releases. This is an essential first stop for
anybody wanting to know about Austria.

■ **City of Graz**
http://www.gcongress.com/graz.htm
Informative guide to Austria's second city. An aerial photo on the
home page leads to comprehensive information on history,
museums, business, and the city's universities. There is also
practical information on hotels, restaurants, and transport.

■ **Innsbruck, Austria**
http://travel.lycos.com/Destinations/Europe/Austria/Innsbruck/
Guide to the Tirolean capital. There is a good description of this
city and its attractions. There are also links to a number of local
institutions and the media.

AZERBAIJAN

Map page 92

National name Azärbaycan
Respublikasi/Republic of Azerbaijan
Area 86,600 sq km/33,436 sq mi
Capital Baku
Major towns/cities Gäncä,
Sumqayit, Naxçivan, Xankändi,
Mingäçevir
Physical features Caspian Sea with rich oil reserves; the
country ranges from semidesert to the Caucasus Mountains
Currency manat (replaced Russian rouble in 1993)
GNP per capita (PPP) (US$) 2,322 (1999)
Resources petroleum, natural gas, iron ore, aluminium, copper,
barytes, cobalt, precious metals, limestone, salt
Population 7,734,000 (2000 est)
Population density (per sq km) 89 (1999 est)
Language Azeri (official), Russian
Religion Shiite Muslim 68%, Sunni Muslim 27%, Russian
Orthodox 3%, Armenian Orthodox 2%
Time difference GMT +4

 ■ CIA ■ LC ■ LP ■ WTG

THE BAHAMAS

Map page 134

National name Commonwealth of
the Bahamas
Area 13,880 sq km/5,383 sq mi
Capital Nassau (on New
Providence island)
Major towns/cities Freeport (on Grand
Bahama)
Physical features comprises 700 tropical coral islands and
about 1,000 cays; the Exumas are a narrow spine of 365 islands;
only 30 of the desert islands are inhabited; Blue Holes of Andros,
the world's longest and deepest submarine caves
Currency Bahamian dollar
GNP per capita (PPP) (US$) 13,955 (1999 est)
Resources aragonite (extracted from seabed), chalk, salt
Population 307,000 (2000 est)
Population density (per sq km) 22 (1999 est)
Language English (official), Creole
Religion Christian 94% (Baptist 32%, Roman Catholic 19%,
Anglican 20%, other Protestant 23%)
Time difference GMT –5

 ■ CIA ■ LP ■ WTG

■ **Bahamas Online**
http://www.bahamas-on-line.com/
One-stop information service for anyone planning to visit the
Bahamas, with sections on such topics as Bahamian history,
shops and services, places to stay, and things to do.

BAHRAIN

Map page 95

National name Dawlat
al-Bahrayn/State of Bahrain
Area 688 sq km/266 sq mi
Capital Al Manāmah (on Bahrain
island)
Major towns/cities Sitra, Al
Muharraq, Jidd Ḥafṣ, Madīnat ʿĪsá
Physical features archipelago of 35 islands in Arabian Gulf,
composed largely of sand-covered limestone; generally poor and
infertile soil; flat and hot; causeway linking Bahrain to mainland
Saudi Arabia
Currency Bahraini dinar
GNP per capita (PPP) (US$) 11,527 (1999 est)
Resources petroleum and natural gas
Population 617,000 (2000 est)
Population density (per sq km) 882 (1999 est)
Language Arabic (official), Farsi, English, Urdu
Religion 85% Muslim (Shiite 60%, Sunni 40%), Christian; Islam
is the state religion
Time difference GMT +3

 ■ CIA ■ LC ■ AN ■ LP ■ WTG

BANGLADESH
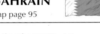

Map page 88

National name Gana Prajatantri
Bangladesh/People's Republic of
Bangladesh
Area 144,000 sq km/55,598 sq mi
Capital Dhaka
Major towns/cities Rajshahi,
Khulna, Chittagong, Sylhet,
Rangpur, Narayanganj
Major ports Chittagong, Khulna
Physical features flat delta of rivers Ganges (Padma) and
Brahmaputra (Jamuna), the largest estuarine delta in the world;
annual rainfall of 2,540 mm/100 in; some 75% of the land is less
than 3 m/10 ft above sea level; hilly in extreme southeast and
northeast
Currency taka
GNP per capita (PPP) (US$) 1,475 (1999)
Resources natural gas, coal, limestone, china clay, glass sand

Population 129,155,000 (2000 est)
Population density (per sq km) 881 (1999 est)
Language Bengali (official), English
Religion Muslim 88%, Hindu 11%; Islam is the state religion
Time difference GMT +6

 ■ CIA ■ LC ■ LP ■ WTG

■ **Bangladesh**
http://www.bangladesh.net/
Online guide to Bangladesh. The site includes information on all
aspects of life and culture in Bangladesh, including the
architecture and history of the country.

BARBADOS

Map page 134

Area 430 sq km/166 sq mi
Capital Bridgetown
Major towns/cities
Speightstown, Holetown, Oistins
Physical features most easterly
island of the West Indies; surrounded by coral reefs; subject to
hurricanes June–November; highest point Mount Hillaby 340 m/
1,115 ft
Currency Barbados dollar
GNP per capita (PPP) (US$) 12,260 (1998)
Resources petroleum and natural gas
Population 270,000 (2000 est)
Population density (per sq km) 625 (1999 est)
Language English (official), Bajan (a Barbadian English dialect)
Religion 40% Anglican, 8% Pentecostal, 6% Methodist, 4%
Roman Catholic
Time difference GMT –4

 ■ CIA ■ LP ■ RG ■ WTG

■ **Barbados – Isle of Dreams**
http://www.barbados.org/
Here are facts and figures about Barbados, weather reports, an
illustrated history and chronology, a feature on Barbados rum,
and links to associated sites.

BELARUS

Map page 70

National name Respublika Belarus/
Republic of Belarus
Area 207,600 sq km/80,154 sq mi
Capital Minsk (Belorussian Mensk)
Major towns/cities Homyel',
Vitsyebsk, Mahilyow, Babruysk,
Hrodna, Brest
Physical features more than 25% forested; rivers Dvina,
Dnieper and its tributaries, including the Pripet and Beresina; the
Pripet Marshes in the east; mild and damp climate
Currency Belarus rouble, or zaichik
GNP per capita (PPP) (US$) 6,518 (1999)
Resources petroleum, natural gas, peat, salt, coal, lignite
Population 10,236,000 (2000 est)
Population density (per sq km) 50 (1999 est)
Language Belorussian (official), Russian, Polish
Religion 80% Eastern Orthodox; Baptist, Roman Catholic
Muslim, and Jewish minorities
Time difference GMT +2

 ■ CIA ■ LC ■ LP ■ WTG

■ **Minsk in Your Pocket Home Page**
http://www.inyourpocket.com/Belarus/Minsk_home.shtml
Guide to everything you ever wanted to know about this
Belarusian capital city. This is an electronic form of a published
guide book and includes sections on such topics as language,
media, what to see, getting there, and where to stay.

BELGIUM
Map page 54

National name Royaume de Belgique
(French), Koninkrijk België (Flemish)/
Kingdom of Belgium
Area 30,510 sq km/11,779 sq mi
Capital Brussels
Major towns/cities Antwerp,
Ghent, Liège, Charleroi, Brugge,
Mons, Namur, Louvain
Major ports Antwerp, Oostende, Zeebrugge
Physical features fertile coastal plain in northwest, central
rolling hills rise eastwards, hills and forest in southeast; Ardennes
Forest; rivers Schelde and Meuse
Currency Belgian franc
GNP per capita (PPP) (US$) 24,200 (1999)
Resources coal, coke, natural gas, iron
Population 10,161,000 (2000 est)
Population density (per sq km) 333 (1999 est)
Language Flemish (a Dutch dialect, known as Vlaams; official)
(spoken by 56%, mainly in Flanders, in the north), French
(especially the dialect Walloon; official) (spoken by 32%, mainly
in Wallonia, in the south), German (0.6%; mainly near the eastern
border)
Religion Roman Catholic 75%, various Protestant
denominations
Time difference GMT +1

 ▪ CIA ▪ LP ▪ RG ▪ WTG

▪ **Antwerp**
http://users.pandora.be/eric.kumiko/
General introduction to the city, including history, art, and culture,
with links to more specific sites.

▪ **Things to see in Brussels**
http://pespmc1.vub.ac.be/BRUSSEL.html
Guide to places of interest to visit in this city, from medieval
houses to futuristic buildings, provided by the Free University of
Brussels.

▪ **Belgium: Overview**
http://pespmc1.vub.ac.be/Belgcul.html
General information about Belgium, its cities and regions, plus a
special focus on its culture, with features on 'typically Belgian
things', such as the Belgian character and Hergé's Tintin.

▪ **Tourist Office for Flanders**
http://www.toervl.be/en/intra_0_en.shtml
Good official source of information on the history, geography, and
culture of the Dutch-speaking region of Belgium. There are
sections on gastronomy, accommodation, attractions, festivals
and celebrations, in addition to profiles of the main cities and
towns of Flanders.

▪ **Belgian Federal Government Online**
http://belgium.fgov.be/pa/ena_frame.htm
Official Belgium site that includes a history of the country and its
organs of state. Visitors can read governmental press releases
and find a wealth of information in the databases of the 'Federal
information service', from photographs of the Belgian royal
family, to electoral results for the last decade.

BELIZE
Map page 134

Area 22,963 sq km/8,866 sq mi
Capital Belmopan
Major towns/cities Belize,
Dangriga, Orange Walk, Corozal,
San Ignacio
Major ports Belize, Dangriga, Punta Gorda
Physical features tropical swampy coastal plain, Maya
Mountains in south; over 90% forested
Currency Belize dollar
GNP per capita (PPP) (US$) 4,492 (1999)
Population 241,000 (2000 est)
Population density (per sq km) 10 (1999 est)
Language English (official), Spanish (widely spoken), Creole
dialects
Religion Roman Catholic 62%, Protestant 30%
Time difference GMT –6

 ▪ CIA ▪ LC ▪ LP ▪ WTG

▪ **Belize Online Tourism and Investment Guide**
http://www.belize.com/
Designed to attract tourists and commerce to the country, with
information grouped under headings such as culture, music,
ancient treasures, and news and information.

BENIN
Map page 104

National name République du
Bénin/Republic of Benin
Area 112,622 sq km/
43,483 sq mi
Capital Porto-Novo (official),
Cotonou (de facto)
Major towns/cities Abomey,
Natitingou, Parakou, Kandi, Ouidah, Djougou, Bohicon, Cotonou
Major ports Cotonou
Physical features flat to undulating terrain; hot and humid in
south; semiarid in north; coastal lagoons with fishing villages on
stilts; Niger River in northeast
Currency franc CFA
GNP per capita (PPP) (US$) 886 (1999)
Resources petroleum, limestone, marble
Population 6,097,000 (2000 est)
Population density (per sq km) 53 (1999 est)
Language French (official), Fon (47%), Yoruba (9%) (both in the
south), six major tribal languages in the north
Religion animist 70%, Muslim 15%, Christian 15%
Time difference GMT +1

 ▪ CIA ▪ LP ▪ NA ▪ WTG

BHUTAN
Map page 88

National name Druk-yul/Kingdom of
Bhutan
Area 47,500 sq km/18,147 sq mi
Capital Thimphu
Major towns/cities Paro,
Punakha, Mongar, Phuntsholing,
Tashigang
Physical features occupies southern slopes of the Himalayas;
Gangkar Punsum (7,529 m/24,700 ft) is one of the world's
highest unclimbed peaks; cut by valleys formed by tributaries of
the Brahmaputra; thick forests in south
Currency ngultrum, although the Indian rupee is also accepted
GNP per capita (PPP) (US$) 1,496 (1999 est)
Resources limestone, gypsum, coal, slate, dolomite, lead, talc,
copper
Population 2,124,000 (2000 est)
Population density (per sq km) 44 (1999 est)
Language Dzongkha (a Tibetan dialect; official), Tibetan,
Sharchop, Bumthap, Nepali, English
Religion 70% Mahayana Buddhist (state religion), 25% Hindu
Time difference GMT +6

 ▪ CIA ▪ LC ▪ LP ▪ WTG

BOLIVIA
Map page 140

National name República de
Bolivia/Republic of Bolivia
Area 1,098,581 sq km/
424,162 sq mi
Capital La Paz (seat of
government), Sucre (legal capital
and seat of the judiciary)
Major towns/cities Santa Cruz,
Cochabamba, Oruro, El Alto, Potosí,
Tarija
Physical features high plateau (Altiplano) between mountain
ridges (cordilleras); forest and lowlands (llano) in east; Andes;
lakes Titicaca (the world's highest navigable lake, 3,800 m/
12,500 ft) and Poopó
Currency boliviano
GNP per capita (PPP) (US$) 2,193 (1999)
Resources petroleum, natural gas, tin (world's fifth-largest
producer), zinc, silver, gold, lead, antimony, tungsten, copper
Population 8,329,000 (2000 est)
Population density (per sq km) 7 (1999 est)
Language Spanish (official) (4%), Aymara, Quechua
Religion Roman Catholic 90% (state-recognized)
Time difference GMT –4

 ▪ CIA ▪ LC ▪ LP ▪ WTG

▪ **Bolivia Web**
http://www.boliviaweb.com/
Whether it's Bolivian history, music and arts, tourism, or sport,
this site should have the answer. There are plenty of photographs,
music to listen to, and links to Bolivian newspapers and radio
stations. Most of it is in English, but some information is only
available in Spanish.

▪ **La Paz, Bolivia**
http://travel.lycos.com/Destinations/South_America/Bolivia/
La_Paz/
Profile of La Paz, Bolivia, the highest capital city in the world.
There is a general introduction to the city's main features, and
four sections – 'Visitors' guide', 'Culture and history', 'News and
weather', and 'Entertainment and photos' – with links to
photographs, and to useful information in English and Spanish
about both the city and the country.

▪ **Potosí, Bolivia**
http://travel.lycos.com/Destinations/South_America/Bolivia/Potosi/
Profile of Potosí, Bolivia, once one of South America's wealthiest
cities. There is a general introduction to its main features, and
four sections – 'Visitors' guide', 'Culture and history', 'News and
weather', and 'Entertainment and photos' – with links to
photographs, and to further useful information in English and
Spanish about both the city and the country.

BOSNIA-HERZEGOVINA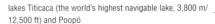
Map page 66

National name Bosna i Hercegovina/
Bosnia-Herzegovina
Area 51,129 sq km/19,740 sq mi
Capital Sarajevo
Major towns/cities Banja
Luka, Mostar, Prijedor, Tuzla,
Zenica, Bihac, Gorazde
Physical features barren, mountainous country, part of the
Dinaric Alps; limestone gorges; 20 km/12 mi of coastline with no
harbour
Currency dinar
GNP per capita (PPP) (US$) 450 (1996 est)
Resources copper, lead, zinc, iron ore, coal, bauxite, manganese
Population 3,972,000 (2000 est)
Population density (per sq km) 75 (1999 est)
Language Serbian, Croat, Bosnian
Religion 40% Muslim, 31% Serbian Orthodox, 15% Roman
Catholic
Time difference GMT +1

 ▪ CIA ▪ LP ▪ WTG

▪ **Bosnia Home Page**
http://www.cco.caltech.edu/~bosnia/bosnia.html
Political and social news about this troubled country, with photo-
essays, a timeline of the conflict, maps of ethnic occupation and
military front lines, features on its culture and daily life, and links
to other Bosnian sites.

BOTSWANA
Map page 108

National name Republic of
Botswana
Area 582,000 sq km/
224,710 sq mi
Capital Gaborone
Major towns/cities Mahalapye,
Serowe, Francistown,

Selebi-Phikwe, Molepolole, Maun

Physical features Kalahari Desert in southwest (70–80% of national territory is desert), plains (Makgadikgadi salt pans) in east, fertile lands and Okavango Delta in north

Currency franc CFA

GNP per capita (PPP) (US$) 6,032 (1999)

Resources diamonds (world's third-largest producer), copper-nickel ore, coal, soda ash, gold, cobalt, salt, plutonium, asbestos, chromite, iron, silver, manganese, talc, uranium

Population 1,622,000 (2000 est)

Population density (per sq km) 3 (1999 est)

Language English (official), Setswana (national)

Religion Christian 50%, animist 50%

Time difference GMT +2

[www.] ■ CIA ■ LP ■ NA ■ WTG

BRAZIL
Map page 138

National name República Federativa do Brasil/Federative Republic of Brazil

Area 8,511,965 sq km/ 3,286,469 sq mi

Capital Brasília

Major towns/cities São Paulo, Belo Horizonte, Nova Iguaçu, Rio de Janeiro, Belém, Recife, Porto Alegre, Salvador, Curitiba, Manaus, Fortaleza

Major ports Rio de Janeiro, Belém, Recife, Porto Alegre, Salvador

Physical features the densely forested Amazon basin covers the northern half of the country with a network of rivers; south is fertile; enormous energy resources, both hydroelectric (Itaipú Reservoir on the Paraná, and Tucuruí on the Tocantins) and nuclear (uranium ores); mostly tropical climate

Currency real

GNP per capita (PPP) (US$) 6,317 (1999)

Resources iron ore (world's second-largest producer), tin (world's fourth-largest producer), aluminium (world's fourth-largest producer), gold, phosphates, platinum, bauxite, uranium, manganese, coal, copper, petroleum, natural gas, hydroelectric power, forests

Population 170,115,000 (2000 est)

Population density (per sq km) 20 (1999 est)

Language Portuguese (official), Spanish, English, French, 120 Indian languages

Religion Roman Catholic 70%; Indian faiths

Time difference GMT –2/5

[www.] ■ CIA ■ LC ■ LP ■ RG ■ WTG

■ **Brasilia's Home Page**
http://www.geocities.com/TheTropics/3416/
Good introduction to the Brazilian capital. There is a history of the construction of the city, a description of its attractions, and a frank listing of its problems. There are a large number of photos.

■ **Belem, Brazil**
http://www.belem.com/
Profile of Brazil's port city of Belém. There is a general introduction to its main features, and four sections – 'visitors' guide', 'culture and history', 'news and weather', and 'entertainment and photos' – with links to photographs, and to further useful information in English and Portuguese about both the city and the country.

■ **Rio de Janeiro, Brazil**
http://www.if.ufrj.br/general/tourist.html
Profile of the colourful Brazilian city of Rio de Janeiro. There is a general introduction to its main features, and four sections – 'visitors' guide', 'culture and history', 'news and weather', and 'entertainment' – with links to photographs, and to further useful information in English and Portuguese about both the city and the country.

■ **São Paolo, Brazil**
http://www.spguia.com.br/Ingles/indexi.html
Profile of São Paolo, Brazil's largest city. There is useful information on areas such as accommodation, transport, and cultural events.

BRUNEI
Map page 86

National name Negara Brunei Darussalam/State of Brunei

Area 5,765 sq km/2,225 sq mi

Capital Bandar Seri Begawan (and chief port)

Major towns/cities Seria, Kuala Belait

Physical features flat coastal plain with hilly lowland in west and mountains in east (Mount Pagon 1,850 m/6,070 ft); 75% of the area is forested; the Limbang valley splits Brunei in two, and its cession to Sarawak in 1890 is disputed by Brunei; tropical climate; Temburong, Tutong, and Belait rivers

Currency Bruneian dollar, although the Singapore dollar is also accepted

GNP per capita (PPP) (US$) 24,824 (1999 est)

Resources petroleum, natural gas

Population 328,000 (2000 est)

Population density (per sq km) 56 (1999 est)

Language Malay (official), Chinese (Hokkien), English

Religion Muslim 66%, Buddhist 14%, Christian 10%

Time difference GMT +8

[www.] ■ CIA ■ LP ■ RG ■ WTG

BULGARIA
Map page 66

National name Republika Bulgaria/ Republic of Bulgaria

Area 110,912 sq km/42,823 sq mi

Capital Sofia

Major towns/cities Plovdiv, Varna, Ruse, Burgas, Stara Zagora, Pleven

Major ports Burgas, Varna

Physical features lowland plains in north and southeast separated by mountains (Balkan and Rhodope) that cover three-quarters of the country; River Danube in north

Currency lev

GNP per capita (PPP) (US$) 4,914 (1999)

Resources coal, iron ore, manganese, lead, zinc, petroleum

Population 8,225,000 (2000 est)

Population density (per sq km) 75 (1999 est)

Language Bulgarian (official), Turkish

Religion Eastern Orthodox Christian, Muslim, Jewish, Roman Catholic, Protestant

Time difference GMT +2

[www.] ■ CIA ■ LC ■ LP ■ RG ■ WTG

■ **All About Bulgaria**
http://www.cs.columbia.edu/~radev/bulginfo.html
Links to more than 700 Bulgarian-related sites, answers to 'Frequently Asked Questions', and an archive of 200 poems make this an impressive page.

■ **Welcome to Sofia**
http://www.sofia.com:8080/realindex.html
Large source of information on past and present life in the Bulgarian capital. The contents include shopping, sightseeing, a good history, a guide to cultural events, accommodation, restaurants, media, and sports. There is also a map and many photographs of the city.

■ **Welcome to Plovdiv!**
http://www.plovdiv.org/
Guide to the second-largest Bulgarian city. A good history of the city and guide to its attractions are illustrated with photographs. There is also information on famous residents, as well as cultural and commercial events.

BURKINA FASO
Map page 104

Area 274,122 sq km/105,838 sq mi

Capital Ouagadougou

Major towns/cities Bobo-Dioulasso, Koudougou, Banfora, Ouahigouya, Tenkodogo

Physical features landlocked plateau with hills in west and southeast; headwaters of the River Volta; semiarid in north, forest and farmland in south; linked by rail to Abidjan in Côte d'Ivoire, Burkina Faso's only outlet to the sea

Currency franc CFA

GNP per capita (PPP) (US$) 898 (1999 est)

Resources manganese, zinc, limestone, phosphates, diamonds, gold, antimony, marble, silver, lead

Population 11,937,000 (2000 est)

Population density (per sq km) 42 (1999 est)

Language French (official), 50 Sudanic languages (90%)

Religion animist 40%, Sunni Muslim 50%, Christian (mainly Roman Catholic) 10%

Time difference GMT+/–0

[www.] ■ CIA ■ LP ■ NA ■ WTG

BURUNDI
Map page 106

National name Republika y'Uburundi/République du Burundi/ Republic of Burundi

Area 27,834 sq km/10,746 sq mi

Capital Bujumbura

Major towns/cities Gitega, Bururi, Ngozi, Muyinga, Ruyigi, Kayanaza

Physical features landlocked grassy highland straddling watershed of Nile and Congo; Lake Tanganyika, Great Rift Valley

Currency Burundi franc

GNP per capita (PPP) (US$) 553 (1999 est)

Resources nickel, gold, tungsten, phosphates, vanadium, uranium, peat, petroleum deposits have been detected

Population 6,695,000 (2000 est)

Population density (per sq km) 236 (1999 est)

Language Kirundi, French (both official), Kiswahili

Religion Roman Catholic 62%, Pentecostalist 5%, Anglican 1%, Muslim 1%, animist

Time difference GMT +2

[www.] ■ CIA ■ LP ■ WTG

CAMBODIA
Map page 84

National name Preah Réaché'anachâkr Kâmpuchéa/ Kingdom of Cambodia

Area 181,035 sq km/69,897 sq mi

Capital Phnum Penh

Major towns/cities Bâtdâmbâng, Kâmpóng Cham, Siëmréab, Prey Vêng

Major ports Kâmpóng Cham

Physical features mostly flat, forested plains with mountains in southwest and north; Mekong River runs north–south; Lake Tonle Sap

Currency Cambodian riel

GNP per capita (PPP) (US$) 1,286 (1999 est)

Resources phosphates, iron ore, gemstones, bauxite, silicon, manganese

Population 11,168,000 (2000 est)

Population density (per sq km) 66 (1999 est)

Language Khmer (official), French

Religion Theravada Buddhist 95%, Muslim, Roman Catholic

Time difference GMT +7

[www.] ■ CIA ■ LC ■ LP ■ WTG

■ **Cambodia Mega Attraction – Angkor**
http://www.asiatour.com/cambodia/e-04angk/ec-ang10.htm
Guide to Cambodia's most impressive attraction. Good photographs accompany a history of the vast complex and details of Angkor Thom, Angkor Wat, and other sites.

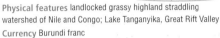

CAMEROON

Map page 104

National name République du Cameroun/Republic of Cameroon
Area 475,440 sq km/ 183,567 sq mi
Capital Yaoundé
Major towns/cities Garoua, Douala, Nkongsamba, Maroua, Bamenda, Bafoussam, Ngaoundéré
Major ports Douala
Physical features desert in far north in the Lake Chad basin, mountains in west, dry savannah plateau in the intermediate area, and dense tropical rainforest in south; Mount Cameroon 4,070 m/ 13,358 ft, an active volcano on the coast, west of the Adamawa Mountains
Currency franc CFA
GNP per capita (PPP) (US$) 1,444 (1999)
Resources petroleum, natural gas, tin ore, limestone, bauxite, iron ore, uranium, gold
Population 15,085,000 (2000 est)
Population density (per sq km) 31 (1999 est)
Language French, English (both official; often spoken in pidgin), Sudanic languages (in the north), Bantu languages (elsewhere); there has been some discontent with the emphasis on French – there are 163 indigenous peoples with their own African languages
Religion animist 50%, Christian 33%, Muslim 16%
Time difference GMT +1

 ■ CIA ■ LP ■ NA ■ WTG

■ **Home Page of the Republic of Cameroon**
http://www.compufix.demon.co.uk/camweb/
Factual data about the country of Cameroon, plus links to a number of associated sites. This site includes a map, an audio clip of the national anthem, and a brief text-only section on tourism in this African country.

CANADA

Map page 122

Area 9,970,610 sq km/3,849,652 sq mi
Capital Ottawa
Major towns/cities Toronto, Montréal, Vancouver, Edmonton, Calgary, Winnipeg, Québec, Hamilton, Saskatoon, Halifax, London, Kitchener, Mississauga, Laval, Surrey
Physical features mountains in west, with low-lying plains in interior and rolling hills in east; St. Lawrence Seaway, Mackenzie River; Great Lakes; Arctic Archipelago; Rocky Mountains; Great Plains or Prairies; Canadian Shield; Niagara Falls; climate varies from temperate in south to arctic in north; 45% of country forested
Currency Canadian dollar
GNP per capita (PPP) (US$) 23,725 (1999)
Resources petroleum, natural gas, coal, copper (world's third-largest producer), nickel (world's second-largest producer), lead (world's fifth-largest producer), zinc (world's largest producer), iron, gold, uranium, timber
Population 31,147,000 (2000 est)
Population density (per sq km) 3 (1999 est)
Language English (60%), French (24%) (both official), American Indian languages, Inuktitut (Inuit)
Religion Roman Catholic 45%, various Protestant denominations
Time difference GMT –3.5/9

 ■ CIA ■ LP ■ RG ■ WTG

■ **Oh Canada!**
http://www.ualberta.ca/~bleeck/canada/
Aims to define, by means of selected annotated links, what it is to be Canadian. It includes information on Canadian history, the constitution, national anthem, and more.

■ **Montreal**
http://www.tourism-montreal.org/
Both historical and contemporary information on Montreal. Visitors can choose from a general presentation of the city and its

---

development, tourist information, specialized overviews of arts, architecture, and business in the city.

■ **Toronto Star City Search**
http://www.starcitysearch.com/
Huge source of information on Canada's largest city. Primarily designed for residents, this site is constantly updated with news of local events, community groups, local government, cultural life, sport, and weather. For visitors there is information on accommodation and tourist attractions. There is also a good search engine.

■ **Welcome to Whitehorse Online**
http://www.city.whitehorse.yk.ca/
Official guide to Canada's most westerly city. There are details of local government services, business activities, and community groups. Information for visitors includes local attractions, suggested drives and hikes, and a guide to the Klondike Bathtub Race and other events.

■ **Québec History at a Glance**
http://www.tourisme.gouv.qc.ca/anglais/menu_a/histoire_a.html
Introduction to the history, culture, and economy of Quebec. It is accompanied by photos of the province and a video. This is part of the official site of the Quebec government which contains a wealth of information on the provincial government, economic opportunities, tourist information, and local news stories.

■ **Government of Canada**
http://infocan.gc.ca/index_e.html
A wealth of information about this country, including numerous fact sheets, a discussion of 'Flag etiquette', and photographs and biographies of Canadian prime ministers between 1867 and 1994. There is also an overview of the government structure, as well as downloadable files containing the full contents of a wide range of laws and acts.

CAPE VERDE

Map page 104

National name República de Cabo Verde/Republic of Cape Verde
Area 4,033 sq km/1,557 sq mi
Capital Praia
Major towns/cities Mindelo, Santa Maria
Major ports Mindelo
Physical features archipelago of ten volcanic islands 565 km/ 350 mi west of Senegal; the windward (Barlavento) group includes Santo Antão, São Vicente, Santa Luzia, São Nicolau, Sal, and Boa Vista; the leeward (Sotovento) group comprises Maio, São Tiago, Fogo, and Brava; all but Santa Luzia are inhabited
Currency Cape Verde escudo
GNP per capita (PPP) (US$) 3,497 (1999 est)
Resources salt, pozzolana (volcanic rock), limestone, basalt, kaolin
Population 428,000 (2000 est)
Population density (per sq km) 104 (1999 est)
Language Portuguese (official), Creole
Religion Roman Catholic 93%, Protestant (Nazarene Church)
Time difference GMT –1

 ■ CIA ■ LP ■ NA ■ WTG

■ **Republic of Cape Verde Home Page**
http://www.umassd.edu/SpecialPrograms/caboverde/capeverdean.html
Information about Cape Verde – its islands, geography and environment, history, culture, and news, plus food aid updates and a 'Did you know...?' section.

CENTRAL AFRICAN REPUBLIC

Map page 106

National name République Centrafricaine/Central African Republic
Area 622,436 sq km/ 240,322 sq mi
Capital Bangui
Major towns/cities Berbérati, Bouar, Bambari, Bossangoa, Carnot, Kaga Bandoro

---

Physical features landlocked flat plateau, with rivers flowing north and south, and hills in northeast and southwest; dry in north, rainforest in southwest; mostly wooded; Kotto and Mbali river falls; the Oubangui River rises 6 m/20 ft at Bangui during the wet season (June–November)
Currency franc CFA
GNP per capita (PPP) (US$) 1,131 (1999 est)
Resources gem diamonds and industrial diamonds, gold, uranium, iron ore, manganese, copper
Population 3,615,000 (2000 est)
Population density (per sq km) 6 (1999 est)
Language French (official), Sangho (national), Arabic, Hunsa, Swahili
Religion Protestant 25%, Roman Catholic 25%, animist 24%, Muslim 15%
Time difference GMT +1

 ■ CIA ■ LP ■ NA ■ WTG

CHAD

Map page 100

National name République du Tchad/Republic of Chad
Area 1,284,000 sq km/ 495,752 sq mi
Capital Ndjamena (formerly Fort Lamy)
Major towns/cities Sarh, Moundou, Abéché, Bongor, Doba, Kélo, Koumra
Physical features landlocked state with mountains (Tibetsi) and part of Sahara Desert in north; moist savannah in south; rivers in south flow northwest to Lake Chad
Currency franc CFA
GNP per capita (PPP) (US$) 816 (1999 est)
Resources petroleum, tungsten, tin ore, bauxite, iron ore, gold, uranium, limestone, kaolin, titanium
Population 7,651,000 (2000 est)
Population density (per sq km) 6 (1999 est)
Language French, Arabic (both official), over 100 African languages
Religion Muslim 50%, Christian 25%, animist 25%
Time difference GMT +1

 ■ CIA ■ LC ■ LP ■ NA ■ WTG

CHILE
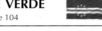
Map page 142

National name República de Chile/Republic of Chile
Area 756,950 sq km/ 292,258 sq mi
Capital Santiago
Major towns/cities Concepción, Viña del Mar, Valparaíso, Talcahuano, Puente Alto, Temuco, Antofagasta
Major ports Valparaíso, Antofagasta, Arica, Iquique, Punta Arenas
Physical features Andes mountains along eastern border, Atacama Desert in north, fertile central valley, grazing land and forest in south
Territories Easter Island, Juan Fernández Islands, part of Tierra del Fuego, claim to part of Antarctica
Currency Chilean peso
GNP per capita (PPP) (US$) 8,370 (1999)
Resources copper (world's largest producer), gold, silver, iron ore, molybdenum, cobalt, iodine, saltpetre, coal, natural gas, petroleum, hydroelectric power
Population 15,211,000 (2000 est)
Population density (per sq km) 20 (1999 est)
Language Spanish (official)
Religion Roman Catholic 80%, Protestant 13%, atheist and nonreligious 6%
Time difference GMT –4

 ■ CIA ■ LC ■ LP ■ WTG

Santiago

http://sunsite.dcc.uchile.cl/chile/turismo/santiago.html

Comprehensive introduction to Chile's capital city, Santiago. The page includes information about historical landmarks, cultural and artistic life, its natural environment, shopping, restaurants, conference centres, and its suburbs, as well as general information about population, climate, language, and transport. There is also a list of useful addresses in the city.

Snapshot of Chile

http://www.gobiernodechile.cl/nuestro_pais/snapshot.htm

This government site, aiming to promote Chile for both investment and tourism purposes, contains a range of detailed information including a thorough explanation of the governmental structure and social policy, and information for visitors.

CHINA
Map page 74

National name Zhonghua Renmin Gongheguo (Zhongguo)/People's Republic of China

Area 9,572,900 sq km/ 3,696,000 sq mi

Capital Beijing (or Peking)

Major towns/cities Shanghai, Hong Kong, Chongqing, Tianjin, Guangzhou (English Canton), Shenyang (formerly Mukden), Wuhan, Nanjing, Harbin, Chengdu, Xi'an

Major ports Tianjin, Shanghai, Hong Kong, Qingdao, Guangzhou

Physical features two-thirds of China is mountains or desert (north and west); the low-lying east is irrigated by rivers Huang He (Yellow River), Chang Jiang (Yangtze-Kiang), Xi Jiang (Si Kiang)

Territories Paracel Islands

Currency yuan

GNP per capita (PPP) (US$) 3,291 (1999)

Resources coal, graphite, tungsten, molybdenum, antimony, tin (world's largest producer), lead (world's fifth-largest producer), mercury, bauxite, phosphate rock, iron ore (world's largest producer), diamonds, gold, manganese, zinc (world's third-largest producer), petroleum, natural gas, fish

Population 1,277,558,000 (2000 est)

Population density (per sq km) 133 (1999 est)

Language Chinese (dialects include Mandarin (official), Yue (Cantonese), Wu (Shanghaiese), Minbai, Minnah, Xiang, Gan, and Hakka)

Religion Taoist, Confucianist, and Buddhist; Muslim 2–3%; Christian about 1% (divided between the 'patriotic' church established in 1958 and the 'loyal' church subject to Rome); Protestant 3 million

Time difference GMT +8

 ■ CIA ■ LC ■ LP ■ RG ■ WTG

Beijing Pages

http://www.flashpaper.com/beijing/

Everything about the Chinese capital, from its location and population to its culture, economy, and government. The site also includes detailed tourism links as well as information about industrial development in the city.

China Today

http://www.chinatoday.com/

Complete guide to China, including culture and ethnology, art and entertainment, education, political organizations, and travel. There is also a section on current events and a basic introduction to this country.

Discover Hong Kong

http://www.discoverhongkong.com/eng/gateway/index.jhtml

Jumping-off point for sources of political, social, and cultural news about Hong Kong. This site is directed at the tourist and includes practical information on such topics as sightseeing, shopping, transportation, where to stay, and local culture, as well as a more practical hotel and restaurant guide.

Tibet in the 20th Century

http://www.tibetinfo.net/tibet-file/chronol.htm

Brief chronology of significant events in Tibet's history over the past century – 1902–90 – prepared by the Tibet Information Network, an independent organization based in the UK and the USA. Click on links at the bottom of the page to access news updates, reports, and basic information.

Inner Mongolia Overview

http://www.bupt.edu.cn/regnet/english/inmon.html

All about Inner Mongolia – its population, climate, education, economy, agriculture, industry, transportation, and cities. The page is illustrated with a few colour photographs, and there are links to others showing features and national customs.

Shanghai

http://www.sh.com/attracti/attracti.htm

Guide to Shanghai. History, geography, and travel information as well as features on festivals make up the majority of the tourist-oriented information on this site, in addition to local transport information and a list of useful telephone numbers.

COLOMBIA
Map page 140

National name República de Colombia/Republic of Colombia

Area 1,141,748 sq km/ 440,828 sq mi

Capital Bogotá

Major towns/cities Medellín, Cali, Barranquilla, Cartagena, Bucaramanga, Cúcuta, Ibagué

Major ports Barranquilla, Cartagena, Buenaventura

Physical features the Andes mountains run north–south; flat coastland in west and plains (llanos) in east; Magdalena River runs north to Caribbean Sea; includes islands of Providencia, San Andrés, and Mapelo; almost half the country is forested

Currency Colombian peso

GNP per capita (PPP) (US$) 5,709 (1999 est)

Resources petroleum, natural gas, coal, nickel, emeralds (accounts for about half of world production), gold, manganese, copper, lead, mercury, platinum, limestone, phosphates

Population 42,321,000 (2000 est)

Population density (per sq km) 36 (1999 est)

Language Spanish (official) (95%)

Religion Roman Catholic

Time difference GMT –5

 ■ CIA ■ LC ■ LP ■ WTG

Colombia

http://www.ddg.com/LIS/aurelia/colombi.htm

General resource on Colombia, with plenty of information on topics such as history, geography, the economy, and politics. There are also two maps to accompany the text.

Bogotá, Colombia

http://travel.lycos.com/Destinations/South_America/Colombia/ Bogota/

Page devoted to Colombia's largest city Bogotá. There is a general introduction to the city's attractions, and four sections – 'Visitor's guide', 'Culture and history', 'News and weather', and 'Entertainment' – each with links to further useful information in both English and Spanish about both the city and the country.

Medellín, Colombia

http://travel.lycos.com/Destinations/South_America/Colombia/ Medellin/

Page devoted to the Colombian city of Medellín, a busy industrial and commercial centre. There is a general introduction to the city's attractions, and four sections – 'Visitors' guide', 'Culture and history', 'News and weather', and 'Entertainment' – each with links to further useful information in English and Spanish about both the city and the country.

COMOROS
Map page 108

National name Jumhuriyyat al-Qumur al-Itthadiyah al-Islamiyah (Arabic), République fédérale islamique des Comores (French)/ Federal Islamic Republic of the Comoros

Area 1,862 sq km/718 sq mi

Capital Moroni

Major towns/cities Mutsamudu, Domoni, Fomboni, Mitsamiouli

Physical features comprises the volcanic islands of Njazídja, Nzwani, and Mwali (formerly Grande Comore, Anjouan, Moheli); at northern end of Mozambique Channel in Indian Ocean between Madagascar and coast of Africa

Currency Comorian franc

GNP per capita (PPP) (US$) 1,360 (1999 est)

Population 694,000 (2000 est)

Population density (per sq km) 363 (1999 est)

Language Arabic, French (both official), Comorian (a Swahili and Arabic dialect), Makua

Religion Muslim; Islam is the state religion

Time difference GMT +3

 ■ CIA ■ LC ■ AN ■ LP ■ WTG

CONGO, DEMOCRATIC REPUBLIC OF
Map page 106

National name République Démocratique du Congo/ Democratic Republic of Congo

Area 2,344,900 sq km/ 905,366 sq mi

Capital Kinshasa

Major towns/cities Lubumbashi, Kananga, Mbuji-Mayi, Kisangani, Kolwezi, Likasi, Boma

Major ports Matadi, Kalemie

Physical features Congo River basin has tropical rainforest (second-largest remaining in world) and savannah; mountains in east and west; lakes Tanganyika, Albert, Edward; Ruwenzori Range

Currency congolese franc

GNP per capita (PPP) (US$) 731 (1999 est)

Resources petroleum, copper, cobalt (65% of world's reserves), manganese, zinc, tin, uranium, silver, gold, diamonds (one of the world's largest producers of industrial diamonds)

Population 51,654,000 (2000 est)

Population density (per sq km) 21 (1999 est)

Language French (official), Swahili, Lingala, Kikongo, Tshiluba (all national languages), over 200 other languages

Religion Roman Catholic 41%, Protestant 32%, Kimbanguist 13%, animist 10%, Muslim 1–5%

Time difference GMT +1/2

 ■ CIA ■ LC ■ LP ■ NA ■ WTG

CONGO
Map page 104

National name République du Congo/Republic of Congo

Area 342,000 sq km/ 132,046 sq mi

Capital Brazzaville

Major towns/cities Pointe-Noire, Nkayi, Loubomo, Bouenza, Mossendjo, Ouésso, Owando

Major ports Pointe-Noire

Physical features narrow coastal plain rises to central plateau, then falls into northern basin; Congo River on the border with the Democratic Republic of Congo; half the country is rainforest

Currency franc CFA

GNP per capita (PPP) (US$) 897 (1999)

Resources petroleum, natural gas, lead, zinc, gold, copper, phosphate, iron ore, potash, bauxite

Population 2,943,000 (2000 est)

Population density (per sq km) 8 (1999 est)

Language French (official), Kongo, Monokutuba and Lingala (both patois), and other dialects

Religion Christian 50%, animist 48%, Muslim 2%

Time difference GMT +1

 ■ CIA ■ LP ■ NA ■ WTG

COSTA RICA

Map page 134

National name República de Costa Rica/Republic of Costa Rica
Area 51,100 sq km/19,729 sq mi
Capital San José
Major towns/cities Alajuela, Cartago, Limón, Puntarenas, San Isidro, Desamparados
Major ports Limón, Puntarenas
Physical features high central plateau and tropical coasts; Costa Rica was once entirely forested, containing an estimated 5% of the Earth's flora and fauna
Currency colón
GNP per capita (PPP) (US$) 5,770 (1999 est)
Resources gold, salt, hydro power
Population 4,023,000 (2000 est)
Population density (per sq km) 77 (1999 est)
Language Spanish (official)
Religion Roman Catholic 95% (state religion)
Time difference GMT –6

 ▪ CIA ▪ LP ▪ WTG

▪ **Costa Rica: Facts**
http://www.centralamerica.com/
Costa Rica for tourists. The site provides a summary of Costa Rican history, geography, and politics, as well as information about the activities you can enjoy in the country.

▪ **Costa Rica TravelWeb**
http://www.crica.com/info/info_intro.html
Information for the traveller and prospective business investor, with details of Costa Rica's government and political parties, healthcare and medical system, plus an overview of its history and culture.

CÔTE D'IVOIRE

Map page 104

National name République de la Côte d'Ivoire/Republic of the Ivory Coast
Area 322,463 sq km/124,502 sq mi
Capital Yamoussoukro
Major towns/cities Abidjan, Bouaké, Daloa, Man, Korhogo, Gagnoa
Major ports Abidjan, San Pedro
Physical features tropical rainforest (diminishing as exploited) in south; savannah and low mountains in north; coastal plain; Vridi canal, Kossou dam, Monts du Toura
Currency franc CFA
GNP per capita (PPP) (US$) 1,546 (1999)
Resources petroleum, natural gas, diamonds, gold, nickel, reserves of manganese, iron ore, bauxite
Population 14,786,000 (2000 est)
Population density (per sq km) 45 (1999 est)
Language French (official), over 60 ethnic languages
Religion animist 17%, Muslim 39% (mainly in north), Christian 26% (mainly Roman Catholic in south)
Time difference GMT +/–0

 ▪ CIA ▪ LC ▪ LP ▪ NA ▪ WTG

▪ **Côte d'Ivoire**
http://www.newafrica.com/profiles/profile.asp?CountryID=17
Informative guide to Côte d'Ivoire that is concerned more with hard facts than information for tourists. The site is divided into a number of sections, such as 'Culture', 'Government', and 'Travel Facts', each offering a large number of facts and statistics about this African country.

CROATIA

Map page 66

National name Republika Hrvatska/Republic of Croatia
Area 56,538 sq km/21,829 sq mi
Capital Zagreb
Major towns/cities Osijek, Split, Dubrovnik, Rijeka, Zadar, Pula

---

Major ports chief port: Rijeka (Fiume); other ports: Zadar, Šibenik, Split, Dubrovnik
Physical features Adriatic coastline with large islands; very mountainous, with part of the Karst region and the Julian and Styrian Alps; some marshland
Currency kuna
GNP per capita (PPP) (US$) 6,915 (1999)
Resources petroleum, natural gas, coal, lignite, bauxite, iron ore, salt
Population 4,473,000 (2000 est)
Population density (per sq km) 79 (1999 est)
Language Croat (official), Serbian
Religion Roman Catholic (Croats) 76.5%; Orthodox Christian (Serbs) 11%, Protestant 1.4%, Muslim 1.2%
Time difference GMT +1

 ▪ CIA ▪ LP ▪ RG ▪ WTG

▪ **Facts about Croatia**
http://www.hr/index_en.shtml
Presentation of Croatia with a variety of focuses on history, culture and media, financial aspects, political issues and government structure, sections on educational institutions, social and health care, a science fact-sheet, and gastronomic guidance. An extra bonus of the site is its extensive list of Web links on contemporary Croatia, including Web sites of ministries, educational and cultural organizations and networks, tourist associations, and media enterprises.

▪ **Government of the Republic of Croatia**
http://www.vlada.hr/eindex.html
Full information about the Croatian government, including biographies and pictures of all the political leaders, documents including the Croatian constitution, and links to other related sites.

▪ **Celebrating 17 Centuries of the City of Split**
http://www.st.carnet.hr/split/
Good source of information on this Croatian port. There are many photos of the city and descriptions of Diocletian's palace and other noted buildings. This site was prepared to mark the 1,700th anniversary of the founding of the city.

▪ **Welcome to Zagreb**
http://www.tel.fer.hr/hrvatska/HRgradovi/Zagreb/Zagreb.html
Guide to the Croatian capital that includes a description and outline of Zagreb's history. This site also includes maps, photos, a Webcam trained on the city centre, and a restaurant guide.

CUBA

Map page 134

National name República de Cuba/Republic of Cuba
Area 110,860 sq km/42,803 sq mi
Capital Havana
Major towns/cities Santiago de Cuba, Camagüey, Holguín, Guantánamo, Santa Clara, Bayamo, Cienfuegos
Physical features comprises Cuba and smaller islands including Isle of Youth; low hills; Sierra Maestra mountains in southeast; Cuba has 3,380 km/2,100 mi of coastline, with deep bays, sandy beaches, coral islands and reefs
Currency Cuban peso
GNP per capita (PPP) (US$) N/A
Resources iron ore, copper, chromite, gold, manganese, nickel, cobalt, silver, salt
Population 11,201,000 (2000 est)
Population density (per sq km) 101 (1999 est)
Language Spanish (official)
Religion Roman Catholic; also Episcopalians and Methodists
Time difference GMT –5

 ▪ CIA ▪ LP ▪ RG ▪ WTG

▪ **CubaWeb**
http://www.cubaweb.com/
Business library, with background information about Cuba for the prospective business investor, and a culture library, covering Cuban history, art, music, literature, food, sport, and collections of photographs.

CYPRUS

Map page 68

National name Kipriakí Dimokratía/Greek Republic of Cyprus (south); Kibris Cumhuriyeti/Turkish Republic of Northern Cyprus (north)
Area 9,251 sq km/3,571 sq mi (3,335 sq km/1,287 sq mi is Turkish-occupied)
Capital Nicosia (divided between Greek and Turkish Cypriots)
Major towns/cities Limassol, Larnaka, Pafos, Lefkosia, Famagusta
Major ports Limassol, Larnaka, and Pafos (Greek); Keryneia and Famagusta (Turkish)
Physical features central plain between two east–west mountain ranges
Currency Cyprus pound and Turkish lira
GNP per capita (PPP) (US$) 18,395 (1999 est)
Resources copper precipitates, beutonite, umber and other ochres
Population 786,000 (2000 est)
Population density (per sq km) 84 (1999 est)
Language Greek, Turkish (both official), English
Religion Greek Orthodox 78%, Sunni Muslim 18%, Maronite, Armenian Apostolic
Time difference GMT +2

 ▪ CIA ▪ LC ▪ LP ▪ WTG

▪ **Cyprus**
http://www.stwing.upenn.edu/~durduran/cyprus2.shtml
Devoted to Cyprus – its news, geography, and culture. Included are picture galleries, Cypriot jokes, and guides to Cypriot and Turkish Cypriot dances.

▪ **Republic of Cyprus**
http://www.pio.gov.cy/
This official Web site contains detailed information about the Cyprus government system (including a full copy of the Cypriot constitution), Cypriot international relations, and documents relating to the 'Cyprus issue'. This site also includes a history of the island and the culture of the people.

CZECH REPUBLIC

Map page 50

National name Ceská Republika/Czech Republic
Area 78,864 sq km/30,449 sq mi
Capital Prague
Major towns/cities Brno, Ostrava, Olomouc, Liberec, Plzen, Hradec Králové, České Budějovice
Physical features mountainous; rivers: Morava, Labe (Elbe), Vltava (Moldau)
Currency koruna (based on the Czechoslovak koruna)
GNP per capita (PPP) (US$) 12,289 (1999)
Resources coal, lignite
Population 10,244,000 (2000 est)
Population density (per sq km) 130 (1999 est)
Language Czech (official), Slovak
Religion Roman Catholic 39%, atheist 30%, Protestant 5%, Orthodox 3%
Time difference GMT +1

 ▪ CIA ▪ LC ▪ LP ▪ RG ▪ WTG

▪ **Czech Info Centre**
http://www.muselik.com/czech/
Updated daily and aimed primarily at the traveller. However, this site also has information on how to trace a Czech ancestor, traditional recipes, and Czech fonts to download.

▪ **Czech Republic**
http://www.czech.cz/
Root page for the official Czech Republic site, with information on history, geography, and politics. It contains a daily news section, photographs, and Czech music, as well as practical information for tourists.

DENMARK

Map page 48

National name Kongeriget Danmark/
Kingdom of Denmark
Area 43,075 sq km/16,631 sq mi
Capital Copenhagen
Major towns/cities Århus,
Odense, Ålborg, Esbjerg,
Randers, Kolding, Horsens
Major ports Århus, Odense, Ålborg, Esbjerg
Physical features comprises the Jutland peninsula and about
500 islands (100 inhabited) including Bornholm in the Baltic Sea;
the land is flat and cultivated; sand dunes and lagoons on the
west coast and long inlets on the east; the main island is Sjælland
(Zealand), where most of Copenhagen is located (the rest is on
the island of Amager)
Territories the dependencies of Faroe Islands and Greenland
Currency Danish krone
GNP per capita (PPP) (US$) 24,280 (1999)
Resources crude petroleum, natural gas, salt, limestone
Population 5,293,000 (2000 est)
Population density (per sq km) 123 (1999 est)
Language Danish (official), German
Religion Evangelical Lutheran 87% (national church), other
Protestant and Roman Catholic 3%
Time difference GMT +1

 ■ CIA ■ LP ■ RG ■ WTG

■ **Aarhus Webben**
http://www.aarhuswebben.dk/index.uk.html
Guide to the Danish city of Aarhus. There is information on the
city's culture, entertainment, restaurants, and hotels. A street map
is also provided and there are links to local Web sites.

■ **Copenhagen, Denmark**
http://travel.excite.com/show/?loc=13648
Comprehensive guide around Copenhagen that offers all the
essential facts plus useful directions concerning hotels, eating
out, transportation, and sightseeing. Its travel tools include
searchable maps, message boards and a 'Yellow pages' section
on things to see and do. The site also features selected links to
useful pages on all aspects of life in Copenhagen.

■ **Greenland Guide**
http://www.greenland-guide.dk/
Official guide to Greenland. The site is highly informative about all
regions of the country and is filled with practical information.
There are also links to several other sites on Greenland.

■ **Faroe Islands Tourist Board**
http://www.tourist.fo/
Comprehensive official source of information on the Faroe
Islands. There are sections on the Faroese language, geography,
history, economy, tourism, and current political controversies in
this autonomous region of Norway.

DJIBOUTI

Map page 100

National name Jumhouriyya
Djibouti/Republic of Djibouti
Area 23,200 sq km/8,957 sq mi
Capital Djibouti (and chief port)
Major towns/cities Tadjoura,
Obock, Dikhil, Ali-Sabieh
Physical features mountains divide
an inland plateau from a coastal plain;
hot and arid
Currency Djibouti franc
GNP per capita (PPP) (US$) 1,200 (1999 est)
Population 638,000 (2000 est)
Population density (per sq km) 27 (1999 est)
Language French (official), Issa (Somali), Afar, Arabic
Religion Sunni Muslim
Time difference GMT +3

 ■ CIA ■ AN ■ LP ■ NA ■ WTG

DOMINICA

Map page 134

National name Commonwealth of
Dominica
Area 751 sq km/290 sq mi
Capital Roseau
Major towns/cities Portsmouth,
Marigot, Mahaut, Atkinson, Grand Bay
Major ports Roseau, Portsmouth, Berekua, Marigot
Physical features second-largest of the Windward Islands,
mountainous central ridge with tropical rainforest
Currency East Caribbean dollar, although the pound sterling and
French franc are also accepted
GNP per capita (PPP) (US$) 4,825 (1999)
Resources pumice, limestone, clay
Population 71,000 (2000 est)
Population density (per sq km) 100 (1999 est)
Language English (official), a Dominican patois (which reflects
earlier periods of French rule)
Religion Roman Catholic 80%
Time difference GMT –4

 ■ CIA ■ LP ■ WTG

DOMINICAN REPUBLIC

Map page 134

National name República
Dominicana/Dominican Republic
Area 48,442 sq km/18,703 sq mi
Capital Santo Domingo
Major towns/cities Santiago,
La Romana, San Pedro de Macorís,
La Vega, San Juan, San Cristóbal
Physical features comprises eastern two-thirds of island of
Hispaniola; central mountain range with fertile valleys; Pico
Duarte 3,174 m/10,417 ft, highest point in Caribbean islands
Currency Dominican Republic peso
GNP per capita (PPP) (US$) 4,653 (1999 est)
Resources ferro-nickel, gold, silver
Population 8,495,000 (2000 est)
Population density (per sq km) 173 (1999 est)
Language Spanish (official)
Religion Roman Catholic
Time difference GMT –4

 ■ CIA ■ LC ■ LP ■ WTG

■ **Dominican Republic on the Internet**
http://www.latinworld.com/caribe/rdominicana/index.html
Resources about the Dominican Republic – its news, culture,
government, sport, travel opportunities, and economy, plus links
to other sites. Please note that some of the information is only
available in Spanish.

ECUADOR

Map page 140

National name República del
Ecuador/Republic of Ecuador
Area 270,670 sq km/
104,505 sq mi
Capital Quito
Major towns/cities Guayaquil,
Cuenca, Machala, Portoviejo, Manta,
Ambato, Santo Domingo
Major ports Guayaquil
Physical features coastal plain rises sharply to Andes
Mountains, which are divided into a series of cultivated valleys;
flat, low-lying rainforest in the east; Galapagos Islands; Cotopaxi,
the world's highest active volcano. Ecuador is crossed by the
Equator, from which it derives its name
Currency sucre
GNP per capita (PPP) (US$) 2,605 (1999)
Resources petroleum, natural gas, gold, silver, copper, zinc,
antimony, iron, uranium, lead, coal
Population 12,646,000 (2000 est)

Population density (per sq km) 46 (1999 est)
Language Spanish (official), Quechua, Jivaro, other indigenous
languages
Religion Roman Catholic
Time difference GMT –5

 ■ CIA ■ LC ■ LP ■ WTG

■ **Guayaquil, Ecuador**
http://travel.lycos.com/Destinations/South_America/Ecuador/
Guayaquil/
Profile of the city of Guayaquil, Ecuador's busiest port. There is a
general introduction to the city's main features, and four sections
– 'Visitors' guide', 'Culture and history', 'News and weather', and
'Entertainment' – each with links to photographs, and further
information in English and Spanish about both the city and the
country.

■ **Quito, Ecuador**
http://travel.lycos.com/Destinations/South_America/Ecuador/Quito/
Profile of the Ecuadorian capital, the beautiful city of Quito. There
is a general introduction to the city's attractions, and four
sections – 'Visitors' guide', 'Culture and history', 'News and
weather', and 'Entertainment' – each with links to further useful
information in English and Spanish about both the city and the
country.

EGYPT

Map page 100

National name Jumhuriyyat Misr
al-'Arabiyya/Arab Republic of Egypt
Area 1,001,450 sq km/
386,659 sq mi
Capital Cairo
Major towns/cities El Giza,
Shubrâ el Kheima, Alexandria, Port
Said, El-Mahalla el-Koubra, El Mansûra,
Suez
Major ports Alexandria, Port Said, Suez, Dumyât, Shubra Al
Khayma
Physical features mostly desert; hills in east; fertile land along
Nile valley and delta; cultivated and settled area is about
35,500 sq km/13,700 sq mi; Aswan High Dam and Lake Nasser;
Sinai
Currency Egyptian pound
GNP per capita (PPP) (US$) 3,303 (1999)
Resources petroleum, natural gas, phosphates, manganese,
uranium, coal, iron ore, gold
Population 68,470,000 (2000 est)
Population density (per sq km) 67 (1999 est)
Language Arabic (official), Coptic (derived from ancient
Egyptian), English, French
Religion Sunni Muslim 90%, Coptic Christian and other Christian
6%
Time difference GMT +2

 ■ CIA ■ LC ■ AN ■ LP ■ NA ■ WTG

■ **Cairo, the Jewel of the Orient**
http://ce.eng.usf.edu/pharos/cairo/
Comprehensive guide to the city's history with a gallery of maps
and pictures. It includes detailed information for visitors – places
to visit (both ancient and modern), where to stay, where to eat,
and details of transportation.

■ **Alexandria, Egypt**
http://ce.eng.usf.edu/pharos/alexandria/
Information about the Egyptian city of Alexandria including an
historical guide, a visitor guide, a picture gallery, maps, and links
to related Web sites.

■ **Aswan**
http://touregypt.net/aswan/
Tourist guide to this relatively undiscovered Egyptian resort. It
contains practical information including maps, weather forecasts,
and hotel listings. Perhaps unsurprisingly, the bulk of the site is
devoted to the museums and monuments, for which there is
plenty of historical information. Part of a collection of guides to all
major and less popular destinations in Egypt.

EL SALVADOR

Map page 134

National name República de El Salvador/Republic of El Salvador
Area 21,393 sq km/8,259 sq mi
Capital San Salvador
Major towns/cities Santa Ana, San Miguel, Nueva San Salvador, Apopa, Delgado
Physical features narrow coastal plain, rising to mountains in north with central plateau
Currency US dollar (replaced Salvadorean colón in 2001)
GNP per capita (PPP) (US$) 4,048 (1999 est)
Resources salt, limestone, gypsum
Population 6,276,000 (2000 est)
Population density (per sq km) 288 (1999 est)
Language Spanish (official), Nahuatl
Religion about 75% Roman Catholic, Protestant
Time difference GMT –6

 ▪ CIA ▪ LC ▪ LP ▪ WTG

EQUATORIAL GUINEA

Map page 104

National name República de Guinea Ecuatorial/Republic of Equatorial Guinea
Area 28,051 sq km/10,830 sq mi
Capital Malabo
Major towns/cities Bata, Mongomo, Ela Nguema, Mbini, Campo Yaunde, Los Angeles
Physical features comprises mainland Río Muni, plus the small islands of Corisco, Elobey Grande and Elobey Chico, and Bioko (formerly Fernando Po) together with Annobón (formerly Pagalu); nearly half the land is forested; volcanic mountains on Bioko
Currency franc CFA
GNP per capita (PPP) (US$) 3,545 (1999 est)
Resources petroleum, natural gas, gold, uranium, iron ore, tantalum, manganese
Population 453,000 (2000 est)
Population density (per sq km) 16 (1999 est)
Language Spanish (official), pidgin English, a Portuguese patois (on Annobón, whose people were formerly slaves of the Portuguese), Fang and other African patois (on Río Muni)
Religion Roman Catholic, Protestant, animist
Time difference GMT +1

 ▪ CIA ▪ LP ▪ NA ▪ WTG

ERITREA

Map page 100

National name Hagere Eretra al-Dawla al-Iritra/State of Eritrea
Area 125,000 sq km/48,262 sq mi
Capital Asmara
Major towns/cities Assab, Keren, Massawa, Adi Ugri, Ed
Major ports Assab, Massawa
Physical features coastline along the Red Sea 1,000 km/620 mi; narrow coastal plain that rises to an inland plateau; Dahlak Islands
Currency Ethiopian nakfa
GNP per capita (PPP) (US$) 1,012 (1999 est)
Resources gold, silver, copper, zinc, sulphur, nickel, chrome, potash, basalt, limestone, marble, sand, silicates
Population 3,850,000 (2000 est)
Population density (per sq km) 30 (1999 est)
Language Tigre, Tigrinya, Arabic, English, Afar, Amharic, Kunama, Italian
Religion mainly Sunni Muslim and Coptic Christian, some Roman Catholic, Protestant, and animist
Time difference GMT +3

 ▪ CIA ▪ LP ▪ NA ▪ WTG

ESTONIA

Map page 48

National name Eesti Vabariik/Republic of Estonia
Area 45,000 sq km/17,374 sq mi
Capital Tallinn
Major towns/cities Tartu, Narva, Kohtla-Järve, Pärnu
Physical features lakes and marshes in a partly forested plain; 774 km/481 mi of coastline; mild climate; Lake Peipus and Narva River forming boundary with Russian Federation; Baltic islands, the largest of which is Saaremaa
Currency kroon
GNP per capita (PPP) (US$) 7,826 (1999)
Resources oilshale, peat, phosphorite ore, superphosphates
Population 1,396,000 (2000 est)
Population density (per sq km) 31 (1999 est)
Language Estonian (official), Russian
Religion Eastern Orthodox, Evangelical Lutheran, Russian Orthodox, Muslim, Judaism
Time difference GMT +2

 ▪ CIA ▪ LC ▪ LP ▪ RG ▪ WTG

▪ **Estonia Country Guide**
http://www.ciesin.ee/ESTCG/
General information and news about Estonia, plus sections on its history, political system, economy, and culture. There is, however, little information of direct use to people wishing to visit the country, except for pages on upcoming events and public transport.

▪ **Tallinn**
http://www.tallinn.ee/english/index.html
Good official guide to the Estonian capital. There is good coverage of the city's rich history, culture, economy, educational and scientific institutions, and transport services. In addition there is a demographic profile of its inhabitants.

ETHIOPIA

Map page 98

National name Ya'Ityopya Federalawi Dimokrasiyawi Repeblik/Federal Democratic Republic of Ethiopia
Area 1,096,900 sq km/423,513 sq mi
Capital Addis Ababa
Major towns/cities Dirē Dawa, Harar, Nazrēt, Desē, Gonder, Mek'ele, Bahir Dar
Physical features a high plateau with central mountain range divided by Rift Valley; plains in east; source of Blue Nile River; Danakil and Ogaden deserts
Currency Ethiopian birr
GNP per capita (PPP) (US$) 599 (1999)
Resources gold, salt, platinum, copper, potash. Reserves of petroleum have not been exploited
Population 62,565,000 (2000 est)
Population density (per sq km) 56 (1999 est)
Language Amharic (official), Arabic, Tigrinya, Orominga, about 100 other local languages
Religion Muslim 45%, Ethiopian Orthodox Church (which has had its own patriarch since 1976) 35%, animist 12%, other Christian 8%
Time difference GMT +3

 ▪ CIA ▪ LC ▪ LP ▪ NA ▪ WTG

▪ **Ethiopia, Land of Zion**
http://www.webstories.co.nz/focus/etiopia/
Fascinating guide to Ethiopia. Divided into three sections – 'Past', 'Land', and 'People' – the site offers a series of illustrated articles, covering topics such as Ethiopian wildlife, Rastafarians, and Haile Selassie.

FIJI

Map page 112

National name Matanitu Ko Viti/Republic of the Fiji Islands
Area 18,333 sq km/7,078 sq mi
Capital Suva
Major towns/cities Lautoka, Nadi, Ba, Labasa, Nausori
Major ports Lautoka, Levuka
Physical features comprises about 844 Melanesian and Polynesian islands and islets (about 100 inhabited), the largest being Viti Levu (10,429 sq km/4,028 sq mi) and Vanua Levu (5,556 sq km/2,146 sq mi); mountainous, volcanic, with tropical rainforest and grasslands; almost all islands surrounded by coral reefs; high volcanic peaks
Currency Fiji dollar
GNP per capita (PPP) (US$) 4,536 (1999)
Resources gold, silver, copper
Population 817,000 (2000 est)
Population density (per sq km) 44 (1999 est)
Language English (official), Fijian, Hindi
Religion Methodist 37%, Hindu 38%, Muslim 8%, Roman Catholic 8%, Sikh
Time difference GMT +12

 ▪ CIA ▪ LP ▪ WTG

▪ **Fiji Online Home Page**
http://www.fiji-online.com.fj
Official Fiji Island Home Page. Visitors will find all the basic facts about the islands, as well as tourism, trade, and finance sections. The site also offers listings of educational institutions, non-profit organizations, and commercial agencies.

FINLAND

Map page 48

National name Suomen Tasavalta (Finnish)/Republiken Finland (Swedish)/Republic of Finland
Area 338,145 sq km/130,557 sq mi
Capital Helsinki (Swedish Helsingfors)
Major towns/cities Tampere, Turku, Espoo, Vantaa, Oulu
Major ports Turku, Oulu
Physical features most of the country is forest, with low hills and about 60,000 lakes; one-third is within the Arctic Circle; archipelago in south includes Åland Islands; Helsinki is the most northerly national capital on the European continent. At the 70th parallel there is constant daylight for 73 days in summer and 51 days of uninterrupted night in winter.
Currency markka
GNP per capita (PPP) (US$) 21,209 (1999)
Resources copper ore, lead ore, gold, zinc ore, silver, peat, hydro power, forests
Population 5,176,000 (2000 est)
Population density (per sq km) 15 (1999 est)
Language Finnish (93%), Swedish (6%) (both official), Saami (Lapp), Russian
Religion Evangelical Lutheran 87%, Greek Orthodox 1%
Time difference GMT +2

 ▪ CIA ▪ LC ▪ LP ▪ RG ▪ WTG

▪ **Virtual Finland**
http://virtual.finland.fi/finfo/english/finnmap.html
Set of maps of Finland which include road, rail, and weather, as well as historical maps. There is also an 'active' map which will take you to pages of information about individual towns, cities, and sites of interest.

▪ **City of Oulu**
http://www.ouka.fi/oulu_ee.html
Large and well-presented trilingual source of information on the largest city in the north of Finland. This site includes history, cultural heritage, local government services and local democracy, local community news, the environment, economy, and employment and investment opportunities. There are a number of photos and an impressive series of links to local institutions and companies.

Welcome to Tampere
http://www.tampere.fi/elke/mato/english/

Information on this Finnish city which is Scandinavia's largest inland community. There is a history of Tampere, description of places of interest, guide to museums, and information on restaurants and accommodation. A number of photos of Tampere are included, which can be sent as electronic 'postcards' across the Internet.

FRANCE
Map page 58

National name République Française/ French Republic

Area (including Corsica) 543,965 sq km/210,024 sq mi

Capital Paris

Major towns/cities Lyon, Lille, Bordeaux, Toulouse, Nantes, Marseille, Nice, Strasbourg, Montpellier, Rennes, Le Havre

Major ports Marseille, Nice, Le Havre

Physical features rivers Seine, Loire, Garonne, Rhône; mountain ranges Alps, Massif Central, Pyrenees, Jura, Vosges, Cévennes; Auvergne mountain region; Mont Blanc (4,810 m/ 15,781 ft); Ardennes forest; Riviera; caves of Dordogne with relics of early humans; the island of Corsica

Territories Guadeloupe, French Guiana, Martinique, Réunion, St. Pierre and Miquelon, Southern and Antarctic Territories, New Caledonia, French Polynesia, Wallis and Futuna, Mayotte, Bassas da India, Clipperton Island, Europa Island, Glorioso Islands, Juan de Nova Island, Tromelin Island

Currency franc

GNP per capita (PPP) (US$) 21,897 (1999)

Resources coal, petroleum, natural gas, iron ore, copper, zinc, bauxite

Population 59,080,000 (2000 est)

Population density (per sq km) 108 (1999 est)

Language French (official; regional languages include Basque, Breton, Catalan, Corsican, and Provençal)

Religion Roman Catholic, about 90%; also Muslim, Protestant, and Jewish minorities

Time difference GMT +1

 ■ CIA ■ LP ■ RG ■ WTG

France
http://www.france.diplomatie.fr/france/index.gb.html

Multilingual resource (French, English, Spanish, and German) on this European country produced by the French Foreign Affairs office. It includes an introduction to the country, history, geography, education, science, and culture. All of these are presented in the form of quite in-depth essays. There is also a section on contemporary news and a source of practical information for visitors.

FranceWay
http://www.franceway.com/

Overview of French culture and heritage, with features on such topics as the French regions and French cuisine and wines, and information for travellers.

Paris Pages
http://www.paris.org/

Essential reference tool for every wanderer around Paris, as it is crammed with information on every aspect of Parisian life. Among its many attractions, the site has features on the culture of the city as well as masses of tourist information.

Tahiti
http://tahiti.com/

Huge source of well-presented information on Tahiti and other islands in French Polynesia. Polynesian history and culture are sympathetically explained. There is also a host of practical information and suggestions for visitors.

New Caledonia Tourism
http://www.new-caledonia-tourism.nc/

Guide to the French Pacific territory. There is a good introduction to local history and Melanesian culture. Visitors are provided with practical information about attractions, transport, and accommodation.

Touring Guide of Provence
http://www.provenceweb.fr/e/provpil.htm

Comprehensive guide to the six départements comprising the region of Provence. There are details of the history and

attractions of all the cities in the region. The site also includes maps and information on accommodation and restaurants.

Bretagne – History and Tradition
http://www.brittany-bretagne.com/level1.cfm?level1=pat

Huge source of information on the history, culture, and heritage of Brittany. There is a history of the region from Neolithic times to the modern day. In addition, this site has information on Brittany's maritime heritage and profiles of famous Bretons.

Strasbourg Online
http://www.strasbourg.com/index.html

Well-presented guide to the seat of the European parliament. There are sections on art, history, culture, business, Alsatian wine and cuisine, and famous residents. This site includes a map of the city, practical information for visitors, and a large number of links to sources of further information in both English and French.

GABON
Map page 104

National name République Gabonaise/Gabonese Republic

Area 267,667 sq km/ 103,346 sq mi

Capital Libreville

Major towns/cities Port-Gentil, Franceville (or Masuku), Lambaréné, Oyem, Mouila

Major ports Port-Gentil and Owendo

Physical features virtually the whole country is tropical rainforest; narrow coastal plain rising to hilly interior with savannah in east and south; Ogooué River flows north–west

Currency franc CFA

GNP per capita (PPP) (US$) 5,325 (1999)

Resources petroleum, natural gas, manganese (one of world's foremost producers and exporters), iron ore, uranium, gold, niobium, talc, phosphates

Population 1,226,000 (2000 est)

Population density (per sq km) 4 (1999 est)

Language French (official), Fang (in the north), Bantu languages, and other local dialects

Religion Christian 60% (mostly Roman Catholic), animist about 4%, Muslim 1%

Time difference GMT +1

 ■ CIA ■ LP ■ NA ■ WTG

THE GAMBIA
Map page 104

National name Republic of the Gambia

Area 10,402 sq km/4,016 sq mi

Capital Banjul

Major towns/cities Brikama, Bakau, Farafenni, Gunjur, Basse

Physical features consists of narrow strip of land along the River Gambia; river flanked by low hills

Currency dalasi

GNP per capita (PPP) (US$) 1,492 (1999)

Resources ilmenite, zircon, rutile, petroleum (well discovered, but not exploited)

Population 1,305,000 (2000 est)

Population density (per sq km) 122 (1999 est)

Language English (official), Mandinka, Fula, Wolof, other indigenous dialects

Religion Muslim 85%, with animist and Christian minorities

Time difference GMT +/−0

 ■ CIA ■ LP ■ RG ■ WTG

Republic of The Gambia
http://www.gambia.com/

Official Web site of The Gambia, with information about the country's history, geography, government, investment opportunities, and economic development, plus a guide for travellers.

GEORGIA
Map page 92

National name Sak'art'velo/Georgia

Area 69,700 sq km/26,911 sq mi

Capital T'bilisi

Major towns/cities K'ut'aisi, Rust'avi, Bat'umi, Zugdidi, Gori

Physical features largely mountainous with a variety of landscape from the subtropical Black Sea shores to the ice and snow of the crest line of the Caucasus; chief rivers are Kura and Rioni

Currency lari

GNP per capita (PPP) (US$) 3,606 (1999)

Resources coal, manganese, barytes, clay, petroleum and natural gas deposits, iron and other ores, gold, agate, marble, alabaster, arsenic, tungsten, mercury

Population 4,968,000 (2000 est)

Population density (per sq km) 72 (1999 est)

Language Georgian (official), Russian, Abkazian, Armenian, Azeri

Religion Georgian Orthodox, also Muslim

Time difference GMT +3

 ■ CIA ■ LC ■ LP ■ WTG

Sakartvelo – former Republic of Georgia
http://www.sakartvelo.com/indexOLD.html

Substantial source of data about Georgia – with maps, statistics, images, audio clips, and information about such topics as its history, architecture, and folklore.

Tbilisi – The Warm Heart of Georgia
http://www.parliament.ge/~nino/tbilis/tbilisi.html

Good introduction to the Georgian capital. The history and cultural traditions of the city are presented with the help of good photographs. This site also contains information on cultural and educational institutions in the city.

GERMANY
Map page 52

National name Bundesrepublik Deutschland/Federal Republic of Germany

Area 357,041 sq km/ 137,853 sq mi

Capital Berlin

Major towns/cities Koln, Hamburg, Munich, Essen, Frankfurt am Main, Dortmund, Stuttgart, Düsseldorf, Leipzig, Dresden, Hannover

Major ports Hamburg, Kiel, Bremerhaven, Rostock

Physical features flat in north, mountainous in south with Alps; rivers Rhine, Weser, Elbe flow north, Danube flows southeast, Oder and Neisse flow north along Polish frontier; many lakes, including Müritz; Black Forest, Harz Mountains, Erzgebirge (Ore Mountains), Bavarian Alps, Fichtelgebirge, Thüringer Forest

Currency Deutschmark

GNP per capita (PPP) (US$) 22,404 (1999)

Resources lignite, hard coal, potash salts, crude oil, natural gas, iron ore, copper, timber, nickel, uranium

Population 82,220,000 (2000 est)

Population density (per sq km) 230 (1999 est)

Language German (official)

Religion Protestant (mainly Lutheran) 38%, Roman Catholic 34%

Time difference GMT +1

 ■ CIA ■ LC ■ LP ■ RG ■ WTG

Munich
http://www.munich-tourist.de/english/englisch/cityinformation/munich-cityinformation-introduction.htm

Overview of the city of Munich, including arts and entertainment facilities, news, weather, places of interest to visit, and travel information.

Bavaria Online
http://www.bavaria.com/

Multilingual site on this area of Germany that includes sections on culture, travel, business, entertainment, and shopping. The site is filled with images and short essays on related subjects like architecture and the Oktoberfest.

■ Berlin

http://userpage.chemie.fu-berlin.de/adressen/berlin.html

City guide to Berlin. Aimed at the tourist, this site details what to do before you go and what to do when you get there. History, geography, and travel information, as well as features on festivals, make up the majority of the remaining information on this site, as well as details of local transport and a list of useful telephone numbers. There are also some images of Berlin, and maps of the city area.

■ Frankfurt am Main

http://expedia.msn.com/wg/Europe/Germany/P14119.asp

Good source of information on Germany's financial capital. There are sections providing an overview of the city's history, culture, tourist attractions, and economic base. There are also a number of photographs.

■ Bundesregierung Deutschland

http://194.94.238.74/tatsachen_ueber_deutschland/englisch/

Lots of factual information about Germany including its history, people, political system, education, and culture. Choose to read the information in German or English. Navigate around the site by using the 'tree' structure, on the left-hand side. The site is also available to view in German, for extra reading comprehension.

■ GermNews

http://www.mathematik.uni-ulm.de/germnews/

Latest news from Germany. This text-based site presents all the latest happenings from a German perspective and also has an archive dating back to 1993. The articles are clear and concise and provide good German reading practice. There is also an English version to help out if the German gets too difficult.

■ Germany

http://eng.bundesregierung.de/frameset/index.jsp

Well-presented official introduction to Germany from the Press and Information Office of the Federal Government. There are thorough overviews of Germany's geography, history, political and judicial system, economy, culture, education, and science. The site also offers links to online versions of information magazines, to federal institutions, and to leading political parties. This is a good first stop for those wanting information about Germany.

GHANA

Map page 104

National name Republic of Ghana
Area 238,540 sq km/92,100 sq mi
Capital Accra
Major towns/cities Kumasi, Tamale, Tema, Sekondi, Takoradi, Cape Coast, Koforidua, Bolgatanga, Obuasi

Major ports Sekondi, Tema
Physical features mostly tropical lowland plains; bisected by River Volta
Currency cedi
GNP per capita (PPP) (US$) 1,793 (1999 est)
Resources diamonds, gold, manganese, bauxite
Population 20,212,000 (2000 est)
Population density (per sq km) 83 (1999 est)
Language English (official), Ga, other African languages
Religion Christian 40%, animist 32%, Muslim 16%
Time difference GMT +/–0

 ■ CIA ■ LC ■ LP ■ RG ■ WTG

■ Republic of Ghana Home Page

http://www.ghana.com/republic/index.html

Introduction to Ghana, with background notes on its geography, regions, and culture, plus maps of the country, links to newspapers, and tourist information.

GREECE

Map page 68

National name Elliniki Dimokratia/Hellenic Republic
Area 131,957 sq km/50,948 sq mi
Capital Athens
Major towns/cities Thessaloniki, Peiraias, Patra,

Iraklion, Larisa, Peristerio, Kallithéa
Major ports Peiraias, Thessaloniki, Patra, Iraklion
Physical features mountainous (Mount Olympus); a large number of islands, notably Crete, Corfu, and Rhodes, and Cyclades and Ionian Islands
Currency drachma
GNP per capita (PPP) (US$) 14,595 (1999)
Resources bauxite, nickel, iron pyrites, magnetite, asbestos, marble, salt, chromite, lignite
Population 10,645,000 (2000 est)
Population density (per sq km) 81 (1999 est)
Language Greek (official)
Religion Greek Orthodox, over 96%; about 1% Muslim
Time difference GMT +2

 ■ CIA ■ LP ■ RG ■ WTG

■ Ancient City of Athens

http://www.indiana.edu/~kglowack/athens/

Photographic archive of the archaeological and architectural remains of ancient Athens, Greece. As the site says, 'It is intended primarily as a resource for students of classical art & archaeology, civilization, languages, and history'. However, there is much here of interest for the general browser.

■ Corfu, Greece

http://travel.lycos.com/Destinations/Europe/Greece/Corfu/

Large source of information on the northernmost of Greece's Ionian Islands. All aspects of the island's history, archaeology, and culture are covered here. There is a map and details of accommodation, places of interest, and local transport.

■ Internet Guide to Greece

http://www.gogreece.com/

Annotated links to Greek-related resources, under headings such as arts and entertainment, culture, music, food, business and finance, news, and travel information.

■ Cultural Map of Hellas

http://www.culture.gr/2/21/maps/hellas.html

'Clickable' map allowing you to browse around contemporary Greece and discover detailed information about the different museums, archaeological sites, and monuments in each region.

■ Rhodes

http://rhodes.helios.gr/

Guide to the largest of Greece's Dodecanese islands. There is a good overall description. Details of the history and attractions of the towns on the island are supported by photographs. There is a wealth of practical information on transport, accommodation, and wining and dining.

■ About Peloponnese – Introduction

http://www.vacation.net.gr/p/pelopon.html

Comprehensive guide to Greece's Peloponnese region. Landscape, history, and attractions are described for all parts of this mountainous peninsula. There is also a map of the region.

GRENADA

Map page 134

Area (including the southern Grenadine Islands, notably Carriacou and Petit Martinique) 344 sq km/ 133 sq mi
Capital St. George's

Major towns/cities Grenville, Sauteurs, Victoria, Gouyave
Physical features southernmost of the Windward Islands; mountainous; Grand-Anse beach; Annandale Falls; the Great Pool volcanic crater
Currency East Caribbean dollar
GNP per capita (PPP) (US$) 5,847 (1999)
Population 94,000 (2000 est)
Population density (per sq km) 286 (1999 est)
Language English (official), some French-African patois
Religion Roman Catholic 53%, Anglican about 14%, Seventh Day Adventist, Pentecostal, Methodist
Time difference GMT –4

 ■ CIA ■ LP ■ WTG

GUATEMALA

Map page 134

National name República de Guatemala/Republic of Guatemala
Area 108,889 sq km/42,042 sq mi
Capital Guatemala

Major towns/cities Quezaltenango, Escuintla, Puerto Barrios (naval base), Chinautla
Physical features mountainous; narrow coastal plains; limestone tropical plateau in north; frequent earthquakes
Currency quetzal
GNP per capita (PPP) (US$) 3,517 (1999 est)
Resources petroleum, antimony, gold, silver, nickel, lead, iron, tungsten
Population 11,385,000 (2000 est)
Population density (per sq km) 102 (1999 est)
Language Spanish (official), 22 Mayan languages (45%)
Religion Roman Catholic 70%, Protestant 10%, traditional Mayan
Time difference GMT –6

 ■ CIA ■ LP ■ WTG

■ About Guatemala

http://www.tradepoint.org.gt/travelguate.html

Lively window onto Guatemala. The site includes extensive sections on the country's ancient history, colonial times, and modern period. Visitors are also treated to a helpful introduction to the people of contemporary Guatemala with colourful visual material, suggestions for fun and adventure, and a short presentation on the country's flora and fauna.

GUINEA
Map page 104

National name République de Guinée/Republic of Guinea
Area 245,857 sq km/94,925 sq mi
Capital Conakry
Major towns/cities Labé, Nzérékoré, Kankan, Kindia, Mamou, Siguiri
Physical features flat coastal plain with mountainous interior; sources of rivers Niger, Gambia, and Senegal; forest in southeast; Fouta Djallon, area of sandstone plateaux, cut by deep valleys
Currency Guinean franc
GNP per capita (PPP) (US$) 1,761 (1999)
Resources bauxite (world's top exporter of bauxite and second-largest producer of bauxite ore), alumina, diamonds, gold, granite, iron ore, uranium, nickel, cobalt, platinum
Population 7,430,000 (2000 est)
Population density (per sq km) 30 (1999 est)
Language French (official), Susu, Pular (Fulfude), Malinke, and other African languages
Religion Muslim 85%, Christian 6%, animist
Time difference GMT +/–0

■ CIA ■ LP ■ NA ■ WTG

GUINEA-BISSAU
Map page 104

National name República da Guiné-Bissau/Republic of Guinea-Bissau
Area 36,125 sq km/13,947 sq mi
Capital Bissau (and chief port)
Major towns/cities Bafatá, Bissorã, Bolama, Gabú, Bubaque, Cacheu, Catió, Farim
Physical features flat coastal plain rising to savannah in east
Currency Guinean peso
GNP per capita (PPP) (US$) 595 (1999)
Resources bauxite, phosphate, petroleum (largely unexploited)
Population 1,213,000 (2000 est)

Population density (per sq km) 33 (1999 est)

Language Portuguese (official), Crioulo (a Cape Verdean dialect of Portuguese), African languages

Religion animist 58%, Muslim 40%, Christian 5% (mainly Roman Catholic)

Time difference GMT +/–0

 ■ CIA ■ LP ■ NA ■ WTG

GUYANA

Map page 140

National name Cooperative Republic of Guyana

Area 214,969 sq km/82,999 sq mi

Capital Georgetown (and chief port)

Major towns/cities Linden, New Amsterdam, Bartica, Corriverton

Major ports New Amsterdam

Physical features coastal plain rises into rolling highlands with savannah in south; mostly tropical rainforest; Mount Roraima; Kaietur National Park, including Kaietur Falls on the Potaro (tributary of Essequibo) 250 m/821 ft

Currency Guyanese dollar

GNP per capita (PPP) (US$) 3,242 (1999 est)

Resources gold, diamonds, bauxite, copper, tungsten, iron, nickel, quartz, molybdenum

Population 861,000 (2000 est)

Population density (per sq km) 4 (1999 est)

Language English (official), Hindi, American Indian languages

Religion Christian 57%, Hindu 34%, Sunni Muslim 9%

Time difference GMT –3

 ■ CIA ■ LC ■ LP ■ WTG

■ Georgetown, Guyana
http://travel.lycos.com/Destinations/South_America/Guyana/Georgetown/

Profile of Guyana's attractive capital, Georgetown. There is a general introduction to the city's main features, and four sections – 'Visitors' guide', 'Culture and history', 'News and weather', and 'Entertainment' – each with links to further useful information about both the city and the country.

■ Guyana Online Tourist Guide
http://www.turq.com/guyana/

Colourful guide to the South American country Guyana. Aimed at the tourist, the site features illustrated pages describing the country's many attractions, as well as information on climate, language, and accommodation. A map of Guyana is also included.

HAITI

Map page 134

National name République d'Haïti/Republic of Haiti

Area 27,750 sq km/10,714 sq mi

Capital Port-au-Prince

Major towns/cities Cap-Haïtien, Gonaïves, Les Cayes, St. Marc, Carrefour, Delmas

Physical features mainly mountainous and tropical; occupies western third of Hispaniola Island in Caribbean Sea

Currency gourde

GNP per capita (PPP) (US$) 1,407 (1999 est)

Resources marble, limestone, calcareous clay, unexploited copper and gold deposits

Population 8,222,000 (2000 est)

Population density (per sq km) 291 (1999 est)

Language French (20%), Creole (both official)

Religion Christian 95% (of which 70% are Roman Catholic), voodoo 4%

Time difference GMT –5

 ■ CIA ■ LC ■ LP ■ WTG

■ Haiti Guide
http://www.haitiguide.com/

Detailed guide to Haiti. The site is divided into a number of

sections, including 'Geography', 'People', and 'Economy', each offering a number of facts and statistics on the country.

HONDURAS

Map page 134

National name República de Honduras/Republic of Honduras

Area 112,100 sq km/43,281 sq mi

Capital Tegucigalpa

Major towns/cities San Pedro Sula, La Ceiba, El Progreso, Choluteca, Juticalpa, Danlí

Major ports La Ceiba

Physical features narrow tropical coastal plain with mountainous interior, Bay Islands, Caribbean reefs

Currency lempira

GNP per capita (PPP) (US$) 2,254 (1999 est)

Resources lead, zinc, silver, gold, tin, iron, copper, antimony

Population 6,485,000 (2000 est)

Population density (per sq km) 56 (1999 est)

Language Spanish (official), English, American Indian languages

Religion Roman Catholic 97%

Time difference GMT –6

 ■ CIA ■ LC ■ LP ■ WTG

■ Honduras.Net
http://www.honduras.net/

Honduran culture, history, and tourist information Web site. Featuring descriptions of the Honduran constitution, a brief history, news, and local recipes, this page has something for everyone interested in this Central American country.

HUNGARY

Map page 50

National name Magyar Köztársaság/Republic of Hungary

Area 93,032 sq km/35,919 sq mi

Capital Budapest

Major towns/cities Miskolc, Debrecen, Szeged, Pécs, Győr, Nyíregyháza, Székesfehérvár, Kecskemét

Physical features Great Hungarian Plain covers eastern half of country; Bakony Forest, Lake Balaton, and Transdanubian Highlands in the west; rivers Danube, Tisza, and Raba; more than 500 thermal springs

Currency forint

GNP per capita (PPP) (US$) 10,479 (1999)

Resources lignite, brown coal, natural gas, petroleum, bauxite, hard coal

Population 10,036,000 (2000 est)

Population density (per sq km) 108 (1999 est)

Language Hungarian (official)

Religion Roman Catholic 65%, Calvinist 20%, other Christian denominations, Jewish, atheist

Time difference GMT +1

 ■ CIA ■ LC ■ LP ■ RG ■ WTG

■ Budapest: A Little Tour
http://www.fsz.bme.hu/hungary/budapest/budapest.html

Comprehensive guide to the city, including its history, detailed information on places of interest, transport, and entertainment. The site contains a gallery of maps and pictures, and some audio clips of Hungarian music.

■ Győr
http://www.arrabonet.gyor.hu/gyor/index-eng.html

Good guide to the Hungarian city. A guided tour of the town is accompanied by a series of photographs. There is a description of the sensitive and extensive post-1945 restoration of the city centre.

■ Hungarian Home Page
http://www.fsz.bme.hu/hungary/homepage.html

Masses of information about Hungary, including a virtual tour of Budapest, Hungarian–English and English–Hungarian dictionaries, and recipes for dishes from goulash to Transylvanian layered cabbage.

ICELAND

Map page 48

National name Lýðveldið Ísland/Republic of Iceland

Area 103,000 sq km/39,768 sq mi

Capital Reykjavík

Major towns/cities Akureyri, Kópavogur, Hafnarfjördur, Keflavík, Vestmannaeyjar

Physical features warmed by the Gulf Stream; glaciers and lava fields cover 75% of the country; active volcanoes (Hekla was once thought the gateway to Hell); geysers, hot springs, and new islands created offshore (Surtsey in 1963); subterranean hot water heats 85% of Iceland's homes; Sidujokull glacier moving at 100 metres a day

Currency krona

GNP per capita (PPP) (US$) 26,283 (1999)

Resources aluminium, diatomite, hydroelectric and thermal power, fish

Population 281,000 (2000 est)

Population density (per sq km) 3 (1999 est)

Language Icelandic (official)

Religion Evangelical Lutheran about 90%, other Protestant and Roman Catholic about 4%

Time difference GMT +/–0

 ■ CIA ■ LP ■ WTG

■ Iceland
http://www.iceland.org/

Official introduction to Iceland. There is easily accessible information on business, education, history, culture, and language. A tourist guide is supported by photos and a video clip. The site also includes a weather report, regularly updated Icelandic news, and an interactive map.

■ Reykjavik – Next Door to Nature
http://tourist.reykjavik.is/

Well-arranged bilingual source of information on the Icelandic capital. The needs of tourists and investors are well provided for, including sections on the history, accommodation, transport, cultural events, and entertainment. There are also a number of photographs.

INDIA

Map page 88

National name Bharat (Hindi)/India; Bharatiya Janarajya (unofficial)/Republic of India

Area 3,166,829 sq km/1,222,713 sq mi

Capital New Delhi

Major towns/cities Mumbai (formerly Bombay), Kolkata (formerly Calcutta), Chennai (formerly Madras), Bangalore, Hyderabad, Ahmadabad, Kanpur, Pune, Nagpur, Bhopal, Jaipur, Lucknow, Surat

Major ports Kolkata, Mumbai, Chennai

Physical features Himalayas on northern border; plains around rivers Ganges, Indus, Brahmaputra; Deccan peninsula south of the Narmada River forms plateau between Western and Eastern Ghats mountain ranges; desert in west; Andaman and Nicobar Islands, Lakshadweep (Laccadive Islands)

Currency rupee

GNP per capita (PPP) (US$) 2,149 (1999 est)

Resources coal, iron ore, copper ore, bauxite, chromite, gold, manganese ore, zinc, lead, limestone, crude oil, natural gas, diamonds

Population 1,013,662,000 (2000 est)

Population density (per sq km) 315 (1999 est)

Language Hindi, English, Assamese, Bengali, Gujarati, Kannada, Kashmiri, Konkani, Malayalam, Manipuri, Marathi, Nepali, Oriya, Punjabi, Sanskrit, Sindhi, Tamil, Telugu, Urdu (all official), more than 1,650 dialects

Religion Hindu 80%, Sunni Muslim 10%, Christian 2.5%, Sikh 2%, Buddhist, Jewish

Time difference GMT +5.5

 ■ CIA ■ LC ■ LP ■ RG ■ WTG

■ AgraOnline

http://www.agraonline.com/

Complete guide to the Indian city of Agra aimed at both tourists and residents alike. For the tourist, there is detailed information about the ways to travel to Agra and also where to stay once you get there. There are also notes on the places to visit, where to go shopping, and the best places to eat out. In a developing section for the resident, there are details of handicrafts and emporiums and also other trade information.

■ Goa

http://travel.indiamart.com/goa/

A useful background aimed mainly at tourists on India's premier holiday resort, which has information on attractions, excursions, shopping, and dining, in addition to a brief historical account of the island.

■ Government of India

http://www.indiagov.org/

Introduction to the politics, history, culture, and society of India. Additional links to relevant sites on the Web are provided. This site is run by the official tourist board and includes descriptions of all the major states, as well as more general background under such headings as 'News', 'Culture', 'Economy', and 'Sport'.

■ Bombay: The Gateway of India

http://www.fhraindia.com/home/cities/mumbai.htm

General outline of the city of Bombay (from 1995 known as Mumbai), including a detailed history section, important institutions, and pictures of landmarks. The introduction claims that the city's squalid reputation is outweighed by its charisma and its safety as a base from which to explore.

■ Calcutta

http://www.nd.edu/~kmukhopa/cal300/calcutta/

Detailed tour of the city of Kolkata (formerly Calcutta), including its people, architecture, economy, and history. There is also an overview of the museums, libraries, and other cultural institutions that can be found in this city.

■ Rajasthan

http://www.rajasthandiary.com/

Rajasthani traditions and spirit are captured at this site, with pictures and information on each of its major cities – Jaipur, Jodhpur, Udaipur, and Jaisalmer. You can also find out about cuisine, travel, accommodation, and historical landmarks.

INDONESIA
Map page 86

National name Republik Indonesia/ Republic of Indonesia
Area 1,904,569 sq km/ 735,354 sq mi
Capital Jakarta
Major towns/cities Surabaya, Bandung, Medan, Semarang, Palembang, Tangerang, Tanjungkarang-Telukbetung, Ujung Pandang, Malang
Major ports Surabaya, Semarang (Java), Ujung Pandang (Sulawesi)
Physical features comprises 13,677 tropical islands (over 6,000 of them are inhabited): the Greater Sundas (including Java, Madura, Sumatra, Sulawesi, and Kalimantan (part of Borneo)), the Lesser Sunda Islands/Nusa Tenggara (including Bali, Lombok, Sumbawa, Flores, Sumba, Alor, Lomblen, Timor, Roti, and Savu), Maluku/Moluccas (over 1,000 islands including Ambon, Ternate, Tidore, Tanimbar, and Halmahera), and Irian Jaya (part of New Guinea); over half the country is tropical rainforest; it has the largest expanse of peatlands in the tropics
Currency rupiah
GNP per capita (PPP) (US$) 2,439 (1999)
Resources petroleum (principal producer of petroleum in the Far East), natural gas, bauxite, nickel (world's third-largest producer), copper, tin (world's second-largest producer), gold, coal, forests
Population 212,107,000 (2000 est)
Population density (per sq km) 110 (1999 est)
Language Bahasa Indonesia (closely related to Malay; official), Javanese, Dutch, over 550 regional languages and dialects
Religion Muslim 87%, Protestant 6%, Roman Catholic 3%, Hindu 2% and Buddhist 1% (the continued spread of Christianity, together with an Islamic revival, have led to greater religious tensions)
Time difference GMT +7/9

 ■ CIA ■ LC ■ LP ■ RG ■ WTG

■ Indonesian Home Page

http://www.uni-stuttgart.de/indonesia/

List of resources relating to Indonesia and its people, with daily news updates, maps, and travel information. The site also contains some general information on this archipelago and regularly updated links to related Indonesian Web sites.

■ Bali

http://werple.mira.net.au/~wreid/bali_p1a.html

Guide to the Indonesian holiday destination of Bali. Aimed at the tourist, this site details what to do before you go, and what to do when you get there. There are also details of the area's history and geography, as well as features on festivals, and some useful travel information. The site also includes many images of Bali, and maps of the area.

IRAN
Map page 90

National name Jomhûrî-ye Eslâmi-ye Îrân/Islamic Republic of Iran
Area 1,648,000 sq km/ 636,292 sq mi
Capital Teheran
Major towns/cities Eşfahân, Mashhad, Tabrīz, Shīrāz, Ahvāz, Kermānshāh, Qom, Karaj
Major ports Abādān
Physical features plateau surrounded by mountains, including Elburz and Zagros; Lake Rezayeh; Dasht-e-Kavir desert; occupies islands of Abu Musa, Greater Tunb and Lesser Tunb in the Gulf
Currency rial
GNP per capita (PPP) (US$) 5,163 (1999)
Resources petroleum, natural gas, coal, magnetite, gypsum, iron ore, copper, chromite, salt, bauxite, decorative stone
Population 67,702,000 (2000 est)
Population density (per sq km) 41 (1999 est)
Language Farsi (official), Kurdish, Turkish, Arabic, English, French
Religion Shiite Muslim (official) 91%, Sunni Muslim 8%; Zoroastrian, Christian, Jewish, and Baha'i comprise about 1%
Time difference GMT +3.5

 ■ CIA ■ LC ■ LP ■ WTG

■ Iran Watch

http://www.harborwatchpub.com/iran/

Reference works about Iran and the country's leaders, government, economy, and culture. The main focus of the current site is 'Iranians in the news' – brief biographies of key Iranians including their career and political tendencies.

■ Iranian Cultural and Information Centre

http://tehran.stanford.edu/

First official Web site of Iran, comprising a wealth of information on Iranian culture and contemporary life. Amongst its attractions are included extensive presentations on literature of and about Iran, the Iranian past, cultural events, and travel opportunities. It also offers an impressive photo gallery with images of Iran and Persian art.

IRAQ
Map page 90

National name al-Jumhuriyya al'Iraqiyya/Republic of Iraq
Area 434,924 sq km/ 167,924 sq mi
Capital Baghdād
Major towns/cities Al Mawşil, Al Başrah, Kirkūk, Al Ḥillah, An Najaf, An Nāşirīyah, Arbīl
Major ports Al Başrah
Physical features mountains in north, desert in west; wide valley of rivers Tigris and Euphrates running northwest-southeast; canal linking Baghdād and The Gulf opened in 1992
Currency Iraqi dinar
GNP per capita (PPP) (US$) N/A
Resources petroleum, natural gas, sulphur, phosphates

Population 23,115,000 (2000 est)
Population density (per sq km) 52 (1999 est)
Language Arabic (80%) (official), Kurdish (15%), Assyrian, Armenian
Religion Shiite Muslim 60%, Sunni Muslim 37%, Christian 3%
Time difference GMT +3

 ■ CIA ■ LC ■ AN ■ LP ■ WTG

IRELAND, REPUBLIC OF
Map page 56

National name Poblacht Na hÉireann/ Republic of Ireland
Area 70,282 sq km/ 27,135 sq mi
Capital Dublin
Major towns/cities Cork, Limerick, Galway, Waterford, Dundalk, Bray
Major ports Cork, Dun Laoghaire, Limerick, Waterford, Galway
Physical features central plateau surrounded by hills; rivers Shannon, Liffey, Boyne; Bog of Allen; Macgillicuddy's Reeks, Wicklow Mountains; Lough Corrib, lakes of Killarney; Galway Bay and Aran Islands
Currency Irish pound, or punt Eireannach
GNP per capita (PPP) (US$) 19,180 (1999)
Resources lead, zinc, peat, limestone, gypsum, petroleum, natural gas, copper, silver
Population 3,730,000 (2000 est)
Population density (per sq km) 53 (1999 est)
Language Irish Gaelic, English (both official)
Religion Roman Catholic 92%, Church of Ireland, other Protestant denominations 3%
Time difference GMT +/–0

■ CIA ■ LP ■ RG ■ WTG

■ Complete Guide to Ireland

http://members.tripod.com/~AndrewGallagher/ireland/

Guide to the geography, history, and politics of Ireland. The site can be viewed with or without frames and also includes sections on sport, tourism, culture, and the Celts.

■ Cork Guide Online

http://www.cork-guide.ie/corkcity.htm

Good source of information on Ireland's third-largest city. A description of the city, its heritage, and attractions is accompanied by some fine photographs. There is also information on accommodation, entertainment, transport, and restaurants

■ Complete Guide to Galway

http://www.wombat.ie/galwayguide/

Thorough and well-arranged source of information on this western Irish county. The needs of residents, tourists, and investors are fully met with sections on attractions, transport, entertainment, accommodation, things to do with children, community groups, and local government services. In addition to a good summary of Galway's history, there are online versions of several detailed history books of the county.

■ Kerry Insight

http://www.kerry-insight.com/

Guide to the Irish county. This site includes sections on fishing, sports, entertainment, accommodation, places of historical interest, events and festivals, an extensive commercial directory, community organizations, guides to towns in the county, maps, and a weather report.

■ Government of Ireland

http://www.irlgov.ie/gov.htm

Complete guide to all the departments of the Irish government, including contact details. The 'Department of the taoiseach' includes a virtual tour of the parliament building, complete with the history of the position of taoiseach, or prime minister.

ISRAEL
Map page 94

National name Medinat Israel/State of Israel
Area 20,800 sq km/8,030 sq mi (as at 1949 armistice)
Capital Jerusalem (not recognized by the United Nations)

Major towns/cities Tel Aviv-Yafo, Haifa, Bat-Yam, Holon, Ramat Gan, Petah Tiqwa, Rishon le Ziyyon, Be'ér Sheva'

Major ports Tel Aviv-Yafo, Haifa, 'Akko (formerly Acre), Elat

Physical features coastal plain of Sharon between Haifa and Tel Aviv noted since ancient times for its fertility; central mountains of Galilee, Samaria, and Judea; Dead Sea, Lake Tiberias, and River Jordan Rift Valley along the east are below sea level; Negev Desert in the south; Israel occupies Golan Heights, West Bank, East Jerusalem, and Gaza Strip (the last was awarded limited autonomy, with West Bank town of Jericho, in 1993)

Currency shekel

GNP per capita (PPP) (US$) 16,867 (1999)

Resources potash, bromides, magnesium, sulphur, copper ore, gold, salt, petroleum, natural gas

Population 6,217,000 (2000 est)

Population density (per sq km) 293 (1999 est)

Language Hebrew, Arabic (both official), English, Yiddish, other European and west Asian languages

Religion Israel is a secular state, but the predominant faith is Judaism 80%; also Sunni Muslim (about 15%), Christian, and Druze

Time difference GMT +2

 ▪ CIA ▪ LC ▪ LP ▪ WTG

▪ Haifa

http://www.infotour.co.il/TourismArea/21001.html

Official site for Haifa and Israel. The top-level page has a historical overview and tourist information as well as a wonderfully illustrated section with practical and historical information for either visiting or learning about Israel's nature reserves and national parks. From this page a related site on Haifa Municipality can be accessed that provides further information on history, the local economy, culture, tourism, and investment opportunities.

▪ Bethlehem University

http://www.bethlehem.edu/

History of the town, guide to churches and religious institutions. This is site is part of the Web site of Bethlehem University.

▪ Applied Resource Institute – Jerusalem

http://www.arij.org/

Comprehensive Palestinian source of up-to-date information on geography, climate, water, agriculture, land use, and settlement activities in the West Bank. This site is indispensable for understanding the Israeli-Palestinian conflict over natural resources.

ITALY
Map page 64

National name Repubblica Italiana/ Italian Republic

Area 301,300 sq km/ 116,331 sq mi

Capital Rome

Major towns/cities Milan, Naples, Turin, Palermo, Genoa, Bologna, Florence

Major ports Naples, Genoa, Palermo, Bari, Catania, Trieste

Physical features mountainous (Maritime Alps, Dolomites, Apennines) with narrow coastal lowlands; continental Europe's only active volcanoes: Vesuvius, Etna, Stromboli; rivers Po, Adige, Arno, Tiber, Rubicon; islands of Sicily, Sardinia, Elba, Capri, Ischia, Lipari, Pantelleria; lakes Como, Maggiore, Garda

Currency lira

GNP per capita (PPP) (US$) 20,751 (1999)

Resources lignite, lead, zinc, mercury, potash, sulphur, fluorspar, bauxite, marble, petroleum, natural gas, fish

Population 57,298,000 (2000 est)

Population density (per sq km) 190 (1999 est)

Language Italian (official), German and Ladin (in the north), French (in the Valle d'Aosta region), Greek and Albanian (in the south)

Religion Roman Catholic 98% (state religion)

Time difference GMT +1

 ▪ CIA ▪ LP ▪ RG ▪ WTG

▪ Windows on Italy – History

http://www.mi.cnr.it/WOI/

Packed with information about the history and culture of Italy's regions and towns. This index leads to pages of information dealing with every major period from prehistoric times to the present day.

▪ History of Venice

http://www.doge.it/storia/storiai.htm

From the first inhabitants to the present day, this is a look at the origins and historical development of the Italian city of Venice. It includes numerous pictures and photographs of the city, and a map of the surrounding area.

▪ History of Sardinia

http://www.crs4.it/~luigi/SARDEGNA/sardegna.html

Illustrated history of Sardinia from prehistoric times to the modern age. There are many pictures of historical artefacts and their locations, as well as explanatory maps of the island.

▪ Florence and Tuscany

http://es.rice.edu/ES/humsoc/Galileo/Student_Work/Florence96/

Web site run by Rice University on Renaissance Florence and Tuscany. The site includes a tour of Florence, details of Florentine music, the Medici family, Florentine architecture, and details of modern life in the city and region.

▪ Sicilia

http://www.mi.cnr.it/WOI/deagosti/regions/sicilia.html#Sicilia

Well-arranged profile of the largest Mediterranean island. There is information on geography, landscape, flora and fauna, population, Sicilian dialects, the island's autonomous status, cultural heritage, and the economy. This site includes a map of the island and suggestions for tourists. There are also descriptions of the sights and history of Palermo, Catania, and other Sicilian cities.

▪ Rome, Italy

http://www.geocities.com/Athens/Forum/2680/

Huge source of information on 'the eternal city'. An offbeat introduction to the 'home of popes and pickpockets' leads to detailed information on the history, monuments, and modern attractions of the Italian capital. There is a weather report, links to local media, and access to a large number of guides to Rome.

▪ Milan, Italy

http://www.smau.it/magellano/english/ciaomi99/

Good source of information on Italy's second-largest city. There is extensive coverage of history, attractions, accommodation, culture, entertainment, and commercial services. There are links to the latest financial information, the weather, an entertainment guide, and the trilingual site of the local football team, A C Milan.

JAMAICA
Map page 134

Area 10,957 sq km/4,230 sq mi

Capital Kingston

Major towns/cities Montego Bay, Spanish Town, Portmore, May Pen

Physical features mountainous tropical island; Blue Mountains (so called because of the haze over them)

Currency Jamaican dollar

GNP per capita (PPP) (US$) 3,276 (1999)

Resources bauxite (one of world's major producers), marble, gypsum, silica, clay

Population 2,583,000 (2000 est)

Population density (per sq km) 234 (1999 est)

Language English (official), Jamaican Creole

Religion Protestant 70%, Rastafarian

Time difference GMT –5

 ▪ CIA ▪ LP ▪ RG ▪ WTG

▪ JamaicaTravel.com

http://www.jamaicatravel.com/

Official site of the Jamaica Tourist Board. A colourful site, this guide covers everything the visitor needs to know, such as where to stay, what to do, and what to see. There is also a calendar to keep you abreast of events in Jamaica, and a visitor's forum to share questions and advice with other visitors.

JAPAN
Map page 82

National name Nihon-koku/State of Japan

Area 377,535 sq km/145,766 sq mi

Capital Tōkyō

Major towns/cities Yokohama, Ōsaka, Nagoya, Fukuoka, Kita-Kyūshū, Kyōto, Sapporo, Kobe, Kawasaki, Hiroshima

Major ports Ōsaka, Nagoya, Yokohama, Kobe

Physical features mountainous, volcanic (Mount Fuji, volcanic Mount Aso, Japan Alps); comprises over 1,000 islands, the largest of which are Hokkaido, Honshu, Kyushu, and Shikoku

Currency yen

GNP per capita (PPP) (US$) 24,041 (1999)

Resources coal, iron, zinc, copper, natural gas, fish

Population 126,714,000 (2000 est)

Population density (per sq km) 335 (1999 est)

Language Japanese (official), Ainu

Religion Shinto, Buddhist (often combined), Christian (less than 1%)

Time difference GMT +9

 ▪ CIA ▪ LC ▪ LP ▪ RG ▪ WTG

▪ Japan Information Network

http://www.jinjapan.org/index.html

Searchable set of links to resources about Japan – its regions, society, culture, current events, and other aspects of Japanese life.

▪ Tokyo

http://www.pandemic.com/tokyo/

City guide to the Japanese capital Tokyo. There are also details of the city's history, geography, and features on festivals. The section on tourist information is supplemented with maps and photographs and contains a list of useful phone numbers.

▪ Kyoto Information

http://www.joho-kyoto.or.jp/Joho-KyotoHome/Infor/Infor/INFOR.html

Good guide to the Japanese port. An overview of Kyoto's 1,200 year history is supported with ample photos. In addition to a guide to the city's traditional crafts and industries, there is information on the contemporary business scene. Details of local attractions are also given at this site.

JORDAN
Map page 90

National name Al-Mamlaka al-Urduniyya al-Hashemiyyah/ Hashemite Kingdom of Jordan

Area 89,206 sq km/34,442 sq mi (excluding the West Bank 5,879 sq km/2,269 sq mi)

Capital Ammān

Major towns/cities Zarqā', Irbid, Ma'ān

Major ports Aqaba

Physical features desert plateau in east; Rift Valley separates east and west banks of River Jordan

Currency Jordanian dinar

GNP per capita (PPP) (US$) 3,542 (1999)

Resources phosphates, potash, shale

Population 6,669,000 (2000 est)

Population density (per sq km) 73 (1999 est)

Language Arabic (official), English

Religion over 90% Sunni Muslim (official religion), small communities of Christians and Shiite Muslims

Time difference GMT +2

▪ CIA ▪ LC ▪ AN ▪ LP ▪ WTG

▪ Hashemite Kingdom of Jordan

http://www.websofjordan.com.jo/

Unofficial site, with links to documents about Jordan's politics, history and culture, economy, tourism, and education opportunities.

▪ Pictures of Jordan

http://www.geocities.com/TheTropics/Cabana/2973/Jordan.html

Impressive collection of photographs from Jordan. This site includes photographs of some of Jordan's most interesting places

such as Petra, Mount Nebo, Wadi Rum, The Dead Sea, and Aquaba, as well as an 'Impressions' section.

KAZAKHSTAN

Map page 76

National name Kazak Respublikasy/Republic of Kazakhstan

Area 2,717,300 sq km/ 1,049,150 sq mi
Capital Astana (formerly Akmola)
Major towns/cities Qaraghandy, Pavlodar, Semey, Petropavl, Shymkent
Physical features Caspian and Aral seas, Lake Balkhash; Steppe region; natural gas and oil deposits in the Caspian Sea
Currency tenge
GNP per capita (PPP) (US$) 4,408 (1999)
Resources petroleum, natural gas, coal, bauxite, chromium, copper, iron ore, lead, titanium, magnesium, tungsten, molybdenum, gold, silver, manganese
Population 16,223,000 (2000 est)
Population density (per sq km) 6 (1999 est)
Language Kazakh (related to Turkish; official), Russian
Religion Sunni Muslim 50–60%, Russian Orthodox 30–35%
Time difference GMT +6

 ■ CIA ■ LC ■ LP ■ WTG

KENYA

Map page 106

National name Jamhuri ya Kenya/ Republic of Kenya
Area 582,600 sq km/ 224,941 sq mi
Capital Nairobi
Major towns/cities Mombasa, Kisumu, Nakuru, Eldoret, Nyeri
Major ports Mombasa
Physical features mountains and highlands in west and centre; coastal plain in south; arid interior and tropical coast; semi-desert in north; Great Rift Valley, Mount Kenya, Lake Nakuru (salt lake with world's largest colony of flamingos), Lake Turkana (Rudolf)
Currency Kenyan shilling
GNP per capita (PPP) (US$) 975 (1999)
Resources soda ash, fluorspar, salt, limestone, rubies, gold, vermiculite, diatonite, garnets
Population 30,080,000 (2000 est)
Population density (per sq km) 51 (1999 est)
Language English, Kiswahili (both official), many local dialects
Religion Roman Catholic 28%, Protestant 8%, Muslim 6%, traditional tribal religions
Time difference GMT +3

 ■ CIA ■ LP ■ RG ■ NA ■ WTG

■ **Kenyaweb**
http://www.kenyaweb.com/
Social, cultural, and political information about Kenya. This site includes travel-oriented information about this African country, including sections on safaris, national parks, key facts, and even a bus route guide.

KIRIBATI

Map page 112

National name Ribaberikan Kiribati/Republic of Kiribati
Area 717 sq km/277 sq mi
Capital Bairiki (on Tarawa atoll)
Major towns/cities principal islands are the Gilbert Islands, the Phoenix Islands, the Line Islands, Banaba
Major ports Bairiki, Betio (on Tarawa)
Physical features comprises 33 Pacific coral islands: the

Kiribati (Gilbert), Rawaki (Phoenix), Banaba (Ocean Island), and three of the Line Islands including Kiritimati (Christmas Island); island groups crossed by Equator and International Date Line
Currency Australian dollar
GNP per capita (PPP) (US$) 3,186 (1999)
Resources phosphate, salt
Population 83,000 (2000 est)
Population density (per sq km) 107 (1999 est)
Language English (official), Gilbertese
Religion Roman Catholic, Protestant (Congregationalist)
Time difference GMT –10/–11

 ■ CIA ■ LP ■ WTG

KUWAIT

Map page 95

National name Dowlat al-Kuwayt/ State of Kuwait

Area 17,819 sq km/6,879 sq mi
Capital Kuwait (and chief port)
Major towns/cities as-Salimiya, Ḥawallī, Al Farwānīyah, Abraq Kheetan, Al Jahrah, Al Aḥmadī, Al Fuḥayḥil
Physical features hot desert; islands of Faylakah, Bubiyan, and Warbah at northeast corner of Arabian Peninsula
Currency Kuwaiti dinar
GNP per capita (PPP) (US$) 24,270 (1997)
Resources petroleum, natural gas, mineral water
Population 1,972,000 (2000 est)
Population density (per sq km) 106 (1999 est)
Language Arabic (78%) (official), English, Kurdish (10%), Farsi (4%)
Religion Sunni Muslim 45%, Shiite Muslim 40%; Christian, Hindu, and Parsi about 5%
Time difference GMT +3

 ■ CIA ■ LC ■ AN ■ LP ■ WTG

KYRGYZSTAN

Map page 76

National name Kyrgyz Respublikasy/Kyrgyz Republic
Area 198,500 sq km/76,640 sq mi
Capital Bishkek (formerly Frunze)
Major towns/cities Osh, Karakol, Kyzyl-Kiya, Tokmak, Djalal-Abad
Physical features mountainous, an extension of the Tien Shan range
Currency som
GNP per capita (PPP) (US$) 2,223 (1999)
Resources petroleum, natural gas, coal, gold, tin, mercury, antimony, zinc, tungsten, uranium
Population 4,699,000 (2000 est)
Population density (per sq km) 24 (1999 est)
Language Kyrgyz (a Turkic language; official), Russian
Religion Sunni Muslim 70%, Russian Orthodox 20%
Time difference GMT +5

 ■ CIA ■ LC ■ LP ■ WTG

■ **Destination Kyrgyzstan**
http://www.peacecorps.gov/wws/guides/kyrgyzstan/
Peace Corps guide, for schoolchildren, to this tiny Central Asian state. There are classroom activities divided by age group and teachers' notes, as well as plentiful maps, illustrations, and guides to other Internet resources.

LAOS

Map page 84

National name Sathalanalat Praxathipatai Paxaxôn Lao/ Democratic People's Republic of Laos

---

Area 236,790 sq km/ 91,424 sq mi

Capital Vientiane
Major towns/cities Louangphrabang (the former royal capital), Pakxé, Savannakhet
Physical features landlocked state with high mountains in east; Mekong River in west; rainforest covers nearly 60% of land
Currency new kip
GNP per capita (PPP) (US$) 1,726 (1999)
Resources coal, tin, gypsum, baryte, lead, zinc, nickel, potash, iron ore; small quantities of gold, silver, precious stones
Population 5,433,000 (2000 est)
Population density (per sq km) 22 (1999 est)
Language Lao (official), French, English, ethnic languages
Religion Theravada Buddhist 85%, animist beliefs among mountain dwellers
Time difference GMT +7

 ■ CIA ■ LC ■ LP ■ WTG

■ **Laos – The Internet Travel Guide**
http://www.pmgeiser.ch/laos/
Written by a traveller for travellers, this is a useful resource for anyone visiting Laos in Southeast Asia. The guide is divided into a number of sections, offering advice on 'Climate', 'Events', 'Border crossing', and so on. A large part of the guide is devoted to the country's numerous attractions, ranging from the Ho Chi Minh trail to the Plain of Jars.

LATVIA
Map page 48

National name Latvijas Republika/ Republic of Latvia
Area 63,700 sq km/24,594 sq mi
Capital Rīga
Major towns/cities Daugavpils, Liepāja, Jūrmala, Jelgava, Ventspils
Major ports Ventspils, Liepāja
Physical features wooded lowland (highest point 312 m/ 1,024 ft), marshes, lakes; 472 km/293 mi of coastline; mild climate
Currency lat
GNP per capita (PPP) (US$) 5,938 (1999)
Resources peat, gypsum, dolomite, limestone, amber, gravel, sand
Population 2,357,000 (2000 est)
Population density (per sq km) 38 (1999 est)
Language Latvian (official)
Religion Lutheran, Roman Catholic, Russian Orthodox
Time difference GMT +2

 ■ CIA ■ LC ■ LP ■ RG ■ WTG

■ **LatviaNet**
http://www.tvnet.lv/en/
Bilingual guide to this Eastern European country, including an overview of the Baltic region, as well as plenty of country-specific information on such topics as the environment, communications, government, tourism, and society.

■ **Riga in Your Pocket Home Page**
http://www.inyourpocket.com/Latvia/Riga_home.shtml
Guide to everything you ever wanted to know about this Baltic capital city. This is an electronic form of a published guide book and includes sections on such topics as language, media, what to see, getting there, and where to stay.

LEBANON
Map page 94

National name Jumhouria al-Lubnaniya/Republic of Lebanon
Area 10,452 sq km/4,035 sq mi
Capital Beirut (and chief port)
Major towns/cities Tripoli, Zahlé, Baabda, Ba'albek, Jezzine
Major ports Tripoli, Soûr, Saïda, Joûnié
Physical features narrow coastal plain; fertile Bekka valley

running north–south between Lebanon and Anti-Lebanon mountain ranges
Currency Lebanese pound
GNP per capita (PPP) (US$) 4,129 (1999)
Resources there are no commercially viable mineral deposits; small reserves of lignite and iron ore
Population 3,282,000 (2000 est)
Population density (per sq km) 310 (1999 est)
Language Arabic (official), French, Armenian, English
Religion Muslim 70% (Shiite 35%, Sunni 23%, Druze 7%, other 5%); Christian 30% (mainly Maronite 19%), Druze 3%; other Christian denominations including Greek Orthodox, Armenian, and Roman Catholic
Time difference GMT +2

 ■ CIA ■ LC ■ AN ■ LP ■ WTG

LESOTHO

Map page 108

National name Mmuso oa Lesotho/ Kingdom of Lesotho
Area 30,355 sq km/11,720 sq mi
Capital Maseru
Major towns/cities Qacha's Nek, Teyateyaneng, Mafeteng, Hlotse, Roma, Quthing
Physical features mountainous with plateaux, forming part of South Africa's chief watershed
Currency loti
GNP per capita (PPP) (US$) 2,058 (1999)
Resources diamonds, uranium, lead, iron ore; believed to have petroleum deposits
Population 2,153,000 (2000 est)
Population density (per sq km) 69 (1999 est)
Language English (official), Sesotho, Zulu, Xhosa
Religion Protestant 42%, Roman Catholic 38%, indigenous beliefs
Time difference GMT +2

 ■ CIA ■ LP ■ RG ■ NA ■ WTG

■ **Lesotho Page**
http://www.sas.upenn.edu/African_Studies/Country_Specific/Lesotho.html
Concise set of resources, including a map, US travel advisories, a database of its languages, and links to further sources of information.

LIBERIA

Map page 104

National name Republic of Liberia
Area 111,370 sq km/42,999 sq mi
Capital Monrovia (and chief port)
Major towns/cities Bensonville, Gbarnga, Voinjama, Buchanan
Major ports Buchanan, Greenville
Physical features forested highlands; swampy tropical coast where six rivers enter the sea
Currency Liberian dollar
GNP per capita (PPP) (US$) N/A
Resources iron ore, diamonds, gold, barytes, kyanite
Population 3,154,000 (2000 est)
Population density (per sq km) 26 (1999 est)
Language English (official), over 20 Niger-Congo languages
Religion animist 70%, Sunni Muslim 20%, Christian 10%
Time difference GMT +/–0

 ■ CIA ■ LP ■ NA ■ WTG

LIBYA

Map page 100

National name Al-Jamahiriyya al-'Arabiyya al-Libiyya ash-Sha'biyya al-Ishtirakiyya al-'Uzma/Great Libyan Arab

---

Socialist People's State of the Masses
Area 1,759,540 sq km/ 679,358 sq mi
Capital Tripoli
Major towns/cities Banghāzī, Miṣrātah, Az Zāwīyah, Tubruq, Ajdābiyā, Darnah
Major ports Banghāzī, Miṣrāta, Az Zāwīyah, Tubruq, Ajdābiyā, Darnah
Physical features flat to undulating plains with plateaux and depressions stretch southwards from the Mediterranean coast to an extremely dry desert interior
Currency Libyan dinar
GNP per capita (PPP) (US$) N/A
Resources petroleum, natural gas, iron ore, potassium, magnesium, sulphur, gypsum
Population 5,605,000 (2000 est)
Population density (per sq km) 3 (1999 est)
Language Arabic (official), Italian, English
Religion Sunni Muslim 97%
Time difference GMT +1

 ■ CIA ■ LC ■ AN ■ LP ■ NA ■ WTG

LIECHTENSTEIN

Map page 62

National name Fürstentum Liechtenstein/Principality of Liechtenstein
Area 160 sq km/62 sq mi
Capital Vaduz
Major towns/cities Balzers, Schaan, Eschen
Physical features landlocked Alpine; includes part of Rhine Valley in west
Currency Swiss franc
GNP per capita (PPP) (US$) 24,000 (1998 est)
Resources hydro power
Population 33,000 (2000 est)
Population density (per sq km) 199 (1999 est)
Language German (official), an Alemannic dialect
Religion Roman Catholic 80%, Protestant 7%
Time difference GMT +1

 ■ CIA ■ LP ■ WTG

■ **Liechtenstein National Tourist Guide**
http://www.news.li/
Official guide to the tiny principality. There is comprehensive information on history, attractions, sporting and recreational pursuits, entertainment, accommodation, and transport. There is a commercial directory, a listing of events, and a guide for philatelists.

LITHUANIA

Map page 48

National name Lietuvos Respublika/ Republic of Lithuania
Area 65,200 sq km/25,173 sq mi
Capital Vilnius
Major towns/cities Kaunas, Klaipėda, Šiauliai, Panevėžys
Physical features central lowlands with gentle hills in west and higher terrain in southeast; 25% forested; some 3,000 small lakes, marshes, and complex sandy coastline; River Nemunas
Currency litas
GNP per capita (PPP) (US$) 6,093 (1999)
Resources small deposits of petroleum, natural gas, peat, limestone, gravel, clay, sand
Population 3,670,000 (2000 est)
Population density (per sq km) 56 (1999 est)
Language Lithuanian (official)
Religion predominantly Roman Catholic; Evangelical Lutheran, also Russian Orthodox, Evangelical Reformist, and Baptist

---

Time difference GMT +2

 ■ CIA ■ LC ■ LP ■ RG ■ WTG

■ **Vilnius in Your Pocket Home Page**
http://www.inyourpocket.com/Lithuania/Vilnius_home.shtml
Guide to everything you ever wanted to know about this Baltic capital city. This is an electronic form of a published guide book and includes sections on such topics as language, media, what to see, getting there, and where to stay.

LUXEMBOURG

Map page 54

National name Grand-Duché de Luxembourg/Grand Duchy of Luxembourg
Area 2,586 sq km/998 sq mi
Capital Luxembourg
Major towns/cities Esch, Differdange, Dudelange, Pétange
Physical features on the River Moselle; part of the Ardennes (Oesling) forest in north
Currency Luxembourg franc
GNP per capita (PPP) (US$) 38,247 (1999)
Resources iron ore
Population 431,000 (2000 est)
Population density (per sq km) 165 (1999 est)
Language Letzeburgisch (a German-Moselle-Frankish dialect; official), English
Religion Roman Catholic about 95%, Protestant and Jewish 4%
Time difference GMT +1

 ■ CIA ■ LP ■ RG ■ WTG

■ **Luxembourg Tourist Office in London**
http://www.luxembourg.co.uk/
Detailed guide to Luxembourg that is aimed primarily at the tourist. The site comprises a number of articles, covering topics such as the country's museums, activities, and culture. Also featured is a directory of hotels, guesthouses, and youth hostels.

MACEDONIA

Map page 68

National name Republika Makedonija/Republic of Macedonia (official internal name); Poranesna Jugoslovenska Republika Makedonija/Former Yugoslav Republic of Macedonia (official international name)
Area 25,700 sq km/9,922 sq mi
Capital Skopje
Major towns/cities Bitola, Prilep, Kumanovo, Tetovo
Physical features mountainous; rivers: Struma, Vardar; lakes: Ohrid, Prespa, Scutari; partly Mediterranean climate with hot summers
Currency Macedonian denar
GNP per capita (PPP) (US$) 4,339 (1999)
Resources coal, iron, zinc, chromium, manganese, lead, copper, nickel, silver, gold
Population 2,024,000 (2000 est)
Population density (per sq km) 78 (1999 est)
Language Macedonian (related to Bulgarian; official), Albanian
Religion Christian, mainly Orthodox 67%; Muslim 30%
Time difference GMT +1

 ■ CIA ■ LP ■ WTG

■ **Macedonia – Frequently Asked Questions**
http://faq.rmacedonia.org/
Large source of well-presented information on the Balkan state. There is comprehensive information about the Macedonian language, literary heritage, history, cuisine, arts, economy, sports, and religion. This site also has regularly updated news of internal and external affairs.

■ **Skopje, Republic of Macedonia**
http://www.skopje.com.mk/angliski/prva.asp
Guide to the Macedonian capital. The economic basis and cultural

life of Skopje are described prior to a summary of the city's long history. There are also a number of photographs.

MADAGASCAR

Map page 108

National name Repoblikan'i Madagasikara/République de Madagascar/Republic of Madagascar
Area 587,041 sq km/ 226,656 sq mi

Capital Antananarivo
Major towns/cities Antsirabe, Mahajanga, Fianarantsoa, Toamasina, Ambatondrazaka
Major ports Toamasina, Antsirañana, Mahajanga
Physical features temperate central highlands; humid valleys and tropical coastal plains; arid in south
Currency Malagasy franc
GNP per capita (PPP) (US$) 766 (1999)
Resources graphite, chromite, mica, titanium ore, small quantities of precious stones, bauxite and coal deposits, petroleum reserves
Population 15,942,000 (2000 est)
Population density (per sq km) 26 (1999 est)
Language Malagasy, French (both official), local dialects
Religion over 50% traditional beliefs, Roman Catholic, Protestant about 40%, Muslim 7%
Time difference GMT +3

www. ▪ CIA ▪ LC ▪ LP ▪ NA ▪ WTG

■ **Madagascar**
http://www.geocities.com/SoHo/Atrium/5431/mad/Index.html
Virtual tour of the island of Madagascar that is aimed at the independent traveller. The tour consists of a series of photographs that follow a trail across the island. There is also a map of the island, as well as an article and fact sheet on Madagascar.

MALAWI

Map page 108

National name Republic of Malawi
Area 118,484 sq km/45,735 sq mi
Capital Lilongwe
Major towns/cities Blantyre, Mzuzu, Zomba
Physical features landlocked narrow plateau with rolling plains; mountainous west of Lake Nyasa
Currency Malawi kwacha
GNP per capita (PPP) (US$) 581 (1999)
Resources marble, coal, gemstones, bauxite and graphite deposits, reserves of phosphates, uranium, glass sands, asbestos, vermiculite
Population 10,925,000 (2000 est)
Population density (per sq km) 90 (1999 est)
Language English, Chichewa (both official), other Bantu languages
Religion Protestant 50%, Roman Catholic 20%, Muslim 2%, animist
Time difference GMT +2

www. ▪ CIA ▪ LP ▪ NA ▪ WTG

■ **Malawi – The Warm Heart of Africa**
http://members.tripod.com/~malawi/
Well-illustrated guide to Malawi. Aimed at the traveller, this site offers advice on the country's attractions and accommodation. Visitors can also learn a few words of Chichewa and sample some of the country's music.

MALAYSIA

Map page 86

National name Persekutuan Tanah Malaysia/Federation of Malaysia
Area 329,759 sq km/127,319 sq mi

Capital Kuala Lumpur
Major towns/cities Johor Bahru, Ipoh, George Town (on Penang island), Kuala Terengganu, Kuala Bahru, Petaling Jaya, Kelang, Kuching (on Sarawak), Kota Kinabalu (on Sabah)

Major ports Kelang
Physical features comprises peninsular Malaysia (the nine Malay states – Johore, Kedah, Kelantan, Negri Sembilan, Pahang, Perak, Perlis, Selangor, Terengganu – plus Malacca and Penang); states of Sabah and Sarawak on the island of Borneo; and the federal territory of Kuala Lumpur; 75% tropical rainforest; central mountain range; Mount Kinabalu, the highest peak in southeast Asia, is in Sabah; swamps in east; Niah caves (Sarawak)
Currency ringgit
GNP per capita (PPP) (US$) 7,963 (1999)
Resources tin, bauxite, copper, iron ore, petroleum, natural gas, forests
Population 22,244,000 (2000 est)
Population density (per sq km) 66 (1999 est)
Language Bahasa Malaysia (Malay; official), English, Chinese, Tamil, Iban, many local dialects
Religion Muslim (official) about 53%, Buddhist 19%, Hindu, Christian, local beliefs
Time difference GMT +8

www. ▪ CIA ▪ LP ▪ RG ▪ WTG

■ **Malaysia Home Page**
http://www.sesrtcic.org/members/mly/mlyhome.shtml
Information about Malaysian history, events, education, economy, politics, tourism, and laws, as well as hyperlinks to other relevant sites.

MALDIVES

Map page 88

National name Divehi Raajjeyge Jumhuriyya/Republic of the Maldives
Area 298 sq km/115 sq mi
Capital Malé
Physical features comprises 1,196 coral islands, grouped into 12 clusters of atolls, largely flat, none bigger than 13 sq km/5 sq mi, average elevation 1.8 m/6 ft; 203 are inhabited

Currency rufiya
GNP per capita (PPP) (US$) 3,545 (1999)
Resources coral (mining was banned as a measure against the encroachment of the sea)
Population 286,000 (2000 est)
Population density (per sq km) 933 (1999 est)
Language Divehi (a Sinhalese dialect; official), English, Arabic
Religion Sunni Muslim
Time difference GMT +5

www. ▪ CIA ▪ LP ▪ WTG

■ **Visit Maldives**
http://www.visitmaldives.com/intro.html
Well-designed guide to the Maldives from their Ministry of Tourism. The site features a 'Travel advisor', offering practical information on health and resorts. There is also a photo gallery, as well as sections devoted to sailing and diving in the Maldives.

MALI

Map page 102

National name République du Mali/Republic of Mali
Area 1,240,142 sq km/ 478,818 sq mi
Capital Bamako
Major towns/cities Mopti, Kayes, Ségou, Tombouctou, Sikasso
Physical features landlocked state with River Niger and savannah in south; part of the Sahara in north; hills in northeast; Senegal River and its branches irrigate the southwest

Currency franc CFA
GNP per capita (PPP) (US$) 693 (1999)
Resources iron ore, uranium, diamonds, bauxite, manganese, copper, lithium, gold
Population 11,234,000 (2000 est)
Population density (per sq km) 9 (1999 est)
Language French (official), Bambara, other African languages
Religion Sunni Muslim 80%, animist, Christian
Time difference GMT +/–0

www. ▪ CIA ▪ LP ▪ NA ▪ WTG

MALTA

Map page 64

National name Repubblika ta'Malta/Republic of Malta
Area 320 sq km/124 sq mi
Capital Valletta (and chief port)
Major towns/cities Rabat, Birkirkara, Qormi, Sliema
Major ports Marsaxlokk, Valletta

Physical features includes islands of Gozo 67 sq km/26 sq mi and Comino 3 sq km/1 sq mi
Currency Maltese lira
GNP per capita (PPP) (US$) 15,066 (1999 est)
Resources stone, sand; offshore petroleum reserves were under exploration 1988–95
Population 389,000 (2000 est)
Population density (per sq km) 1,206 (1999 est)
Language Maltese, English (both official)
Religion Roman Catholic 98%
Time difference GMT +1

www. ▪ CIA ▪ LP ▪ WTG

■ **Official Web Site of the Maltese Government**
http://www.magnet.mt/
Good source of official information on the Mediterranean island state. There are sections on the complex history, culture, government services, and the economy. The needs of tourists are also well catered for with a host of practical information.

MARSHALL ISLANDS
Map page 112

National name Majol/Republic of the Marshall Islands
Area 181 sq km/70 sq mi
Capital Dalap-Uliga-Darrit (on Majuro atoll)
Major towns/cities Ebeye (the only other town)
Physical features comprises the Ratak and Ralik island chains in the West Pacific, which together form an archipelago of 31 coral atolls, 5 islands, and 1,152 islets
Currency US dollar
GNP per capita (PPP) (US$) 1,860 (1999 est)
Resources phosphates
Population 64,000 (2000 est)
Population density (per sq km) 343 (1999 est)
Language Marshallese, English (both official)
Religion Christian (mainly Protestant) and Baha'i
Time difference GMT +12

www. ▪ CIA ▪ LP

■ **Internet Guide to the Republic of the Marshall Islands**
http://www.rmiembassyus.org/
Comprehensive official guide to the Micronesian state. The history, culture, cuisine, economy, government services, and democratic system of the Marshall Islands are fully explained with the help of maps and photos. RMI concerns about global warming, from a state whose highest elevation is a mere six metres, are set out.

MAURITANIA

Map page 102

National name Al-Jumhuriyya al-Islamiyya al-Mawritaniyya/ République Islamique Arabe et Africaine de Mauritanie/Islamic Republic of Mauritania

Area 1,030,700 sq km/ 397,953 sq mi

Capital Nouakchott (and chief port)

Major towns/cities Nouâdhibou, Kaédi, Zouérat, Kiffa, Rosso, Atâr

Major ports Nouâdhibou

Physical features valley of River Senegal in south; remainder arid and flat

Currency ouguiya

GNP per capita (PPP) (US$) 1,522 (1999 est)

Resources copper, gold, iron ore, gypsum, phosphates, sulphur, peat

Population 2,670,000 (2000 est)

Population density (per sq km) 3 (1999 est)

Language Hasaniya Arabic (official), Pulaar, Soninke, Wolof (all national languages), French (particularly in the south)

Religion Sunni Muslim (state religion)

Time difference GMT +/−0

 ■ CIA ■ LC ■ AN ■ LP ■ NA ■ WTG

MAURITIUS

Map page 108

National name Republic of Mauritius

Area 1,865 sq km/720 sq mi

Capital Port Louis (and chief port)

Major towns/cities Beau Bassin, Rose Hill, Curepipe, Quatre Bornes, Vacoas-Phoenix

Physical features mountainous, volcanic island surrounded by coral reefs; the island of Rodrigues is part of Mauritius; there are several small island dependencies

Currency Mauritian rupee

GNP per capita (PPP) (US$) 8,652 (1999)

Population 1,158,000 (2000 est)

Population density (per sq km) 616 (1999 est)

Language English (official), French, Creole (36%), Bhojpuri (32%), other Indian languages

Religion Hindu over 50%, Christian (mainly Roman Catholic) about 30%, Muslim 17%

Time difference GMT +4

 ■ CIA ■ LC ■ LP ■ WTG

MEXICO

Map page 134

National name Estados Unidos Mexicanos/United States of Mexico

Area 1,958,201 sq km/ 756,061 sq mi

Capital Mexico City

Major towns/cities Guadalajara, Monterrey, Puebla, Ciudad Juárez, Tijuana

Major ports 49 ocean ports

Physical features partly arid central highlands; Sierra Madre mountain ranges east and west; tropical coastal plains; volcanoes, including Popocatepetl; Rio Grande

Currency Mexican peso

GNP per capita (PPP) (US$) 7,719 (1999)

Resources petroleum, natural gas, zinc, salt, silver, copper, coal, mercury, manganese, phosphates, uranium, strontium sulphide

Population 98,881,000 (2000 est)

Population density (per sq km) 50 (1999 est)

Language Spanish (official), Nahuatl, Maya, Zapoteco, Mixteco, Otomi

Religion Roman Catholic about 90%

Time difference GMT −6/8

 ■ CIA ■ LC ■ LP ■ RG ■ WTG

■ Amigo! Mexico Online

http://www.mexonline.com/

Although a membership-based service, this page also offers lots of free information for the casual browser – with sections on activities, arts and culture, pre-Columbian history, and help for prospective travellers.

■ Mexico

http://www.trace-sc.com/index1.htm

Wide variety of fully-searchable information on Mexico. It includes pages about the ancient Aztec culture, including examples of some historical documents. On a more contemporary note, there is a current news section, as well as information on places for the tourist to visit.

■ Acapulco Today

http://accessmexico.com/acapulco/

Cornucopia of images, maps, news, and general information on this Mexican seaside resort – its culture, nightlife, food, and events. This site also includes details of local archaeological digs and an exploration of the Mayan world, with many links to other Mexican sites.

MICRONESIA, FEDERATED STATES OF

Map page 112

National name Federated States of Micronesia (FSM)

Area 700 sq km/270 sq mi

Capital Palikir (in Pohnpei island state)

Major towns/cities Kolonia (in Pohnpei), Weno (in Truk), Lelu (in Kosrae)

Physical features an archipelago of 607 equatorial, volcanic islands in the West Pacific

Currency US dollar

GNP per capita (PPP) (US$) 3,860 (1999 est)

Population 119,000 (2000 est)

Population density (per sq km) 165 (1999 est)

Language English (official), eight officially recognized local languages (including Trukese, Pohnpeian, Yapese, and Kosrean), a number of other dialects

Religion Christianity (mainly Roman Catholic in Yap state, Protestant elsewhere)

Time difference GMT +10 (Chuuk and Yap); +11 (Kosrae and Pohnpei)

 ■ CIA ■ LP ■ WTG

■ Welcome to the Federated States of Micronesia

http://www.fsmgov.org/

Official site of the four Pacific islands comprising the Federated States of Micronesia. The contents include a good history, information on culture, language, natural resources, and government structures. The tourist attractions of the four states of Micronesia are listed, together with practical information for visitors.

MOLDOVA

Map page 66

National name Republica Moldova/ Republic of Moldova

Area 33,700 sq km/13,011 sq mi

Capital Chişinău (Russian Kishinev)

Major towns/cities Tiraspol, Bălţi, Tighina

Physical features hilly land lying largely between the rivers Prut and Dniester; northern Moldova comprises the level plain of the Bălţi Steppe and uplands; the climate is warm and moderately continental

Currency leu

GNP per capita (PPP) (US$) 2,358 (1999)

Resources lignite, phosphorites, gypsum, building materials; petroleum and natural gas deposits discovered in the early 1990s were not yet exploited in 1996

Population 4,380,000 (2000 est)

Population density (per sq km) 130 (1999 est)

Language Moldovan (official), Russian, Gaganz (a Turkish dialect)

Religion Eastern Orthodox 98.5%; remainder Jewish

Time difference GMT +2

 ■ CIA ■ LC ■ LP ■ WTG

■ Chisinau, Moldova

http://www.beebware.com/directory/Regional/Europe/Moldova/ Localities/Chisinau/

Good introduction to the Moldovan capital. There is a description of the city, its economy, and history. Among the useful links are those to the Moldovan government site and one describing the revival of the Jewish community in Chisinau.

MONACO

Map page 58

National name Principauté de Monaco/ Principality of Monaco

Area 1.95 sq km/0.75 sq mi

Physical features steep and rugged; surrounded landwards by French territory; being expanded by filling in the sea

Currency French franc

GNP per capita (PPP) (US$) 27,000 (1999 est)

Population 34,000 (2000 est)

Population density (per sq km) 16,074 (1999 est)

Language French (official), Monégasgne (a mixture of the French Provençal and Italian Ligurian dialects), Italian

Religion Roman Catholic about 90%

Time difference GMT +1

 ■ CIA ■ LP ■ WTG

■ Monaco Online

http://www.monaco.mc

Colourful site on the Principality of Monaco. There are sections on all major aspects of life in the principality including the history of Monaco, the Grand Prix, financial advice, a business directory, the annual television festival, and a panorama of impressive shots of the cliffs and shores of Monaco.

MONGOLIA

Map page 78

National name Mongol Uls/ State of Mongolia

Area 1,565,000 sq km/ 604,246 sq mi

Capital Ulaanbaatar

Major towns/cities Darhan, Choybalsan, Erdenet

Physical features high plateau with desert and steppe (grasslands); Altai Mountains in southwest; salt lakes; part of Gobi desert in southeast; contains both the world's southernmost permafrost and northernmost desert

Currency tugrik

GNP per capita (PPP) (US$) 1,496 (1999)

Resources copper, nickel, zinc, molybdenum, phosphorites, tungsten, tin, fluorospar, gold, lead; reserves of petroleum discovered in 1994

Population 2,662,000 (2000 est)

Population density (per sq km) 2 (1999 est)

Language Khalkha Mongolian (official), Kazakh (in the province of Bagan-Ölgiy), Chinese, Russian, Turkic languages

Religion there is no state religion, but traditional lamaism (Mahayana Buddhism) is gaining new strength; the Sunni Muslim Kazakhs of Western Mongolia have also begun the renewal of their religious life, and Christian missionary activity has increased

Time difference GMT +8

 ■ CIA ■ LC ■ LP ■ WTG

■ Mongolia Page

http://www.ozemail.com.au/~mongolei/ENGLISH/engindex.html

Account of the geography, history, politics, and culture of Mongolia. It includes an overview of the country's art, music, and festivals, and a collection of images. This site also has information on travel and even some useful contacts in this country.

MOROCCO

Map page 102

National name Al-Mamlaka al-Maghribyya/Kingdom of Morocco
Area 458,730 sq km/ 177,115 sq mi (excluding Western Sahara)
Capital Rabat

Major towns/cities Casablanca, Marrakech, Fès, Oujda, Kénitra, Tétouan, Meknès
Major ports Casablanca, Tanger, Agadir
Physical features mountain ranges, including the Atlas Mountains northeast–southwest; fertile coastal plains in west
Currency dirham
GNP per capita (PPP) (US$) 3,190 (1999)
Resources phosphate rock and phosphoric acid, coal, iron ore, barytes, lead, copper, manganese, zinc, petroleum, natural gas, fish
Population 28,351,000 (2000 est)
Population density (per sq km) 61 (1999 est)
Language Arabic (75%) (official), Berber dialects (25%), French, Spanish
Religion Sunni Muslim; Christian and Jewish minorities
Time difference GMT +/–0

www. ▪ CIA ▪ AN ▪ LP ▪ RG ▪ WTG

▪ **Kingdom of Morocco**
http://www.mincom.gov.ma/
Morocco's official bilingual window on the World Wide Web. It offers articles on Moroccan identity, lifestyle, and culture, overviews of the different regions of the country, a fauna and flora section, a financial and investment guide, and information on the government.

MOZAMBIQUE

Map page 108

National name República de Moçambique/Republic of Mozambique
Area 799,380 sq km/ 308,640 sq mi
Capital Maputo (and chief port)
Major towns/cities Beira, Nampula, Nacala, Chimoio
Major ports Beira, Nacala, Quelimane
Physical features mostly flat tropical lowland; mountains in west; rivers Zambezi and Limpopo
Currency metical
GNP per capita (PPP) (US$) 797 (1999 est)
Resources coal, salt, bauxite, graphite; reserves of iron ore, gold, precious and semi-precious stones, marble, natural gas (all largely unexploited in 1996)
Population 19,680,000 (2000 est)
Population density (per sq km) 24 (1999 est)
Language Portuguese (official), 16 African languages
Religion animist 48%, Muslim 20%, Roman Catholic 16%, Protestant 16%
Time difference GMT +2

www. ▪ CIA ▪ LP ▪ NA ▪ WTG

▪ **Mozambique Home Page**
http://www.mozambique.mz/eindex.htm
Informative guide to Mozambique available in both English and Portuguese. The site consists of a number of sections, such as 'Government', 'Environment', 'Tourism', each of which contains a number of articles. The tourist guide is well worth a visit, and offers a useful insight into Mozambique's provinces and attractions.

MYANMAR (BURMA)

Map page 84

National name Pyedawngsu Myanma Naingngan/Union of Myanmar
Area 676,577 sq km/ 261,226 sq mi
Capital Yangon (formerly Rangoon) (and chief port)

Major towns/cities Mandalay, Moulmein, Bago, Bassein, Taung-gyi, Sittwe,
Physical features over half is rainforest; rivers Irrawaddy and Chindwin in central lowlands ringed by mountains in north, west, and east
Currency kyat
GNP per capita (PPP) (US$) 1,200 (1999 est)
Resources natural gas, petroleum, zinc, tin, copper, tungsten, coal, lead, gems, silver, gold
Population 45,611,000 (2000 est)
Population density (per sq km) 70 (1999 est)
Language Burmese (official), English, tribal dialects
Religion Hinayana Buddhist 89%, Christian 5%, Muslim 4%, animist 1.5%
Time difference GMT +6.5

www. ▪ CIA ▪ LP ▪ WTG

▪ **Shan People of Burma**
http://pw2.netcom.com/~burma/tai/pride.html
Pages devoted to the history, language, culture, and present situation of the Shan, or Tai, people of Burma. There is also a link to the Panglong Agreement that led to Burma's independence in 1948.

NAMIBIA

Map page 108

National name Republic of Namibia
Area 824,300 sq km/318,262 sq mi
Capital Windhoek
Major towns/cities Swakopmund, Rehoboth, Rundu
Major ports Walvis Bay
Physical features mainly desert (Namib and Kalahari); Orange River; Caprivi Strip links Namibia to Zambezi River; includes the enclave of Walvis Bay (area 1,120 sq km/432 sq mi)
Currency Namibian dollar
GNP per capita (PPP) (US$) 5,369 (1999 est)
Resources uranium, copper, lead, zinc, silver, tin, gold, salt, semi-precious stones, diamonds (one of the world's leading producers of gem diamonds), hydrocarbons, lithium, manganese, tungsten, cadmium, vanadium
Population 1,726,000 (2000 est)
Population density (per sq km) 2 (1999 est)
Language English (official), Afrikaans, German, Ovambo (51%), Nama (12%), Kavango (10%), other indigenous languages
Religion about 90% Christian (Lutheran, Roman Catholic, Dutch Reformed Church, Anglican)
Time difference GMT +1

www. ▪ CIA ▪ LP ▪ NA ▪ WTG

▪ **Namibia Online Travel Guide**
http://www.southafrica-travel.net/namibia/enamib.htm
Colourful and informative guide to Namibia. Not only are there descriptions of the country's history and government, but the site also covers Namibia's climate and vegetation as well as its many popular attractions.

NAURU

Map page 112

National name Republic of Nauru
Area 21 sq km/8.1 sq mi
Capital Yaren District (seat of government)
Physical features tropical coral

island in southwest Pacific; plateau encircled by coral cliffs and sandy beaches
Currency Australian dollar
GNP per capita (PPP) (US$) 11,800 (1994 est)
Resources phosphates
Population 12,000 (2000 est)
Population density (per sq km) 524 (1999 est)
Language Nauruan, English (both official)
Religion majority Protestant, Roman Catholic
Time difference GMT +12

www. ▪ CIA ▪ LP ▪ WTG

▪ **Nauru**
http://www.tbc.gov.bc.ca/cwgames/country/Nauru/nauru.html
Official guide to Nauru sponsored by the Commonwealth. The site provides information on the geography, history, culture, economy, government, and judicial system of this phosphate-rich island.

NEPAL

Map page 88

National name Nepál Adhirajya/ Kingdom of Nepal
Area 147,181 sq km/56,826 sq mi
Capital Kathmandu
Major towns/cities Biratnagar, Lalitpur, Bhadgaon, Pokhara, Birganj, Dahran Bazar

Physical features descends from the Himalayas in the north through foothills to the River Ganges plain in the south; Mount Everest, Mount Kanchenjunga
Currency Nepalese rupee
GNP per capita (PPP) (US$) 1,219 (1999)
Resources lignite, talcum, magnesite, limestone, copper, cobalt
Population 23,930,000 (2000 est)
Population density (per sq km) 159 (1999 est)
Language Nepali (official), Tibetan, numerous local languages
Religion Hindu 90%; Buddhist 5%, Muslim 3%, Christian
Time difference GMT +5.5

www. ▪ CIA ▪ LC ▪ LP ▪ RG ▪ WTG

NETHERLANDS

Map page 54

National name Koninkrijk der Nederlanden/Kingdom of the Netherlands
Area 41,863 sq km/16,163 sq mi
Capital Amsterdam (official), The Hague (legislative and judicial)

Major towns/cities Rotterdam, Utrecht, Eindhoven, Groningen, Tilburg, Maastricht, Apeldoorn, Nijmegen, Breda
Major ports Rotterdam
Physical features flat coastal lowland; rivers Rhine, Schelde, Maas; Frisian Islands
Territories Aruba, Netherlands Antilles (Caribbean)
Currency guilder
GNP per capita (PPP) (US$) 23,052 (1999)
Resources petroleum, natural gas
Population 15,786,000 (1999 est)
Population density (per sq km) 376 (1999 est)
Language Dutch (official)
Religion atheist 39%, Roman Catholic 31%, Dutch Reformed Church 14%, Calvinist 8%
Time difference GMT +1

www. ▪ CIA ▪ LP ▪ RG ▪ WTG

▪ **Amsterdam Channel Home Page**
http://www.channels.nl/adam.html
Provides an innovative 'tour' through Amsterdam through a wealth of images of the city – select the direction you wish to follow next and a view of that area is called up. There are links to details of some sites and a street map is also available.

▪ **Directorate IJsselmeer Region**
http://www.waterland.net/rdij/indexen.html

Well-presented official information from the Dutch Ministry of Works on 'the wet heart of the Netherlands'. There is a good history of the IJsselmeer polders and the scheme to tame the Zuider Zee. The operation of the complex water management scheme is fully explained. Several environmental aspects of the scheme are also covered.

■ **General Information on the Netherlands**
http://www.netherlands-embassy.org/
Well-organized official introduction to Holland from the Dutch embassy in Washington DC. The easily accessed sections include information on the country's history, economy, industry, defence, political structure, social policy, tourism, health, education, environment, and the media. There are a large number of useful links making this site a starting point for finding further information on Holland.

NEW ZEALAND

Map page 116

National name Aotearoa/
New Zealand
Area 268,680 sq km/
103,737 sq mi
Capital Wellington
Major towns/cities Auckland,
Hamilton, Christchurch, Manukau
Major ports Auckland, Wellington

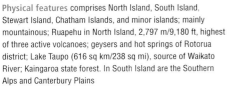

Physical features comprises North Island, South Island, Stewart Island, Chatham Islands, and minor islands; mainly mountainous; Ruapehu in North Island, 2,797 m/9,180 ft, highest of three active volcanoes; geysers and hot springs of Rotorua district; Lake Taupo (616 sq km/238 sq mi), source of Waikato River; Kaingaroa state forest. In South Island are the Southern Alps and Canterbury Plains
Territories Tokelau (three atolls transferred in 1926 from former Gilbert and Ellice Islands colony); Niue Island (one of the Cook Islands, separately administered from 1903: chief town Alafi); Cook Islands are internally self-governing but share common citizenship with New Zealand; Ross Dependency in Antarctica
Currency New Zealand dollar
GNP per capita (PPP) (US$) 16,566 (1999)
Resources coal, clay, limestone, dolomite, natural gas, hydroelectric power, pumice, iron ore, gold, forests
Population 3,862,000 (2000 est)
Population density (per sq km) 14 (1999 est)
Language English (official), Maori
Religion Christian (Anglican 18%, Roman Catholic 14%, Presbyterian 13%)
Time difference GMT +12

 ■ CIA ■ LP ■ WTG

■ **New Zealand on the Web**
http://nz.com/
Aimed at the prospective visitor, this site includes a virtual tour of New Zealand, a guidebook, and background information on its history and culture. There is also some information about trade and commerce.

■ **Welcome to Paradise – the Cook Islands**
http://www.ck/index.html
Very thorough guide to the Cook Islands in English and French. The many pages are packed with information on the geography, culture, economy, and government of the fifteen far-flung islands. The differing needs of tourists and investors are both met by this well-organized site.

■ **Hamilton – Heart of the Mighty Waikato**
http://www.chemistry.co.nz/waikato.htm
Well-arranged guide to the city of Hamilton and the Waikato region. The attractions, economy, and lifestyle of New Zealand's productive agricultural region are set out. There is also a history and practical information for visitors.

■ **Bay of Plenty**
http://www.bayofplenty.co.nz/
Guide to the towns, beaches, and other natural attractions of this New Zealand region. There is practical information for visitors and a suggested itinerary. There are also a number of links to other sites about towns and places around the inlet.

■ **NZHistory.net.nz**
http://www.nzhistory.net.nz/index.html
Site for anyone interested in the recent history of New Zealand, with illustrated extracts from history books and biographies

---

spanning the 19th and 20th centuries, and exhibitions on military, social, and government history. There are also links to other relevant sites and a discussion group.

NICARAGUA

Map page 134

National name República de Nicaragua/Republic of Nicaragua
Area 127,849 sq km/49,362 sq mi
Capital Managua
Major towns/cities León, Chinandega, Masaya, Granada, Estelí
Major ports Corinto, Puerto Cabezas, El Bluff
Physical features narrow Pacific coastal plain separated from broad Atlantic coastal plain by volcanic mountains and lakes Managua and Nicaragua; one of the world's most active earthquake regions
Currency cordoba
GNP per capita (PPP) (US$) 2,154 (1999)
Resources gold, silver, copper, lead, antimony, zinc, iron, limestone, gypsum, marble, bentonite
Population 5,074,000 (2000 est)
Population density (per sq km) 39 (1999 est)
Language Spanish (official), English, American Indian languages
Religion Roman Catholic 95%
Time difference GMT –6

 ■ CIA ■ LC ■ LP ■ WTG

■ **Experience Nicaragua**
http://library.thinkquest.org/17749/
Well-designed and in-depth resource for the study of Nicaragua. The site is divided into three main sections – 'History', 'Economy', and 'Culture' – with numerous articles and graphics in each. Travel advice is also included, as well as a number of video and audio clips that offer a sample of Nicaraguan society and culture.

NIGER

Map page 102

National name République du Niger/Republic of Niger
Area 1,186,408 sq km/
458,072 sq mi
Capital Niamey
Major towns/cities Zinder, Maradi, Tahoua, Agadez, Birnin Konni, Arlit
Physical features desert plains between hills in north and savannah in south; River Niger in southwest, Lake Chad in southeast
Currency franc CFA
GNP per capita (PPP) (US$) 727 (1999)
Resources uranium (one of world's leading producers), phosphates, gypsum, coal, cassiterite, tin, salt, gold; deposits of other minerals (including petroleum, iron ore, copper, lead, diamonds, and tungsten) have been confirmed
Population 10,730,000 (2000 est)
Population density (per sq km) 9 (1999 est)
Language French (official), Hausa (70%), Djerma, other ethnic languages
Religion Sunni Muslim 95%; also Christian, and traditional animist beliefs
Time difference GMT +1

 ■ CIA ■ LP ■ NA ■ WTG

■ **Margaret Rehm's Niger Page**
http://www.davison.k12.mi.us/academic/rehm1.htm
Photographic panorama of Niger with photos taken by a volunteer from the Peace Corps. The site is divided into four categories, related to agriculture, village life, livestock, and water.

NIGERIA

Map page 104

National name Federal Republic of Nigeria
Area 923,773 sq km/356,668 sq mi

Capital Abuja
Major towns/cities Ibadan, Lagos, Ogbomosho, Kano, Oshogbo, Ilorin, Abeokuta, Zaria, Port Harcourt
Major ports Lagos, Port Harcourt, Warri, Calabar

Physical features arid savannah in north; tropical rainforest in south, with mangrove swamps along coast; River Niger forms wide delta; mountains in southeast
Currency naira
GNP per capita (PPP) (US$) 744 (1999)
Resources petroleum, natural gas, coal, tin, iron ore, uranium, limestone, marble, forest
Population 111,506,000 (2000 est)
Population density (per sq km) 118 (1999 est)
Language English, French (both official), Hausa, Ibo, Yoruba
Religion Sunni Muslim 50% (in north), Christian 35% (in south), local religions 15%
Time difference GMT +1

 ■ CIA ■ LC ■ LP ■ NA ■ LP

NORTH KOREA

Map page 82

National name Chosun Minchu-chui Inmin Konghwa-guk/Democratic People's Republic of Korea
Area 120,538 sq km/
46,539 sq mi
Capital P'yŏngyang
Major towns/cities Hamhŭng, Ch'ŏngjin, Namp'o, Wŏnsan, Sinŭiji
Physical features wide coastal plain in west rising to mountains cut by deep valleys in interior
Currency won
GNP per capita (PPP) (US$) 950 (1999 est)
Resources coal, iron, lead, copper, zinc, tin, silver, gold, magnesite (has 40–50% of world's deposits of magnesite)
Population 24,039,000 (2000 est)
Population density (per sq km) 197 (1999 est)
Language Korean (official)
Religion Buddhist (predominant religion), Chondoist, Christian, traditional beliefs
Time difference GMT +9

 ■ CIA ■ LC ■ LP ■ WTG

■ **Korea Central News Agency**
http://www.kcna.co.jp/
Site of the Korea Central News Agency. This online propaganda from the North Korean regime provides a fascinating insight into the outlook of one of the world's most isolated regimes.

NORWAY

Map page 48

National name Kongeriket Norge/
Kingdom of Norway
Area 387,000 sq km/149,420 sq mi (including Svalbard and Jan Mayen)
Capital Oslo
Major towns/cities Bergen, Trondheim, Stavanger, Kristiansand, Drammen
Physical features mountainous with fertile valleys and deeply indented coast; forests cover 25%; extends north of Arctic Circle
Territories dependencies in the Arctic (Svalbard and Jan Mayen) and in Antarctica (Bouvet and Peter I Island, and Queen Maud Land)
Currency Norwegian krone
GNP per capita (PPP) (US$) 26,522 (1999)
Resources petroleum, natural gas, iron ore, iron pyrites, copper, lead, zinc, forests
Population 4,465,000 (2000 est)
Population density (per sq km) 14 (1999 est)
Language Norwegian (official), Saami (Lapp), Finnish

Religion Evangelical Lutheran (endowed by state) 88%; other Protestant and Roman Catholic 4%

Time difference GMT +1

 ■ CIA ■ LP ■ RG ■ WTG

■ Welcome to Bergen – The Gateway to the Fjords of Norway

http://www.uib.no/Bergen/reiseliv/tourist/index.html

Well-arranged guide to the Norwegian city. This site includes a history, a guide to local attractions, and information about cultural life. There are also details of how to visit nearby fjords.

■ Stavanger

http://www.stavanger-web.com/

Good introduction to the Norwegian seaport. There are over 1,800 links to sites about Stavanger, including information on history, accommodation, transport, cultural events, and entertainment.

■ Official Documentation and Information from Norway

http://odin.dep.no/odin/engelsk/index-b-n-a.html

Well-presented official introduction to all aspects of Norwegian life. There are sections on geography, economy, foreign policy, the political system, the royal family, culture, education, health, sport, and Norway's position within the European Union. Assistance is provided for those wishing to trace their Norwegian ancestry. The site is frequently updated with official Foreign Ministry information and news articles on Norwegian life.

■ Tromsø, Norway

http://www.destinasjontromso.no/eng_default.htm

Information on the northern Norwegian 'gateway to the Arctic'. An introduction to the city includes a weather report. A large number of photos are included of Tromso in all seasons including the midnight sun and northern lights.

OMAN
Map page 90

National name Saltanat `Uman/ Sultanate of Oman

Area 272,000 sq km/ 105,019 sq mi

Capital Muscat

Major towns/cities Sallālah, Ibrī, Suḥār, Al Buraymī, Nazwā, Sūr, Maṭraḥ

Physical features mountains to the north and south of a high arid plateau; fertile coastal strip; Jebel Akhdar highlands; Kuria Muria Islands

Currency Omani rial

GNP per capita (PPP) (US$) 8,690 (1997)

Resources petroleum, natural gas, copper, chromite, gold, salt, marble, gypsum, limestone

Population 2,542,000 (2000 est)

Population density (per sq km) 9 (1999 est)

Language Arabic (official), English, Urdu, other Indian languages

Religion Muslim 75% (predominantly Ibadhi Muslim), about 25% Hindu

Time difference GMT +4

 ■ CIA ■ LC ■ AN ■ LP ■ WTG

■ Oman Infoworld

http://Home.InfoRamp.Net/~emous/oman/about.htm

Variety of information on Oman. The site includes a useful fact sheet and a brief overview of the history of the country, sections on its art and architecture, heritage, traditions and customs, fashion and crafts, and sports pages, a presentation of the economic structure including pages on industry, trading, finance, banking, and transport, and a separate tourist information page.

PAKISTAN
Map page 90

National name Islami Jamhuriyya e Pakistan/Islamic Republic of Pakistan

Area 803,940 sq km/ 310,321 sq mi

Capital Islamabad

Major towns/cities Lahore,

Rawalpindi, Faisalabad, Karachi, Hyderabad, Multan, Peshawar, Gujranwala, Quetta

Major ports Karachi

Physical features fertile Indus plain in east, Baluchistan plateau in west, mountains in north and northwest; the 'five rivers' (Indus, Jhelum, Chenab, Ravi, and Sutlej) feed the world's largest irrigation system; K2 mountain; Khyber Pass

Currency Pakistan rupee

GNP per capita (PPP) (US$) 1,757 (1999)

Resources iron ore, natural gas, limestone, rock salt, gypsum, silica, coal, petroleum, graphite, copper, manganese, chromite

Population 156,483,000 (2000 est)

Population density (per sq km) 189 (1999 est)

Language Urdu (official), English, Punjabi, Sindhi, Pashto, Baluchi, other local dialects

Religion Sunni Muslim 90%, Shiite Muslim 5%; also Hindu, Christian, Parsee, Buddhist

Time difference GMT +5

 ■ CIA ■ LC ■ LP ■ WTG

PALAU
Map page 112

National name Belu'u era Belau/Republic of Palau

Area 508 sq km/196 sq mi

Capital Koror (on Koror island)

Physical features more than 350 (mostly uninhabited) islands, islets, and atolls in the west Pacific; warm, humid climate, susceptible to typhoons

Currency US dollar

GNP per capita (PPP) (US$) N/A

Population 19,000 (2000 est)

Population density (per sq km) 39 (1999 est)

Language Palauan, English (both official in most states)

Religion Christian, principally Roman Catholic; Modekngei (indigenous religion)

Time difference GMT +9

 ■ CIA ■ LP ■ WTG

■ Welcome to Palau

http://visit-palau.com/

Guide to the Pacific state. Information on local history and Palaun culture is supported by good photographs. There is practical information for tourists and for those interested in fishing and diving.

PANAMA
Map page 134

National name República de Panamá/Republic of Panama

Area 77,100 sq km/29,768 sq mi

Capital Panamá

Major towns/cities San Miguelito, Colón, David, La Chorrera, Santiago, Chitré, Changuinola

Major ports Colón, Cristóbal, Balboa

Physical features coastal plains and mountainous interior; tropical rainforest in east and northwest; Archipelago de las Perlas in Gulf of Panama; Panama Canal

Currency balboa

GNP per capita (PPP) (US$) 5,016 (1999)

Resources limestone, clay, salt; deposits of coal, copper, and molybdenum have been discovered

Population 2,856,000 (2000 est)

Population density (per sq km) 36 (1999 est)

Language Spanish (official), English

Religion Roman Catholic 93%

Time difference GMT –5

 ■ CIA ■ LC ■ LP ■ WTG

■ Welcome to the Panama Canal

http://www.pancanal.com/

Good source of information on the organization, operation, and

history of the Panama Canal from its operating authority. Photographs and diagrams help explain the workings of the canal and its system of locks.

PAPUA NEW GUINEA
Map page 112

National name Gau Hedinarai ai Papua-Matamata Guinea/ Independent State of Papua New Guinea

Area 462,840 sq km/178,702 sq mi

Capital Port Moresby (on East New Guinea)

Major towns/cities Lae, Madang, Arawa, Wewak, Goroka, Rabaul

Major ports Port Moresby, Rabaul

Physical features mountainous; swamps and plains; monsoon climate; tropical islands of New Ireland, New Britain, and Bougainville; Admiralty Islands, D'Entrecasteaux Islands, and Louisiade Archipelago; active volcanoes Vulcan and Tavurvur

Currency kina

GNP per capita (PPP) (US$) 2,263 (1999 est)

Resources copper, gold, silver; deposits of chromite, cobalt, nickel, quartz; substantial reserves of petroleum and natural gas (petroleum production began in 1992)

Population 4,807,000 (2000 est)

Population density (per sq km) 10 (1999 est)

Language English (official), pidgin English, over 700 local languages

Religion Christian 97%, of which 3% Roman Catholic; local pantheistic beliefs

Time difference GMT +10

 ■ CIA ■ LP ■ WTG

■ Papua New Guinea Information Site

http://www.niugini.com/

Guide to Papua New Guinea. The ethnic and linguistic diversity of the country and its complex history are well presented. A 'clickable' map accesses information on each of the country's twenty provinces.

PARAGUAY
Map page 142

National name República del Paraguay/Republic of Paraguay

Area 406,752 sq km/ 157,046 sq mi

Capital Asunción (and chief port)

Major towns/cities Ciudad del Este, Pedro Juan Caballero, San Lorenzo, Fernando de la Mora, Lambare, Luque, Capiatá

Major ports Concepción

Physical features low marshy plain and marshlands; divided by Paraguay River; Paraná River forms southeast boundary

Currency guaraní

GNP per capita (PPP) (US$) 4,193 (1999 est)

Resources gypsum, kaolin, limestone, salt; deposits (not commercially exploited) of bauxite, iron ore, copper, manganese, uranium; deposits of natural gas discovered in 1994; exploration for petroleum deposits ongoing mid-1990s

Population 5,496,000 (2000 est)

Population density (per sq km) 13 (1999 est)

Language Spanish (official), Guaraní (an indigenous Indian language)

Religion Roman Catholic (official religion) 85%; Mennonite, Anglican

Time difference GMT –3/4

 ■ CIA ■ LC ■ LP ■ WTG

■ Asuncion, Paraguay

http://travel.lycos.com/Destinations/South_America/Paraguay/Asuncion/

Profile of Asunción, capital of Paraguay. There is a general introduction to its main features, and four sections – 'Visitors' guide', 'Culture and history', 'News and weather', and

'Entertainment' – with links to photographs, and to further useful information in English and Spanish about the city and the country.

PERU

Map page 140

National name República del Perú/Republic of Peru
Area 1,285,200 sq km/ 496,216 sq mi
Capital Lima
Major towns/cities Arequipa, Iquitos, Chiclayo, Trujillo, Huancayo, Piura, Chimbote
Major ports Callao, Chimbote, Salaverry
Physical features Andes mountains running northwest–southeast cover 27% of Peru, separating Amazon river-basin jungle in northeast from coastal plain in west; desert along coast north–south (Atacama Desert); Lake Titicaca
Currency nuevo sol
GNP per capita (PPP) (US$) 4,387 (1999)
Resources lead, copper, iron, silver, zinc (world's fourth-largest producer), petroleum
Population 25,662,000 (2000 est)
Population density (per sq km) 20 (1999 est)
Language Spanish, Quechua (both official), Aymara, many indigenous dialects
Religion Roman Catholic (state religion) 95%
Time difference GMT –5

 ▪ CIA ▪ LC ▪ LP ▪ WTG

▪ **Peru Home Page**
http://www.rcp.net.pe/peru/peru_ingles.html
Basic information about Peru, including links to audio clips of Peruvian music and a section on ecotourism.

▪ **Arequipa, Peru**
http://travel.lycos.com/Destinations/South_America/Peru/Arequipa/
Profile of the 'white city' of Arequipa in southern Peru. There is a general introduction to the city's main features, and four sections – 'Visitors' guide', 'Culture and history', 'News and weather', and 'Entertainment' – each with links to further useful information in English and Spanish about both the city and the country.

▪ **Cuzco, Peru**
http://travel.lycos.com/Destinations/South_America/Peru/Cuzco/
Page devoted to the ancient Peruvian city of Cuzco. There is a general introduction to the city's main features, and four sections – 'Visitors' guide', 'Culture and history', 'News and weather', and 'Entertainment' – each with links to further useful information in English and Spanish about both the city and the country.

▪ **Lima, Peru**
http://travel.lycos.com/Destinations/South_America/Peru/Lima/
Profile of the historic city of Lima, capital of Peru. There is a general introduction to the city's main features, and four sections – 'Visitors' guide', 'Culture and history', 'News and weather', and 'Entertainment' – each with links to further useful information in English and Spanish about both the city and the country.

PHILIPPINES

Map page 84

National name Republika Ñg Pilipinas/Republic of the Philippines
Area 300,000 sq km/115,830 sq mi
Capital Manila (on Luzon island) (and chief port)
Major towns/cities Quezon City, Davao, Caloocan, Cebu, Bacolod, Cagayan de Oro, Iloilo
Major ports Cebu, Davao (on Mindanao), Iloilo, Zamboanga (on Mindanao)
Physical features comprises over 7,000 islands; volcanic mountain ranges traverse main chain north–south; 50% still forested. The largest islands are Luzon 108,172 sq km/ 41,754 sq mi and Mindanao 94,227 sq km/36,372 sq mi; others include Samar, Negros, Palawan, Panay, Mindoro, Leyte, Cebu, and the Sulu group; Pinatubo volcano (1,759 m/5,770 ft); Mindanao has active volcano Apo (2,954 m/9,690 ft) and mountainous rainforest

Currency peso
GNP per capita (PPP) (US$) 3,815 (1999)
Resources copper ore, gold, silver, chromium, nickel, coal, crude petroleum, natural gas, forests
Population 75,967,000 (2000 est)
Population density (per sq km) 248 (1999 est)
Language Filipino, English (both official), Spanish, Cebuano, Ilocano, more than 70 other indigenous languages
Religion Christian 94%, mainly Roman Catholic (84%), Protestant; Muslim 4%, local religions
Time difference GMT +8

 ▪ CIA ▪ LC ▪ LP ▪ WTG

▪ **Philippine History**
http://www.tribo.org/history.html
Well organized source of information about Philippine history, with sections on such topics as the islands' ancient past, the colonial period, the Spanish and US occupations, and the Philippine republic.

▪ **Kalayaan – A Celebration of the 100 Glorious Years of Philippine Independence**
http://www.abs-cbn.com/centennial/index.html
Information on the celebrations surrounding the centennial of Philippine independence. The Web site includes information on events taking place during the celebrations and in particular the Mythical Island exhibition site. Two further areas of the Web site which are still under construction describe heroes of the Philippines and provide images of the country.

POLAND

Map page 50

National name Rzeczpospolita Polska/ Republic of Poland
Area 312,683 sq km/120,726 sq mi
Capital Warsaw
Major towns/cities Łódź, Kraków, Wroclaw, Poznan, Gdansk, Szczecin, Katowice, Bydgoszcz, Lublin
Major ports Gdansk (Danzig), Szczecin (Stettin), Gdynia (Gdingen)
Physical features part of the great plain of Europe; Vistula, Oder, and Neisse rivers; Sudeten, Tatra, and Carpathian mountains on southern frontier
Currency zloty
GNP per capita (PPP) (US$) 7,894 (1999)
Resources coal (world's fifth-largest producer), copper, sulphur, silver, petroleum and natural gas reserves
Population 38,765,000 (2000 est)
Population density (per sq km) 124 (1999 est)
Language Polish (official)
Religion Roman Catholic 95%
Time difference GMT +1

 ▪ CIA ▪ LC ▪ LP ▪ RG ▪ WTG

▪ **Welcome to Warsaw**
http://www.geocities.com/Heartland/9413/warszawa.html
General guide to the city of Warsaw, its university, its weather, and additional information about other sights and attractions in Poland.

▪ **Cracow**
http://www.krakow.pl/en/
Official guide to the Polish World Heritage city. There are sections on the government structure, local economy, cultural life, and local attractions. There is practical information for visitors.

▪ **Polish National Tourist Office**
http://www.polandtour.org/
Well-designed guide to Poland that is available in English, French, and German. Choose from five different sections – 'About Poland', 'Travel information', 'Regions and cities', 'Recreation and sports', and 'Culture and arts' – each of which offers a number of in-depth articles about the country.

PORTUGAL

Map page 60

National name República Portuguesa/Republic of Portugal
Area 92,000 sq km/35,521 sq mi (including the Azores and Madeira)
Capital Lisbon
Major towns/cities Porto, Coimbra, Amadora, Setúbal, Funchal, Braga, Vila Nova de Gaia
Major ports Porto, Setúbal
Physical features mountainous in the north (Serra da Estrêla mountains); plains in the south; rivers Minho, Douro, Tagus (Tejo), Guadiana
Currency escudo
GNP per capita (PPP) (US$) 15,147 (1999)
Resources limestone, granite, marble, iron, tungsten, copper, pyrites, gold, uranium, coal, forests
Population 9,875,000 (2000 est)
Population density (per sq km) 107 (1999 est)
Language Portuguese (official)
Religion Roman Catholic 97%
Time difference GMT +/–0

 ▪ CIA ▪ LC ▪ LP ▪ RG ▪ WTG

▪ **Lisbon**
http://www.EUnet.pt/Lisboa/i/lisboa.html
Bilingual site with information about the 'city of the seven hills' including its history, a town map, and information on museums, restaurants, bars, and hotels. It also includes plenty of pictures and some audio clips from Portuguese artists.

▪ **Porto, Portugal**
http://travel.lycos.com/Destinations/Europe/Portugal/Porto/
Good source of practical, historical, and cultural information on Portugal's second city. The attractions of the city are well-presented. There is also information on the celebrated 'vinho do Porto' – port – which takes it name from the city.

▪ **Welcome to the Algarve**
http://www.nexus-pt.com/algarve.htm
Comprehensive source of information on the region of southern Portugal. A 'clickable' map gives access to information on the history, culture, and facilities of all the communities of the Algarve. There is a weather report and links to local newspapers, as well as more practical information for tourists and residents.

▪ **Madeira Web**
http://www.madeira-web.com/PagesUK/index.html
Guide to the Portuguese island group. There are sections on history, culture, food, and government services, in addition to practical information for visitors to Madeira and Porto Santo. There is also a bibliography giving links to further sources of information.

▪ **Portugal's National Tourism Service**
http://www.portugal-live.net/
Travel guide dedicated to those planning a holiday or business trip to Portugal. The site features a directory of hotels and resorts, together with information on the country's attractions and a number of maps to help you locate them! The site is kept up to date, especially the useful sections on current events and weather.

QATAR

Map page 95

National name Dawlat Qatar/ State of Qatar
Area 11,400 sq km/4,401 sq mi
Capital Doha (and chief port)
Major towns/cities Dukhān, ad Dawhah, ar-Rayyan, Umm Salal, Musay'īd, aš-Šahniyah
Physical features mostly flat desert with salt flats in south
Currency Qatari riyal
GNP per capita (PPP) (US$) N/A
Resources petroleum, natural gas, water resources
Population 599,000 (2000 est)
Population density (per sq km) 52 (1999 est)
Language Arabic (official), English
Religion Sunni Muslim 95%
Time difference GMT +3

▪ CIA ▪ LC ▪ AN ▪ LP ▪ WTG

ROMANIA

Map page 66

National name România/Romania
Area 237,500 sq km/91,698 sq mi
Capital Bucharest
Major towns/cities Brasov, Timisoara, Cluj-Napoca, Iaşi, Constanta, Galati, Craiova
Major ports Galati, Constanta, Brăila
Physical features mountains surrounding a plateau, with river plains in south and east. Carpathian Mountains, Transylvanian Alps; River Danube; Black Sea coast; mineral springs
Currency leu
GNP per capita (PPP) (US$) 5,647 (1999)
Resources brown coal, hard coal, iron ore, salt, bauxite, copper, lead, zinc, methane gas, petroleum (reserves expected to be exhausted by mid- to late 1990s)
Population 22,327,000 (2000 est)
Population density (per sq km) 94 (1999 est)
Language Romanian (official), Hungarian, German
Religion Romanian Orthodox 87%; Roman Catholic and Uniate 5%, Reformed/Lutheran 3%, Unitarian 1%
Time difference GMT +2

 ▪ CIA ▪ LC ▪ LP ▪ RG ▪ WTG

▪ **Virtual Romania**
http://internettrash.com/users/adrian/vromania.html
Canadian-based page with a large interactive map, links to news sources, and essays on aspects of Romanian history and culture.

▪ **Romania & Constitutional Monarchy**
http://www.geocities.com/CapitolHill/Lobby/8957/
Historical information, facts, and stories about Romania. The history of the Romanian Monarchy and, in particular, His Majesty, King Michael I, are described here. The Web site features interviews with the king and many photographs of members of the Romanian royal family.

▪ **Bucharest Online – Your Complete Guide to the Capital of Romania**
http://bucharest.com/bol/
Well-presented guide to the Romanian capital. Descriptions of the city and its history are accompanied by photographs. There is also transport and commercial information. This site also includes a search engine.

▪ **Cluj-Napoca**
http://travel.lycos.com/destinations/location.asp?pid=334499
Good guide to the Transylvanian capital. There is a description and history of the city in addition to information on museums, accommodation, and entertainment. There are a large number of useful links to other sources of information.

RUSSIA

Map page 74

National name Rossiiskaya Federatsiya/Russian Federation
Area 17,075,400 sq km/ 6,592,811 sq mi
Capital Moscow
Major towns/cities St. Petersburg, Nizhniy Novgorod, Samara, Yekaterinburg, Novosibirsk, Chelyabinsk, Kazan, Omsk, Perm', Ufa
Physical features fertile Black Earth district; extensive forests; the Ural Mountains with large mineral resources; Lake Baikal, world's deepest lake
Currency rouble
GNP per capita (PPP) (US$) 6,339 (1999)
Resources petroleum, natural gas, coal, peat, copper (world's fourth-largest producer), iron ore, lead, aluminium, phosphate rock, nickel, manganese, gold, diamonds, platinum, zinc, tin
Population 146,934,000 (2000 est)
Population density (per sq km) 9 (1999 est)
Language Russian (official) and many East Slavic, Altaic, Uralic, Caucasian languages
Religion traditionally Russian Orthodox; significant Muslim and Buddhist communities
Time difference GMT +2–12

 ▪ CIA ▪ LC ▪ LP ▪ RG ▪ WTG

▪ **Saint Petersburg, Russia**
http://www.geocities.com/TheTropics/Shores/6751/
Introduction to the city of St Petersburg, including a walking tour and a map, a guide to the city's museums, a history, and a regularly updated 'What's new' section.

▪ **Russia Alive!**
http://www.alincom.com/russ/index.htm
Guide to the new Russia, with links to related sites and a virtual tour of Moscow.

▪ **SovInform Bureau**
http://www.siber.com/sib/index.html
Dedicated to all things Russian, including information about Russian art, culture, humour, politics, communication and technology, travel, and visas. Advice and tools are also offered which enable you to 'Russify' your PC.

▪ **Russia Today**
http://www.russiatoday.com/
Extensive general information magazine on Russia. As well as daily press reviews and business news, the site provides sections on the government, the constitution, and coverage of hot current issues. Russia Today has a reputation for being on top of the news and getting its readers involved: it even offered them a chance to select the next Russian president in a mock election. A must for everyone wanting to make sense of the bewildering developments in the region.

▪ **Exploring Moscow**
http://www.interknowledge.com/russia/moscow01.htm
Walk about Moscow with stops at the Kremlin, Red Square, Lenin's Mausoleum, St Basil's cathedral, old Moscow, and other highlights of the Russian capital. The site also offers separate sections on fine art and theatrical life in the city, a calendar of events, and advice on accommodation.

▪ **Kalingrad in Your Pocket Home Page**
http://www.inyourpocket.com/Kaliningrad/index.shtml
Guide to everything you ever wanted to know about this Russian enclave. This is an electronic form of a published guide book and includes sections on such topics as language, media, what to see, getting there, and where to stay.

▪ **Novgorod the Great**
http://www.adm.nov.ru/web.nsf/pages/englishhome
Good guide to the culture and history of the Russian World Heritage city. There are descriptions and photos of the many historical buildings in Novgorod. This site includes sections on Novgorodian artistic and musical traditions.

RWANDA

Map page 106

National name Republika y'u Rwanda/Republic of Rwanda
Area 26,338 sq km/10,169 sq mi
Capital Kigali
Major towns/cities Butare, Ruhengeri, Gisenyi, Kibungo, Cyangugu
Physical features high savannah and hills, with volcanic mountains in northwest; part of lake Kivu; highest peak Mount Karisimbi 4,507 m/14,792 ft; Kagera River (whose headwaters are the source of the Nile)
Currency Rwandan franc
GNP per capita (PPP) (US$) 690 (1998)
Resources cassiterite (a tin-bearing ore), wolframite (a tungsten-bearing ore), natural gas, gold, columbo-tantalite, beryl
Population 7,733,000 (2000 est)
Population density (per sq km) 275 (1999 est)
Language Kinyarwanda, French (both official), Kiswahili
Religion about 50% animist; about 40% Christian, mainly Roman Catholic; 9% Muslim
Time difference GMT +2

 ▪ CIA ▪ LP ▪ NA ▪ WTG

ST. KITTS AND NEVIS

Map page 134

National name Federation of St. Christopher and St. Nevis
Area 262 sq km/101 sq mi (St. Kitts 168 sq km/65 sq mi, Nevis 93 sq km/36 sq mi)
Capital Basseterre (on St. Kitts) (and chief port)
Major towns/cities Charlestown (Nevis), Newcastle, Sandy Point Town, Dieppe Bay Town
Physical features both islands are volcanic; fertile plains on coast; black beaches
Currency East Caribbean dollar
GNP per capita (PPP) (US$) 9,801 (1999)
Population 38,000 (2000 est)
Population density (per sq km) 160 (1999 est)
Language English (official)
Religion Anglican 36%, Methodist 32%, other Protestant 8%, Roman Catholic 10%
Time difference GMT –4

 ▪ CIA ▪ LP ▪ WTG

▪ **St Kitts and Nevis Government**
http://www.stkittsnevis.net/index.html
The 'How we are governed' section provides a detailed explanation of the structure of this twin-island nation. There is also regularly updated information about the hurricanes that may affect the islands, as well as a biography of the 'Hero of the nation', Robert L Bradshaw, who was instrumental in securing their independence.

ST. LUCIA

Map page 134

Area 617 sq km/238 sq mi
Capital Castries
Major towns/cities Soufrière, Vieux Fort, Choiseul, Gros Islet
Major ports Vieux-Fort
Physical features mountainous island with fertile valleys; mainly tropical forest; volcanic peaks; Gros and Petit Pitons
Currency East Caribbean dollar
GNP per capita (PPP) (US$) 5,022 (1999)
Resources geothermal energy
Population 154,000 (2000 est)
Population density (per sq km) 252 (1999 est)
Language English (official), French patois
Religion Roman Catholic 85%; Anglican, Protestant
Time difference GMT –4

 ▪ CIA ▪ LP ▪ RG ▪ WTG

▪ **St Lucia Travel Guide**
http://www.stluciaguide.com/
Guide offering information on and reservations for accommodation and car rental in the Caribbean island of St Lucia. The site also includes advice on the country's many attractions, which include the national rainforest, sulphur springs, and scuba-diving.

ST. VINCENT AND THE GRENADINES

Map page 134

Area 388 sq km/150 sq mi (including islets of the Northern Grenadines 43 sq km/17 sq mi)
Capital Kingstown
Major towns/cities Georgetown, Châteaubelair, Dovers
Physical features volcanic mountains, thickly forested; La Soufrière volcano
Currency East Caribbean dollar
GNP per capita (PPP) (US$) 4,667 (1999)
Population 114,000 (2000 est)

Population density (per sq km) 355 (1999 est)
Language English (official), French patois
Religion Anglican, Methodist, Roman Catholic
Time difference GMT –4

 ■ CIA ■ LP ■ WTG

■ **St Vincent and the Grenadines – Jewels of the Caribbean**
http://www.svgtourism.com/
From the Department of Tourism, this guide offers detailed
information on St Vincent and the Grenadines. It includes advice
on travel information and accommodation, as well as sections on
the islands' attractions, sports, and current events. Be sure to visit
the site's photo album, which highlights the beauty of the islands.

SAMOA
Map page 112

National name 'O la Malo Tu
To'atasi o Samoa/Independent
State of Samoa
Area 2,830 sq km/1,092 sq mi
Capital Apia (on Upolu island)
(and chief port)
Major towns/cities Lalomanu,
Tuasivi, Falealupo, Falelatai, Taga
Physical features comprises South Pacific islands of Savai'i and
Upolu, with two smaller tropical islands and uninhabited islets;
mountain ranges on main islands; coral reefs; over half forested
Currency tala, or Samoan dollar
GNP per capita (PPP) (US$) 3,915 (1999)
Population 180,000 (2000 est)
Population density (per sq km) 63 (1999 est)
Language English, Samoan (both official)
Religion Congregationalist; also Roman Catholic, Methodist
Time difference GMT –11

 ■ CIA ■ LP ■ WTG

SAN MARINO
Map page 64

National name Serenissima Repubblica
di San Marino/Most Serene Republic of
San Marino
Area 61 sq km/24 sq mi
Capital San Marino
Major towns/cities
Serravalle, Faetano, Fiorentino,
Borgo Maggiore, Domagnano
Physical features the slope of Mount Titano
Currency Italian lira
GNP per capita (PPP) (US$) 20,000 (1997 est)
Resources limestone and other building stone
Population 27,000 (2000 est)
Population density (per sq km) 417 (1999 est)
Language Italian (official)
Religion Roman Catholic 95%
Time difference GMT +1

 ■ CIA ■ WTG

■ **Welcome to the Republic of San Marino**
http://inthenet.sm/rsm/intro.htm
Good official guide to the world's smallest and oldest nation state.
The history of San Marino is interestingly presented. There is a
wealth of practical information on attractions, accommodation,
and restaurants, as well as coverage of all aspects of political,
economic, and cultural life. The pride of the 25,000 Sammarinese
shines through this well-organized site.

SÃO TOMÉ AND PRÍNCIPE
Map page 104

National name República Democrática de São Tomé e Príncipe/
Democratic Republic of São Tomé and Príncipe
Area 1,000 sq km/386 sq mi
Capital São Tomé

Major towns/cities Santo António,
Sant Ana, Porto Alegre, Neves,
Santo Amaro
Physical features comprises two
main islands and several smaller
ones, all volcanic; thickly forested
and fertile
Currency dobra
GNP per capita (PPP) (US$) 1,335 (1999)
Population 147,000 (2000 est)
Population density (per sq km) 161 (1999 est)
Language Portuguese (official), Fang (a Bantu language),
Lungwa São Tomé (a Portuguese Creole)
Religion Roman Catholic 80%, animist
Time difference GMT +/–0

 ■ CIA ■ LP ■ NA ■ WTG

SAUDI ARABIA
Map page 90

National name Al-Mamlaka
al-'Arabiyya as-Sa'udiyya/Kingdom
of Saudi Arabia
Area 2,200,518 sq km/
849,620 sq mi
Capital Riyadh
Major towns/cities Jedda, Mecca, Medina, Ad Dammām,
Tabūk, Buraydah
Major ports Jedda, Ad Dammām, Jīzān, Yanbu
Physical features features desert, sloping to The Gulf from a
height of 2,750 m/9,000 ft in the west
Currency riyal
GNP per capita (PPP) (US$) 10,472 (1999 est)
Resources petroleum, natural gas, iron ore, limestone, gypsum,
marble, clay, salt, gold, uranium, copper, fish
Population 21,607,000 (2000 est)
Population density (per sq km) 9 (1999 est)
Language Arabic (official), English
Religion Sunni Muslim 85%; there is a Shiite minority
Time difference GMT +3

 ■ CIA ■ LC ■ AN ■ LP ■ WTG

■ **All Saudi**
http://www.all-saudi.com/en
A dedicated search engine for all things related to Saudi Arabia,
with maps, recipes, a travel guide, and useful Arabic phrases.

SENEGAL
Map page 104

National name République du
Sénégal/Republic of Senegal
Area 196,200 sq km/75,752 sq mi
Capital Dakar (and chief port)
Major towns/cities Thiès,
Kaolack, Saint-Louis, Ziguinchor,
Diourbel, Mbour
Physical features plains rising to
hills in southeast; swamp and tropical forest in southwest; River
Senegal; The Gambia forms an enclave within Senegal
Currency franc CFA
GNP per capita (PPP) (US$) 1,341 (1999)
Resources calcium phosphates, aluminium phosphates, salt,
natural gas; offshore deposits of petroleum to be developed
Population 9,481,000 (2000 est)
Population density (per sq km) 47 (1999 est)
Language French (official), Wolof, other ethnic languages
Religion mainly Sunni Muslim; Christian 4%, animist 1%
Time difference GMT +/–0

 ■ CIA ■ LP ■ NA ■ WTG

SEYCHELLES
Map page 108

National name Republic of
Seychelles
Area 453 sq km/174 sq mi
Capital Victoria (on Mahé island)
(and chief port)
Major towns/cities Cascade, Anse
Boileau, Takamaka
Physical features comprises two
distinct island groups: one, the Granitic group, concentrated, the
other, the Outer or Coralline group, widely scattered; totals over
100 islands and islets
Currency Seychelles rupee
GNP per capita (PPP) (US$) 10,381 (1999)
Resources guano; natural gas and metal deposits were being
explored mid-1990s
Population 77,000 (2000 est)
Population density (per sq km) 174 (1999 est)
Language Creole (an Asian, African, European mixture) (95%),
English, French (all official)
Religion Roman Catholic 90%
Time difference GMT +4

 ■ CIA ■ LC ■ LP ■ NA ■ WTG

■ **Seychelles Super Site**
http://www.sey.net/
Immodestly-named guide to the Seychelles that lives up to its
title. The site contains a wealth of information about the islands,
including sections on 'Accommodation', 'What to see & do', and
'Activities'. The 'Travellers' information' section is particularly
useful for locating advice about visas, money, and health.

SIERRA LEONE
Map page 104

National name Republic of Sierra
Leone
Area 71,740 sq km/27,698 sq mi
Capital Freetown
Major towns/cities Koidu, Bo,
Kenema, Makeni
Major ports Bonthe
Physical features mountains in east;
hills and forest; coastal mangrove swamps
Currency leone
GNP per capita (PPP) (US$) 414 (1999)
Resources gold, diamonds, bauxite, rutile (titanium dioxide)
Population 4,854,000 (2000 est)
Population density (per sq km) 66 (1999 est)
Language English (official), Krio (a Creole language), Mende,
Limba, Temne
Religion animist 45%, Muslim 44%, Protestant 8%, Roman
Catholic 3%
Time difference GMT +/–0

 ■ CIA ■ LP ■ NA ■ WTG

SINGAPORE
Map page 86

National name Repablik Singapura/
Republic of Singapore
Area 622 sq km/240 sq mi
Capital Singapore
Physical features comprises
Singapore Island, low and flat,
and 57 small islands; Singapore
Island is joined to the mainland by
causeway across Strait of Johore
Currency Singapore dollar
GNP per capita (PPP) (US$) 27,024 (1999)
Resources granite
Population 3,567,000 (2000 est)
Population density (per sq km) 5,662 (1999 est)

Language Malay, Mandarin Chinese, Tamil, English (all official), other Indian languages, Chinese dialects
Religion Buddhist, Taoist, Muslim, Hindu, Christian
Time difference GMT +8

 ▪ CIA ▪ LC ▪ LP ▪ RG ▪ WTG

▪ Singapore
http://www.stb.com.sg/
Guide to Singapore. History, geography, and travel information, as well as features on festivals, make up the majority of the tourist- and business-oriented information on this site. However, there is also a useful 'Tourist news' features with regularly updated information on events in and around Singapore.

▪ Singapore – The People
http://www.sg/flavour/people.html
Comprehensive page devoted to the people of Singapore, their origins, religion, and customs. Scroll through the information, or click on headings, to find out about early immigration; birth, marriage and death; language and literacy; religions; and numerous local festivals.

▪ Singapore Government
http://www.gov.sg/
Official Web site of the Singapore government that includes an overview of the government departments, and a section dedicated to recent government campaigns. There is also the opportunity to send the government your comments and suggestions.

SLOVAK REPUBLIC

Map page 50

National name Slovenská Republika/ Slovak Republic
Area 49,035 sq km/18,932 sq mi
Capital Bratislava
Major towns/cities Košice, Nitra, Prešov, Banská Bystrica, Zilina, Trnava, Martin
Physical features Western range of Carpathian Mountains, including Tatra and Beskids in north; Danube plain in south; numerous lakes and mineral springs
Currency Slovak koruna (based on Czechoslovak koruna)
GNP per capita (PPP) (US$) 9,811 (1999)
Resources brown coal, lignite, copper, zinc, lead, iron ore, magnesite
Population 5,387,000 (2000 est)
Population density (per sq km) 110 (1999 est)
Language Slovak (official), Hungarian, Czech, other ethnic languages
Religion Roman Catholic (over 50%), Lutheran, Reformist, Orthodox, atheist 10%
Time difference GMT +1

 ▪ CIA ▪ LP ▪ RG ▪ WTG

▪ Slovakia Document Store
http://slovakia.eunet.sk/
Collection of resources in Slovak and English, including a traveller's guide and information about the country's geography, natural resources, history, culture, and religion.

SLOVENIA

Map page 62

National name Republika Slovenija/ Republic of Slovenia
Area 20,251 sq km/7,818 sq mi
Capital Ljubljana
Major towns/cities Maribor, Kranj, Celje, Velenje, Koper, Novo Mesto
Major ports Koper
Physical features mountainous; Sava and Drava rivers
Currency tolar
GNP per capita (PPP) (US$) 15,062 (1999)
Resources coal, lead, zinc; small reserves/deposits of natural gas, petroleum, salt, uranium
Population 1,986,000 (2000 est)
Population density (per sq km) 98 (1999 est)

Language Slovene (related to Serbo-Croat; official), Hungarian, Italian
Religion Roman Catholic 70%; Eastern Orthodox, Lutheran, Muslim
Time difference GMT +1

 ▪ CIA ▪ LP ▪ RG ▪ WTG

▪ Slovenia – Country Information
http://www.matkurja.com/eng/country-info/
Index of pages covering Slovenia. There is information about history, culture, food and drink, and places to visit, as well as Slovenia's economy and government.

▪ Ljubljana
http://www.ijs.si/slo/ljubljana/
Well-presented guide to the Slovenian capital. A 'clickable' map highlights points of interest in the city. There is history and a large number of photographs in addition to practical information for visitors.

SOLOMON ISLANDS

Map page 112

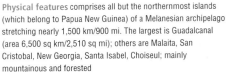

Area 27,600 sq km/ 10,656 sq mi
Capital Honiara (on Guadalcanal island) (and chief port)
Major towns/cities Gizo, Auki, Kirakira, Buala
Major ports Yandina
Physical features comprises all but the northernmost islands (which belong to Papua New Guinea) of a Melanesian archipelago stretching nearly 1,500 km/900 mi. The largest is Guadalcanal (area 6,500 sq km/2,510 sq mi); others are Malaita, San Cristobal, New Georgia, Santa Isabel, Choiseul; mainly mountainous and forested
Currency Solomon Island dollar
GNP per capita (PPP) (US$) 1,793 (1999)
Resources bauxite, phosphates, gold, silver, copper, lead, zinc, cobalt, asbestos, nickel
Population 444,000 (2000 est)
Population density (per sq km) 16 (1999 est)
Language English (official), pidgin English, more than 80 Melanesian dialects (85%), Papuan and Polynesian languages
Religion more than 80% Christian; Anglican 34%, Roman Catholic 19%, South Sea Evangelical, other Protestant, animist 5%
Time difference GMT +11

 ▪ CIA ▪ LP ▪ WTG

▪ Solomon Islands – Pearl of the Pacific
http://www.solomons.com/
Good source of information on the far-flung islands, atolls, and reefs comprising the state of the Solomon Islands. The contents include a good history, map, and information on the culture, investment opportunities, and government structures. There is also practical information for tourists.

SOMALIA

Map page 106

National name Jamhuuriyadda Soomaaliya/Republic of Somalia
Area 637,700 sq km/ 246,215 sq mi
Capital Mogadishu (and chief port)
Major towns/cities Hargeysa, Berbera, Kismaayo, Marka
Major ports Berbera, Marka, Kismaayo
Physical features mainly flat, with hills in north
Currency Somali shilling
GNP per capita (PPP) (US$) 600 (1999 est)
Resources chromium, coal, salt, tin, zinc, copper, gypsum, manganese, iron ore, uranium, gold, silver; deposits of petroleum and natural gas have been discovered but remain unexploited
Population 10,097,000 (2000 est)
Population density (per sq km) 15 (1999 est)
Language Somali, Arabic (both official), Italian, English

Religion Sunni Muslim; small Christian community, mainly Roman Catholic
Time difference GMT +3

 ▪ CIA ▪ LC ▪ AN ▪ LP ▪ NA ▪ WTG

SOUTH AFRICA

Map page 108

National name Republiek van Suid-Afrika/Republic of South Africa
Area 1,222,081 sq km/ 471,845 sq mi
Capital Cape Town (legislative), Pretoria (administrative), Bloemfontein (judicial)
Major towns/cities Johannesburg, Durban, Port Elizabeth, Vereeniging, Pietermaritzburg, Kimberley, Soweto, Tembisa
Major ports Cape Town, Durban, Port Elizabeth, East London
Physical features southern end of large plateau, fringed by mountains and lowland coastal margin; Drakensberg Mountains, Table Mountain; Limpopo and Orange rivers
Territories Marion Island and Prince Edward Island in the Antarctic
Currency rand
GNP per capita (PPP) (US$) 8,318 (1999)
Resources gold (world's largest producer), coal, platinum, iron ore, diamonds, chromium, manganese, limestone, asbestos, fluorspar, uranium, copper, lead, zinc, petroleum, natural gas
Population 40,377,000 (2000 est)
Population density (per sq km) 33 (1999 est)
Language English, Afrikaans, Xhosa, Zulu, Sesotho (all official), other African languages
Religion Dutch Reformed Church and other Christian denominations 77%, Hindu 2%, Muslim 1%
Time difference GMT +2

 ▪ CIA ▪ LC ▪ LP ▪ RG ▪ NA ▪ WTG

▪ South Africa.com – News & Information
http://www.southafrica.com/
South African site with general information about, and maps of, the country and links to over ten different newspapers, related organizations, and the South African yellow pages. You can also get hourly weather reports from various weather stations across the country. There are also links back to large sections on 'Travel & tourism', 'Business & finance', and 'Society & culture'.

▪ Cape Town
http://www.toptentravel.com/capetown.html
City guide to Cape Town, South Africa. Aimed at the tourist, this site details what to do before you go, and what to do when you get there. History, geography, and travel information, as well as features on festivals, make up the majority of the remaining information on this site, but there are also details of local transport and a list of useful telephone numbers. It also includes images of Cape Town, and maps of the city area.

SOUTH KOREA

Map page 82

National name Daehan Minguk/ Republic of Korea
Area 98,799 sq km/38,146 sq mi
Capital Seoul
Major towns/cities Pusan, Taegu, Inch'ŏn, Kwangju, Taejŏn, Songnam
Major ports Pusan, Inch'ŏn
Physical features southern end of a mountainous peninsula separating the Sea of Japan from the Yellow Sea
Currency won
GNP per capita (PPP) (US$) 14,637 (1999)
Resources coal, iron ore, tungsten, gold, molybdenum, graphite, fluorite, natural gas, hydroelectric power, fish
Population 46,844,000 (2000 est)
Population density (per sq km) 473 (1999 est)
Language Korean (official)
Religion Buddhist 48%, Confucian 3%, Christian 47%, mainly

Protestant; Chund Kyo (peculiar to Korea, combining elements of Shaman, Buddhist, and Christian doctrines)

Time difference GMT +9

 ▪CIA ▪LC ▪LP ▪WTG

▪ **Welcome to Pusan**

http://pusanweb.com/

Comprehensive guide to Korea's main port. There is useful information on Pusan's history, culture, cuisine, transport, and facilities for visitors.

SPAIN
Map page 60

National name España/Spain

Area 504,750 sq km/194,883 sq mi (including the Balearic and Canary islands)

Capital Madrid

Major towns/cities Barcelona, Valencia, Zaragoza, Sevilla, Málaga, Bilbao, Las Palmas (on Gran Canarias island), Murcia, Palma (on Mallorca)

Major ports Barcelona, Valencia, Cartagena, Málaga, Cádiz, Vigo, Santander, Bilbao

Physical features central plateau with mountain ranges, lowlands in south; rivers Ebro, Douro, Tagus, Guadiana, Guadalquivir; Iberian Plateau (Meseta); Pyrenees, Cantabrian Mountains, Andalusian Mountains, Sierra Nevada

Territories Balearic and Canary Islands; in North Africa: Ceuta, Melilla, Alhucemas, Chafarinas Islands, Peñón de Vélez

Currency peseta

GNP per capita (PPP) (US$) 16,730 (1999)

Resources coal, lignite, anthracite, copper, iron, zinc, uranium, potassium salts

Population 39,630,000 (2000 est)

Population density (per sq km) 79 (1999 est)

Language Spanish (Castilian; official), Basque, Catalan, Galician

Religion Roman Catholic 98%

Time difference GMT +1

 ▪CIA ▪LC ▪LP ▪RG ▪WTG

▪ **Barcelona, Spain**

http://travel.lycos.com/Destinations/Europe/Spain/Barcelona/

Guide to the Catalan capital. Information on the history, culture, traditions, churches, museums, architectural sites, cafes, transport system, and restaurants of Barcelona is well-presented. There is also a weather report, maps, and links to local media.

▪ **Bilbao, Spain**

http://www.bizkaia.net/bizkaia/English/General_information/Routes_and_places/I1VILLA.HTM

Good source of information on the northern Spanish city. This site includes a history of Bilbao, an introduction to Basque culture, details of local attractions, and information on transport and other government services. There is also practical information for visitors, a map, a weather report, and links to local newspapers.

▪ **Seville, Spain**

http://www.sol.com/

Substantial source of information on the Andalusian capital. The history, culture, and cuisine of Seville are well-presented. There is a wealth of practical information about accommodation, restaurants, the Alcazar and other local attractions, the famous fiesta, and cultural events.

▪ **Costa del Sol, Spain**

http://travel.lycos.com/Destinations/Europe/Spain/Costa_del_Sol/

Comprehensive source of information on the 300 km long Spanish coastal region. There is information on all the main resorts as well as the history and culture of the region. The needs of tourists, residents, and investors are all catered for. This site also includes a weather report and links to local media.

▪ **Balearic Islands, Spain**

http://travel.lycos.com/Destinations/Europe/Spain/Balearic_Islands/

Source of information on all of the Balearic Islands. The history, culture, and political status of this Mediterranean island chain are well-presented and there is a wealth of practical information for visitors and residents. This site also includes a weather report and links to local media and other sources of local information.

▪ **Turespaña**

http://www.tourspain.es/

Official site of the Spanish National Tourist Office, available in English, Spanish, French, and German. The site features articles on the country's cities and islands, arts and culture, and landscapes and beaches. There is also an accommodation directory containing listings of hotels, apartments, and campsites.

SRI LANKA
Map page 88

National name Sri Lanka Prajatantrika Samajavadi Janarajaya/Democratic Socialist Republic of Sri Lanka

Area 65,610 sq km/25,332 sq mi

Capital Sri Jayewardenapura Kotte

Major towns/cities Colombo, Kandy, Dehiwala-Mount Lavinia, Moratuwa, Jaffna, Galle

Major ports Colombo, Jaffna, Galle, Negombo, Trincomalee

Physical features flat in north and around coast; hills and mountains in south and central interior

Currency Sri Lankan rupee

GNP per capita (PPP) (US$) 3,056 (1999)

Resources gemstones, graphite, iron ore, monazite, rutile, uranium, iemenite sands, limestone, salt, clay

Population 18,827,000 (2000 est)

Population density (per sq km) 284 (1999 est)

Language Sinhala, Tamil (both official), English

Religion Buddhist 69%, Hindu 15%, Muslim 8%, Christian 8%

Time difference GMT +5.5

 ▪CIA ▪LC ▪LP ▪WTG

▪ **Sri Lanka Info Page**

http://www.lacnet.org/srilanka/

Host of links grouped under headings such as news, issues, culture, nature, food and cooking, and travel and tourism.

SUDAN
Map page 100

National name Al-Jumhuryyat es-Sudan/Republic of Sudan

Area 2,505,800 sq km/967,489 sq mi

Capital Khartoum

Major towns/cities Omdurman, Port Sudan, Juba, Wad Medani, El Obeid, Kassala, Gedaref, Nyala

Major ports Port Sudan

Physical features fertile Nile valley separates Libyan Desert in west from high rocky Nubian Desert in east

Currency Sudanese dinar

GNP per capita (PPP) (US$) 1,298 (1999)

Resources petroleum, marble, mica, chromite, gypsum, gold, graphite, sulphur, iron, manganese, zinc, fluorspar, talc, limestone, dolomite, pumice

Population 29,490,000 (2000 est)

Population density (per sq km) 12 (1999 est)

Language Arabic (51%) (official), 100 local languages

Religion Sunni Muslim 70%; also animist 25%, and Christian 5%

Time difference GMT +2

 ▪CIA ▪LC ▪AN ▪LP ▪NA ▪WTG

SURINAME
Map page 140

National name Republiek Suriname/Republic of Suriname

Area 163,820 sq km/63,250 sq mi

Capital Paramaribo

Major towns/cities Nieuw Nickerie, Moengo, Brokopondo, Nieuw Amsterdam, Albina, Groningen

---

Physical features hilly and forested, with flat and narrow coastal plain; Suriname River

Currency Suriname guilder

GNP per capita (PPP) (US$) 3,820 (1998 est)

Resources petroleum, bauxite (one of the world's leading producers), iron ore, copper, manganese, nickel, platinum, gold, kaolin

Population 417,000 (2000 est)

Population density (per sq km) 3 (1999 est)

Language Dutch (official), Spanish, Sranan (Creole), English, Hindi, Javanese, Chinese, various tribal languages

Religion Christian 47%, Hindu 28%, Muslim 20%

Time difference GMT −3.5

 ▪CIA ▪LP ▪WTG

▪ **Paramaribo, Suriname**

http://travel.lycos.com/Destinations/South_America/Suriname/Paramaribo/

Profile of Surinam's historic capital, Paramaribo. There is a general introduction to the city's main features, and four sections – 'Visitors' guide', 'Culture and history', 'News and weather', and 'Entertainment' – each with links to further information in English and Dutch about both the city and the country.

SWAZILAND
Map page 108

National name Umbuso wakaNgwane/Kingdom of Swaziland

Area 17,400 sq km/6,718 sq mi

Capital Mbabane, Lobamba

Major towns/cities Manzini, Big Bend, Mhlume, Nhlangano

Physical features central valley; mountains in west (Highveld); plateau in east (Lowveld and Lubombo plateau)

Currency lilangeni

GNP per capita (PPP) (US$) 4,200 (1999)

Resources coal, asbestos, diamonds, gold, tin, kaolin, iron ore, talc, pyrophyllite, silica

Population 1,008,000 (2000 est)

Population density (per sq km) 56 (1999 est)

Language Swazi, English (both official)

Religion about 60% Christian, animist

Time difference GMT +2

 ▪CIA ▪LP ▪RG ▪NA ▪WTG

▪ **Swaziland Internet**

http://www.directory.sz/internet/

Searchable guide to aspects of life in Swaziland today. Type in a word in the search box, or click on links to find out about the country's information technology, food and agriculture, religious organizations, tourism and leisure, and government and diplomatic institutions.

SWEDEN
Map page 48

National name Konungariket Sverige/Kingdom of Sweden

Area 450,000 sq km/173,745 sq mi

Capital Stockholm

Major towns/cities Göteborg, Malmö, Uppsala, Norrköping, Västerås, Linköping, Örebro, Helsingborg

Major ports Helsingborg, Malmö, Göteborg, Stockholm

Physical features mountains in west; plains in south; thickly forested; more than 20,000 islands off the Stockholm coast; lakes, including Vänern, Vättern, Mälaren, and Hjälmaren

Currency Swedish krona

GNP per capita (PPP) (US$) 20,824 (1999)

Resources iron ore, uranium, copper, lead, zinc, silver, hydroelectric power, forests

Population 8,910,000 (2000 est)

Population density (per sq km) 20 (1999 est)

Language Swedish (official), Finnish, Saami (Lapp)

Religion Evangelical Lutheran, Church of Sweden (established national church) 90%; Muslim, Jewish

Time difference GMT +1

 ▪ CIA ▪ LP ▪ RG ▪ WTG

▪ **Stockholm**

http://travel.excite.com/show/?loc=2693

Guide to the city of Stockholm. This site includes local news and weather, as well as details of places to visit, hotels, transportation, and maps of the area.

▪ **Sweden – Provincial Information**

http://www.sverigeturism.se/smorgasbord/

Guide to all 27 regions of Sweden from an active map on the home page. Each region contains sections of useful tourist information, such as 'History', 'Culture', 'Events and festivities', 'Family', and 'Major cities'. There is also a separate section called 'Swedish image gallery'.

▪ **Visby – World Heritage City**

http://www.ovpm.org/ville.asp?v=88

Information about the capital of Gotland and World Heritage site. There is a history of the Hanseatic League city and a description of its sights. There is also a link to information about UNESCO's criteria for World Heritage status.

▪ **Göteborg Tourist Information**

http://centralen.gp.se/tourist/

Good guide to the Swedish port city. This site includes a description, and detailed guides to attractions, history, restaurants, and accommodation. There is also a useful search engine.

SWITZERLAND
Map page 62

National name Schweizerische Eidgenossenschaft (German)/ Confédération Suisse (French)/ Confederazione Svizzera (Italian)/ Confederaziun Svizra (Romansch)/Swiss Confederation

Area 41,300 sq km/15,945 sq mi

Capital Bern

Major towns/cities Zürich, Geneva, Basel, Lausanne, Luzern, St. Gallen, Winterthur

Major ports river port Basel (on the Rhine)

Physical features most mountainous country in Europe (Alps and Jura mountains); highest peak Dufourspitze 4,634 m/ 15,203 ft in Apennines

Currency Swiss franc

GNP per capita (PPP) (US$) 27,486 (1999)

Resources salt, hydroelectric power, forest

Population 7,386,000 (2000 est)

Population density (per sq km) 178 (1999 est)

Language German (65%), French (18%), Italian (10%), Romansch (1%) (all official)

Religion Roman Catholic 46%, Protestant 40%

Time difference GMT +1

 ▪ CIA ▪ LP ▪ RG ▪ WTG

▪ **Geneva**

http://www.geneva-guide.ch/

An attractive 'alternative guide' to Geneva, affording an unusual glimpse of this Swiss city by means of four virtual tours of its streets. The site contains sections on local history as well as maps and guides to accommodation, local customs, language, and currency. There are also links to information on the country's other major cities.

▪ **Basel Online**

http://www.bsonline.ch/english/index.cfm

Large source of information on the Swiss city. There are sections on the history, culture, traditions, museums, nightlife, transport system, accommodation, and cuisine of the city. There are also a number of photos and links to regularly updated information on local events.

▪ **Welcome to Berne**

http://www.berntourismus.ch/

Large source of well-arranged official information on the Swiss federal capital. There are sections on the city's history, attractions, accommodation, as well as some lesser known facts.

This site also offers maps, a guide to the local cuisine, and a listing of restaurants.

SYRIA
Map page 90

National name al-Jumhuriyya al-Arabiyya as-Suriyya/Syrian Arab Republic

Area 185,200 sq km/ 71,505 sq mi

Capital Damascus

Major towns/cities Aleppo, Homs, Al Lādhiqīyah, Hamāh, Ar Raqqah, Dayr az Zawr

Major ports Al Lādhiqīyah

Physical features mountains alternate with fertile plains and desert areas; Euphrates River

Currency Syrian pound

GNP per capita (PPP) (US$) 2,761 (1999)

Resources petroleum, natural gas, iron ore, phosphates, salt, gypsum, sodium chloride, bitumen

Population 16,125,000 (2000 est)

Population density (per sq km) 85 (1999 est)

Language Arabic (89%) (official), Kurdish (6%), Armenian (3%), French, English, Aramaic, Circassian

Religion Sunni Muslim 74%; other Islamic sects 16%, Christian 10%

Time difference GMT +2

 ▪ CIA ▪ LC ▪ AN ▪ LP ▪ WTG

▪ **Cafe Syria**

http://www.cafe-syria.com/

Portal dedicated to promoting all things to do with Syria. Included here is descriptions of all major cities, facts and information for the tourist, and an overview of the history and government of the country.

TAIWAN
Map page 104

National name Chung-hua Min-kuo/ Republic of China

Area 36,179 sq km/13,968 sq mi

Capital T'aipei

Major towns/cities Kaohsiung, T'aichung, T'ainan, Panch'iao, Chungho, Sanch'ung

Major ports Kaohsiung, Chilung

Physical features island (formerly Formosa) off People's Republic of China; mountainous, with lowlands in west; Penghu (Pescadores), Jinmen (Quemoy), Mazu (Matsu) islands

Currency New Taiwan dollar

GNP per capita (PPP) (US$) 18,950 (1998 est)

Resources coal, copper, marble, dolomite; small reserves of petroleum and natural gas

Population 22,113,000 (1999 est)

Population density (per sq km) 685 (1999 est)

Language Chinese (dialects include Mandarin (official), Min, and Hakka)

Religion officially atheist; Buddhist 23%, Taoist 18%, I-Kuan Tao 4%, Christian 3%, Confucian and other 3%

Time difference GMT +8

 ▪ CIA ▪ LP ▪ WTG

▪ **Visitor's Guide to Taiwan**

http://peacock.tnjc.edu.tw/ADD/TOUR/main.html

Detailed guide to Taiwan. The site includes sections on the major attractions of Taiwan, including Lion's Head Mountain, black sand beaches, and 'Aborigine country'. There are also a selection of articles on Taiwan's culture, sports, and wildlife.

TAJIKISTAN
Map page 100

National name Jumhurii Tojikston/Republic of Tajikistan

Area 143,100 sq km/55,250 sq mi

Capital Dushanbe

Major towns/cities Khŭjand, Qŭrghonteppa, Kŭlob, Ŭroteppa, Kofarnihon

Physical features mountainous, more than half of its territory lying above 3,000 m/10,000 ft; huge mountain glaciers, which are the source of many rapid rivers

Currency Tajik rouble

GNP per capita (PPP) (US$) 981 (1999)

Resources coal, aluminium, lead, zinc, iron, tin, uranium, radium, arsenic, bismuth, gold, mica, asbestos, lapis lazuli; small reserves of petroleum and natural gas

Population 6,188,000 (2000 est)

Population density (per sq km) 43 (1999 est)

Language Tajik (related to Farsi; official), Russian

Religion Sunni Muslim; small Russian Orthodox and Jewish communities

Time difference GMT +5

 ▪ CIA ▪ LC ▪ LP ▪ WTG

TANZANIA
Map page 106

National name Jamhuri ya Muungano wa Tanzania/United Republic of Tanzania

Area 945,000 sq km/ 364,864 sq mi

Capital Dodoma (official), Dar es Salaam (administrative)

Major towns/cities Zanzibar, Mwanza, Mbeya, Tanga, Morogoro

Major ports Dar es Salaam

Physical features central plateau; lakes in north and west; coastal plains; lakes Victoria, Tanganyika, and Nyasa; half the country is forested; comprises islands of Zanzibar and Pemba; Mount Kilimanjaro, 5,895 m/19,340 ft, the highest peak in Africa; Olduvai Gorge; Ngorongoro Crater, 14.5 km/9 mi across, 762 m/ 2,500 ft deep

Currency Tanzanian shilling

GNP per capita (PPP) (US$) 478 (1999)

Resources diamonds, other gemstones, gold, salt, phosphates, coal, gypsum, tin, kaolin (exploration for petroleum in progress)

Population 33,517,000 (2000 est)

Population density (per sq km) 35 (1999 est)

Language Kiswahili, English (both official), Arabic (in Zanzibar), many local languages

Religion Muslim, Christian, traditional religions

Time difference GMT +3

 ▪ CIA ▪ LP ▪ NA ▪ WTG

▪ **Tanzania**

http://www.tanzania-online.gov.uk/tourism/tourism.html

Official Web site of the Tanzania High Commission in London, England. The site features articles on Tanzania's national parks, game reserves, and mountains, and also includes more general information on visa requirements, currency, and the best time of year to visit.

THAILAND
Map page 84

National name Ratcha Anachak Thai/ Kingdom of Thailand

Area 513,115 sq km/198,113 sq mi

Capital Bangkok (and chief port)

Major towns/cities Chiang Mai, Hat Yai, Khon Kaen, Songkhla, Nakhon Ratchasima, Nonthaburi, Udon Thani

Major ports Nakhon Sawan

Physical features mountainous, semi-arid plateau in northeast, fertile central region, tropical isthmus in south; rivers Chao Phraya, Mekong, and Salween

Currency baht

GNP per capita (PPP) (US$) 5,599 (1999)

Resources tin ore, lignite, gypsum, antimony, manganese, copper, tungsten, lead, gold, zinc, silver, rubies, sapphires, natural gas, petroleum, fish

Population 61,399,000 (2000 est)

Population density (per sq km) 119 (1999 est)

Language Thai, Chinese (both official), English, Lao, Malay, Khmer

Religion Buddhist 95%; Muslim 5%

Time difference GMT +7

 ▪ CIA ▪ LC ▪ LP ▪ RG ▪ WTG

▪ Bangkok
http://www.bu.ac.th/thailand/bangkok.html

Aspects of life in this thriving Thai city, described by some as the Venice of the East. This site, run by Bangkok University, is equally appropriate for the business traveller and the tourist, with maps, photographs, accommodation and embassy details, in addition to cultural background and culinary information.

▪ Thailand Information
http://www.bu.ac.th/thailand/thailand.html

Cultural background and tourist information combine with beautiful photographs to make this site the best starting point for a virtual tour of the 'Land of Smiles'. From Thai boxing to road distances, this Bangkok University run site has a whole range of facts about the country.

TOGO
Map page 104

National name République Togolaise/Togolese Republic

Area 56,800 sq km/21,930 sq mi

Capital Lomé

Major towns/cities Sokodé, Kpalimé, Kara, Atakpamé, Bassar, Tsévié

Physical features two savannah plains, divided by range of hills northeast–southwest; coastal lagoons and marsh; Mono Tableland, Oti Plateau, Oti River

Currency franc CFA

GNP per capita (PPP) (US$) 1,346 (1999 est)

Resources phosphates, limestone, marble, deposits of iron ore, manganese, chromite, peat; exploration for petroleum and uranium was under way in the early 1990s

Population 4,629,000 (2000 est)

Population density (per sq km) 79 (1999 est)

Language French (official), Ewe, Kabre, Gurma, other local languages

Religion animist about 50%, Catholic and Protestant 35%, Muslim 15%

Time difference GMT +/–0

 ▪ CIA ▪ LP ▪ NA ▪ WTG

TONGA
Map page 112

National name Pule'anga Fakatu'i 'o Tonga/Kingdom of Tonga

Area 750 sq km/290 sq mi

Capital Nuku'alofa (on Tongatapu island)

Major towns/cities Neiafu, Vaini

Physical features three groups of islands in southwest Pacific, mostly coral formations, but actively volcanic in west; of the 170 islands in the Tonga group, 36 are inhabited

Currency pa'anga, or Tongan dollar

GNP per capita (PPP) (US$) 4,281 (1999)

Population 99,000 (2000 est)

Population density (per sq km) 131 (1999 est)

Language Tongan (official), English

Religion mainly Free Wesleyan Church; Roman Catholic, Anglican

Time difference GMT +13

 ▪ CIA ▪ LP ▪ WTG

▪ Welcome to the Royal Kingdom of Tonga
http://www.vacations.tvb.gov.to/

Well-presented official guide to the Polynesian monarchy. There is a map, history, and guide to local culture and investment opportunities. The needs of tourists are met with practical information on attractions and accommodation. This site also includes an audio welcome message from Tonga's Crown Prince.

TRINIDAD AND TOBAGO
Map page 134

National name Republic of Trinidad and Tobago

Area 5,130 sq km/1,980 sq mi (Trinidad 4,828 sq km/ 1,864 sq mi and Tobago 300 sq km/115 sq mi)

Capital Port of Spain (and chief port)

Major towns/cities San Fernando, Arima, Point Fortin

Major ports Scarborough

Physical features comprises two main islands and some smaller ones in Caribbean Sea; coastal swamps and hills east–west

Currency Trinidad and Tobago dollar

GNP per capita (PPP) (US$) 7,262 (1999)

Resources petroleum, natural gas, asphalt (world's largest deposits of natural asphalt)

Population 1,295,000 (2000 est)

Population density (per sq km) 251 (1999 est)

Language English (official), Hindi, French, Spanish

Religion Roman Catholic 33%, Hindu 25%, Anglican 15%, Muslim 6%, Presbyterian 4%

Time difference GMT –4

 ▪ CIA ▪ LP ▪ RG ▪ WTG

▪ Welcome to Trinidad and Tobago!
http://www.visittnt.com/

Official Web site of Trinidad and Tobago tourism. This site provides information on the 'cool, serene, and green' country, divided into four main sections: 'General information', 'How to get here?', 'Where to stay?', and 'What to do here?'. Particularly worth a visit is the section on the annual carnival, which includes photographs and audio clips from previous years.

TUNISIA
Map page 102

National name Al-Jumhuriyya at-Tunisiyya/Tunisian Republic

Area 164,150 sq km/63,378 sq mi

Capital Tunis (and chief port)

Major towns/cities Sfax, L'Ariana, Bizerte, Gabès, Sousse, Kairouan

Major ports Sfax, Sousse, Bizerte

Physical features arable and forested land in north graduates towards desert in south; fertile island of Jerba, linked to mainland by causeway (identified with island of lotus-eaters); Shott el Jerid salt lakes

Currency Tunisian dinar

GNP per capita (PPP) (US$) 5,478 (1999)

Resources petroleum, natural gas, phosphates, iron, zinc, lead, aluminium fluoride, fluorspar, sea salt

Population 9,586,000 (2000 est)

Population density (per sq km) 58 (1999 est est)

Language Arabic (official), French

Religion Sunni Muslim (state religion); Jewish and Christian minorities

Time difference GMT +1

 ▪ CIA ▪ AN ▪ LP ▪ NA ▪ WTG

TURKEY
Map page 92

National name Türkiye Cumhuriyeti/Republic of Turkey

Area 779,500 sq km/300,964 sq mi

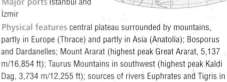

Capital Ankara

Major towns/cities İstanbul, İzmir, Adana, Bursa, Gaziantep, Konya, Mersin, Antalya, Diyarbakırduringr

Major ports İstanbul and İzmir

Physical features central plateau surrounded by mountains, partly in Europe (Thrace) and partly in Asia (Anatolia); Bosporus and Dardanelles; Mount Ararat (highest peak Great Ararat, 5,137 m/16,854 ft); Taurus Mountains in southwest (highest peak Kaldi Dag, 3,734 m/12,255 ft); sources of rivers Euphrates and Tigris in east

Currency Turkish lira

GNP per capita (PPP) (US$) 6,126 (1999)

Resources chromium, copper, mercury, antimony, borax, coal, petroleum, natural gas, iron ore, salt

Population 66,591,000 (2000 est)

Population density (per sq km) 84 (1999 est)

Language Turkish (official), Kurdish, Arabic

Religion Sunni Muslim 99%; Orthodox, Armenian churches

Time difference GMT +3

 ▪ CIA ▪ LC ▪ LP ▪ RG ▪ WTG

▪ Time Out Guide to Istanbul
http://www.ddg.com/ISTANBUL/

Virtual tour of Istanbul including a description of all the important sites, a library of pictures, and both 2D and 3D maps of the city.

▪ Discover Turkey
http://www.turkishnews.com/DiscoverTurkey/

Collection of pages on Turkey, its culture, and people. There is a country map, as well as sections on tourism, business, poetry, politics, and even carpets.

▪ Turkey
http://www.turkey.org/start.html

Guide to Turkey and Turkish culture, with links to the country's history as well as a detailed biography of Turkish leader Mustafa Kemal Ataturk.

▪ Pamukkale
http://www.exploreturkey.com/pamukkal.htm

Good guide to the history of Turkey's 'Holy City' and the current attractions of Pamukkale. Information on recent archaeological discoveries is presented here and there are also good pictures of the ruins and the spectacular geological formations in the area.

▪ Ankara
http://www.hitit.co.uk/regions/Ankara/About.html

Tourist guide to the Turkish capital. The history of the city is summarized and its public buildings, institutions, and attractions described. There is also a section outlining places of interest outside the capital.

▪ Izmir
http://www.turkey.org/tourism/izmir/izmir.htm

Good guide to Turkey's third biggest city – 'the pearl of the Aegean'. There is an outline of the city's history and heritage, and a guide to hotels, museums, and other places of interest. Information on nearby recreational areas is supported by photographs.

▪ NatureKey Online Travel Magazine
http://www.naturekey.com/

Devoted, not to the towns and cities of Turkey, but to the country's natural areas. The monthly issues of this online magazine include regular features such as 'news' and links to related outdoor pursuits sites. It also contains an image gallery, a 'clickable' map of Turkey's regions, and features on specific areas written by both visitors and local inhabitants.

TURKMENISTAN
Map page 76

National name Türkmenistan/ Turkmenistan

Area 488,100 sq km/ 188,455 sq mi

Capital Ashkhabad

Major towns/cities Chardzhev, Mary, Nebitdag, Dashkhovuz, Turkmenbashi

Major ports Turkmenbashi

Physical features about 90% of land is desert including the

173

Kara Kum 'Black Sands' desert (area 310,800 sq km/120,000 sq mi)
Currency manat
GNP per capita (PPP) (US$) 3,099 (1999)
Resources petroleum, natural gas, coal, sulphur, magnesium, iodine-bromine, sodium sulphate and different types of salt
Population 4,459,000 (2000 est)
Population density (per sq km) 9 (1999 est)
Language Turkmen (a Turkic language; official), Russian, Uzbek, other regional languages
Religion Sunni Muslim
Time difference GMT +5

 ■ CIA ■ LC ■ LP ■ WTG

TUVALU
Map page 112

National name Fakavae Aliki-Malo i Tuvalu/ Constitutional Monarchy of Tuvalu
Area 25 sq km/9.6 sq mi
Capital Fongafale (on Funafuti atoll)

Physical features nine low coral atolls forming a chain of 579 km/650 mi in the Southwest Pacific
Currency Australian dollar
GNP per capita (PPP) (US$) 970 (1998 est)
Population 12,000 (2000 est)
Population density (per sq km) 423 (1999 est)
Language Tuvaluan, English (both official), a Gilbertese dialect (on Nui)
Religion Protestant 96% (Church of Tuvalu)
Time difference GMT +12

 ■ CIA ■ LP ■ WTG

■ **Tuvalu Travel Guide**
http://www.pi-travel.co.nz/tuvalu/index.html
Travel guide to the islands of Tuvalu, one of the world's smallest and most isolated countries. The guide is divided into a number of sections, offering information on the country's attractions, a directory of accommodation, and practical advice on topics such as entry requirements and health risks.

UGANDA
Map page 106

National name Republic of Uganda
Area 236,600 sq km/ 91,351 sq mi
Capital Kampala
Major towns/cities Jinja, Mbale, Entebbe, Masaka, Mbarara, Soroti

Physical features plateau with mountains in west (Ruwenzori Range, with Mount Margherita, 5,110 m/16,765 ft); forest and grassland; 18% is lakes, rivers, and wetlands (Owen Falls on White Nile where it leaves Lake Victoria; Lake Albert in west); arid in northwest
Currency Ugandan new shilling
GNP per capita (PPP) (US$) 1,136 (1999 est)
Resources copper, apatite, limestone; believed to possess the world's second-largest deposit of gold (hitherto unexploited); also reserves of magnetite, tin, tungsten, beryllium, bismuth, asbestos, graphite
Population 21,778,000 (2000 est)
Population density (per sq km) 89
Language English (official), Kiswahili, other Bantu and Nilotic languages
Religion Christian 65%, animist 20%, Muslim 15%
Time difference GMT +3

 ■ CIA ■ LC ■ LP ■ NA ■ WTG

UKRAINE
Map page 70

National name Ukrayina/ Ukraine
Area 603,700 sq km/ 233,088 sq mi
Capital Kiev

Major towns/cities Kharkiv, Donets'k, Dnipropetrovs'k, L'viv, Kryvyy Rih, Zaporizhzhya, Odessa
Physical features Russian plain; Carpathian and Crimean Mountains; rivers: Dnieper (with the Dnieper dam 1932), Donetz, Bug
Currency hryvna
GNP per capita (PPP) (US$) 3,142 (1999)
Resources coal, iron ore (world's fifth-largest producer), crude oil, natural gas, salt, chemicals, brown coal, alabaster, gypsum
Population 50,456,000 (2000 est)
Population density (per sq km) 84 (1999 est)
Language Ukrainian (a Slavonic language; official), Russian (also official in Crimea), other regional languages
Religion traditionally Ukrainian Orthodox; also Ukrainian Catholic; small Protestant, Jewish, and Muslim communities
Time difference GMT +2

 ■ CIA ■ LP ■ WTG

■ **EuroScope: Ukraine**
http://pages.prodigy.net/euroscope/guidetoc.html
Tourist guide to Ukraine. This in-depth site features profiles of Ukraine's major towns and cities, with information on hotels and restaurants in each. Make sure you visit the photo galleries, which offer an insight into Hutsul folk art and Ukrainian Jewry.

■ **Kiev, Ukraine**
http://travel.lycos.com/Destinations/Europe/Ukraine/Kiev/
Large source of information on the Ukrainian capital. There are descriptions of the city, its history, attractions, entertainment, and cultural events. There are also links to a number of sources of information on Ukraine.

■ **Odessa Web**
http://www.odessit.com/tours/tours/english/overview.htm
Guide to this Ukrainian seaport. Dealing with both the old and the new, this site has sections on the history and cultural traditions and also the night life. There are also a number of photographs of notable buildings.

UNITED ARAB EMIRATES
Map page 95

National name Dawlat Imarat al-'Arabiyya al Muttahida/State of the Arab Emirates (UAE)
Area 83,657 sq km/32,299 sq mi
Capital Abu Dhabi
Major towns/cities Dubai, Sharjah, Ra's al Khaymah, Ajmān, Al 'Ayn
Major ports Dubai
Physical features desert and flat coastal plain; mountains in east
Currency UAE dirham
GNP per capita (PPP) (US$) 18,825 (1999 est)
Resources petroleum and natural gas
Population 2,441,000 (2000 est)
Population density (per sq km) 29 (1999 est)
Language Arabic (official), Farsi, Hindi, Urdu, English
Religion Muslim 96% (of which 80% Sunni); Christian, Hindu
Time difference GMT +4

 ■ CIA ■ LC ■ AN ■ LP ■ WTG

■ **Tourism – United Arab Emirates**
http://www.ecssr.ac.ae/tourism.html
Guide to the tourist attractions of the United Arab Emirates, with basic practical information for visitors. It is largely text-based but has some good images of local wildlife.

■ **Ras al Khaimah**
http://www.uaeforever.com/RasAlKhaimah/
Guide to the most traditional of the United Arab Emirates. There is a good description of the history and attractions of the small

strategically placed emirate. There are also good photos of Ras al Khaimah and its leader.

■ **Abu Dhabi**
http://www.uaeforever.com/AbuDhabi/
Well-presented guide to the largest and richest of the United Arab Emirates. There is a good description of the history, cultural heritage, attractions, and local economy. There are a number of good photos of Abu Dhabi and its ruler, the UAE president.

■ **Dubai**
http://www.uaeforever.com/Dubai/
Well-presented guide to the second-largest of the United Arab Emirates. There is a good description of the history of the trading entrepot, the role of the Makhtoum family, as well as details of it's cultural heritage, attractions, and the local economy. There are a number of good photos of Dubai and its ruler.

UNITED KINGDOM
Map page 56

National name United Kingdom of Great Britain and Northern Ireland (UK)
Area 244,100 sq km/94,247 sq mi
Capital London
Major towns/cities Birmingham, Glasgow, Leeds, Sheffield, Liverpool, Manchester, Edinburgh, Bradford, Bristol, Coventry, Belfast, Cardiff
Major ports London, Grimsby, Southampton, Liverpool
Physical features became separated from European continent in about 6000 BC; rolling landscape, increasingly mountainous towards the north, with Grampian Mountains in Scotland, Pennines in northern England, Cambrian Mountains in Wales; rivers include Thames, Severn, and Spey
Territories Anguilla, Bermuda, British Antarctic Territory, British Indian Ocean Territory, British Virgin Islands, Cayman Islands, Falkland Islands, Gibraltar, Montserrat, Pitcairn Islands, St. Helena and Dependencies (Ascension, Tristan da Cunha), South Georgia, South Sandwich Islands, Turks and Caicos Islands; the Channel Islands and the Isle of Man are not part of the UK but are direct dependencies of the crown
Currency pound sterling
GNP per capita (PPP) (US$) 20,883 (1999)
Resources coal, limestone, crude petroleum, natural gas, tin, iron, salt, sand and gravel
Population 58,830,000 (2000 est)
Population density (per sq km) 240 (1999 est)
Language English (official), Welsh (also official in Wales), Gaelic
Religion about 46% Church of England (established church); other Protestant denominations, Roman Catholic, Muslim, Jewish, Hindu, Sikh
Time difference GMT +/–0

 ■ CIA ■ LP ■ RG ■ WTG

■ **Gateway to Scotland**
http://www.geo.ed.ac.uk/home/scotland/scotland.html
Guide to all things Scottish, including an 'active map', a guide to the major cities, and information on the language, as well as sections on famous residents and history.

■ **UK Travel Guide**
http://www.uktravel.com/index.html
Essential resource for anyone planning to travel in the UK. It includes an A–Z of practical information from accommodation to the weather. The site also includes a 'clickable' map with features on towns and cities as well as several images.

■ **Lake District National Park Authority**
http://www.lake-district.gov.uk/index.htm
Official guide to the attractions of Britain's largest national park. There are sections on geology, history, conservation activities, and exhibitions in the Park's visitor's centre. There is a daily weather report for keen walkers. There are also some fabulous photographs of Lakeland beauty spots.

■ **Cardiff, Capital City of Wales**
http://www.cardiff.gov.uk/
Official guide to the Welsh capital. Local government functions are fully explained and investment opportunities outlined. There are many photos of the city and a listing of local amenities and historic sites.

■ **States of Jersey**
http://www.jersey.gov.uk/

Official information about the largest of the Channel Islands. This well organized site caters for the needs of residents and visitors. There is good coverage of the history and cultural heritage of Jersey. Information for visitors is first-rate with details of local attractions, events, and even the weather.

■ **LondonNet – The Net Magazine Guide to London**
http://www.londonnet.co.uk/
Informative guide to London, suitable for both tourists and residents alike. There are notes on accommodation in London, covering hotels, apartments, and even places for the 'cost conscious'. Other areas covered here include the museums to visit, the best ways to travel, and the pick of the London nightlife. In addition, there are also notes on the places to shop and eat.

■ **Northern Ireland Tourist Board**
http://www.ni-tourism.com/index.asp
This site covers the needs of anyone planning to visit Northern Ireland, from accommodation to events and attractions. It also features a virtual tour covering history, activities, food and drink, and places to stay.

UNITED STATES OF AMERICA

Map page 124

National name United States of America (USA)
Area 9,372,615 sq km/ 3,618,766 sq mi
Capital Washington D.C.
Major towns/cities New York, Los Angeles, Chicago, Philadelphia, Detroit, San Francisco, Dallas, San Diego, San Antonio, Houston, Boston, Phoenix, Indianapolis, Honolulu, San José
Physical features topography and vegetation from tropical (Hawaii) to arctic (Alaska); mountain ranges parallel with east and west coasts; the Rocky Mountains separate rivers emptying into the Pacific from those flowing into the Gulf of Mexico; Great Lakes in north; rivers include Hudson, Mississippi, Missouri, Colorado, Columbia, Snake, Rio Grande, Ohio
Territories the commonwealths of Puerto Rico and Northern Marianas; Guam, the US Virgin Islands, American Samoa, Wake Island, Midway Islands, Johnston Atoll, Baker Island, Howland Island, Jarvis Island, Kingman Reef, Navassa Island, Palmyra Island
Currency US dollar
GNP per capita (PPP) (US$) 30,600 (1999)
Resources coal, copper (world's second-largest producer), iron, bauxite, mercury, silver, gold, nickel, zinc (world's fifth-largest producer), tungsten, uranium, phosphate, petroleum, natural gas, timber
Population 278,357,000 (2000 est)
Population density (per sq km) 29 (1999 est)
Language English, Spanish
Religion Protestant 58%; Roman Catholic 28%; atheist 10%; Jewish 2%; other 4% (1998)
Time difference GMT –5–11

 ■ CIA ■ LP ■ RG ■ WTG

■ **Best of Hawaii**
http://www.bestofhawaii.com/
Jumping-off point for visitors seeking information about the best of Hawaii. This site includes a wealth of information aimed at the tourist – including maps, food, weather, accommodation, and even an online version of the Hawaiian phone directory.

■ **Grand Canyon**
http://www.kaibab.org/
Visitors to this site will find an outline of the geological and human history tracing the gradual conquest of the Canyon, and a spectacular photo gallery with close-ups and panoramas. There are also details of recommended hikes and trails, and you can discover valuable tips on hiking and backpacking.

■ **New York**
http://newyork.citysearch.com/
Impressive, user-friendly guide to New York City, filled with practical information. There are interesting feature articles and constant updates on what's on in the Big Apple. If the pace of life gets too hectic, the search engine can even provide a comprehensive listing of mind and body healing centres.

■ **Washington DC**
http://www.washington.org/
Site of the Washington DC Convention and Visitors' Association. This is a helpful guide filled with practical information for tourists and details of the attractions in the Washington area. There is also a useful set of maps.

■ **Niagara Falls Convention and Visitors Bureau**
http://www.nfcvb.com/
Official guide to the Niagara area in the state of New York. In addition to interesting facts about the falls, there is extensive information on local tours, transport, accommodation, places to eat, local festivals, and events.

■ **Prehistory of Alaska**
http://www.nps.gov/akso/akarc/
Alaska's prehistory divided into five sections: 'early prehistory', 'tundra and Arctic Alaska', 'southeast Alaska', 'southwest Alaska and Pacific coast', and 'interior Alaska'. there are also links to Alaska's 15 national parks and preserves – click on the acronym to access a general description of each park's cultural resources.

URUGUAY

Map page 142

National name República Oriental del Uruguay/Eastern Republic of Uruguay
Area 176,200 sq km/68,030 sq mi
Capital Montevideo
Major towns/cities Salto, Paysandú, Las Piedras, Rivera, Tacuarembó
Physical features grassy plains (pampas) and low hills; rivers Negro, Uruguay, Río de la Plata
Currency Uruguayan peso
GNP per capita (PPP) (US$) 8,280 (1999)
Resources small-scale extraction of building materials, industrial minerals, semi-precious stones; gold deposits are being developed
Population 3,337,000 (2000 est)
Population density (per sq km) 19 (1999 est)
Language Spanish (official), Brazilero (a mixture of Spanish and Portuguese)
Religion mainly Roman Catholic
Time difference GMT –3

 ■ CIA ■ LP ■ WTG

■ **Uruguay – General Information**
http://www.embassy.org/uruguay/
Comprehensive information about Uruguay. There are links to a profile of the country detailing its main features, as well as to its history, geography and climate, culture, cuisine, and wine. The site includes a map and a list of new Uruguay telephone numbers.

UZBEKISTAN

Map page 76

National name Özbekiston Respublikasi/Republic of Uzbekistan
Area 447,400 sq km/ 172,741 sq mi
Capital Tashkent
Major towns/cities Samarkand, Bukhara, Namangan, Andijon, Nukus, Karshi
Physical features oases in deserts; rivers: Amu Darya, Syr Darya; Fergana Valley; rich in mineral deposits
Currency som
GNP per capita (PPP) (US$) 2,092 (1999)
Resources petroleum, natural gas, coal, gold (world's seventh-largest producer), silver, uranium (world's fourth-largest producer), copper, lead, zinc, tungsten
Population 24,318,000 (2000 est)
Population density (per sq km) 54 (1999 est)
Language Uzbek (a Turkic language; official), Russian, Tajik
Religion predominantly Sunni Muslim; small Wahhabi, Sufi, and Orthodox Christian communities
Time difference GMT +5

 ■ CIA ■ LC ■ LP ■ WTG

VANUATU

Map page 112

National name Ripablik blong Vanuatu/République de Vanuatu/Republic of Vanuatu
Area 14,800 sq km/5,714 sq mi
Capital Port-Vila (on Efate island) (and chief port)
Major towns/cities Luganville (on Espíritu Santo)
Physical features comprises around 70 inhabited islands, including Espíritu Santo, Malekula, and Efate; densely forested, mountainous; three active volcanoes; cyclones on average twice a year
Currency vatu
GNP per capita (PPP) (US$) 2,771 (1999 est)
Resources manganese; gold, copper, and large deposits of petroleum have been discovered but have hitherto remained unexploited
Population 190,000 (2000 est)
Population density (per sq km) 13 (1999 est)
Language Bislama (82%), English, French (all official)
Religion Christian 80%, animist about 8%
Time difference GMT +11

⊕ **www.** ■ CIA ■ LP ■ WTG

■ **Vanuatu Online**
http://www.vanuatu.net.vu/VanuatuOnlineDirectory.html
Source of information on the Melanesian state. There is a history of the islands, information on government services, the local economy, and attractions. This is in addition to practical information for tourists which includes a special section for philatelists.

■ **Port-Vila, Vanuatu**
http://travel.lycos.com/Destinations/Australia_and_Pacific/Vanuatu/Port_Vila/
Guide to the capital of Vanuatu. There is coverage of local attractions, culture, and history. The site also has practical information for visitors and those planning to reside in the city, and the text is improved by the inclusion of several photographs of Port-Vila.

VATICAN CITY
Map page 64

National name Stato della Città del Vaticano/Vatican City State
Area 0.4 sq km/0.2 sq mi
Physical features forms an enclave in the heart of Rome, Italy
Currency Vatican City lira and Italian lira
GNP per capita (PPP) see Italy
Population 1,000 (2000 est)
Population density (per sq km) 2,500 (2000 est)
Language Latin (official), Italian
Religion Roman Catholic
Time difference GMT +1

⊕ **www.** ■ CIA ■ LP ■ WTG

■ **Holy See (Vatican City)**
http://www.vatican.va/
Multilingual, searchable page, with recent news reports and press releases from the Vatican Information Service. As well as the latest news from the Vatican City State, it also includes information about the Vatican museums and their plans for celebrating the year 2000.

VENEZUELA

Map page 140

National name República de Venezuela/Republic of Venezuela
Area 912,100 sq km/352,161 sq mi
Capital Caracas

Major towns/cities Maracaibo, Maracay, Barquisimeto, Valencia, Ciudad Guayana, Petare

Major ports Maracaibo

Physical features Andes Mountains and Lake Maracaibo in northwest; central plains (llanos); delta of River Orinoco in east; Guiana Highlands in southeast

Currency bolívar

GNP per capita (PPP) (US$) 5,268 (1999)

Resources petroleum, natural gas, aluminium, iron ore, coal, diamonds, gold, zinc, copper, silver, lead, phosphates, manganese, titanium

Population 24,170,000 (2000 est)

Population density (per sq km) 26 (1999 est)

Language Spanish (official), Indian languages (2%)

Religion Roman Catholic 92%

Time difference GMT –4

 ■ CIA ■ LC ■ LP ■ WTG

■ Fodor's Trip Planner – Caracas

http://www.fodors.com/ptpshort.cgi?Caracas

Create your own personal mini-guide to the Venezuelan capital with this handy on-line tourist guide. By choosing price ranges of accommodation and restaurants, and selecting options such as transport, currency and languages, a detailed pamphlet can be quickly compiled. If you select the language option, a link will appear to a site that provides useful phrases.

■ Venezuela Yours

http://www.venezuelatuya.com/eng.htm

Guide to Venezuela that is available in six languages, including English. The site features profiles of a number of the country's attractions, including the Andes, Caracas, and La Gran Sabana. There is also a selection of beautifully-illustrated articles on Venezuela's history and wildlife.

VIETNAM
Map page 84

National name Công-hòa xã-hôi chu-nghia Viêt Nam/Socialist Republic of Vietnam

Area 329,600 sq km/127,258 sq mi

Capital Hanoi

Major towns/cities Ho Chi Minh (formerly Saigon), Hai Phong, Da Nẵng, Cân Tho, Nha Trang, Biên Hoa, Huê

Major ports Ho Chi Minh (formerly Saigon), Da Nẵng, Hai Phong

Physical features Red River and Mekong deltas, centre of cultivation and population; tropical rainforest; mountainous in north and northwest

Currency dong

GNP per capita (PPP) (US$) 1,755 (1999)

Resources petroleum, coal, tin, zinc, iron, antimony, chromium, phosphate, apatite, bauxite

Population 79,832,000 (2000 est)

Population density (per sq km) 237 (1999 est)

Language Vietnamese (official), French, English, Khmer, Chinese, local languages

Religion mainly Buddhist; Christian, mainly Roman Catholic (8–10%); Taoist, Confucian, Hos Hoa, and Cao Dai sects

Time difference GMT +7

 ■ CIA ■ LC ■ LP ■ WTG

■ Administrative Structure Of Vietnam

http://www.batin.com.vn/vninfo/asv.htm

Fascinating insight into Vietnamese government and politics: at times it almost feels as if you are privy to state secrets! There are few multimedia frills on this site, but the colourful propaganda easily makes up for that.

■ Vietnam Pictures

http://sunsite.unc.edu/vietnam/

Multimedia archive of Vietnam, including photographs, audio clips, video footage, and text articles covering many aspects of Vietnamese life. The many hypertext links included on this page can take you on a virtual tour of this Southeast Asian country.

YEMEN
Map page 90

National name Al-Jumhuriyya al Yamaniyya/Republic of Yemen

Area 531,900 sq km/ 205,366 sq mi

Capital Şan'ā

Major towns/cities Aden, Ta'izz, Al Mukallā, Al Ḩudaydah, Ibb, Dhamār

Major ports Aden

Physical features hot, moist coastal plain, rising to plateau and desert

Currency riyal

GNP per capita (PPP) (US$) 688 (1999)

Resources petroleum, natural gas, gypsum, salt; deposits of copper, gold, lead, zinc, molybdenum

Population 18,112,000 (2000 est)

Population density (per sq km) 33 (1999 est)

Language Arabic (official)

Religion Sunni Muslim 63%, Shiite Muslim 37%

Time difference GMT +3

 ■ CIA ■ AN ■ LP ■ WTG

■ Yemen

http://www.al-bab.com/yemen/

Impressive source of comprehensive information on Yemen. There is coverage of history, culture, archaeology, tourism, economics, the political scene, international relations, and the local media. A large number of photographs include some stunning satellite images.

YUGOSLAVIA
Map page 66

National name Savezna Republika Jugoslavija/Federal Republic of Yugoslavia

Area 58,300 sq km/22,509 sq mi

Capital Belgrade

Major towns/cities Priština, Novi Sad, Niš, Kragujevac, Podgorica (formerly Titograd), Subotica

Physical features federation of republics of Serbia and Montenegro and two former autonomous provinces, Kosovo and Vojvodina

Currency new Yugoslav dinar

GNP per capita (PPP) (US$) 5,880 (1997 est)

Resources petroleum, natural gas, coal, copper ore, bauxite, iron ore, lead, zinc

Population 10,640,000 (2000 est)

Population density (per sq km) 182 (1999 est)

Language Serbo-Croat (official), Albanian (in Kosovo)

Religion Serbian and Montenegrin Orthodox; Muslim in southern Serbia

Time difference GMT +1

 ■ CIA ■ LC ■ LP ■ WTG

ZAMBIA
Map page 108

National name Republic of Zambia

Area 752,600 sq km/ 290,578 sq mi

Capital Lusaka

Major towns/cities Kitwe, Ndola, Kabwe, Mufulira, Chingola, Luanshya, Livingstone

Physical features forested plateau cut through by rivers; Zambezi River, Victoria Falls, Kariba Dam

Currency Zambian kwacha

GNP per capita (PPP) (US$) 686 (1999)

Resources copper (world's fourth-largest producer), cobalt, zinc, lead, coal, gold, emeralds, amethysts and other gemstones, limestone, selenium

Population 9,169,000 (2000 est)

Population density (per sq km) 12 (1999 est)

Language English (official), Bantu languages

Religion about 64% Christian, animist, Hindu, Muslim

Time difference GMT +2

 ■ CIA ■ LP ■ NA ■ WTG

■ Travel Guide to Zambia

http://www.africa-insites.com/zambia/travel/Default.htm

Comprehensive, illustrated guide to travelling in Zambia. There is information on the country's cities, towns, and game reserves, as well as a series of articles on the safaris and other adventure holidays possible in Zambia, which include surfing on the Zambezi beneath Victoria Falls, house-boating on Lake Kariba, and white-water rafting.

ZIMBABWE
Map page 108

National name Republic of Zimbabwe

Area 390,300 sq km/ 150,694 sq mi

Capital Harare

Major towns/cities Bulawayo, Gweru, Kwekwe, Mutare, Kadoma, Chitungwiza

Physical features high plateau with central high veld and mountains in east; rivers Zambezi, Limpopo; Victoria Falls

Currency Zimbabwe dollar

GNP per capita (PPP) (US$) 2,470 (1999)

Resources gold, nickel, asbestos, coal, chromium, copper, silver, emeralds, lithium, tin, iron ore, cobalt

Population 11,669,000 (2000 est)

Population density (per sq km) 30 (1999 est)

Language English, Shona, Ndebele (all official)

Religion 50% follow a syncretic (part Christian, part indigenous beliefs) type of religion, Christian 25%, animist 24%, small Muslim minority

Time difference GMT +2

 ■ CIA ■ LP ■ NA ■ WTG

INDEX

HOW TO USE THE INDEX

This is an alphabetically arranged index of the places and features that can be found on the maps in this atlas. Each name is generally indexed to the largest scale map on which it appears. If that map covers a double page, the name will always be indexed by the left-hand page number.

Names composed of two or more words are alphabetized as if they were one word.

All names appear in full in the index, except for 'St.' and 'Ste.', which, although abbreviated, are indexed as though spelled in full.

Where two or more places have the same name, they can be distinguished from each other by the country or province name that immediately follows the entry. These names are indexed in the alphabetical order of the country or province.

Alternative names, such as English translations, can also be found in the index and are cross-referenced to the map form by the '=' sign. In these cases the names also appear in brackets on the maps.

Settlements are indexed to the position of the symbol; all other features are indexed to the position of the name on the map.

Abbreviations and symbols used in this index are explained in the list opposite.

FINDING A NAME ON THE MAP

Each index entry contains the name, followed by a symbol indicating the feature type (for example, settlement, river), a page reference and a grid reference:

Name —	Owosso	● 128 D2
	Owyhee	● 126 C2
Symbol —	Owyhee	✦ 126 C2
	Oxford, *New Zealand*	■ 116 D6
	Oxford, *United Kingdom*	● 38 G4
Page reference —	Oxnard	● 132 C2
	Oxted	● **38** J4
	Oyama	● 82 K5
Grid reference —	Oyapock	✦ 140 G3
	Oyem	● 104 G4

The grid reference locates a place or feature within a rectangle formed by the network of lines of longitude and latitude. A name can be found by referring to the red letters and numbers placed around the maps. First find the letter, which appears along the top and bottom of the map, and then the number, down the sides. The name will be found within the rectangle uniquely defined by that letter and number. A number in brackets preceding the grid reference indicates that the name is to be found within an inset map.

ABBREVIATIONS

Ak.	Alaska	*N.D.*	North Dakota
Al.	Alabama	*Nebr.*	Nebraska
Ariz.	Arizona	*Nev.*	Nevada
Ark.	Arkansas	*Nfld.*	Newfoundland
B.C.	British Columbia	*N.H.*	New Hampshire
Calif.	California	*N. Ire.*	Northern Ireland
Colo.	Colorado	*N.J.*	New Jersey
Conn.	Connecticut	*N. Mex.*	New Mexico
Del.	Delaware	*N.W.T.*	Northwest Territories
Dem. Rep. of Congo		*N.Y.*	New York
. . . Democratic Republic of Congo		*Oh.*	Ohio
Eng.	England	*Okla.*	Oklahoma
Fla.	Florida	*Ont.*	Ontario
Ga.	Georgia	*Oreg.*	Oregon
Ia.	Iowa	*Orkney Is.*	Orkney Islands
Id.	Idaho	*Pa.*	Pennsylvania
Ill.	Illinois	*R.G.S.*	Rio Grande do Sul
Ind.	Indiana	*R.I.*	Rhode Island
Kans.	Kansas	*S.C.*	South Carolina
Ky.	Kentucky	*Scot.*	Scotland
La.	Louisiana	*S.D.*	South Dakota
Man.	Manitoba	*Shetland Is.*	Shetland Islands
Mass.	Massachusetts	*Tenn.*	Tennessee
Md.	Maryland	*Tex.*	Texas
Me.	Maine	*Ut.*	Utah
M.G.	Mato Grosso	*Va.*	Virginia
Mich.	Michigan	*Vt.*	Vermont
Minn.	Minnesota	*Wash.*	Washington
Miss.	Mississippi	*Wis.*	Wisconsin
Mo.	Missouri	*W. Va.*	West Virginia
Mont.	Montana	*Wyo.*	Wyoming
N.B.	New Brunswick	*Y.T.*	Yukon Territory
N.C.	North Carolina		

SYMBOLS

X	Continent name	**↗**	Lake, salt lake
A	Country name	**▷**	Gulf, strait, bay
a	State or province name	**⌣**	Sea, ocean
■	Country capital	**▷**	Cape, point
▢	State or province capital	**⊙**	Island or island group, rocky or coral reef
●	Settlement		
▲	Mountain, volcano, peak	**✳**	Place of interest
▲▲	Mountain range	**♠**	National park or other protected area
⬰	Physical region or feature		
✦	River, canal	**ℋ**	Historical or cultural region

GLOSSARY

This is an alphabetically arranged glossary of the geographical terms used on the maps and in this index. The first column shows the map form, the second the language of origin and the third the English translation.

A

açude . . . . Portuguese . . . . reservoir
adası . . . . Turkish . . . . island
akra . . . . Greek . . . . peninsula
alpen . . . . German . . . . mountains
alpes . . . . French . . . . mountains
alpi . . . . Italian . . . . mountains
älven . . . . Swedish . . . . river
archipiélago . . . . Spanish . . . . archipelago
arquipélago . . . . Portuguese . . . . . . archipelago

B

bab . . . . Arabic . . . . strait
bahía . . . . Spanish . . . . bay
bahir, bahr . . . . Arabic . . . . bay, lake, river
baía . . . . Portuguese . . . . bay
baie . . . . French . . . . bay
baja . . . . Spanish . . . . lower
bandar . . . . Arabic, Somalian,
                        Malay, Persian . . harbour, port
baraji . . . . Turkish . . . . dam
barragem . . . . Portuguese . . . . reservoir
ben . . . . Gaelic . . . . mountain
Berg(e) . . . . German . . . . mountain(s)
boğazı . . . . Turkish . . . . strait
Bucht . . . . German . . . . bay
buḥayrat . . . . Arabic . . . . lake
burnu, burun . . . . Turkish . . . . cape

C

cabo . . . . Spanish . . . . cape
canal . . . . French, Spanish . . canal, channel
canale . . . . Italian . . . . canal, channel
cerro . . . . Spanish . . . . mountain
chott . . . . Arabic . . . . . . marsh, salt lake
co . . . . Tibetan . . . . lake
collines . . . . French . . . . hills
cordillera . . . . Spanish . . . . range

D

dağ(ı) . . . . Turkish . . . . mountain
dağlar(ı) . . . . Turkish . . . . mountains
danau . . . . Indonesian . . . . lake
daryacheh . . . . Persian . . . . lake
dasht . . . . Persian . . . . desert
djebel . . . . Arabic . . . . mountain(s)
-do . . . . Korean . . . . island

E

embalse . . . . Spanish . . . . reservoir
erg . . . . Arabic . . . . sandy desert
estrecho . . . . Spanish . . . . strait

F

feng . . . . Chinese . . . . mountain
-fjördur . . . . Icelandic . . . . fjord
-flói . . . . Icelandic . . . . bay

G

Gebirge . . . . German . . . . range
golfe . . . . French . . . . bay, gulf

golfo . . . . Italian, Portuguese,
                        Spanish . . . . bay, gulf
göl, gölü . . . . Turkish . . . . lake
gora . . . . Russian . . . . mountain
gory . . . . Russian . . . . mountains
gunong . . . . Malay . . . . mountain
gunung . . . . Indonesian . . . . mountain

H

hai . . . . Chinese . . . . lake, sea
hāmūn . . . . Persian . . . . lake, marsh
hawr . . . . Arabic . . . . lake
hu . . . . Chinese . . . . . . lake, reservoir

I

île(s) . . . . French . . . . island(s)
ilha(s) . . . . Portuguese . . . . island(s)
isla(s) . . . . Spanish . . . . island(s)

J

jabal . . . . Arabic . . . . mountain(s)
-järvi . . . . Finnish . . . . lake
jaza'ir . . . . Arabic . . . . islands
jazīrat . . . . Arabic . . . . island
jbel . . . . Arabic . . . . mountain
jebel . . . . Arabic . . . . mountain
jezero . . . . Serbo-Croatian . . . . lake
jezioro . . . . Polish . . . . lake
jiang . . . . Chinese . . . . river
-jima . . . . Japanese . . . . island
-joki . . . . Finnish . . . . river
-jökull . . . . Icelandic . . . . glacier

K

kepulauan . . . . Indonesian . . . . islands
khrebet . . . . Russian . . . . . . mountain range
-ko . . . . Japanese . . . . lake
kolpos . . . . Greek . . . . bay, gulf
körfezi . . . . Turkish . . . . bay, gulf
kryazh . . . . Russian . . . . ridge
küh(ha) . . . . Persian . . . . mountain(s)

L

lac . . . . French . . . . lake
lacul . . . . Romanian . . . . lake
lago . . . . Italian, Portuguese,
                        Spanish . . . . lake
lagoa . . . . Portuguese . . . . lagoon
laguna . . . . Spanish . . . . lagoon, lake
limni . . . . Greek . . . . lake
ling . . . . Chinese . . . . mountain(s), peak
liqeni . . . . Albanian . . . . lake
loch, lough . . . . Gaelic . . . . lake

M

massif . . . . French . . . . mountains
-meer . . . . Dutch . . . . lake, sea
mont . . . . French . . . . mount
monte . . . . Italian, Portuguese,
                        Spanish . . . . mount
montes . . . . Portuguese,
                        Spanish . . . . mountains
monts . . . . French . . . . mountains
muntii . . . . Romanian . . . . mountains
mys . . . . Russian . . . . cape

N

nafud . . . . Arabic . . . . desert
nevado . . . . Spanish . . snow-capped mountain
nuruu . . . . Mongolian . . . . mountains

nuur . . . . Mongolian . . . . lake

O

ostrov(a) . . . . Russian . . . . island(s)
ozero . . . . Russian . . . . lake

P

pegunungan . . . . Indonesian . . . . mountains
pelagos . . . . Greek . . . . sea
pendi . . . . Chinese . . . . basin
pesky . . . . Russian . . . . sandy desert
pic . . . . French . . . . peak
pico . . . . Portuguese, Spanish . . . . . peak
planalto . . . . Portuguese . . . . plateau
planina . . . . Bulgarian . . . . mountains
poluostrov . . . . Russian . . . . peninsula
puerto . . . . Spanish . . . . harbour, port
puncak . . . . Indonesian . . . . peak
punta . . . . Italian, Spanish . . . . point
puy . . . . French . . . . peak

Q

qundao . . . . Chinese . . . . archipelago

R

ras, rås, ra's . . . . Arabic . . . . cape
represa . . . . Portuguese . . . . . dam, reservoir
-rettō . . . . Japanese . . . . archipelago
rio . . . . Portuguese . . . . river
río . . . . Spanish . . . . river

S

sahra . . . . Arabic . . . . desert
salar . . . . Spanish . . . . salt flat
-san . . . . Japanese, Korean . . . . . mountain
-sanmaek . . . . Korean . . . . mountains
sebkha . . . . Arabic . . . . salt flat
sebkhet . . . . Arabic . . . . salt marsh
See . . . . German . . . . lake
serra . . . . Portuguese . . . . range
severnaya, severo- . . . . Russian . . . . northern
shan . . . . Chinese . . . . mountain(s)
-shima . . . . Japanese . . . . island
-shotō . . . . Japanese . . . . islands
sierra . . . . Spanish . . . . range

T

tanjona . . . . Malagasy . . . . cape
tanjung . . . . Indonesian . . . . cape
teluk . . . . Indonesian . . . . bay, gulf
ténéré . . . . Berber . . . . desert
-tō . . . . Japanese . . . . island

V

vârful . . . . Romanian . . . . mountain
-vesi . . . . Finnish . . . . lake
vodokhranilishche . . . . . Russian . . . . reservoir
volcán . . . . Spanish . . . . volcano

W

wādī . . . . Arabic . . . . watercourse
Wald . . . . German . . . . forest

Z

-zaki . . . . Japanese . . . . cape
zaliv . . . . Russian . . . . bay, gulf

chen 54 J4
en 52 F8
st 54 G4
rau 62 D3
re 62 C3
rschot 54 G4
a 104 F3
ādān 95 C1
ādeh 95 E1
adla 102 E2
aji 104 F3
akaliki 104 F3
akan 76 S7
Anbar 95 E1
ancay 140 C6
ano Terme 62 G5
arqū 95 E1
ashiri 82 N1
ava 48 M8
aya Hāyk' 106 F2
ay Wenz 100 G5
beville, *France* 54 D4
beville, *United States* 130 C4
beyfeale 35 B4
beyleix 35 D4
d al Kūrī 90 F7
éché 100 D5
engourou 104 D3
enójar 60 F6
enrå 52 E1
ensberg 52 G8
eokuta 104 E3
eraeron 38 D3
erdare 38 E4
erdeen, *South Africa* 108 C6
erdeen, *United Kingdom* 36 F4
erdeen, *Miss., United States* 130 D3
erdeen, *S.D., United States* 126 G1
erdeen, *Wash., United States* 126 B1
erdeen Lake 122 M4
erfeldy 36 E5
ergavenny 38 E4
ertillery 38 E4
erystwyth 38 D3
ez' 70 M1
ıā 100 H4
ar 92 N5
djan 104 D3
llene 132 G2
ngdon, *United Kingdom* 38 G4
ngdon, *United States* 130 E2
nūb 100 F2
isso 104 D3
mey 104 E3
ng Mbang 104 G4
u Déia 100 C5
yne 36 F4
aiq 95 C4
antes 60 B5
ud 66 L3
aroka Range 126 E1
al Abayḑ 95 E4
Aweigîla 94 B6
Ballâs 100 E3
Dhabi = Abū Ẕabī 95 F4
Hamed 100 F4
ja 104 F3
mombazi 106 C3
ne Yosēf 100 G5
Nujaym 100 C1
Qarin 100 C1
ro 106 E3
Simbel 100 F3
t Head 116 B6
ye Meda 106 F1
Ẕabī 95 F4
poneta 124 E7
pulco 134 E5
rá 140 H4
rigua 140 D2
ra 104 D3
ington 38 F2
aguas 134 L7
ayvayam 78 W4
eng 80 H1
enkirch 62 G3
en See 62 G3
ill 35 A3
ill Head 35 A3
im 52 E3
insk 76 S6
it 70 L3
nasheen 36 C4
Göl 68 M7
hanbeyli 68 Q6
eale 64 K11
ins Island 134 K4
ncagua 138 D7
res 102 (1)B2
oruña 60 B1
uarossa 62 D4
ui Terme 62 D6
e 140 C5
64 L9
United States 130 B3
Yugoslavia 50 K12
k Island 132 (3)C1
m 90 G5
mas 68 G8
ms Island 116 (2)B1
in 90 E7
na 92 F5
re 35 C4
a 62 E5
Dafrah 95 E5
Dahnā 95 B3
Dakhla 102 B4
Dammām 95 D3
Dawādimī 90 D5
Dawḩah 95 D4
Dilam 95 B5
Dir'īyah 95 B4
s Ababa = Ādīs Ābeba 106 F2
Ad Dīwānīyah 90 D3
Adel 128 B2
Adelaide 114 G6
Adelaide Peninsula 122 M3
Adelaide River 114 F2
Aden = Adan 90 E7
Aderbissinat 104 F1
Adh Dhayd 95 F4
Adi 87 D3
Adige 62 G5
Adīgrat 100 G5
Adilabad 88 C5
Adin 126 B2
Adīrī 100 B2
Ādīs Ābeba 106 F2
Adi Ugri 100 G5
Adıyaman 92 H5
Adjud 66 Q3
Adler 92 H2
Admiralty Island 122 E5
Admiralty Islands 112 E6
Adoni 88 C5
Adour 58 F10
Adra 60 H8
Adrano 64 J11
Adrar 102 E3
Adrar des Ifôghas 102 F5
Adrar Tamgak 102 G5
Adria 62 H5
Adriatic Sea 64 H4
Adwick le Street 38 G2
Adycha 78 P3
Adygeya 92 J1
Adygeysk 92 H1
Adzopé 104 D3
Adz'vavom 70 L1
Aegean Sea 68 H5
A Estrada 60 B2
Afghanistan 90 H3
Afgooye 106 H3
'Afīf 100 H3
Afikpo 104 F3
Afmadow 106 G3
Afognak Island 132 (1)G4
A Fonsagrada 60 C1
Afragola 64 J8
Africa 98 F5
'Afrīn 92 G5
Afuá 140 G4
'Afula 94 C4
Afyon 68 N6
Agadez 102 G5
Agadir 102 D2
Agadyr' 76 N8
Agalega Islands 98 J7
Agan 78 B4
Āgaro 106 F2
Agartala 88 F4
Agathonisi 68 J7
Agattu Island 78 W6
Ağcabädi 92 M3
Agde 58 J10
Agen 58 F9
Agia Triada 68 D7
Ağin 92 H4
Aginskoye 76 S6
Agiokampos 68 E5
Agios Efstratios 68 H5
Agios Georgios 68 F7
Agios Nikolaos 68 H9
Agnibilekrou 104 D3
Agnita 66 M4
Agra 88 C3
Agrakhanskiy Poluostrov 92 M2
Ağri 92 K4
Agri 64 L8
Agrigento 64 H11
Agrinio 68 D6
Agropoli 64 K8
Agryz 70 K3
Ağsu 92 N3
Agua Prieta 132 E2
Aguascalientes 134 D4
A Gudiña 60 C2
Aguelhok 102 F5
Águilas 60 J7
Agulhas Negras 140 H8
Ağva 68 M3
Ahar 92 M4
Ahaura 116 C6
Ahaus 54 K2
Ahititi 116 E4
Ahlen 54 K3
Ahmadabad 88 B4
Ahmadnagar 88 B5
Ahmadpur East 88 B3
Ahr 52 B6
Ahram 95 D2
Ahrensburg 52 F3
Ahvāz 90 E3
Aichach 52 G8
Aigialousa 92 F6
Aigina 68 F7
Aigina 68 F7
Aigio 68 E6
Aigosthena 68 F6
Aiguillon 58 F9
Aihui 78 M6
Ailsa Craig 36 C6
Aim 78 N5
Ain 58 L7
Aïn Beïda 102 G1
'Aïn Ben Tili 102 D3
Aïn Bessem 60 P8
Aïn el Hadjel 60 P9
Aïn Oussera 102 F1
Ainsa 60 L2
Aïn Sefra 102 E2
Aïn Taya 60 P8
Aïn-Tédélès 60 L8
Aïn Témouchent 60 J9
Airão 140 E4
Airdrie 36 E6
Aire 38 G2
Air Force Island 122 S3
Airolo 62 D4
Airpanas 87 C4
Aisne 54 F5
Aitape 87 F3
Aitkin 128 B1
Aitutaki 112 K7
Aiud 66 L3
Aix-en-Provence 58 L10
Aix-les-Bains 58 L8
Aizawl 88 F4
Aizkraukle 48 N8
Aizpute 48 L8
Aizu-wakamatsu 82 K5
Ajaccio 64 C7
Aj Bogd Uul 80 B2
Ajdābiyā 100 D1
Ajigasawa 82 L3
Ajka 50 G10
Ajlun 94 C4
Ajmān 95 F4
Ajmer 88 B3
Ajo 132 D2
Ajtos 66 Q7
Akanthou 94 A1
Akaroa 116 D6
Akasha 100 F3
Akashi 82 H6
Akbalyk 76 P8
Akbasty 76 L8
Akçakale 92 H5
Akçakoca 68 P3
Akdağmadeni 92 F4
Aken 52 H5
Aketi 106 C3
Akhalk'alak'i 92 K3
Akhisar 68 K6
Akhmīm 100 F2
Akhty 92 M3
Akimiski Island 122 Q6
Akita 82 L4
Akjoujt 102 C5
Akka 102 D3
Akkajaure 48 J3
Akkeshi 82 N2
'Akko 94 C4
Akmeqit 90 L2
Akobo 106 E2
Akola 88 C4
Akonolinga 104 G4
Akordat 100 G4
Akpatok Island 122 T4
Akqi 76 P9
Akra Drepano 68 G5
Akranes 48 (1)B2
Akra Sounio 68 F7
Akra Spatha 68 F9
Akra Trypiti 68 G9
Åkrehamn 48 C7
Akron 128 D2
Aksaray 92 E4
Aksarka 76 M4
Akşehir 68 P6
Akseki 68 P7
Aksha 78 J6
Akshiy 76 P9
Aksu 76 Q9
Aksuat 76 Q8
Āksum 100 G5
Aktau, *Kazakhstan* 46 K3
Aktau, *Kazakhstan* 76 N7
Aktogay, *Kazakhstan* 76 N8
Aktogay, *Kazakhstan* 76 P8
Aktuma 76 M8
Aktyubinsk 70 L4
Akula 106 C3
Akulivik 122 R4
Akune 82 F8
Akure 104 F3
Akureyri 48 (1)E2
Akwanga 104 F3
Alabama 130 D3
Alaçam 92 F3
Alaejos 60 E3
Alagoas 140 K5
Alagoinhas 140 K6
Alagón 60 J3
Al Ahmadi 95 C2
Al 'Amārah 90 E3
Alaminos 84 F3
Alamo 126 C3
Alamogordo 132 E2
Alamo Lake 132 D2
Åland 48 K6
Alanya 92 E5
Alappuzha 88 C7
Al Argoub 102 B4
Al Arţāwīyah 90 E4
Alaşehir 68 L6
Al 'Ashurīyah 100 H1
Alaska 132 (1)F2
Alaska Peninsula 132 (1)E4
Alaska Range 132 (1)G3
Alassio 62 D6
Alatri 64 H7
Alatyr' 70 J4
Alaverdi 92 L3
Alavus 48 M5
Al 'Ayn 95 F4
Alazeya 78 S2
Alba, *Italy* 62 D6
Alba, *Spain* 60 E4
Albacete 60 J5
Alba Iulia 66 L3
Albania 68 B3
Albany 122 Q6
Albany, *Australia* 114 C6
Albany, *Ga., United States* 130 E3
Albany, *Ky., United States* 130 E2
Albany, *N.Y., United States* 128 F2
Albany, *Oreg., United States* 126 B2
Albardão do João Maria 142 L4
Al Bardī 100 D1
Al Başrah 90 E3
Albatross Bay 114 H2
Albatross Point 116 E4
Al Baydā' 100 D1
Albenga 62 D6
Albert 54 E4
Alberta 122 H6
Albertirsa 50 J10
Albert Kanaal 54 G3
Albert Lea 128 B2
Albert Nile 106 E3
Albertville 58 M8
Albi 58 H10
Albina 140 G2
Albino 62 E5
Albion 126 F1
Ålborg 48 E8
Ålborg Bugt 48 F8
Albox 60 H7
Albstadt 52 E8
Albufeira 60 B7
Āl Bū Kamāl 92 J6
Albuquerque 132 E1
Al Burayj 94 D2
Al Buraymī 90 G5
Alburquerque 60 D5
Albury 114 J7
Al Buşayyah 95 B1
Alcácer do Sal 60 B6
Alcala de Guadaira 60 E7
Alcala de Henares 60 G4
Alcalá la Real 60 G7
Alcamo 64 G11
Alcañiz 60 K3
Alcantarilla 60 J7
Alcaraz 60 H6
Alcaudete 60 F7
Alcazar de San Juan 60 G5
Alcobendas 60 G4
Alcoi 60 K6
Alcolea del Pinar 60 H3
Alcorcón 60 G4
Alcoutim 60 C7
Aldabra Islands 108 (2)A2
Aldan 78 M5
Aldan 78 N5
Aldeburgh 38 K3
Alderley Edge 38 F2
Alderney 38 (1)F6
Aldershot 38 H4
Aleg 102 C5
Aleksandrov-Sakhalinskiy 78 Q6
Aleksandrovskiy Zavod 78 K6
Aleksandrovskoye 70 Q2
Alekseyevka 76 N7
Aleksinac 66 J6
Alençon 58 F5
Aleppo = Ḩalab 92 G5
Aléria 64 D6
Alès 58 K9
Aleşd 50 M10
Alessandria 62 D6
Ålesund 48 D5
Aleutian Islands 132 (3)B1
Aleutian Range 132 (1)F4
Aleutian Trench 74 W5
Alexander Archipelago 132 (1)K4
Alexander Bay 108 B5
Alexander City 130 D3
Alexandra 116 B7
Alexandreia 68 E4
Alexandria = El Iskandarîya, *Egypt* 100 E1
Alexandria, *Romania* 66 N6
Alexandria, *La., United States* 130 C3
Alexandria, *Minn., United States* 128 A1
Alexandria, *Va., United States* 128 E3
Alexandroupoli 68 H4
Alexis Creek 122 G6
'Āley 94 C3
Aley 76 Q7
Aleysk 76 Q7
Al Farwānīyah 95 B2
Al Fāw 95 C2
Alfeld 52 E5
Alföld 66 H2
Alfonsine 62 H6
Alfreton 38 G2
Al Fuḩayḩīl 95 C2
Al-Fujayrah 95 G4
Algeciras 60 E8
Algemes 60 K5
Algena 100 G4
Alger 102 F1
Algeria 102 E3
Al Ghāţ 95 A3
Al Ghayḑah 90 F6
Alghero 64 C8
Algiers = Alger 102 F1
Algona 128 B2
Al Hadīthah 94 E5
Alhama de Murcia 60 J7
Al Ḩamar 95 B5
Al Ḩamīdīyah 94 C2
Al Ḩammādah al Ḩamrā' 102 G3
Al Harūj al Aswad 100 C2
Al Ḩasakah 92 J5
Alhaurmín el Grande 60 F8
Al Ḩijāz 100 G2
Al Ḩillah 90 D3
Al Ḩilwah 95 B5
Al Hoceima 102 E1
Al Ḩudaydah 100 H5
Al Hufūf 95 C4
Al Ḩumayḑah 90 C4
Aliabad 95 F2
Aliağa 68 J6
Aliakmonas 68 E4
Ali Bayramlı 92 N4
Alicante 60 K6
Alice 130 B4
Alice Springs 114 F4
Alicudi 64 J10
Aligarh 88 C3
Alindao 106 C2
Alingsås 48 G8
Alisos 132 D2
Aliwal North 108 D6
Al Jabal al Akhḑar 100 D1
Al Jaghbūb 100 D2
Al Jālamīd 100 G1
Al Jarah 95 B2

Al Jawf, *Libya* 100 D3
Al Jawf, *Saudi Arabia* 100 G2
Aljezur 60 B7
Al Jifārah 95 A5
Al Jubayl 95 C3
Aljustrel 60 B7
Al Kāmil 90 G5
Al Khābūrah 95 G5
Al Khālis 92 L7
Al Kharj 95 B4
Al Khaşab 95 G3
Al Khawr 95 D4
Al Khubar 95 D3
Al Khufrah 100 D3
Al Khums 102 H2
Al Khuwayr 95 D3
Al Kir'ānah 95 D4
Alkmaar 54 G2
Al Kūt 90 E3
Al Kuwayt 95 C2
Al Lādhiqīyah 92 F6
Allahabad 88 D3
Allakh-Yun' 78 P4
Alldays 108 D4
Allen 84 G4
Allendale 130 E3
Allentown 128 E2
Aller = Cabañaquinta 60 E1
Aller 52 E4
Alliance 126 F2
Allier 58 J8
Allinge 50 D2
Al Lith 100 H3
Alloa 36 E5
Alma, *Canada* 128 F1
Alma, *Nebr., United States* 126 G2
Alma, *Wis., United States* 128 B2
Almada 60 A6
Almadén 60 F6
Al Madīnah 100 G3
Al Mahbas 102 D3
Al Majma'ah 90 E4
Almalyk 76 M9
Al Manāmah 95 D3
Almansa 60 J6
Al Ma'qil 95 B1
Al Marj 100 D1
Almaty 76 P9
Al Mawşil 92 K5
Al Mazāḩimīyah 95 B4
Almazán 60 H3
Almeirim 140 G4
Almelo 54 J2
Almendralejo 60 D6
Almería 60 H8
Al'met'yevsk 76 J7
Almiros 68 E5
Al Mish'āb 95 C2
Almonte 60 D7
Almora 88 C3
Almosa 126 E3
Al Mubarraz 95 C4
Al Mudawwara 94 D7
Al Mukallā 90 E7
Al Mukhā 100 H5
Almuñécar 60 G8
Al Muqdādīyah 92 L7
Al Nu'ayrīyah 95 C3
Alnwick 36 G6
Alonnisos 68 F5
Alor 87 B4
Alor Setar 84 C5
Alotau 114 K2
Alpena 128 D1
Alphen 54 G2
Alpi Lepontine 62 D4
Alpine 132 E2
Alpi Orobie 62 E4
Alps 62 B5
Al Qadmūs 94 D1
Al Qalībah 100 G2
Al Qāmishlī 92 J5
Al Qar'ah 95 B3
Al Qarqar 94 E5
Al Qaryāt 100 B1
Al Qaryatayn 94 E2
Al Qaţif 95 C3
Al Qaţrūn 100 B3
Al Qunayţirah 94 C3
Al Qunfudhah 100 H4
Al Qurayyāt 100 G1
Al Qurnah 95 B1
Al 'Quşayr, *Iraq* 95 A1
Al 'Quşayr, *Syria* 94 D2
Al Quţayfah 94 D3
Als 52 E1
Alsask 122 K6
Alsasua 60 H2
Alsfeld 52 E6
Alston 36 F7
Alta 48 M2
Altaelva 48 M2
Altai Mountains 80 A1
Al Tamīnī 100 D1
Altamira 140 G4
Altamura 64 L8
Altanbulag 78 H6
Altay 76 R7
Altay, *China* 76 R8
Altay, *Mongolia* 80 B1
Altdorf 62 D4
Alte Mellum 52 D3
Altenberg 52 J6
Altenburg 52 H6
Altenkirchen 52 J2
Altkirch 62 C3
Alto Garças 140 G7
Alto Molócuè 108 F3
Alton, *United Kingdom* 38 H4
Alton, *United States* 128 B3
Altoona 128 E2
Alto Parnaíba 140 H5
Altötting 62 H2
Altun Shan 76 S10
Alturas 126 B2
Altus 130 B3
Al 'Ubaylah 90 F5
Alūksne 48 P8
Alupka 92 E1
Al 'Uqaylah 100 C1
Alushta 92 F1
Al 'Uthmānīyah 95 C4
Al 'Uwaynāt, *Libya* 100 B2
Al 'Uwaynāt, *Libya* 100 D3
Al 'Uwayqīlah 100 H1
Al 'Uzayr 95 B1
Alva 130 B2
Alvarães 140 E4
Älvdalen 48 H6
Älvsbyn 48 L4
Al Wafrā' 95 B2
Al Wajh 100 G2
Al Wannān 95 C3
Alwar 88 C3
Al Wari'ah 95 B3
Alxa Zouqi 80 D3
Alytus 50 P3
Alzey 52 D7
Alzira 60 K5
Amadi 106 E2
Amādīyah 92 K5
Amadjuak Lake 122 S4
Amadora 60 A6
Amahai 87 C3
Amakusa-Shimo-shima 82 E7
Amaliada 68 D7
Amalner 88 C4
Amamapare 87 E3
Amambaí 142 K3
Amami-Ōshima 74 S7
Amanab 87 F3
Amandola 64 H6
Amantea 64 L9
Amapá 140 G3
Amapá 140 G3
Amarante 140 J5
Amarapura 84 B2
Amareleja 60 C6
Amarillo 132 F1
Amasya 92 F3
Amay 54 H4
Amazar 78 L6
Amazon = Amazonas 138 F4
Amazonas 140 D4
Amazonas 140 E4
Ambala 88 C2
Ambanjā 108 H2
Ambarchik 78 U3
Ambato 140 B4
Ambato Boeny 108 H3
Ambatondrazaka 108 H3
Amberg 52 G7
Ambikapur 88 D4
Ambilobe 108 H2
Amble 36 G6
Ambleside 36 F7
Ambohimahasoa 108 H4
Amboise 58 G6
Ambon 87 C3
Ambositra 108 H4
Ambovombe 108 H5
Amchitka Island 132 (3)B1
Amderma 76 L4
Amdo 88 F2
Ameland 54 H1
Amengel'dy 76 M7
American Falls 126 D2
American Samoa 112 J7
Americus 130 E3
Amersfoort 54 H2
Amery 122 N5
Amery Ice Shelf 144 (2)M2
Ames 128 B2
Amesbury 38 G4
Amfilochia 68 D6
Amfissa 68 E6
Amga 78 N4
Amga 78 L5
Amguid 102 G3
Amgun' 78 P6
Amherst 122 U7
Amiens 54 E5
Amirante Islands 108 (2)B2
Amistad Reservoir 132 F3
Amlekhganj 88 D3
Åmli 48 E7
Amlwch 38 D2
'Amm Adam 100 G4
'Ammān 94 C5
Ammanford 38 E4
Ammassalik 122 Z3
Ammerland 54 K1
Ammersee 62 F2
Ammochostos 92 E6
Ammochostos Bay 94 A1
Amo 84 C2
Amol 90 F2
Amorgos 68 H8
Amos 128 E1
Amourj 102 D5
Ampana 87 B3
Ampanihy 108 G4
Amparai 88 D7
Ampezzo 62 H4
Amposta 60 L4
Amrān 90 D6
Amravati 88 C4
Amritsar 88 B2
Amroha 88 C3
Amrum 52 D2
Amsterdam, *Netherlands* 54 G2
Amsterdam, *United States* 128 F2
Amstetten 62 K2
Am Timan 100 D5
Amudar'ya 76 L9
Amundsen Gulf 122 G2
Amundsen Sea 144 (2)GG3
Amungen 48 H6
Amuntai 86 F3
Amur 78 P6
Amursk 78 P6
Amvrakikos Kolpos 68 C6
Anabanua 87 B3
Anabar 78 J2
Anaconda 126 D1
Anacortes 126 B1
Anadarko 126 G3
Anadolu Dağları 92 H3
Anadyr' 78 X4
Anadyrskaya Nizmennost' 78 X3
Anadyrskiy Zaliv 78 Y3
Anafi 68 H8
'Ānah 92 J6
Anaheilt 36 C5
Anaheim 132 C2
Anáhuac 132 F3
Analalava 108 H2
Anamur 92 E5
Anan 82 H7
Anantapur 88 C6
Anan'yiv 66 T2
Anapa 92 G1
Anápolis 140 H7
Anār 95 F1
Anārak 90 F3
Anardara 90 H3
Anatolia 68 M6
Añatuya 142 J4
Anchorage 132 (1)H3
Ancona 64 H5
Ancud 142 G7
Anda 80 H1
Andalgalá 142 H4
Åndalsnes 48 D5
Andalusia 130 D3
Andaman Islands 84 A4
Andaman Sea 84 A4
Andapa 108 H2
Andarāb 90 J2
Andenne 54 H4
Andéramboukane 104 E1
Andermatt 62 D4
Andernach 54 K4
Anderson 130 E3
Anderson 122 F3
Andes 138 D5
Andfjorden 48 J2
Andilamena 108 H3
Andipsara 68 H6
Andizhan 76 N9
Andkhvoy 90 J2
Andoas 140 B4
Andong 82 E5
Andorra 60 L2
Andorra la Vella 60 M2
Andover 38 G4
Andøya 48 H2
Andradina 142 L3
Andreanof Islands 132 (3)C1
Andrews 132 F2
Andria 64 L7
Andriamena 108 H3
Andros 68 G7
Andros, *Greece* 68 G7
Andros, *The Bahamas* 130 F5
Andros Town 130 F5
Andrott 88 B6
Andrychów 50 J8
Andûjar 60 F6
Andulo 108 B2
Aneto 60 L2
Angara 78 G5
Angarsk 78 G6
Ånge 48 H5
Angel de la Guarda 132 D3
Angeles 84 G3
Ängelholm 48 G8
Angeln 52 E2
Angermünde 52 K4
Angern 62 M2
Angers 58 E6
Anglesey 38 D2
Angmagssalik = Ammassalik 122 Z3
Ango 106 D3
Angoche 108 F3
Angohrān 95 G3
Angol 142 G6
Angola 98 E7
Angola 128 D2
Angostura Reservoir 126 F2
Angoulême 58 F8
Angren 76 M9
Anguilla 134 M5
Aniak 132 (1)F3
Anina 66 J4
Ankang 80 D4
Ankara 92 E4
Ankazoabo 108 G4
Anklam 52 J3
Ankpa 104 F3
Ånn 48 G5
Anna 70 H4
Annaba 102 G1
Annaberg-Buchholz 52 H6
An Nabk, *Saudi Arabia* 94 E5
An Nabk, *Syria* 94 D2
An Nafud 100 G2
An Nāirīyah 90 E3
An Najaf 90 D3
Annan 36 E7
Annapolis 128 E3
Annapurna 88 D3
Ann Arbor 128 D2
An Nāşirīyah 100 J1
Annecy 62 B5
Annemasse 62 B4
Anniston 130 D3
Annobón 104 F5
Annonay 58 K8
An Nukhayb 90 D3
Anqing 80 F4
Ansbach 52 F7
Anshan 82 B3
Anshun 80 D5
Ansley 126 G2
Anson 130 B3
Ansongo 102 F5
Antakya 92 G5
Antalaha 108
Antalya 68
Antalya Körfezi 68
Antananarivo 108
Antarctic Peninsula 144
Antequera 60
Anti-Atlas 102
Antibes 62
Antigo 128
Antigua 134
Antigua and Barbuda 134
Antikythira 68
Antiparos 68
Antipaxoi 68
Antipayuta 76
Antipodes Islands 116
Antlers 130
Antofagasta 142
Antonito 126
Antrim 35
Antrim Hills 35
Antropovo 70
Antsalova 108
Antsirabe 108
Antsirañana 108
Antu 82
Antwerp = Antwerpen 54
Antwerpen 54
Anuradhapura 88
Anveh 95
Anxi 80
Anyang, *China* 80
Anyang, *South Korea* 82
Anyuysk 78
Anzhero-Sudzhensk 76
Anzi 106
Anzio 64
Aoga-shima 82
Aomori 82
Aosta 62
Aoukâr 102
Aoukoukar 104
Apalachee Bay 130
Apalachicola 130
Aparri 84
Apatin 66
Apatity 70
Ape 48
Apeldoorn 54
Api 88
Apia 112
Apoera 140
Apolda 52
Apollo Bay 114
Aporé 140
Apostle Islands 128
Apoteri 140
Appalachian Mountains 130
Appennino 64
Appennino Abruzzese 64
Appennino Calabro 64
Appennino Lucano 64
Appennino Tosco-Emiliano 62
Appennino Umbro-Marchigiano 64
Appleby-in-Westmorland 36
Appleton 128
Aprilia 64
Apure 140
Apurimac 140
Āqā 90
'Aqaba 94
Aquidauana 140
Ara 88
Arabian Sea 90
Aracaju 140
Aracati 140
Araçatuba 140
Aracuca 134
Arad 66
Arādah 90
Arafura Sea 87
Aragarças 140
Araguaia 138
Araguaína 140
Araguari 140
Araguatins 140
Arāk 90
Arak 102
Aral Sea 76
Aral'sk 70
Aran 35
Aranda de Duero 60
Aranđjelovac 66
Aran Islands 35
Aranjuez 60
Aranos 108
Aranyaprathet 84
Araouane 102
Arapahoe 126
Arapiraca 140
'Ar'ar 90
Araras 140
Ararat 92
Arauca 140
Araxá 140
Araz 92
Arbīl 92
Arbon 62
Arbre du Ténéré 102
Arbroath 36
Arcachon 58
Arcadia 130
Arcata 126
Archidona 60
Archipelago of the Recherche 114
Archipel de la Société 112
Archipel des Tuamotu 112
Archipiélago de Camagüey 134
Archipiélago de la Reina Adelaida 142
Archipiélago de los Chonos 142
Arco, *Italy* 62
Arco, *United States* 126
Arcos de la Frontera 60
Arctic Bay 122
Arctic Ocean 42
Arctic Red River 122

Name	Page	Grid
da	68	H3
da	68	J3
dabīl	92	N4
dahan	92	K3
dalstangen	48	D6
datov	70	J4
dee	35	E3
dennes	54	G4
destān	90	F3
dila	60	C6
dmore	124	G5
drossan	36	D6
ds Peninsula	35	F2
edo	87	D3
eia Branca	140	K5
endal	48	E7
enys de Mar	60	N3
eopoli	68	E8
equipa	140	C7
ere	140	G4
évalo	60	F3
ezzo	64	F5
gan	76	R9
genta	62	G6
gentan	54	B6
gentera	62	B6
gentina	142	H6
genton-sur-Creuse	58	G7
geş	66	N5
golikos Kolpos	68	E7
gos	68	E7
gos Orestiko	68	D4
gostoli	68	C6
gun'	78	K6
gungu	104	E2
gunsk	78	L6
gyll	36	C5
Horqin Qi	80	G2
hus	48	F8
iano Irpino	64	K7
i Atoll	88	B8
ica	140	C7
iège	58	G11
ihge	60	M2
inos	140	F6
ipuanã	140	E5
ipuanã	140	E5
iquemes	140	E5
izona	132	D2
jäng	48	G7
jasa	86	F4
ka	78	Q5
kadak	70	H4
kadelphia	130	C3
kalyk	76	M7
kansas	130	C3
kansas	130	C3
kansas City	130	B2
khalts'ikhe	92	K3
khangel'sk	70	H2
khipelag Nordenshel'da	76	R2
klow	35	E4
koudi	68	C6
les	58	K10
lington, *Oreg., United States*	126	B1
lington, *Tex., United States*	130	B3
lington, *Va., United States*	128	E3
lit	102	G5
lon	54	H4
magh	35	E2
mavir	92	J1
menia	92	K3
menia	140	B3
mentières	54	E4
midale	114	K6
mstrong	122	P6
myans'k	70	F5
nedo	60	H2
nett	130	B2
nhem	54	H3
nhem Land	114	F2
no	62	F7
nold	38	G2
nøy	48	G3
nøya	48	L1
nprior	128	E1
nsberg	54	L3
nstadt	52	F6
oab	108	B5
olsen	52	E5
oma	100	G4
orae	112	H6
quipélago dos Bijagós	104	A2
Ramādī	90	D3
Ramlah	94	C7
ran	36	C6
Raqqah	92	H6
ras	54	E4
rasate	60	H1
Rastan	94	D2
Rawḑah	90	E7
Rayn	95	A5
recife	102	C3
Riyāḑ	90	E5
row Lake	126	C1
royo Grande	132	B1
Ruşāfah	92	H6
Rustāq	90	G5
Ruţba	90	D3
Ruways	90	F5
sandøy	48	G4
ta, *Greece*	68	C5
ta, *Mallorca*	60	P5
tem	82	G2
temovsk	76	S7
temovskiy	78	K5
tesia	132	F2
thur	126	F2
thur's Town	130	F5
tigas	142	K5
tillery Lake	122	J4
tsyz	66	S4
tux	76	P10
tvin	92	J3
tyk	78	Q4
u	112	D6
Arua	106	E3
Aruba	134	K6
Arumã	140	E4
Arusha	106	F4
Arvayheer	80	C1
Arviat	122	N4
Arvidsjaur	48	K4
Arvika	48	G7
Ary	76	Y3
Aryta	78	M4
Arzamas	70	H3
Arzew	60	K9
Arzignano	62	G5
Asahi-dake	82	M2
Asahikawa	82	M2
Åsalë	100	G5
Asansol	88	E4
Asarum	50	D1
Asbest	70	M3
Ascea	64	K8
Ascensión	140	E7
Ascension	98	B6
Aschaffenburg	52	E7
Aschersleben	52	G5
Ascoli Piceno	64	H6
Åsela	106	F2
Åsele	48	J4
Asenovgrad	68	G3
Asha	70	L3
Ashbourne, *Republic of Ireland*	35	E3
Ashbourne, *Eng., United Kingdom*	38	G2
Ashburton	116	C6
Ashby-de-la-Zouch	38	G3
Ashdod	94	B5
Asherton	130	B4
Asheville	128	D3
Ashford	38	J4
Ash Fork	132	D1
Ashgabat	90	G2
Ashington	36	G6
Ashizuri-misaki	82	G7
Ashkhabad = Ashgabat	90	G2
Ashland, *Kans., United States*	126	G3
Ashland, *Ky., United States*	128	D3
Ashland, *Mont., United States*	126	E1
Ashland, *Oreg., United States*	126	B2
Ashland, *Wis., United States*	128	B1
Ashoro	82	M2
Ashqelon	94	B5
Ash Shadādah	92	J5
Ash Shāriqah	95	F4
Ash Sharqāt	92	K6
Ash Shiḩr	90	E7
Ash Shu'bah	95	A2
Ash Shuqayq	100	H4
Ash Shurayf	100	G2
Ash Shuwayrif	102	H3
Ashtabula	128	D2
Ashton-under-Lyne	38	F2
Ashuanipi	122	T6
Ashuanipi Lake	122	T6
Asia	74	M5
Āsika	88	D5
Asilah	102	D1
Asinara	64	C7
Asino	76	R6
Asīr	100	H3
Aşkale	92	J4
Askim	48	F7
Askot	88	D3
Asmara	100	G4
Åsnen	48	H8
Āsosa	106	E1
Aspang Markt	62	M3
Aspe	60	K6
Aspermont	132	F2
As Pontes de Garcia Rodriguez	60	C1
As Sa'an	94	E1
Assab	100	H5
As Şalīf	90	D6
As Salmān	90	E3
As Salwā	95	D4
Assamakka	102	G5
As Samāwah	100	J1
Aş Şanamayn	94	D3
As Sarīr	100	D2
Asse	54	G4
Assemini	64	C9
Assen	54	J2
Assens	52	E1
As Sīb	95	H5
As Sidrah	100	C1
Assiniboia	122	K7
Assiniboine	122	M7
Assis	142	L3
Assisi	64	G5
As Sukhnah	92	H6
As Sulaymānīyah	92	L6
As Sulayyil	90	E5
Assumption	106	H5
As Suwaydā'	94	D4
As Suwayh	90	G5
Astakida	68	J9
Astana	76	N7
Astara	90	E2
Asti	62	D6
Astorga	60	D2
Astoria	126	B1
Astove	106	H6
Astrakhan'	70	J5
Astypalaia	68	J8
Asunción	142	K4
Aswân	100	F3
Aswân Dam	100	F3
Asyût	100	F2
As Zaydīyah	100	H4
Ata	112	J8
Atafu	112	J6
Atakpamé	104	E3
Atalaia do Norte	140	C4
Atâr	102	C4
Atasu	76	N8
Atbara	100	F4
Atbasar	70	N4
Atchison	130	B2
Aterno	64	H6
Ath	54	F4
Athabasca	122	J5
Athens = Athina	68	F7
Athens, *Al., United States*	130	D3
Athens, *Ga., United States*	130	E3
Athens, *Oh., United States*	130	E2
Athens, *Tenn., United States*	130	E2
Athens, *Tex., United States*	130	B3
Athina	68	F7
Athlone	35	D3
Ath Thāyat	94	D7
Athy	35	E4
Ati	100	C5
Atiamuri	116	F4
Atico	140	C7
Atikokan	128	B1
Atka	78	S4
Atka Island	132	(3)C1
Atlanta	130	E3
Atlantic, *Ia., United States*	130	B1
Atlantic, *N.C., United States*	130	F3
Atlantic City	128	F3
Atlantic Ocean	42	E2
Atlas Bogd	80	B2
Atlas Mountains	60	N9
Atlasovo	78	T5
Atlas Saharien	102	E2
Atlin	122	E5
Atmakur	88	C5
Atmore	130	D3
Atoka	130	B3
Atokos	68	C6
Atol das Rocas	140	L4
Atri	64	H6
Aţ Ţā'if	90	D5
Attapu	84	D4
Attawapiskat	122	Q6
Attersee	62	J3
Attica	128	C2
Attleborough	38	K3
Attu Island	132	(3)A1
Attur	88	C6
At Turbah	100	H5
Atyrau	70	K5
Aubagne	58	L10
Aubange	54	H5
Aube	58	K5
Aubenas	58	K9
Aubry Lake	122	F3
Auburn, *Al., United States*	130	D3
Auburn, *Calif., United States*	126	B3
Auburn, *Nebr., United States*	126	G2
Auburn, *Wash., United States*	126	B1
Aubusson	58	H8
Auce	50	M1
Auch	58	F10
Auchi	104	F3
Auchterarder	36	E5
Auckland	116	E3
Auckland Islands	116	(2)B1
Aude	58	H10
Aue	52	H6
Auerbach	52	H6
Augathella	114	J5
Augsburg	62	F2
Augusta, *Australia*	114	C6
Augusta, *Italy*	64	K11
Augusta, *Ga., United States*	130	E3
Augusta, *Me., United States*	128	G2
Augustów	50	M4
Aulla	62	E6
Aurangābād	88	C5
Auray	58	C6
Aurich	54	K1
Aurillac	58	H9
Aurora, *Colo., United States*	126	F3
Aurora, *Ill., United States*	128	C2
Aurora, *Mo., United States*	130	C2
Aurukun	114	H2
Aus	108	B5
Auschwitz = Oświęcim	50	J7
Austin, *Minn., United States*	128	B2
Austin, *Nev., United States*	126	C3
Austin, *Tex., United States*	130	B3
Australia	114	E4
Australian Alps	112	E9
Australian Capital Territory	114	J7
Austria	62	J3
Autun	58	K7
Auxerre	58	J6
Auxonne	58	L6
Avallon	58	J6
Avam	78	E2
Åvārsin	92	M4
Aveiro	60	B4
Avellino	64	J8
Averøya	48	D5
Avesnes-sur-Helpe	54	F4
Avesta	48	J6
Avezzano	64	H6
Aviemore	36	E4
Avignon	58	K10
Ávila	60	F4
Avilés	60	E1
Avion	54	E4
Avola	64	K12
Avon, *Eng., United Kingdom*	38	G3
Avon, *Eng., United Kingdom*	38	G4
Avonmouth	38	F4
Avranches	58	D5
Avrig	66	M4
Awaji-shima	82	H6
Awanui	116	D2
Awat	76	Q9
Awatere	116	D5
Awbārī	100	B2
Aweil	106	D2
Awjilah	100	D2
Awka	104	F3
Ax-les-Thermes	58	G11
Ayacucho	140	C6
Ayaguz	76	Q8
Ayakkuduk	76	M9
Ayamonte	60	C7
Ayan	78	P5
Ayan	78	E3
Aya Napa	94	A2
Ayancık	92	F3
Ayanka	78	V4
Ayaviri	140	C6
Aydin	92	B5
Aydıncık	68	R8
Ayers Rock = Uluru	114	F5
Aykhal	78	J3
Aykino	76	H5
Aylesbury	38	H4
Aylmer Lake	122	K4
Aylsham	38	K3
'Ayn al Baida'	94	D5
Ayní	76	M10
Ayn 'Isá	92	H5
Ayoûn el 'Atroûs	102	D5
Ayr, *Australia*	114	J3
Ayr, *United Kingdom*	36	D6
Ayutthaya	84	C4
Ayvalik	68	J5
Azaila	60	K3
Azaouâd	102	E5
Āzarān	92	M5
Azare	104	G2
Azauri	140	G3
A'zāz	92	G5
Azdavay	68	R3
Azerbaijan	92	M3
Aziza	60	H3
Azogues	140	B4
Azores = Açores	102	(1)B2
Azov	70	G5
Azpeitia	60	H1
Azrou	102	D2
Aztec	126	E3
Azuaga	60	E6
Azul	142	K6
Az Zabadānī	94	D3
Aẓ Ẓahrān	95	D3
Az Zāwīyah	100	B1
Az Zubayr	95	B1

B

Name	Page	Grid
Ba'albek	94	D2
Baaqline	94	C3
Baardheere	106	G3
Babadag	66	R5
Babaeski	68	K3
Bāb al Mandab	90	D7
Babana	87	A3
Babanusa	106	D1
Babar	87	C4
Babayevo	70	G3
Babayurt	92	M2
Babo	87	D3
Bābol	90	F2
Babruysk	70	E4
Babura	104	F2
Babushkin	78	H6
Babuyan Islands	84	G3
Bacaadweyn	106	H2
Bacabal	140	J4
Bacan	87	C3
Bacău	66	P3
Baccarat	62	B2
Bachu	90	L2
Back	122	M3
Bačka Palanka	66	G4
Bačka Topola	66	G4
Backnang	62	E2
Bac Liêu	84	D5
Bacolod	84	G4
Badajós	140	H4
Badajoz	60	D6
Bad al Milḩ	92	K7
Badalona	60	N3
Bad Ausee	62	J3
Bad Bentheim	54	K2
Bad Berleburg	52	D5
Bad Doberan	52	G2
Bad Dürkheim	52	D7
Bad Ems	54	K4
Baden	50	F9
Baden-Baden	62	D2
Badenoch	36	D5
Baderna	64	H3
Bad Freienwalde	52	K4
Badgastein	62	J3
Badgingarra	114	C6
Bad Harzburg	52	F5
Bad Hersfeld	52	E6
Bad Homburg	52	D6
Bad Honnef	54	K4
Badin	88	A4
Bad Ischl	62	J3
Bādiyat ash Shām	94	D4
Bad Kissingen	52	F6
Bad Kreuznach	54	K5
Bad Langensalza	52	F5
Bad Lauterberg	52	F5
Bad Liebenwerda	52	J5
Bad Mergentheim	52	E7
Bad Nauheim	52	D6
Bad Neuenahr-Ahrweiler	54	K4
Bad Neustadt	52	F6
Bad Oeynhausen	52	D4
Badong	80	E4
Bad Reichenhall	62	H3
Badr Ḩunayn	100	G3
Bad Säckingen	52	C9
Bad Salzuflen	52	D4
Bad Salzungen	52	F6
Bad Schwartau	52	F3
Bad Segeberg	52	F3
Bad Sobernheim	54	K5
Bad Urach	62	E2
Bad Vöslau	66	D2
Bad Waldsee	62	E3
Bad Wilbad	62	D2
Bad Wildungen	52	E5
Bad Windsheim	52	F7
Bad Wurzach	62	E3
Baena	60	F7
Bærum	48	F7

Baeza 60 G6
Baffin Bay 120 J2
Baffin Island 122 R2
Bafia 104 G4
Bafoulabé 104 B2
Bafoussam 104 G3
Bāfq 90 G3
Bafra 92 F3
Bafra Burun 92 G3
Bāft 95 G2
Bafwasende 106 D3
Baga 100 B5
Bagani 108 C3
Bagansiapiapi 86 C2
Bagaroua 104 E2
Bagdad 132 D2
Bagdarin 78 J6
Bagé 142 L5
Bagenalstown 35 E4
Baggs 126 E2
Baghdād 90 D3
Bagheria 64 H10
Baghlān 90 J2
Bagnères-de-Bigorre 58 F10
Bagno di Romagna 62 G7
Bagnols-sur-Cèze 58 K9
Bago 84 G4
Baguio 84 G3
Bagun Datuk 86 C2
Baharampur 88 E4
Bahawalnagar 88 B3
Bahawalpur 88 B3
Bahçe 92 G5
Bahia 140 J6
Bahía Blanca 142 J6
Bahía Blanca 142 J6
Bahía de Banderas 134 C4
Bahía de Campeche 134 F4
Bahía de Manta 140 A4
Bahía de Petacalco 134 D5
Bahía de Pisco 140 B6
Bahía de Santa Elena 140 A4
Bahía de Sechura 140 A5
Bahía Grande 142 H9
Bahía Kino 124 D6
Bahía Negra 142 K3
Bahía Samborombón 142 K6
Bahir Dar 100 G5
Bahraich 88 D3
Bahrain 95 D4
Baḩrat Ḩimş 94 D2
Bahr el Abiad 100 F5
Bahr el Azraq 100 F5
Bahr el Ghazal 100 C5
Bahr el Ghazal 106 D2
Bahr el Jebel 106 E2
Bahr el Nîl = Nile 100 F4
Baia 66 R5
Baía de Marajó 140 H4
Baía de Todos os Santos 140 K6
Baía do Bengo 104 G6
Baia Mare 66 L2
Baião 140 H4
Baia Sprie 66 L2
Baïbokoum 106 B2
Baicheng, *China* 80 G1
Baicheng, *China* 76 Q9
Baie Comeau 128 G1
Baie de la Seine 54 B5
Baie de la Somme 54 D4
Baie-du-Poste 122 S6
Baie St. Paul 128 F1
Baiji 92 K6
Baile Ailein 36 B2
Baile Átha Cliath = Dublin 35 E3
Bailén 60 G6
Bailleul 54 E4
Bailundo 108 B2
Bainbridge 130 E3
Bairiki 112 H5
Bairin Yuoqi 80 F2
Bairin Zuoqi 80 F2
Bairnsdale 114 J7
Bais 84 G5
Baja 66 F3
Baja California 124 C5
Bajram Curri 68 B2
Bakchar 76 Q6
Bakel 104 B2
Baker 112 J5
Baker, *Calif., United States* 126 C3
Baker, *Mont., United States* 126 F1
Baker, *Oreg., United States* 126 C2
Baker Lake 122 M4
Baker Lake 122 N4
Bakersfield 132 C1
Bakewell 38 G2
Bakharden 76 K10
Bakhta 78 D4
Baki 90 E1
Bakkafjörður 48 (1)F1
Bakkaflói 48 (1)F1
Baku = Baki 90 E1
Balâ 92 E4
Bala 38 E3
Balabac 84 F5
Balabac 84 F5
Balabac Strait 84 F5
Balagansk 78 G6
Balaghat 88 D4
Balaguer 60 L3
Balakhta 76 S6
Balaklava 92 E1
Balakovo 70 J4
Bālā Morghāb 76 L10
Bălan 66 N3
Balāngīr 88 D4
Balashov 70 H4
Balassagyarmat 66 G1
Balaton 66 E3
Balatonfüred 66 E3
Balatonlelle 66 E3
Balbina 140 F4
Balbriggan 35 E3
Balčik 92 C2
Balclutha 116 B8
Bald Knob 128 B3
Baldwin 130 E3
Balearic Islands = Islas Baleares 60 N5
Baler 84 G3
Bāleshwar 88 E4
Baley 78 K6
Baléyara 104 E2
Balguntay 76 R9
Bali 86 F4
Balige 86 B2
Balıkesir 68 K5
Balikpapan 86 F3
Balimo 87 F4
Balingen 62 D2
Balintang Channel 84 G3
Balkhash 76 N8
Ballachulish 36 C5
Balladonia 114 D6
Ballaghaderreen 35 C3
Ballantrae 36 C6
Ballarat 114 H7
Ballater 36 E4
Balleny Island 144 (2)Y3
Ballina, *Australia* 114 K5
Ballina, *Republic of Ireland* 35 B2
Ballinasloe 35 C3
Ballincollig 35 C5
Ballinger 132 G2
Ballinrobe 35 B3
Ballinskelligs Bay 35 A5
Ball's Pyramid 114 L6
Ballum 54 H1
Ballybofey 35 D2
Ballycastle 35 E1
Ballyclare 35 F2
Ballygar 35 C3
Ballygawley 35 D2
Ballyhaunis 35 C3
Ballymena 35 E2
Ballymoney 35 E1
Ballynahinch 35 F2
Ballyshannon 35 C2
Balmazújváros 66 J2
Balotra 88 B3
Balranald 114 H6
Balş 66 M5
Balsas 140 H5
Balsas 134 D5
Balta 66 S2
Bălţi 66 Q2
Baltic Sea 48 J8
Baltimore 128 E3
Baltiysk 50 J3
Balvi 48 P8
Balykchy 76 P9
Balykshi 70 K5
Bam 90 G4
Bamaga 114 H2
Bamako 104 C2
Bamba 102 E5
Bambari 106 C2
Bamberg 52 F7
Bambesa 106 D3
Bambouk 102 C6
Bambouk Kaarta 104 B2
Bamda 80 B4
Bamenda 104 G3
Bāmīān 90 J3
Banaba 112 G6
Bañados del Izozog 140 E7
Banalia 106 D3
Banana, *Australia* 114 K4
Banana, *Dem. Rep. of Congo* 106 A5
Banaz 68 M6
Ban Ban 84 C3
Ban Betong 86 C1
Banbridge 35 E2
Banbury 38 G3
Banchory 36 F4
Banda 88 D3
Banda Aceh 84 B5
Bandama 104 C3
Bandarbeyla 106 J2
Bandar-e 'Abbās 95 G3
Bandar-e Anzalī 90 E2
Bandar-e Deylam 95 D1
Bandar-e Ganāveh 95 D2
Bandar-e Khoemir 95 F3
Bandar-e Lengeh 95 F3
Bandar-e Ma'shur 95 C1
Bandar-e Torkeman 90 F2
Bandar Khomeynī 95 C1
Bandar Seri Begawan 86 E2
Banda Sea 87 C3
Band-e Chārak 95 F3
Band-e Moghūyeh 95 F3
Bandirma 68 K4
Bandundu 106 B4
Bandung 86 D4
Băneasa 66 Q5
Bāneh 92 L6
Banff, *Canada* 122 H6
Banff, *United Kingdom* 36 F4
Bangalore 88 C6
Bangangté 104 G3
Bangassou 106 C3
Bangbong 87 B3
Banggi 86 F1
Banghāzī 100 D1
Bangka 86 D3
Bangkalan 86 E4
Bangkok = Krung Thep 84 C4
Bangladesh 88 E4
Bangor, *N. Ire., United Kingdom* 35 F2
Bangor, *Wales, United Kingdom* 38 D2
Bangor, *United States* 128 G2
Bangor Erris 35 B2
Bang Saphan Yai 84 B4
Bangued 84 G3
Bangui, *Central African Republic* 106 B3
Bangui, *Philippines* 84 G3
Ban Hua Hin 84 B4
Bani-Bangou 104 E1
Banī Walīd 102 H2
Bāniyās 92 F6
Banja Luka 66 E5
Banjarmasin 86 E3
Banjul 104 A2
Ban Khemmarat 84 D3
Banks Island = Moa, *Australia* 114 H2
Banks Island, *B.C., Canada* 122 E6
Banks Island, *N.W.T., Canada* 122 G2
Banks Lake 126 C1
Banks Peninsula 116 D6
Banks Strait 114 J8
Bann, *N. Ire., United Kingdom* 35 E2
Bann, *N. Ire., United Kingdom* 35 E2
Bannerman Town 130 F5
Bannu 88 B2
Bánovce 50 H9
Banská Bystrica 50 J9
Banská Štiavnica 50 H9
Bansko 68 F3
Bantry 35 B5
Bantry Bay 35 B5
Banyo 104 G3
Banyoles 60 N2
Banyuwangi 86 E4
Baode 80 E3
Baoding 80 F3
Baoji 80 D4
Bao Lôc 84 D4
Baoro 106 B2
Baoshan 84 B1
Baotou 80 E2
Baoying 80 F4
Bap 88 B3
Bapaume 54 E4
Ba'qūbah 90 D3
Baquedano 142 H3
Bar 66 G7
Barabai 86 F3
Barabhas 36 E2
Baraboo 128 C2
Barakaldo 60 H1
Baramati 88 B5
Baramula 88 B2
Baran 88 C3
Baranavichy 70 E4
Baraolt 66 N3
Barbados 140 F1
Barbastro 60 L2
Barbate 60 E8
Barbuda 134 M5
Barcaldine 114 J4
Barcău 66 K2
Barcellona Pozzo di Gotto 64 K10
Barcelona, *Spain* 60 N3
Barcelona, *Venezuela* 134 M6
Barcelos, *Brazil* 140 E4
Barcelos, *Spain* 60 B3
Barclayville 104 C4
Barco de Valdeorras = O Barco 60 D2
Barcs 66 E4
Bārdā 92 M3
Bardai 100 C3
Barddhamān 88 E4
Bardejov 50 L8
Bardonecchia 62 B5
Bardsey 38 D3
Bareilly 88 C3
Barentin 54 C5
Barents Sea 76 E3
Barentu 100 G4
Bareo 86 F2
Barga 88 D2
Bargaal 106 J1
Bargteheide 52 F3
Barguzin 78 H6
Bar Harbor 128 G2
Bari 64 L7
Barikot 88 B1
Barinas 140 C2
Bârîs 100 F3
Barisal 88 F4
Barito 87 A3
Barkam 80 C4
Barkava 48 P8
Barkly Tableland 114 F3
Barkol 76 S9
Bârlad 66 Q3
Bârlad 66 Q3
Bar-le-Duc 54 H6
Barletta 64 L7
Barmer 88 B3
Barmouth 38 D3
Barmouth Bay 38 D3
Barnard Castle 36 G7
Barnaul 76 Q7
Barnet 38 H4
Barnoldswick 38 F2
Barnsley 38 G2
Barnstaple 38 D4
Barnstaple Bay 38 D4
Barpeta 88 F3
Barquisimeto 140 D1
Barr 62 C2
Barra, *Brazil* 140 J6
Barra, *United Kingdom* 36 A4
Barracão do Barreto 140 G5
Barracas 60 K5
Barra do Bugres 140 F7
Barra do Corda 140 H5
Barra do Cuanza 106 A5
Barra do Garças 140 G7
Barra do São Manuel 140 G5
Barragem de Santa Clara 60 B7
Barragem de Sobradinho 140 J5
Barragem do Castelo de Bode 60 B5
Barragem do Maranhão 60 C6
Barranca, *Peru* 140 B4
Barranca, *Peru* 140 B6
Barranquilla 134 K6
Barreiras 140 H6
Barreiro 60 A6
Barretos 140 H8
Barrhead 36 D6
Barrie 128 E2
Barron 128 B1
Barrow 132 (1)F1
Barrow 35 E4
Barrow Creek 114 F4
Barrow-in-Furness 36 E7
Barrow Island 114 B4
Barrow Strait 122 N2
Barry 38 E4
Barshatas 76 P8
Barsi 88 C5
Barstow 132 C2
Bar-sur-Aube 58 K5
Bar-sur-Seine 58 K5
Barth 52 H2
Bartın 92 E3
Bartle Frere 112 E7
Bartlesville 130 B2
Bartlett 126 G2
Barton-upon-Humber 38 H2
Bartoszyce 50 K3
Barus 86 B2
Baruun Urt 80 E1
Barwani 88 B4
Barysaw 70 E4
Basaidu 95 F3
Basankusu 106 B3
Basarabeasca 66 R3
Basarabi 66 R5
Basca 64 C2
Basco 84 G2
Basel 62 C3
Bashkiriya 70 K4
Bāsht 95 D1
Basilan 87 B1
Basildon 38 J4
Basiluzzo 64 K10
Basingstoke 38 G4
Başkale 92 K4
Basoko 106 C3
Bassano 124 D1
Bassano del Grappa 62 G5
Bassar 104 E3
Bassas da India 108 F4
Bassein 84 A3
Basse Santa Su 102 C6
Basse-Terre 134 M5
Bassett 126 G2
Bassikounou 102 D5
Bass Strait 114 H7
Bassum 52 D4
Bastak 95 F3
Bastānābād 92 M5
Basti 88 D3
Bastia 64 D6
Bastogne 54 H4
Bastrop, *La., United States* 130 C3
Bastrop, *Tex., United States* 130 B3
Bata 104 F4
Batagay 78 N3
Batagay-Alyta 78 N3
Batak 68 G3
Batamay 78 M4
Batang 80 B5
Batangas 84 G4
Batan Islands 84 G2
Batanta 87 C3
Batchelor 114 F2
Batemans Bay 114 K7
Batesville 130 D3
Bath, *United Kingdom* 38 F4
Bath, *United States* 128 E2
Bathinda 88 B2
Bathurst, *Australia* 114 J6
Bathurst, *Canada* 122 T7
Bathurst Inlet 122 K3
Bathurst Island, *Australia* 114 E2
Bathurst Island, *Canada* 122 M1
Batman 90 D2
Batna 102 G1
Baton Rouge 130 C3
Bátonyterenye 66 G2
Batouri 104 G4
Batroûn 94 C2
Batticaloa 88 D7
Battipaglia 64 J8
Battle 122 J6
Battle 38 J5
Battle Creek 128 C2
Battle Harbour 122 V6
Battle Mountain 126 C2
Batu 106 F
Batui 87 B3
Bat'umi 92 J3
Batu Pahat 86 C2
Baturino 76 R6
Baubau 87 B4
Bauchi 104 F
Baudette 128 B
Baukau 87 C
Baume-les-Dames 58 M6
Bauru 142 M
Bauska 48 N
Bautzen 50 D
Bawean 86 E
Bawiti 100 E
Bawku 104 D
Bayamo 134 J
Bayanaul 76 P
Bayandelger 78 H
Bayan Har Shan 80 B
Bayanhongor 80 C
Bayan Mod 80 C
Bayan Obo 80 D
Bayansumküre 76 Q
Bayburt 92 J
Bay City, *Mich., United States* 128 D
Bay City, *Tex., United States* 130 B
Baydhabo 106 G
Bayerische Alpen 62 G
Bayeux 54 B
Bayfield 128 B
Bayindir 68 K
Bāyir 94 D
Baykit 76 T
Baykonur 76 M
Bay Minette 130 D
Bay of Bengal 88 E
Bay of Biscay 58 C
Bay of Fundy 122 T
Bay of Islands 116 E

Bay of Plenty	116	F3
Bayonne	58	D10
Bayramaly	90	H2
Bayramiç	68	J5
Bayreuth	52	G7
Baysun	90	J2
Bayt al Faqīh	100	H5
Bay View	116	F4
Baza	60	H7
Bazas	58	E9
Bazdar	90	J4
Beach	126	F1
Beachy Head	38	J5
Beaconsfield	38	H4
Beagle Gulf	114	E2
Bealanana	108	H2
Bear Island = Bjørnøya, *Norway*	76	B3
Bear Island, *Republic of Ireland*	35	B5
Bear Lake	126	D2
Bearsden	36	D6
Beasain	60	H1
Beas de Segura	60	H6
Beatrice	130	B1
Beatty	132	C1
Beaufort, *Malaysia*	86	F1
Beaufort, *N.C., United States*	130	F3
Beaufort, *S.C., United States*	130	E3
Beaufort Sea	120	Q2
Beaufort West	108	C6
Beaumont, *New Zealand*	116	B7
Beaumont, *United States*	130	C3
Beaune	58	K6
Beauvais	54	E5
Beaver	126	D3
Beaver Creek	132	(1)J3
Beaver Dam	128	C3
Beaver Falls	128	D2
Beawar	88	B3
Beazley	142	H5
Bebington	38	E2
Bebra	52	E6
Beccles	38	K3
Bečej	66	H4
Béchar	102	E2
Beckley	130	E2
Becks	116	B7
Beckum	54	L3
Beclean	66	M2
Bedale	36	G7
Bedelē	106	F2
Bedford, *United Kingdom*	38	H3
Bedford, *United States*	130	D2
Bedworth	38	G3
Beenleigh	114	K5
Beer Menuha	94	C6
Beer Ora	94	C7
Be'ér Sheva'	94	B5
Beeston	38	G3
Beeville	130	B4
Behbehān	95	D1
Bei'an	78	M7
Beihai	84	D2
Beijing	80	F3
Beipan	80	D5
Beipiao	80	G2
Beira	108	E3
Beirut = Beyrouth	94	C3
Beith	36	D6
Beiuş	66	K3
Beizhen	82	A3
Béja	102	G1
Bejaïa	102	G1
Béjar	60	E4
Bekdash	90	F1
Békés	50	L11
Békéscsaba	66	J3
Bekily	108	H4
Bekkai	82	N2
Bela	90	J4
Bela Crkva	66	J5
Belaga	86	E2
Belarus	46	G2
Bela Vista	108	E5
Belaya	70	K3
Belaya Gora	78	R3
Bełchatów	50	J6
Belcher Islands	122	Q5
Beledweyne	106	H3
Belek	76	J10
Belém	140	H4
Belen	134	C2
Belfast	35	F2
Belfield	126	F1
Belfort	62	B3
Belgazyn	76	T7
Belgium	54	G4
Belgorod	70	G4
Belgrade = Beograd	66	H5
Beli	104	G3
Belice	64	H11
Beli Manastir	66	F4
Belinyu	86	D3
Belitung	86	D3
Belize	134	G5
Belize	134	G5
Bellac	58	G7
Bella Coola	122	F6
Bellary	88	C5
Belleek	35	C2
Bellefontaine	128	D2
Belle Fourche	126	F2
Belle Glade	130	E4
Belle Île	58	B6
Belle Isle	122	V6
Bellême	58	F5
Belleterre	128	E1
Belleville, *Canada*	128	E2
Belleville, *United States*	130	B2
Bellingham	126	B1
Bellingshausen Sea	144	(2)JJ4
Bellinzona	62	E4
Bello	140	B2
Belluno	62	H4
Bellyk	78	E6
Belmont	128	E2
Belmonte, *Brazil*	140	K7

Belmonte, *Spain*	60	H5
Belmopan	134	G5
Belmullet	35	B2
Belogorsk	78	M6
Belogradčik	66	K6
Beloha	108	H5
Belo Horizonte	140	J7
Beloit, *Kans., United States*	130	B2
Beloit, *Wis., United States*	128	C2
Belo Monte	140	G4
Belomorsk	70	F2
Belorechensk	92	H1
Beloretsk	70	L4
Belo Tsiribihina	108	G3
Belovo	76	R7
Beloyarskiy	76	M5
Beloye More	70	G1
Belozersk	70	G2
Belozerskoye	70	N3
Belper	38	G2
Belye Vody	76	M9
Belyy Yar	76	Q6
Belzig	52	H4
Bembibre	60	D2
Bemidji	128	A1
Bena Dibele	106	C4
Ben Alder	36	D5
Benavente	60	E3
Benbecula	36	A4
Bend	126	B2
Bendorf	54	K4
Bene	108	E3
Benešov	50	D8
Benevento	64	J7
Bengbu	80	F4
Bengkalis	86	C2
Bengkulu	86	C3
Benguela	108	A2
Benguerir	102	D2
Benha	100	F1
Ben Hope	36	D3
Beni	106	D3
Beni	140	D6
Beni Abbès	102	E2
Benicarló	60	L4
Benidorm	60	K6
Benî Mazâr	100	F2
Beni Mellal	102	D2
Benin	104	E2
Benin City	104	F3
Beni Saf	60	J9
Beni Slimane	60	P8
Beni Suef	100	F2
Benito Juaréz	142	K6
Benjamin Constant	140	D4
Benkelman	126	F2
Ben Klibreck	36	D3
Benkovac	62	L6
Ben Lawers	36	D5
Ben Lui	36	D5
Ben Macdui	36	E4
Ben More	36	B5
Ben More Assynt	36	D3
Ben Nevis	36	D5
Bennington	128	F2
Benoud	102	F2
Bensheim	52	D7
Benson, *Ariz., United States*	132	D2
Benson, *Minn., United States*	124	G2
Benteng	87	B4
Bentinck Island	114	G3
Bent Jbail	94	C3
Bentley	38	G2
Bentonville	130	C2
Bentung	86	C2
Benue	104	G3
Ben Wyvis	36	D4
Benxi	80	G2
Beo	86	H6
Beograd	66	H5
Bepazarı	92	D3
Berat	68	B4
Beravina	108	H3
Berber	100	F4
Berbera	100	H5
Berbérati	106	B3
Berchtesgaden	62	J3
Berck	54	D4
Berdigestyakh	78	M4
Berdyans'k	70	G5
Berdychiv	70	E5
Bereeda	106	J1
Berehove	66	K1
Bererreá	60	C2
Berettyóújfalu	66	J2
Berettys	50	L10
Bereznik	70	H2
Berezniki	70	L3
Berezovo	70	N2
Berezovyy	78	P6
Berga	60	M2
Bergama	68	K5
Bergamo	62	E5
Bergara	60	H1
Bergby	48	J6
Bergedorf	52	F3
Bergen, *Germany*	52	J2
Bergen, *Germany*	52	E4
Bergen, *Netherlands*	54	G2
Bergen, *Norway*	48	C6
Bergen op Zoom	54	G3
Bergerac	58	F9
Bergheim	54	J4
Bergisch Gladbach	52	C6
Bergsfjordhalvøya	48	L1
Beringen	54	H3
Beringovskiy	78	X4
Bering Sea	132	(1)C4
Bering Strait	132	(1)C2
Berīzak	95	G3
Berkeley	132	B1
Berkner Island	144	(2)A2
Berkovica	66	L6
Berlin, *Germany*	52	J4
Berlin, *United States*	128	F2
Bermejillo	132	F3

Bermejo	142	K4
Bermeo	60	H1
Bermuda	120	H6
Bern	62	C4
Bernado	132	E2
Bernalda	64	L8
Bernau	52	J4
Bernay	54	C5
Bernburg	52	G5
Berner Alpen	62	C4
Berneray	36	A4
Beroun	50	D8
Berounka	52	J7
Berovo	68	E3
Berrouaghia	60	N8
Berry Islands	130	F4
Bertoua	104	G4
Bertram	128	D1
Beruni	76	L9
Berwick-upon-Tweed	36	F6
Besalampy	108	G3
Besançon	58	M6
Besbay	76	K8
Beshneh	95	F2
Bessemer	130	D3
Bestamak	76	P8
Bestuzhevo	70	H2
Bestyakh, *Russia*	78	L3
Bestyakh, *Russia*	78	M4
Betanzos	60	B1
Bětdâmbâng	84	C4
Bethany	128	B2
Bethel, *Ak., United States*	132	(1)E3
Bethel, *Pa., United States*	128	F2
Bethlehem, *Israel*	94	C5
Bethlehem, *South Africa*	108	D5
Béthune	54	E4
Betioky	108	G4
Betoota	114	H5
Betpak-Dala	76	M8
Betroka	108	H4
Bet-She'an	94	C4
Bettiah	88	D3
Bettyhill	36	D3
Betul	88	C4
Betws-y-Coed	38	E2
Betzdorf	52	C6
Beulah	128	C2
Beverley	38	H2
Beverungen	52	E5
Bexhill	38	J5
Bey Dağlari	68	M8
Beykoz	68	M3
Beyla	104	C3
Beyneu	76	J8
Beypazarı	68	P4
Beyra	106	H2
Beyrouth	94	C3
Beyşehir	68	P7
Beyşehir Gölü	68	P7
Bezhetsk	70	G3
Béziers	58	J10
Bhadgaon	88	E3
Bhadrakh	88	E4
Bhadravati	88	C6
Bhagalpur	88	E3
Bhairab Bazar	88	F4
Bhakkar	88	B2
Bhamo	84	B2
Bharuch	88	B4
Bhatpara	88	E4
Bhavnagar	88	B4
Bhawanipatna	88	D5
Bhilai	88	D4
Bhilwara	88	B3
Bhīmavaram	88	D5
Bhind	88	C3
Bhiwandi	88	B5
Bhopal	88	C4
Bhubaneshwar	88	E4
Bhuj	88	A4
Bhusawal	88	C4
Bhutan	88	E3
Biak	87	E3
Biak	87	E3
Biała	50	K8
Biała Podlaska	50	N5
Białogard	50	F3
Białystok	50	N4
Biarritz	58	D10
Biasca	62	D4
Bibbiena	62	G7
Biberach	62	E2
Bicaz	66	P3
Bicester	38	G4
Bickerton Island	114	G2
Bicske	66	F2
Bida	104	F3
Bidar	88	C5
Bidbid	95	H5
Biddeford	128	F2
Bideford	38	D4
Bideford Bay = Barnstaple Bay	38	D4
Biedenkopf	52	D6
Biel	62	C3
Bielefeld	52	D4
Biella	62	D5
Bielsko-Biała	50	J8
Bielsk Podlaski	50	N5
Biên Hoa	84	D4
Bietigheim-Bissingen	62	E2
Big	122	G2
Biga	68	K4
Bigadiç	68	L5
Big Desert	114	H7
Big Falls	128	B1
Biggar	36	E6
Biggleswade	38	H3
Bighorn	124	E2
Bighorn Lake	126	E1
Bighorn Mountains	126	E2
Bight of Bangkok	84	C4
Bight of Benin	104	E3
Bight of Biafra	104	F4
Big Lake	132	(1)H2
Bignona	102	B6

Big Pine	130	E5
Big Rapids	128	C2
Big River	122	K6
Big Sandy	126	D1
Big Sioux	126	G2
Big Spring	132	F2
Big Sur	132	B1
Big Trout Lake	122	P6
Bihać	62	L6
Bihoro	82	N2
Bijapur	88	C5
Bījār	92	M6
Bijeljina	66	G5
Bijelo Polje	66	G6
Bijie	80	D5
Bikaner	88	B3
Bikin	78	N7
Bikini	112	G4
Bilaspur	88	D4
Biläsuvar	92	N4
Bila Tserkva	70	F5
Bilbao	60	H1
Bileća	66	F7
Bilecik	68	M4
Bilečko Jezero	66	F7
Biled	66	H4
Biłgoraj	50	M7
Bilhorod-Dnistrovs'kyy	70	F5
Bilibino	78	V3
Bilina	52	J6
Billericay	38	J4
Billings	126	D1
Billingshurst	38	H4
Bill of Portland	38	F5
Bilma	100	B4
Biloela	114	K4
Biloxi	130	D3
Bimini Islands	130	F4
Bina-Etawa	88	C4
Binche	54	G4
Bindi Bindi	114	C6
Bindura	108	E3
Bingen	52	C7
Binghamton	128	E2
Bingley	38	G2
Bingöl	92	J4
Binongko	87	B4
Bintuhan	86	C3
Bintulu	86	E2
Bintuni	87	D3
Binyang	84	D2
Binzhou	80	F3
Biograd	62	L7
Birāk	102	H3
Birao	100	D5
Biratnagar	88	E3
Bi'r Bazīrī	94	E2
Birdsville	114	G5
Bireun	86	B1
Bir Gandouz	102	B4
Bîr Gifgâfa	94	A6
Birhan	100	G5
Bîr Hasana	94	A6
Birjand	90	G3
Birkenfeld	54	K5
Birkenhead	38	E2
Birmingham, *United Kingdom*	38	G3
Birmingham, *United States*	130	D3
Bîr Mogreïn	102	C3
Birnie	112	J6
Birnin-Gwari	104	F2
Birnin Kebbi	104	E2
Birnin Konni	104	F2
Birnin Kudu	104	F2
Birobidzhan	78	N7
Birr	35	D3
Birsk	70	L3
Bîr Tâba	94	B7
Biržai	50	P1
Bi'r Zalţan	100	C2
Bisbee	132	E2
Bisceglie	64	L7
Bischofshofen	62	J3
Bischofswerda	50	D6
Biševo	64	L6
Bishkek	76	N9
Bishop	126	C3
Bishop Auckland	36	G7
Bishop's Cleeve	38	F4
Bishop's Stortford	38	J4
Biskra	102	G2
Bislig	84	H5
Bismarck	124	F2
Bismarck Sea	112	E6
Bissau	102	B6
Bistcho Lake	122	H5
Bistrița	66	M2
Bistrița	66	P3
Bitburg	54	J5
Bitche	52	C7
Bitkine	100	C5
Bitlis	92	K4
Bitola	68	D3
Bitonto	64	L7
Bitterfeld	52	H5
Bitterroot Range	126	C1
Bitti	64	D8
Bitung	87	C2
Biu	104	G2
Biwa-ko	82	H6
Bixby	128	B3
Biyāvra	88	C4
Biysk	76	R7
Bizerte	102	G1
Bjala, *Bulgaria*	66	N6
Bjala, *Bulgaria*	66	Q7
Bjala Slatina	66	L6
Bjelovar	66	D4
Bjerkvik	48	J2
Bjørnøya	76	B3
B-Köpenick	52	J4
Bla	104	C2
Blaby	38	G3
Blackall	60	J4
Blackburn	38	F2
Blackfoot	126	D2

Blackfoot Reservoir 126 D2
Black Hills 126 F2
Black Isle 36 D4
Black Mountains 38 E3
Blackpool 38 E2
Black Range 132 E2
Black River Falls 128 B2
Black Rock Desert 126 C2
Blacksburg 128 D3
Black Sea 92 D2
Blacks Harbour 128 G1
Blacksod Bay 35 A2
Black Sugarloaf 114 K6
Black Volta 104 D3
Blackwater 35 C4
Blackwater 114 J4
Blaenau Ffestiniog 38 E3
Blagodarnyy 92 K1
Blagoevgrad 68 F3
Blagoveshchenka 76 P7
Blagoveshchensk 78 M6
Blain 58 D6
Blair 128 A2
Blairgowrie 36 E5
Blairsden 126 B3
Blairsville 130 E3
Blaj 66 L3
Blakely 130 E3
Blanco 140 E6
Blandford Forum 38 F5
Blanding 132 E1
Blangy-sur-Bresle 54 D5
Blankenberge 54 F3
Blankenburg 52 F5
Blankenheim 54 J4
Blantyre 108 F3
Blasket Islands 35 A4
Blaubeuren 62 E2
Blaye-et-Sainte-Luce 58 E8
Bled 62 K4
Blenheim 116 D5
Blessington Lakes 35 E3
Bletchley 38 H3
Blevands Huk 52 D1
Blida 102 F1
Blind River 124 K2
Bloemfontein 108 D5
Bloemhof 108 D5
Blois 58 G6
Blönduós 48 (1)C2
Błonie 50 K5
Bloody Foreland 35 C1
Bloomfield 130 D2
Bloomington, *Ill., United States* 128 C2
Bloomington, *Ind., United States* 128 C3
Bloxwich 38 F3
Bludenz 62 E3
Blue Earth 128 B2
Bluefield 128 D3
Bluefields 134 H6
Blue Mountain Lake 128 F2
Blue Mountains 126 C2
Blue Nile = Bahr el Azraq 100 F5
Bluenose Lake 122 H3
Blue Stack Mountains 35 C2
Bluff, *New Zealand* 116 B8
Bluff, *United States* 132 E1
Blumenau 142 M4
Blyth 36 G6
Blythe 132 D2
Blytheville 130 D2
Bo 104 B3
Boac 84 G4
Boa Vista, *Brazil* 140 E3
Boa Vista, *Cape Verde* 104 (1)B1
Bobbili 88 D5
Bobbio 62 E6
Bobigny 54 E6
Bobingen 62 F2
Böblingen 62 E2
Bobo-Dioulasso 104 D2
Bobolice 50 F4
Bobr 50 E6
Bobrov 70 H4
Bôca do Acre 140 D5
Boca Grande 138 E3
Boca Grande 134 M7
Bocaiúva 140 J7
Bocaranga 106 B2
Bochart 128 F1
Bochnia 50 K8
Bocholt 52 B5
Bochum 52 C5
Bockenem 52 F4
Bodaybo 78 J5
Bode 52 G4
Bodélé 100 C4
Boden 48 L4
Bodham 88 C5
Bodmin 38 D5
Bodmin Moor 38 D5
Bodø 48 H3
Bodrog 50 L9
Bodrum 68 K7
Boende 106 C4
Boffa 104 B2
Bogale 84 B3
Bogalusa 130 D3
Boggabilla 114 K5
Boggeragh Mountains 35 C4
Boghni 60 P8
Bognor Regis 38 H5
Bogo 84 G4
Bog of Allen 35 E3
Bogor 86 D4
Bogorodskoye 78 Q6
Bogotá 140 C3
Bogotol 76 R6
Bogra 88 E4
Boguchany 78 F5
Bogué 102 C5
Bo Hai 80 F3
Bohmerwald 52 H7
Bohol 84 G5
Bohumin 50 H8
Boiaçu 140 E4
Boise 126 C2
Boise City 132 F1
Bojnūrd 76 K10
Bokatola 106 B4
Boké 104 B2
Bokoro 104 H2
Bokspits 108 C5
Bokungu 106 C4
Bolbec 54 C5
Boldu 66 Q4
Bole, *China* 76 Q9
Bole, *Ghana* 104 D3
Bolechiv 50 N8
Bolesławiec 50 E6
Bolgatanga 104 D2
Bolhrad 66 R4
Bolintin-Vale 66 N5
Bolivar 128 B3
Bolivia 140 D7
Bollène 58 K9
Bollnäs 48 J6
Bolmen 48 G8
Bolnisi 92 L3
Bolobo 104 H5
Bologna 62 G6
Bolognesi 140 C5
Bolomba 104 H4
Bolotnoye 76 Q6
Bol'shaya Pyssa 70 J2
Bol'sherech'ye 70 P3
Bol'shezemel'skaya Tundra 76 J4
Bol Shirta 78 C4
Bolshoy Atlym 70 N2
Bol'shoy Osinovaya 78 W3
Bol'shoy Vlas'evo 78 Q6
Bolshoy Yugan 70 P2
Bolsover 38 G2
Bolton 38 F2
Bolu 92 D3
Bolvadin 68 P6
Bolzano 62 G4
Boma 104 G6
Bombala 114 J7
Bombay = Mumbai 88 B5
Bomili 106 D3
Bom Jesus da Lapa 140 J6
Bømlo 48 C7
Bomnak 78 M6
Bomossa 104 H4
Bonāb 92 M5
Bonaparte Archipelago 114 B2
Bonavista Bay 122 W7
Bondeno 62 G6
Bondo 106 C3
Bondokodi 114 C1
Bondoukou 104 D3
Bondowoso 86 E4
Bonerate 87 B4
Bongaigaon 88 F3
Bongandanga 106 C3
Bongao 87 A1
Bongor 104 H2
Bonifacio 64 D7
Bonn 52 C6
Bonners Ferry 126 C1
Bonneville 62 B4
Bonnie Rock 114 C6
Bonorva 64 C8
Bonthe 104 B3
Bontoc 84 G3
Bontosunggu 87 A4
Bonyhád 66 F3
Boone 128 D3
Boonville 130 C2
Boorama 106 G2
Boosaaso 106 H1
Boothia Peninsula 122 M2
Bootle 36 E7
Booué 104 G5
Boppard 52 C6
Bor, *Russia* 78 D4
Bor, *Sudan* 106 E2
Bor, *Turkey* 68 S7
Bor, *Yugoslavia* 66 K5
Borah Peak 126 C3
Borås 48 G8
Borāzjān 95 D2
Bordeaux 58 E9
Bordeira 60 B7
Borden Peninsula 122 Q2
Border Town 114 H7
Bordj Bou Arréridj 102 F1
Bordj Bounaam 60 M9
Bordj Flye Sante Marie 102 E3
Bordj Messaouda 102 G2
Bordj Mokhtar 102 F4
Bordj Omar Driss 102 G3
Borgarnes 48 (1)C2
Borger 132 F1
Borgholm 48 J8
Borgomanero 62 D5
Borgo San Dalmazzo 62 C6
Borgo San Lorenzo 62 G7
Borgosesia 62 D5
Borgo Val di Taro 62 E6
Bori Jenein 102 H2
Borislav 50 N8
Borisoglebsk 70 H4
Borjomi 92 K3
Borken 54 J3
Borkou 100 C4
Borkum 54 J1
Borkum 54 J1
Borlänge 48 H6
Bormida 62 D6
Bormio 62 F4
Borna 52 H5
Borne 54 J2
Borneo 86 E3
Bornholm 48 H9
Borodino 76 R5
Borodinskoye 48 Q6
Boromo 104 D2
Borongan 84 H4
Borovichi 70 F3
Borovskoy 70 M4
Borriana 60 K5
Borrisokane 35 C4
Borroloola 114 G3
Borşa 66 M2
Borshchiv 66 P1
Borshchovochnyy Khrebet 78 J7
Borðeyri 48 (1)C2
Borūjerd 90 E3
Borzya 78 K6
Bosa 64 C8
Bosanska Dubica 66 D4
Bosanska Gradiška 66 E4
Bosanska Kostajnica 62 M5
Bosanska Krupa 66 D5
Bosanski Brod 66 F4
Bosanski Novi 66 D4
Bosanski Petrovac 66 D5
Bosansko Grahovo 62 M6
Bośca 66 J4
Bose 84 D2
Bosilegrad 66 K7
Boskovice 50 F8
Bosna 66 F5
Bosnia-Herzegovina 66 E5
Bosobolo 106 B3
Bosporus = İstanbul Boğazı 68 M3
Bosporus 90 A1
Bossambélé 106 B2
Bossangoa 106 B2
Bossier City 130 C3
Bosten Hu 76 R9
Boston, *United Kingdom* 38 H3
Boston, *United States* 128 F2
Botevgrad 66 L7
Botlikh 90 E1
Botna 66 R3
Botoşani 66 P2
Botou 80 F3
Botrange 54 J4
Botswana 108 C4
Bottrop 54 J3
Bou Ahmed 60 F9
Bouaké 104 C3
Bouar 106 B2
Bouârfa 102 E2
Boufarik 60 N8
Bougainville Island 112 F6
Bougainville Reef 114 J3
Bougouni 104 C2
Bougzoul 60 N9
Bouira 102 F1
Bou Ismaïl 60 N8
Bou Izakarn 102 D3
Boujdour 102 C3
Bou Kadir 60 M8
Boukra 102 C3
Boulder 126 E2
Boulder City 132 D1
Boulia 114 G4
Boulogne-sur-Mer 54 D4
Bouna 104 D3
Boundiali 104 C3
Bounty Islands 112 H10
Bourem 102 E5
Bourg 58 E8
Bourg-de-Piage 58 L9
Bourg-en-Bresse 58 L7
Bourges 58 H6
Bourgoin-Jallieu 58 L8
Bourke 114 J6
Bourne 38 H3
Bournemouth 38 G5
Bou Saâda 102 F1
Bousso 100 C5
Boussu 54 F4
Boutilimit 102 C5
Bouzghaïa 60 M8
Bowbells 126 F1
Bowen 114 J4
Bowie, *Ariz., United States* 132 E2
Bowie, *Tex., United States* 132 G2
Bowkan 92 M5
Bowling Green, *Fla., United States* 130 E4
Bowling Green, *Ky., United States* 130 D2
Bowling Green, *Mo., United States* 130 C2
Bowman 126 F1
Bowman Bay 122 R3
Bowmore 36 B6
Bo Xian 80 F4
Boxwood Hill 114 C6
Boyabat 92 F3
Boyang 80 F5
Boyarka 78 F2
Boyle 35 C3
Boyne 35 E3
Boysen Reservoir 126 E2
Boyuibe 142 J3
Bozcaada 68 H5
Boz Dağ 68 M7
Bozeman 126 D1
Bozkır 68 Q7
Bozoum 106 B2
Bozova 92 H5
Bozüyük 68 N5
Bra 62 C6
Brač 66 D6
Bracciano 64 G6
Bräcke 48 H5
Brackley 38 G3
Bracknell 38 H4
Brad 66 K3
Bradano 64 L8
Bradford 38 G2
Brady 130 B3
Brae 36 (1)G1
Braemar 36 E4
Braga 60 B3
Bragança, *Brazil* 140 H4
Bragança, *Portugal* 60 D3
Brahmapur 88 D5
Brahmaputra 88 F3
Braich y Pwll 38 D3
Brăila 66 Q4
Brainerd 128 B1
Braintree 38 J4
Brake 52 D3
Bramming 52 D1
Brampton 128 E2
Brampton 36 F7
Bramsche 52 D4
Branco 140 E3
Brandberg 108 A4
Brandenburg 52 H4
Brandenton 130 E4
Brandon 122 M7
Brandon Mountain 35 A4
Brandvlei 108 C5
Brandýs 50 D7
Braniewo 50 J3
Brasileia 140 D6
Brasília 140 H7
Braslaw 48 P9
Braşov 66 N4
Bratislava 50 G9
Bratsk 78 G5
Bratskoye Vodokhranilishche 78 G5
Brattleboro 128 F2
Braţul 66 R4
Bratunac 66 G5
Braunau 62 J2
Braunschweig 52 F4
Braunton 38 D4
Brawley 132 C2
Bray 35 E3
Brazil 138 F4
Brazzaville 106 B4
Brčko 66 F5
Brda 50 G4
Bream Bay 116 E2
Brechin 36 F5
Breckenridge 132 G2
Břeclav 50 F9
Brecon Beacons National Park 38 E4
Breda 54 G3
Bredasdorp 108 C6
Bredstedt 52 E2
Bredy 70 M4
Bree 54 H3
Bregenz 62 E3
Breiðafjörður 48 (1)A2
Bremangerlandet 48 B6
Bremen, *Germany* 52 D3
Bremen, *United States* 130 D3
Bremerhaven 52 D3
Bremerton 126 B1
Bremervörde 52 E3
Brenham 130 B3
Brennero 62 G4
Breno 62 F5
Brentwood 38 J4
Brescia 62 F5
Breslau = Wrocław 50 G6
Bressanone 62 G4
Bressay 36 (1)H1
Bressuire 58 E7
Brest, *Belarus* 70 D4
Brest, *France* 58 A5
Breteuil 54 E5
Bretten 52 D7
Breves 140 G4
Brewarrina 114 J5
Brewton 130 D3
Brežice 66 C4
Brézina 102 F2
Brezno 50 J9
Bria 106 C2
Briançon 62 B6
Briceni 66 Q1
Bridgend 38 E4
Bridgeport, *Calif., United States* 132 C1
Bridgeport, *Conn., United States* 128 F2
Bridgeport, *Nebr., United States* 126 F2
Bridgetown 140 F1
Bridgewater 122 U8
Bridgnorth 38 F3
Bridgwater 38 E4
Bridgwater Bay 38 E4
Bridlington 38 H1
Bridport 38 F5
Brienzer See 62 D4
Brig 62 C4
Brigg 38 H2
Brigham City 126 D2
Brighouse 38 G2
Brighton, *United Kingdom* 38 H5
Brighton, *United States* 126 F3
Brignoles 62 B7
Brikama 104 A2
Brilon 52 D5
Brindisi 64 M8
Brinkley 130 C3
Brisbane 114 K5
Bristol, *United Kingdom* 38 F4
Bristol, *United States* 130 E2
Bristol Bay 132 (1)E4
Bristol Channel 38 E4
British Columbia 122 F5
Britstown 108 C6
Brive-la-Gaillarde 58 G8
Briviesca 60 G2
Brixham 38 E5
Brlik 76 N9
Brno 50 F8
Broadford 36 C4
Broadlaw 36 E6
Broad Sound 114 J4
Broadstairs 38 K4
Broadus 126 E1
Brockton 128 F2
Brockville 128 E2
Brod 66 J9
Brodeur Peninsula 122 P2
Brodick 36 C6
Brodnica 50 J4
Broken Arrow 134 E1
Broken Bow 130 C3
Broken Hill 114 H6
Brokopondo 140 F2
Bromley 38 J4
Bromölla 50 D1
Bromsgrove 38 F3
Brønderslev 48 E8

roni 62 E5
rooke's Point 84 F5
rookhaven 130 C3
rookings, *Oreg., United States* 126 B2
rookings, *S.D., United States* 126 G2
rooks 122 J6
rooks Range 132 (1)F2
ooksville 130 E4
oome 114 D3
ora 36 E3
ösarp 48 H9
ough 38 H2
oughton Island 122 U3
ovary 70 F4
ownfield 132 F2
ownhills 38 G3
owning 126 D1
ownsville, *Tenn., United States* 130 D2
ownsville, *Tex., United States* 130 B4
ownwood 130 B3
uchsal 52 D7
uck, *Austria* 62 L3
uck, *Austria* 62 M2
uck an der Mur 66 C2
ugge 54 F3
ühl 54 J4
uint 88 G3
umado 140 J6
umath 62 C2
uneau 126 C2
unei 86 E2
unflo 48 H5
unico 64 F2
unsbüttel 52 E3
unswick, *Ga., United States* 130 E3
unswick, *Me., United States* 128 G2
untal 50 G8
ush 126 F2
ussels = Bruxelles 54 G4
uxelles 54 G4
yan 130 B3
yanka 76 S6
yansk 70 F4
zeg 50 G7
zeg Dolny 50 F6
zeziny 50 J6
Spandau 50 C5
bi 108 E4
cak 92 D5
caramanga 140 C2
chan 36 F4
chanan 104 B3
chan Gulf 122 S2
charest = Bucureşti 66 P5
chen 52 E7
chholz 52 E3
chy 58 M5
ckeburg 52 E4
ckie 36 F4
ckingham 38 H3
čovice 50 F8
cureşti 66 P5
dapest 66 G2
de 38 D5
de Bay 38 D5
dennovsk 92 L1
dingen 52 E6
doni 64 D8
drio 62 G6
dva 66 F7
enaventura, *Colombia* 140 B3
enaventura, *Mexico* 132 E3
ena Vista 126 E3
enos Aires 142 K5
ffalo, *Okla., United States* 130 B2
ffalo, *N.Y., United States* 128 E2
ffalo, *S.D., United States* 126 F1
ffalo, *Tex., United States* 130 B3
ffalo, *Wyo., United States* 126 E2
ffalo Lake 122 J4
ffalo Narrows 122 K5
ftea 66 N5
g 50 L5
gojno 66 E5
grino 76 H4
gsuk 84 F5
gul'ma 70 K4
guruslan 70 K4
ḩayrat al Asad 92 H5
ḩayrat ath Tharthār 92 K6
huşi 66 P3
ilth Wells 38 E3
insk 70 J3
ir Nuur 80 F1
janovac 66 J7
je 62 J5
jumbura 106 D4
kachacha 78 K6
kavu 106 D4
khara 90 H2
kittinggi 86 C3
koba 106 E4
la, *Indonesia* 87 D3
la, *Papua New Guinea* 87 F4
lach 62 D3
lan 84 G4
lâq 100 F2
lawayo 108 D4
ldir Island 78 X6
lgan 78 G7
lgaria 66 M7
li 87 C2
lle 62 C4
llhead City 132 D1
lls 116 E5
lukumba 87 B4
lun 78 M2
mba 106 C3
mbeşti Jiu 66 L4
na 106 F3
nbury 114 C6
ncrana 35 D1
nda 106 E4
ndaberg 114 K4
nde 52 D4
ngunya 114 J5
Bunia 106 E3
Bunkie 130 C3
Bunnell 130 E4
Bünyan 92 F4
Bu ol Kheyr 95 D2
Buôn Mê Thuột 84 D4
Buotama 78 M4
Bura 106 F4
Buran 76 R8
Buranj 88 D2
Burāq 94 D3
Buraydah 90 D4
Burco 106 H2
Burdur 92 D5
Burdur Gölü 68 N7
Burë 100 G5
Büren 54 L3
Burg 52 G4
Burgas 66 Q7
Burgaski Zaliv 66 Q7
Burgdorf 62 C3
Burgess Hill 38 H5
Burghausen 62 H2
Burglengenfeld 52 H7
Burgos 60 G2
Burgsvik 48 K8
Burhaniye 68 K5
Burhanpur 88 C4
Burjassot 60 K5
Burj Şāfitā 94 D2
Burketown 114 G3
Burkeville 128 E3
Bur-Khaybyt 78 P3
Burkina Faso 104 D2
Burlin 70 K4
Burlington, *Colo., United States* 132 F1
Burlington, *Ia., United States* 128 B2
Burlington, *Vt., United States* 128 F2
Burma = Myanmar 84 B2
Burnet 130 B3
Burney 126 B2
Burnie 114 J8
Burnley 38 F2
Burns 126 C2
Burns Junction 126 C2
Burns Lake 122 F6
Burqin 76 R8
Burra 114 G6
Burrel 68 C3
Burrow Head 36 D7
Bursa 68 M4
Bûr Safâga 100 F2
Bûr Sa'îd 100 F1
Burscough Bridge 38 F2
Bur Sudan 100 G4
Burtnieks 48 N8
Burton upon Trent 38 G3
Buru 87 C3
Burundi 106 D4
Bururi 106 D4
Burwell 126 G2
Bury 38 F2
Buryatiya 78 J6
Bury St. Edmunds 38 J3
Būshehr 95 D2
Bushey 38 H4
Bushire = Būshehr 95 D2
Businga 106 C3
Busira 106 C4
Buşrá ash Shām 94 D4
Bussum 54 H2
Busto Arsizio 62 D5
Buta 106 C3
Butare 106 D4
Butaritari 112 H5
Bute 36 C6
Butembo 106 D3
Búðardalur 48 (1)C2
Buton 87 B3
Butte, *Mont., United States* 126 D1
Butte, *Nebr., United States* 126 G2
Butt of Lewis 36 B3
Butuan 84 H5
Butwal 88 D3
Butzbach 52 D6
Bützow 52 G3
Buulobarde 106 H3
Buur Gaabo 106 G4
Buurhabaka 106 G3
Buxtehude 52 E3
Buxton 38 G2
Buy 70 H3
Buynaksk 92 M2
Büyükada 68 L4
Büyükçekmece 68 L4
Buzai Gumbad 90 K2
Buzançais 58 G7
Buzău 66 P4
Buzău 66 Q4
Buzuluk 70 K4
Byam Martin Island 122 L2
Byaroza 48 N10
Bydgoszcz 50 H4
Bygdin 48 D6
Bygland 48 D7
Bykovskiy 78 M2
Bylot Island 122 R2
Byskeälven 48 L4
Bystřice 50 G8
Bystrzyca Kłodzka 50 F7
Bytča 50 H8
Bytom 50 H7
Bytów 50 G3
Bzura 50 J5

C

Caaguazú 142 K4
Caballococha 140 C5
Caballo Reservoir 132 E2
Cabañaquinta 60 E1
Cabanatuan 84 G3
Cabano 128 G1
Cabdul Qaadir 100 H5
Cabeza del Buey 60 E6
Cabezas 140 E7
Cabimas 140 C1
Cabinda 104 G6
Cabinda 104 G6
Cabo Bascuñán 142 G4
Cabo Beata 134 K5
Cabo Camarón 134 G5
Cabo Carvoeiro 60 A5
Cabo Catoche 134 G4
Cabo Corrientes, *Colombia* 140 B2
Cabo Corrientes, *Mexico* 134 C4
Cabo Corrubedo 60 A2
Cabo Cruz 134 J5
Cabo de Espichel 60 A6
Cabo de Gata 60 H8
Cabo de Hornos 142 H10
Cabo de la Nao 60 L6
Cabo Delgado 108 G2
Cabo de Palos 60 K7
Cabo de São Roque 140 K5
Cabo de Sao Tomé 142 N3
Cabo de São Vicente 60 A7
Cabo de Trafalgar 60 D8
Cabo dos Bahías 142 H8
Cabo Fisterra 60 A2
Cabo Frio 142 N3
Cabo Gracias a Dios 134 H6
Cabo Mondego 60 A4
Cabo Norte 140 H3
Cabo Orange 140 G3
Cabo Ortegal 60 B1
Cabo Peñas 60 E1
Caborca 132 D2
Cabo Rojo 134 E4
Cabo Roxo 104 A2
Cabo San Diego 142 H9
Cabo San Francisco de Paula 142 H8
Cabo San Juan 104 F4
Cabo San Lucas 124 D7
Cabo Santa Elena 134 J7
Cabo Tortosa 60 L4
Cabo Tres Puntas 142 H8
Cabot Strait 122 U7
Cabrera 60 N5
Čačak 66 H6
Cáceres, *Brazil* 140 F7
Cáceres, *Spain* 60 D5
Cacheu 104 A2
Cachimbo 140 G5
Cachoeira do Sul 142 L4
Cachoeiro de Itapemirim 140 J8
Cacola 108 B2
Caconda 108 B2
Čadca 50 H8
Cader Idris 38 E3
Cadillac, *Mich., United States* 128 C2
Cadillac, *Mont., United States* 124 E2
Cádiz 60 D8
Caen 54 B5
Caernarfon 38 D2
Caernarfon Bay 38 D2
Caerphilly 38 E4
Cagayan de Oro 84 G5
Cagli 62 H7
Cagliari 64 D9
Cagnes-sur-Mer 62 C7
Caguas 134 L5
Cahama 108 A3
Caha Mountains 35 B5
Caher 35 D4
Cahersiveen 35 A5
Cahors 58 G9
Cahuapanas 140 B5
Cahul 66 R4
Caia 108 F3
Caianda 108 C2
Caicos Islands 134 K4
Cairinis 36 A4
Cairngorm Mountains 36 E4
Cairns 114 J3
Cairo = El Qâhira, *Egypt* 100 F1
Cairo, *United States* 130 D2
Cairo Montenotte 62 D6
Caister-on-Sea 38 K3
Caithness 36 E3
Caiundo 108 B3
Cajamarca 140 B5
Čakovec 66 D3
Calabar 104 F3
Calabozo 140 D2
Calabro 64 L9
Calafat 66 K6
Calagua Islands 84 G4
Calahorra 60 J2
Calais 54 D4
Calama, *Brazil* 140 E5
Calama, *Peru* 142 H3
Calamar 140 C3
Calamian Group 84 F4
Calamocha 60 J4
Călan 66 L4
Calanscio Sand Sea 100 D2
Calapan 84 G4
Călăraşi, *Moldova* 66 R2
Călăraşi, *Romania* 66 Q5
Calatafim 64 G11
Calatayud 60 J3
Calauag 84 G4
Calbayog 84 G4
Calçoene 140 G3
Calcutta = Kolkata 88 E4
Caldas da Rainha 60 A5
Caldera 142 G4
Caldicot 38 F4
Caldwell, *Id., United States* 126 C2
Caldwell, *Kans., United States* 130 B2
Calf of Man 36 D7
Calgary 122 J6
Calhoun 130 E3
Calhoun City 130 D3
Calhoun Falls 130 E3
Cali 140 B3
Calicut = Kozhikode 88 C6
Caliente 126 D3
California 124 B4
Calilabad 92 N4
Callan 35 D4
Callander 36 D5
Callao 140 B6
Caloundra 114 K5
Caltagirone 64 J11
Caltanissetta 64 J11
Caluquembe 108 A2
Caluula 106 J1
Calvi 64 C6
Calvin 130 B3
Calvinia 108 B6
Calw 62 D2
Camaçari 140 K6
Camacupa 108 B2
Camagüey 134 J4
Camaiore 62 F7
Camana 140 C7
Camargue 58 K10
Camariñas 60 A1
Camarones 142 H7
Ca Mau 84 D5
Camberley 38 H4
Cambodia 84 C4
Camborne 38 C5
Cambrai 54 F4
Cambre 60 B1
Cambria 126 B3
Cambrian Mountains 38 E3
Cambridge, *New Zealand* 116 E3
Cambridge, *United Kingdom* 38 J3
Cambridge, *Md., United States* 128 E3
Cambridge, *Mass., United States* 128 F2
Cambridge, *Oh., United States* 128 D3
Cambridge Bay 122 K3
Cambrils 60 M3
Camden, *Ark., United States* 130 C3
Camden, *S.C., United States* 130 E3
Cameron, *La., United States* 130 C4
Cameron, *Mo., United States* 130 C2
Cameron, *Tex., United States* 130 B3
Cameroon 104 G3
Cametá 140 H4
Çamiçigölü 68 K7
Caminha 60 B3
Camiranga 140 H4
Camocim 140 J4
Camooweal 114 G3
Camopi 140 G3
Campbell Island 116 (2)C2
Campbell River 122 F7
Campbellsville 128 C3
Campbellton 128 G1
Campbeltown 36 C6
Campeche 134 F5
Câmpeni 66 L3
Câmpia Turzii 66 L3
Câmpina 66 N4
Campina Grande 140 L5
Campinas 142 M3
Campobasso 64 J7
Campo de Criptana 60 G5
Campo de Diauarum 140 G6
Campo Gallo 142 J4
Campo Grande 142 L3
Campo Maior 140 J4
Campo Mourão 142 L3
Campos 142 N3
Câmpulung 66 N4
Câmpulung Moldovenesc 66 N2
Cam Ranh 84 D4
Çan 68 K4
Canada 120 M4
Canadian 132 F1
Canadian 132 F1
Çanakkale 68 J4
Çanakkale Boğazı 68 J4
Canal de Panamá 134 J7
Cananea 132 D2
Canary Islands = Islas Canarias 102 B3
Cañaveras 60 H4
Canberra 114 J7
Cancún 134 G4
Çandarli Körfezi 68 J6
Candelaro 66 C8
Candlemas Island 138 J9
Cangamba 108 B2
Cangas 60 B2
Cangas de Narcea 60 D1
Cangyuan 84 B2
Cangzhou 80 F3
Canicattì 64 H11
Canindé 140 K4
Çankiri 92 E3
Canna 36 B4
Cannanore 88 C6
Cannanore 88 B6
Cannes 62 C7
Cannock 38 F3
Canon City 132 E1
Cantanduanes 84 G4
Canterbury 38 K4
Canterbury Bight 116 C7
Canterbury Plains 116 C6
Cân Tho 84 D5
Canto do Buriti 140 J5
Canton, *Miss., United States* 130 D3
Canton, *Oh., United States* 130 E1
Canton, *S.D., United States* 126 G2
Canumã 140 F4
Canumã 140 F5
Canutama 140 E5
Canvey Island 38 J4
Canyon 132 F1
Canyon Ferry Lake 126 D1
Cao Bāng 84 D2
Caorle 62 H5
Cap Blanc 64 D11
Cap Bon 102 H1
Cap Corse 64 D5
Cap d'Agde 58 J10
Cap d'Antifer 54 C5
Cap de Fer 102 G1
Cap de Formentor 60 P5
Cap de la Hague 58 D4
Cap-de-la-Madeleine 128 F1
Cap de Nouvelle-France 122 S4

Cap de ses Salines	60	P5
Cap des Trois Fourches	60	H9
Cape Agulhas	108	C6
Cape Alexandra	142	P9
Cape Andreas	90	B2
Cape Apostolos Andreas	92	F6
Cape Arid	114	D6
Cape Arnaoutis	92	D6
Cape Arnhem	114	G2
Cape Barren Island	114	J8
Cape Bauld	122	V6
Cape Blanco	126	B2
Cape Borda	114	G7
Cape Breton Island	122	U7
Cape Brett	116	E2
Cape Byron	114	K5
Cape Campbell	116	E5
Cape Canaveral	130	E4
Cape Canaveral	130	E4
Cape Carnot	114	F6
Cape Charles	128	E3
Cape Chidley	122	U4
Cape Christian	122	T2
Cape Churchill	122	N5
Cape Clear	35	B5
Cape Cleare	132	(1)H4
Cape Coast	104	D3
Cape Cod	128	G2
Cape Columbine	108	B6
Cape Colville	116	E3
Cape Comorin	88	C7
Cape Constantine	132	(1)E4
Cape Coral	130	E4
Cape Crawford	114	G3
Cape Croker	114	F2
Cape Dalhousie	132	(1)L1
Cape Direction	114	H2
Cape Disappointment	142	P9
Cape Dominion	122	R3
Cape Dorchester	122	R3
Cape Dorset	122	R4
Cape Dyer	122	U3
Cape Egmont	116	D4
Cape Eleaia	94	B1
Cape Farewell, *Greenland*	120	F4
Cape Farewell, *New Zealand*	116	D5
Cape Fear	130	F3
Cape Finisterre = Cabo Fisterra	60	A2
Cape Flattery, *Australia*	114	J2
Cape Flattery, *United States*	126	A1
Cape Forestier	114	J8
Cape Foulwind	116	C5
Cape Fria	108	A3
Cape Girardeau	128	C3
Cape Greko	92	F6
Cape Grenville	114	H2
Cape Grim	114	H8
Cape Harrison	122	V6
Cape Hatteras	130	F2
Cape Henrietta Maria	122	Q5
Cape Horn = Cabo de Hornos	142	H10
Cape Howe	114	K7
Cape Inscription	114	B5
Cape Jaffa	114	G7
Cape Karikari	116	D2
Cape Kellett	122	F2
Cape Kidnappers	116	F4
Cape Leeuwin	114	B6
Cape Lévêque	114	D3
Cape Londonderry	114	E2
Cape Lookout	134	J2
Cape May	128	F3
Cape Melville	114	H2
Cape Mendenhall	132	(1)D4
Cape Mendocino	126	A2
Cape Mercy	122	U4
Cape Meredith	142	J9
Cape Naturaliste	114	B6
Capenda-Camulemba	108	B1
Cape Negrais	84	A3
Cape Nelson	114	H7
Cape Newenham	132	(1)E4
Cape of Good Hope	108	B6
Cape Palliser	116	E5
Cape Palmas	104	C4
Cape Parry	122	G2
Cape Providence	116	A8
Cape Race	120	G5
Cape Ray	122	V7
Cape Reinga	116	D2
Cape Romanzof	132	(1)D3
Cape Runaway	116	G3
Cape Sable	122	T8
Cape St. Elias	132	(1)J4
Cape St. Francis	108	C6
Cape San Agustin	84	H5
Cape San Blas	130	D4
Cape Saunders	116	C7
Cape Scott	114	E2
Cape Stephens	116	D5
Cape Terawhiti	116	E5
Cape Three Points	104	D4
Cape Town	108	B6
Cape Turnagain	116	F5
Cape Verde	104	(1)B2
Cape Wessel	114	G2
Cape Wrangell	78	W6
Cape Wrath	36	D3
Cape York	114	H2
Cape York Peninsula	114	H2
Cap Figalo	60	J9
Cap Fréhel	58	C5
Cap Gris-Nez	54	D4
Cap-Haïtien	134	K5
Cap Juby	102	C3
Čapljina	66	E6
Cap Lopez	104	F5
Cap Negro	60	E9
Capo Carbonara	64	D10
Capo Colonna	64	M9
Capo Gallo	64	H10
Capo Granitola	64	G11
Capo Murro di Porco	64	K11
Capo Palinuro	64	J8
Capo Passero	64	K12
Capo Santa Maria di Leuca	64	N9
Capo San Vito	64	G10
Capo Spartivento, *Italy*	64	C10
Capo Spartivento, *Italy*	64	L11
Capo Vaticano	64	K10
Capraia	64	D5
Cap Rhir	102	C2
Capri	64	J8
Capri	64	J8
Capricorn Group	114	K4
Cap Rosa	64	C11
Cap Serrat	64	D11
Cap Spartel	60	E9
Cap Timiris	102	B5
Capua	64	J7
Cap Verga	104	B2
Cap Vert	104	A2
Caquetá	140	C4
Caracal	66	M5
Caracarai	140	E3
Caracas	140	D1
Caransebeș	66	K4
Carauari	140	D4
Caravaca de la Cruz	60	J6
Caravelas	140	K7
Carazinho	142	L4
Carballiño	60	B2
Carballo	60	B1
Carbondale, *Ill., United States*	130	D2
Carbondale, *Pa., United States*	130	F1
Carboneras	60	J7
Carbonia	64	C9
Carcar	84	G4
Carcassonne	58	H10
Cardabia	114	B4
Cardiff	38	E4
Cardigan	38	D3
Cardigan Bay	38	D3
Cardston	126	D1
Carei	66	K2
Carentan	58	D4
Cariacica	142	N3
Cariati	64	L9
Caribbean Sea	134	J6
Caripito	140	E1
Carlet	60	K5
Carleton Place	128	E1
Carlisle, *United Kingdom*	36	F7
Carlisle, *United States*	128	E2
Carlow	35	E4
Carlsbad	132	F2
Carluke	36	E6
Carlyle	126	F1
Carmacks	122	D4
Carmagnola	62	C6
Carmarthen	38	D4
Carmarthen Bay	38	D4
Carmaux	58	H9
Carmel Head	38	D2
Carmen	134	B3
Carmona	60	E7
Carnarvon, *Australia*	114	B4
Carnarvon, *South Africa*	108	C6
Carn Bàn	36	D4
Carnforth	36	F7
Car Nicobar	88	F7
Carnot	106	B2
Carnsore Point	35	E4
Carolina	140	H5
Carolina Beach	130	F3
Caroline Island	112	L6
Caroline Islands	112	E5
Carpathian Mountains	50	J8
Carpații Meridionali	66	K4
Carpentras	58	L9
Carpi	62	F6
Carrabelle	130	E4
Carrara	62	F6
Carrickfergus	35	F2
Carrickmacross	35	E3
Carrick-on-Shannon	35	C3
Carrick-on-Suir	35	D4
Carrington	126	G1
Carrizozo	132	E2
Carroll	128	B2
Carrollton, *Ky., United States*	128	D3
Carrollton, *Mo., United States*	130	C1
Carryduff	35	F2
Çarşamba	92	G3
Carson City	126	C3
Cartagena, *Colombia*	140	B1
Cartagena, *Spain*	60	K7
Carthage	130	C3
Cartwright	122	V6
Caruarú	140	K5
Carúpano	140	E1
Casablanca	102	D2
Casa Grande	132	D2
Casale Monferrato	62	D5
Casalmaggiore	62	F6
Casamozza	64	D6
Casarano	64	N9
Cascade, *Id., United States*	126	C2
Cascade, *Mont., United States*	126	C1
Cascade Range	126	B2
Cascade Reservoir	126	C2
Cascais	60	A6
Cascavel	142	L3
Caserta	64	J7
Cashel, *Republic of Ireland*	35	D4
Cashel, *Zimbabwe*	108	E3
Casiguran	84	G3
Casino	114	K5
Čàsma	62	M5
Caspe	60	K3
Casper	126	E2
Caspian Sea	46	J3
Cassiar	122	F5
Cassino	64	H7
Castanhal	140	H4
Castelbuono	64	J11
Castèl di Sangro	64	J7
Castelfidardo	64	H5
Castellammare del Golfo	64	G10
Castellane	62	B7
Castellaneta	64	L8
Castelli	142	J4
Castelló de la Plana	60	K5
Castelnaudary	58	G10
Castelo Branco	60	C5
Castelsarrasin	58	G10
Castelvetrano	64	G11
Castets	58	D10
Castiglion Fiorentino	62	G7
Castlebar	35	B3
Castlebay	36	A5
Castleblayney	35	E2
Castle Douglas	36	E7
Castleford	38	G2
Castleisland	35	B4
Castle Point	116	F5
Castlerea	35	C3
Castletown, *Isle of Man*	36	D7
Castletown, *Republic of Ireland*	35	D4
Castlewellan	35	F2
Castres	58	H10
Castricum	54	G2
Castries	134	M6
Castro	142	M3
Castro Verde	60	B7
Castrovillari	64	L9
Castuera	60	E6
Çatak	92	K5
Catamarca	142	H4
Catandica	108	E3
Catania	64	K11
Catanzaro	64	L10
Catanzaro Marina	64	L10
Catarman	84	G4
Catbalogan	84	H4
Catió	104	A2
Cat Island	130	F5
Cat Lake	122	N6
Cato Island	114	L4
Catriló	142	J6
Catrimani	140	E3
Catskill Mountains	124	M3
Cattolica	62	H7
Cauayan	84	G5
Cauca	140	C2
Caucaia	140	K4
Caucasia	140	B2
Caucasus	92	K2
Caudry	54	F4
Cauquenes	142	G6
Caura	140	E2
Causapscal	128	G1
Căușeni	66	S3
Cavaillon	58	L10
Cavalese	62	G4
Cavan	35	D3
Cavarzere	62	H5
Cave	116	C7
Cavinas	140	D6
Cavtat	66	F7
Caxias	140	J4
Caxias do Sul	142	L4
Caxito	104	G6
Çay	68	P6
Cayce	130	E3
Çaycuma	68	Q3
Cayenne	140	G3
Cayman Islands	134	H5
Caynabo	106	H2
Cayos Miskitos	134	H6
Cay Sal Bank	130	E5
Cazorla	60	H7
Ceará	140	J4
Cebu	84	G4
Cebu	84	G4
Cecina	62	F7
Cedar City	126	D3
Cedar Falls	128	B2
Cedar Lake	122	L6
Cedar Rapids	128	B2
Cedros	124	C6
Ceduna	114	F6
Ceerigaabo	106	H1
Cefalù	64	J10
Cegléd	66	G2
Celaya	134	D4
Celebes = Sulawesi	87	A3
Celebes Sea	87	B2
Celje	66	C3
Celldömölk	66	E2
Celle	52	F4
Celtic Sea	56	E10
Centerville	128	B2
Cento	62	G6
Central African Republic	106	C2
Central City	126	G2
Centralia, *Ill., United States*	128	C3
Centralia, *Wash., United States*	126	B1
Central Range	87	F3
Central Siberian Plateau = Srednesibirskoye Ploskogor'ye	78	H4
Cenxi	84	E2
Cerea	62	G5
Ceres, *Argentina*	142	J4
Ceres, *Brazil*	140	H7
Cerezo de Abajo	60	G3
Cerignola	64	K7
Çerikli	92	E4
Çerkes	68	Q4
Çerkezköy	68	K3
Cerknica	62	K5
Cernavodă	66	R5
Cero Champaqui	142	J5
Cerralvo	124	E7
Cërrik	68	C3
Cerritos	132	F4
Cerro Aconcagua	142	G5
Cerro Bonete	142	H4
Cerro de la Encantada	124	C5
Cerro de Pasco	140	B6
Cerro Huehuento	134	C4
Cerro Las Tórtolas	142	H5
Cerro Marahuaca	140	D3
Cerro Mercedario	142	G5
Cerro Murallón	142	G8
Cerro Nevado	142	H6
Cerro Pena Nevade	134	D4
Cerro San Lorenzo	142	G8
Cerro San Valentín	142	
Cerros de Bala	140	
Cerro Tres Picos	142	
Cerro Tupungato	142	
Cerro Yaví	140	
Cerro Yogan	142	
Certaldo	62	
Cervaro	64	
Červen Brjag	66	
Cervia	62	
Cervionne	64	
Cervo	60	
Cesano	62	
Cesena	62	
Cesenatico	62	
Cēsis	48	
Česka Lípa	52	
České Budějovice	62	
Český Krumlov	62	
Çeşme	68	
Česna	62	
Cessnock	114	
Cestas	58	
Cetate	66	
Cetinje	66	
Cetraro	64	
Ceuta	102	
Cevizli	68	
Chachapoyas	140	
Chaco Boreal	142	
Chad	100	
Chadan	76	
Chadron	126	
Chagai	90	
Chagda	78	
Chaghcharān	90	
Chagyl	90	
Chāh Bahār	90	
Chāībāsa	88	
Chainat	84	
Chaiyaphum	84	
Chalais	58	
Chalhuanca	140	
Chalinze	106	
Chalki	68	
Chalkida	68	
Chalkidiki	68	
Challans	58	
Challapata	140	
Challenger Deep	112	
Challis	126	
Châlons-sur-Marne	54	
Chalon-sur-Saône	58	
Cham	52	
Chama	108	
Chamba	88	
Chambal	88	
Chamberlain	126	
Chambersburg	128	
Chambéry	62	
Chambly	54	
Chamonix	62	
Champagnole	62	
Champaign	128	
Champaubert	54	
Champlitte	62	
Chañaral	142	
Chandalar	122	
Chandeleur Islands	134	
Chandigarh	88	
Chandler	132	
Chandrapur	88	
Changane	108	
Changara	108	
Changchun	82	
Changde	80	
Chang-hua	80	
Chang Jiang	80	
Changsha	80	
Changshou	80	
Changshu	80	
Changting	80	
Changzhi	80	
Changzhou	80	
Chania	68	
Channel Islands, *United Kingdom*	38	(1)[illegible]
Channel Islands, *United States*	124	
Channel-Port aux Basques	122	
Chanthaburi	84	
Chantilly	54	
Chanute	130	
Chao Phraya	84	
Chaouèn	102	
Chao Xian	80	
Chaoyang	80	
Chaozhou	80	
Chapada Diamantina	140	
Chapais	128	
Chapayev	70	
Chapayevo	78	
Chapayevskoye	76	
Chapecó	142	
Chapeltown	38	
Chapleau	128	
Chara	78	
Charcas	132	
Chard	122	
Chard	38	
Chardara	90	
Chardzhev	90	
Chari	100	
Chārīkār	90	
Charleroi	54	
Charlesbourg	128	
Charleston, *New Zealand*	116	
Charleston, *S.C., United States*	130	
Charleston, *W. Va., United States*	130	
Charlestown	130	
Charlestown	35	
Charlestown of Aberlour	36	
Charleville	114	
Charleville-Mézières	54	
Charlevoix	128	
Charlotte, *Mich., United States*	128	
Charlotte, *N.C., United States*	130	
Charlottesville	130	

Charlottetown	122	U7
Charlton Island	122	Q6
Charlton Kings	38	F4
Charrat	62	C4
Charsk	76	Q8
Charters Towers	114	J4
Chartres	58	G5
Charymovo	70	Q3
Chasel'ka	78	C3
Chastyye	70	K3
Châteaguay	128	F1
Châteaubriant	58	D6
Châteaudun	58	G5
Châteaulin	58	A5
Châteauneuf-sur-Loire	58	H6
Châteauroux	58	G7
Château-Thierry	54	F5
Châtellerault	58	F7
Châtenois	62	A2
Chatham	128	D2
Chatham	38	J4
Chatham Island	116	(1)B1
Chatham Islands	116	(1)B1
Châtillon-sur-Seine	58	K6
Chattanooga	124	J4
Chatteris	38	J3
Chauffayer	62	B6
Chauk	88	F4
Chaumont	58	L5
Chaunskaya Guba	78	V3
Chauny	54	F5
Chaves, *Brazil*	140	G4
Chaves, *Portugal*	60	C3
Chavuma	108	C2
Cheb	52	H6
Cheboksary	70	J3
Chechnya	92	L2
Cheddar	38	F4
Cheduba Island	88	F5
Cheektowaga	128	E2
Chegdomyn	78	N6
Chegga	102	D3
Chegutu	108	E3
Chehalis	126	B1
Cheju	82	D7
Cheju do	82	D7
Chekhov	78	Q7
Chelan	126	C1
Cheleken	90	F2
Chélif	60	L8
Chelkar	76	K8
Chełm	50	N6
Chełmno	50	H4
Chelmsford	38	J4
Chełmza	50	H4
Cheltenham	38	F4
Chelyabinsk	70	M3
Chelyuskin	76	U2
Chemnitz	52	H6
Chenab	88	B2
Chenachane	102	E3
Cheney Reservoir	130	B2
Chengde	80	F2
Chengdu	80	C4
Chengshan Jiao	82	B5
Chennai	88	D6
Chenzhou	80	E5
Chepes	142	H5
Chepstow	38	F4
Cher	58	G6
Cheraw	130	F3
Cherbaniani Reef	88	B6
Cherbourg	58	D4
Cherchell	60	N8
Cherdyn	70	L2
Cheremkhovo	78	G6
Cherepovets	70	G3
Cherkasy	70	F5
Cherkessk	92	K1
Chermoz	70	L3
Chernihiv	70	F4
Chernivtsi	70	E5
Chernushka	70	L3
Chernyakhovsk	50	L3
Chernyayevo	78	M6
Chernyshevsk	78	K6
Chernyshevskiy	78	J4
Chernyye Zemli	70	J5
Cherokee	128	A2
Cherskiy	78	U3
Chervonohrad	70	D4
Chesapeake	130	F2
Cheshskaya Guba	70	J1
Cheshunt	38	H4
hester, *United Kingdom*	38	F2
hester, *Calif., United States*	126	B2
hester, *Mont., United States*	126	D1
hesterfield	38	G2
hesterfield Inlet	122	N4
hester-le-Street	36	G7
hetumal	134	G5
hetwynd	122	G5
heviot	116	D6
h'ew Bahir	106	F3
heyenne	126	F2
heyenne	126	F2
heyenne Wells	132	F1
heyne Bay	114	C6
hhapra	88	D3
hhatarpur	88	C4
hhindwara	88	C4
hhuka	88	E3
hiai	80	G6
hiang Khan	84	C3
hiang-Mai	84	B3
hiang Rai	84	B3
hiavari	62	E6
hiavenno	62	E4
hiba	82	L6
hibougamau	122	S6
hibuto	108	E4
hicago	128	C2
hicapa	106	C5
hichagof Island	132	(1)K4
hichaoua	102	D2
hichester	38	H5
Chickasha	130	B3
Chiclana de la Frontera	60	D8
Chiclayo	140	B5
Chico	142	H8
Chicopee	128	F2
Chicoutimi	122	S7
Chicualacuala	108	E4
Chiemsee	62	H3
Chieri	62	C5
Chiese	62	F5
Chieti	64	J6
Chifeng	80	F2
Chiganak	76	N8
Chigubo	108	E4
Chihuahua	132	E3
Chiili	76	M9
Chikwa	108	E2
Chilas	88	B1
Childress	132	F2
Chile	138	D8
Chile Chico	142	G8
Chilik	76	P9
Chilika Lake	88	D4
Chillán	142	G6
Chillicothe, *Mo., United States*	128	B3
Chillicothe, *Oh., United States*	128	D3
Chilliwack	126	B1
Chiloquin	126	B2
Chilpancingo	134	E5
Chiltern Hills	38	H4
Chilung	80	G5
Chimbay	76	K9
Chimborazo	140	B4
Chimbote	140	B5
Chimchememel'	78	V3
Chimec	66	J1
Chimoio	108	E3
China	74	N6
Chincha Alta	140	B6
Chincilla de Monte-Aragón	60	J6
Chinde	108	F3
Chin do	82	C6
Chindwin	84	A2
Chingola	108	D2
Chinguetti	102	C4
Chinhoyi	108	E3
Chiniot	88	B2
Chinju	82	E6
Chinmen	84	F2
Chinnur	88	C5
Chino	82	K6
Chioggia	62	H5
Chios	68	J6
Chios	68	H6
Chipata	108	E2
Chippenham	38	F4
Chippewa Falls	128	B2
Chipping Norton	38	G4
Chipping Sodbury	38	F4
Chirala	88	D5
Chirchik	76	M9
Chirikof Island	132	(1)F5
Chiromo	108	F3
Chirripo	134	H7
Chişinău	66	R2
Chişineu-Criş	66	J3
Chita	78	J6
Chitado	108	A3
Chitato	106	C5
Chitembo	108	B2
Chitipa	106	E5
Chitradurga	88	C6
Chitral	88	B1
Chitré	134	H7
Chittagong	88	F4
Chittaurgarh	88	B4
Chittoor	88	C6
Chitungwiza	108	E3
Chiume	108	C3
Chivasso	62	C5
Chizha	70	H1
Chodov	52	H6
Chodzież	50	F5
Choiseul	112	F6
Chojnice	50	G4
Chojnów	50	F6
Chokurdakh	78	R2
Chókwé	108	E4
Cholet	58	E6
Choma	108	D3
Chomutov	50	C7
Chona	78	H4
Chonan	82	D5
Chone	140	A4
Ch'ŏngjin	82	E3
Ch'ŏngju	82	D6
Chŏngju	82	C4
Chŏngp'yŏng	82	D4
Chongqing	74	P7
Chŏngŭp	82	D6
Ch'ŏnju	82	D5
Chonogol	80	F1
Chon Thanh	84	D4
Chop	50	M9
Chorley	38	F2
Chornobyl'	70	F4
Chornomors'ke	70	F5
Ch'osan	82	C3
Chōshi	82	L6
Choszczno	50	E4
Choteau	126	D1
Chott el Hodna	102	F1
Chott el Jerid	102	G2
Chott Melrhir	102	G2
Choûm	102	C4
Choybalsan	78	J7
Choyr	80	D1
Chre	58	H9
Christchurch	116	D6
Christchurch	38	G5
Christiansburg	128	D3
Christiansø	50	E2
Christmas Island	86	D5
Chrudim	50	E8
Chrysi	68	H10
Chrysoupoli	66	M9
Chu	76	N9
Chubut	142	H7
Chugach Mountains	122	B4
Chūgoku-sanchi	80	J3
Chugwater	126	F2
Chukchi Sea	132	(1)C2
Chukotskiy Khrebet	78	W3
Chukotskiy Poluostrov	78	Z3
Chula Vista	132	C2
Chulucanas	140	A5
Chulym	76	R6
Chum	70	M1
Chumikan	78	P6
Chum Phae	84	C3
Chumphon	84	B4
Ch'unch'ŏn	82	D5
Chunchura	88	E4
Chundzha	76	P9
Ch'ungju	82	D5
Chuquicamata	142	H3
Chur	62	E4
Churapcha	78	N4
Churchill	122	N5
Churchill, *Man., Canada*	122	M5
Churchill, *Nfld., Canada*	122	U6
Churchill Falls	122	U6
Churchill Peak	122	F5
Church Stretton	38	F3
Churu	88	B3
Chuska Mountains	132	E1
Chusovoy	70	L3
Chute des Passes	122	S7
Chuuk	112	F5
Chuvashiya	70	J3
Chuxiong	84	C2
Chuya	78	J5
Ciadîr-Lunga	66	R3
Cide	92	E3
Ciechanów	50	K5
Ciechocinek	50	H5
Ciego de Avila	134	J4
Cienfuegos	134	H4
Cieza	60	J6
Cihanbeyli	92	E4
Cijulang	86	D4
Cilacap	86	D4
Cili	80	E5
Cimarron	130	B2
Cimişlia	66	R3
Cîmpeni	50	N11
Cinca	60	L3
Cincinnati	128	D3
Çine	68	L7
Ciney	54	H4
Cintalapa	134	F5
Circle, *Ak., United States*	132	(1)J2
Circle, *Mont., United States*	126	E1
Circleville	128	D3
Cirebon	86	D4
Cirencester	38	G4
Cirò Marina	64	M9
Çirpan	68	H2
Cisco	130	B3
Cistierna	60	E2
Čitluk	66	E6
Citronelle	130	D3
Cittadella	62	G5
Città di Castello	62	H7
Ciucea	66	K3
Ciudad Acuña	132	F3
Ciudad Bolívar	140	E2
Ciudad Camargo	132	E3
Ciudad del Carmen	134	F5
Ciudad del Este	142	L4
Ciudad Delicias	132	E3
Ciudad del Maíz	132	G4
Ciudad de México	134	E5
Ciudad de Valles	134	E4
Ciudad Guayana	140	E2
Ciudad Juárez	132	E2
Ciudad Madero	132	G4
Ciudad Mante	134	E4
Ciudad Obregón	134	C3
Ciudad Real	60	G6
Ciudad-Rodrigo	60	D4
Ciudad Valles	132	G4
Ciudad Victoria	124	G7
Ciutadella	60	P4
Cividale del Friuli	62	J4
Civita Castellana	64	G6
Civitanova Marche	64	H5
Civitavecchia	64	F6
Cizre	92	K5
Clacton-on-Sea	38	K4
Clair Engle Lake	126	B2
Clairview	114	J4
Clamecy	58	J6
Clare	35	A3
Claregalway	35	C3
Claremorris	35	C3
Clarence	116	D6
Clarence Strait	114	E2
Clarendon	132	F2
Clarkdale	132	D2
Clarksburg	130	E2
Clarksdale	130	C3
Clarks Junction	116	C7
Clarkston	126	C1
Clarksville, *Ark., United States*	130	C2
Clarksville, *Tenn., United States*	130	D2
Claro	140	G7
Clausthal-Zellerfeld	52	F5
Claveria	84	G3
Clayton	132	F1
Clear Island	35	B5
Clear Lake	128	B2
Clear Lake Reservoir	126	B2
Clearwater	130	E4
Clearwater	126	C1
Clearwater Mountains	126	C1
Cleburne	130	B3
Cleethorpes	38	H2
Clermont, *Australia*	114	J4
Clermont, *France*	54	E5
Clermont-Ferrand	58	J8
Clervaux	54	J4
Cles	62	F4
Clevedon	38	F4
Cleveland, *Oh., United States*	128	D2
Cleveland, *Tenn., United States*	130	E2
Cleveland, *Tex., United States*	130	B3
Cleveleys	38	E2
Clew Bay	35	B3
Clifden	116	A7
Clifden	35	A3
Clifton	132	E2
Climax	126	E1
Clines Corners	132	E2
Clinton, *Canada*	122	G6
Clinton, *New Zealand*	116	B8
Clinton, *Ark., United States*	128	B3
Clinton, *Ia., United States*	124	H3
Clinton, *Miss., United States*	130	C3
Clinton, *Mo., United States*	128	B3
Clinton, *N.C., United States*	130	F3
Clinton, *Okla., United States*	130	B2
Clipperton Island	134	C6
Clitheroe	38	F2
Cloghan	35	D3
Clogher Head	35	E3
Clonakilty	35	C5
Clonakilty Bay	35	C5
Cloncurry	114	H4
Clones	35	D2
Clonmel	35	D4
Cloppenburg	52	D4
Cloquet	128	B1
Cloud Peak	126	E2
Clovis, *Calif., United States*	126	C3
Clovis, *N. Mex., United States*	132	F2
Cluj-Napoca	66	L3
Cluny	58	K7
Cluses	62	B4
Clyde	36	E6
Clydebank	36	D6
Clyde River	122	T2
Coaldale	126	C3
Coalville	126	C2
Coalville	38	G3
Coari	140	E4
Coast Mountains	122	E5
Coast Range	126	B3
Coatbridge	36	D6
Coats Island	122	Q4
Coatzacoalcos	134	F5
Cobalt	122	R7
Cobán	134	F5
Cobar	114	J6
Cobh	35	C5
Cobija	140	D6
Cobourg	124	L3
Cobourg Peninsula	114	F2
Cóbuè	108	E2
Coburg	52	F6
Cochabamba	140	D7
Cochin = Kochi	88	C7
Cochrane	128	D1
Cockburn Town	130	G5
Cockermouth	36	E7
Coco	134	H6
Cocoa	130	E4
Cocobeach	104	F4
Coco Channel	84	A4
Coco Island	84	A4
Codajás	140	E4
Codigoro	62	H6
Cod Island	122	U5
Codlea	66	N4
Codó	140	J4
Codogno	62	E5
Codroipo	62	J5
Cody	126	E2
Coen	114	H2
Coesfeld	52	C5
Coëtivy	98	J6
Coeur d'Alene	126	C1
Coeur d'Alene Lake	126	C1
Coevorden	54	J2
Coffs Harbour	114	K6
Cofrents	60	J5
Coggeshall	38	J4
Cognac	58	E8
Cogne	62	C5
Coiba	138	C3
Coihaique	142	G8
Coimbatore	88	C6
Coimbra	60	B4
Colchester	38	J4
Coldstream	36	F6
Colebrook	128	F1
Coleman	130	B3
Coleraine	35	E1
Colesberg	108	D6
Colfax	126	C1
Colibaşi	66	M5
Colico	62	E4
Coll	36	B5
Collado-Villalba	60	F4
Collecchio	62	F6
College Station	130	B3
Collier Bay	114	D3
Collingwood	128	E2
Collins	130	D3
Collooney	35	C2
Colmar	62	C2
Colmenar Viejo	60	G4
Colne	38	F2
Colombia	140	C3
Colombo	88	C7
Colomiers	58	G10
Colón	126	J7
Colonia Las Heras	142	H8
Colonial Heights	128	E3
Colonsay	36	B5
Colorado	126	E3
Colorado, *Colo., United States*	132	E1
Colorado, *Tex., United States*	132	G2
Colorado Plateau	132	D1
Colorado Springs	126	F3
Columbia	126	C1
Columbia, *La., United States*	130	C3
Columbia, *Md., United States*	130	F2

Columbia, Mo., United States — 130 C2
Columbia, S.C., United States — 130 E3
Columbia, Tenn., United States — 130 D2
Columbia Mountains — 122 E2
Columbus, Ga., United States — 130 E3
Columbus, Ind., United States — 130 D2
Columbus, Miss., United States — 130 D3
Columbus, Mont., United States — 126 E1
Columbus, Nebr., United States — 126 G2
Columbus, N. Mex., United States — 132 E2
Columbus, Oh., United States — 130 E1
Columbus, Tex., United States — 130 B4
Colville — 132 (1)G2
Colville — 116 E3
Colville Lake — 132 (1)M2
Colwyn Bay — 38 E3
Comacchio — 62 H6
Comănești — 66 P3
Comarnic — 66 N4
Combarbalá — 142 G5
Combeaufontaine — 58 M6
Comber — 35 F2
Comilla — 84 A2
Comino = Kemmuna — 64 J12
Commentry — 58 H7
Commercy — 54 H6
Como — 62 E5
Comodoro Rivadavia — 142 H8
Comoé — 104 D3
Comondú — 124 D6
Comoros — 108 G2
Compiègne — 54 E5
Comrat — 66 R3
Comstock — 132 F3
Conakry — 104 B3
Concarneau — 58 B6
Conceição do Araguaia — 140 H5
Concepción, Bolivia — 140 E7
Concepción, Chile — 142 G6
Conches-en-Ouche — 54 C6
Conchos — 134 C3
Concord, Calif., United States — 132 B1
Concord, N.H., United States — 128 F2
Concord, N.C., United States — 130 E2
Concordia, Argentina — 142 K5
Concordia, United States — 130 B2
Condé-sur-Noireau — 54 B6
Condobolin — 114 J6
Condom — 58 F10
Conegliano — 62 H5
Conggar — 88 F3
Congleton — 38 F2
Congo — 104 G5
Congo — 98 G2
Coningsby — 38 H2
Conisbrough — 38 G2
Connah's Quay — 38 E2
Connaught — 35 C3
Connecticut — 128 F2
Connemara — 35 B3
Connemara National Park — 35 B3
Conrad — 126 D1
Consett — 36 G7
Côn Son — 84 D5
Constanța — 92 C1
Constantina — 60 E7
Constantine — 102 G1
Consul — 126 E1
Contact — 126 D2
Contamana — 140 B5
Contwoyto Lake — 122 J3
Conway — 130 F3
Conway — 130 C2
Conwy — 38 E2
Conwy Bay — 38 E2
Coober Pedy — 114 F5
Cookeville — 128 C3
Cook Inlet — 132 (1)G4
Cook Islands — 112 K7
Cookstown — 35 E2
Cook Strait — 116 E5
Cooktown — 114 J3
Coolabah — 114 J6
Coolgardie — 114 D6
Cooma — 114 J7
Coonabarabran — 114 J6
Coon Rapids — 128 B1
Coopers Town — 130 F4
Coorabie — 114 F6
Coos Bay — 126 B2
Cootamundra — 114 J6
Copenhagen = København — 48 G9
Copertino — 64 N8
Copiapó — 142 G4
Copper Harbor — 128 C1
Côqen — 88 D2
Coquille — 126 B2
Coquimbo — 142 G4
Corabia — 66 M6
Coral — 124 K1
Coral Harbour — 122 Q4
Coral Sea — 114 K2
Coral Sea Islands Territory — 114 K2
Coral Springs — 130 E4
Corantijn — 140 F3
Corbeil-Essonnes — 58 H5
Corbigny — 58 J6
Corbridge — 36 F7
Corbu — 66 R5
Corby — 38 H3
Cordele — 130 E3
Cordillera Cantábrica — 60 D2
Cordillera Central — 138 E5
Cordillera del Condor — 140 B5
Cordillera de Mérida — 138 D3
Cordillera de Oliva — 142 G4
Cordillera Isabella — 134 G6
Cordillera Occidental — 138 E5
Cordillera Oriental — 138 D5
Cordillera Penibética — 60 F8
Cordillera Vilcabamba — 140 C6
Córdoba, Argentina — 142 J5
Córdoba, Spain — 60 F7
Corfu = Kerkyra — 68 B5
Coria — 60 D5
Corinth — 130 D3

Corinto — 140 H7
Cork — 35 C5
Cork Harbour — 35 C5
Corleone — 64 H11
Çorlu — 68 K3
Corn Islands — 138 C2
Cornwall — 124 M2
Cornwallis Island — 122 M2
Coro — 140 D1
Corocoro — 140 D7
Coromandel — 116 E3
Coromandel Coast — 88 D6
Coromandel Peninsula — 116 E3
Coron — 84 G4
Coronation Gulf — 122 J3
Coronel Oviedo — 142 K4
Coronel Pringles — 142 J6
Coronel Suárez — 142 J6
Corpus Christi — 130 B4
Corraun Peninsula — 35 B3
Corrientes — 142 K4
Corrigan — 130 C3
Corriverton — 140 F2
Corse — 64 D6
Corsham — 38 F4
Corsica = Corse — 64 D6
Corsicana — 130 B3
Corte — 64 D6
Cortegana — 60 D7
Cortez — 132 E1
Cortina d'Ampezzo — 62 H4
Cortland — 128 E2
Cortona — 64 F5
Coruche — 60 B6
Çorum — 92 F3
Corumbá — 140 F7
Corvallis — 126 B2
Corvo — 102 (1)A2
Cosenza — 64 L9
Cosmoledo Group — 108 (2)A2
Cosne-sur-Loire — 58 H6
Cossato — 62 D5
Costa Blanca — 60 K7
Costa Brava — 60 P3
Costa del Sol — 60 F8
Costa de Mosquitos — 134 H6
Costa Dorada — 60 M4
Costa do Sol — 60 A6
Costa Rica — 134 G7
Costa Smeralda — 64 D7
Costa Verde — 60 D1
Costești — 66 M5
Coswig — 52 H5
Cotabato — 84 G5
Côte d'Ivoire — 104 C3
Cotonou — 104 E3
Cotswold Hills — 38 F4
Cottage Grove — 126 B2
Cottbus — 50 D6
Cotulla — 130 B4
Couhe — 58 F7
Coulommiers — 54 F6
Council Bluffs — 126 F2
Coupar Angus — 36 E5
Courland Lagoon — 50 L2
Courtacon — 54 F6
Courtenay — 124 B2
Coushatta — 130 C3
Coutances — 58 D4
Couvin — 54 G4
Covasna — 66 P4
Coventry — 38 G3
Covilhã — 60 C4
Covington, Ga., United States — 130 E3
Covington, Ky., United States — 130 E2
Covington, Va., United States — 128 D3
Cowbridge — 38 E4
Cowell — 114 G6
Cowes — 38 G5
Cowra — 114 J6
Cox's Bazar — 88 F4
Coy Aike — 142 H9
Cradock — 108 D6
Craig — 126 E2
Craigavon — 35 E2
Crail — 36 F5
Crailsheim — 52 F7
Craiova — 66 L5
Cranbrook, Australia — 114 C6
Cranbrook, United States — 124 C2
Crater Lake — 126 B2
Crato — 140 K5
Crawford — 126 F2
Crawfordsville — 128 C2
Crawley — 38 H4
Cray — 36 E5
Crediton — 38 E5
Cree Lake — 122 K5
Creil — 54 E5
Crema — 62 E5
Cremona — 62 F5
Crépy-en-Valois — 54 E5
Cres — 62 K6
Cres — 62 K6
Crescent City — 126 B2
Crest — 58 L9
Creston — 128 B2
Crestview — 124 J5
Crete = Kriti — 68 H10
Créteil — 54 E6
Creuse — 58 G7
Crevillent — 60 K6
Crewe — 38 F2
Crewkerne — 38 F5
Crianlarich — 36 D5
Criciúma — 142 M4
Crieff — 36 E5
Cristalina — 140 H7
Cristóbal Colón — 120 J8
Crna Gora — 66 F7
Croatia — 66 C4
Crockett — 130 B3
Croker Island — 114 F2
Cromer — 38 K3
Cromwell — 116 B7
Crook — 36 G7

Crooked Island — 134 K4
Crookston — 124 G2
Crosby — 38 H2
Cross City — 130 E3
Cross Fell — 36 F7
Cross Lake — 122 M6
Crossville — 128 C3
Crotone — 64 M9
Crowborough — 38 J4
Crowley — 130 C3
Crownest Pass — 124 D2
Crown Point — 128 C2
Croydon — 38 H4
Croydon — 114 H3
Cruz Alta — 142 L4
Cruz del Eje — 142 J5
Cruzeiro do Sul — 140 C5
Crvenka — 66 G4
Crystal City — 130 B4
Crystal Falls — 128 C1
Crystal River — 130 E4
Crystal Springs — 130 C3
Csorna — 66 E2
Csurgó — 62 N4
Cuamba — 108 F2
Cuando — 108 C3
Cuangar — 108 B3
Cuango — 106 B5
Cuanza — 106 B5
Cuatro Ciénegas — 132 F3
Cuauhtémoc — 132 E3
Cuba — 134 H4
Cuba — 126 E3
Cubal — 106 A6
Cubali — 108 A2
Cubango — 108 B3
Çubuk — 68 R4
Cucuí — 140 D3
Cúcuta — 140 C2
Cuddalore — 88 C6
Cuddapah — 88 C6
Cuemba — 108 B2
Cuenca, Ecuador — 140 B4
Cuenca, Spain — 60 H4
Cuernavaca — 134 E5
Cuero — 130 B4
Cuiabá — 140 F7
Cuillin Hills — 36 B4
Cuilo — 106 B5
Cuio — 106 A6
Cuito — 108 B3
Cuito Cuanavale — 108 B3
Culbertson — 126 E1
Culfa — 92 L4
Culiacán — 134 C4
Cullen — 36 F4
Cullera — 60 K5
Cullman — 130 D3
Culpepper — 140 (1)A1
Culuene — 140 G6
Culverden — 116 D6
Cumaná — 140 E1
Cumberland — 128 E3
Cumberland Peninsula — 122 T3
Cumberland Sound — 122 T3
Cumbernauld — 36 E6
Cumbrian Mountains — 36 E7
Cummings — 126 B3
Cumnock — 36 D6
Cumpas — 132 E2
Çumra — 68 Q7
Cunderdin — 114 C6
Cunene — 108 A3
Cuneo — 62 C6
Cunnamulla — 114 J5
Cuorgne — 62 C5
Cupar — 36 E5
Čuprija — 66 J6
Cure — 58 J6
Curicó — 142 G5
Curitiba — 142 M4
Currais Novos — 140 K5
Curral Velho — 104 (1)B1
Currie — 114 H7
Curtea de Argeş — 66 M4
Curtici — 66 J3
Curtis Island — 114 K4
Curuá — 140 G5
Curup — 86 C3
Curuzú Cuatiá — 142 K4
Curvelo — 140 J7
Cusco — 140 C6
Cushendall — 35 E1
Cuthbert — 130 E3
Cutro — 64 L9
Cuttack — 88 E4
Cuvier Island — 116 E3
Cuxhaven — 52 D3
Cuya — 140 C7
Cuyuni — 140 F2
Cwmbran — 38 E4
Cyclades = Kyklades — 68 G7
Cypress Hills — 124 D2
Cyprus — 92 E6
Czarnków — 50 F5
Czech Republic — 50 C8
Częstochowa — 50 J7
Człuchów — 50 G4

D

Da'an — 80 G1
Dab'a — 94 D5
Dabas — 66 G2
Dabat — 100 G5
Dabola — 104 B2
Dabra — 88 C3
Dăbuleni — 66 M6
Dachau — 62 G2
Dadu — 88 A3
Daet — 84 G4
Dagana — 102 B5
Dagestan — 92 M2

Dagupan — 84 G…
Dahabān — 100 C…
Da Hinggan Ling — 80 G…
Dahlak Archipelago — 100 …
Dahlonega — 130 E…
Dahn — 54 K…
Dahod — 88 B…
Dahongliutan — 90 L…
Dahūk — 92 K…
Daimiel — 60 G…
Dai Xian — 80 E…
Dakar — 104 A…
Dakoro — 104 F…
Dakota City — 126 G…
Dakovica — 66 H…
Dakovo — 66 F…
Dala — 106 C…
Dalai Nur — 80 F…
Dalälven — 48 H…
Dalaman — 92 C…
Dalandzadgad — 80 C…
Dalap-Uiiga-Darrit — 112 H…
Da Lat — 84 D…
Dalbandin — 90 H…
Dalbeattie — 36 E…
Dalby — 114 K…
Dalgän — 90 G…
Dalhart — 132 F…
Dalhousie — 88 C…
Dali — 84 C…
Dalian — 80 G…
Dalizi — 82 D…
Dalkeith — 36 E…
Dalkey — 35 E…
Dallas — 130 B…
Dalmā — 95 E…
Dalmellington — 36 D…
Daloa — 104 C…
Dalry — 36 D…
Dalrymple Lake — 114 J…
Dāltenganj — 88 D…
Dalton — 130 E…
Dalvík — 48 (1)D…
Daly Waters — 114 F…
Daman — 88 B…
Damanhūr — 100 F…
Damar — 87 C…
Damara — 104 H…
Damasak — 104 G…
Damascus = Dimashq — 94 D…
Damaturu — 104 G…
Dāmiya — 94 C…
Damoh — 88 C…
Damqawt — 90 F…
Damxung — 88 F…
Da Näng — 84 D…
Danau Poso — 87 A…
Danau Toba — 86 B…
Danau Towuti — 87 B…
Danba — 80 C…
Dandeldhura — 88 D…
Dandong — 82 C…
Daneți — 66 M…
Dangara — 90 J…
Danger Islands — 112 K…
Danghe Nanshan — 80 B…
Daniel — 126 D…
Danilov — 70 H…
Dank — 95 G…
Dankov — 70 G…
Dannenberg — 52 G…
Dannevirke — 116 F…
Dansville — 128 E…
Danube — 46 H…
Danville, Ill., United States — 130 D…
Danville, Ky., United States — 130 E…
Danville, Va., United States — 130 E…
Dan Xian — 84 D…
Dao Phu Quôc — 84 C…
Dapa — 84 H…
Dapaong — 104 E…
Da Qaidam — 80 B…
Daqing — 78 M…
Dar'ā — 94 D…
Dārāb — 95 F…
Darabani — 66 P…
Daraj — 100 B…
Dārākūyeh — 95 F…
Darazo — 104 G…
Dar Ben Karricha el Behri — 60 E…
Darbhanga — 88 E…
Dardanelles = Çanakkale Boğazı — 68 J…
Darende — 92 G…
Dar es Salaam — 106 F…
Darfo Boario Terme — 62 F…
Dargan-Ata — 76 L…
Dargaville — 116 D…
Darham — 78 H…
Darjeeling — 88 E…
Darling — 114 H…
Darlington — 36 G…
Darłowo — 48 J…
Dărmănești — 66 P…
Dar Mazār — 95 H…
Darmstadt — 52 D…
Darnah — 100 D…
Darnley Bay — 122 G…
Daroca — 60 J…
Darß — 52 H…
Dartford — 38 J…
Dartmoor National Park — 38 E…
Dartmouth, Canada — 122 U…
Dartmouth, United Kingdom — 38 E…
Daru — 87 E…
Daruba — 87 C…
Daruvar — 62 N…
Darvaza — 76 K…
Darvel — 36 D…
Darwen — 38 F…
Darwin — 114 F…
Daryācheh-ye Bakhtegan — 95 E…
Daryācheh-ye Orūmīyeh — 92 L…
Daryācheh-ye Tashk — 95 H…
Dārzīn — 95 H…
Dashizhai — 80 G…
Dashkhovuz — 76 K…

Dasht-e Kavir 90 F3
Dasht-e Lut 95 H1
Datça 68 K8
Datça 92 B5
Date 82 L2
Datong 80 E2
Datong 80 C3
Daugava 70 E3
Daugavpils 70 E3
Daun 54 J4
Dauphin 122 M6
Daura 104 F2
Dausa 88 C3
Dăvăci 92 N3
Davangere 88 C6
Davao 84 H5
Davenport 128 B2
Daventry 38 G3
David 134 H7
Davis Sea 144 (2)Q3
Davis Strait 122 V3
Davlekanovo 76 J7
Davos 62 E4
Dawa 80 G2
Dawqah, *Oman* 90 F6
Dawqah, *Saudi Arabia* 100 H4
Dawson 122 D4
Dawson Creek 122 G5
Dawu 80 C4
Dax 58 D10
Daxian 80 D4
Dayong 80 E5
Dayr az Zawr 92 J6
Dayton, *Oh., United States* 128 D3
Dayton, *Tenn., United States* 128 C3
Dayton, *Tex., United States* 130 C4
Dayton, *Wash., United States* 126 C1
Daytona Beach 130 E4
Dayu 80 E5
Dazhu 80 D4
De Aar 108 C6
Dead Sea 94 C5
Deakin 114 E6
Deal 38 K4
De'an 80 F5
Deán Funes 142 J5
Dease Lake 132 (1)M4
Dease Strait 122 J3
Death Valley 126 C3
Deba Habe 104 G2
Debar 68 C3
Dębica 50 L7
Debin 78 S4
Dęblin 50 L6
Dębno 50 D5
Debre Birhan 106 F2
Debrecen 66 J2
Debre Markos 100 G5
Debrešte 68 D3
Debre Tabor 100 G5
Decatur, *Al., United States* 128 C4
Decatur, *Ill., United States* 128 C3
Decazeville 58 H9
Deccan 88 C5
Děčín 50 D7
Decize 58 J7
De Cocksdorp 54 G1
Decorah 128 B2
Dedoplis 92 M3
Dédougou 104 D2
Dedza 108 E2
Dee, *Eng., United Kingdom* 38 E2
Dee, *Scot., United Kingdom* 36 F4
Deering 132 (1)E2
Deer Lake 122 V7
Deer Lodge 126 D1
Deer Park 126 C1
De Funiak Springs 130 D3
Dêgê 80 B4
Degeh Bur 106 G2
Degema 104 F4
Deggendorf 62 J2
Dehaj 95 F1
Dehalak Desēt 90 D6
Deh Bid 95 E1
Deh-Dasht 95 D1
Dehiba 102 H2
Dehküyeh 95 F3
Dehlonān 90 E3
Dehra 90 L3
Dehra Dun 88 C2
Dehri 88 D4
Deh Shū 90 H3
Deinze 54 F4
Dej 66 L2
De Kalb 130 C3
De-Kastri 78 Q6
Dekese 106 C4
Delano 132 C1
Delaware 130 F2
Delaware 128 D2
Delbrück 52 D5
Delémont 62 C3
Delfoi 68 E6
Delft 54 G2
Delfzijl 54 J1
Delgo 100 F3
Delhi, *India* 88 C3
Delhi, *United States* 128 F2
Delingha 80 B3
Delitzsch 52 H5
Dellys 60 P8
Delmenhorst 52 D3
Delnice 62 K5
Delray Beach 130 E4
Del Rio 132 F3
Delta, *Colo., United States* 126 E3
Delta, *Ut., United States* 126 D3
Delta del Orinoco 140 E2
Delta Junction 132 (1)H3
Deming 132 E2
Demirci 68 L5
Demmin 52 J3
Democratic Republic of Congo 106 C4
Demopolis 130 D3
Demyanka 70 P3
Dem'yanskoye 70 N3
Denain 54 F4
Denau 90 J2
Denbigh 128 E1
Denbigh 38 E2
Den Burg 54 G1
Dendang 86 D3
Dender 54 F4
Dendi 106 F2
Dengkou 80 D2
Denham 114 B5
Den Helder 54 G2
Dénia 60 L6
Deniliquin 114 H7
Denio 126 C2
Denison, *Ia., United States* 128 A2
Denison, *Tex., United States* 130 B3
Denizli 92 C5
Denmark 46 E2
Denmark 114 C6
Denmark Strait 120 D3
Denpasar 86 E4
Denton 132 G2
Denton 38 F2
D'Entrecasteaux Islands 114 K1
Denver 126 F3
Deogarh, *India* 88 B3
Deogarh, *India* 88 D4
Deoghar 88 E4
Déols 58 G7
De Panne 54 E3
Depok 86 D4
Dépression du Mourdi 100 D4
Deputatskiy 78 P3
Dêqên 84 B1
Dera Ghazi Khan 90 K3
Dera Ismail Khan 90 K3
Derbent 90 E1
Derby, *Australia* 114 D3
Derby, *United Kingdom* 38 G3
De Ridder 130 C3
Dermott 130 C3
Derryveagh Mountains 35 C1
Dersingham 38 J3
Derudeb 100 G4
Derventa 66 E5
Desborough 38 H3
Desē 100 G5
Deseado 142 H8
Deseado 142 H8
Desert Center 132 C2
Des Moines, *Ia., United States* 124 H3
Des Moines, *N. Mex., United States* 132 F1
Desna 70 F4
Dessau 52 H5
Desvres 54 D4
Deta 66 J4
Detmold 52 D5
Detroit 124 K3
Detroit Lakes 128 A1
Det Udom 84 C4
Detva 50 J9
Deurne 54 H3
Deva 66 K4
Deventer 54 J2
Devikot 88 B3
Devils Lake 126 G1
Devil's Lake 122 L7
Devil's Point 130 F5
Devizes 38 G4
Devnja 66 Q6
Devon Island 122 P1
Devonport 114 J8
Dewangiri 88 F3
Dewas 88 C4
Dewsbury 38 G2
Deyang 80 C4
Deyhuk 90 G3
Deyyer 95 E3
Dezfūl 90 E3
Dezhou 80 F3
Dhahran = Aẓ Ẓahrān 95 D3
Dhaka 88 F4
Dhamār 100 H5
Dhamtri 88 D4
Dhanbad 88 E4
Dhar 88 C4
Dhārwād 88 B5
Dhaulagiri 88 D3
Dhekelia 94 A2
Dhībān 94 C5
Dhoraji 88 B4
Dhule 88 B4
Dhulian 88 E4
Dhuudo 106 J2
Dhuusa Marreeb 106 H2
Dia 68 H9
Diaca 106 G6
Diamantina 140 H7
Diamantino 140 F6
Diamond Islets 114 K3
Diane Bank 114 J3
Dianópolis 140 H6
Dibā al Ḥiṣn 95 G4
Dibbiena 64 F5
Dibrugarh 88 F3
Dickens 132 F2
Dickinson 126 F1
Dickson 130 D2
Didcot 38 G4
Diéléni 104 C2
Didymoteicho 68 J3
Die 58 L9
Diébougou 104 D2
Dieburg 52 D7
Diéma 104 C2
Diemel 52 E5
Diemeringen 52 C8
Diepholz 52 D4
Dieppe 54 D5
Diest 54 H4
Diffa 104 G2
Digne-les-Bains 62 B6
Digoin 58 J7
Dijon 58 L6
Dikhil 100 H5
Dikili 68 J5
Diklosmta 92 L2
Diksmuide 54 E3
Dikson 76 Q3
Dikwa 104 G2
Dīla 106 F2
Dili 87 C4
Dilijan 92 L3
Dillenburg 52 D6
Dilling 100 E5
Dillingen, *Germany* 52 F8
Dillingen, *Germany* 52 B7
Dillingham 132 (1)F4
Dillion 124 D2
Dillon 126 D1
Dillon Cone 116 D6
Dilolo 108 C2
Dimapur 88 F3
Dimashq 94 D3
Dimitrovgrad, *Bulgaria* 66 N7
Dimitrovgrad, *Russia* 70 J4
Dimitrovgrad, *Yugoslavia* 66 K7
Dimona 94 C5
Dinagat 84 H4
Dinajpur 88 E3
Dinan 58 C5
Dinant 54 G4
Dinar 92 D4
Dinard 58 C5
Dinaric Alps 62 L6
Dindigul 88 C6
Dindori 88 D4
Dingle 35 A4
Dingle Bay 35 A4
Dingolfing 62 H2
Dinguiraye 104 B2
Dingwall 36 D4
Dingxi 80 C3
Dinkelsbühl 52 F7
Dinosaur 126 E2
Diomede Islands 78 AA3
Dioriga Kointhou 68 F7
Diourbel 102 B6
Dipolog 84 G5
Dir 88 B1
Dirē Dawa 106 G2
Dirk Hartog Island 114 B5
Dirranbandi 114 J5
Disko = Qeqertarsuaq 122 V2
Disko Bugt = Qeqertarsuup Tunua 122 V3
Diss 38 K3
Distrito Federal 140 H7
Dithmarschen 52 D2
Dīvāndarreh 92 M6
Divinópolis 142 N3
Divo 104 C3
Divriği 92 H4
Dixon 128 C2
Dixon Entrance 132 (1)L5
Diyarbakır 92 J5
Dja 104 G4
Djado 102 H4
Djamâa 102 G2
Djambala 104 G5
Djanet 102 G4
Djelfa 102 F2
Djéma 106 D2
Djenné 102 E6
Djibo 104 D2
Djibouti 100 H5
Djibouti 100 H5
Djolu 106 C3
Djougou 104 E3
Djúpivogur 48 (1)F2
Dnestrovsc 66 S3
Dnieper 70 F5
Dniester 66 Q1
Dniprodzerzhyns'k 70 F5
Dnipropetrovs'k 70 F5
Dnister = Dniester 66 Q1
Dno 70 E3
Doba, *Chad* 106 B2
Doba, *China* 88 E2
Dobbiaco 62 H4
Döbeln 52 J5
Döbern 52 K5
Doboj 66 F5
Dobre Miasto 50 K4
Dobrič 66 Q6
Dobryanka 70 L3
Doctor Arroyo 132 F4
Dodecanese = Dodekanisos 68 J8
Dodge City 126 F3
Dodoma 106 F5
Doetinchem 54 J3
Dofa 87 C3
Doğanşehir 92 G4
Dōgo 82 G5
Dogondoutchi 104 E2
Doğubeyazıt 92 L4
Doha = Ad Dawḥah 95 D4
Doka 87 D4
Dokkum 52 B3
Dolak 87 E4
Dolbeau 128 F1
Dole 62 A3
Dolgany 78 E2
Dolgellau 38 E3
Dolinsk 78 Q7
Dollard 52 C3
Dolný Kubrín 50 J8
Dolomiti 62 G4
Dolores 142 K6
Dolphin and Union Strait 122 H3
Domar 88 D2
Domažlice 52 H7
Dombås 48 E5
Dombóvár 66 F3
Domfront 58 E5
Dominica 138 E2
Dominican Republic 138 D1
Domodossola 62 D4
Domokos 68 E5
Dompu 87 A4
Domžale 62 K4
Don 46 H2
Donau = Danube 62 H2
Donaueschingen 62 D3
Donauwörth 52 F8
Don Benito 60 E6
Doncaster 38 G2
Dondra Head 88 D7
Donegal 35 C2
Donegal Bay 35 C2
Donets 46 H3
Donets'k 70 G5
Dongara 114 B5
Dongco 88 D2
Dongfang 84 D3
Donggala 87 A3
Donggou 82 C4
Dongguan 84 E2
Dông Hôi 84 D3
Dongjingcheng 82 E1
Donglük 76 R10
Dongning 82 F2
Dongo 104 H4
Dongola 100 F4
Dongou 104 H4
Dongsha Qundao 84 F2
Dongsheng 80 E3
Dong Ujimqin Qi 80 F1
Dongying 80 F3
Doniphan 130 C2
Donji Vakuf 62 N6
Donner Pass 126 B3
Donostia 60 J1
Donousa 68 H7
Doolow 106 G3
Dora 62 C5
Dorchester 38 F5
Dordrecht 54 G3
Dorfen 62 H2
Dori 104 D2
Doring 108 B6
Dorion 128 C1
Dorking 38 H4
Dormagen 54 J3
Dornbirn 62 E3
Dornoch 36 D4
Dornoch Firth 36 E4
Doro 104 D1
Dorog 50 H10
Dorohoi 66 P2
Döröö Nuur 76 S8
Dorotea 48 J4
Dorsten 54 J3
Dortmund 52 C5
Doruma 106 D3
Dos Hermanas 60 E7
Dosse 52 H4
Dosso 104 E2
Dothan 130 D3
Douai 54 F4
Douala 104 F4
Douarnenez 58 A5
Doubs 62 B3
Douentza 104 C2
Douglas, *Isle of Man* 36 D7
Douglas, *Republic of Ireland* 35 C5
Douglas, *South Africa* 108 C5
Douglas, *Scot., United Kingdom* 36 E6
Douglas, *Ariz., United States* 132 E2
Douglas, *Ga., United States* 130 E3
Douglas, *Wyo., United States* 126 E2
Doullens 54 E4
Dourados 142 L3
Douro 60 B3
Dover, *United Kingdom* 38 K4
Dover, *United States* 130 F2
Dover, *Australia* 114 J8
Dover-Foxcroft 128 G1
Dowlatābād, *Iran* 95 E2
Dowlatābād, *Iran* 95 G2
Downham Market 38 J3
Downpatrick 35 F2
Downpatrick Head 35 B2
Dowshī 90 J2
Drac 62 B6
Drachten 54 J1
Dragan 48 H4
Drăgănești-Olt 66 M5
Drăgășani 66 M5
Draguignan 62 B7
Drakensberg 108 D6
Drake Passage 142 G10
Drama 68 G3
Drammen 48 F7
Drasenhofen 62 M2
Drau 62 J4
Drava 66 E4
Dravograd 64 K2
Drawsko Pomorskie 50 E4
Dresden 52 J5
Dreux 54 D6
Drezdenko 50 E5
Driffield 38 H2
Drina 66 G5
Driva 48 E5
Drjanovo 66 N7
Drniš 66 D6
Drobeta-Turnu Severin 66 K5
Drochia 66 Q1
Drogheda 35 E3
Drohobych 50 N8
Droitwich 38 F3
Drôme 58 K9
Dromore 35 D2
Dronfield 38 G2
Dronne 58 F8
Dronten 54 H2
Drummondville 128 F1
Drumnadrochit 36 D4
Druskininkai 48 M9
Druzhina 78 Q3
Drvar 66 D5
Dryden 124 H2
Drymen 36 D5
Drysdale River 114 E3
Dschang 104 G3
Ḍubā 100 G2
Dubai = Dubayy 95 F4

Dubăsari 66 S2
Dubawnt Lake 122 L4
Dubayy 95 F4
Dubbo 114 J6
Dübendorf 62 D3
Dublin, *Republic of Ireland* 35 E3
Dublin, *United States* 130 E3
Dublin Bay 35 E3
Dubna 70 G3
Dubnica 50 H9
Du Bois 128 E2
Dubois, *Id., United States* 126 D2
Dubois, *Wyo., United States* 126 E2
Dubovskoye 70 H5
Dubreka 104 B3
Dubrovnik 66 F7
Dubuque 128 B2
Duchesne 126 D2
Ducie Island 112 P8
Dudelange 54 J5
Duderstadt 52 F5
Dudinka 76 R4
Dudley 38 F3
Duero 60 F3
Dugi Otok 66 B6
Duifken Point 114 H2
Duisburg 54 J3
Duiveland 54 F3
Dukat 78 T4
Duk Faiwil 106 E2
Dukhān 95 D4
Dukla 50 L8
Dukou 80 C5
Dulan 80 B3
Dulce 132 E1
Dulce 142 J4
Dul'Durga 78 J6
Dullewala 88 B2
Dülmen 52 C5
Dulovo 66 Q6
Duluth 128 B1
Dūmā 94 D3
Dumaguete 84 G5
Dumai 86 C2
Dumas, *Ark., United States* 130 C3
Dumas, *Tex., United States* 126 F3
Ḑumayr 94 D3
Dumbarton 36 D6
Ďumbier 50 J9
Dumboa 104 G2
Dumfries 36 E6
Dümmer 52 D4
Dumont d'Urville Sea 144 (2)U3
Dumyât 100 F1
Duna = Danube 66 E2
Dunaj = Danube 50 G10
Dunajská Streda 66 E2
Dunakeszi 66 G2
Dunărea = Danube 66 K5
Dunaújváros 66 F3
Dunav = Danube 66 J5
Dunayivtsi 70 E5
Dunbar, *Australia* 114 H3
Dunbar, *United Kingdom* 36 F5
Dunblane 36 E5
Duncan 126 B1
Duncan Passage 84 A4
Duncansby Head 36 F3
Dundaga 48 M8
Dundalk 35 E2
Dundalk Bay 35 E3
Dundee, *South Africa* 108 E5
Dundee, *United Kingdom* 36 F5
Dundrum Bay 35 F2
Dunedin 116 C7
Dunfanaghy 35 D1
Dunfermline 36 E5
Dungannon 35 E2
Dungarvan 35 D4
Dungarvan Harbour 35 D4
Dungeness 38 J5
Dungiven 35 E2
Dungu 106 D3
Dungun 84 C6
Dungunab 100 G3
Dunhua 82 E2
Dunhuang 80 A2
Dunkeld 36 E5
Dunkerque 54 E3
Dunkirk 128 E2
Dunkwa 104 D3
Dun Laoghaire 35 E3
Dunmanus Bay 35 B5
Dunnet Head 36 E3
Dunoon 36 D6
Duns 36 F6
Dunseith 126 G1
Dunshaughlin 35 E3
Dunsmuir 126 B2
Dunstable 38 H4
Dunvegan 36 B4
Duque de Caxias 142 N3
Du Quoin 130 D2
Durance 58 L10
Durango, *Mexico* 132 F4
Durango, *Spain* 60 H1
Durango, *United States* 126 E3
Durankurak 66 R6
Durant 130 B3
Durazno 142 K5
Durban 108 E5
Durban-Corbières 58 H10
Düren 54 J4
Durgapur 88 E4
Durham, *Canada* 128 D2
Durham, *United Kingdom* 36 G7
Durham, *United States* 130 F2
Duri 86 C2
Durmā 95 B4
Durmanec 66 C3
Durmitor 66 G6
Durness 36 D3
Durrës 68 B3
Durrow 35 D4
Dursey 35 A5
Dursunbey 68 L5
D'Urville Island 116 D5
Dushanbe 90 J2
Düsseldorf 54 J3
Duvno 62 N7
Duyun 80 D5
Düzce 68 P4
Dvina 46 H2
Dvinskaya Guba 70 G1
Dwarka 88 A4
Dworshak Reservoir 126 C1
Dyat'kovo 70 F4
Dyersburg 130 D2
Dyje 62 M2
Dzamīn Üüd 78 J8
Dzavhan 76 S8
Dzerzhinsk 70 H3
Dzhalinda 78 L6
Dzhambeyty 70 K4
Dzhankoy 70 F5
Dzhardzhan 78 L3
Dzharkurgan 90 J2
Dzhetygara 70 M4
Dzhezkazgan 70 N5
Dzhigudzhak 78 T4
Dzhizak 76 M9
Dzhusaly 70 M5
Działdowo 50 K4
Dzüünbulag 80 F1
Dzuunmod 80 D1

E

Eads 126 F3
Eagle 132 (1)J3
Eagle Lake 126 B2
Eagle Pass 132 F3
East Antarctica 144 (2)P2
Eastbourne 38 J5
East Cape 116 G3
East China Sea 80 H4
East Dereham 38 J3
Easter Island 112 Q8
Eastern Cape 108 D6
Eastern Ghats 88 C6
Easter Ross 36 D4
East Falkland 142 K9
East Grinstead 38 H4
East Kilbride 36 D6
Eastleigh 38 G5
East Liverpool 130 E1
East London 108 D6
Eastmain 122 R6
Eastmain 122 S6
East Point 130 E3
East Retford 38 H2
East St. Louis 128 B3
East Siberian Sea = Vostochno-Sibirskoye More 78 U2
East Timor = Timor Timur 87 C4
Eatonton 130 E3
Eau Claire 128 B2
Ebbw Vale 38 E4
Ebensee 62 J3
Eberbach 52 D7
Ebersbach 50 D6
Ebersberg 62 G2
Eberswalde 52 J4
Ebinur Hu 76 Q9
Eboli 64 K8
Ebolowa 104 G4
Ebro 60 K3
Eceabat 68 J4
Ech Chélif 102 F1
Echinos 68 G3
Echo Bay 122 H3
Écija 60 E7
Eckernförde 52 E2
Ecuador 140 B4
Ed 100 H5
Edam 54 H2
Eday 36 F2
Ed Da'ein 100 E5
Ed Damazin 100 F5
Ed Debba 100 F4
Eddrachillis Bay 36 C3
Ed Dueim 100 F5
Ede, *Netherlands* 54 H2
Ede, *Nigeria* 104 E3
Edéa 104 G4
Edelény 50 K9
Eden 36 F7
Eden, *Australia* 114 J7
Eden, *United States* 132 G2
Edendale 116 B8
Eder 52 D5
Edersee 52 E5
Edessa 68 E4
Edgecumbe 116 F3
Edinburgh 36 E6
Edineț 66 Q1
Edirne 68 J3
Edmonds 126 B1
Edmonton 122 J6
Edmundson 124 N2
Edmundston 128 G1
Edolo 62 F4
Edremit 68 J5
Edremit Körfezi 68 H5
Edwards 132 C2
Edwards Plateau 132 F2
Eeklo 54 F3
Eemshaven 54 J1
Éfaté 112 G7
Eferding 50 D9
Effingham 130 D2
Eganville 128 E1
Eger 66 H2
Eger 52 G6
Egersund 48 D7
Eggenfelden 62 H2
Egilsstaðir 48 (1)F2
Egremont 36 E7
Eğridir 68 N7
Eğridir Gölü 68 N6
Egvekinot 78 Y3
Egypt 100 E2
Ehingen 62 E2
Eibar 60 H1
Eichstätt 62 G2
Eider 52 D2
Eidfjord 48 D6
Eidsvold 114 K5
Eidsvoll 48 F6
Eifel 54 J4
Eigg 36 B5
Eight Degree Channel 88 B7
Eilenburg 52 H5
Einbeck 52 E5
Eindhoven 54 H3
Eirunepé 140 D5
Eiseb 108 C4
Eisenach 52 F6
Eisenerz 62 K3
Eisenhüttenstadt 50 D5
Eisenstadt 62 M3
Eisleben 52 G5
Eivissa 60 M5
Eivissa 60 M6
Ejea de los Caballeros 60 J2
Ejido Insurgentes 124 D6
Ejin Horo Qi 80 D3
Ejin Qi 80 C2
Ejmiadzin 92 L3
Ekalaka 126 F1
Ekenäs 48 M7
Eketahuna 116 E5
Ekibastuz 76 P7
Ekimchan 78 N6
Ekonda 76 V4
Eksjo 48 H8
Ekwan 122 Q6
Elafonisos 68 E8
El 'Alamein 100 E1
El Amria 60 J9
El 'Arîsh 94 A5
Elat 94 B7
Elazığ 92 H4
El Azraq 94 D5
Elba 64 E6
El Banco 140 C2
Elbasan 68 C3
El Baúl 140 D2
Elbe 52 F3
Elbeuf 54 D5
Elbistan 92 G4
Elbląg 50 J3
El Borj 60 E9
Elbow 124 E1
Elbrus 92 K2
El Burgo de Ebro 60 K3
El Burgo de Osma 60 G3
El Cajon 132 C2
El Callao 140 E2
El Campo 130 B4
El Centro 132 C2
El Cerro 140 E7
Elch 60 K6
Elda 60 K6
El'dikan 78 P4
Eldorado 142 L4
El Dorado, *Mexico* 124 E7
El Dorado, *Ark., United States* 130 C3
El Dorado, *Kans., United States* 130 B2
El Dorado, *Venezuela* 140 E2
Eldoret 106 F3
Elefsina 68 F6
Elektrėnai 50 P3
El Encanto 140 C4
Elephant Butte Reservoir 132 E2
Eleuthera 124 L6
El Fahs 64 D12
El Faiyûm 100 F2
El Fasher 100 E5
El Geneina 100 D5
Elgin, *United Kingdom* 36 E4
Elgin, *Ill., United States* 128 C2
Elgin, *N.D., United States* 126 F1
El'ginskiy 78 Q4
El Gîza 100 F1
El Goléa 102 F2
El Homr 102 F3
Elhovo 68 J2
El Iskandarîya 100 E1
Elista 70 H5
Elizabeth 128 F2
Elizabeth City 130 F2
Elizabethton 130 E2
El Jadida 102 D2
El Jafr 94 D6
El Jafr 94 D6
Ełk 50 M4
Ełk 50 M4
El Kala 64 C12
Elk City 132 G1
El Kef 64 C12
El Kelaâ des Srarhna 102 D2
El Khandaq 100 F4
El Khârga 100 F2
Elkhart, *Ind., United States* 128 C2
Elkhart, *Kans., United States* 130 A2
El Khartum 100 F4
El Khartum Bahri 100 F4
Elkhorn 128 C2
Elkhorn 126 G2
Elkins 128 E3
Elko, *Canada* 126 C1
Elko, *United States* 126 C2
Elk River 128 B1
El Kuntilla 94 B7
Ellendale 124 G2
Ellensburg 126 B1
Ellesmere 38 F3
Ellesmere Island 120 K1
Ellesmere Port 38 F2
Ellice Islands 112 H6
Elliot 108 D6
Ellis 122 J8
Ellisras 108 D4
Elliston 114 F6
Ellon 36 F4
Ellsworth 128 G2
Ellwangen 62 F2
Elmadağ 68 R5
Elmali 68 M8
El Manşûra 100 F1
El Mazâr 94 A5
El Minya 100 F2
Elmira 128 E2
Elmshorn 52 E3
El Muglad 100 E5
El Nido 84 F4
El Obeid 100 F5
El Odaiya 100 E5
El Oued 102 G2
El Paso 132 E2
Elphin 36 C3
El Portal 132 C1
El Potosi 132 F4
El Prat de Llobregat 60 N3
El Puerto de Santa María 60 D8
El Qâhira 100 F1
El Qasr 100 E2
El Quşeima 94 B6
El Quweira 94 C7
El Reno 130 B2
El Sahuaro 132 D2
El Salvador 134 F6
Elster 52 H5
Elsterwerda 52 J5
Elstree 38 H4
El Sueco 132 E3
El Suweis 100 F2
Eltanin Bay 144 (2)JJ2
El Tarf 64 C12
El Thamad 94 B7
El Tigre 140 E2
El Turbio 142 G9
Eluru 88 D5
Elvas 60 C6
Elverum 48 F6
Elvira 140 C5
El Wak 106 G3
Ely, *United Kingdom* 38 J3
Ely, *United States* 126 D3
Emajõgi 48 P7
Emāmrūd 90 F2
Emba 70 L5
Emba 70 L5
Embalse de Alarcon 60 H5
Embalse de Alcántara Uno 60 D5
Embalse de Almendra 60 D3
Embalse de Contreras 60 J5
Embalse de Gabriel y Galán 60 D4
Embalse de Garcia Sola 60 E5
Embalse de Guadalhorce 60 F8
Embalse de Guadalmena 60 G6
Embalse de Guri 140 E2
Embalse de la Serena 60 E6
Embalse de la Sotonera 60 K2
Embalse del Bembézar 60 E6
Embalse del Ebro 60 G1
Embalse del Río Negro 138 F7
Embalse de Negratín 60 G7
Embalse de Ricobayo 60 E3
Embalse de Santa Teresa 60 E4
Embalse de Yesa 60 J2
Embalse Toekomstig 140 F3
Embarcación 142 J3
Emden 52 C3
Emerald 114 J4
Emi Koussi 100 C4
Emin 76 Q8
Emirdağ 68 P5
Emmeloord 54 H2
Emmen 54 J2
Emmendingen 62 C2
Emmerich 54 J3
Emory Peak 132 F3
Empalme 132 D3
Empangeni 108 E5
Empoli 62 F7
Emporia 130 B2
Empty Quarter = Rub' al Khālī 90 E6
Ems 54 J1
Ems-Jade-Kanal 52 C3
Enafors 70 B2
Encarnación 142 K4
Encs 66 J1
Ende 87 B4
Enderby Island 116 (2)B1
Energetik 70 L4
Enewetak 112 F4
Enez 68 J4
Enfida 64 E12
Enfield 38 H4
Engel's 70 J4
Enggano 86 C4
Enghien 54 G4
England 56 L9
English Channel 56 J12
English Channel 38 H5
Engozero 48 S4
'En Hazeva 94 C6
Enid 130 B2
Enkhuizen 54 H2
Enköping 48 J7
Enna 64 J11
En Nahud 100 E5
Enngonia 114 J5
Ennis, *Republic of Ireland* 35 C4
Ennis, *United States* 126 D1
Enniscorthy 35 E4
Enniskillen 35 D2
Ennistymon 35 B4
Enn Nâqoûra 94 C3
Enns 62 K2
Enns 62 K3
Enschede 54 J2
Ensenada 132 C2
Enshi 80 D4
Entebbe 106 E3
Enterprise 126 C1
Entrevaux 62 B7
Entroncamento 60 B5
Enugu 104 F3
Enurmino 78 Z3
Envira 140 C5

nz 62 D2
nza 62 F6
panomi 68 E4
péna 106 B3
pernay 58 J4
pinal 62 B2
piskopi 68 Q10
psom 38 H4
qlīd 95 E1
quatorial Guinea 104 F4
rbach 52 D7
rçek 92 K4
rciş 92 K4
rcolano 64 J8
rd 66 F2
rdek 68 K4
rdemli 68 S8
rdenet 78 G7
rding 62 G2
rechim 142 L4
reğli, *Turkey* 92 D3
reğli, *Turkey* 92 F5
reikoussa 68 B5
renhot 80 E2
rfurt 52 G6
rgani 92 H4
rg Chech 102 D4
rg du Ténéré 102 H5
rgel 80 D2
rgene 68 J3
rg Iguidi 102 D3
Hai 80 C5
rie 128 D2
rimo 82 M2
rimo-misaki 82 M3
riskay 36 A4
ritrea 100 G4
rlangen 52 G7
rmenek 92 E5
rmoupoli 68 G7
rnard Bay 36 C3
rode 88 C6
Rachidia 102 E2
Rahad 100 F5
Renk 106 E1
rris Head 35 A2
rrol 128 F2
Ruseifa 94 D4
rsekë 68 C4
rskine 128 A1
rtai 76 S8
rtix 76 R8
rzgebirge 52 H6
rzin 76 S7
rzincan 92 H4
rzurum 92 J4
san-misaki 82 L3
sashi, *Japan* 82 L3
sashi, *Japan* 82 M1
sbjerg 48 E9
scanaba 128 C1
scárcega 134 F5
sch 54 J5
schwege 52 F5
schweiler 54 J4
scondido 132 C2
séka 104 G4
şfahān 90 F3
skifjörður 48 (1)G2
skilstuna 48 J7
skimo Lakes 132 (1)L2
skişehir 92 D4
sla 60 E3
slāmābād e Gharb 92 M6
slamshahr 90 F2
sler Dağ 68 M7
slö 50 C2
smeraldas 140 B3
sneux 54 H4
spalion 58 H9
spanola, *Canada* 128 D1
spanola, *United States* 126 E3
spelkamp 52 D4
sperance 114 D6
sperance Bay 114 D6
speranza 140 C5
spinho 60 B4
spírito Santo 140 J7
spíritu Santo 112 G7
splanada 140 K6
spoo 48 N6
spungebera 108 E4
s Samrā 94 D4
ssaouira 102 D2
s Semara 102 C3
ssen, *Belgium* 54 G3
ssen, *Germany* 54 K3
ssequibo 140 F2
sslingen 62 E2
ştahbānāt 95 F2
ste 62 G5
stella 60 H2
stepona 60 E8
steros 142 J3
stevan 124 F2
stonia 48 M7
storil 60 A6
strecho de Le Maire 142 H10
strecho de Magallanes 142 G9
strela 60 C4
stremoz 60 C6
stuário do Rio Amazonaz 140 H3
sztergom 66 F2
ain 54 H5
ampes 58 H5
ang de Berre 58 L10
aples 54 D4
awah 88 C3
hiopia 98 G5
olin Strait 132 (1)D3
osha Pan 108 B3
retat 54 C5
telbruck 52 B7
tlingen 52 D8
ucla 114 E6
uclid 128 D2
Eufala 130 D3
Eufaula Lake 130 B2
Eugene 126 B2
Eupen 52 B6
Euphrates = Fırat 92 H4
Eure 54 D6
Eureka, *Calif., United States* 126 B2
Eureka, *Mont., United States* 126 C1
Eureka, *Nev., United States* 132 C1
Eureka, *Ut., United States* 126 D3
Europe 48 G2
Europoort 54 F3
Euskirchen 52 B6
Eutin 52 F2
Eutsuk Lake 122 F6
Evans Strait 122 Q4
Evanston, *Ill., United States* 128 C2
Evanston, *Wyo., United States* 126 D2
Evansville 130 D2
Evaz 95 F3
Everett 126 B1
Everglades City 130 E4
Evergreen 130 D3
Evesham 38 G3
Évora 60 C6
Évreux 54 D5
Evron 58 E5
Evvoia 68 F6
Ewo 104 G5
Exaltación 140 D6
Exe 38 E5
Exeter 38 E5
Exmoor National Park 38 E4
Exmouth, *Australia* 114 B4
Exmouth, *United Kingdom* 38 E5
Exuma Sound 124 L7
Eyemouth 36 F6
Eyl 106 H2
Eyre Peninsula 114 G2
Ezine 68 J5

F

Faadippolu Atoll 88 B8
Fåborg 52 F1
Fabriano 62 H7
Fachi 102 H5
Fada 100 D4
Fada Ngourma 104 E2
Faenza 62 G6
Færingehavn = Kangerluarsoruseq 122 W4
Faeroes 46 D1
Fafanlap 87 D3
Făgăraș 66 M4
Fagernes 48 E6
Fagersta 48 H6
Făget 66 K4
Fagurhólsmýri 48 (1)E3
Fahraj 95 H2
Faial 102 (1)B2
Fairbanks 132 (1)H3
Fair Head 35 E1
Fair Isle 36 (1)G2
Fairlie 116 C7
Fairmont 128 B2
Faisalabad 88 B2
Faith 126 F1
Faizabad 88 D3
Fakenham 38 J3
Fakfak 87 D3
Fakse 52 H1
Fakse Bugt 48 G9
Faku 80 G2
Falaise 54 B6
Falaise de Tiguidit 102 G5
Falconara Marittima 62 J7
Falcon Lake 130 B4
Fălești 66 Q2
Falfurrias 130 B4
Falkenberg 48 G8
Falkensee 52 J4
Falkirk 36 E6
Falkland Islands 142 K9
Falkland Sound 142 J9
Falköping 48 G7
Fallingbostel 52 E4
Fallon 126 C3
Fall River 128 F2
Falls City 124 G3
Falmouth, *United Kingdom* 38 C5
Falmouth, *United States* 128 F2
Falmouth Bay 38 C5
Falster 52 H2
Fălticeni 66 P2
Falun 48 H6
Famagusta = Ammochostos 94 A1
Fanchang 80 F4
Fandriana 108 H4
Fangzheng 80 H1
Fannūj 90 G4
Fano 62 J7
Fanø 52 D1
Fanø Bugt 52 D1
Faradje 106 D3
Farafangana 108 H4
Farāh 90 H3
Farah Rud 90 H3
Faranah 104 B2
Fareham 38 G5
Farewell Spit 116 D5
Fargo 124 G2
Faribault 128 B2
Faridabad 88 C3
Farihy Alaotra 108 H3
Färjestaden 50 F1
Farmington, *Me., United States* 128 F2
Farmington, *N. Mex., United States* 132 E1
Farnborough 38 H4
Farne Islands 36 G6
Farnham 38 H4
Fårö 48 K8
Faro, *Brazil* 140 F4
Faro, *Portugal* 60 C7
Fårösund 48 K8
Farquhar Group 108 (2)B3
Farrāshband 95 E2
Farson 126 E2
Fasā 95 E2
Fasano 64 M8
Fatehgarh 88 C3
Fatehpur 88 D3
Făurei 66 Q4
Fauske 48 H3
Fauville-en-Caux 54 C5
Favara 64 H11
Faversham 38 J4
Favignana 64 G11
Faxaflói 48 (1)B2
Faya 100 C4
Fayette 130 D3
Fayetteville, *Ark., United States* 130 C2
Fayetteville, *N.C., United States* 128 E3
Fayetteville, *Tenn., United States* 130 D2
Faylakah 95 C2
Fažana 64 H4
Fdérik 102 C4
Featherston 116 E5
Fécamp 54 C5
Federated States of Micronesia 112 E5
Fedorovka 70 M4
Fehmarn 52 G2
Feijó 140 C5
Feilding 116 E5
Feira de Santana 140 K6
Feistritz 62 L3
Fejø 52 G2
Feldbach 62 L4
Feldkirch 62 E3
Feldkirchen 62 K4
Felidu Atoll 88 B8
Felixstowe 38 K4
Feltre 62 G4
Femø 52 G2
Femund 48 F5
Fengcheng 82 C3
Fenghua 80 G5
Fengning 80 F2
Feng Xian 80 D4
Feni 88 F4
Fenyang 80 E3
Feodosiya 92 F1
Feres 68 J4
Fergana 90 K1
Fergus Falls 124 G2
Ferkessédougou 104 C3
Ferlach 62 K4
Fermo 64 H5
Fermoy 35 C4
Fernandina Beach 130 E3
Fernandópolis 142 L3
Ferndown 38 G5
Ferrara 62 G6
Ferreira do Alentejo 60 B7
Ferrol 60 B1
Ferryhill 36 G7
Ferry Lake 130 C2
Fès 102 E2
Festus 128 B3
Fetești 66 Q5
Fethiye 68 M8
Fetisovo 90 F1
Fetlar 36 (1)H1
Feucht 52 G7
Feuchtwangen 52 F7
Feyzābād 90 K2
Ffestiniog 38 E3
Fianarantsoa 108 H4
Fianga 106 B2
Fichē 106 F2
Fidenza 62 F6
Fieni 66 N4
Fier 68 B4
Fife Ness 36 F5
Figari 64 D7
Figeac 58 G9
Figline Valdarno 62 G7
Figueira da Foz 60 B4
Figueres 60 N2
Figuig 102 E2
Figuil 104 G3
Fiji 112 H8
Filadélfia 142 J3
Fil'akovo 50 J9
Filey 36 H7
Filiași 66 L5
Filicudi 64 J10
Fīltu 106 G2
Finale Ligure 62 D6
Findlay 128 D2
Fingoè 108 E3
Finike 68 N8
Finland 48 P3
Finlay 122 F5
Finley 114 J7
Finnsnes 48 K2
Finsterwalde 52 J5
Fionnphort 36 B5
Fırat 92 H4
Firenze 62 G7
Firminy 58 K8
Firozabad 88 C3
Firozpur 88 B2
Firth of Clyde 36 D6
Firth of Forth 36 F5
Firth of Lorn 36 C5
Firth of Thames 116 E3
Fish 108 B5
Fisher Strait 122 Q4
Fishguard 38 D4
Fiskenæsset = Qeqertarsuatsiaat 122 W4
Fismes 54 F5
Fitzroy Crossing 114 E3
Fivizzano 62 F6
Fizi 106 D4
Flå 48 E6
Flamborough Head 38 H1
Flaming Gorge Reservoir 126 E2
Flamingo 130 E4
Flannan Islands 36 A3
Flåsjön 48 H4
Flateyri 48 (1)B1
Flathead Lake 126 D1
Flat Point 116 E5
Fleetwood 38 E2
Flekkefjord 48 D7
Flensburg 52 E2
Flensburg Fjord 52 E2
Flers 54 B6
Flinders Island 114 J7
Flinders Ranges 114 G6
Flinders Reefs 114 J3
Flin Flon 122 L6
Flint, *United Kingdom* 38 E2
Flint, *United States* 128 D2
Flint Island 112 L7
Flirey 62 A2
Flöha 52 J6
Florac 58 J9
Florence = Firenze, *Italy* 62 G7
Florence, *Al., United States* 130 D3
Florence, *S.C., United States* 130 F3
Florencia 140 B3
Florennes 54 G4
Florenville 54 H5
Flores, *Azores* 102 (1)A2
Flores, *Indonesia* 87 B4
Flores Sea 87 A4
Florești 66 R2
Floriano 140 J5
Florianópolis 142 M4
Florida 130 E4
Florida 142 K5
Florida Keys 120 K7
Florina 68 D4
Florissant 128 B3
Florø 48 C6
Floydada 132 F2
Flumendosa 64 D9
Fly 87 F4
Foča 66 F6
Foça 68 J6
Focșani 66 Q4
Foggia 64 K7
Fogo 104 (1)B1
Fogo Island 122 W7
Fohnsdorf 62 K3
Föhr 52 D2
Foix 58 G11
Folegandros 68 G8
Foleyet 128 D1
Foligno 64 G6
Folkestone 38 K4
Folkston 130 E3
Follonica 64 E6
Fomboni 108 G2
Fond du Lac 128 C2
Fondi 64 H7
Fongafale 112 H6
Fontainebleau 58 H5
Fontana 64 M8
Fonte Boa 140 D4
Fontenay-le-Comte 58 E7
Fontur 48 (1)F1
Fonyód 64 M2
Forbach, *France* 54 J5
Forbach, *Germany* 54 L6
Forchheim 52 G7
Førde 48 C6
Fordingbridge 38 G5
Fordyce 130 C3
Foreland Point 38 E4
Forest, *Canada* 128 D2
Forest, *United States* 130 D3
Forest of Bowland 38 F2
Forest of Dean 38 F4
Forestville 128 G1
Forfar 36 F5
Forges-les-Eaux 54 D5
Forks 126 B1
Forlì 62 H6
Formazza 62 D4
Formby 38 E2
Formentera 60 M6
Formia 64 H7
Formiga 142 M3
Formosa, *Brazil* 140 H7
Formosa, *Paraguay* 142 K4
Fornovo di Taro 62 F6
Forres 36 E4
Forsayth 114 H3
Forssa 48 M6
Forst 52 K5
Forsyth 126 E1
Fort Abbas 88 B3
Fortaleza 140 K4
Fort Augustus 36 D4
Fort Bayne 128 C4
Fort Beaufort 108 D6
Fort Benton 126 D1
Fort Bragg 132 B1
Fort Chipewyan 122 J5
Fort Cobb Reservoir 130 B2
Fort Collins 126 E2
Fort-de-France 134 M6
Fort Dodge 128 B2
Forte dei Marmi 62 F7
Fortezza 62 G4
Fort Frances 128 B1
Fort George 122 R6
Fort Gibson Lake 130 B2
Fort Good Hope 122 F3
Forth 36 D5
Fort Hope 122 P6
Fortín Coronel Eugenio Garay 142 J3
Fort Kent 128 G1
Fort Lauderdale 130 E4
Fort Liard 122 G4
Fort Mackay 122 J5
Fort Macleod 126 D1
Fort McMurray 122 J5
Fort McPherson 132 (1)L2
Fort Munro 90 J4
Fort Myers 130 E4
Fort Nelson 122 G5
Fort Norman 132 (1)M3
Fort Payne 130 D3
Fort Peck Reservoir 126 E1

Fort Pierce — 130 E4
Fort Pierre — 126 F2
Fort Portal — 106 E3
Fort Providence — 122 H4
Fortrose — 116 B8
Fort Rupert — 122 R6
Fort St. John — 122 G5
Fort Saint Lucie — 130 E4
Fort Scott — 130 C2
Fort Severn — 122 P5
Fort Shevchenko — 76 J9
Fort Simpson — 122 G4
Fort Smith, *Canada* — 122 J4
Fort Smith, *United States* — 130 C2
Fort Stockton — 132 F2
Fort Summer — 132 F2
Fortuna — 126 F1
Fortune Bay — 122 V7
Fortuneswell — 38 F5
Fort Vermilion — 122 H5
Fort Wayne — 130 D1
Fort William — 36 C5
Fort Worth — 130 B3
Fort Yates — 126 F1
Foshan — 84 E2
Fosna — 48 F5
Fossano — 62 C6
Fossombrone — 62 H7
Fougamou — 104 G5
Fougères — 58 D5
Foula — 36 (1)F1
Foulness — 38 K4
Foumban — 104 G3
Fourmies — 54 G4
Fournoi — 68 J7
Fouta Djallon — 104 B2
Foveaux Strait — 116 A8
Fowey — 38 D5
Foxe Basin — 122 R3
Foxe Channel — 122 R4
Foxe Peninsula — 122 R4
Fox Glacier — 116 B6
Fox Islands — 132 (1)D5
Foz — 60 C1
Foz do Cunene — 108 A3
Foz do Iguaçu — 142 L4
Fraga — 60 L3
Franca — 142 M3
Francavilla al Mare — 64 J6
France [A] — 58 G4
Franceville — 104 G5
Francisco I. Madero — 132 F4
Francistown — 108 D4
Francs Peak — 126 E2
Franeker — 54 H1
Frankenberg — 52 D5
Frankenthal — 52 D7
Frankfort, *Ind., United States* — 130 D1
Frankfort, *Ky., United States* — 130 E2
Frankfurt, *Germany* — 52 K4
Frankfurt, *Germany* — 52 D6
Franklin, *N.C., United States* — 128 D3
Franklin, *Tenn., United States* — 128 C3
Franklin Bay — 122 F2
Franklin D. Roosevelt Lake — 126 C1
Franklin Mountains — 122 F3
Franklin Strait — 122 M2
Franz Josef Glacier — 116 C6
Franz Josef Land = Zemlya Frantsa-Iosifa — 76 J2
Fraser — 122 G6
Fraserburg — 108 C6
Fraserburgh — 36 F4
Fraser Island — 114 K5
Frasertown — 116 F4
Frater — 128 D1
Frauenfeld — 62 D3
Fredensborg — 50 B2
Frederick, *Md., United States* — 128 E3
Frederick, *Okla., United States* — 130 B3
Fredericksburg, *Tex., United States* — 130 B3
Fredericksburg, *Va., United States* — 128 E3
Fredericktown — 128 B3
Fredericton — 122 T7
Frederikshåb = Paamiut — 122 X4
Frederikshavn — 48 F8
Frederikssund — 50 B2
Frederiksværk — 48 G9
Fredrikstad — 48 F7
Freeport, *Ill., United States* — 128 C2
Freeport, *Tex., United States* — 130 B4
Freeport City — 130 F4
Freer — 130 B4
Free State — 108 D5
Freetown — 104 B3
Fregenal de la Sierre — 60 D6
Freiberg — 52 J6
Freiburg — 62 C3
Freilassing — 62 H3
Freising — 62 G2
Freistadt — 62 K2
Fréjus — 58 M10
Fremantle — 114 C6
Fremont, *Calif., United States* — 132 B1
Fremont, *Nebr., United States* — 124 G3
Frenchglen — 126 C2
French Guiana — 140 G3
French Pass — 116 D5
French Polynesia — 112 L7
Frenda — 102 F1
Fresnes-sur-Apances — 62 A3
Fresnillo — 134 D4
Fresno — 132 C1
Fresno Reservoir — 126 E1
Freudenstadt — 62 D2
Freyung — 52 J8
Frías — 142 H4
Fribourg — 62 C4
Friedburg — 62 G2
Friedrichshafen — 62 E3
Friesach — 62 K4
Friesoythe — 52 C3
Frisian Islands — 54 H1
Fritzlar — 52 E5
Frobisher Bay — 122 T4
Frodsham — 38 F2

Frolovo — 70 H5
Frome — 38 F4
Frontera — 134 F5
Frontignan — 58 J10
Frosinone — 64 H7
Frøya — 48 D5
Frýdek Místek — 50 H8
Fudai — 82 L4
Fuding — 80 G5
Fuengirola — 60 F8
Fuentesauco — 60 E3
Fuerte Olimpo — 142 K3
Fuerteventura — 102 C3
Fugu — 80 E5
Fuhai — 76 R8
Fujieda — 82 K6
Fujin — 78 N7
Fuji-san [▲] — 82 K6
Fukuchiyama — 82 H6
Fukue — 82 E7
Fukue-jima — 82 E7
Fukui — 82 J5
Fukuoka — 82 F7
Fukushima — 82 L5
Fukuyama — 82 G6
Fulda — 52 E6
Fulda — 52 E6
Fuling — 80 D5
Fulton — 130 D2
Funabashi — 82 L6
Funafuti — 112 H6
Funchal — 102 B2
Fundão — 60 C4
Funing — 84 D2
Funtua — 104 F2
Furano — 82 M2
Fürg — 95 F2
Furmanovka — 76 N9
Furmanovo — 70 J5
Furneaux Group — 114 J8
Furqlus — 94 E2
Fürstenberg — 52 J3
Fürstenfeldbruck — 62 G2
Fürstenwalde — 52 K4
Fürth — 52 F7
Furukawa — 82 L4
Fushun — 82 B3
Fusong — 82 D2
Füssen — 62 F3
Futog — 66 G4
Fuxhou — 80 F5
Fu Xian — 80 D3
Fuxin — 80 G2
Fuyang — 80 F4
Fuyu — 80 G1
Fuyun — 76 R8
Fuzhou — 84 F1
Fyn — 52 F1
Fynshav — 52 F2

G

Gaalkacyo — 106 H2
Gabès — 102 H2
Gabon [A] — 104 G5
Gaborone [■] — 108 D4
Gäbrik — 95 H4
Gabrovo — 66 N7
Gacé — 54 C6
Gacko — 66 F6
Gäddede — 48 H4
Gadsden — 130 D3
Găeşti — 66 N5
Gaeta — 64 H7
Gafsa — 102 G2
Gaggenau — 62 D2
Gagnoa — 104 C3
Gagra — 92 J2
Gaildorf — 62 E2
Gaillac — 58 G10
Gainesville, *Fla., United States* — 130 E3
Gainesville, *Ga., United States* — 130 E3
Gainesville, *Mo., United States* — 130 C2
Gainesville, *Tex., United States* — 130 B3
Gainsborough — 38 H2
Gairloch — 36 C4
Gai Xian — 82 B3
Gala — 88 E3
Galana — 106 F4
Galanta — 62 N2
Galapagos Islands = Islas Galápagos — 140 (1)B1
Galashiels — 36 F6
Galatas — 68 F7
Galaţi — 66 R4
Galdhøpiggen — 48 D6
Galena — 132 (1)F3
Galesburg — 128 B2
Galich — 70 H3
Gallabat — 100 G5
Gallan Head — 36 A3
Galle — 88 D7
Gallipoli — 64 N4
Gallipolis — 130 E2
Gällivare — 48 L3
Galloway — 36 D6
Gallup — 132 E1
Galtat Zemmour — 102 C3
Galveston Bay — 124 G6
Galway — 35 B3
Galway Bay — 35 B3
Gamalakhe — 108 E6
Gambēla — 106 E2
Gambell — 78 Z4
Gambier Islands — 112 N8
Gamboma — 106 B4
Gamboula — 106 B3
Gan — 78 L7
Ganado — 132 E1
Gâncă — 92 M3
Gandajika — 106 C5
Gander — 122 W7
Ganderkesee — 52 D3
Gandesa — 60 L3
Gāndhīdhām — 88 B4

Gandhinagar — 88 B4
Gandia — 60 K6
Gandu — 140 K6
Ganganagar — 88 B3
Gangara — 104 F2
Gangdise Shan [▲] — 88 D2
Ganges — 58 J10
Ganges [⇗] — 88 E3
Gangi — 64 J11
Gangtok — 88 E3
Gannett Peak [▲] — 126 E2
Ganta — 104 C3
Ganye — 104 G3
Ganzhou — 80 E5
Gao — 102 E5
Gaoual — 102 C6
Gap — 62 B6
Gapan — 84 G3
Garanhuns — 140 K5
Garba — 104 J3
Garbsen — 52 E4
Gardelegen — 52 G4
Garden City — 126 F3
Gardēz — 90 J3
Gardone Val Trompia — 62 F5
Gargždai — 50 L2
Gariau — 87 D3
Garies — 108 B6
Garissa — 106 F4
Garland — 130 B3
Garlasco — 62 D5
Garliava — 50 N3
Garmisch-Partenkirchen — 62 G3
Garnett — 130 B2
Garonne — 58 E9
Garoowe — 106 H2
Garoua — 104 G3
Garoua Boulaï — 104 G3
Garron Point — 35 F1
Garry Lake — 122 L3
Garsen — 106 G4
Garut — 86 D4
Garwa — 88 D4
Garwolin — 50 L6
Gary — 124 J3
Garyarsa — 88 D2
Garzê — 80 B4
Gasan Kuli — 90 F2
Gasht — 90 H4
Gashua — 104 G2
Gastonia — 130 E2
Gastre — 142 H7
Gatchina — 70 F3
Gatehouse of Fleet — 36 D7
Gateshead — 36 G7
Gatesville — 130 B3
Gatineau — 128 E1
Gatley — 38 F2
Gatrüyeh — 95 F2
Gauja — 48 N8
Gaula — 48 F5
Gaurella — 88 D4
Gauteng — 108 D5
Gava — 60 N3
Gävbandī — 95 E3
Gavdos — 68 G10
Gävle — 48 J6
Gawler — 114 G6
Gawler Ranges — 114 G6
Gaxun Nur — 80 C2
Gaya, *India* — 88 E4
Gaya, *Niger* — 104 E2
Gaylord — 128 D1
Gayndah — 114 K5
Gayny — 70 K2
Gaywood — 38 J3
Gaza — 94 B5
Gaz-Achak — 76 L9
Gazandzhyk — 76 K10
Gaza Strip — 94 B5
Gaziantep — 92 G5
Gazipaşa — 68 Q8
Gazli — 76 L9
Gaz Şāleb — 95 G2
Gbaaka — 104 C3
Gbarnga — 104 C3
Gdańsk — 50 H3
Gdov — 48 P7
Gdyel — 60 K9
Gdynia — 50 H3
Gebel el Tīh — 94 A7
Gebel Halāl — 94 A6
Gebel Katherina [▲] — 100 F2
Gebel Yi'allaq [▲] — 94 A6
Gebze — 68 M4
Gedaref — 100 G5
Gediz — 68 M6
Gediz — 68 K6
Gedser — 52 G2
Geel — 54 H3
Geelong — 114 H7
Geesthacht — 52 F3
Ge'gyai — 88 D2
Geidam — 104 G2
Geilenkirchen — 54 J4
Geilo — 48 E6
Geinhausen — 52 E6
Geislingen — 62 E2
Geita — 106 E4
Gejiu — 84 C2
Gela — 64 J11
Geladī — 106 H2
Geldern — 54 J3
Geleen — 54 H4
Gelendzhik — 92 H1
Gelibolu — 68 J4
Gelibolu Yarimadasi — 68 J4
Gelsenkirchen — 54 K3
Gembloux — 54 G4
Gembu — 104 G3
Gemena — 106 B3
Gemlik — 68 M4
Gemlik Körfezi — 68 L4
Gemona del Friuli — 62 J4
Genalē Wenz — 106 G2
General Acha — 142 J6

General Alvear — 142
General Pico — 142
General Pinedo — 142
General Roca — 142
General Santos — 84 H5
Geneva — 128
Genève — 62
Gengma — 84
Genil — 60
Genk — 54
Genoa = Genova — 62
Genova — 62
Gent — 54
Genteng — 86
Genthin — 52
Geographe Bay — 114
George — 108
George — 122
George Town, *Australia* — 114
George Town, *Malaysia* — 86
George Town, *The Bahamas* — 130
Georgetown, *Australia* — 114
Georgetown, *Guyana* — 140
Georgetown, *The Gambia* — 104
Georgetown, *Ky., United States* — 130
Georgetown, *S.C., United States* — 130
Georgetown, *Tex., United States* — 130
George West — 130
Georgia [A] — 92
Georgia — 130
Georgian Bay — 128
Gera — 52
Geraldine — 116
Geraldton, *Australia* — 114
Geraldton, *Canada* — 124
Gérardmer — 62
Geräsh — 95
Gerede — 92
Gerefsried — 62
Gereshk — 90
Gérgal — 60
Gerik — 86
Gerlach — 126
Germantown — 128
Germany [A] — 52
Germencik — 68
Germering — 62
Germersheim — 54
Gernika — 60
Gerolzhofen — 52
Gêrzê — 88
Geser — 87
Getafe — 60
Gettysburg — 126
Getxo — 60
Geugnon — 58
Gevaş — 92
Gevelija — 68
Gewanē — 100
Geyik Dağ [▲] — 68
Geyser — 126
Geyve — 68
Ghabāghib — 94
Ghadāmis — 102
Ghadīr Minqār — 94
Ghana [A] — 104
Ghanzi — 108
Gharandal — 94
Ghardaïa — 102
Gharo — 90
Gharyān — 100
Ghāt — 100
Ghazaouet — 102
Ghaziabad — 88
Ghazipur — 88
Ghazni — 90
Gheorgheni — 66
Gherla — 66
Ghizar — 88
Ghotāru — 88
Ghōwrī — 95
Ghunthur — 94
Giannitsa — 68
Giannutri — 64
Giarre — 64 K11
Gibraleón — 60
Gibraltar — 60
Gibson Desert — 114
Gideån — 48
Gien — 58
Gießen — 52
Gifhorn — 52
Gifu — 82
Giga — 36
Giglio — 64
Giglio Castello — 64
Gijón — 60
Gila — 132
Gila Bend — 132
Gilan Garb — 92
Gilău — 66
Gilazi — 92
Gilbert Islands — 112
Gilbués — 140
Gilching — 62
Gilf Kebir Plateau — 100
Gilgandra — 114
Gilgit — 88
Gilimanuk — 86
Gillam — 122
Gillette — 126
Gillingham — 38
Gills Rock — 128
Gilroy — 126
Gimbī — 106
Gimli — 122
Gimol'skoe Ozero — 48
Ginīr — 106
Gioia del Colle — 64
Gioia Tauro — 64 K11
Gioura — 68
Girdle Ness — 36
Giresun — 92
Girga — 100
Girona — 60
Gironde — 58

Girvan 36 D6
Gisborne 116 G4
Gisenyi 106 D4
Gitega 106 D4
Giurgiu 66 N6
Givet 54 G4
Givors 58 K8
Giyon 106 F2
Gizhiga 78 U4
Gizhiginskaya Guba 78 T4
Giżycko 50 L3
Gjiri i Vlorës 68 B4
Gjirokaster 68 C4
Gjoa Haven 122 M3
Gjøvik 48 F6
Glacier Peak 126 B1
Gladstone 114 K4
Glamoč 66 D5
Glan 87 C1
Glan 52 C7
Glarner Alpen 62 D4
Glasgow, *United Kingdom* 36 D6
Glasgow, *Ky., United States* 128 C3
Glasgow, *Mont., United States* 126 E1
Glastonbury 38 F4
Glauchau 52 H6
Glazov 76 J6
Gleisdorf 62 L3
Glen Affric 36 D4
Glendale, *Ariz., United States* 132 D2
Glendale, *Calif., United States* 132 C2
Glendambo 114 G6
Glendive 126 F1
Glenfinnan 36 C5
Glengormley 35 F2
Glen Mor 36 D4
Glenmorgan 114 J5
Glennallen 132 (1)H3
Glenn Innes 114 K5
Glenrothes 36 E5
Glens Falls 128 F2
lenveagh National Park 35 D1
lenwood, *Ark., United States* 128 B4
lenwood, *Minn., United States* 128 A1
lenwood, *N. Mex., United States* 132 E2
lenwood Springs 126 E3
lidden 128 B1
lina 62 M5
liwice 50 H7
lodeni 66 Q2
łogów 50 F6
lomfjord 48 H3
lomma 48 F5
lorieuses 98 H7
lossop 38 G2
loucester, *United Kingdom* 38 F4
loucester, *United States* 128 F2
owno 50 J6
uchołazy 50 G7
ückstadt 52 E3
münd, *Austria* 62 J4
münd, *Austria* 62 L2
munden 62 J3
niezno 50 G5
njilane 68 D2
noien 52 H3
oalpara 88 F3
oba 106 F2
obabis 108 B4
obernador Gregores 142 G8
obi Desert 80 C2
obo 82 H7
obustan 90 E1
oce Delčev 68 F3
och 54 J3
ochas 108 B4
odalming 38 H4
odbout 128 G1
odé 106 G2
oderich 128 D2
odhra 88 B4
odöllő 66 G2
ods Lake 122 N6
odthåb = Nuuk 122 W4
eree 54 F3
es 54 F3
gama 128 D1
iânia 140 H7
iás 140 G6
iás 140 G7
kçeada 68 H4
kova Körfezi 68 K8
ksun 92 G5
laghat 88 F3
lan Heights 94 C3
lbāf 95 G2
lbasi 92 G5
l'chikha 76 Q3
cük 68 K5
dap 50 M3
ld Coast 114 K5
lden Bay 116 D5
ldendale 126 B1
lden Gate 132 B1
lden Vale 35 C4
dfield 126 C3
dsboro 128 E3
ldsworthy 114 C4
le 92 K3
eniów 50 D4
estānak 95 F1
fe d'Ajaccio 64 C7
fe de Gabès 102 H2
fe de Hammamet 102 H1
fe de Porto 64 C6
fe de Sagone 64 C6
fe de Saint-Malo 58 C5
fe de Tunis 64 E11
fe de Valinco 64 C7
fe du Lion 58 J10
fo de Almería 60 H8
fo de Batabanó 134 H4
fo de Cádiz 60 C7
fo de California 134 B3
fo de Chiriquí 134 H7
fo de Corcovado 142 F7
Golfo de Cupica 140 B2
Golfo de Fonseca 134 G6
Golfo de Guayaquil 140 A4
Golfo de Honduras 134 G5
Golfo del Darién 140 B2
Golfo dell' Asinara 64 C7
Golfo de los Mosquitos 140 A2
Golfo de Mazarrón 60 J7
Golfo de Morrosquillo 140 B1
Golfo de Panamá 134 J7
Golfo de Penas 142 F8
Golfo de San Jorge 142 H8
Golfo de Santa Clara 132 D2
Golfo de Tehuantepec 134 E5
Golfo de València 60 L5
Golfo de Venezuela 140 C1
Golfo di Augusta 64 K11
Golfo di Catania 64 K11
Golfo di Gaeta 64 H7
Golfo di Gela 64 J11
Golfo di Genova 64 C4
Golfo di Manfredonia 64 L7
Golfo di Olbia 64 D8
Golfo di Oristano 64 C9
Golfo di Orosei 64 D8
Golfo di Palmas 64 C10
Golfo di Policastro 64 K9
Golfo di Salerno 64 J8
Golfo di Sant'Eufemia 64 K10
Golfo di Squillace 64 L10
Golfo di Taranto 64 L8
Golfo di Trieste 62 J5
Golfo di Venezia 62 H5
Golfo San Matías 142 J6
Gölhisar 68 M8
Golin Baixing 82 A1
Gölköy 92 G3
Gölmarmara 68 K6
Golyshmanovo 76 M6
Goma 106 D4
Gombe 104 G2
Gombi 104 G2
Gomera 102 B3
Gómez Palacio 132 F3
Gonam 78 M5
Gonbad-e Kavus 90 G2
Gonda 88 D3
Gonder 100 G5
Gondia 88 D4
Gondomar 60 B3
Gönen 68 K4
Gonfreville-Orcher 54 C5
Gongga Shan 80 C5
Gonghe 80 C3
Gongliu 76 Q9
Gongpoquan 80 B2
Gongshan 84 B1
Gonzáles 124 G7
Gonzales 130 B4
González 132 G4
Goodland 126 F3
Goodwick 38 B3
Goole 38 H2
Goolgowi 114 J6
Goomalling 114 C6
Goondiwindi 114 K5
Goose Lake 126 B2
Göppingen 62 E2
Góra 50 F6
Gora Bazardyuzi 92 M3
Gora Kamen 76 S4
Gorakhpur 88 D3
Gora Ledyanaya 78 W4
Gora Pobeda 78 R4
Gora Yenashimskiy Polkan 76 S6
Goražde 66 F6
Gorbitsa 78 K6
Goré 104 H3
Gorē 106 F2
Gore 116 B8
Gorey 35 E4
Gorgān 90 F2
Gorgona 62 E7
Gori 92 L2
Gorinchem 54 H3
Goris 92 M4
Gorizia 62 J5
Gorki 70 N1
Gorlice 50 L8
Görlitz 50 D6
Gorna Orjakhovica 66 N6
Gornji Milanovac 66 H5
Gorno-Altaysk 76 R7
Gorodets 70 H3
Gorontalo 87 B2
Gort 35 C3
Gorumna 35 B3
Goryachiy Klyuch 92 H1
Gory Belukha 76 R8
Gory Ulutau 70 N5
Gorzów Wielkopolski 50 E5
Goslar 52 F5
Gospić 64 K4
Gosport 38 G5
Gossau 62 E3
Gossi 104 D1
Gostivar 68 C3
Gostyń 50 G6
Gostynin 50 J5
Göteborg 48 F8
Gotha 52 F6
Gothèye 104 E2
Gotland 48 K8
Gotō-rettō 82 E7
Gotska Sandön 48 K7
Göttingen 52 E5
Gouda 54 G2
Gough Island 98 B10
Goundam 102 E5
Gouraya 60 M8
Gourcy 104 D2
Gourdon 58 G9
Gournay-en-Bray 54 D5
Gourock 36 D6
Governador Valadares 140 J7
Governor's Harbour 130 F4
Govorovo 78 M3
Gowārān 90 J4
Gower 38 D4
Goya 142 K4
Gozha Co 88 D1
Gozo = Gwardex 64 J12
Graaff-Reinet 108 C6
Grabovica 66 K5
Gračac 62 L6
Gračanica 66 F5
Gradačac 66 F5
Gräfenhainichen 52 H5
Grafton, *Australia* 114 K5
Grafton, *United States* 126 G1
Graham Island 132 (1)L5
Grajaú 140 H5
Grajewo 50 M4
Gram 52 E1
Gramat 58 G9
Grampian Mountains 36 D5
Granada, *Nicaragua* 134 G6
Granada, *Spain* 60 G7
Granard 35 D3
Granby 128 F1
Gran Canaria 102 B3
Grand Bahama 130 F4
Grand Ballon 58 N6
Grand Bank 122 V7
Grand Canal 35 D3
Grand Canyon 126 D3
Grande, *Bolivia* 140 E7
Grande, *Brazil* 140 J6
Grande Cache 122 H6
Grande Prairie 122 H5
Grand Erg de Bilma 102 H5
Grand Erg Occidental 102 E3
Grand Erg Oriental 102 F3
Grand Falls, *N.B., Canada* 128 G1
Grand Falls, *Nfld., Canada* 122 V7
Grand Forks, *Canada* 124 C2
Grand Forks, *United States* 126 G1
Grand Haven 128 C2
Grand Island 126 G2
Grand Junction 126 E3
Grand Marais, *Mich., United States* 128 C1
Grand Marais, *Minn., United States* 128 B1
Grand-Mère 128 F1
Grândola 60 B6
Grand Portage 128 C1
Grand Rapids, *Canada* 122 M6
Grand Rapids, *Mich., United States* 128 C2
Grand Rapids, *Minn., United States* 128 B1
Grand Teton 126 D2
Grange 35 C2
Grangemouth 36 E5
Grangeville 126 C1
Granite Falls 128 A2
Granollers 60 N3
Gran Paradiso 62 C5
Grantham 38 H3
Grantown-on-Spey 36 E4
Grants 132 E1
Grants Pass 126 B2
Granville 58 D5
Granville Lake 122 M5
Gräsö 48 K6
Grasse 62 B7
Grassrange 126 E1
Grass Valley 126 B3
Graulhet 58 G10
Graus 60 L2
Gravelines 54 E3
Gravenhurst 128 E2
Gravesend 38 J4
Gravina in Puglia 64 L8
Gray 58 L6
Grayling 128 D2
Grays 38 J4
Grays Lake 126 D2
Grayville 128 C3
Graz 62 L3
Great Abaco 130 F4
Great Artesian Basin 114 H4
Great Australian Bight 114 E6
Great Bahama Bank 134 J4
Great Barrier Island 116 E3
Great Barrier Reef 114 J2
Great Basin 126 C3
Great Bear Lake 132 (1)M2
Great Bend 132 G1
Great Dividing Range 114 J4
Greater Antilles 134 J5
Greater Sunda Islands 112 B6
Great Exhibition Bay 116 D2
Great Exuma 124 L7
Great Falls 126 D1
Great Inagua 134 K4
Great Karoo 108 C6
Great Malvern 38 F3
Great Nicobar 88 F7
Great Ormes Head 36 E2
Great Ouse 38 J3
Great Plains 126 F2
Great Rift Valley 106 E5
Great Salt Lake 126 D2
Great Salt Lake Desert 126 D2
Great Sand Sea 100 D2
Great Sandy Desert 114 D4
Great Slave Lake 120 N3
Great Torrington 38 D5
Great Victoria Desert 114 E5
Great Wall 80 C3
Great Yarmouth 38 K3
Greece 68 D5
Greeley 126 F2
Green 126 D3
Green Bay 128 C2
Greenfield 130 D2
Greenland 120 G2
Greenland Sea 120 B2
Greenlaw 36 F6
Greenock 36 D6
Green River, *Wyo., United States* 126 E2
Green River, *Ut., United States* 126 D3
Greensboro 130 F2
Greensburg, *Ind., United States* 130 D2
Greensburg, *Pa., United States* 128 E2
Greenvale 114 J3
Green Valley 134 B2
Greenville, *Liberia* 104 C3
Greenville, *Al., United States* 130 D3
Greenville, *Fla., United States* 130 E3
Greenville, *Miss., United States* 130 C3
Greenville, *N.C., United States* 128 E3
Greenville, *S.C., United States* 130 E3
Greenwood, *Miss., United States* 130 C3
Greenwood, *S.C., United States* 130 E3
Gregory 126 G2
Gregory Lake 114 E4
Greifswald 52 J2
Greifswalder Bodden 52 J2
Greiz 52 H6
Grenada 140 E1
Grenada 124 J5
Grenchen 62 C3
Grenoble 58 L8
Gretna 130 C4
Gretna 36 E7
Greve in Chianti 62 G7
Greven 54 K2
Grevena 68 D4
Grevenbroich 54 J3
Grevesmühlen 52 G3
Greybull 126 E2
Greymouth 116 C6
Grey Range 114 H5
Griesheim 52 D7
Grieskirchen 62 J2
Grigoriopol 66 S2
Grimma 52 H5
Grimmen 52 J2
Grimsby 38 H2
Grímsey 48 (1)D1
Grímsstaðir 48 (1)E2
Grímsvötn 48 (1)E2
Grindsted 48 E9
Grobina 50 L1
Gröbming 62 J3
Grodekovo 80 J2
Grodzisk Wielkopolski 50 F5
Grójec 50 K6
Gronau 52 C4
Groningen 52 B3
Groote Eylandt 114 G2
Grootfontein 108 B3
Großenhain 52 J5
Großer Arber 52 J7
Großer Beerberg 52 F6
Grosseto 64 F6
Groß-Gerau 52 D7
Großglockner 62 H3
Groß Mohrdorf 52 H2
Groswater Bay 122 V6
Grottaglie 64 M8
Groupe Actéon 112 N8
Grove Hill 130 D3
Groznyy 92 L2
Grubišno Polje 66 E4
Grudovo 68 K2
Grudziądz 50 H4
Gruinard Bay 36 C4
Grünau 108 B5
Grünberg 52 D6
Gryazi 70 G4
Gryazovets 70 H3
Gryfice 50 E4
Gryfino 52 K3
Grytøya 48 J2
Grytviken 142 P9
Gstaad 62 C4
Guadalajara, *Mexico* 134 D4
Guadalajara, *Spain* 60 G4
Guadalcanal 112 F7
Guadalope 60 K4
Guadalquivir 60 E7
Guadalupe 134 E3
Guadalupe 134 A3
Guadeloupe 138 E2
Guadiana 60 C7
Guadix 60 G7
Guaíra 142 L3
Guajará Mirim 140 D6
Guajarraã 140 D5
Guam 112 E4
Guanambi 140 J6
Guanare 140 D2
Guane 134 H4
Guangshui 80 E4
Guangyuan 80 D4
Guangzhou 84 E2
Guanipa 140 E2
Guanling 80 D5
Guantánamo 134 J4
Guanyun 80 F4
Guaporé 140 E6
Guaqui 140 D7
Guarabira 140 K5
Guarda 60 C4
Guardo 60 F2
Guasave 124 E6
Guastalla 62 F6
Guatemala 134 F5
Guatemala 134 F6
Guaviare 140 D3
Guayaquil 140 B4
Guayaramerín 140 D6
Guaymas 132 D3
Guba, *Dem. Rep. of Congo* 106 D6
Guba, *Ethiopia* 100 G5
Guba Buorkhaya 78 N2
Gubakha 70 L3
Guban 106 G2
Gubbi 88 C6
Gubbio 62 H7
Guben 52 K5
Gubin 50 D6
Gudaut'a 92 J2
Gudbrandsdalen 48 E6
Gudermes 92 M2
Gudvangen 48 D6
Guebwiller 52 C9
Guéckédou 104 B3

Name	Page	Grid
Guelma	102	G1
Guelph	128	D2
Guérande	58	C6
Guéret	58	B7
Guernsey	126	F2
Guernsey	38	(1)F6
Guérou	102	C5
Guerrero Negro	132	D3
Gugē	106	F2
Güh Küh	90	G4
Guiana	134	L7
Guiana Highlands	140	F3
Guider	104	G3
Guiglo	104	C3
Guijuelo	60	E4
Guildford	38	H4
Guilianova	64	H6
Guilin	84	E1
Guillaumes	62	B6
Guillestre	62	B6
Guimarães	60	B3
Guinea	104	B2
Guinea-Bissau	104	A2
Günes	134	H4
Guingamp	58	B5
Güiria	140	E1
Guisborough	36	G7
Guise	54	F5
Guitiriz	60	C1
Guiyang	80	D5
Gujranwala	88	B2
Gujrat	88	B2
Gulang	80	C3
Gulbarga	88	C5
Gulbene	48	P8
Gulf of Aden	90	E7
Gulf of Alaska	132	(1)H4
Gulf of Aqaba	90	B4
Gulf of Boothia	122	N2
Gulf of Bothnia	48	K6
Gulf of Carpentaria	114	G2
Gulf of Finland	48	M7
Gulf of Gdansk	50	J3
Gulf of Guinea	104	D4
Gulf of Mannar	88	C7
Gulf of Martaban	84	B3
Gulf of Mexico	134	F3
Gulf of Oman	95	G4
Gulf of Riga	48	M8
Gulf of St. Lawrence	122	U7
Gulf of Santa Catalina	132	C2
Gulf of Thailand	84	C4
Gulf of Tongking	84	D3
Gulfport	130	D3
Gulistan	76	M9
Gülsehir	68	S6
Gulu	106	E3
Gülübovo	68	H2
Gumdag	90	F2
Gumel	104	F2
Gumla	88	D4
Gummersbach	54	K3
Gummi	104	F2
Gümüshane	92	H3
Guna	88	C4
Guna Terara	100	G5
Gungu	106	B5
Gunib	92	M2
Gunnbjørns Fjeld	144	(1)U2
Gunnedah	114	K6
Gunnison, Colo., United States	126	E3
Gunnison, Ut., United States	126	D3
Gunong Kinabalu	86	F1
Guntakal	88	C5
Guntur	88	D5
Gunung Kerinci	86	C3
Gunung Korbu	86	C2
Gunung Kwoka	87	D3
Gunung Leuser	86	B2
Gunung Mekongga	87	B3
Gunung Mulu	86	E2
Gunung Pangrango	86	D4
Gunungsitoli	86	B2
Gunung Togwomeri	87	D3
Günzburg	62	F2
Gunzenhausen	52	F7
Guoyang	80	F4
Gura Humorului	66	N2
Gurk	62	K4
Gurskøye	78	P6
Gürün	92	G4
Gurupi	140	H4
Gusau	104	F2
Gusev	50	M3
Gushgy	90	H2
Gusinoozersk	78	H6
Guspini	64	C9
Güssing	62	M3
Güstrow	50	B4
Gütersloh	52	D5
Guthrie, Okla., United States	126	G3
Guthrie, Tex., United States	132	F2
Gutsuo	88	E3
Guttenberg	128	B2
Guwahati	88	F3
Guyana	140	F2
Guyang	80	E2
Guymon	132	F1
Guyuan	80	D3
Guzar	90	J2
Gvardeysk	50	L3
Gwadar	90	H4
Gwalior	88	C3
Gwanda	108	D4
Gwardex	64	J12
Gwda	50	F4
Gweebarra Bay	35	C2
Gweru	108	D3
Gyangzê	88	E3
Gyaring Hu	80	B4
Gyaros	68	G7
Gyda	76	P3
Gydanskiy Poluostrov	76	P3
Gyirong	88	E3
Gyldenløves Fjord	122	Y4
Gympie	114	K5
Gyomaendrőd	66	H3
Gyöngyös	66	G2
Győr	66	E2
Gypsumville	122	M6
Gytheio	68	E8
Gyula	66	J3
Gyumri	92	K3
Gyzylarbat	90	G2

H

Name	Page	Grid
Haapajärvi	48	N5
Haapsalu	48	M7
Haar	62	G2
Haarlem	54	G2
Haast	116	B6
Habahe	76	R8
Habarūt	90	F3
Habaswein	106	F3
Habbān	90	E7
Habbānīyah	92	K7
Habirag	80	F2
Habomai-Shoto	78	R8
Haboro	82	L1
Hachijō-jima	82	K7
Hachinohe	82	L3
Hachiōji	82	K6
Hadadong	76	Q9
Haddington	36	F6
Hadejia	104	G2
Hadejia	104	F2
Hadera	94	B4
Haderslev	52	E1
Haḍhramaut	90	E6
Hadhunmathi Atoll	88	B8
Hadilik	76	R10
Hadjout	60	N8
Hadleigh	38	J3
Hadrian's Wall	36	F6
Haeju	82	C4
Haenam	82	D6
Hafar al Bāṭin	95	A2
Hafik	92	G4
Hafnarfjörður	48	(1)C2
Haft Gel	95	C1
Hagen	54	K3
Hagenow	52	G3
Hägere Hiywet	106	F2
Hagerstown	128	E3
Ha Giang	80	C6
Haguenau	54	K6
Haicheng	82	B3
Haifa = Hefa	94	B4
Haikou	84	E3
Hā'il	90	D4
Hailar	78	K7
Hailey	126	D2
Hailong	82	C2
Hailsham	38	J5
Hailuoto	48	N4
Hainan	84	D3
Haines Junction	132	(1)K3
Haining	80	G4
Hai Phong	84	D2
Haiti	134	K5
Haiya	100	G4
Hajdúböszörmény	66	J2
Hajdúhadház	50	L10
Hajdúnánás	50	L10
Hajdúszoboszló	50	L10
Hajipur	88	E3
Ḥājjīābād	95	F2
Hajmah	90	G6
Hajnówka	50	N5
Haka	88	F4
Hakkâri	92	K5
Hakodate	82	L3
Halab	92	G5
Ḥalabān	100	H3
Halabja	92	L6
Halaib	100	G3
Halba	94	D2
Halberstadt	52	G5
Halden	48	F7
Haldensleben	52	G4
Halesowen	38	F3
Halifax	122	U8
Halifax	38	G2
Halifax Bay	114	J3
Halkirk	36	E3
Hall	62	G3
Hall Beach	122	Q3
Halle	54	G4
Hallein	62	J3
Halligen	52	D2
Hallock	126	G1
Hall Peninsula	122	T4
Halls Creek	114	E3
Halmahera	87	C2
Halmahera Sea	87	C3
Halmstad	50	B1
Halstead	38	J4
Haltern	54	K3
Haltwhistle	36	F7
Hamada	82	G6
Hamadān	90	E3
Hamaguir	102	E2
Hamāh	92	G6
Hamamatsu	82	J6
Hamar	48	H2
Hamarøy	48	H2
Hamatonbetsu	82	M1
Hambantota	88	D7
Hamburg, Germany	52	E3
Hamburg, Ark., United States	130	C2
Hamburg, N.Y., United States	128	E2
Hämeenlinna	48	N6
Hameln	52	E4
Hamersley Range	114	C4
Hamhŭng	82	D4
Hami	76	S9
Hamīd	100	D3
Hamilton, Australia	114	H7
Hamilton, Bermuda	134	M2
Hamilton, Canada	128	E2
Hamilton, New Zealand	116	E3
Hamilton, United Kingdom	36	D6
Hamilton, Al., United States	130	D3
Hamilton, Mont., United States	126	D1
Hamilton, Oh., United States	128	D3
Hamina	48	P6
Hamirpur	88	D3
Hamm	52	C5
Hammada du Drâa	102	D3
Hammam Bou Hadjar	60	K9
Hammamet	64	E12
Hammam Lif	102	H1
Hammelburg	52	E6
Hammerfest	48	M1
Hammer Springs	116	D6
Hampden	116	C7
Hampshire Downs	38	G4
Hämün-e Jaz Mūrīān	95	H3
Ḩanalc	100	G2
Hanamaki	82	L4
Hanau	52	D6
Hancheng	80	E3
Hancock	128	C1
Handan	80	E3
Handeni	106	F5
Handerslev	48	E9
Handlová	50	H9
Hanford	132	C1
Hangayn Nuruu	76	T3
Hangu	80	F3
Hangzhou	80	F4
Hanidh	95	C3
Hanko	48	M7
Hanksville	126	D3
Hanna	122	K6
Hannibal	130	C2
Hannover	52	E4
Hanö	50	D2
Hanöbukten	50	D2
Hanoi = Hà Nôi	84	D2
Hanover	128	F2
Han Shui	80	D4
Hanson Bay	116	(1)B1
Hanumangarh	88	B3
Hanzhong	80	D4
Hao	112	M7
Hāora	88	E4
Haouza	102	C3
Haparanda	48	N4
Hāpoli	88	F3
Hapur	88	C3
Ḥaraḍ, Saudi Arabia	90	E5
Ḥaraḍ, Yemen	100	H4
Haramachi	82	L5
Harare	108	E3
Harbour Breton	122	V7
Harburg	52	F3
Hardangerfjorden	48	C7
Hardangervidda	48	D6
Hardenberg	54	J2
Harderwijk	54	H2
Hardin	126	E1
Hardy	130	C2
Haren	54	K2
Härer	106	G2
Hargeysa	106	G2
Har Hu	80	B3
Haridwar	88	C3
Harihari	116	C6
Harima-nada	82	H6
Hari Rud	90	H3
Harlan	128	A2
Härläu	66	P2
Harlech	38	D3
Harlem	126	E1
Harlingen, Netherlands	54	H1
Harlingen, United States	130	B4
Harlow	38	J4
Harlowtown	126	E1
Harmanli	68	H3
Harney Basin	124	B3
Harney Lake	126	C2
Härnösand	48	J5
Har Nur	78	K7
Har Nuur	76	S8
Haro	60	H2
Haroldswick	36	(1)H1
Harpenden	38	H4
Harricanaw	122	R6
Harrisburg, Ill., United States	128	C3
Harrisburg, Pa., United States	130	F1
Harrison	128	B3
Harrison Bay	132	(1)G1
Harrisville	128	D2
Harrogate	38	G2
Harrow	38	H4
Har Saggi	94	B6
Harsin	92	M6
Hârşova	66	Q5
Harstad	48	J2
Hartberg	62	L3
Hartford	128	F2
Hartland Point	38	D4
Hartlepool	36	G7
Har Us Nuur	76	S8
Harvey	126	G1
Harwich	38	K4
Harz	52	F5
Hāsā	94	C6
Haselünne	54	C4
Hashtpar	92	N5
Hāsik	90	G6
Haskell	130	B3
Haskovo	68	H3
Haslemere	38	H4
Hassan	88	C6
Hasselfelde	52	F5
Hasselt	54	H4
Haßfurt	52	F6
Hassi Bel Guebbour	102	G3
Hassi Messaoud	102	G2
Hässleholm	50	C1
Hastings, New Zealand	116	F4
Hastings, United Kingdom	38	J5
Hastings, Minn., United States	128	
Hastings, Nebr., United States	126	
Hateg	66	
Hatfield	38	
Hatgal	78	
Ha Tinh	84	
Hatteras	130	
Hattiesburg	130	
Hatvan	66	
Hat Yai	84	
Haud	100	
Haud Ogadēn	106	
Haugesund	48	
Hauraki Gulf	116	
Haut Atlas	102	
Hauts Plateaux	102	
Havana = La Habana	134	
Havana	130	
Havant	38	
Havel	50	
Havelock, New Zealand	116	
Havelock, United States	130	
Havelock North	116	
Havenby	52	
Haverfordwest	38	
Haverhill	38	
Havlíčkův Brod	50	
Havre	126	
Havre-St-Pierre	122	
Havrylivtsi	66	
Havza	92	
Hawaii	132	(2)
Hawaii	132	(2)
Hawaiian Islands	112	
Hawera	116	
Hawes	36	
Hawi	132	(2)
Hawick	36	
Hawke Bay	116	
Hawker	114	
Hawr al'Awdah	95	
Hawr al Ḩammar	95	
Hawthorne	126	
Hay	114	
Hay	122	
Hayange	54	
Haydarābād	92	
Hayden	132	
Hayrabolu	68	
Hay River	122	
Hays	130	
Haywards Heath	38	
Hazard	128	
Hazārībāg	88	
Hazebrouck	54	
Hazel Grove	36	
Hazelton, Canada	122	
Hazelton, United States	128	
Head of Bight	114	
Hearne	130	
Hearst	128	
Hebbronville	132	
Hebgen Lake	126	
Hebi	80	
Hebron, Canada	122	
Hebron, Israel	94	
Hebron, Nebr., United States	126	
Hebron, N.D., United States	126	
Hecate Strait	122	
Hechi	84	
Hechingen	62	
Hede	48	
Heerenveen	54	
Heerlen	54	
Hefa	94	
Hefei	80	
Hegang	80	
Hegura-jima	82	
Hegyfalu	62	M
Heide	52	
Heidelberg	52	
Heidenheim	62	
Heilbad Heiligenstadt	52	
Heilbronn	52	
Heiligenhafen	52	
Heimaey	48	(1)
Heinola	48	
Hejing	76	
Hekla	48	(1)
Helagsfjället	48	
Helena, Ark., United States	130	
Helena, Mont., United States	126	
Helen Reef	87	
Helensburgh	36	
Helensville	116	
Helgea	50	
Helgoland	52	
Helgoländer Bucht	52	
Hellín	60	
Helmand	90	
Helmond	54	
Helmsdale	36	
Helmsley	36	
Helmstedt	52	
Helodrano Antongila	108	
Helong	82	
Helsinge	50	
Helsingborg	48	
Helsingør	48	
Helsinki	48	
Helston	38	
Helwan	100	
Hemel Hempstead	38	
Hemsworth	36	
Henashi-zaki	82	
Hendek	68	
Henderson, Ky., United States	128	
Henderson, Nev., United States	126	
Henderson, N.C. United States	130	
Henderson Island	112	
Hendersonville	128	
Hendijarn	95	
Hengelo	54	
Hengyang	80	
Henichesk	70	
Hénin-Beaumont	54	